Economic Policy in the Age of Glc

In the age of globalisation, both domestic and foreign economic policies play an important role in determining firms' strategies. Understanding such policies is an essential part of the cultural background of managers at all levels of a firm. At the same time, firms' choices have a greater impact on economic policymaking in a global economy, as the range of alternatives open to them expands. In this book, Nicola Acocella analyses both sides of this relationship. Special emphasis is placed on current issues in policymaking on the basis of social choice principles and the normative and positive theory of economic policy, and on issues concerning the establishment of international public institutions that can match the global reach of the private institutions (markets and firms) that generate many of today's economic challenges. Broad in scope, this book is aimed at students who have completed an introductory course in both microeconomics and macroeconomics.

NICOLA ACOCELLA is Professor of Economic Policy in the Department of Public Economics at the University of Rome 'La Sapienza'. His publications include *Foundations of Economic Policy: Values and Techniques* (Cambridge, 1998).

Economic Policy in the Age of Globalisation

Nicola Acocella

Translated from the Italian by

Brendan Jones

CAMBRIDGE
UNIVERSITY PRESS

CAMBRIDGE UNIVERSITY PRESS
Cambridge, New York, Melbourne, Madrid, Cape Town, Singapore, São Paulo, Delhi

Cambridge University Press
The Edinburgh Building, Cambridge CB2 8RU, UK

Published in the United States of America by Cambridge University Press, New York

www.cambridge.org
Information on this title: www.cambridge.org/9780521540384

Originally published in Italian as *Politica economica e strategie aziendali,*
2nd edn., by Carocci, Roma, 2003.

First published in English by Cambridge University Press 2005 as
Economic Policy in the Age of Globalisation
English Translation © Nicola Acocella 2005

First published 2005

A catalogue record for this publication is available from the British Library

Library of Congress Cataloguing in Publication data
Acocella, Nicola, 1939–
[Politica economica e strategie aziendali. English]
Economic policy in the age of globalization / Nicola Acocella ; translated from the Italian
by Brendan Jones.
    p.   cm.
Includes bibliographical references and index.
ISBN 0 521 83282 9 (alk. paper) – ISBN 0 521 54038 0 (pbk. : alk. paper)
1. Economic policy.   2. Globalization – Economic aspects.   I. Title.
HD87.A28513   2005
338.9 – dc22   2004051110

ISBN 978-0-521-83282-3 hardback
ISBN 978-0-521-54038-4 paperback

Transferred to digital printing 2009

To Valerio and Roberta

Contents

Boxes

xv

Tables

Symbols, abbreviations and acronyms

Symbols

a	coefficient measuring sensitivity of investment to interest rate
A	autonomous expenditure
b_a	cyclically adjusted budget balance as a percentage of GDP
b_s	total budget deficit or surplus as a ratio of GDP
b_t	benefits at time t
B	total discounted benefits; in a different setting, public debt
B_s	total budget deficit or surplus
BMB	bank monetary base (bank reserves)
BP	deficit or surplus on the balance of payments in real terms
BP_m	deficit or surplus on the balance of payments in monetary terms
c	marginal (and average) propensity to consume
c_t	costs at time t
C	total discounted costs; in a different setting, consumption
C_g	government consumption
CA	current and capital account (movements of good) in real terms
CA_m	current and capital account (movements of goods) in monetary terms
CR	loans
D	deposits
e	nominal exchange rate
e_r	real exchange rate
ε_m	import elasticity
ε_x	export elasticity
g	gross mark-up rate
G	government expenditure
G_p	primary government expenditure
h	ratio between currency in circulation and deposits
i	nominal interest rate
I	private investment
I_g	government net investment

INT	interest on public debt
j	ratio between bank monetary base and deposits
k	fraction of income held as monetary balances
K	capital
KA	net capital movements
l	government spending multiplier
L_s	money supply
LF	labour force
M	imports
m	propensity to import
M_w	Rest of the World imports
m_w	Rest of the World propensity to import
MB	monetary base; in a different setting, marginal benefit
MC	marginal cost
MR	marginal revenue
MRS	marginal rate of substitution
$MRTS$	marginal rate of technical substitution
MRT	marginal rate of transformation
N	employment
p	price or absolute price level (in the home country)
$\dot{p}$	inflation rate
p^e	expected price
$\dot{p}^e$	expected inflation rate
p_m	import price expressed in terms of foreign currency
p_x	export price expressed in terms of domestic currency
p_w	absolute price level in the foreign country
P	population
PMB	the public's monetary base or currency in circulation
π	average labour productivity
q	quantity consumed or supplied in a given period
q_x	quantity exported
q_m	quantity imported
Q	quantity produced since the beginning of production
r	real interest rate
R	profits
S	savings
t	time; in a different setting, tax rate
T	time horizon; in a different setting, total transactions; in still another setting, taxes or current revenues; sometimes used to indicate taxes less transfers
Tr	total government transfers
Tr_c	current transfers less interest on public debt
Tr_k	capital transfers

Tr_h	transfers to households
TT	terms of trade
u	unemployment rate
U	total unemployment
v	sensitivity of speculative demand for money to interest rate
V	money velocity of circulation
w	wage rate or unit labour cost
W	welfare function (or level); in a different setting, wages
X	percentage decided by the regulator to be subtracted to the rate of change in the retail price index; exports in a macroeconomic setting
Y	income as output or demand
Y_n	natural rate of employment income
Y_w	Rest of the World income
$\overline{Y}$	Full employment income

Abbreviations and acronyms

ACP	African, Caribbean and Pacific
ASEAN	Association of South East Asian Nations
BIS	Bank for International Settlements
BIT	Bureau International du Travail
CAP	Common Agricultural Policy
CBA	Cost-benefit analysis
CET	Common external tariff
CSF	Community Support Framework
CVM	Contingent valuation method
DCE	Domestic credit expansion
DSB	Dispute Settlement Body (GATT)
EAGGF	European Agricultural Guidance and Guarantee Fund
EC	European Community
ECB	European Central Bank
ECSC	European Coal and Steel Community
EEA	European Economic Area
EEA	European Environment Agency
EEC	European Economic Community
EFF	Extended Fund Facility (IMF)
EIA	Environmental impact assessment
EIB	European Investment Bank
EMI	European Monetary Institute
EMS	European Monetary System
EMU	European Monetary Union
EONIA	Euro Overnight Index Average
EP	European Parliament

ERDF	European Regional Development Fund
ERM	Exchange Rate Mechanism
ESCB	European System of Central Banks
ESF	European Social Fund
EU	European Union
FDI	Foreign direct investment
FIFG	Financial Instrument for Fisheries Guidance
FSA	Financial Services Authority
FTA	Free trade area
FTAA	Free Trade Area of the Americas
GATS	General Agreement on Trade in Services
GATT	General Agreement on Tariffs and Trade
GDP	Gross domestic product
GEF	Global Environmental Facility
GRA	General Resources Account (IMF)
GHG	Greenhouse gas
GNP	Gross national product
HDI	Human Development Index
IBRD	International Bank for Reconstruction and Development
ICN	International Competition Network
ICT	Information and communication technology
IDA	International Development Association
IFC	International Finance Corporation
ILO	International Labour Office
IMF	International Monetary Fund
IPR	Intellectual property rights
IRR	Internal rate of return
IT	Information technology
LDC	Less-developed country
MFA	Multifibre Agreement
MFN	Most favoured nation
MIGA	Multilateral Investment Guarantee Agency
MNC	Multinational corporation
NAFTA	North American Free Trade Area
NBFI	Non-bank financial intermediary
NCB	National Central Banks
NCM	New classical macroeconomics
NPV	Net present value
NTB	Non-tariff barrier
OECD	Organisation for Economic Cooperation and Development
OMA	Orderly market agreement
OMO	Open market operation
PPP	Purchasing power parity

QMV	Qualified majority voting
QR	Quantitative restriction
R&D	Research and development
REH	Rational expectations hypothesis
SDR	Special Drawing Rights (IMF)
SEA	Single European Act
SEM	Single European Market
SGP	Stability and Growth Pact
SRF	Supplemental Reserve Facility (IMF)
SSA	Sub-Saharan Africa
SWF	Social welfare function
TARGET	Trans-European Automated Real-time Gross Settlement Express Transfer
TEU	Treaty on European Union
TFP	Total factor productivity
TIP	Tax-tied incomes policies/Tax-based incomes policies
TNC	Transnational corporation
TRIMs	Trade-Related Investment Measures
TRIPS	Trade-Related Aspects of Intellectual Property Rights
UN	United Nations
UNCTAD	United Nations Conference on Trade and Development
UNDP	United Nations Development Programme
UNEP	United Nations Environment Programme
VER	Voluntary export restraint
WTO	World Trade Organisation

Preface

Some forty years ago, there were rather simple and commonly accepted justifications for government intervention in the economy.

Market failures at both the microeconomic and the macroeconomic level were considered so widespread and deep as to justify programmed action by government. In the late 1940s authors such as R. Frisch, J. Tinbergen, H. Theil and others began to develop the so-called 'theory of economic policy'. On the basis of fixed targets or a social preference function, as well as an analytical model of the economy and the assumption of rational policymakers, consistent levels of policy instruments were derived for static and dynamic settings.

This theory had to face two main challenges. The first was advanced on theoretical grounds by economists such as Coase, Friedman, Lucas and adherents of the theory of 'public choice', who tended to reaffirm the virtues of the 'invisible hand' while underscoring numerous 'non-market failures'. This challenge was largely met by the theory of economic policy, which, on the one hand, recognised the possible existence of government failures and, on the other, was reformulated in a way to overcome charges of inconsistency.

The second challenge to the theory of economic policy has come more recently from the evolution of reality, with the globalisation of markets and production. Globalisation has induced major changes in society, the economy and economic policy. Globalisation has given rise to a considerable change in the distribution of income both among and within countries, often creating economic and social problems that governments have struggled to address. In addition, globalisation has increased the exposure of economies to external shocks by increasing their degree of international openness. Most importantly, globalisation tends to reduce the *decisionmaking independence* of a country, since its economic conditions cannot diverge significantly from those in other economies. A specific aspect of this reduction in national policymakers' independence derives from the fact that almost no policy has only domestic effects. Exposure to the global market thus constrains divergent behaviour by public (as well as private) agents in the country in question. In particular, countries are exposed to the negative consequences of *permissive economic policies* in other countries that seek to encourage consumers and firms to move in. More generally, each national government faces constraints in the short term on its freedom to expand demand or to adopt structural policy measures that increase the short-term costs of agents located in that country, even if such measures could produce positive effects in the long term.

At the root of the problems that globalisation poses to the effectiveness of public corrective action to remedy microeconomic and macroeconomic market failures is the separation that it creates between the geographical scope of private institutions (markets and firms), which are increasingly planetary in reach, and that of public institutions, which largely remain national – or, at most, regional – often hampering the effectiveness of their action at the global (multilateral) level. This separation underlies the growing problems of controlling public action, but these problems do not leave firms unscathed, as they may reduce performance, at least in the long term.

This book has a dual purpose: first, to assess the impact on public conduct of private action in a global context; second, to offer an overview of the difficulties of public action in a globalised environment, and of trends within national governments and regional and multilateral international organisations. It is addressed to students of business courses, seeking to give them a framework in which to set corporate strategies with an awareness of the terms on which public choices are made.

Part I of the book is devoted to a brief discussion of the arguments both for and against the market. The analysis of microeconomic failures is completed by a discussion of market failures that, given the present state of the discipline, can be best analysed from a macroeconomic standpoint.

Part II of the book is devoted to a restatement of the 'classic' normative theory of economic policy developed by Frisch, Tinbergen, Theil and others and to examining criticism of this position, from the Lucas critique to the theory of political business cycles and the theory of bureaucracy. Non-market failures are then discussed and, to a certain extent, compared with market failures.

Taking both market and non-market failures into account, an analysis of specific policy targets and instruments follows in part III, which deals with microeconomic policies. The problems analysed in this part concern property rights, corporate governance, public enterprises and privatisation; competition policies; policies for externalities and public goods; industrial and regional policies, redistributive policies; social choice and cost-benefit analysis (CBA).

Part IV considers macroeconomic policies in an open economy, dealing with monetary policy, fiscal policy, incomes and price policies and general balance of payments policies.

Part V is concerned with the role of public institutions in an international setting. It analyses public institutions, in both the multilateral sphere (such as international monetary systems and exchange rate regimes; development and trade organisations) and at the regional level (the European Union).

Part VI deals with the internationalisation of private institutions – i.e. the globalisation of markets and production, the challenges of globalisation for public policies and the quest for a new institutional setting.

This textbook is intended for students who have completed at least a full year's study of both microeconomics and macroeconomics. No calculus is required, except for a very few passages. Some boxes are added to most chapters to deal with specific issues, often of a practical nature. Each chapter is completed by a summary. A detailed subject index makes the book a helpful resource for consultation by the educated public in general. A list of symbols, abbreviations and acronyms used in the text is provided at the beginning of the book.

The terms **emboldened** in the text are key economic terms that the reader must absorb as fundamental building blocks for their understanding of the subject.

This English edition owes much to a number of people or institutions who contributed to it in various ways. Maria Pianta wrote one of the boxes. For other boxes, I drew extensively on works by Scott Barrett, Massimo Florio, Vito Tanzi and Jelle Visser. Other boxes reproduce parts of official documents of the ECB, IMF, UNCTAD, World Bank and WTO. Luciano Milone, Alessandro Noce and Pietrantonio Valentino read parts of the text or gave their advice for improving it.

This book would have been impossible without the financial support of the Cassa di Risparmio di Pescara in meeting the costs of translation.

Veronica Fedeli contributed her time and effort with generosity. Brendan Jones translated the book with care and skill. Nicola Burton efficiently assisted in preparing the volume and Chris Harrison carefully steered the book along its path and provided me with valuable suggestions. I give my heartfelt thanks to all.

The book is dedicated to my children, Valerio and Roberta, who, as globetrotters, can be thought of as living examples of globalisation.

I would be very grateful to readers who report any errors they may find or who wish to offer suggestions and comments (nicola.acocella@uniroma1.it).

Nicola Acocella
University of Rome 'La Sapienza'

1 Introduction

1.1 Economic policy

The reader about to embark on the study of economic policy will very probably already be familiar with the principles of economic analysis, and it is to this discipline that we will turn to introduce our subject.

Economic analysis examines the *individual or aggregate decisions of private economic agents* about what they produce, exchange and consume. These decisions are taken with specific objectives in mind, objectives that represent criteria for ordering the various possible situations in which agents might find themselves. For example, according to neoclassical theory consumers choose the combination of goods that maximises their utility, while entrepreneurs choose the quantity of output and the combination of inputs for each good that maximises their profit.

Economic analysis does not usually examine the behaviour of 'public' economic agents, which are attributed with collective aims. The choices of the latter – for example, government decisions regarding the level of expenditure or taxation – enter the macroeconomic and microeconomic models of economic analysis as simple data. At most, alternative hypotheses regarding the level of government expenditure or taxation[1] are considered in order to acquire some indication of what changes there would be in the performance of individual economic agents or the economy as a whole. Our study of economic policy must therefore complete many aspects of this analysis on three different levels:

(1) First and foremost, we must seek to understand the process by which government makes its choices, taking as given its objectives and the roles and scope of different institutions[2] and assuming that we know how the economy functions. This is the **'current' choices level**.

---

[1] In this case the variables are said to vary parametrically.

[2] The term '*institution*' has been given a variety of meanings in the social sciences. However, these can be reduced essentially to the following two. First, the term may indicate a set of 'rules' that regulate, in a lasting manner, the relationships within a group of agents; in this sense, for example, marriage, private property and the market are all institutions. A second meaning extends the definition to include the *agents* involved in implementing the rules and the *resources* necessary to do so; in this second sense, the government, the family and the Mafia are all institutions. We will use the term in both senses.

(2) A second level of analysis concerns the very existence and respective structures of government and the market. In standard economic analysis both of these institutions are considered 'natural', the latter perhaps more so than the former. The scope of each is given and possible areas of overlap and relationships of substitutability or complementarity do not emerge. In other words, economic analysis does not address questions about the extent to which government replaces the market – and vice versa – or the degree to which government is necessary for the market or reinforces it. Beyond the specific case of government and the market, a more general issue regards the types of higher-level economic institutions that are necessary or useful in governing a society. This is the level of **institutional (constitutional) choices**, which we reach once we know society's objectives and how the economy functions under different possible institutions.

(3) The final level of analysis concerns the identification of socially desirable goals. A similar problem is dealt with in economic analysis when the firm is realistically conceived as a combination of diverse interests rather than in terms of the classic figure of the entrepreneur (who is both owner and manager). Simplifying, it can be argued that a firm is composed of the owner, who seeks to maximise profits; the manager, who instead seeks to increase the firm's size (sales) or its rate of growth, since his income, power and prestige (the manager's ultimate objectives) depend on these variables; and workers, who are primarily concerned with the level of their real wages. An attempt to define a preference function for the firm must take account of the preference functions of the economic agents that operate within it. Similarly, for society as a whole we seek to derive a system of preferences (and hence objectives) from the preferences (objectives) of the various components of the community. This level of our study of economic policy therefore seeks to identify social goals (the **social choices level**).

Without going into further detail here, we can define **economic policy** as the discipline that studies public economic action, inasmuch as it studies all three levels: the 'current' choices of the government, the choice of higher-level institutions (i.e. the definition of society's 'economic constitution') and the identification of social preferences or objectives. Economic policy thus complements the analysis of the behaviour of economic agents and the functioning of economic systems conducted in economic analysis. Economic policy and economic analysis have in fact been conceived as separate disciplines for the sake of convenience within the more general framework of economic science to enable a more in-depth analysis of the issues involved. Just as in economic analysis it is essential to understand government action, drawing from the discipline of economic policy, in the latter it is equally crucial to understand the functioning of the private economic system, borrowing this knowledge from economic analysis.

Two clarifications are in order. First, economic policy can serve as a guide to public action only with the help of a variety of disciplines: in addition to economic analysis, these include philosophy, political science, constitutional and administrative law, statistics, econometrics and many others. With this in mind, we must caution that the knowledge provided by economic analysis cannot usually be used as a guide to action without the qualifying and mediating contributions of these other disciplines.[3]

The second clarification regards the possibility (or necessity, as some would argue) of widening the definition of economic policy to include any conceptualisation that uses the knowledge of economic analysis (and other disciplines) as a guide to action for any economic agent whatsoever, especially the largest and most powerful. This would comprise not only government and other public bodies but also big business and industrial associations or lobbies, as well as 'big labour' (Caffè, 1966, I, pp. 13–14). Such a broad range of study would correspond to the second of the two ultimate tasks of economic science identified by Knight (1952): first, understanding and explaining certain phenomena, and, second, using that understanding to guide our action.

This broader definition has only recently received significant attention, but it will be largely reappraised in the light of the approach we adopt in chapter 9, where we characterise economic policy as a *strategic game*.

1.2 Economic reality and social preferences

A question that will recur throughout this book is why and under what conditions we require the presence of an economic agent with social or collective objectives in an economic system composed of individuals who essentially pursue their own interests. The need for such an agent is clearly related to the possibility that the operation of the economy may be judged unsatisfactory in some way; that is, it fails to satisfy certain wants. Such a judgement requires a comparison of reality and desires: if, for example, we have (involuntary) unemployment in a system based entirely on private action and this state of affairs is considered socially undesirable, intervention by an agent that pursues social aims is required.

This text has no intention of explaining further how economic systems work. Although we will draw on the relevant areas in economic analysis, our focus will be on social (or public or collective) *desiderata*, especially the way in which these are (can be, must be) formulated, which is the subject of social choice theory. We can then proceed with a comparison of desires and reality to derive society's institutional choices (what role to assign to different institutions) and government's current choices (the specific economic measures to be taken).

Bear in mind that the validity of many of our conclusions regarding institutional and current choices closely depends on the validity of the analytical tools employed, in particular the theories adopted to explain the performance of the economic system. At least as much as other sciences, economic analysis does not offer, nor can it offer, a body of objectively true statements (Myrdal, 1953, 1958). Each economic theory highlights

---

[3] For example, in Keynesian economic theory an increase in investment, whether public or private, causes income to increase by some multiple. Income could be increased by raising public investment. However, the precise amount of such investment can be established only if we know the value of certain parameters, which calls for statistical or econometric investigation; at the same time, the feasibility of increasing public investment must be assessed in both political terms (the possibility of winning parliamentary approval) and administrative terms (the possibility of effective and timely implementation).

certain more or less important aspects of reality, and the economic policy scholar must exercise special care in choosing a reference model. More specifically, we will see that two opposing 'visions' underlie the different theories: one that casts its gaze on economic reality through 'Panglossian' lenses, emphasising the 'harmony' and the ability to adjust (perhaps hidden but undoubtedly present) of certain institutions, such as the market; and another more pessimistic (or simply more realistic) view that underscores the negative aspects of those institutions in terms of 'failures' and instability.

1.3   Outline of the text and organisation of the discipline

In introducing the issues of economic policy, the three levels of choice examined by the discipline were presented in the following order in section 1.1:

(a) current choices
(b) institutional choices
(c) social choices.

Note, however, that the logical order of these issues is precisely the reverse. No institutional or current decision can be taken without first establishing social preferences; given these, institutional choices at the various levels can be taken. Once our higher-level institutions have been established, current choices can then be made.

The text normally follows the logical order. However, we do not deal with social choices, for which we refer the reader to Acocella (1998). Part I (chapters 2 and 3) deals in a highly abstract way with the institutional choices consequent upon the various possible social aims, principally with reference to the government–market dichotomy. We frequently return to the question in more realistic fashion later in the text. Social choices and institutional choices constitute the branch of economic policy known in the literature as **welfare economics**.

Part II (chapters 4 and 5) also examines general issues regarding institutional choices. More specifically, it examines policy models: given the social preferences that are to guide public action, as well as the analytical models developed by economic analysis, we must deal with the problem of planning – i.e. coordinating the use of available tools to satisfy those preferences, achieving the multiple objectives of government action. This (normative) approach to public intervention is then compared with the actual process of public decisionmaking (the 'positive' theory of economic policy). This part belongs to the **theory of economic policy**, which addresses questions regarding the definition and structure of government intervention.

Current choices can be divided into:

(a) 'structural' choices (such as those regarding the type of financial system), which are decisions on institutional, but not constitutional, matters; and
(b) 'corrective' choices (for example, a change in income tax brackets).

The *theory of current decisions* is examined in the remainder of the book. In parts III, IV, V and VI we examine, respectively: microeconomic policies (chapters 6, 7, 8

Table 1.1 *An overview of the discipline of economic policy*

Part of discipline	Subject matter	Parts and chapters of the book
(1) Welfare economics	(1) Identification of social preferences	Part I Chapters 2, 3 (brief references)
	(2) Identification of optimal institutions at the constitutional level	Part I Chapters 2, 3
(2) Theory of economic policy	(1) Planning criteria (design and structure of public intervention)	Part II Chapter 4
	(2) The actual process of public decisionmaking	Part II Chapter 5
(3) Theory of current decisions (corrective and structural)	(1) Microeconomic policies	Part III Chapters 6, 7, 8, 9
	(2) Macroeconomic policies	Part IV Chapters 10, 11, 12, 13, 14, 15
	(3) Private and public institutions in an international setting	Part V Chapters 16, 17, 18
	(4) Globalisation and the quest for a new institutional setting	Part VI Chapters 19, 20

and 9); macroeconomic policies (chapters 10, 11, 12, 13, 14 and 15); issues involving existing public institutions at the world or regional level (chapters 16, 17 and 18). In part VII we consider the globalisation of markets and production and the quest for a new institutional setting (chapters 19 and 20).

An overview of the content of the discipline is given in table 1.1. The plan of the book and its division into parts and chapters is also presented here.

1.4 Summary

1 Strictly speaking, economic policy is the discipline that studies *public economic action*. It examines the process through which social preferences are formed (social choices), the choice of institutions and the current decisions of government.
2 More generally, the field of economic policy comprises any discipline that uses the knowledge of economic analysis and other disciplines as a *guide to action for any economic agent*.
3 The question that recurs at each of the levels noted in point 1 above is that regarding the foundations of a *social (or collective) point of view* distinct from individual preferences.
4 These foundations are to be sought in *economic analysis* and other social sciences.

5   The parts of this book are arranged in decreasing order of abstraction. Part I deals with the process through which social institutions can be defined, in particular as far as the choice between government and the market is concerned. Part II outlines the structure of rational public action and provides a more realistic picture of the agents that form society and the process of defining and implementing government action. Parts III and V examine government action in various fields at both the microeconomic and macroeconomic levels and in closed and open economies. Part VI deals with the adaptation of existing international public institutions required by the globalisation of markets and production.

I   The market, efficiency and equity

2 Market failures: microeconomic aspects

2.1 The role of the market and government

This part of the book addresses the problem of how different economic institutions – i.e. different 'rules' or procedures governing economic interactions among individuals – enable society to best satisfy those principles and the objectives derived from them. Limiting our discussion to the 'constitutional' aspects of economic institutions (setting aside consideration of current choices), we find two principal 'rules' of social interaction: the *market* and *government*. Obviously, other institutions may also have economic importance, such as *firms*[1] and **non-profit organisations** other than households and government. Focusing on the market and government, we intend to direct our attention to the extreme aspects of the contrast between institutions oriented towards the pursuit of individual and collective interests, respectively. In reality, the contrast is not as sharp as it might seem. There are organisations, such as firms, that in their most abstract form also pursue private aims, or other organisations with social ends that do not share the features of government, such as voluntary non-profit groups. We address non-profit institutions only briefly (see sections 6.5 and 8.5).

This part of the book offers a preliminary examination of how and under what conditions the economic results that can be achieved through the market (intended as a specific expression of private interests) or government (intended as a particular expression of collective interests) ensure that the principles of efficiency and equity are respected.

At this point in our analysis the distinction between market and government can be made only with regard to the private or public nature of the interests represented by the institution. Later (from chapter 5 on) we will also consider the difference between the two in terms of the nature of the *allocative mechanism* and, more generally, the *decision process* typical of – but not exclusive to – the institution: voluntary in the case of the market, coercive in the case of government (see, among others, Hirschman, 1970; Stiglitz, 1989; Holcombe, 1994). In any case we use the term 'market' to include

---

[1] Firms do not play any substantial (realistic) role in general equilibrium theory, even if this formally takes account of them. The problem was first raised by Coase (1937) and, more than sixty years on, we still do not have a comprehensive framework for the analysis of the market, the firm and other institutions.

private firms (unless otherwise specified), whereas the term 'state' includes all public organisations. We deal specifically with non-profit institutions in section 6.5.

2.2   Criteria for the choice of institutions: efficiency and equity

Social institutions can be assessed on the basis of two essential criteria: efficiency and equity.[2] In choosing between institutions directed at the pursuit of individual interests and those directed at the achievement of collective interests, we might therefore prefer the market or government on the basis of one or the other criterion.

One position broadly favourable of the market was expressed by Adam Smith. As is well known, the founder of economic science was a convinced believer in the 'virtue' of the (competitive) market as a social institution. His 'invisible hand' aphorism sought to express the ability of the market to ensure that economic choices made by individuals in the pursuit of their personal interests and preferences would have a beneficial effect for society as a whole. Smith (1776, p. 409) argued:

> As every individual, therefore, endeavours ... to employ his capital ... and so to direct that industry that its produce may be of the greatest value; every individual necessarily labours to render the annual revenue of the society as great as he can. He ... neither intends to promote the publick interest, nor knows how much he is promoting it ... he intends only his own gain, and he is in this ... led by an invisible hand to promote an end which was no part of his intention. (Smith, 1776, book IV, chapter II, p. 456)

Smith does not specify either the meaning of 'public interest' (efficiency or equity) or the type of market that would ensure pursuit of the public interest itself. Before we can analyse the terms of the choice of institutions in detail, we must clarify the concepts of efficiency and equity, and the types of market.

There are many concepts of **efficiency**. Among others, we can name allocative (or Pareto) efficiency, '*x*' efficiency and dynamic efficiency.

In order to define **allocative efficiency**, we need to introduce the concept of the *Pareto principle*. According to this principle, a *group* of individuals increases its welfare in moving from *a* to *b* if at least one individual is better off in *b* and no individual is worse off. This proposition allows us to classify the two situations *a* and *b* from the point of view of society as a whole.

It should be emphasised that this proposition is a value judgement;[3] it is a valuation *criterion* that might not be shared by everybody.[4] For example, before accepting the proposition, we might want to know something about who will benefit (e.g. whether the beneficiary is rich or poor), or how much some individuals (e.g. the rich) might

---

[2] We clarify the meaning of these terms shortly. For the moment, we appeal to the reader's intuition.

[3] **Value judgements** are ethical, religious or political judgements of a personal nature. They express a subjective view of *how things should be*; by contrast, **factual judgements** are claims (whether correct or not) about *what is*.

[4] Sen (1970a, p. 57) argues that a value judgement remains a value judgement even if nearly everyone in a society accepts it.

expect to benefit. However, the way the criterion is formulated does not allow us to take account of such additional information. Moreover, the Pareto principle implicitly assumes that the community must tend to satisfy the preferences of individuals however these are formed and whatever their content (the **liberal-democratic principle**, or **ethical individualism**, or **welfarism**, as Sen (1987) terms it). In other words, there are no needs worthy of protection other than those expressed by individuals. This is a postulate that some would not be willing to accept in every case.

Despite its status of a value judgement, the Pareto principle has an important role in economic science in that it represents a concept of **efficiency**: the possibility of one or more individuals obtaining more of something (in our case, utility) without forcing other individuals to do with less (and perhaps giving them even more) of the available resources.

From the concept of Pareto *principle* we can derive that of a **Pareto optimum** (see Pareto, 1906). A social state *a* is Pareto 'optimal' if in moving from that state *to any other state* it is not possible to increase the welfare of one member of society without worsening the condition of at least one other.

We can show that a Pareto optimum in a production and consumption economy requires:

(a) the *efficient allocation of consumption of goods*, which is achieved when the marginal rates of substitution (MRS)[5] for each pair of goods of all the consumers in society are equal

(b) the *efficient allocation of production inputs*, which is achieved when the marginal rates of technical substitution (MRTS) between each pair of inputs in the production of different goods are equal

(c) *general efficiency*, which is achieved when the marginal rate of substitution between each pair of goods for all individuals is equal to the marginal rate of transformation (MRT).[6]

We should note that the term 'optimum' is an entirely unsatisfactory choice of terminology (see Cornwall, 1984, p. 402). Since it is derived from the Pareto principle, so-called 'Pareto optimality' carries with it all of the limitations of the principle itself, limitations that are masked by the use of a term ('optimality') that implies desirability. We will see that such an association is not well founded. The use of a less value-loaded term, such as 'Pareto efficiency' or **allocative efficiency**, would have been more appropriate. Nevertheless, we will follow the dominant usage in this text, using 'optimality' rather than 'efficiency'.

'X'-efficiency is the ability of firms to select technically efficient production plans: after having chosen efficient production techniques (in particular, after having selected

---

[5] The **MRS** between, say, cloth and bread, can be defined as the reduction in the quantity of bread needed to offset the increased utility of an infinitesimal rise in the quantity of cloth if we wish to maintain the satisfaction of an individual unchanged.

[6] The **MRT** between cloth and bread is the reduction in the amount of bread that can be produced for each infinitely small extra unit of cloth production, given the quantity of inputs.

the efficient combination of capital and labour, given the prices of these inputs), production must be organised so as to maximise output. This requires the precise specification of a firm's objectives in order to prevent discretionary behaviour on the part of workers at all levels, who could be induced to pursue their own objectives to the detriment of the interests of the firm (Leibenstein, 1966).

The concept of efficiency has also been conceived in a number of ways in the field of dynamic analysis (**dynamic efficiency**).

At the microeconomic level we first have the concept of **adaptive efficiency** (Alchian, 1950), which involves a learning process leading to the gradual understanding of problems and the 'correct' responses to those problems. In particular, the problem may involve the ability to reduce production costs over time or identify the demand curve.

Another concept of dynamic efficiency is given by **innovative ability**, which regards the capacity to develop *process innovations* (aimed at reducing costs) or *product innovations* (aimed at developing new products).

Many economists and philosophers, beginning with Aristotle, have also developed differing conceptions of **equity**. While we will defer our examination of the question, we can say that in general the distribution of income or wealth is considered equitable if it ensures equality of opportunity (or starting points) or equality of final positions (i.e. the results of the economic process) for the members of a community. However, some argue that a distribution is equitable if it is arrived at in accordance with procedures that ensure the enjoyment of fundamental individual rights and liberties (Nozick, 1974).

2.3   Pareto efficiency and competitive equilibrium: the first fundamental theorem of welfare economics

To begin, we will refer to the principle of efficiency as given by the Pareto criterion. The reason for this will be immediately clear.[7] The correspondence between Pareto optimality and equilibrium in a perfectly competitive market has been demonstrated in the economic literature.

The correspondence between competitive equilibrium and the Pareto optimum is based on the set of hypotheses, conceptual tools and methodologies of general equilibrium theory. In many respects, the correspondence is thus a development of Adam Smith's 'invisible hand' aphorism, which underscores the virtues of the market in achieving the 'public good'.

We deal now with the theorem that expresses the equivalence between competitive equilibrium and the Pareto optimum.

The **first 'fundamental' theorem of welfare economics** says that in an economic system with perfect competition and complete markets, a competitive equilibrium, *if it exists*, will be Pareto optimal.

A competitive equilibrium, in fact, satisfies the analytical condition for the Pareto optimality indicated in section 2.2: in particular, the ratio between the equilibrium

---

[7] We are not arguing that the Pareto principle should be given greater weight than fairness or other efficiency criteria. Note that although we begin our discussion with the Pareto principle we will also examine other possible social choice criteria.

prices of two goods (e.g. bread and cloth) equals the MRS and the MRT between bread and cloth (see Acocella, 1998).

In order to understand the implications of the first theorem we need to provide a precise definition of the central concepts it expresses.

By **perfect competition** we mean a regime in which there are:
(a) homogeneous goods; (b) a large (hypothetically, infinite) number of agents; (c) no agreements between agents; (d) free entry and exit; (e) full information about prices.

While we will give greater space to this subject later; let us first take an intuitive look at what these conditions mean in relation to achieving a Pareto optimal state. The condition of homogeneous goods enables us to define markets precisely. Together with the requirement for a large number of agents, the absence of agreements and free entry and exit, it also ensures that agents regard market prices as given (i.e. they are **price-takers**). Full information on the set of prices in all markets is a transparency requirement needed to avoid market segmentation and ensure that a single price holds over the entire market for a given good.

Complete markets imply the absence of **externalities**. These are the advantages or disadvantages caused to other agents (producers or consumers) by the activity of a given agent (producer or consumer) for which the latter does not, respectively, receive or pay a price. An example of a (negative) externality is pollution. Externalities would place agents in a relationship that does not involve an economic exchange and for which, therefore, there would be no market.[8]

A (Walrasian) **competitive equilibrium** is a situation (not necessarily unique or stable) in which there is a set of prices such as to cause excess demand in all markets to be zero. An equilibrium certainly exists if agents' utility functions have the standard properties (continuity, non-satiability of preferences, etc.) and increasing returns to scale are ruled out (production sets are convex).[9] Note that increasing returns to scale mean constantly decreasing long-run average costs, which would be an obstacle to the presence of more than one firm in the market since each firm would seek to increase its size until it saturated the market.[10]

There can also be more than one competitive equilibrium position. This creates analytical difficulties for anyone attempting to identify a single equilibrium point, but can prove useful from the standpoint of economic policy, providing a range of efficient positions that can be chosen on the basis of other criteria, such as equity or political feasibility.

---

[8] We will see later that the problem is more general, since it includes the case of public goods, forward markets and other markets (see sections 2.9 and 2.10).

[9] The conditions were formulated, among others, by Arrow and Debreu (1954) and by Arrow and Hahn (1971).

[10] The numerosity of agents (one of the conditions for perfect competition) requires that there are no increasing returns to scale. The presence of numerous agents means that each represents a small fraction of the market. In particular, each firm reaches its equilibrium point at a relatively low level of output. The cost curve is therefore initially decreasing and then increasing or constant. This would be impossible in the case of increasing returns to scale. In this case Pareto efficiency would require that the price be equal to marginal cost, but the steady decline in unit costs implies that they are higher than marginal cost at each point. Meeting the efficiency condition would therefore require the price to be lower than average costs, i.e. the firm should operate at a *loss*.

The most problematic aspect of a competitive equilibrium concerns its stability – e.g. the possibility of reaching and maintaining such an equilibrium. There is still no satisfactory proof that ensures such an outcome (see, in particular, Kirman, 1989; see also Hahn, 1982, pp. 73 ff.; F. M. Fisher, 1983).

2.4   Efficiency and equity: the second fundamental theorem

The scope of the first fundamental theorem is fairly limited, not only because the conditions for the existence (and stability) of a competitive equilibrium are very restrictive, but also because of the special nature of Pareto 'optimality' itself. Let us consider the two issues in turn.

The first theorem can be interpreted as a precise statement of the 'invisible hand', with reference to the market features that lead to positive outcomes (Pareto efficiency) for the economic system. Since such features are very restrictive and unrealistic, the first theorem can, however, be interpreted as a precise statement of the limits of the invisible hand in real situations.

As regards the nature of the optimality generated by the market, it has been demonstrated that perfectly competitive markets can produce equilibrium situations that are Pareto efficient but in which some consumers do not have the resources necessary for survival (Coles and Hammond, 1995) or which are dictatorial; even slavery can be Pareto efficient (Bergstrom, 1971). Thus, Pareto 'optimality' does not assume or imply any judgement about the desirability of a given situation. To say that a certain state of the economic system is Pareto optimal does not mean that it is 'good', but only that it ensures production efficiency, consumption efficiency and 'general' efficiency *in relation to a given initial distribution of resources.* As Sen (1970a, p. 22) argues, a social state can be Pareto optimal but still be 'perfectly disgusting'.

The question then arises of whether a social planner who judges certain Pareto optimal states with sharply divergent utility levels to be undesirable can avoid them and reach more egalitarian positions through the market mechanism. The **second fundamental theorem of welfare economics** enables us to say that he can. It says that every Pareto optimal state can be obtained as a competitive equilibrium if certain conditions are met and as long as resources are redistributed appropriately. This should be carried out with transfers that do not interfere with the properties of the market as a mechanism for resource allocation.

The second theorem has been interpreted as suggesting a clear division of roles between government and the market: the former would have a *redistributive* function while the latter would have an *allocative* function. It establishes a foundation for state intervention in distributive issues.

2.5   Market failures and the first theorem of welfare economics

We have seen that the principal result of specifying the conditions which must be satisfied for the 'invisible hand' to produce a social optimum (as well as identifying

Table 2.1 *Limitations of justifications of the market economy based on the first theorem of welfare economics*

Underlying hypothesis of the first theorem		Reason for criticism		Section in the book
1	Complete competitive markets			
	1.1 Competitive markets	1	Non-competitive regimes	2.6
	1.2 Complete markets	1	Externalities	2.7–2.8
		2	Public goods	2.9
		3	Transaction costs and asymmetric information	2.10
2	Pareto principle	1	Income distribution	2.12
		2	Merit wants	2.13
		3	Specificity of the efficiency concept	2.14

it with the Pareto optimum) is negative. Indeed, the conditions are so restrictive, and the nature of the optimal state that can be achieved under them is so special, that one could say the first theorem of welfare economics clarifies the reasons why the market does *not* usually guarantee an efficient and equitable social state. Table 2.1 summarises these reasons.

The remaining part of this chapter will examine the reasons for **market failures** at the microeconomic level. Chapter 3 will deal with failures at the macroeconomic level, which the literature does not normally include in the category of market failures. Almost all economists use this term to refer to the situations in which the conditions of Pareto optimality are not satisfied (thus excluding failures associated with distributive inequalities and merit goods), and in any case exclude any consideration of macroeconomic aspects. We prefer to follow Stiglitz (1988) and broaden the category of market failures to include those that arise when the conditions of Pareto optimality are satisfied and macroeconomic performance is involved.

2.6   Perfect competition and markets in the real world

We have already pointed out the unrealistic nature of the assumptions of perfect competition. Real-life markets feature imperfect or monopolistic competition, oligopoly and monopoly. In all of these real-market situations the condition that ensures **Pareto optimality** under perfect competition – i.e. **equality of price and marginal cost** – is violated.

The following subsections will examine the realism of the various conditions of perfect competition.

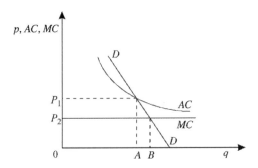

Figure 2.1

2.6.1 *Numerosity of agents and returns to scale*

Let us first examine the case in which the requirement for a large number of agents is not met on the supply side. In particular, suppose we have a monopoly situation that does not depend on historical or legal factors or on barriers to entry but solely on the nature of the *returns to scale* in the industry. If returns are increasing with reference to the relevant tract of the demand curve, we face what is called a ***natural monopoly***: minimising costs for the quantity demanded by the market can be achieved only when there is one firm.[11] This is shown in figure 2.1 (DD = demand function; AC = average cost; MC = marginal cost, which is assumed to be constant).[12]

Let us examine what price a private monopolist will set with an eye to the possibility of achieving an efficient allocation. We already know from microeconomics that the most profitable solution is found at the point where the marginal cost is equal to the marginal revenue, not to the price. Let us try to understand why a solution respecting Pareto efficiency would not be possible. If the monopolist chooses price P_2, equal to marginal cost, producing the quantity $0B$ (which would satisfy the condition for Pareto efficiency) it would suffer a loss, as unit costs are higher than marginal costs. The only way to avoid a loss without distorting the allocation of resources is to set the price equal to marginal cost and cover the loss (equal to fixed costs) by charging all consumers of the good a lump-sum (and hence non-distortional) fee. But how is the firm to divide the total extra payment among its customers? Assume that the number of consumers is not known before the firm is established. If there were only one consumer, that person would have to bear the entire fixed cost; if there were two, they would each bear half the cost; n consumers would pay $1/n$ of the total surcharge. The firm could estimate a minimum number of consumers, n^*, among whom it would divide the fixed cost, charging any additional consumers a price equal to marginal cost only, if it is not to be distortional.[13] Having already covered fixed costs with the surcharge imposed on the first n^* consumers, subsequent consumers will not have to bear the extra burden.

[11] If there were two or more firms, they would have an incentive to merge; or each could seek to increase output in order to reduce costs.
[12] Any decrease in unit cost is therefore due to the existence of fixed costs.
[13] In practice, the charge for fixed costs in addition to the marginal cost is paid by all consumers, but this is not an efficient solution either.

However, given these conditions it is possible that no consumer will want to be one of the first n^* consumers who must pay the surcharge. Each consumer will have an incentive to engage in *free riding* behaviour.

It is equally unlikely that a firm can discover who its customers are by committing them to purchasing a given quantity of goods before it begins production; consumers will avoid signing one of the first, more expensive, contracts (see also Inman, 1987, p. 659).[14]

The free rider problem could be avoided only if the firm were in a position to set discriminatory prices. This would require:

(a) the necessary information to set an *appropriate price* for each consumer, taking account of all the factors (preferences, income, etc.) that determine the price elasticity of each consumer's demand;
(b) no possibility for consumers to *resell the goods on secondary markets.*

However, these are difficult conditions to meet.

In conclusion, we can say that it is not possible for the 'natural' monopolist to set its price equal to marginal cost. Decreasing costs therefore lead to market failure, making it impossible to satisfy Pareto optimality.

Another problem emerges if scale economies are not so great as to lead to monopoly but give rise to oligopoly instead. This is a situation common to many industries – e.g. mining, steel, rubber, chemical, transportation, domestic appliances, telephone services. In this case, rather than responding automatically to the price set by the market, as in perfect competition, each firm is involved in a game in which it sets its price or level of output by taking account of the reaction of its competitors, thus engaging in 'strategic' behaviour,[15] with the consequence that not all possible equilibria will be Pareto efficient.

With monopoly or oligopoly, market failure can be eliminated or reduced by government action in the form of regulation (antitrust legislation, price controls, etc.) or the creation of state-owned firms. We will discuss these measures in sections 6.4, 7.3 and 7.4.

2.6.2   *Free market entry and exit*

Economies of scale have traditionally been considered the most important cause of market failure. More recently, some authors (see Baumol, Panzar and Willig, 1982) have argued that equilibria similar to those produced by competitive markets are possible even in a monopoly or oligopoly situation created by the existence of increasing returns

---

[14] This failure, pointed out by Dupuit (1844) and later by Marshall (1890) and Pigou (1920), was re-examined in great detail by Hotelling (1938). We will return to this issue in section 2.9, which will present an important parallel between market failures due to increasing returns and those caused by public goods.
[15] This is a difficult term to define for those who are not familiar with game theory. Briefly, we can say that strategic behaviour is any behaviour that takes into consideration the possible decisions of others and also seeks to influence them, which is not possible in perfect competition.

to scale. This result depends on the **'contestability' of markets**, i.e. the *possibility* that firms can enter and exit a market freely and without costs.

Assume that the (small number of) firms in the market earn *extra* profits, setting their prices above average cost. If entry and exit are free and costless, new firms will enter the market. They can divide part of the extra profits with the existing firms, gaining market share by setting a lower price until the existing firms react by lowering their own prices. In order to avoid the losses of a possible price war, the new entrants can always exit the market (by assumption, at no cost) having earned net extra profits in the meantime.

The 'hit and run' tactics employed by the new entrants would be possible if entry and exit were completely free and costless; this, then, would be the main condition for competition, and ensuring it would produce outcomes similar to those obtained under perfect competition, despite the presence of scale economies. These tactics would in fact induce incumbent firms to set a price no higher than average cost, thus eliminating any extra profit; it would also reduce costs to a minimum.

Two comments are in order. First, the condition of total absence of entry and exit costs is not satisfied in the real world,[16] where these costs are quite significant. For example, take the specificity of capital (whether human or physical), which gives rise to training, design and adaptation costs for the performance of specific functions; take also the costs involved in promoting specific products. All such costs are **sunk costs** if capital (even its most apparently fungible components) is re-employed in a different use.[17] This means that markets are hardly contestable in real life.

Second, we must stress that if markets were contestable there might still be a distortion in the allocation of resources. Recall that Pareto efficiency requires that price equal marginal (not average) cost. The efficiency that can be achieved in contestable markets is thus generally different from Pareto efficiency and consists simply in the fact that the monopoly firm sets output at a level implying absence of profits and minimisation of costs.

Only in a special case will this situation be Pareto efficient. This is shown in figure 2.2, where the demand curve intersects the unit cost curve at its lowest point, and hence in correspondence to marginal cost. In other cases (figures 2.3 and 2.4) this does not occur: the equilibrium positions are efficient, in the sense that we have production efficiency (minimisation of costs), but they are not Pareto efficient, since price is not equal to marginal cost. The equilibrium in figure 2.4 is efficient (in the sense we have discussed) but is not stable. The incumbent cannot produce $0Q_2$ setting price at $0P_2$; if the market is contestable, new competitors will enter, trying to satisfy part of the demand at a lower price. Nevertheless, given the pattern of costs, there is no room for more than one firm: however output is divided, two firms will have higher costs than a single firm

---

[16] Only in this case, and assuming (unrealistically) that the incumbent reacts slowly to the new entrant, would 'hit and run' tactics work. A relatively simple exposition of this point is given in Vickers and Yarrow (1988). This is a case of 'non-robustness' of the model to even small changes (in a more realistic sense) in the hypotheses.

[17] In some cases, these costs can be partially recovered by appropriately managing human and physical capital.

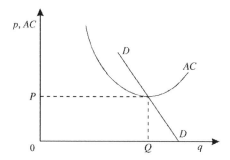

Figure 2.2

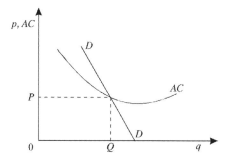

Figure 2.3

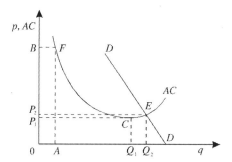

Figure 2.4

(**subadditivity of costs**). This can be illustrated very clearly by imagining a market in which one firm produces $0Q_1$ and the other produces Q_1Q_2 (equal to $0A$). The area $0Q_2EP_2$, which gives the cost of producing $0Q_2$ for a single firm, is less than the sum of the areas $0Q_1CP_1$ and $0AFB$, which give the cost of producing $0Q_1$ and Q_1Q_2 ($=0A$), respectively. This will hold for any division of $0Q_2$.[18] Subadditivity is a generalisation of the concept of scale economies: at point E there are no scale economies, but the unit

---

[18] Obviously, this outcome depends on the exact shape of the cost curve and the level of output. If output were significantly more than $0Q_2$, this would no longer be valid.

cost for one firm is less than that which two or more firms would bear to produce the same quantity $0Q_2$.

Even if contestable markets are not sufficient to ensure Pareto efficient outcomes, considering the other positive features of these markets it may be desirable for the government to seek to reduce entry and exit barriers as much as possible. This is particularly the case for legal barriers such as licences and authorisations to engage in an activity. The objective is especially warranted when these requirements have no other well-founded justification. This is particularly important when alternative solutions, such as nationalisation, are considered inappropriate (for example, because of budget difficulties or the incentive problems arising with public sector managers). We must bear in mind, however, that in many cases entry and exit barriers, such as advertising costs, are a part of firms' strategies. In this case it may be necessary to control the behaviour of dominant firms through antitrust legislation.

2.6.3   *The other assumptions of perfect competition*

Briefly examining the other conditions for perfect competition, note that the presence of a *large number of agents* does not ensure a competitive market if there are *agreements* between them to limit competition. This indicates another possible task for the government: preventing such agreements, which is normally done through antitrust legislation.

The requirement for *homogeneous* goods may not be met, first because of company strategies aimed at differentiating products so as to create specific markets for a given firm's goods in which it holds a monopoly position. Differentiation is accentuated by advertising, which should therefore be controlled by government intervention when it does not convey any real information. Others argue that it is a form of free speech (rather than an instrument of persuasion) and as such merits protection.[19]

Full information about the prices set in the various transactions involving the same good is an equally, if not more, important requirement for perfect competition. Partial information creates one or more largely independent submarkets for the same good (*market segmentation*) and gives rise to the possibility of excess demand in some and excess supply in others, with no tendency towards equilibrium. Section 2.10 examines in detail one aspect of partial information often encountered in the real world: asymmetric information.

2.7   Incomplete markets and externalities

The first fundamental theorem of welfare economics postulates the existence of complete markets, i.e. markets for all existing goods and services at a given time (in a one-period equilibrium) or in all periods covered by the decision horizon (in the intertemporal equilibrium). However, in the real world markets may be **incomplete**

---

[19] The reader might find it interesting to verify the actual information content of the advertising to which we are exposed.

(or missing) due to: (a) externalities; (b) the existence of public goods; or (c) the absence of some spot or forward markets due to transaction costs and asymmetric information in a world of uncertainty (Magill and Quinzii, 1996).

In this section and in section 2.8 we examine externalities. Section 2.9 looks at public goods. Section 2.10 investigates the consequences of transaction costs and the asymmetric nature of information.

The definition of externality allows us to deduce that the absence of payment for the benefit (positive externality or **external economy**) or harm (negative externality or **external diseconomy**) caused to others signifies the absence of a market. This may be due to:

(a) The lack of individual **property rights**[20] over certain goods, which are instead 'common property'; this may induce each individual user to overexploit[21] the goods and to act as a free rider, ignoring the common rights of other individuals and raising these individuals' access costs to the common property: think of air and water and their use in travel, hunting or fishing.

(b) **Jointness in production or consumption**: an individual produces or consumes, creating a benefit (or disadvantage) for others owing to the way in which the activity is carried out. Typical cases of negative externalities caused by joint consumption (*consumption externalities*) are the noise pollution caused by someone listening to a radio at full volume or the air pollution produced by automobiles;[22] examples of activities that can give rise to external consumption economies are tending one's garden or getting an education. Production diseconomies include factory waste disposal (industrial pollution), while examples of external economies are the technological knowledge imparted by staff training programmes, the free dissemination of technological information or the construction of communications infrastructure open to all (*production externalities*).[23] A now famous example of production external economies is that of the reciprocal advantages accruing to the bee keeper and fruit farmer operating on neighbouring plots of land (see Boadway and Bruce, 1984).[24]

---

[20] 'A property right is a socially enforced right to select uses of an economic good' (Alchian, 1987, p. 1031) – or any other good, we might add.

[21] The standard of comparison is the use an individual would make of the good in a certain period if there were individual property rights; this use might be moderated by a variety of considerations, such as the depletion of the goods and maintenance or repair costs.

[22] This externality, like the others we will examine shortly, can also be attributed to the lack of individual property rights. The two causes of externality are not mutually exclusive; they can in fact be considered as two aspects – one legal, the other economic – of the relationships that can exist among the members of a society.

[23] These and similar reasons are why, according to Marshall, it would be possible for an *industry* to produce at decreasing costs while the individual *firms* in that industry face increasing costs: think of the reciprocal advantages created in '**industrial districts**' – areas specialising in a particular line of business, which are still important in a number of countries, such as Italy (see Brusco, 1986; Pyke *et al.*, 1990; Sengenberger and Pyke, 1992). For Marshall, then, external economies made perfect competition consistent with the reality of scale economies at an industry level. However, apart from the case of industrial districts, Marshall used externalities as a purely analytical expedient in order to continue to use a competitive framework even if in the real world the number of industries facing increasing returns to scale was rising, which undermined one of the conditions for perfect competition (numerosity of agents).

[24] The small selection of examples presented here does not give a true picture of the pervasiveness of externalities, which has been underscored by authors such as Hunt (1980).

In general, the effect externalities produce with respect to the Pareto efficiency conditions is to require different MRSs between the various individuals (consumption externalities) and, similarly, different MRTSs across industries (production externalities).

Take consumption externalities, for example. Let the goods being consumed be bread and compact discs. Owing to the condition of her stereo (which can play only at high volume), Alice's music playing causes significant noise pollution for Bob, while his music has no external effect on Alice's utility. If Alice chooses her bundle of consumption goods only with regard to her own utility function (*private* welfare),[25] she will set her MRS between CDs and bread equal to the ratio of their market prices and will have no incentive to move from this position. However, she will thereby consume 'too many' CDs from Bob's point of view, reducing his utility: each of her CDs is a cause of disutility for him. Taking a social point of view would mean changing perspective: each person should take account of all of the effects of his choices, both the impact on his individual utility and that on the utility of others. Hence, in choosing her consumption bundle Alice should also consider the noise pollution suffered by Bob. This would cause her to reduce her consumption of CDs below the level she would choose if she were to take account of her utility alone. The fact is that Alice has no incentive to take account of the harm her consumption of CDs causes Bob, as she does not have to pay a price for that harm; instead, acting on purely private criteria, she equalises the MRS between CDs and bread and the ratio of their prices.

We can show that the condition for an efficient allocation of consumption in the absence of externalities leads to an inefficient allocation if there are externalities. Referring to the previous example, starting from a situation in which the MRSs of the two individuals are equal and are also equal to the price ratio and the marginal rate of transformation (MRT) – e.g. 4 units of bread against 1 CD – the utility of at least one of the two could increase. In particular, if we took one disc from Alice and gave it to Bob in return for an extra 4 loaves of bread for Alice, Alice's utility would remain the same while Bob's would increase, as he would be less bothered by Alice's music. We can conclude that:

(a) the initial allocation was not optimal, as Bob was able to increase his satisfaction at no loss to Alice; and
(b) since everyone's endowment of goods has changed, the MRSs are not equal in the new Pareto superior situation.

We can add that an efficient allocation of consumption requires the MRS between CDs and bread for the person causing a diseconomy to be higher than the price ratio and the MRT. Let us return to our example. Acting on the basis of social criteria (i.e. taking account of externalities), Alice should reduce her consumption of CDs. Doing so, her MRS between CDs and bread increases, since the MRS is decreasing as the consumption of CDs rises. Since the price ratio and the MRT are unchanged, the MRS

---

[25] That is, we assume that she takes no account of the consequences of her choice on Bob's utility.

for the person causing a diseconomy (which was equal to the other person's MRS, the price ratio and the MRT in the purely private situation) is now higher than this common value. In the case of a positive externality, the MRS for the person generating the externality would instead be lower than the other person's MRS, the price ratio and the MRT.[26]

Similar considerations hold for production externalities. Achieving Pareto efficiency in the presence of production externalities requires that the MRTS between the two factors in the production of the different goods be different. This is easily seen if we apply the reasoning we used with consumption externalities.[27]

We can express the same concept in another way. Externalities cause divergences between private costs and social costs or, equivalently, between the *marginal private product* and the *marginal social product*. In the presence of external economies, the marginal private cost is greater than the marginal social cost. By contrast, external diseconomies result in higher marginal social costs than marginal private costs. The opposite holds for the marginal product.

This has important consequences. Take the example of a polluting factory. The polluter does not have to bear the social cost of the pollution and, therefore, in equalising his (private) marginal cost and price he will produce a higher level of output than he would if the social cost of pollution were also included in his calculations. The opposite would occur in the case of external economies. We can thus conclude that industries that generate negative externalities produce more than the social optimum, while those generating positive externalities produce less.[28]

Government intervention can remove the divergence between social and private cost (or product) by internalising the cost or benefit to society caused by the activity of a firm or individual. It can do this in a variety of ways, which we will discuss more fully in section 7.6. In particular, the government can levy taxes (known as Pigovian taxes, as they were initially suggested by Pigou; see Pigou, 1920, chapter XI; 1928) on those who create external diseconomies or it can use regulation to prevent the creation of diseconomies.

2.8 Externalities and the Coase theorem

It has been pointed out that both forms of government intervention (taxes and regulation) assume that some members of society have a right and others do not

---

[26] The reader will easily note the fact that in the presence of externalities, the analytical conditions presented in section 2.2 would not ensure Pareto optimality. With regard, for example, to general efficiency, in such circumstances the position of at least one individual (the person affected by the external diseconomy or the external economy) could improve if we produced, respectively, 1 unit less or more of the good that generates the externality, and correspondingly reduced or increased the quantity of the good assigned to the person who causes the externality.

[27] Take the same example and replace bread and CDs with labour and machinery and utilities *A* and *B* with products *a* and *b* (e.g. oil and fish), assuming that the output of fish is negatively affected by the quantity of machinery used to produce oil.

[28] This argument was originally advanced by Pigou in his discussion of the factors determining the size of the national 'dividend'.

(for example, citizens have a right to breathe clean air, while firms do not have a right to pollute). This particular assignment of property rights is not apparently controversial today with regard to externalities generated by pollution, but disagreement can arise over other forms of externality.

For example, let us take a problem that has served as the basis of innumerable Westerns: the relationship between farmers and ranchers. If property rights are assigned to farmers, the passage of a herd of cattle over a planted field constitutes an injury caused by the rancher to the farmer and therefore calls for corrective public intervention (e.g. a tax on cattle). Were property rights assigned to ranchers, trampling a crop would not give rise to a diseconomy for farmers; in fact, if the cultivation of the land were to hinder the passage of the herd, a diseconomy would arise for ranchers. Hence, the very existence of uncompensated disadvantages or advantages and the identity of those who cause them depend on how property rights are assigned.

According to Coase, the real problem a society must solve is the **choice of institutions**, and therefore the criteria for **assigning property rights**. In his view, institutions should be designed so as to guarantee the maximum possible efficiency. In this regard he makes the following two propositions:

(1) If a number of conditions are satisfied (including prior assignment of property rights and absence of **transaction costs**),[29] agents affected by externalities can reach mutually beneficial agreements without government intervention; moreover, if there is only one position that maximises social wealth, the agents involved will reach that position regardless of the way property rights are assigned.

(2) If there *are* transaction costs, the possibility of reaching the most efficient position through the market can depend on how property rights are assigned; therefore, property rights should be assigned in such a way as to ensure that the most efficient position (which is not necessarily unique) will be reached (see Coase, 1960).

Stigler (1966) labelled proposition (1) the **'Coase theorem'**; this is the most well-known and debated element of Coase's arguments. In addition to the prior assignment of property rights and no (or negligible) transaction costs, the other necessary conditions for this proposition to hold are: the presence of an external authority that ensures the performance of contracts; and a freely transferable *numéraire* good, such as money. Given these conditions, the only role for the government in dealing with externalities should be to assign property rights and ensure that contracts are honoured. In reality, this is not a minor role, since the assignment of property rights, which would in any case require a governmental political mechanism, will determine the final distribution of wealth.[30]

According to proposition (2), transaction costs can have a significant impact on the possibility of producing an efficient allocation of resources. If transaction costs are

---

[29] These are costs for establishing and using markets as a mechanism for resource allocation; they include costs for discovering quoted prices, goods available and the potential partner to a transaction as well as those of negotiating, drafting and enforcing contracts.

[30] Coase does not give much importance to this role, since his aim is only to find the most efficient institutions.

low, their impact will be negligible, but if they exceed the potential net benefit they will discourage those who do not have property rights from proposing an agreement to adopt measures to prevent the damage.

The importance of Coase's work cannot be overstated. First, it underscores the fact that Pigovian analysis of externalities and the proposed policy (taxation) implicitly assume a specific institutional context (i.e. a certain assignment of property rights), without examining the problem of whether an alternative assignment of rights could enhance efficiency.[31] Second, Coase's work underpins the now extensive literature on property rights covering a vast range of institutional issues (see, for example, Pagano, 1992). Nevertheless, his work has received criticism, especially from those who have focused on the interpretation given to it by Stigler, which is based on proposition (1) (the 'Coase theorem').[32]

One important criticism of Coase's work is that the theorem is tautological (Calabresi, 1968). Consider it again: if we assume that agents act rationally and that there are no transaction costs or legal barriers to exchange, in a situation where property rights have been assigned any inefficient resource allocation will be completely eliminated through agreements between economic agents. This statement is tautological if by 'inefficient allocation of resources' we mean (as we normally do) a situation that can be improved for some without worsening the condition of others: such an improvement is always obtainable through bargaining if there are no transaction costs.[33]

A second criticism (Cooter, 1982) considers the possibility that, in the absence of an authority to force individuals to negotiate, they might adopt reciprocal hostile positions such as those envisaged by Hobbes (threats, attacks, attempts to eliminate adversaries, etc.) rather than cooperative behaviour. This criticism apparently misses the mark, since Coase does not argue that, even with no transaction costs, we can do without the government, which among other things would be entrusted with protecting individual rights. However, there is one sense in which Cooter's critique is on target: cooperative behaviour among the members of a society may not depend only on the possibility of procuring economic gain for oneself; there might be no cooperation even when there is an economic gain for the cooperating agents if other, non-economic, considerations prevail. In addition, cooperation can depend on the overall distribution of income.[34]

---

[31] However, with reference to pollution, if we have the polluter pay compensation for the damage caused (and therefore grant other people a right to clean air) it is not only for historical reasons, but also because we feel that this institutional solution is more efficient than the other (attributing property rights to the polluter): in short, we feel it is less costly for society to solve the problem at the source rather than downstream (e.g. by wearing gas masks). The value of Coase's work is that of having demanded explicit – and therefore clearer and more effective – consideration of the terms of the problem.

[32] Coase himself sought to clarify a number of erroneous interpretations in one of his rare but penetrating essays (see Coase, 1988).

[33] Regan (1972) notes that the Coase theorem also establishes the invariance of the final position with respect to the assignment of property rights. However, this invariance is ensured only if certain specific hypotheses are satisfied (for example, 'quasi-linear' preferences; for the significance of this hypothesis, see Varian, 1987).

[34] The sign of the relationship is uncertain. There are reasons to support both a direct and inverse relationship between the degree of cooperation and the degree of inequality of incomes.

A further problem concerns the effects of the way property rights are assigned (proposition (2)). It is certainly true that assigning property rights can have an impact on efficiency. However, this does not imply either that historically prevailing institutions are the most efficient ones (see Pagano and Rowthorn, 1997) or that public action should be geared to such an objective, since – as we have said – the assignment of property rights is relevant also for income distribution.

The last and most important question raised by the Coase propositions regards the possibility that they (especially proposition (1)) can be interpreted as a way of limiting the effects of market failures caused by externalities. Coase's argument (especially proposition (2)) is not unattractive and underscores clearly interesting problems; however, the most important issues arising from the existence of externalities are:

(a) that they conflict with the conditions required by the second fundamental theorem of welfare economics (convex production sets); and
(b) that externalities create analytical difficulties that can jeopardise the existence of a market equilibrium, since they can give rise to discontinuities in the supply functions of goods (Starrett (1972) and Laffont (1976)).

2.9   Public goods

In the competitive markets considered in the theorems of welfare economics, goods are characterised by *rivalry* in their use (for consumers and producers): the use of a good by one person restricts the availability of the good for another. In real-life markets, however, there are also non-rival goods: that is, goods for which an increase in one person's consumption does not reduce its availability for others ('more for you means no less for me'). These are known as **public goods**. Examples of public goods are national defence, monuments, street lighting, lighthouses or radio and television broadcasts. In all of these cases the use of the good by an additional person raises the cost of providing it by (virtually) nothing – i.e. the marginal cost is (virtually) zero. In some cases, such as pollution, it would probably be more accurate to speak of public 'bads', but we will generally use the term 'public goods'.

Global public goods have assumed specific relevance in relation to globalisation (see chapter 19 and box 2.1). These are public goods whose benefits extend beyond national boundaries, such as peace, the environment, biodiversity, health, scientific and technical knowledge, financial stability and shared technical standards[35] (Kaul, Grunberg and Stern, 1999; Kaul *et al.* 2003).[36]

---

[35] Such standards display the typical public good characteristics of non-rivalry and non-excludability. *Standardisation* reduces the costs associated with an excessive variety of goods or artificial product differentiation that can reduce or distort competition. The areas in which standards can be employed are numerous, ranging from accounting rules to weights and measures and technical standards (electrical sockets are just one example).

[36] The typical characteristics of global public goods are described in box 2.1

Box 2.1.   Global public goods: the environment and sustainable development

The **natural environment** consists of everything not built by human beings. Obviously, the action of mankind has always modified the environment, which can sometimes make it difficult to distinguish the natural world from the handiwork of humans. However, we can develop the concept of the *natural environment* to include everything, including that which has been modified to some degree by us, that is directed by laws and dynamics that are not governed by human beings and yet has a decisive impact on the living conditions of current and future generations.

Exploiting the environment means consuming *renewable* and *non-renewable* resources. Renewable resources are biological entities, such as plants and animals, that can reproduce and grow. Their use therefore does not damage the functioning of the **ecosystem** (i.e. animals, plants and minerals and their intrinsic reciprocal relationships), at least as long as the equilibrium stock of such resources is maintained – i.e. as long as we do not exploit resources beyond the point where additions to the stock exactly offset losses. Fishing, forestry, fruit harvesting and animal husbandry are acceptable because the resources involved can reproduce themselves. However, there are minimum and maximum levels of exploitation within which stocks of resources can vary: if stocks should drop below the minimum level of sustainability, extinction becomes a danger; stocks in excess of the maximum can threaten the survival of other resources. Excessive losses of a resource can harm the reproductive capacity of the entire system, altering its physical characteristics in such a manner as to reduce its use in both aesthetic and material terms. Such *environmental degradation* is often irreversible, meaning that any subsequent action on the part of man to restore the resource to its original state is doomed to failure. This is especially true in the modern world, where pressure on the environment is especially intense. There are well-known instances of damage being reversed: the cleaning of the Thames and other British rivers is a case in point. However, in many situations the primary danger is massive, irreversible harm to the environment.

The main limit to the survival of the ecosystem is non-renewable resources. These include fossil fuels (oil, natural gas, coal) and minerals. Such resources cannot be regenerated and every use results in their partial depletion, which in some cases can be extremely rapid. For example, oil reserves have been estimated at 25–30 years, although the likely discovery of new oil fields could extend this by another 8–10 years. Similarly, natural gas reserves are expected to run down in about 30 years, although in this case proven reserves are expanding more rapidly; reserves of uranium should last another 60 years.

The scarcity of natural resources can jeopardise our ability to provide the quantity and quality of supply in the future. In qualitative terms, the destruction of the environment deprives future generations of certain types of enjoyment. In quantitative terms, depletion may limit the volume of goods that they will be able to produce. **Development** should therefore be **sustainable**, i.e. it should not compromise the capacity of future generations to satisfy their needs (United Nations, 1987; World Bank, 2002).

In truth, 'sustainability' is a highly imprecise concept and can be interpreted in a number of ways, giving rise to more or less restrictive definitions. The greatest limit to sustainability is imposed by non-renewable resources. Two approaches are possible, each of which represents a different world view.

Under **weak sustainability**, we can replace natural resources with *renewable capital*. In this case, it is sufficient to avoid reducing aggregate environmental wealth, leaving future generations a stock of aggregate capital at least equal to the stock available to the current generation. One measure of weak sustainability is given by non-negative **effective** or **net saving** of natural resources.[a]

Under **strong sustainability**, which is rooted in ecology, it is necessary to preserve a minimum physical stock of natural capital in order to ensure the availability of certain 'services' essential to the survival of the economic system. Only part of the natural resources in excess of this minimum level can be used for production. Should this minimum stock be tapped, we would risk a catastrophe that could threaten the very survival of the human race.[b]

Notes:
a   This concept of saving – according to the principles of **green accounting**, i.e. national accounts that reflect the effects of economic activity on the environment – considers the consumption of natural resources and the accumulation of pollution.
b   For a more extensive discussion of strong and weak sustainability, see Pearce, Markandya and Barbier (1989); Solow (1992); Pearce and Barbier (2000).

Public goods are a special form of externality, since the producer of such goods does not benefit himself alone but also benefits others, who can use it *for free*: if, for example, a shipping line builds a lighthouse to guide its ships through a dangerous stretch of water, it also creates a benefit for all the ships that sail through the area without receiving any payment from other ships.

Every good produces some externalities, but in many cases these have little impact, such as the admiration or envy the colour of my neighbour's car might arouse (in which case we speak of private goods). In cases such as the lighthouse the external effect is much more significant, perhaps accounting for the entire value of the good. These are public goods.[37] There is a broad spectrum of goods between these two extremes.

---

[37] This is the meaning of *non-rivalry*: the full value of a public good can be used by everyone. For example, let the value of the lighthouse be F. The utility (or profit) function of other ships will include the full value F. By contrast, the colour of my neighbour's car is a negligible factor in the car's value, and I can easily omit it from my utility function.

Curing contagious diseases, road building, parks and sports facilities are all goods with varying degrees of public and private characteristics.

A public good, then, has only fixed costs. Take the lighthouse. Construction and running costs are largely invariant to changes in the amount of services provided to ships.[38] This is in fact an extreme case of increasing returns to scale. We saw in section 2.6 that the existence of increasing returns to scale owing to high fixed costs in a natural monopoly can lead to market failure; considering the dominance of fixed costs in public goods, the two forms of market failure can be thought of as one. In both cases, it is the presence of fixed costs and decreasing average costs that leads to market failure (see Foley, 1970; Heller, 1972; Starrett, 1988; Mueller, 2003), creating an incentive for a cooperative solution: if the supply of one unit of a good to individual A and another unit to individual B costs twice as much as it costs to produce one unit for A (or B), there would be no reason to cooperate: each consumer could choose *independently* whether or not to acquire that good and there would be no benefit from a cooperative decision to provide (consume) the good (Mueller, 2003, p. 11). Cooperation is in principle possible only if provision (consumption) of two units of the good costs less than twice as much as one unit. In practice, cooperation is difficult to obtain since private agents have an incentive to free ride.

We can state the reasons for market failure in the case of public goods even more clearly: if A bears the fixed cost for the production of a public good, both A and B will benefit, and in a competitive economy B could not be charged more than the marginal cost, which for a pure public good is equal to zero. A would therefore have to pay the full cost of the public good, which may well reduce (or eliminate) any incentive to produce the good. In such conditions, each agent will prefer to act as a free rider, waiting for others to produce the good.

There is another aspect of public goods to consider. In some cases, it is impossible to exclude others from the use of public goods owing to the nature of the goods themselves and/or technical reasons: national defence and lighthouses are examples. It is possible to exclude some from using other goods, such as television signals, but exclusion adds to the cost.

The difficulty or impossibility of exclusion accentuates the free rider problem and the impracticability of the market,[39] making the production of public goods a less attractive

---

[38] Note that we have defined the amount produced in terms of the number of services rendered to other ships. A taller or more powerful lighthouse might provide more services, but the effective variability of the size and power of the lighthouse is in reality relatively limited; in any case, for a given size and power, costs do not vary however many ships pass through the area.

[39] Oakland (1987, p. 486) stresses that 'while the inability to exclude costlessly exacerbates the efficiency problem of private provision of public goods, it is not essential for market failure'. We can add that exclusion, although possible in some cases of public good, is not desirable because consumption of the public good by an individual does not preclude consumption by another (apart from possible problems of congestion). There is therefore no reason to set a price (a form of exclusion) for the public good (at least as long as congestion is not a problem). More precisely, since the marginal cost of using a public good is zero, making the marginal user pay a price greater than zero (i.e. practising some form of exclusion) would violate the conditions of Pareto efficiency in a competitive economy, where price is equal to marginal cost.

proposition. If others could be excluded from consumption of a public good,[40] the benefits accruing to its supplier would be equal to any direct benefit from the good itself plus the amount paid by others for the use they have been *allowed* to make of the good. By contrast, if it is not possible to exclude others the only benefits will be those deriving from the direct use of the good.

In other words, since the decision to produce a private or public good by a private economic agent depends on the existence of a non-negative expected profit, by reducing expected profit, non-excludability makes the production of public goods by private agents less attractive. In fact, everyone will have an incentive to free ride, seeking to use the public good that others might decide to produce. This becomes increasingly likely as the number of agents who would benefit from the good increases.

Non-excludability is important because it can explain why some natural public goods are ruined: this is the **'tragedy of the commons'** – i.e. the over-exploitation of common property such as air, water and other natural resources (see Hardin, 1968; Cornes and Sandler, 1996). The two properties of public goods – the essential condition of non-rivalry and the non-essential but very common condition of non-excludability[41] – provide the justification for government intervention to produce such goods directly or stimulate production by others and to finance their production through taxation or to regulate their use in order to prevent the plundering of natural resources.

As demonstrated by Samuelson (1954), the conditions for 'general' Pareto optimality in the presence of public goods are different from those we presented in section 2.3 (the MRS between two goods for all individuals equal to the MRT). Assume there exist only two goods, bread and a lighthouse. With a MRT of 2, we could give up 2 units of bread in order to build a lighthouse. To obtain 'general' Pareto efficiency it is not necessary for each consumer to be willing to reallocate consumption of the two goods in the same proportion – i.e. to have a MRS equal to 2: if there are four consumers, it is sufficient for each to give up 0.5 units of bread in order to have an additional lighthouse with no change in his utility. More precisely, the condition that must be satisfied for 'general' efficiency in the allocation of resources in the presence of public goods is not $MRS^i_{a,b} = MRT_{a,b}$, but rather $\sum_i MRS^i_{a,b} = MRT_{a,b}$, where i denotes individuals and a and b are the goods.[42]

We can present the substance of our discussion so far in terms of a simple **'prisoner's dilemma'** game (table 2.2).[43]

---

[40] Obviously, the ability to exclude also means the ability to demand payment for the use of the good, if one wishes to do so.

[41] Public goods with both characteristics are called **pure public goods**. If exclusion is possible, they are called **impure** or **mixed public goods**. Those who consider both non-rivalry and non-excludability to be necessary conditions of public goods define mixed or impure public goods as those that lack *one* of the two characteristics (not necessarily non-excludability).

[42] Given the similarities between externalities and public goods, it is not surprising that a similar condition holds in the case of external economies. This gives value to the statement in section 2.7 on the conditions for efficiency in the case of externalities: for the person who creates a positive externality the MRS should be less than the MRT and the price ratio. The reader might find it helpful to consult Mueller (2003, p. 26).

[43] The game was initially used to illustrate the situation of two prisoners who cannot cooperate, i.e. they cannot make a *binding* commitment. Take the case of two prisoners accused of the same crime in a situation

Table 2.2 *Prisoner's dilemma and public goods*

		B	
		Build	Don't build
	Build	1 (8, 8)	4 (5, 11)
A	Don't build	2 (11, 5)	3 (6, 6)

Let there be two shipping lines, *A* and *B*, that have the same number of ships operating a given route. Each assesses the consequences of its decision to build or not to build a lighthouse and, at the same time, of the possibility that the other will build it (or not). The first number of each pair shown in the cells of the matrix in table 2.2 indicates the net benefit to *A* from the four possible combinations of the two strategies that *A* and *B* can follow. The second number gives the net benefit to *B*. Thus, if they adopted a *cooperative strategy* and both decided to build they could share the costs and reap a high net benefit (8 each). However, this is not an equilibrium solution *in a private system* because each can expect to benefit more from a non-cooperative strategy. For example, *A* finds it profitable not to build, since by doing so (i.e. acting as a free rider) he would gain 11 (rather than 8) if *B* decides to build and bear the entire cost of the construction. On the other hand, *A* would gain 6 if *B* also decided not to build (compared with a gain of 5 if he decided to build and *B* did not). *A*'s payoff from playing 'Don't build' is in both cases higher than that from playing 'Build'. The same holds for *B*[44] and, therefore, both find it advantageous not to build (cell 3), although this outcome is Pareto inefficient compared with that produced by the cooperative solution (cell 1). The latter cannot be reached except through cooperative action that can only be enforced (or facilitated) by the intervention of a third operator whose objective is to maximise the benefit for the entire society, i.e. a public body.[45] This provides a justification for government financing

where the prosecutor is not sure of obtaining a conviction. Each prisoner is told that if he confesses he will receive a reduced sentence while the other will serve the full term; if both confess, they will receive a less-than-full sentence but the penalty will still be longer than if only one were to confess. If neither confesses, both might be convicted of lesser crimes only. Given these conditions, both prisoners have an incentive to confess. The reader can use the matrix shown in table 2.2, replacing 'Build' and 'Don't build' with 'Confess', and 'Don't confess' respectively, and taking the results of the game to be the length of the sentence.

Public goods can give rise to (or be represented by) different games from that shown (for example, the game of 'chicken', where cooperation is again better than non-cooperation). For both games, see Rasmusen (1994).

[44] In the technical jargon of game theory we would say that the non-cooperative **solution** ('Don't build') is **dominant** for both players. In other words, each has an incentive not to build because the benefit of this strategy is greater no matter what the other decides to do.

[45] Cooperative outcomes may emerge spontaneously when the game is repeated an infinite number of times. Such outcomes are linked to the possibility that an agent will adopt non-cooperative behaviour in response to similar behaviour on the part of others (see, for example, J. Friedman, 1990 and Fudenberg and Tirole, 1991).

or production of public goods, funded by tax receipts rather than the payment of a price.

We must still deal with the problem of the optimal output of the public good, which is difficult to establish for two major reasons: the complexity of mechanisms for measuring preferences and problems of congestion.

As regards the revelation of preferences, if it is not possible to exclude users there is no way to discover the value of the public good for individuals through the price they are prepared to pay. To encourage truthful revelation of preferences, a number of alternative mechanisms have been devised; they are, however, complex and open to manipulation by coalitions. We will return to this issue in subsection 7.5.1.

As regards congestion, we have already said that there are public goods for which non-rivalry is absolute (hence the problem of congestion does not arise). However, there are also public goods for which use by one does not hinder use by another only up to a certain point, beyond which the utility to initial users may decline, probably owing to a decline in quality.[46]

When congestion is particularly severe (i.e. when it becomes a problem for a relatively small number of users), it may be profitable to produce the good through a decentralised system of relatively small communities, such as local authorities (see Tiebout, 1956) or even clubs, hence the name **club goods** given to goods such as swimming pools, tennis courts, etc. (Buchanan, 1965). Each person can choose among the different levels and qualities of public goods and the different financial contributions in the various communities, **voting with one's feet** – i.e. by moving to the community that offers the best conditions (Tiebout, 1956). The existence of congestion in production of public goods lies at the heart of fiscal federalism.

2.10   Transaction costs and asymmetric information

Since the seminal contribution of Coase (1937),[47] economists have been aware of the existence of transaction costs. Such costs are pervasive and relevant for both **spot markets** (those for goods to be delivered in the initial period) and **forward markets** (those for goods whose price is determined in the initial period, which are to be delivered in a subsequent period).[48]

In forward (especially contingent) markets transaction costs may be substantial owing to the high degree of uncertainty about future contingencies which make some

---

[46] However, it is often difficult to distinguish between a reduction in the quality of a public good and a reduction in its quantity.

[47] Later contributions include, among others, Demsetz (1968) and Williamson (1975, 1985, 1989). The approach inaugurated by Coase has been mainly interested in analysing the relative performance of alternative institutions such as markets and firms. According to Coase the choice between coordination – possibly in an occasional way – though the market and continuous coordination through the firm's hierarchy (or the choice between **buy** and **make** for getting some input) depends on the relative transaction costs of the two institutions. We will see in chapter 5 that an application to public institutions has also been suggested.

[48] *Forward markets* are used for securities, commodities and currencies. Forward transactions in the foreign exchange market will be dealt with in subsection 10.1.2. If the performance of a contract is tied to some contingency (e.g. survival, or, alternatively, death of the person insured or occurrence of some damage), we have **contingent markets**.

of them 'uninsurable'. That is why in the real world we find very few forward and contingent markets (commodity forward markets, credit, insurance). In both spot and forward markets, transaction costs are greater in the presence of asymmetric information.

Asymmetric information refers to the different amount of information available to the two parties to a transaction, one of whom is called the *principal* (the party without full information) and the other the *agent* (that with full information). The terms were coined in order to convey the idea that the party without full information relies on the other to carry out transactions with hidden features. Problems of asymmetric information are also known as **agency problems**.

Asymmetric information can give rise to two different situations: (a) *adverse selection*; and (b) *moral hazard*.

Adverse selection occurs when one of the parties (the principal) is unable to observe the situation of the agent or important *exogenous* characteristics of the agent or the good involved in the transaction. It is important to emphasise that the characteristics referred to here already exist at the time the decision to undertake a transaction is made; this is why they are called 'exogenous'.

One problem of adverse selection was first noted by Akerlof (1970) with reference to the used car market, where there is considerable asymmetry of information. Very few buyers have the knowledge to assess the condition and reliability of a used car. When they do have such knowledge, they may still find it difficult to spot hidden defects, unlike the owner, who has gained a thorough knowledge of the car through use. Suppose the market price of a used car refers to one in average condition, with an average number of defects, etc. Only owners of cars in equal or worse condition will have an incentive to sell their cars. The person assessing the value of used cars will consequently adjust the price of an average car downwards, lowering the standard even further and so on, until there are only 'lemons' left or the market disappears altogether. This is a Pareto inefficient situation, because it is likely that the missing transactions would have been mutually beneficial: in other words, there are people willing to purchase a car with certain characteristics at a price (demand price) that is higher than that at which others are willing to sell (supply price). Similar difficulties arise in the exchange of technological knowledge. This is hindered, on the one hand, by the lack of information on the demand side, preventing full assessment of the technological characteristics of the good supplied. On the other hand, should the supplier reveal the characteristics of the good (in order to persuade the counterparty that the exchange is appealing), the potential buyer might no longer be interested in the transaction.

Similarly, insurance companies cannot distinguish between risky and less risky customers or events, which may 'empty' some markets.[49] The same thing can occur when

---

[49] The reader with some knowledge of actuarial mathematics can consider a standard life or health insurance contract offered on fair terms to customers with a different probability of having an accident, falling ill, etc. in the case where each person is perfectly informed about her own probability of experiencing such an event but where the insurance company does not know the individual probabilities of any given customer having an accident, falling ill, etc. Those with a lower risk will not insure themselves, which raises the

patients are unable to distinguish between competent and incompetent doctors, or when financial intermediaries are unable to assess the insolvency risk of potential customers.

Let us take a brief look at bank lending. Suppose that banks are unable to determine the riskiness of specific borrowers and that they charge a uniform interest rate that includes a premium to cover the risk of insolvency. Assume also that the potential borrowers expect a uniform rate of profit net of the risk premium, with higher expected gross returns for riskier lines of business: under these conditions, only customers in the riskiest undertakings will find it profitable to borrow from the banks, thus inducing the latter to raise the risk premium. Each rise in the interest rate (either due to this mechanism or to some exogenous factor such as a credit squeeze) discourages loan demand from less risky customers. An increase in the interest rate would thus have a perverse effect on banks, one that they seek to avoid by closely evaluating the economic and financial condition of their customers and by placing a ceiling on credit supplied to each customer or denying credit to some borrowers, thus rationing credit this way rather than by raising its price (i.e. the interest rate). The behaviour of banks can have a negative effect on the allocation of resources: we cannot assume that the bank allocates credit to projects with the highest expected return (see Ordover and Weiss, 1981; Stiglitz and Weiss, 1981).

The second situation of asymmetric information, the **moral hazard** (or incentive) problem[50], arises when the principal is unable to monitor the actions carried out by the agent or the characteristics of the good conferred (controllable by the agent) following the decision to go ahead with the transaction in a situation where the agent has no incentive to act in the principal's interest. We will give only three examples: (a) the failure of a holder of an insurance policy to take appropriate risk reduction measures; (b) *shirking* by a worker (or manager) in the performance of a contractual duty; (c) the incentive for borrowers to undertake riskier projects as an effect of higher interest rates. In all three cases, the agent has no incentive to perform the contract in the way he would in the case of symmetric information. The term **incentive problems** is thus used to denominate this situation of asymmetric information.

There are various steps that can be taken by private agents to avoid the negative consequences of adverse selection: contracts in which payment is linked to approval of the *quality* of the good or to the *results* obtained using the good; pledges of *collateral*; quality *certification* by professional associations; establishing a reputation (e.g. through trademarks); *signalling* the characteristics of the good or one's own qualities (e.g. being willing to accept conditional contracts that provide for repayment in the case of malfunction). A solution to moral hazard is the use of incentives (e.g. partial insurance, so that the agent has an interest in preventing fire, illness, etc.; higher wages to raise the expected loss of workers to avoid shirking). One solution to the problems raised by both forms of asymmetric information is to abandon prices as an instrument

---

average probability of the event occurring for the remaining people and thus increases the premium rate charged by the insurance company. The effect is to reduce the number of insured people even further. This goes on until the premium rate (including administration costs and a profit margin) is so high as to discourage even the riskiest person.

[50] This is sometimes called the **hidden action** problem.

of rationing and make recourse to *direct rationing* (e.g. credit rationing). However, it is highly doubtful that these or other private solutions can systematically overcome the incompleteness of markets caused by asymmetric information. Take product certification: this has all the characteristics of a public good, giving individual agents an incentive to engage in free riding behaviour (Inman, 1987, pp. 660–1).[51]

The solution is therefore public action in various guises, ranging – in the field of microeconomic actions – from regulation imposing certain behaviour in order to produce better information to the creation of government-owned enterprises to produce public goods or to overcome asymmetric information. There are many examples of such intervention around the world in the areas of insurance,[52] banking[53] and certification.[54]

2.11   Perfect competition and 'imperfections': the theory of the second best

We have frequently remarked on the divergence of real-world conditions and the hypotheses used to obtain certain results, such as the first theorem of welfare economics.

Of course, any scientific proposition must to some degree abstract from certain aspects of reality: to take an example from geography, a 1:1-scale map of the world would not give us a better understanding of reality; it would be a description rather than an attempt to identify key features and, in our field, important connections, causes and effects. Such a map would be at least as awkward as reality itself. The key to scientific abstraction is to set aside features that are less important for the purposes at hand (whether analytical or prescriptive), so that the conclusions reached with the simplified model broadly correspond to the aspects of the economic system that we wish to emphasise or influence. We can thus accept theories that use unrealistic hypotheses where the perspective chosen justifies this choice.[55]

---

[51] Certification has been compared to **network externalities**, i.e. the external effects created in situations such as telephone networks, where the advantages of joining the network increase as the number of people already connected increases. No one has an incentive to join a network with few users, as this would mean bearing a large share of fixed costs.

   Private networks are limited to very large-scale projects, in which, however, there are initially a relatively small number of participants and other circumstances also work to counter the problem of free riding (personal ties, location, etc.). For more on the concept of network externalities, see Economides (1996).

[52] Various forms of public insurance are common in many countries (life insurance, export credit, deposit insurance, etc.). These also partly serve a redistributive purpose in favour of certain categories (small savers, exporters, small depositors, etc.) (see Stiglitz, 1988, pp. 121–2).

[53] Examples are public financial intermediaries, subsidised loans, government-guaranteed student loans and so forth.

[54] For example, the rules and public bodies for supervising weights and measures, quality certification and the certification of financial statements.

[55] According to M. Friedman (1953) the realism of hypotheses is irrelevant and what counts is the *predictive power* of the model. This position has been widely criticised, especially by Samuelson (1963), who argues that it is necessary to use realistic assumptions in any case. The position taken here is very similar to that of Sen (1980) who, after asserting that the description (analysis) of a phenomenon calls for the selection of its most important features, correctly argues that correspondence with reality is neither a sufficient nor a necessary condition for the description (analysis) of the phenomenon. For example, the statement 'Michelangelo produced the statue of David' is not true, since quarry workers and others also played a role, but it is nonetheless useful since it gives us information about the source of the inspiration expressed in the statue, which is the most interesting aspect of a sculpture.

A corollary of this argument is that 'small' changes in real life and/or in the theory do not modify greatly the conclusions of the model, which remain attached to the 'core' of reality: the model is 'robust' with respect to small variations in the hypotheses.[56]

The central idea of the first theorem of welfare economics is that a competitive equilibrium is Pareto optimal. We could therefore argue that small divergences from perfect competition do not lead us far from the Pareto optimum, and that the smaller any divergence is the less we stray from Pareto optimality.

The **theory of the second best** argues the exact opposite: it is not true that 'a situation in which more, but not all, of the optimum conditions are fulfilled is necessarily, or is even likely, to be superior to a situation in which fewer are fulfilled' (Lipsey and Lancaster, 1956, p. 12).

Let us try to understand why. First we must emphasise that where at least one of the conditions necessary for Pareto optimality is not met, we will have an inferior outcome; that is, we can only achieve a second-order optimum with respect to a 'first best' Pareto optimum. Hence the term 'second best'.

Let us consider a situation in which, for simplicity, we wish to assess only one aspect of the general efficiency of an economic system, production efficiency. We know that profit maximising firms in a competitive economy will achieve such efficiency; that is, they will allocate scarce resources among various uses in the most efficient way. One of the ways the conditions of production efficiency can be expressed in a perfectly competitive market is the equality of price and marginal cost. To say that firms fulfil this condition means that they will use resources in the production of a good until the value of the resources used to produce an additional unit (i.e. marginal cost) is equal to the value society assigns the good (i.e. price). If this condition is met throughout the economy, given consumer preferences, the price of each good (say, bread) will exactly reflect the resources necessary (wheat, transportation services, energy, etc.) to obtain the good itself (or rather, the last unit produced); in turn, resources will have been produced following analogous criteria.

If perfect competition in a sector is 'unattainable' (for example, owing to the impossibility of eliminating monopoly in the provision of transportation services),[57] it is clearly impossible to achieve a Pareto optimal situation. However, we might think that the second best outcome would require that optimum conditions for resource allocation be met in the other $n - 1$ sectors (where n can be very large). The theorem of the second best tells us that this is not the case, and it is easy to see why.

Let us consider bread production. If the level of bread output were established by equalising price and marginal cost, too few resources might be used in the production of bread: the cost of transportation services used in making bread is high, not because of the natural scarcity of these services (or the resources needed to produce them) but because providers of these services can exercise their market power. Underproduction

---

[56] If the analytical purpose of the statement concerning the person responsible for the David is to show the source of inspiration, our argument in n. 55 would remain valid even if Michelangelo had delegated part of the execution of the sculpture to others.

[57] We will return later to the nature of such a distortion.

of bread would mean that a distortion in one sector unconnected with any scarcity of resources had been allowed to curtail output in another sector. In our example, if there were no other goods, achieving the social optimum would necessitate setting the output of bread at a level where marginal cost was higher than the market price; this position could be achieved with government subsidies for bread production. We could apply the same reasoning to problems regarding *substitutability in consumption* rather than complementarity in production.[58]

Our example shows how divergence from *one* of the efficiency conditions causes a divergence from *all* the other conditions, in some *non-specifiable* way, given the numerous and complex relationships of complementarity and substitutability among goods. This conclusion is of great importance in the analysis of Pareto efficiency in markets where there are even small divergences from the conditions for perfect competitive equilibrium: the fundamental theorems of welfare economics are not robust.

Nevertheless, the reason a sector may feature an *irremovable* divergence from perfect competition may not be equally clear. The problem is to determine if government intervention can eliminate the divergence and if that intervention should be aimed at this goal, rather than at encouraging (or discouraging) the production of other goods. Let us assume that the cause is in fact 'irremovable': for example, a natural monopoly.[59] It could be argued that nationalisation or regulation allow the state to guarantee non-monopolistic behaviour, even when the causes of the monopoly cannot be removed; for example, efficiency would be ensured if a government-owned monopoly determined output by setting price equal to marginal cost.

Only if the government could not or would not act to achieve this end would we need a generalised divergence from perfect competition in other sectors in order to ensure a second best situation. And there are many reasons why the government might be unable or unwilling to establish, for example, a public enterprise: an excessively high level of public spending, large budget deficits or problems of management control.

An entirely different application of the theory of the second best involves public action itself. With reference to our earlier example, let there be two government agencies, one of which is responsible for competition policy (in particular in the transportation sector) and the other for the supply of essential goods (bread). The problem is whether the two agencies can act separately; that is, can they take decisions in isolation from each other, implementing *piecemeal* policies? We can ask if the bread supply agency can

---

[58] Suppose that there exists an irremovable monopoly in the supply of road transportation services only. What is the efficient pricing policy for the railways, supposing that there are no other industries? Given the substitutability of the two services, we could argue that the purchase of rail services should be encouraged by setting rail prices below marginal cost.

There is a large literature on the theory of the second best. Some contributions were made before the Lipsey and Lancaster article and regard problems with the theory of customs unions (see Viner, 1950; Meade, 1955), 'optimal' production (see McKenzie, 1951) and excess burden of taxation (Corlett and Hague, 1953).

[59] The reader will recall that this exists when a single firm is able to produce at lower cost than that at which two or more firms would produce any level of output. We will discuss natural monopoly at greater length in section 7.3.

act in isolation from the other agency to ensure that the efficiency condition (price equal to marginal cost) is met in its sector regardless of the actions of the other agency, which might in turn seek to fulfil the same conditions in its own industry. In the light of the theory of the second best, the answer is, in general, clearly 'no'. 'Separability' conditions for which the distortions in one sector do not affect the Pareto optimality conditions in others have been identified, but they are extremely restrictive. Nevertheless, these conditions are important for dealing with a number of practical questions of economic policy, such as cost-benefit analysis (CBA) of projects (see chapter 9).

2.12   Income distribution and equity

Having concluded our microeconomic analysis of the causes of market failure due to failure to respect the Pareto optimality conditions, we must now present the remaining two causes, which may occur even when a state is Pareto optimal. In this section, we examine issues relating to equity.

Before beginning, we must note that *'equity'* can assume a variety of meanings. For example, we can distinguish between the *ability* (or productivity) principle (which invokes equality of opportunity or equal starting points) and the *need* (or redistributive) principle (which seeks to equalise outcomes). Liberal doctrine adopts the former, underscoring the need for common rules (procedures) and for everyone to be able to participate in the game, which, however, can end with different outcomes for the participants according to their abilities and their determination. Socialist and catholic doctrines emphasise the latter, underscoring the desirability of equal welfare (or in any case a levelling of certain outcomes) for the members of society, regardless of abilities or procedures.

These are two extreme views that influence to varying degrees the positions actually taken by individuals, political parties and governments in Western democracies. Both visions are part of the 'culture' and ideology of these democracies and any differences, as great as they may be, are nevertheless only differences of degree.[60]

We are particularly interested in the economic aspects of equity (i.e. economic equality). One indicator of this is the *distribution of income*.[61] Even a partial acceptance of the principle of need, in economic terms, means that we must pay attention to the distribution of economic 'values' (i.e. income, wealth, consumption, etc.) among different individuals.

We have noted that a Pareto optimal situation may exist even when the final allocation of goods does not enable certain individuals to survive. These are extreme cases. However, they underscore the possibility that Pareto efficient states may feature income distributions that some, or many or even a majority of the community, consider unjust. This would be an entirely special approach to equity, however: we would be accepting

---

[60] Roemer (1996) offers a review of the existing theories of distributive justice.

[61] This can be examined from different points of view. In a microeconomic context personal (or family) and regional distribution are mostly important. The **functional distribution of income** (i.e. distribution among factors of production) is also relevant in a macroeconomic context.

the idea that equity and efficiency are separable features of reality, namely that one is independent of the other, as in the second theorem of welfare economics.

One criticism of the separation of efficiency and equity concerns the impossibility of making non-distortive re-allocations of resources (Acocella, 1998).[62] The fact that redistribution may 'disturb' efficiency, together with the administrative costs of implementing redistribution, is the basis of the argument that equity can be achieved only to the detriment of efficiency (there is a ***trade-off* between efficiency and equity**).[63]

However, there are many reasons to argue the opposite: an increase in equity can in fact increase efficiency (both static and dynamic). First, the elimination of malnutrition and other forms of privation that weaken the body and limit the potential of human capital all increase the social product and the growth rate of the economy (see sections 3.6 and 8.5; in addition, see Putterman, Roemer and Silvestre, 1998). But inequality also has a negative impact on the social product if certain conventions of community life are violated: the belief that an unequal distribution of income violates some social convention can be a cause of 'moral indignation' in the majority of community members. The inadequate distribution of consumption associated with 'excessive' income inequality will thus generate external diseconomies that may find expression in reduced productivity, social unrest (Caffè, 1948) or other forms of social disruption.[64]

For material or psychological reasons, then, equity may represent a necessary condition for the 'viability' of an economic system. However, it is impossible to specify the extent to which greater equity increases rather than decreases efficiency, precisely because of the conventional nature of equity itself.

Equity can be measured with reference to income or other indicators. Deferring our discussion of some other indicators of 'values' to our examination of development (section 3.5), we will limit ourselves here to a consideration of some data on poverty and the degree of income inequality between 'rich' and 'poor' countries and within the 'rich' countries themselves.

In 2000 1.1 billion people had an annual *per capita* income of no more than $350, or about $1 per day[65] (World Bank, 2004). This is fewer than in 1987 and 1990, but mainly because of reduced poverty in China (see table 2.3).

The $1 per day **poverty line** – i.e. a level of income below which a person is considered to be poor – is a measure appropriate for situations of extreme poverty in less developed countries (LDCs). In developed countries the state of poverty must be evaluated with

---

[62] Taxation and transfers can both affect incentives to work or save.

[63] This trade-off is summed up in the **parable of the leaky bucket**: according to Okun (1975), transferring wealth from the rich to the poor is like carrying water in a leaky bucket: some of the contents are spilled during the transfer, owing to the disincentives to work and saving created.

[64] In this case, 'equity' is intended as *fairness*, meaning the perception of what is considered equitable. For more on the concept of fairness and the possibility that the existence of fair-minded people can force selfish agents to cooperate see Fehr and Schmidt (1999). On concepts of fairness see also Kolm (1984) and Fleurbaey and Maniquet (1999).

[65] The United Nations Millennium Declaration of September 2000 (see United Nations, 2000) specified a set of goals (the so-called 'Millennium Development Goals' (MDGs), for which see United Nations Development Programme, 2003). Goal 1 seeks to eradicate extreme poverty and hunger, by halving between 1990 and 2015 the proportion of people whose income is less than $1 a day as well as the proportion of people who suffer from hunger.

Table 2.3 *Global poverty regional breakdown, 1987, 1990, 2000*

	(%)			No.		
Region	1987	1990	2000	1987	1990	2000
East Asia and the Pacific	26.6	29.4	14.5	418	470	261
Excluding China	23.9	24.1	10.6	114	110	57
Europe and Central Asia	0.2	1.4	4.2	1	6	20
Latin America and the Caribbean	15.3	11.0	10.8	64	48	56
Middle East and North Africa	4.3	2.1	2.8	9	5	8
South Asia	44.9	41.5	31.9	474	466	432
Sub-Saharan Africa (SSA)	46.6	47.4	49.0	217	241	323
Total	**28.3**	**28.3**	**21.6**	**1,183**	**1,237**	**1,100**
Excluding China	28.5	27.2	23.3	880	877	896

Source: World Bank (2004).

reference to higher poverty lines. In 1998 the United States, which although it does not have the highest *per capita* income is unanimously considered the most economically advanced country in the world, had 32.4 million people (or 12.0 per cent of the population) living below the poverty line set for that country, about the same as in 1968 (12.8 per cent) (see Burtless and Smeeding, 2001).[66]

There has been a rise in inequality at the world level among national average incomes over the last four centuries (Williamson, 2002), but the increase seems to have slowed since the 1980s. The distribution of world income among the world's people also worsened over the nineteenth century and through to the end of the Second World War (1945). It appears to have stabilised or deteriorated more slowly since (Bourguignon and Morrisson, 2002). In the 1980s and 1990s inequality within countries has normally increased in most developed and at least some developing countries such as China and India (Forster and Person, 2002; Atkinson, 2003).

Government redistributive action can be carried out through public spending (in particular, transfers to households and/or firms), taxation (especially progressive taxes) and price controls (fixing both minimum and maximum prices; see section 7.6).

2.13 Merit wants

We have already presented the criticism of welfarism (section 2.2), showing among other things that very few people in modern Western society would be prepared to support fully the idea that each person is always the best judge of his own needs under

---

[66] The US official poverty line was defined in the mid-1960s on an *absolute* basis, reflecting the different consumption requirements of households based on their size and composition. The poverty thresholds fixed in monetary terms are updated every year to reflect changes in the Consumer Price Index (CPI).

By contrast, the European Commission, following the approval of the first Community Action Programme to Combat Poverty (see Commission of the European Communities, 1989), has indicated a *relative* poverty line, equal to 50 per cent of the average disposable income per equivalent adult in the member country in question.

all possible circumstances. For example, there is broad agreement that this assumption does not hold for minors or the mentally infirm. The replacement of individual choices with those of some external entity (the essence of *paternalism*) can be extended to other situations.

Paternalism is a feature of much government action, especially through regulation in areas such as safety (mandatory crash helmets, seat belts, earthed electrical sockets, earthquake-proof construction techniques, etc.); health (ban on use of narcotics or, during Prohibition in the United States, alcohol); education (compulsory school attendance up to the age of sixteen); art (conservation of artistic heritage, art subsidies, etc.). Government-run compulsory insurance schemes also have a paternalistic foundation.

Needs whose satisfaction the government wishes to promote regardless of individual preferences are known as **'merit wants'** (Musgrave, 1959). Goods that enable satisfaction of merit wants are called **'merit goods'**.[67]

Such an approach can be justified on two counts:

(a) people may not have information about important aspects of the situation needed to make a choice, or their information (and preferences) may be distorted by advertising or other external influences
(b) their decisionmaking processes do not follow the normal canons of rationality.

Note that the paternalistic argument in support of government intervention in these areas may be supplemented by other forms of justification, such as the presence of externalities or of public goods (as is the case of compulsory education or the prohibition of alcohol consumption). Some might be willing to support certain measures only when this second level of justification predominates. For example, laws such as the prohibition on driving while drunk (given the risk of injuring others) might be acceptable but not those that primarily or exclusively safeguard the health of the individual concerned (e.g. seat belt requirements). In countries with a system of social insurance, a similar justification given for individual safety regulations is the desire to reduce public expenditure – and thus the negative effects on other people – needed to cope with the consequences of injuries (medical care, disability pensions and so on).

2.14 Dynamic efficiency and market failures

The theoretical foundations of market failures from the point of view of dynamic efficiency are often less apparent than those regarding the inability of the market to ensure *allocative efficiency*. The interested reader can consult specialised texts for a more extensive discussion of these issues (see, for example, Hay and Morris, 1991, chapter 18). We briefly mention market failures in particular in terms of innovative efficiency, due to seven key factors:

---

[67] The shift in focus from individuals' needs to objects (goods) is, however, open to criticism: it is claimed that in many cases what is safeguarded is the (consumption of) the good, when in most cases we wish to (or should) promote the welfare of the individual.

(1) the existence of significant *external diseconomies* or the absence of external economies (environmental pollution, exploitation of non-renewable resources, lack of infrastructure and services, crime), of specific relevance if simultaneously present in a given area

(2) **dynamic external economies**, i.e. the benefits or incentives that investment in one industry (e.g. electricity supply) generates for the growth of the market of other industries operating down-stream (e.g. electrical appliances) or up-stream (e.g. generator turbines) (see Rosenstein-Rodan, 1943: 207; Nurkse, 1953: 14)

(3) *asymmetric information* (see section 2.10)

(4) the great *uncertainty* in many basic research projects and technologies applied to sectors such as aerospace, nuclear energy, biotechnology, information and communication technology (ICT)

(5) the existence of **learning-by-doing**, i.e. learning through experience gained during the production process, which prevents newcomers from exploiting dynamic economies of scale (see Arrow, 1962)

(6) *inertia in skills* (the competence trap), which risks firms being locked into a given technological context in the event of technological discontinuities and rapid changes in the environment in which they operate (see Levinthal, 1996)

(7) *financial constraints*, which have an impact on firms with regard to their investment plans, especially research and development (R&D), and on consumers with regard to their decisions about education and human capital formation. We examine this in greater detail in section 3.6.

2.15 Dynamic efficiency and market forms

Our discussion of the negative effects of monopoly in section 2.6 concerned allocative efficiency. With a different success criterion, the assessment of monopoly could differ. This would be the case, according to Schumpeter (1943), were the criterion that of innovative efficiency. In Schumpeter's analysis, innovation is greatest in monopolistic markets. This is so for two reasons:

(1) on the one hand, profits – which are the main source of funds for investment in R&D – are higher

(2) on the other, there is a larger stimulus to invention from the prospect of reaping its fruits in full, an incentive which is missing in competitive markets, where an innovative firm would immediately be imitated by others and would not earn any extra profits.

This position has been criticised on theoretical grounds, and the empirical evidence is contradictory (see Scherer, 1980). In any case Schumpeter's position is indicative of the fact that different optimality criteria (and different theoretical hypotheses) can lead to different conclusions about the desirability of the various market regimes.[68]

We could say that non-competitive market regimes are Pareto inefficient, but they may be efficient in the sense that under certain conditions (contestability) unit costs can be minimised; or they *may* stimulate innovation and hence dynamic efficiency. There are therefore arguments both for and against non-competitive markets. The presence of public enterprises in industries facing increasing returns to scale could help reconcile these different aims. We will discuss this issue in section 6.4.

2.16   Summary

1   The main institutions, in the sense of 'rules' governing social interaction, are the *market* and *government*. Their relative merits can be assessed in the light of the principles of efficiency and equity.

2   A good starting point for our analysis is the criterion of *Pareto efficiency*, owing to the correspondence between equilibrium in a perfectly competitive market and Pareto optimality.

3   The correspondence is expressed by the two fundamental *theorems of welfare economics*. The first states that in an economic system with perfect competition and complete markets, a competitive equilibrium, *if it exists*, will be Pareto optimal. The second states that under certain conditions every Pareto optimal state can be achieved as the outcome of a competitive equilibrium through an appropriate redistribution of resources.

4   The two theorems are a specification of *Smith's 'invisible hand' concept*, which emphasises the virtues of the market in achieving the 'public interest'. However, the unrealistic and particularly restrictive nature of the hypotheses on which the theorems rest points to the limits of the conception and the existence of market 'failures'.

5   As regards the first fundamental theorem, the limits regard:
   (a) the markets that enable the achievement of Pareto optimality (there must be a complete set of perfectly competitive markets)
   (b) the criterion used to assess the 'goodness' of outcomes (Pareto optimality).

6   As regards the second theorem, we should note the weakness of its prescriptive content in favour of the capitalist market. The same Pareto optimal results could be attained with different institutional arrangements, notably *government intervention in the allocative process*.

7   The existence of *non-competitive markets* can be attributed to the invalidity of the assumptions of perfect competition. Two differences are of particular importance: the small number of suppliers, owing to economies of scale, and barriers to entry or exit from the market.

---

[68] Vickers (1995) has stated different concepts of competition and correspondingly different ways through which it can promote economic efficiency (through *incentives* to reduce organisational inefficiency, *selection* of efficient organisations and *stimulus* to innovation).

8 It is not profitable for a private monopolist to set price *equal to marginal cost*, which means that the Pareto optimality conditions are not met.

9 According to the theory of *contestable markets*, free market entry and exit is the most important factor in ensuring quasi-competitive market results; however, entry and exit costs make it difficult for a potential entrant to 'hit and run'.

10 *Incomplete markets* are associated with externalities, public goods, transaction costs and asymmetric information.

11 *Externalities* cause a divergence between private costs (or benefits) and social costs (or benefits). The conditions for achieving Pareto efficiency in the presence of externalities differ from those that hold without externalities, and meeting them requires public intervention.

12 According to Coase, government intervention is not necessary to reach the most efficient state: if there are no transaction costs, it will be possible for agents to reach mutually beneficial agreements. However, if there are *transaction costs*, government intervention is needed to assign property rights in such a way as to ensure that the most efficient outcome is reached. There have been many specific criticisms of Coase's position. The most general criticism underscores the fact that the theorem does not narrow the range of market failures: the presence of externalities conflicts with the second theorem since it implies non-convex production sets and jeopardises the very existence of a market equilibrium.

13 *Public goods*, characterised by non-rivalry and non-excludability in use, are a special category of externality. Non-rivalry gives rise to free riding behaviour, which leads to market failure and the need for government intervention for the production, financing or regulation of such goods. A prisoner's dilemma game can be used to illustrate the nature of public goods.

14 *Private, asymmetric information* gives rise to agency problems in the form of 'adverse selection' and 'moral hazard', which can prevent the formation of both spot and forward markets (by raising transaction costs) and thereby hinder the efficient allocation of resources. Incompleteness of markets can be overcome by public intervention.

15 Even small disparities between reality and the hypotheses used in the fundamental theorems of welfare economics can give rise to very large modifications of the conditions needed to achieve a Pareto optimum and, in particular, can *reduce the desirability of perfect competition*.

16 The free operation of the market does not ensure acceptable *income distributions*. Acceptability can be judged on the basis of different principles that influence government action to varying degrees.

17 Rejection of the welfarist assumption introduces a further example of (microeconomic) market failure: it may be felt necessary to act on behalf of individuals *regardless of their preferences* (merit wants).

18 Market failures also arise from the point of view of *dynamic efficiency*. Some economists argue that monopoly, which reduces allocative efficiency, can increase innovative efficiency.

3　Market failures: macroeconomic aspects

3.1　The instability of a capitalist market economy: macroeconomic failures

In chapter 2, we examined traditional market failures in the light of microeconomic theory.

However, a more complete assessment of the ability of real-life markets to act as an 'invisible hand' cannot neglect numerous recurring 'crisis' situations of unemployment, inflation, external payments imbalances or underdevelopment, which do not appear to be immediately explainable in terms of the classic microeconomic market failures. These situations are manifestations of the **'instability'** of capitalist market economies.[1] 'Instability' here does not simply mean the failure of the economy to converge towards equilibrium but also the possibility that the economy may evolve along a *non-optimal path* from the point of view of efficiency and/or equity and may remain in such a non-optimal state.

These aspects of reality are difficult to model using general equilibrium theory – and, often, even with other existing microeconomic theories. Let us examine some of the reasons for this conclusion, focusing on general equilibrium theory.

It is difficult to believe that persistent mass unemployment, often experienced by market economies, is a voluntary phenomenon. *Involuntary unemployment*, however, cannot arise in models of general competitive equilibrium: if all markets are in equilibrium, the labour market will also be in equilibrium and any unemployment must be voluntary.

Microeconomic theories explain relative prices, not the absolute price level; they have never succeeded in modelling a monetary economy in a satisfactory way. For these reasons, they cannot take account of inflation. Since models are developed in real terms, such theories have limited explanatory power in dealing with problems of imbalances in the balance of payments, since this is expressed in monetary terms. Finally, problems such as underdevelopment are difficult to tackle with static theories such as general equilibrium theory.

Advocates of the virtues of the 'invisible hand' have attempted to account for some of these features of reality (unemployment, for example) using general equilibrium theory

---

[1] See, among others, Robinson (1962b); Minsky (1975); Vicarelli (1984).

and introducing hypotheses that explain the malfunctioning of prices (*price rigidity*); in this context, a central role has been given to the assertion that government intervention has contributed to this rigidity and, therefore, to the crises we are examining.

A more convincing analysis has been advanced by others who have argued that the cause of the instability is to be sought in *structural features* of the markets that prevent them from operating in the way and with the results predicted by general equilibrium theory.

Adopting this approach, we will define as *'macroeconomic' failures* those failures associated with the instability of market economies. More specifically, unemployment, inflation, balance of payments disequilibria and underdevelopment can be considered macroeconomic market failures for the following three reasons:

(a) they are **failures**, since they reflect the presence of inefficiencies and/or injustice, raising the same problems we encountered in our analysis of microeconomic failures
(b) they are **market** failures, since they are intrinsic to the working of actual markets, as we will show in the following sections; there can also be *government failures* of the kind emerging in relation to the political business cycle, but these are of a different nature and we defer our analysis of them until chapter 5
(c) they are **macroeconomic** failures, since the theory that best explains them currently appears not to be a microeconomic theory, but rather a macroeconomic one.

The macroeconomic aspect of failures connected with 'instability' should not be misleading, preventing us from associating them with the more traditional microeconomic failures. In the light of point (a) above, we can see that the problems arising from the operation of the market are much the same and can always be expressed in terms of inefficiency and injustice, even if some are microeconomic in nature and others are macroeconomic.

Let us now examine in greater detail the main forms of instability both individually and in relation to each other. The following two sections describe the characteristics of unemployment and inflation, clarifying the problems of efficiency and equity they are associated with. Section 3.4 presents the main economic theories that have dealt with these phenomena in a short-run framework and that identify the roots of such kinds of instability in the operation of the private or public economic system.

Section 3.5 deals with the problems of slow growth and underdevelopment from a purely descriptive point of view; the explanations for this form of market failure and its consequences for employment are analysed briefly in section 3.6. For expository reasons, the definition and description of the balance of payments is given in section 3.7 and the discussion of the underlying theories is deferred to chapter 10.

3.2   Unemployment

By unemployment we essentially mean **involuntary unemployment**. This arises when there are (potential) workers willing to accept employment at, or even slightly below, the prevailing (real) wage rate (Keynes, 1936), but the demand for labour is insufficient

Table 3.1 *Unemployment as a percentage of the total labour force in selected industrial countries, various years[a]*

	Canada	France	Germany[b]	Italy	Japan	Sweden	United Kingdom	United States
1950	3.6	2.3	8.2	6.9	1.9	1.7	2.5	5.2
1955	4.3	2.4	4.3	7.0	2.5	1.8	2.1	4.2
1960	6.8	1.8	1.0	3.9	1.7	1.7	2.2	5.4
1965	3.6	1.3	0.5	5.0	1.1	1.2	2.2	4.4
1970	5.6	2.4	0.6	4.9	1.1	1.5	3.1	4.9
1975	6.9	4.0	3.6	5.8	1.9	1.6	4.3	8.3
1980	7.5	6.2	2.9	7.5	2.0	2.0	6.4	7.0
1985	10.7	9.8	7.2	8.1	2.6	2.9	11.2	7.2
1990	8.1	8.6	4.8	8.9	2.1	1.7	6.9	5.6
1995	9.4	11.4	8.2	11.5	3.1	8.8	8.5	5.6
2000	6.8	9.3	7.9	10.4	4.7	5.9	5.3	4.0
2001	7.2	8.6	7.9	9.5	5.0	5.1	5.0	4.8
2002	7.7	8.8	8.6	9.0	5.4	4.9	5.1	5.8
2003	7.6	9.4	9.7	8.6	5.3	5.6	5.0	6.0

Notes:
[a] After 1985 data are adjusted to ensure comparability over time and to conform to the guidelines of the International Labour Office (ILO).
[b] Prior to 1995 data refers to Western Germany.
Sources: Maddison (1991), until 1985; OECD (2004) for subsequent years.

to provide them all with jobs: the supply of labour is therefore '*rationed*'. We will not discuss either *voluntary* or *frictional unemployment*.[2]

In the post-war experience of market economies we can distinguish two different phases of employment and unemployment: before 1973 (the year of the first oil crisis) and after 1973. In the pre-1973 period, unemployment was in steady decline in various countries; in the subsequent phase, it increased significantly, the most notable exception being that of the United States (table 3.1).

Unemployment in market economies is certainly well below the levels seen during the Great Depression, when the unemployment rate[3] reached 24 per cent in the United States (1932) and 20 per cent in Great Britain (January 1933). Nevertheless, the return to double-digit unemployment rates is an indication of the relevance of a problem that many had thought solved from both an analytical and a policy point of view.

[2] On Keynes' definition, **voluntary unemployment** occurs when, for various reasons, a worker does not accept a wage rate equal to the marginal productivity of his labour; **frictional unemployment** is caused by errors of calculation, unexpected changes, etc. that give rise to temporary imbalances in the supply and demand for labour in given fields and areas. The data available are not normally able to distinguish the various types of unemployment.
[3] The *unemployment rate* is defined as the ratio between the number of unemployed and the labour force (people who offer their services in the labour market and find – or do not find – employment). If U denotes the unemployed, N the employed and LF the labour force, $LF = N + U$. The unemployment rate is $u = U/LF$.

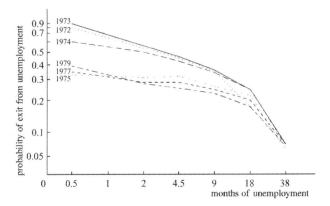

Figure 3.1
Source: Malinvaud (1984).

The existence of involuntary unemployment represents a loss of efficiency in static and dynamic terms. In static terms, it means that it is possible to improve the situations of some individuals (the unemployed themselves) without making others worse off.[4] Moreover, unemployment of human resources for a prolonged period may cause these resources to deteriorate: the deterioration of skills is one of the reasons why the probability of an unemployed person finding work declines as the period of unemployment lengthens (look at figure 3.1, which refers to France). Although the various curves refer to different years and reflect the different macroeconomic conditions prevailing in each year, they are all clearly decreasing, indicating a decline in the probability of finding a job as the period of unemployment lengthens.

In addition to causing a loss of efficiency, unemployment usually increases the inequality of *income distribution*. The economic and social consequences of unemployment can be eased at an individual level by government action to redistribute income, such as paying unemployment benefits or guaranteeing a minimum income.

Although unemployment benefits have been introduced in all developed countries, both their level relative to wages and their duration vary markedly across countries.[5] No **basic income** or **citizen's income system** has so far been introduced.

When unemployment benefits are sufficiently high, it is easier to fire or lay off workers, as the benefits reduce the cost of these actions to both the worker and the firm. Although the latter bears part of the cost, it faces less worker resistance. Unemployment benefits are therefore both an instrument for supplementing personal incomes and for increasing the flexibility of the economic system and **industrial relations** – i.e. relations between employers and employees.

Some economists oppose unemployment benefits because they supposedly create *labour supply disincentives*. However, according to the available evidence, only the

[4] At least some of the unemployed have a marginal productivity that is higher than the *'reservation wage'* – i.e. the wage they are willing to accept.
[5] A fairly comprehensive survey of unemployment benefits in various countries is provided by Layard, Nickell and Jackman (1991, tables A1 and A2, pp. 514–16).

maximum duration of benefits, not their relative amount, seems to have an impact on the labour supply and, then, on the duration of unemployment and the effectiveness of unemployment in reducing wages (Barr, 1992).

Unemployment represents an *economic cost for society as a whole* in terms of lost output. This cost must be added to the non-economic costs of unemployment, which come in the form of frustration, social exclusion and the possibility of social unrest and higher crime levels.[6] The existence of all these costs explains the commitment to achieving 'full' employment taken on by the governments of many market economies in the post-war period, partly under the influence of solutions suggested by Keynesian theory.[7]

Nevertheless, this commitment was hedged by at least two considerations:

(1) First, the term 'full' employment was not intended literally as 100 per cent of the labour force. The commitment concerned involuntary unemployment in excess of frictional unemployment, since the latter was considered a normal consequence of 'imperfections' in the markets. In reality, frictional unemployment corresponds to vacancies that would be extremely difficult to fill immediately owing to a lack of information and short-term inertia (e.g. the time needed to change jobs, which frequently involves moving from one place to another).[8]

(2) The full employment position is akin to a 'precipice': 'The point of full employment, so far from being an equilibrium resting place, seems to be a precipice over which, once it has reached the edge, the value of money must plunge into a bottomless abyss' (Robinson, 1937, p. 24). One explanation is that the effects of the pressure of demand for goods operate on supply, which in full employment is completely inelastic. Perhaps more important is another argument emphasised by Robinson: the incompatibility of full employment with the traditional wage system of liberal capitalism (Robinson, 1962b, p. 118). Such incompatibility is associated with the 'discipline' exerted by unemployment on wage demands (Marx, 1867; Kalecki, 1943; Shapiro and Stiglitz, 1984; Bowles, 1985). The absence of a (large) pool of unemployed able to compete with employed workers lessens fears of redundancy and, thus, undermines worker effort while encouraging demands for wage rises. In other words, it is possible for the objective of full employment to conflict with 'factory discipline' or the social and political stability of the market economy. Such conflict tends to emerge in the form of inflation, which we examine in the following section.

---

[6] We could also add workers' greater dependence and vulnerability to blackmail by employers. However, this is not a net cost to society, since it is offset by a benefit to employers. It is nevertheless an important feature of unemployment, since it plays a role in the 'disciplinary' function of unemployment, which we will discuss shortly.

[7] This occurred in the United Kingdom with the White Paper on employment policy of 1944 and in the United States with the Employment Act of 1946. These important changes in public policies reflected the work not only of Keynes but also of other reformers, such as William Beveridge.

[8] There are other situations in which unemployment coexists with vacant jobs. For example, there may be *mismatching* between the supply and demand for certain skills, which can be eliminated only with (re)training.

3.3   Inflation

It is well known that the term 'inflation' normally refers to a (sustained) rise in the *general level of prices* and, therefore, a *decline in the value of money*. There are many types of inflation, which can be distinguished by:

(a) their immediate causes: demand-pull inflation, financial inflation, credit inflation, supply inflation, cost-push inflation, profit inflation and imported inflation
(b) the pace of price increases: creeping inflation, moderate inflation, galloping inflation, hyperinflation.

Demand-pull inflation is caused by the pressure of demand exceeding supply when the economy is making full use of its physical and human resources.[9] Financial and credit inflation are forms of demand-pull inflation triggered, respectively, by an increase in government deficit spending (i.e. without a corresponding increase in tax revenues) and by excessive bank lending when the economy is operating at the full employment level.[10]

Supply inflation is a consequence of shocks that reduce supply (natural disasters, war, major restructurings of production that temporarily reduce productive capacity).[11]

Cost-push inflation consists in the shift of higher production costs (in particular, variable costs) onto prices. **Profit inflation** is specifically associated with an increase in *profit margins* made possible by imperfectly competitive markets. An effective way to analyse the effects of changes in costs and profit margins on prices is offered by the **full cost principle** (mark-up theory).[12]

---

[9] If there are no sectoral supply bottlenecks (as there are in real life), the rise in prices should begin to emerge only when aggregate demand exceeds supply.

[10] The best known example of this occurred in 1929 in the United States, when bank credit fuelled stock market speculation that ended in October of that year with the collapse of share prices. For more on this type of inflation and the related problems, see Minsky (1975).

[11] One important case occurred around 1990 with the destruction of productive capacity in Eastern European countries in the wake of institutional and political upheaval, the opening of markets, the abandonment of price controls and industrial reconversion and restructuring.

[12] The full cost principle states that prices are formed by adding to variable (or direct or prime) costs (unit labour costs, or the ratio of labour costs to average labour productivity; raw materials; energy, specific taxes) a gross **mark-up** rate including the normal industry-wide (net) profit margin as well as provision for indirect (fixed) costs (depreciation, etc.). If for simplicity we consider unit labour costs only, we have $p = (w/\pi)(1 + g)$, where p is price, w is unit labour costs, π average labour productivity and g the gross profit margin or gross mark-up rate. Taking the logarithms of the two terms of the price equation and differentiating with respect to time, we have the following relation: $\dot{p} = \dot{w} - \dot{\pi} + (1 + g)$ where the dot over the variable indicates the rate of change of the variable per (infinitesimal) unit of time – e.g. $\dot{p} \equiv (dp/dt)/p$. The same relation holds approximately for discrete changes.

 The reader not familiar with calculus can consider that for any variable z which is the product of two other variables, x and y (i.e. $z = x \cdot y$) it is true that $\dot{z} \cong \dot{x} + \dot{y}$, where $\dot{z} \equiv (\Delta z/\Delta t)/z$ and similarly, the dot on each of the other variables indicates the percentage rate of change of that variable. This can be demonstrated rather easily if we first put $z_{t+1} = z_t + \Delta z$ and similarly for the other variables. If $z_t = x_t \cdot y_t$ is subtracted from $z_t + \Delta z = (x_t + \Delta x) \cdot (y_t + \Delta y)$ and the difference is divided by $z_t = x_t \cdot y_t$ we obtain $\dot{z} = \dot{x} + \dot{y} + \dot{x}\dot{y}$, where $\dot{x}\dot{y}$ is a higher-order term, negligible for small changes in the variables. Similarly, one can show that, if $z = \frac{x}{y}$, $\dot{z} \cong \dot{x} - \dot{y}$. From the combination of these two rules (the one for a variable that is the product of two other variables; the other for a variable equal to the ratio of two other variables) the expression indicated above for changes in prices can be obtained.

Imported inflation has various possible roots: a prolonged increase in a country's exports fuelled by excess foreign demand (which may give rise to inflation in the foreign country, hence the term *imported* inflation); a large capital inflow that expands the monetary base and stimulates demand; or, finally, an increase in the prices of imported raw materials and semifinished goods due either to autonomous decisions by their producers (as in the oil crisis) or to a currency depreciation.

The distinction between the various types of inflation should not be overemphasised, since there are often situations in which the various causes *interact*, as is the case with cost-push and demand-pull inflation: an increase in aggregate demand, in addition to provoking a rise in prices on its own, brings the labour market closer to full employment, thereby causing a rise in wages[13] that further boosts prices.

As regards the rate at which prices increase, we can categorise inflation as:

- **creeping**, when prices rise slowly (say 2–3 per cent annually)
- **moderate**, if the rate of increase is less than 10 per cent annually
- **galloping**, when prices rise at double or even triple digit rates
- **hyperinflation**, an annual rate of at least 300 per cent.[14]

Inflation can be measured with one of the various price indices available[15]: the *implicit GDP deflator* or its components (*consumption deflator, investment deflator*, etc.), *wholesale prices, producer prices, consumer prices*, etc. As we know, these indicators refer to different baskets of goods.[16]

Inflation in the post-war period has been very different in the industrial and developing countries. In certain of the latter (for example, in Latin America) galloping inflation or even hyperinflation are usual, although they do not necessarily cause the value of a currency to collapse, creating the need for its replacement – i.e. the need for another instrument able to act as a *medium of exchange*. Except for the years immediately following the Second World War, inflation in the industrial countries was normally of the creeping sort, at least until the 1973 oil crisis. The increase in oil prices caused inflation to rise almost everywhere, although it never evolved into hyperinflation (table 3.2).

By contrast, there were many cases of galloping inflation prior to the Second World War. Moreover, periods of inflation were frequently followed by periods of *deflation*

---

[13] According to the Phillips curve, a reduction in the unemployment rate causes an increase in the *rate of change* in money wages.

[14] These figures are indicative only. Cagan (1956) offers a study of the most important cases of hyperinflation. For an analysis of inflation in Germany after the First World War, which in November 1923 saw prices reach 1,422.9 billion times their pre-war level, see Bresciani Turroni (1937).

[15] We must bear in mind, however, that certain potentially inflationary situations are imperfectly measured by changes in prices. For example, excess demand, rather than raising prices, may be reflected in an increase in imports or activate other rationing mechanisms (e.g. lines at the cash register or delivery delays). This is called **'repressed'** or **'hidden' inflation**.

[16] Each indicator can be worked out differently to emphasise the dynamics of inflation over time. For example, we can divide the change in the index in the last year (e.g. from April 2003 to April 2004) by the value of the index at the beginning of the period (April 2003) to calculate the **twelve-month** (end-of-period) rate of change; if the change in the index in the last 12 months (from May 2003 to April 2004) with respect to the previous 12 months (May 2002 to April 2003) is divided by the average value of the index in these 12 months (May 2002–April 2003), we obtain the **average inflation** rate for the last year.

Table 3.2 *Average annual percentage change in consumer prices in selected industrial countries, various years[a]*

	Canada	France	Germany[b]	Italy	Japan	Sweden	United Kingdom	United States
1951–5	2.5	5.4	1.9	4.3	6.4	5.6	5.5	2.1
1956–60	1.9	5.9	1.8	1.7	1.5	3.7	2.6	2
1961–5	1.5	3.8	2.8	4.9	6.2	3.6	3.6	1.3
1966–70	3.8	4.3	2.6	2.9	5.4	4.5	4.6	4.2
1971–5	7.3	8.8	6.1	11.3	11.5	8	13	6.7
1976–80	8.6	10.7	4.2	16.6	6.6	10.5	14.1	8.4
1981–5	7.4	9.6	3.9	13.7	2.7	9	7.2	5.4
1986–90	4.4	3.1	1	5.6	0.8	5.8	4.9	3.7
1991–5	1.5	2.2	3.4	5	1.4	3.8	3.6	3.1
1996–2000	1.6	1.2	1.1	2.3	0.3	0.6	2.5	2.4
2003	2.8	1.2	1.0	2.8	−0.3	1.49	1.4	2.3

Notes:
[a] After 1985 data are adjusted to ensure comparability over time and to conform to the guidelines of the International Labour Office (ILO).
[b] Prior to 1995 data refers to Western Germany.
Sources: Our calculations from sources quoted in table 3.1.

(especially before 1914), an example of the **'classical' cycle** in which prices rise during expansionary phases before falling during recessions. Since 1945, not only have the (rare) recessions not been accompanied by falling prices, but there have even been situations in which stagnant demand and inflation have coexisted (hence the term **'stagflation'**).[17]

Inflationary pressure emerges whenever the recipients of money income (wages, profits, rents) seek to increase their own share of real income at the expense of others (i.e. consumers).[18] The resistance of others and/or constant real output (which may

[17] In comparing the figures in tables 3.1 and 3.2, note that after 1973 many countries have recorded a rise in both unemployment and inflation. See Acocella and Ciccarone (1994, 1997) on stagflation as a breakdown in the classical cycle and the regularities underlying the Phillips curve.

[18] Obviously every income earner is also a consumer. Nevertheless, one may try to be a free rider, since the benefit he receives from an increase in income may be greater than his loss as a consumer.

For example, take a 10 per cent increase in wages in the bread industry, which for simplicity we assume is not accompanied by an increase in productivity. If bread factory owners do not want to see their profit margins reduced, the wage rise originates a 10 per cent rise in bread prices in the absence of other direct costs, as we can see from the full cost principle. This increase harms all consumers, including workers in the bread industry. The latter, however, receive a net benefit, since their incomes have increased by 10 per cent while their costs have risen by less. The 10 per cent rise in the price of bread causes the cost of a typical basket of goods to rise by less: for example, if spending on bread accounts for 20 per cent of overall consumption expenditure, then the increase in spending is equal to 20 per cent × 10 per cent = 2 per cent.

We can present the same argument in another way. By definition, redistributing income means that the advantage to some is equal to the disadvantage of others. Even though the agent responsible for the redistribution can be both beneficiary and victim, the redistribution may still be worthwhile if the benefit accrues to a relatively small number of agents while the cost is spread over a larger number. Obviously,

be physically impossible to increase in the short run) causes an increase in prices. This definition of inflation covers the basic cost-push and demand-pull types of inflation. It shows that inflation is a symptom of social conflict and, at times, in its more extreme and uncontrolled forms, of social collapse.

The struggle for income distribution of which inflation is an expression is never neutral, in the sense that it always involves some change in the distribution itself, since an increase in the general (or absolute) price level is always accompanied by a *change in relative prices*: some can only keep their prices unchanged (if they are exposed to fierce competition) or succeed in raising their prices by less than the average rise, while others are able to raise their prices by more than the average.

Not only income but also wealth is redistributed by inflation. For example, the value of a bond with a fixed nominal value declines in real terms in an inflationary setting, to the advantage of debtors (typically firms and, often, the government) and the detriment of creditors (typically households).[19]

Obviously, the extent of the redistribution of income and wealth depends on many factors, including the degree to which inflation has been *anticipated* by agents and their *bargaining power*[20] and, therefore, their ability to adjust the price of the good they offer. In order to protect themselves from unexpected rises in the general price level, some agents are able to introduce **indexation** mechanisms that link their income to changes in the general price level, as sometimes occurs with money wages and yields on securities.

The costs to some agents of the redistribution of income and wealth caused by inflation are cancelled out for society as a whole because they are offset by gains for others. There are therefore *no net costs* from inflation for the whole economic system as far as redistributive aspects are concerned. Some have even argued that moderate inflation can benefit the entire economic system owing to the stimulus it gives to investment: firms, which are generally debtors, see the cost of the capital they raise in the financial market decline in real terms and, at the same time, the rise in prices enables them to increase total revenue (turnover), while other costs may not rise to the same extent owing to inertial factors.[21]

Inflation has positive net costs for society as a whole, however, since it gives rise to specific costs generated by the need to adjust price lists or automatic payment machines (called **menu costs** and **slot machine costs**, respectively) or by the reduction in real money holdings, due to the increase in interest rates that normally accompanies

---

this is likely to be the case if the changes regard a single industry and are not transmitted to other sectors. Nevertheless, even if transmission is likely, any single agent may find it profitable to try and increase his income, acting as a free rider.

[19] Government can also benefit from inflation if it imposes progressive taxes ('fiscal drag': see chapter 12).

[20] This is a function of all the elements of the productive structure that determine effective competition. The international openness of the economy *can* have some influence. In reality, in certain cases (such as the government and other public bodies) we cannot speak of bargaining power, since their power is based, for example, on a direct ability to affect prices – e.g. through fiscal or monetary policy – that cannot properly be considered to fall within the framework of negotiations.

[21] A rapid survey of the literature that, for various reasons, has pointed out the advantages of a positive inflation rate is given by Drèze (1993, pp. 32–3). Modigliani, Baldassarri and Castiglionesi (1996) argue the opposite view.

an increase in the inflation rate, thereby raising the opportunity cost of holding money. People therefore make more frequent visits to the bank to withdraw cash, incurring what are known as **shoeleather costs**. Some argue that these costs, while perhaps small in themselves, cause inflexibility that has harmful effects in terms of unemployment.

Apart from these considerations, the costs to society of creeping or moderate inflation are relatively modest, especially compared with those associated with unemployment, with which there can be a trade-off. On the other hand, reducing inflation can become an economic policy objective, for essentially two reasons:

(a) to reduce the social conflict associated with it
(b) to reduce the risk of experiencing the uncontrollable growth of prices in the form of hyperinflation.

The social costs of galloping inflation and hyperinflation are certainly much larger. In this case, there is less transparency in the working of the mechanism of relative prices, which underlies resource allocation, and distortions and inefficiencies arise. In some cases, there is also a risk that an economy afflicted by hyperinflation might even have to do without the benefits of money, which would not be able to fulfil its essential functions as a unit of account, medium of exchange and store of value.[22]

3.4   The short-run analysis of unemployment and inflation

This section examines unemployment associated with the level of aggregate demand from a short-run perspective as well as inflation that can emerge in the same short-run time frame. We defer an analysis of the long-run causes of unemployment to section 3.6.

3.4.1   *The theory of Keynes and Kalecki*

First of all, it is important that we understand the 'vision' of 'classical' macroeconomics,[23] which is very similar to that underlying Smith's 'invisible hand': a capitalist system is driven by forces, generated by individual interests, that on their own can produce an equilibrium showing some kind of optimality. On this view, economic phenomena appear as the manifestations of natural laws (Vercelli, 1991) rather than the product (at least in part) of the existing institutional context, which is reduced by the 'classical' economists to the operation of a pure *barter economy*. With reference to

---

[22] See Dornbusch and Fischer, 1994 on the costs of galloping inflation and hyperinflation.
[23] Macroeconomics – as we understand this term today – essentially began with Keynes. If by the 'classics' we intend – as he did – all those who preceded him (i.e. the 'classical' economists proper plus the neoclassical or marginalist school), it is clear that a true 'classical' macroeconomic theory does not exist precisely because macroeconomics came into being with Keynes. Nevertheless, we can use the term with reference to a *reconstruction* of classical thought in terms of aggregate variables. This is in part an arbitrary operation, both as an *ex post* reconstruction and as a summing together of a wide variety of schools. For example, our discussion does not apply to the work of Malthus, Marx and Sismondi, who did not at all believe that the capitalist economic system was immune to economic crises.

the concepts introduced in section 3.1, according to this vision the economic system has a *natural order* that gives it 'stability', especially in the sense of ensuring full employment of resources.

We said that the market is virtually the only institution considered by the 'classics'. Obviously, they were aware of the existence of money, but they believed that the essence of the functioning of the *real* economy could be represented without considering money itself. **Say's law**, which asserts that supply creates its own demand, certainly holds in a barter economy: saving is in itself an act of investment which ensures equilibrium in the goods market. In a *monetary economy*, Say's law no longer holds,[24] for reasons we will examine shortly. Planned saving and investment in a monetary economy could still be considered to match if we thought that there was a mechanism to rebalance them – i.e. to coordinate the related decisions. That is, we could assume the existence of a price for saving (the interest rate), whose movements would balance planned saving and investment. Such a hypothesis is, however, not realistic and evades the important question of coordinating different agents' decisions in a monetary economy and, with it, the question of *uncertainty*, dominating all economic choices.

Keynes' *General Theory* (1936) is the crowning achievement of decades of research, stimulated by the problems of his time, on the fundamental and distinctive features of an economic system based on competition and private capital accumulation. Keynesian analysis[25] focuses on the changes in employment caused by changes in aggregate demand.

Compared with the classical argument that changes in *relative* prices would always be able to ensure that aggregate demand was at the full employment level, the Keynesian view is that *nominal* price movements are slow relative to changes in quantities. The *stickiness* of *nominal* prices (especially their downward *rigidity*) is a consequence of the distributive conflict between the various classes of income earner: each individual will tend at least not to reduce the price of the good he supplies, fearing that the prices of the goods he purchases will remain unchanged or will rise. Paradoxically, a monetary economy makes it more difficult to coordinate the decisions that determine the income distribution.

Nevertheless, this should not lead us to think that ensuring greater price flexibility would enhance the ability of the system to re-establish equilibrium. Take the rigidity of money wages. According to the 'classics', the flexibility of real wages, obtained by reducing money wages in conjunction with a (less-than-proportional) reduction in prices, would allow an economy to attain a full employment level of income. However,

---

[24] Say's law can be seen as one of the first analytical statements of the concept of the 'invisible hand'.

[25] The analysis in the *General Theory* incorporates a number of simplifying assumptions, of which we should mention:

   (a) the existence of a *closed economic system*, or a situation in which net exports are zero; this assumption was later dropped by other authors
   (b) a *short-run outlook*, which means that productive capacity and technology, consumer preferences and the degree of competition are given.

apart from the stability problems that can arise, this position is based on an incomplete vision of the real wage that focuses on its role as a cost (to the firm) while neglecting its role as income (for the worker). This is an unjustifiable extension of a proposition valid at the microeconomic level to the system as a whole.[26]

According to Keynes, a reduction in money and real wages will increase employment only if *aggregate demand* does not fall, which depends on the effect of the wage reduction on the variables that determine demand: the propensity to consume, the marginal efficiency of capital and interest rates. Changes in money (and real) wages affect these three variables in many ways. It is worth reviewing the most important arguments, since they give us an idea of the complexity of Keynes' analysis of a matter that is often dealt with in a schematic and oversimplified way:

(1) The fall in real wages causes a *redistribution of income from workers to other classes*, including *rentiers*, that have a lower propensity to consume.
(2) The reduction of wages in a country relative to foreign wages improves the *international competitiveness* of its goods.[27]
(3) The reduction in prices associated with the fall in money wages causes the *real value of debts to rise*, with the consequent possibility of bankruptcies – or, in any case, a reduction in investment demand.[28]
(4) The fall in real wages may induce expectations of either further reductions or, by contrast, an increase in subsequent periods. This will have corresponding negative or positive effects on *investment*.
(5) The reduction in money wages accompanied by some reduction in prices lowers the *transactions demand for money* associated with the payment of wages themselves. If the nominal quantity of money remains unchanged, this is equivalent to an increase in the real money supply, which leads to a fall in the interest rate. This should have a positive impact on investment unless it triggers expectations of future rises in long-term interest rates and wages owing to the increase in investment (Keynes, 1936, chapter 19).[29]

In general, the multiplicity of effects produced by changes in the real wage raises doubts about the ability of this mechanism to ensure equilibrium in the labour market. The inadequacy of the real wage as a price capable of returning the labour market to equilibrium is compounded by the inexistence of a price that can match saving

---

[26] For an individual industry the reduction in monetary wages shifts the labour supply curve to the right and produces a new equilibrium at a lower price level and a higher level of output and demand.
[27] This is one of the few cases in which Keynes goes beyond the hypothesis of a closed economy in the *General Theory*. Strictly speaking, we should ignore these effects, but they are significant in economies with a high degree of international openness.
[28] At the same time, there may be an increase in the propensity to consume of agents with a surplus of savings (creditors), but it is unlikely that this increase can offset the decline in investment for many reasons, which include: greater awareness on the part of entrepreneurs of the effects of price changes; the 'epidemic' nature of the fall in investment, including that due to bankruptcies (the **Fisher effect**). Note that the effect described by Fisher (1932, 1933) implies a direct relationship between aggregate demand and the price level. The reader should be aware that some authors give a different content to the Fisher effect, referring to Fisher's analysis of the relationship between interest rates and inflation (e.g. see Summers, 1983).
[29] The increase in investment could generate expectations of future price rises.

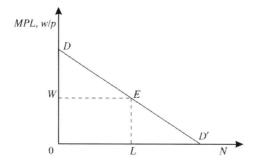

Figure 3.2

and investment decisions. In a monetary economy saving is separated from investment and the two functions are carried out by two correspondingly distinct classes of agents, unlike the barter economy of the classical world, where saving and investment always coincide because at every moment one decision exactly corresponds to the other. In a monetary economy, the separation of saving and investment decisions introduces an element of uncertainty about the likely return on the new capital (investment). This return is linked to *expectations* about many aspects of the future, such as the level of demand and cost conditions. The decision process behind investment choices thus depends on the expectations underlying the **marginal efficiency of capital** as well as on the **'animal spirits'** of entrepreneurs.[30] If entrepreneurs are not optimistic about future returns on investment, they will not invest profits, and aggregate demand will tend to fall. This can be shown with the help of a simple diagram, based on the analysis of Kalecki (1933), which has a number of points in common with that of Keynes.

In figure 3.2, the line DD' shows how the marginal productivity of labour (MPL) changes as the number of employed workers, N, changes. If the number of workers in a given period is L, equal to full employment, and the current real wage is $0W$, the value of output, $DEL0$, will be distributed between workers (who receive $EL0W$) and capitalists (who receive the remainder, equal to DEW).

Now suppose, for simplicity, that the workers consume all of their income and capitalists do not consume anything, investing instead.[31] If investment is exactly equal to profits (DEW), demand will be equal to output at full employment. However, nothing guarantees that this will happen: investment could be less than profits if the outlook for future profitability were poor. In this situation, a fall in money wages that was not accompanied by a proportional fall in prices (for example, owing to monopoly production in the goods market) could also contribute to reducing effective demand

---

[30] As is well known, investment in Keynes normally depends on the interest rate, *given* the marginal efficiency of capital. Here we have sought to underscore the uncertain character of the assessments that generate the latter variable. Shortly we will deal with the uncertain and conventional nature of the former.

[31] This hypothesis, typical of the classics, is compatible with the Keynesian hypothesis that the marginal propensity to consume of the system as a whole is less than 1.

further, since it would depress the level of the real wage, $0W$ – and, by hypothesis, the level of consumption.

In a monetary economy the capital value of financial wealth is also intrinsically unstable. This introduces a further source of uncertainty, which may induce individuals to avoid holding wealth in forms that do not allow them to protect its value – that is, they may attempt to remain 'liquid' (i.e. demand money). As Keynes points out, in this framework the **interest rate** 'is the reward for parting with liquidity' for a certain period of time and is therefore the price that brings demand for and supply of money into equilibrium. The interest rate has little to do with saving decisions and therefore cannot function as the price that equilibrates saving and investment.

What is the source of the instability in the value of financial wealth? As is well known, it is due to expectations of possible fluctuations in the interest rate.[32] This underscores the entirely *conventional* nature of this variable. The interest rate is the compensation demanded by someone in return for not holding his wealth in liquid form; it will rise as the number of people who think that in the future its level will be high increases; on the other hand, '*any* level of interest rates which is accepted with sufficient conviction as *likely* to be durable, *will* be durable' (Keynes, 1936, p. 203, emphasis in original).

For all of these reasons, aggregate demand and employment in a capitalist system are unstable and may be far below the full employment level. In Keynes' view, government intervention through monetary policy and, above all, fiscal policy is the only force that can bring the system to full employment.

The tools of Keynesian analysis have helped to explain not only shortfalls in aggregate demand and unemployment, but also situations of excess demand, providing specific recommendations on how to avoid inflationary pressures. In his pamphlet *How to Pay for the War* (Keynes, 1940), Keynes himself analysed such situations in relation to the problems caused by the Second World War. Under wartime conditions, demand tends to increase excessively, primarily owing to the stimulus of military expenditure which, together with ordinary consumption and investment demand, usually gives rise to excess demand and inflation. This had happened during the First World War: government deficit spending was initially financed by issuing bonds, while authorities sought to curb private spending with higher interest rates. The attempt to avoid or contain inflation was not successful, however, as overall spending was not reduced at all: financing the war effort with public debt coupled with a restrictive monetary policy increased households' disposable income (thanks to the interest they received), thereby sustaining a high level of consumption and causing price inflation. It also increased the public debt burden. Governments were thus induced to finance their deficits with monetary base. However, the small rise in nominal interest rates that resulted, together with high inflation, reduced the real interest rate and, therefore, provided an incentive to

---

[32] In particular, the idea that the interest rate might rise in the future generates fears of capital losses from holding unredeemable fixed-interest securities.

invest, stimulating demand through this channel as well. The increase in the quantity of money together with the constraint on output growth imposed by the full employment of resources therefore had further inflationary consequences.

Keynes' suggested recipe during the Second World War was to ration private consumption, prohibit certain uses of savings (such as the purchase of durable or luxury goods and the securities of firms producing civilian goods) and channel savings into bank deposits, which would be used to subscribe government securities issued at low interest rates in order to reduce financing costs.[33]

Keynes' analysis contains a wealth of considerations on the functioning of a capitalist economy and, as we have seen, shines light on the many fundamental reasons why it is difficult to believe that the *normal* condition of such an economy is one of full employment. Many economists have sought to identify specific situations that can give rise to (involuntary) unemployment, casting it as the result of *exceptions* and *imperfections* with respect to a normal state of full employment.

The absorption of Keynes' thought into orthodox 'classical' theory began just a few months after the publication of the *General Theory* with the work of Hicks (1937), to whom we owe the *IS-LM* model familiar to anyone with at least an elementary grounding in macroeconomics. In this model, only a liquidity trap could prevent the system from reaching full employment. The liquidity trap would render monetary policy ineffective, making it necessary to use fiscal policy to return the economy to full employment.

The *IS-LM* model is an excellent teaching tool for arriving at an initial approximate characterisation of the functioning of an economy in the short run and of the effects of using various instruments of macroeconomic policy. This is one of the reasons why the model has gained such wide acceptance. Indeed, we too make use of it, given the lack of more satisfactory models that would enable us to express at least some of the most significant aspects of the Keynesian analysis in formal terms.

The *IS-LM* model was the starting point for the so-called 'neoclassical synthesis'. Many authors contributed to its development, with a leading role being played by Modigliani (1944), who identified the rigidity of nominal wages as an additional special case that would give rise to unemployment.

The absorption of Keynes' thought into the 'classical' framework continued with Patinkin's (1956) work. This provided the analytical foundation for the *monetarist models* rejecting the effectiveness of Keynesian policies. We will examine this development in the next two subsections. A different strand of analysis has been developed more recently by a number of economists linked in some way to Keynesian thought (the New Keynesians), who pursue the analysis of market 'imperfections' or, more generally, situations that give rise to involuntary unemployment. This group frequently employs concepts introduced and used in microeconomics, such as scale economies, market power and informational asymmetry, thus explaining unemployment in terms

---

[33] This technique of channeling savings was called the **'monetary circuit'**.

of certain types of *microeconomic failure*. We will examine this line of analysis in subsection 3.4.3.

3.4.2   'Natural' unemployment and the limits of government according to Friedman

Milton Friedman and the monetarists conceive the market economy as intrinsically stable, unlike Keynes and the Keynesians.[34] They do not deny the instability shown in numerous real-life situations, but they attribute it to *government action* rather than to the private sector.[35]

Friedman revives the *quantity theory of money*, adapting it to take account of Keynesian innovations. This theory (of which the Fisher equation – also called the quantity equation – is the most complete expression) postulates a causal, direct and proportional relationship between the *quantity of money* and the *price level*, assuming a constant level of money velocity (i.e. a constant demand for money) and of transactions (which corresponds to full employment). Friedman argues that changes in the money supply are the principal systematic determinants of the growth of nominal income.[36] Nevertheless, the seemingly greater openness of neo-quantity theorists to the possibility that money does not affect just prices but also real income is in practice very limited, as we will see shortly.

M. Friedman (1968), in fact, argues that these effects are normally temporary and associated with inflation. More precisely, he argues that monetary policy cannot peg the market interest rate[37] or the current (or market) unemployment rate below the natural interest rate and the natural rate of unemployment, respectively, for more than very short periods without triggering rising inflation. Let us see why.

First, we must clarify the meaning of a number of concepts introduced by Friedman. The **natural interest rate** is basically the equilibrium price between the demand for capital (investment) and the supply of capital (saving). The **natural rate of unemployment** is that where the number of job vacancies is in a certain equilibrium relation with the number of unemployed; since there is a broad balance between supply and demand for labour, wages tend to remain constant. The natural unemployment rate is determined by *structural factors*, such as the level of economic development, the value placed

---

[34] It is possible to argue that a homogeneous Keynesian strand of analysis does not exist. Although well aware of the large differences of positions, we feel it is still possible to use the term.

[35] For example, Schwartz (1975, 1981) argues that the depression of 1929 is largely attributable to the Federal Reserve's excessive concern about stock market speculation, which prompted a monetary tightening. For a rebuttal of this position, see Temin (1976).

[36] Consider the identity known as the **equation of exchange** or the **Fisher equation**: $L_s V = pT$, where L_s is the quantity of money, V velocity, p the price level and T transactions. If we exclude financial transactions from T – money is defined as the medium of exchange for goods and services – and consider the structure of the real economy as given (especially the degree of vertical integration), we can replace T with income, Y (which the reader will recall is equal to market output net of the double counting for intermediate goods). In this case, V would no longer denote the *transactions* velocity of money, but rather the *income* velocity of money. In addition, if we replace velocity with the fraction of income individuals desire to hold as money balances, k (the inverse of velocity), we can rewrite the Fisher equation as $L_s = kpY$. If k is constant (as Milton Friedman basically assumes), changes in L_s will be reflected in nominal income, pY.

[37] It is more accurate to speak of an *interest rate structure*, given the variety of financial assets.

on leisure and the characteristics of the labour market (e.g. flexibility, segmentation, availability of job information). M. Friedman (1968) emphasises that 'natural' does not mean constant over time or that economic policy cannot influence the natural rate, but simply that government action can be directed only at the *structural factors* that determine it. As we will see shortly, monetary or fiscal macroeconomic policies do not affect these structural elements.

Imagine that the market interest rate and unemployment rate are at their natural levels; the goods market and the labour market are therefore in equilibrium. An increase in the quantity of money, causing an increase in the level of real balances, will initially lead to a reduction in the interest rate and an increase in the demand for goods, especially capital goods, with an accompanying rise in output. At the same time employment will rise, owing to the simultaneous rise in supply and demand for labour. This is apparently a contradiction: the increase in the demand for labour can occur only if we assume a *decline* in the real wage; while an increase in the supply of labour occurs only if there is a *rise* in the real wage. We can overcome the inconsistency by assuming that:

(a) Expectations are adaptive (i.e. agents adjust them on the basis of the past value of the reference variables).[38]
(b) The various agents have different information and reaction times to information: in particular, firms are better informed than workers of past or current price increases. Firms expect a fall in the real wage (valued in terms of their product) and correspondingly increase investment and their demand for labour. For their part, workers, noting an increase in nominal wages and not in prices (i.e. incorrectly predicting the increase in the prices of consumer goods), expect an increase in real wages and therefore increase their supply of labour.

However, the *money illusion* of workers is only temporary, and in the long run the unemployment rate should rise to its natural level. At the same time, the market interest rate will rise due to the increase in prices, until it is again at its natural level.

Let us examine in detail the behaviour of the market unemployment rate using the *'expectations-augmented' Phillips curve*. The original **Phillips curve** (which was statistically observed in Phillips, 1958, and is widely used by Keynesians) is the inverse relationship between the rate of change in money wage rates, $\dot{w}$, and the unemployment rate, u: $\dot{w} = \varphi(u)$, with $\varphi' < 0$. According to Friedman, this relation is unlikely to remain stable over time.

To understand the reasons why the curve tends to shift, Friedman first draws attention to the fact that workers are not interested in the nominal wage but rather in the *real*

---

[38] More precisely, under this hypothesis, expectations for a variable are revised in each period in proportion to the difference between the actual value of the variable in the previous period and the value expected for the same period, i.e. in proportion to the error in the forecast made in the previous period. In formal terms, the expected price at time t can be expressed as: $p_t^e = p_{t-1}^e + \gamma(p_{t-1} - p_{t-1}^e)$, where p_{t-1}^e is the expected price at time $t-1$, while p_{t-1} is the actual price and $0 < \gamma \leq 1$ is a constant. If, in place of the price level at time t, p_t we consider the inflation rate in period t, $\dot{p}_t$, expectations regarding the inflation rate in period t are adaptive if: $\dot{p}_t^e = \dot{p}_{t-1}^e + \gamma(\dot{p}_{t-1} - \dot{p}_{t-1}^e)$. In the special case where $\gamma = 1$, we have: $\dot{p}_t^e = \dot{p}_{t-1}$; i.e. the expected inflation rate for period t is equal to the actual rate in the previous period (static expectations). This simple relation will be used shortly.

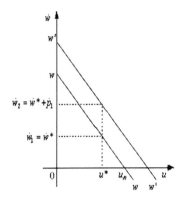

Figure 3.3

wage. Therefore if they want to ensure a certain increase in the real wage (say, 5 per cent), they will be satisfied with a 5 per cent increase in the nominal wage only if they expect no rise in prices. The original Phillips curve implicitly incorporates the hypothesis that the expected rise in prices, $\dot{p}_t^e$, is nil (or that the nominal wage rate matters). However, this hypothesis is not necessarily valid. In our example, it certainly does not hold if the 5 per cent increase is inflationary[39] because the consequent increase in prices will affect expectations about future price changes.

Hence, we can replace the equation $\dot{w}_t = \varphi(u_t)$ with the more general equation: $\dot{w}_t = \varphi(u_t) + \dot{p}_t^e$. We therefore cannot speak of a single Phillips curve, but rather a map of (short-run) Phillips curves, each with a different value for expected inflation. If the expected inflation rate for period t is equal to the effective inflation rate in the previous period, $\dot{p}_{t-1}$, substituting we have $\dot{w}_t = \varphi(u_t) + \dot{p}_{t-1}$.

This relationship is shown in figure 3.3, where for simplicity we have drawn only two Phillips curves. Assume that in period zero the system has been at u_N for some undefined time: the rate of wage change in the current period is $\dot{w}_0 = 0$; since $\dot{w}_{-1} = 0$ as well, if we assume $\dot{\pi}_{-1} = 0$ and $(1+g)_{-1} = 0$, we have $\dot{p}_{-1} = 0$ and, therefore, $\dot{p}_0^e = 0$, for the specific hypothesis of adaptive expectations. Hence, $\dot{w}_0 = \varphi(u_N) + \dot{p}_{-1} = 0 + 0 = 0$ and $\dot{p}_0 = \dot{w}_0 - \dot{\pi}_0 + (1+g)_0 = 0 - 0 + 0 = 0$.

This situation will last as long as there are no shocks. An expansionary monetary policy would shift the system from u_N to $u_1 = u^*$ in period 1, causing a wage increase $\dot{w}_1 = \dot{w}^* + \dot{p}_0$. If $\dot{w}^* = 5\%$, then $\dot{w}^* = 5\% + 0 = 5\%$. Hence, in period 1, immediately following the monetary action the system moves along the initial Phillips curve ww. If we continue to have $\dot{\pi}_1 = (1+g)_1 = 0$, we will have $\dot{p}_1 = \dot{w}_1 = 5\%$. This means that if the system remains at $u_1 = u^*$ in period 2, we have $\dot{w}_2 = \varphi(u_1) + \dot{p}_1 = 5\% + 5\% = 10\%$. Since this holds for every value of $u \neq u_N$, it follows that in period 2 the valid Phillips

---

[39] The possibility that the wage increase is inflationary can be analysed in terms of the full-cost principle (see section 3.3), according to which $\dot{p} = \dot{w} - \dot{\pi} + (1+g)$. Since we can, as a first approximation, consider $\dot{\pi}$ and $(1+g)$ as constants, we can express the rate of change in prices as a function of the rate of change in wages alone: $\dot{p} = \dot{w} + \text{constant}$, and, if the rate of change in wages depends on the unemployment rate (as in the original Phillips curve), we can write $\dot{p} = f(u)$. This relation is called the **derived Phillips curve**. In our example, we will assume for simplicity that $\dot{\pi} = (1+g) = 0$, hence $\dot{p} = \dot{w} = \varphi(u)$.

curve is the initial curve augmented by inflation expectations – i.e. the curve $w'w'$. Summarising, the variables would have the following values in the various periods:

t	$\dot{p}^e$	u	$\dot{w}$	$\dot{p}$
0	0	u_N	0	0
1	0	$u^* < u_N$	5%	5%
2	5%	$u^* < u_N$	10%	10%

In this light, we can also understand how – according to Friedman – monetary policy can trigger a *self-fuelling inflationary process*. Is there a limit to the rise in the inflation rate? Actually, such a limit must exist. Recall that the process was triggered by the rise in real balances caused by an increase in the money supply with prices (initially) unchanged. When prices have risen by as much as the money supply (if the rise was a one-time increase) the expansionary effect of real balances will dissipate and there is therefore no reason for the unemployment rate to be less than the natural rate. If, however, there has been an increase in the *rate* of money supply growth, the expansionary effect of real balances will end when the *rate* of increase in prices has risen by the same amount.[40] Nevertheless, at that point, since an inflationary process is already under way (at a rate equal to the growth in the money supply), agents will expect prices to rise at the same rate in the future and the rate of wage change will also be positive (and equal to the expected inflation rate), despite the fact that the unemployment rate is at its natural level.

We can draw the following two conclusions from our analysis.

(1) According to the modern quantity theorists, monetary policy is effective only in the *short term*; it can keep the market unemployment rate below the natural unemployment rate for a short period only. Doing so for a longer period would require the quantity of money (or its rate of growth) to be increased even further, which will generate inflation higher than that initially anticipated by workers, thus creating scope for holding the unemployment rate below the natural level. Therefore, we can guarantee an unemployment rate below the natural rate only at the cost of rising inflation.

(2) Again according to the monetarists, the long-run **Phillips curve** is **vertical** – i.e. for any inflation rate unemployment will remain at its natural rate. There is therefore *no trade-off between unemployment and inflation*, except in the short run.

What positive role do neo-quantity theorists attribute to monetary policy? In the words of M. Friedman (1968), it must keep the economic machine 'well-oiled': the change in the money supply must be equal to the average variation in money demand which, if there is no change in the velocity of circulation, is equal to the change in

---

[40] At the same time, workers will have noted the increase in the inflation rate.

real income in a stable price environment.[41] Therefore, if aggregate demand grows by an annual average of 3 per cent over a sufficiently long period, the money supply must also increase by 3 per cent annually.[42] This is the essence of the so-called **simple rule** (a case of predetermined government behaviour or, as we will see in section 4.4, an automatic rule), which Friedman contrasts with *discretionary intervention* by monetary authorities, especially the use of countercyclical monetary policy, which consists in policy measures decided on a case-by-case basis by the authorities: when demand is weak, the central bank takes expansionary action; in situations of excess demand it adopts a restrictive stance.

The superiority of automatic rules over discretionary measures is not solely due to the temporary nature of the effects of discretionary policy on employment and its cost in terms of inflation,[43] but also to the possibility that it might have perverse effects, owing to the length and variability of the *effect time lag* of monetary policy – i.e. the delay with which the effects of this policy feed through to the economy: the economy could start responding to a monetary expansion or contraction in a phase of the business cycle that is completely different from that in which the policy action was originally undertaken. The consequence would be an *aggravation*, instead of a moderation of the cycle.

Friedman is equally sceptical of fiscal policy. First, a change in government spending can turn out to be ineffective even in the short run if it is perceived to be temporary. In this case, the change would have no effect on permanent income and therefore on consumption. Even if it were effective in the short term, it would not be so in the long run, since an increase in deficit-financed government spending without issuing money would **crowd out** interest rate-sensitive private spending – i.e. investment. By shifting the *IS* curve (from IS^0 to IS' in figure 3.4), the increase in public spending would initially raise income above the corresponding natural level of unemployment (Y_n in figure 3.4) but would also cause:

(a) An increase in the *interest rate* (see point *B* in the figure), given that the money supply is constant while income increases, reducing the money available to meet speculative demand.
(b) An increase in the *price level or inflation rate*, for the reasons given in our discussion of the expectations-augmented Phillips curve. Inflation reduces the real money supply, causing *LM* to shift to the left, thus determining a further rise in interest rates, until demand returns to the level corresponding to the natural rate of unemployment (*C* in figure 3.4).

---

[41] Taking the version of the quantity theory presented in n. 36 ($L_s = kpY$), we have $\dot{L}_s = \dot{k} + \dot{p} + \dot{Y}$. If $\dot{k} = 0$, i.e. the velocity of circulation is constant, since we want $\dot{p} = 0$, then $\dot{L}_s = \dot{Y}$, as we have argued.

[42] Friedman had initially suggested a 2 per cent annual increase in the money supply, assuming a decline in velocity of 1 per cent per year. This hypothesis seemed to be supported by econometric evidence (although this was later refuted) and was consistent with the conception of money as a luxury good, i.e. a good with an income elasticity of demand greater than unity.

[43] Friedman argues that one of the greatest costs of inflation is a consequence of the difficulty of gauging relative prices, which can give rise to an inefficient allocation of resources.

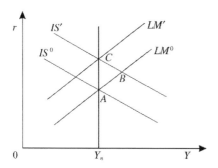

Figure 3.4

The dual conception underlying the monetarist position is that:

(a) The private economic system is *intrinsically stable*, obeying forces that return it to full employment (or to the 'natural' rate of unemployment) even if hit by external shocks; important stabilising factors are the exogenous character of money,[44] the long-run outlook of consumption decisions (based on the permanent income hypothesis) and the 'adaptive' nature of expectations.
(b) In contrast, government action is *ineffective beyond the short term* and does not affect the structural features of the economic system. For example, lowering the market unemployment rate does not lower the natural unemployment rate: in fact, government action may even be destabilising if, for example, it causes an increase in prices that reduces agents' ability to assess their situation.

As we will see in subsection 3.4.3, this view of the operation of the private economic system and government action is carried to extremes by the so-called 'second-generation monetarists', the theorists of new classical macroeconomics (NCM). We will therefore not criticise Friedman's monetarism here, reserving our critique for subsection 3.4.3 with reference to certain aspects of his position shared by the monetarism of new classical macroeconomics.

3.4.3 The ineffectiveness of government intervention in new classical macroeconomics

NCM shares and in fact strengthens the first-generation monetarist approach, basing its arguments on even more optimistic hypotheses about the intrinsic re-equilibrating capacity of a market economic system and, on the other hand, reaching even more pessimistic conclusions about the effectiveness of government intervention in the economy. It is founded on two essential hypotheses:

(a) agents form their expectations *rationally*
(b) markets are constantly returned to equilibrium by the movement of *perfectly flexible prices*.

---

[44] That is, money is determined in a rigid way by some external authority.

We will deal with these assumptions in turn.

Agents form **rational expectations** in the sense that they use all available information, which is not necessarily complete (Muth, 1961). For example, an agent may know the price of his own product, but not those of other products; there is, in other words, *asymmetric information* between different 'islands'.[45] In making decisions, the agent will form his expectations of the relevant variables (in the previous example, of the prices of the other products) using all information at his disposal. A rational prediction will be correct *on average*. The agent can make errors, but these will be random, not systematic. The presence of systematic errors would imply a less-than-complete use of certain information, especially past prediction errors, which is excluded by the rational expectations hypothesis (REH).

Expectations of this sort are forward-looking, rather than backward-looking as in the case of adaptive expectations. The introduction of rational expectations is equivalent to the hypothesis that agents act *as if* they knew the theory underlying the model. From this point of view, the REH is necessary for the consistency of the model (the agents whose decisions underpin the model cannot forecast results different from those predicted by the model). However, the process by which agents form rational expectations – i.e. the way they learn the functioning of the economic system and thus the model that represents it – is not clear. Moreover, it is implicitly assumed that the economic model does not change, or that it has adapted to every possible past change (the *stationarity condition*), which necessarily makes the rational expectations theory a long-run theory (B. Friedman, 1979).

The introduction of *rational expectations* into an economic model is a powerful tool, ensuring that agents' expectations are consistent with the results generated by the model. In a model that incorporates the REH, the 'vision' underlying the model is extremely important. If the model adopts a 'classical' viewpoint – i.e. it postulates the existence of a more or less 'natural' equilibrium – then the REH reinforces the existence of a natural equilibrium. If, however, the model views the private economic system as unstable, the REH makes economic policy even more effective, as we will see shortly.[46] Thus, of the two hypotheses put forward by NCM, the REH does not appear to characterise the school's stance since it is also now used by economists who hold very different views.

Moving to the second, and key, hypothesis, NCM postulates the existence of markets that are *rapidly clearing* or always in equilibrium. In particular, the labour market is always in full employment equilibrium and any unemployment is voluntary. Unemployment can decline if there is an *unexpected* increase in the general price level that is noted only by firms and not by workers. For example, assume that there is an unexpected increase in demand. The prices of goods will tend to rise, reducing the real wage

---

[45] This hypothesis, utilised by Lucas (1973), is exemplified by a reference to a situation in which each agent lives on his own 'island' and knows the price of his good and not those of goods produced by other agents on other islands.

[46] It can be argued that it is difficult to imagine how rational expectations could be formed in this case (Davidson, 1982–3).

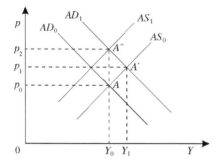

Figure 3.5

level expected by firms, thus increasing their demand for labour and, at the same time, the supply of goods. The increase in the demand for labour causes expected money and real wages to rise, since workers are unaware of the simultaneous rise in prices; they will be willing to increase their supply of labour services, which will reduce (voluntary) unemployment. But these effects cannot last.

Let us take a closer look at the effects of an expansionary monetary policy. The situation in the goods market is shown in figure 3.5. Similarly to what happens in a market for a single good, suppose that we can define an aggregate[47] demand curve, AD, and an aggregate supply curve, AS. Y_0 is the long-run equilibrium, where actual and expected price levels coincide; the unemployment rate is the natural rate. Now imagine there is an *unexpected* increase in the money supply; this causes aggregate demand to increase, shifting AD to the right from AD_0 to AD_1. As a result, the price level for all goods rises above the expected level, but, since we have asymmetric information,[48] each agent initially perceives only the increase in the price of the good he sells and will therefore increase the amount of the good he is willing to supply. Equilibrium output will therefore rise from Y_0 to Y_1.

However, the expansionary effect of an increase in demand and prices is due to the element of surprise. It cannot last, since not only the price of each agent's own good is at an unexpected level, but also the prices of other goods and labour, and the discrepancy will induce agents to modify their expectations. The only consistent equilibrium is therefore that where expected prices equal actual prices. If the increase in the money supply is *transitory*, after the initial surprise output will return to a level corresponding to the natural rate of unemployment. Agents will maintain their expectations regarding prices – leaving the position of AS unchanged – and, since in subsequent periods the money supply will return to the normal level, the AD curve will return to AD_0. So, output is still that corresponding to the natural rate of unemployment, Y_0, and prices are at the initial level, p_0. In summary, if the increase in the money supply is *unexpected but transitory*, it will raise employment and prices, but only temporarily.

---

[47] These have become a normal feature of major macroeconomics textbooks (see, for example, Dornbusch and Fischer, 1994), even if they are based on debatable hypotheses about the functioning of the economy.

[48] Recall the 'islands' example mentioned earlier.

If, however, the increase in the money supply is permanent, sooner or later agents will revise their price expectations upwards, shifting the supply curve to the left, as shown in figure 3.5.[49] Thus, the positive effects in real terms of an *unexpected but permanent* increase in the money supply will be short-lived, with the only long-run effect being an increase in the price level to p_2.

By contrast, an *expected* increase in the money supply will not have any effect on output because it *simultaneously* generates expectations of an increase in the prices of other goods and therefore induces agents (firms and workers) to safeguard their income by raising the price of their product. If everyone raises their prices, the general price level rises, thus confirming expectations. This can be illustrated by referring again to figure 3.5. The only result of the increase in aggregate demand from AD_0 to AD_1 is the rise in the price level from p_0 to p_2, with no change in real income from its initial level at Y_0, which corresponds to the natural unemployment rate, since there is a simultaneous shift in aggregate supply from AS_0 to AS_1. The difference with respect to the case of an unexpected but permanent increase in the money supply is that there are no real effects, even in the short run.

Fiscal policy also fails to produce real effects. If fiscal measures are expected – either because they are announced by policymakers or simply deduced on the basis of available information – they leave the general equilibrium of the system unchanged, immediately affecting prices alone. The Phillips curve is vertical not only in the long run but also in the short run. An expansionary fiscal policy will therefore be entirely ineffective or even harmful due to resulting inflation. Only fiscal measures that are unexpected – and, note, unpredictable, given available information – can be effective, but this success would necessarily be sporadic. Such a policy could not be systematic,[50] since agents would otherwise incorporate their knowledge of the habitual behaviour of policymakers into their information set, rendering government action predictable: a one-off surprise effect is allowed, but the REH makes it impossible for policymakers to surprise (or fool) agents systematically. The effects of monetary policy can be examined in similar terms, by considering that an increase in money supply determines an increase in aggregate demand and, therefore, a shift toward the right of AD. The consequence will be that any expected increase in money supply will have the effect of raising prices only.

In this light, the implications of NCM for economic policy are drastic and negative: there is no systematic possibility for economic policy to change the level of output and employment. In other words, we have **policy neutrality** or **policy invariance**.

The theoretical approach of NCM is in many respects a clear advance, thanks to its introduction of refined and innovative conceptual tools and analytical techniques. However, some of the basic hypotheses and the underlying vision of the economic

---

[49] To understand the reasons for this last shift, consider that each agent, for each given price level of his good, expecting a general increase in the price level of other goods and labour as a result of the increase in demand, will be willing to supply less of that good.

[50] Policy would have to be systematic if it were aimed at certain objectives: for example, if the government wants to ensure an unemployment rate of 5 per cent, it must act systematically, i.e. increase (reduce) demand when the actual unemployment rate is higher (lower) than the target rate.

process are essentially the same as those of the 'classical' economists, and as such are open to the same criticisms. In particular, we can refer to:

(a) The *perfect flexibility of prices and wages*, whereas the reality presents situations of stickiness of a non-accidental nature (see subsection 3.4.4).

(b) The *continuous re-equilibrating tendency of markets*, as in general Walrasian equilibrium, despite the imperfect flexibility of prices[51] in the real world (see subsection 3.4.4 for more on this problem).[52]

(c) The *type of information available* (as postulated in the 'island' parable), which seems very peculiar and, once again, at odds with reality: quite often agents can learn of changes in the general price level at the same time, or even before, they learn of changes in the price of the good they sell.[53]

(d) More generally, the simplistic approach to the numerous problems associated with the real-world scarcity of information, the limitations of our calculating and optimising abilities and the complexity of learning the parameters of the model. These are essential matters, and different approaches entail different consequences for economic policy. For example, NCM's neglect of *learning processes* conflates the long run with the short run; as a result, conclusions valid only for the long run are also attributed to the short run, where they are unacceptable. Introducing rational expectations into macroeconomic schemes based on Walrasian general equilibrium thereby renders neutral, and hence innocuous, the expectations themselves.

(e) The fact that the economic system depicted by NCM appears to reproduce the operation of a *stationary society* and the behaviour of individuals whose rationality excludes 'the highest, specifically human form of rationality: creative rationality [which] aims at transforming the environment into more satisfactory forms, necessarily violating the conditions of stationarity which the new classical economists consider indispensable for the applicability of rational expectations' (Vercelli, 1991, p. 105).

Obviously, with such hypotheses and such a vision of the economic process it is possible to obtain results that border on the absurd: 'we are asked to believe that three and a half million unemployed, give or take half a million searchers, are to be explained by their desire to substitute present for future leisure' (Hahn, 1985, p. 16).

3.4.4 *Some recent theories of involuntary unemployment*

We have said that one of the main macroeconomic problems is *involuntary unemployment*. This is a salient feature of the 'instability' of market capitalism underscored by Keynes. Despite the lively, penetrating and technically sound criticisms levelled by the

---

[51] As an alternative to perfect price flexibility, one could argue that the price elasticities of supply and demand are high enough to ensure the readjustment of markets. Nevertheless, the empirical evidence on elasticities does not appear to support values high enough for this to occur.

[52] This Panglossian vision of economic reality is criticised in Buiter (1980).

[53] The island model – initially proposed by Phelps (1970) – seems appropriate for a society where the most rapid form of communication is a floating coconut (see Maddock and Carter, 1982).

neo-quantity school and NCM at the Keynesian analysis, this central problem remains. We have seen that the first- and second-generation monetarists focus instead on voluntary unemployment and its variations. However, voluntary unemployment is *not* the problem. Economists, workers and the public want to understand why someone is involuntarily made redundant or cannot find a job, even if he is willing to work at the current wage rate. We are less interested in understanding why someone else might resign voluntarily (or in any case not work) in order to sit in the sun in the Bahamas or otherwise have more leisure.

The inability of monetarists to come to grips with the problem of involuntary unemployment – as with other aspects of the instability of a market economy – can be explained (as we noted in section 3.1) by the failure to consider those aspects of the system, such as the insufficient re-equilibrating capacity of prices, uncertainty, etc. that, despite being an essential element of its practical operation, are automatically eliminated from the analysis of long-run equilibrium positions.

At the time the efforts to restore the 'classical' approach were in full bloom, awareness of these problems led to a number of attempts to formulate new analytical approaches. Some of these adopt the vision of Keynes and Kalecki, while others limit their scope to removing certain of the hypotheses of orthodox neoclassical models; still others take a sharply different tack, agreeing on the underlying problem (the causes of involuntary unemployment), but giving it a very different explanation.

The main themes of this research are the following:

(1) the operation of an economy with *essentially fixed prices*
(2) the explanation of the *rigidity of prices and wages*
(3) the explanation of the *high level of real wages* as a possible cause of involuntary unemployment
(4) the identification of *strategic complementarities* between individual decisions that could lead to a long-run equilibrium with involuntary unemployment.

(1) The **fixed price or disequilibrium models** first introduced by Clower (1965) and Leijonhufvud (1968) have been refined in more recent years. They mark a move away (at least in a short-run perspective) from the concept of Walrasian equilibrium, especially in their elimination of the auctioneer who ensures that decisions are coordinated and transactions carried out at equilibrium prices only. If prices are rigid, it is possible that some agents will find themselves 'rationed' – i.e. they cannot effectively express the demand or supply that maximises their position. And this can happen simultaneously in different markets, especially the goods and labour markets, creating an interdependence between excess demand (or supply) in both. If, for example, prices are too high with respect to wages, a vicious circle of excess supply of goods and excess supply of labour is created, which corresponds to Keynesian unemployment: in a decentralised economy, it is possible that no one will have an incentive to act so as to return the system to full employment (see Barro and Grossman, 1971; Malinvaud, 1977; Benassy, 1992).

(2) Explaining the rigidity of prices and wages (*nominal rigidities*), to which the economists of the neoclassical synthesis attribute the existence of unemployment (see

subsection 3.4.2), plays an important role in the new-Keynesian research programme. It has been noted that there can be considerable resistance to price changes under imperfect competition, even when the costs involved are very low, such as those incurred in changing price lists or adjusting automatic payment machines (see Mankiw, 1985; Blanchard and Kiyotaki, 1987).

The **theory of implicit contracts** (Baily, 1974; Azariadis, 1975) can account for wage rigidity, but it has difficulty in explaining *unemployment*. This theory assumes different degrees of risk aversion and informational asymmetry between workers and firms. Workers are also assumed to have less access to insurance markets. Under these conditions both groups of agents have an incentive to agree to labour contracts that incorporate a form of insurance from the firm, which agrees to pay an essentially constant wage regardless of the economic situation. The worker gives up part of his potential wage when economic conditions are good in exchange for a commitment from his employer to pay the same wage in less favourable conditions, when the worker might otherwise lose his job and, consequently, receive no wage at all. The reduction in the wage initially received by the worker constitutes the premium paid to ensure that he is not fired later. However, the insurance contract is *implicit*, not explicit. Firms prefer implicit contracts when there is informational asymmetry: for example, in order to avoid shirking by workers, which would be more likely if there were an explicit contractual guarantee against redundancy and the firm could not effectively monitor the effort made by the worker (moral hazard).

Nevertheless, by its very nature this approach does not account for unemployment very well. In fact, it is intuitively clear that implicit insurance agreements in labour contracts would tend to reduce unemployment in otherwise negative social states as compared with the level that would prevail in a competitive labour market. There could therefore even be 'socially excessive' (i.e. inefficient) employment. Rosen (1985, p. 1155) has noted: 'the only way a risk-averse worker can partially insure against the utility loss of layoff and unemployment in this problem is by working in circumstances where it is socially inefficient to do so.'

(3) Depending on the circumstances, high real wages may or may not create unemployment, as we know from Keynesian analysis. However, it is also important to understand the possible *causes* of high real wages, in addition to their effects. Among the many such causes, we will limit our discussion here to two: efficiency wages and the insider–outsider problem.

The hypothesis of **efficiency wages** (see, among others, Shapiro and Stiglitz, 1984) is based on the idea that the wage level influences the productivity of workers: not in the fairly obvious sense in which a higher wage increases the physical and psychological capabilities of the worker by raising his standard of living, but rather that it induces the worker to refrain from shirking since it raises the value of the income the worker would have to forgo as a result of the inevitable loss of his job if the shirking were discovered. The higher wage results because the worker and the firm have asymmetric information about the worker's effort (the worker has private information), which means that it is difficult for the firm to monitor the worker's performance. The firm therefore has an incentive to increase his wage, which acts as an incentive for the worker, thus inducing him to make a greater effort in performing his job. If this behaviour is practised by many firms, the higher wage level can create unemployment (in the long run or, in an open economy, even the short run).

Insider–outsider models (Lindbeck and Snower, 1984; Blanchard and Summers, 1986) attribute high unemployment to the high wage level imposed by employed workers (*insiders*).[54] These workers can force firms to pay higher wage rates than those requested by unemployed workers (*outsiders*) for two major reasons: first, there are hiring, training costs and redundancy costs, which segment the labour market; second, insiders can decide to cooperate among themselves but not with would-be outsiders hired to replace fired insiders. Firms respond to the higher wage rate imposed by insiders by moving along the labour demand curve, thus reducing the level of employment.[55]

This model has a number of important consequences. In particular, it implies that there is little worker turnover: both the employed and unemployed tend to remain employed or unemployed and there is little movement between the two groups. If employed workers behave as the model assumes and do not have an interest in defending the unemployed, deflationary policies (or external shocks of the same sign) cause a fall in employment and an increase in unemployment for any given level of inflation; the equilibrium unemployment rate therefore tends to rise. The effect can be accentuated by a prolonged reduction in aggregate demand, which leads to an increase in the proportion of long-term unemployed. This increases the power of insiders, since in practice the long-term unemployed are not effective competitors of those with jobs (see section 3.2). The increase in the equilibrium unemployment rate can explain the persistence of unemployment (**hysteresis**) even when there is an increase in aggregate demand if this occurs after prolonged deflationary policies.

(4) There are many theoretical hypotheses based on the existence of **strategic complementarities** in otherwise imperfect markets.[56] They emphasise the existence of *reciprocal external economies* among the decisions of the various economic agents: one agent tends to do what the other does; for example he increases or reduces production if others do the same. A model of strategic complementarities is offered by Weitzman (1982). The presence of *increasing returns to scale* means that firms are large relative to the size of their market and therefore face a decreasing demand curve with respect to price. Each firm, whether an existing firm or a new one created with unemployed factors, fears saturating the market with its output and therefore seeks some way to limit production. But if all the firms took a bolder approach and increased their output in a coordinated manner, the demand of each firm would create a market for the others and the economy could attain full employment.

---

[54] Others, such as McDonald and Solow (1981) emphasise the role of unions.
[55] This might not happen if workers' utility functions take account of both their wage and the level of unemployment.
[56] On this approach, and the opposite view of strategic substitutability, see Cooper and John (1988).

Despite their considerable diversity, the explanations of unemployment offered by these theories concur in arguing that real-life markets can have adverse effects on the level of employment, making corrective government action necessary.

Some of the approaches discussed here develop ideas and results in the spirit of Keynes and Kalecki (especially the Weitzman model). Almost all offer explanations of the possible causes of unemployment that might be relevant to certain countries or historical periods. However, their generality and analytical development do not yet appear satisfactory. Nevertheless, they are a good starting point for resuming the debate on the reasons for the instability of capitalism following the rehabilitation of market economies by the monetarists with models generally based on the assumptions of complete markets, full information, no transaction costs and representative economic agents (see Kirman, 1992; Greenwald and Stiglitz, 1993).

An especially interesting element of these analyses is that they are all conducted in *microeconomic* terms, drawing inspiration from the microeconomic failures analysed in chapter 2, and seek to overcome at this level some of the restrictive hypotheses employed by the monetarists. Some of these analyses could be used to provide appropriate microeconomic foundations to theories of involuntary unemployment. As mentioned, however, their current development seems insufficient, and until more progress is made we think it is legitimate to continue to use macroeconomic models that are not based on microeconomic foundations.

Although at the moment there is no comprehensive and widely-accepted Keynesian theory (see Romer, 1993), we think that the discussion so far shows that the Keynesian vision of capitalism appears to be the most suitable for explaining some market failures at the macroeconomic level, specifically unemployment, and the need for government intervention to mitigate, if not eliminate, its effects. Friedman's monetarist school is to be lauded for having clarified, or emphasised, factors and mechanisms that can contribute to understanding inflation: among the factors, the creation of an 'excessive' money supply; among the mechanisms, expectations of future inflation.

3.5   Growth and development

Growth is an increase in the *income and material wealth of a country*. **Development** is a more general concept that usually includes growth but also considers other aspects of economic and social change. Development occurs when *human well-being improves*.

The distinction is important, since growth does not always imply development and development does not always imply growth. In the most backward countries there is a high risk that an increase in total income, or even in *per capita* income, may not be accompanied by a reduction in poverty or improvements in health, life expectancy, education, the environment, etc. However, there are also considerable differences in definitions of development (see Desai, 1991).

The considerations of the United Nations (see United Nations, 1990) seem especially well founded. They are based on the Aristotelian idea that societies should be judged according to the extent that they promote 'human good'. This leads to a definition of human development as a 'process of enlarging people's choice', which amounts to expanding human **'capabilities'** (see Sen, 1987).[57] The 1990 United Nations report underscores the reasons why income cannot be considered a good criterion for measuring our range of choice:

(1) income is a means, not an end; it may be used equally for essential medicines and superfluous or even harmful goods (such as illegal drugs)
(2) experience provides examples of high levels of human development at low income levels, and vice versa
(3) the present income of a country may be a poor indicator of its future prospects for growth, which largely depend on how much is being invested in human capital
(4) current measures of *per capita* income, which are often used for comparisons through time and across countries, often hide major problems: first, as they are averages, they do not take account of inequalities in income distribution; second, expressing *per capita* income in terms of a common currency (dollars, for example) overlooks *purchasing power* differences, which are not reflected in market or official exchange rates.

Measuring human development therefore requires the use of a range of indicators. Nevertheless, for reasons of simplicity and the availability of data, the *human development index (HDI)* concentrates on three essential elements of human life: longevity, level of knowledge and living standards. Longevity is indicated by *life expectancy at birth*; knowledge is measured by *adult literacy* and the average number of years of schooling; living standards are given as the *logarithm of per capita income at purchasing power parity*.[58]

The level of development of countries as given by the HDI differs considerably from that suggested by the traditional gross domestic product GDP (or gross national, product, GNP) indicator. The most striking examples (on 2000 data) are Armenia, Tajikistan, Georgia and Congo, which rise by 41, 39, 34 and 27 places, respectively, according to the former index, and by Equatorial Guinea, Botswana, Namibia and Gabon, which fall by 73, 62, 54 and 44 places, respectively (United Nations, 2002).

Beyond this, we must recall the large and growing gap in *per capita* incomes between countries noted in section 2.12. We can also observe that domestic income disparities

---

[57] Desai (1989) first used the idea of capabilities to develop a poverty index. The difference between Sen's theory and alternative ethical approaches is discussed in Crocker (1992).

[58] The use of logarithms is based on the idea that there are 'decreasing returns' in the transformation of income into human capabilities. In other words, people do not need excessive financial resources to ensure themselves a decent standard of living. The logarithmic transformation was partially abandoned in subsequent United Nations reports in favour of a more complex transformation, partly based on a formula developed by Atkinson (see Atkinson, 1970; United Nations, 1993, pp. 110 ff.).

To calculate dollar income at purchasing power parity (PPP), we do not use market or official exchange rates, i.e. the price of a currency (say, the dollar) in terms of another currency (say, the yen), expressed by the foreign exchange market or set by policymakers. We instead use the exchange rate – whether higher or lower – corresponding to an equal level of domestic purchasing power of the two currencies of the countries being compared (i.e. the exchange rate thereby obtained – called the **purchasing power parity exchange rate** – should strictly reflect the ratio between the general domestic price levels in the countries concerned).

are less marked than those between countries, and we can add that inequality is greater in developing countries than in the industrial world.

From a dynamic point of view (which underlies concepts such as growth and development), the problems of employment are especially insidious. It is not sufficient to compare actual income with the full employment level of income in a certain time period: even if the two are the same during that period, it does not mean that they will remain so over a longer span. In particular, it is not enough to maintain the same level of effective income in order to ensure continued full employment. In dynamic terms the full employment level of income is a moving target, expressed by the concept of *potential GNP* (or *output*) introduced by Okun (1962), which is an important extension of the Keynesian concept of full employment income.[59] More precisely, **potential output** is that which can be obtained in a given time period by making 'full' use of physical and human resources. The term 'full' refers to a 'normal' level corresponding to a system operating without strains or bottlenecks,[60] which may mean (frictional) unemployment of, say, 4 per cent for a given country and time.

The variability of potential output over time is clear if we consider that the level of 'full' employment under the above definition, the labour force and average labour productivity change. We can define:

$$Y = \pi N \tag{3.1}$$

where Y is output, π is average output per employed person (average labour productivity) and N the number of employed.

Equation (3.1) can also be written as:

$$Y = \pi \cdot \frac{N}{LF} \cdot \frac{LF}{P} \cdot P \tag{3.2}$$

where N/LF is the complement to 1 of the unemployment rate,[61] LF is the labour force, P is the population and LF/P is the labour force participation rate. Equation (3.2) emphasises the variables associated with the variability of potential output over time: average labour productivity, the unemployment rate, the labour force participation rate and population.[62] Obviously each of these variables changes in relation to many factors, which we do not have space to examine here.

Equation (3.2) shows why a change in income and a change in the unemployment rate are not proportional: first, if income and the participation rate are constant, the ratio between employment and the labour force declines owing to the simple fact that productivity and population tend to rise over time. The decline in the ratio between

---

[59] This became one of the objectives of US economic policy connected with the 'New Frontier' programme of President Kennedy in the 1960s. Tax reduction was used as a new instrument in achieving this goal.

[60] This means that reference to a 'normal' level of employment is a way of expressing both an employment objective and an inflation objective.

[61] Note that this is not the **employment rate**, which is defined as the *ratio between the number of employed and the (active) population*.

[62] Multiplying the participation rate by the population gives the labour force; we can therefore write (3.2) as $Y = \pi \cdot (N/LF) \cdot LF$; we have chosen the version given by (3.2) since it shows more clearly the variables that change over time.

employment and the labour force means that the unemployment rate rises. Income must increase more rapidly than the sum of productivity and population growth (which represents the long-run growth trend in income) in order for unemployment to fall.

This is the essence of **Okun's law**. It is not in fact a law but rather an empirical regularity that links the unemployment rate with the variation in real GDP. For example, the ratio between the percentage rise in GDP (above the long-run growth trend) and the reduction in the unemployment rate for the United States has been estimated at about 2.5 to 1 (initially 3 to 1): i.e. GDP must grow by 2.5 percentage points more than its long-run trend in order to reduce the unemployment rate by 1 percentage point.

3.6   Market failure in growth theories

In the few pages that remain in this chapter we analyse market failures in relation to problems of economic growth. We do not deal explicitly with economic development issues, not because we think that these are less important, but rather for reasons of brevity and because we think that the widespread conviction that the market can solve growth problems (and more so than it can development problems) is erroneous. In the following subsections we intend to show that there are many possible market failures related to growth (and development).

3.6.1   The Harrod–Domar growth model

Modern growth theory is largely based on the work of Harrod (1939) and Domar (1946, 1947), which sought to complete the work of Keynes in dynamic terms and in a longer-term perspective. In order to overcome the short-term outlook of Keynesian analysis, investment must be considered not only as a component of aggregate demand (as in Keynes) but also as a factor in the creation of *productive capacity* and, therefore, supply. Harrod identifies the ratio between the average propensity to save, s, and the capital output ratio, v, as the **warranted rate of growth** (i.e. the rate of increase in investment that will maintain equilibrium in the goods market), noting, however, that nothing guarantees that actual investment will equal the investment needed to meet the actual increase in demand.

If all firms expect demand to grow at the warranted rate and invest appropriately to meet that demand, then their expectations will be fulfilled. If, however, they expect demand to grow more quickly than the warranted rate, the actual *rate of growth* will be greater than the expected rate and there will be excess demand. By contrast, if expectations are pessimistic, the actual rate of growth will be less than the expected rate and there will be excess supply. This is the essence of **Harrod's instability**, which can be considered a statement of the implausibility of a market economy ensuring dynamically stable conditions of equal supply and demand.[63]

---

[63] We have presented the problem of Harrod's instability following Sen (1970b).

A further problem has been highlighted by Harrod's analysis. If the labour force is growing at the rate n, in the absence of labour-augmenting technical progress the actual rate of output growth cannot exceed n (the **natural rate of growth**). With technical progress the natural rate of growth is equal to $n + \lambda$, where λ is the rate of output growth per employed person due to technical progress. The second problem identified by Harrod consists in the fact that there are no mechanisms in a capitalist market economy that can also ensure that the warranted and natural rates of growth will be equal. Therefore, there is no guarantee that the labour force created through natural population growth and technological innovation (with the consequent rise in labour efficiency) can be absorbed in a long-run dynamic context (*technological unemployment*).

3.6.2   Neoclassical and post-Keynesian growth models

The problem of the existence of automatic mechanisms for ensuring the convergence of the warranted and natural rates of growth was the object of theoretical work until relatively recently.

Neoclassical economists identified the variation of the capital–output ratio as just such a mechanism. In their view such change is induced by the substitutability of productive factors associated with changes in their relative prices. As in general equilibrium theory, price flexibility in perfectly competitive and complete markets would ensure the attainment of an efficient position, which in this case would be the maximum growth rate possible given the dynamic constraints on the availability of resources. Removing Harrod's assumption of a fixed capital coefficient, Solow (1956) shows that the warranted rate of growth would tend to converge to the natural rate. However, Solow assumes that investment decisions are always based on the relative availability of capital and labour and not on firms' expectations about the future. Under such a hypothesis, the goods market can never be in disequilibrium, thus removing the problem underlying the Keynesian analysis (i.e. the independence of investment decisions), which in its dynamic version gave rise to Harrod's instability.

'Post-Keynesian' growth theories tend to develop the analysis of the relationship between capital accumulation and income distribution.[64] They solve the problem of convergence between the warranted and natural rates of growth by assuming the possibility of changes in the average propensity to save caused by changes in income distribution. However, by specifying the convergence condition in this way, post-Keynesian analysis does not introduce – as does neoclassical theory – hypotheses that deny the existence of a problem of effective demand. Joan Robinson (1962a) argues that *capital accumulation* is the driving force of capitalist economies, since it permits the creation of jobs and profits. Nevertheless, its erratic nature – strongly emphasised by Keynes – is the principal limitation of market capitalism.

---

[64] In addition to the economists we will mention later, other contributors to this strand of analysis are Garegnani, Harcourt and Pasinetti. The latter in particular has analysed the problems of economic growth (most recently, see Pasinetti, 1981, 1993).

In the effort to identify factors that can limit the growth of the manufacturing sector and the world economic system as a whole, Kaldor (1976) considers the inability of the **terms of trade** (i.e. the relative price) between manufactures and primary products to rebalance the growth rates of their respective industries.[65] This incapacity is attributed to the fact that while the prices of primary products vary with changes in their demand, the prices of manufactured goods are independent of demand and obey the logic of oligopoly (**administered prices**). Consequently, the burden of adjustment of an imbalance between demand and supply lies entirely on the prices of primary products (commodities). However, large swings in these prices tend to have a depressive effect on the demand for industrial goods. This is fairly clear in the case of a reduction in commodities prices which, since it reduces the purchasing power of producers in those industries, also reduces demand for industrial goods. The depressive effect also emerges in the opposite case of a rise in commodities prices, since this creates scope for a more than proportional increase in the prices of industrial goods and, therefore, profits. The increase in profits may have a dampening effect on aggregate demand, since it is not normally accompanied by an equally large increase in spending. On the other hand, the inflation triggered by the rise in commodities prices is not tolerated by the political authorities of the industrial countries, who intervene with restrictive measures.

3.6.3 Endogenous growth theories

Regardless of their differences, the theories discussed in the previous two subsections share a common approach: they argue that the long-run rate of growth of an economy is equal to the natural rate and make no attempt to investigate the forces that determine long-run growth, assuming them to be known and given (*exogenous growth*). This is one limitation of these theories.

A second limitation specific to the neoclassical growth theory is the unrealistic nature of the consequences of this theoretical approach. Neoclassical growth theory implies, in clear contrast with reality, the long-run convergence of different economies towards the same growth rate and, if saving propensities are the same, the same level of *per capita* income.

In order to overcome these limitations, there have since the 1990s been numerous contributions to what are known as **theories of endogenous growth**. They draw their name from the attempt to explain the various, and often complementary, factors that determine the growth of an economy. Among these, *technological progress* plays an important role. Endogenous growth models develop, in a particular setting, some concepts used by earlier economists, such as Smith (1776), Young (1928) and others. A central role is played by the explanation of technological progress as the outcome of

---

[65] The rates of growth in the two sectors are linked by *sectoral interdependencies*: for example, agricultural and industrial raw materials are inputs for the manufacturing sector, while the primary goods sector uses industrial goods such as plant and machinery.

'**learning by doing**', i.e. learning linked to experience, along the lines developed by Arrow (1962).

According to Romer (1986), who has developed this theoretical approach to growth in recent years, learning gives rise to increasing returns to scale, which are incompatible with the assumptions of perfect competition. He thus revives the problem already tackled by Marshall (see section 2.7) and his explanation is very similar to that proposed by Marshall himself: individual firms are assumed to face production functions with constant returns to scale while the economy as a whole faces increasing returns to scale owing to the external economies *unintentionally* generated by the past accumulation of knowledge. Government spending can reinforce technological progress and the increase in productivity produced by private investment. This is one justification for government intervention aimed at fostering growth: since it is not possible for private sector agents to capture all the benefits of the accumulation of knowledge, the growth rate of a market economy is lower than the *socially efficient level*, which can be reached only with the aid of government intervention.

In later endogenous growth models, this form of technological progress is supplemented by the progress generated by specific R&D *activity* aimed at appropriating all of the benefits deriving from a monopoly on knowledge (Romer, 1987, 1990; Grossman and Helpman, 1991), along lines reminiscent of Schumpeter (1934). In this context, the possibility arises of a conflict between two different ways of accelerating the introduction of technological progress into an economy: that produced by the search for *new* knowledge, which gives rise to monopoly positions, and that of the diffusion of *available* knowledge and, consequently, the erosion of existing monopolies. A possible role for government would be to mediate between these opposing needs by creating a framework of rules and incentives to encourage new knowledge without hindering its diffusion, thereby maximising the rate of productivity growth.

Human capital plays an important role in endogenous growth. It is simultaneously the result of a productive process and the source of technological progress. Assuming that human capital is reproduced with a technology yielding constant returns to scale, it can be shown that capital itself and the economy have a positive rate of growth (Lucas, 1988). While Lucas argues that the market is capable of ensuring an efficient accumulation of human (and physical) capital, the most recent literature (see, for example, Glomm and Ravikumar, 1992; Galor and Zeira, 1993; Bénabou, 1996; Cozzi, 1997) has underscored the many market failures associated with its formation: imperfect information; the influence of cultural, religious and social factors that often act cumulatively to produce virtuous or vicious circles; lack of the means needed to form human capital; imperfections in the financial markets to which agents could, in theory, turn in order to supplement their insufficient personal resources. Again, government intervention may therefore be necessary to foster human capital formation in such a way as to increase an economy's rate of growth. And, for the reasons we have cited, this would in many cases require *income redistribution*, which would have the dual effect of increasing equity and the dynamic efficiency of the economy.

3.7   The balance of payments

The **balance of payments** ('external accounts') is the systematic record of the economic transactions[66] in a specific period of time between the residents of a country and non-residents. Such transactions normally give rise to outflows and inflows of foreign exchange.[67] A *debit entry* is recorded for any transaction involving an *outflow* of foreign exchange (imports of goods and services, unilateral – or unrequited – transfers abroad, capital outflows); a *credit entry* is recorded for any transaction involving an *inflow* of foreign exchange (exports of goods and services, unrequited transfers from abroad, capital inflows).

The balance of payments is now prepared in accordance with the Fifth Manual of the International Monetary Fund (IMF) and is composed of three accounts: the *current* account, the *capital* account and the *financial* account.

The **current account** records exports and imports of goods, or rather goods, services (such as freight, insurance, tourism) and income (compensation of employees and investment income abroad),[68] as well as current transfers.[69] Within the current account, the record of goods transactions gives the trade balance, while other transactions are called 'invisible items'. The **capital account** records commercial transactions and transfers associated with investment activities: the sale and purchase of intangible assets such as patents, copyrights, goodwill and transfers for the purpose of, or dependent on, transactions involving capital assets (for example, contributions for the purchase of industrial equipment). Together, the two accounts record *goods movements (merchandise and services)*, except for transfers. We will refer to the overall balance of these two accounts as the *balance of goods movements*.

The **financial account** records short, medium and long-term capital movements, divided into:

- *direct investment* (the purchase or sale of shares and equity interests that give control of firms located abroad)
- *portfolio investment* (the purchase or sale of shares and other equity participations that do not give control of firms; purchases of bonds and government securities)
- *derivatives* (see section 10.1.2.)
- *other investments* (public and private loans, short-, medium- and long-term trade credit, bank capital and other short-term assets)
- changes in *official reserves*.

---

[66] According to the *Balance of Payments Manual* of the International Monetary Fund (IMF), an economic transaction is a transfer of an economic value, with or without a quid pro quo, between one economic agent and another. An economic value is a good, service, income or financial item (IMF, 1993).

[67] Foreign exchange consists of banknotes and other financial assets representing a claim on residents of a foreign country expressed in the currency of that country.

[68] Investment income and income from labour (of temporary emigrants), considered as separate items, in fact constitute income from services.

[69] Unrequited transfers can be official (contributions to and from international organisations, such as the United Nations; government aid to developing countries, etc.) or private (gifts, remittances from permanent emigrants, which are treated as donations as since such persons are no longer considered residents).

The reader should note that an increase in official reserves should be considered a loan of national capital in a foreign currency. However, for reasons that we will clarify shortly, when we talk about capital movements we mean the *balance of the financial account excluding official reserves*.

In addition to monetary gold – i.e. gold that can be used to settle international transactions – the **official reserves** of a country or group of countries[70] also include liquid, marketable and high-quality foreign currency claims (in the case of the euro area, currencies other than the euro) on non-residents.

The sum of the three accounts should in theory be equal to zero. In reality, this does not occur because, for example, not all exporters report payments by non-residents into foreign accounts. The discrepancy is posted under the 'errors and omissions' item, which can be quite large. Since the balances on current account and capital account always add up to zero, if 'errors and omissions' is equal to zero, *the change in official reserves* should correspond to the sum of the balances of the current account and the capital account (that is, the goods movement balance), plus capital movements as defined earlier. In substance, *it is the net balance of all the other items in the balance of payments, even if the balance is technically equal to zero.*[71]

The change in reserves corresponds to a change in monetary base[72] in the economy, which is the credit or debit entry offsetting to official foreign currency movements. For example, an exporter may grant credit to the foreign party to the transaction (and in this case, in addition to the recording in the current account, we also register a use of foreign currency in the financial account under 'Other investments'), or may be paid with some foreign currency financial instrument (which gives rise to the same registration) or may receive foreign currency that is then exchanged with the central bank (in which case, in addition to the entry in the current account the transaction also gives rise to the recording of the use of foreign currency capital by the central bank in the financial account under 'Change in official reserves'). *Obviously, if the exporter sells its foreign currency to the central bank, it receives domestic currency in exchange, which increases the monetary base.*

Both increases and decreases in official reserves are to be considered positions of *disequilibrium*, albeit for different reasons. First, a reduction in reserves signals a deterioration in the ability to finance any future excess of payments over receipts, which would not be able to be settled. By contrast, an increase in reserves is difficult to sustain

---

[70] A single balance of payments is prepared for countries in a monetary union, such as the euro area, recording economic transactions between residents of the area countries and residents in other countries.

[71] The balance of payments used to be divided into two sections: current items and capital movements. The former corresponded to the sum of the current and capital accounts, while the capital movements section corresponded to the financial account, excluding changes in reserves. This change, taking account of errors and omissions, was the balance of the external accounts, equal to the algebraic sum of the movements in the two sections (current items and capital movements).

[72] This will be defined in section 11.5. For the moment, the reader can think of it as the banknotes and coins issued by the monetary authorities.

in the long term for different, although generally less pressing reasons – namely, it could give rise to undesirable monetary base creation.[73]

Table 3.3 shows the balance of payments of the euro area using the new methodology for the years 1997–2002.

More generally, however, the balance of payments can be seen as a mirror of relations between a given country and the rest of the world, and can be linked to national accounting concepts.

From this point of view, abstracting from the public sector, the excess of exports over imports reflects an excess of savings over domestic investment.[74] With a current account surplus, equilibrating the balance of payments would require a deficit on the other two accounts, namely a deficit (assuming that the capital account is in balance) on the financial account – i.e. a net outflow of capital representing a loan through which the country makes its excess savings available to the rest of the world. By contrast, positive net imports and overall balance of payments equilibrium indicate that the country is borrowing savings from the rest of the world. Obviously, equilibrium in the balance of payments with a current account imbalance[75] is difficult to sustain in the long run, since it implies that the country is not able to foster independent growth, remaining dependent on the rest of the world for the savings needed to support domestic investment.

Monetary union between two or more countries (like that launched on 1 January 1999 between the countries participating in European Monetary Union, EMU) would eliminate the formal balance of payments problem for economic relations among the countries, but it would leave untouched the problem of the performance of the *real economy* in each country. Monetary union does not eliminate the importance of tracking movements of goods and services between the various countries, precisely because they are indicative of savings flows: for example, some countries could be steady net importers. Sustaining this situation depends on a constant net inflow of capital or transfers from the rest of the world, especially other countries from the area.[76] However, such a situation cannot continue for long. On the one hand other countries find it difficult to maintain a steady outflow of unrequited transfers (in effect, donations). On the other, inflows of private capital into the country in question could generate income[77] that in the long term should create sufficient productive capacity to reverse the sign of net imports of goods and services; were relative underdevelopment to last, their persistence would be difficult to explain.

[73] Under certain conditions, however, this can be offset through other channels of monetary base creation or destruction. We discuss these issues in chapter 11.
[74] As we know from national accounting, in this case $S - I = X - M$. If we specify the public sector, $S - I = X - M + G - T$, where S, I, X, M, G and T, respectively, stand for saving, investment, exports, imports, government spending and taxes.
[75] In this case, the balance of payments is not in *full* equilibrium, which requires that all accounts balance separately.
[76] From the point of view of Germany, for example, the rest of the world is made up of the other euro area countries as well as all the countries not participating in the union.
[77] This would happen when they finance investment, thus increasing productive capacity in the host country.

Table 3.3 *Balance of payments of the euro area, 1997–2002*[a,b]

	Current Account					Capital account	Financial Account						Errors and omissions
	Total	Goods	Services	Income	Current transfers		Total	Direct investment	Portfolio investment	Financial derivatives	Other investment	Reserve assets	
	1	2	3	4	5	6	7	8	9	10	11	12	13
1997	62.1	116.4	3.1	−15.2	−42.2	13.0	−68.4	−44.5	−24.3	−8.2	123.0	8.2	24.1
1998	31.9	109.0	−1.1	−28.8	−47.2	12.4	11.7	−81.3	−110.0	3.8	160.8	10.1	−5.4
1999	−19.0	75.7	−10.7	−37.3	−46.7	12.8	70.0	−120.1	−43.0	−2.2	182.0	17.6	−19.4
2000	−60.4	31.6	−11.5	−27.0	−53.4	9.8	−40.5	−12.3	−115.2	−3.7	8.8	17.8	45.4
2001	−13.8	75.8	0.9	−39.7	−50.8	8.9	−171.3	−101.5	38.1	−13.8	−184.4	−2.5	97.5
2002	62.0	132.7	13.3	−39.2	−44.8	11.9		−21.0	50.4				

Notes:
[a] EUR billion (ECU billion to end-1998), net flows.
[b] Inflows (+); outflows (−); Reserve assets: increase (−); decrease (+).
Source: European Central Bank (2003a).

3.8 Summary

1 A complete assessment of real markets cannot ignore a number of important phenomena that are not immediately apparent at a microeconomic level, or in any case are difficult to account for with general equilibrium theory. We refer to the instances of '*instability*' *in market economies*: involuntary unemployment, inflation, underdevelopment, balance of payments disequilibria.

2 According to some theories, these phenomena – which imply inefficiency and inequality – are to be attributed to *structural features* of markets that prevent them from operating as implied by the abstract hypotheses of the theory of general equilibrium. We therefore refer to them as 'market failures'. Since these phenomena are best described by macroeconomic theories, we call them 'macroeconomic market failures'.

3 *Involuntary unemployment* is an especially important example of instability, implying inefficiency and inequality.

4 Whatever form it takes, *inflation* represents a competition for the distribution of income. It normally gives rise to a redistribution of income and wealth and costs for society as a whole, which will be large or small depending on the level of inflation.

5 The 'classical' macroeconomic vision is very similar to that underlying the 'invisible hand': a market economy has a natural order that endows it with stability. In particular, *full employment* is assured by re-equilibrating movements in interest rates and real wages.

6 Keynes calls into question the capacities of market economies to re-equilibrate through *changes in relative prices*, especially the interest rate and the real wage rate. The uncertainty that pervades a monetary economy creates instability for new capital formation (investment) and the capital value of financial wealth, with possible negative effects on aggregate demand and employment.

7 Milton Friedman and the monetarists conceive the market economy as inherently *stable*. Monetary policy is effective only in the short run; in the long run there is no trade-off between inflation and unemployment (the Phillips curve is vertical). On the other hand, fiscal policy crowds out private expenditure. This view of the operation of a market economy is brought to extremes by the theorists of NCM, who postulate rational expectations and markets that are always in equilibrium. The Phillips curve is vertical in the short run as well. Fiscal and monetary policy are therefore at best useless, and may even be harmful owing to the inflation they generate.

8 The conclusion that *government action is 'neutral'* reached by the NCM school and Friedman's monetarists is the result of a simplistic and misleading treatment of the many problems of the real world related to the scarcity of information, limits on individuals' powers of calculation and optimisation and the complexity of learning processes.

9 There have been many attempts to find new approaches to explaining *involuntary unemployment*. They have considered:

(a) examining the operation of an economy with rigid prices

(b) explaining the rigidity of prices and wages

(c) explaining the high level of real wages

(d) identifying strategic complementarities between the choices of various agents that might lead to a long-run unemployment equilibrium.

10 An increase in income is an indicator of *growth*. *Development* is a different concept that considers other causes of economic and social progress. The Human Development Index (HDI) suggested by the United Nations is an indicator that seeks to measure the capability of people to choose.

11 In a dynamic framework, the problems of employment can be addressed by referring to the concept of *potential output*: the objective of long-run full employment income leads us to attempt to minimise the divergence between that level and actual production.

12 The analysis of the problems of economic growth has underscored the possibility of numerous *market failures*. First, Harrod's instability is a reformulation in a dynamic framework of the problems pointed out by Keynes, stemming from the autonomous nature of investment decisions. In addition, Harrod shows that it is unlikely that the warranted rate of growth will be equal to the natural rate of growth and, therefore, that a growing labour force will be able to find jobs. Neoclassical and post-Keynesian economists offer different answers to the possibility that there are mechanisms ensuring that the two rates of growth converge. Endogenous growth theories identify numerous cumulative factors that explain technological progress and economic growth (unintentional learning, intentional R&D activities, human capital formation) and determine the possibility that market economies will grow at an insufficient rate.

13 The *balance of payments* records international economic transactions. Balance of payments surpluses and deficits are both disequilibrium positions. The balance of payments is composed of three accounts: the current account, the capital account and the financial account. The first two record movements of goods; the financial account registers capital movements and changes in official reserves. Goods surpluses and deficits represent excessive or insufficient saving with respect to domestic investment, and are difficult to sustain in the long run.

II Normative and positive theory of economic policy

4   The normative theory of economic policy

4.1   The government as a rational agent

In chapters 2 and 3 we identified market failures at both the microeconomic and macroeconomic levels, thus showing the need for intervention by an agent that, having collective motives and objectives, would be able to transcend these failures.

Our analysis in this chapter focuses on the abstract potential for action by such an agent in a market economy with the aim of correcting the market's operation or replacing it altogether. We develop a theory about what this agent, acting rationally, *should* do to compensate for market inadequacies. From this point of view, we will be in a position similar to that held by much of neoclassical theory, which deduces the optimal (maximising) behaviour of various (private) agents on the basis of certain postulates.

In chapter 5 we examine the actual behaviour of government, comparing it with the abstract structure we intend to sketch out here, so as to identify 'non-market' failures in the same way we illustrated market failures in our earlier discussion.

Both steps – i.e. the formulation of both a normative and a positive theory of public involvement in the economy – are necessary if we wish to reach some sort of conclusion regarding the relative roles to assign to government and the market in 'regulating' the economic activity of individuals. In particular, the normative theory is needed as a yardstick for assessing the reality of government intervention and the possibility of improving the way it is carried out and its results. This theory has helped raise the debate about government involvement in economic life above the level of slogans, as one of its progenitors had hoped (see Tinbergen, 1956). In addition, the development of a logical structure to verify the internal consistency, and therefore the *rationality*, of a system of economic policy ensures that it is not based solely on intuition, experience and the forecasting abilities of policymakers.

4.2   Planning

4.2.1   Meaning and foundation

Planning means taking *coordinated and consistent economic policy decisions*. In the area of government intervention this means avoiding piecemeal measures and considering the full range of policy aims (targets or objectives) and the set of possible actions (instruments) for every problem.

The need for coordinated action is a consequence of at least three factors:

(1) There are normally a variety of instruments available to achieve the various possible objectives. Choosing the appropriate instrument for each objective involves considering the relative effectiveness of each alternative, the time required for the effects of each instrument to operate and the presence of any *constraints* on their use.

(2) The existence of *multiple objectives* and the fact that each instrument can influence more than one (even all of them; see subsection 4.5.2) means that in general policy problems are interdependent. In solving one problem (or hitting a target) the instrument will also affect other issues (other targets), and not necessarily in the desired way. Accordingly, the various policy problems must generally be solved *simultaneously*, as we will see. A special case in which it is possible under certain conditions to solve individual problems separately (or in a *decentralised* manner) will be examined later (see section 14.10 on the 'appropriate' assignment of instruments to objectives).

(3) Policy problems are *intertemporal*: the solution of a problem in the present is tied to the solution of the same problem in subsequent periods. An especially important aspect of planning in this context is the 'time consistency' of public choices. For the precise meaning of this concept we refer to Acocella (1998).

4.2.2   The constituent elements of the plan

We have already referred to the elements of a plan in section 4.2.1, mentioning two of them explicitly: targets (or objectives) and instruments. More precisely, a **target** is an economic policy aim that we can usually measure in terms of an economic variable, such as income or employment. An **instrument** is a 'lever' – represented by another variable – that policymakers can use to achieve the target – i.e. to change the value of an objective variable in the desired way. We will see later the characteristics that an economic variable must have in order to be used as an instrument.

The ability of instruments to influence targets is inferred from economic analysis, which identifies the relationships between economic variables, thereby giving us an idea of the possibility that adjusting certain variables (the instruments) will have an effect on others (the targets). The 'structure of information' on the relationships between economic variables can be expressed as a mathematical model that describes the functioning of the economy at an aggregate level (a macroeconomic model) or a disaggregated level (a microeconomic model). Obviously, the **analytical model** will differ according to the school of economic thought that most influences the economist.

In summary, a plan (or programme) is formed of three elements: targets, instruments and analytical models. In the coming pages we will examine each in detail.

4.2.3 *An example*

We have seen that the essence of planning is the coordinated use of multiple instruments to achieve a variety of objectives. We will return to the problem of coordination later, after having introduced additional concepts. For the moment, we will show how a simple economic policy problem involving only one target can be framed and then solved. This case will serve as an introduction to the subsequent analysis of more realistic situations in which policymakers wish to pursue multiple objectives.

Observing real-life situations allows policymakers to identify the aspects of reality that they consider to be unsatisfactory and whose correction could become a policy objective. Using the lens of economic analysis, they will also be able to identify the causal relationships between different economic variables (analytical models).

In examining the world around them, policymakers may decide, say, that employment is too low, which reduces social welfare. In such a situation, policymakers will propose specific targets for employment (N), which can be expressed in a number of ways: as increments of N ($\triangle N$) or as a fixed value of $N(N = \overline{N})$. We will here assume that the target is expressed as $N = \overline{N}$.

For their part, economists will have developed a model of the sort shown by (4.1), which specifies the variables on which employment, N, depends (e.g. following the Keynesian approach, the components of autonomous demand, A);

$$Y = \pi N$$
$$Y = C + A \tag{4.1}$$
$$C = cY$$

In model (4.1), Y is income, π is average labour productivity, C and A denote consumption and autonomous expenditure, respectively, and c is the average and marginal propensity to consume. Substituting the second and third equations into the first, (4.1) can be rewritten in the following way, which specifies N as a function of the other variables:

$$N = \frac{1}{\pi} \cdot \frac{1}{(1 - c)} A \tag{4.2}$$

Our next step is to identify the instruments, i.e. the variables in (4.2) that can be adjusted by policymakers to influence the target variable.

Examining (4.2), more than one variable emerges as a possible candidate for the role of instrument: they may be variables that can be considered true instruments under policymakers' control, or others that are not true instruments but, for simplicity, can be considered as such since they reflect, with varying degrees of immediacy and effectiveness, movements in the real instruments.

For example, A is composed of, among other things, government consumption and investment spending, G, which is directly controllable, and private investment, I, which we will initially take as given but which can be indirectly influenced by controlling liquidity (see chapter 11). However, even c can be considered a policy instrument, since it reflects income redistribution induced by government action, which could influence the marginal propensity to consume of the economy as a whole if the propensities to consume of individuals, groups or classes are different (see subsection 4.5.1).

In our example, in abstract terms we have certain degrees of freedom in choosing the instrument. Once we have established which instrument should be used, we can solve the policy problem. If we assume that only one instrument will be used (for example, government expenditure), I and c will be considered given and the policy problem consists in finding the value for G that will generate the desired value of N, i.e. that will yield $N = \overline{N}$.

We first rewrite 4.2 as:

$$N = \frac{1}{\pi} \cdot \frac{1}{(1-c)}(\bar{I} + G) \qquad (4.2')$$

and then write the instrument, G, as a function of the target, N:

$$G = [\pi(1-c)N] - \bar{I} \qquad (4.3)$$

Equation (4.3) tells us in general how G changes as N changes, with the other variables taken as given.

Finally, we assign N the desired value $\overline{N}$

$$G = [\pi(1-c)\overline{N}] - \bar{I} \qquad (4.4)$$

This gives us the only value of G consistent with the data and the desired target ($N = \overline{N}$) In the real world, then, knowing the values of $\bar{I}$, π and c, as well as that of the target, we can immediately determine the level of G that, given our hypotheses, will allow us to reach the employment target.

4.3   Economic policy objectives

The individual policy objectives were identified in the previous chapters. They belong to microeconomic or macroeconomic policy. Expressing them is the task of politicians, who are accountable to the public for their choices.

The importance of the political system in defining the relationship between policy-makers' preferences and individual preferences is clear. The problem lies in identifying the *objectives* to pursue and the *weight* to give to each. The choice of certain objectives rather than others by policymakers can reflect the preferences of at least a part (preferably a majority) of the electorate to a greater or lesser degree. This depends to a considerable extent on the operation of the democratic political mechanism. For the moment, we assume that such a mechanism exists and functions perfectly. We also assume that there are no bureaucratic barriers or distortions in the implementation of the policies adopted to achieve the objectives. We will drop both of these assumptions in chapter 5.

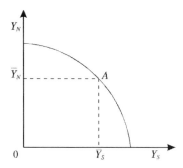

Figure 4.1

The various objectives that policymakers seek to achieve in a given period of time could be **consistent** among themselves (in the sense that a certain policy measure leads to the achievement of various objectives simultaneously) or **substitute** for each other (a measure that leads to the achievement of one objective makes it more difficult to achieve another objective). In the second situation, we have a **trade-off between objectives**.

There are four ways to express targets:

(a) the *fixed-target* approach
(b) the *priority* approach
(c) the *flexible-target* approach with a *variable* marginal rate of substitution (MRS)
(d) the *flexible-target* approach with a *constant* MRS.

We first examine these approaches in diagrammatic form before proceeding to a more rigorous analytical treatment.

4.3.1 Fixed targets

The first method for expressing policy objectives was developed by Tinbergen (1952, 1956) and consists in assigning fixed values to the variables chosen as economic policy targets.

Let the targets be income in two geographical areas (call them North and South): Y_N and Y_S; the possibility of producing income with existing resources in the two areas is expressed as $Y_N = f(Y_S)$, which is shown in figure 4.1 as a 'transformation' curve.

Expressing the objectives as fixed targets is equivalent to taking a point on the curve, such as A, where

$$Y_N = \overline{Y}_N \quad Y_S = \overline{Y}_S$$

If the pair of desired values for the two income levels were outside the transformation curve, the politician would have to decide between two alternatives: either reduce the value of at least one of his targets or attempt to shift the transformation curve up (i.e. ease the constraint). Given that the second option may take time to achieve, even a

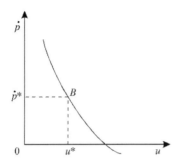

Figure 4.2

stubborn and far-sighted politician could well decide to choose the first option, at least until he was able to engineer a shift in the transformation curve.

A second example of a fixed target problem is reconciling an employment target (expressed in terms of the unemployment rate, u) and monetary stability (expressed in terms of $\dot{p} \equiv (\Delta p/\Delta t)/p$ the rate of change in prices per unit of time, or the inflation rate). These two targets can be linked by a relation or 'transformation' curve, $\dot{p} = f(u)$, shown in figure 4.2 (the 'derived' Phillips curve). As we saw in chapter 3, this is a much debated relationship; we use it here to illustrate one possible type of constraint on economic policy choices.

Expressing the desired objectives as fixed targets means selecting a point on the derived Phillips curve (B, for example) where $\dot{p} = \dot{p}^*$ and $\dot{u} = u^*$.

The analytical design of a planning problem with fixed targets is given in section 4.5.

4.3.2   The priority approach

Setting fixed targets may not be feasible if policymakers do not know the exact position of the 'transformation' curve (or, more precisely, the relationship that links one target with another). In this case it may be more appropriate to specify *priorities* in reaching objectives. For example, policymakers may wish to ensure a certain volume of income in the less-developed area of the country (the South), then seek to maximise income in the more advanced area (the North) consistent with the actual position of the transformation curve. With reference to figure 4.3, the transformation curve can either be at A or B. However, policymakers want $Y_S = \overline{Y}_S$; they then wish to maximise Y_N, which will be $\overline{Y}'_N$ or $\overline{Y}''_N$, depending on the position of the transformation curve.

If employment and price stability are the objectives and policymakers wish to give priority to the former, they will set a certain unemployment rate as their target and then seek to minimise the inflation rate. We leave it to the reader to diagram this case.

In analytical terms, the operation involves maximising (or minimising, if we are dealing with a 'bad') the value of the non-priority target, subject to the desired value of the priority target and the constraint of the transformation curve or the model that represents the functioning of the economy.

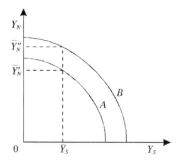

Figure 4.3

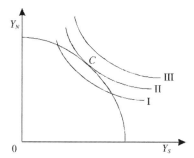

Figure 4.4

4.3.3   Flexible targets: social welfare function with variable MRS

Approaching a policy problem in terms of flexible targets is equivalent to the way the consumer problem is set in standard microeconomics.

The consumer, rather than setting the quantities of goods and services he wishes to consume in rigid terms (or rather than setting priorities), indicates his objectives in flexible terms by expressing his *preferences*. Referring to a map of indifference curves representing those preferences, the consumer compares the map with the budget constraint (or 'transformation' curve), thereby determining his choices (i.e. the quantity of goods and services that he must acquire to maximise his utility) at the point of tangency, rather than specifying them *a priori*.

Similarly, the policymaker, perhaps with the help of an economist, will construct a map of 'social' indifference curves reflecting the preferences of society (a **social welfare function**, SWF). He will superimpose the map on the transformation curve between the variables that are arguments of his utility function, thus determining the choice of objectives. Figure 4.4 shows the map of social indifference curves between Y_N and Y_S and the transformation curve introduced in figure 4.1. Obviously, the solution to the problem is given at the point of tangency, C.

As we can see, in this case the indifference curves associated with the SWF are identical to those associated with the consumer's utility function. If the arguments of

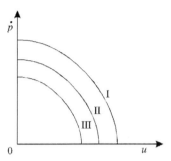

Figure 4.5

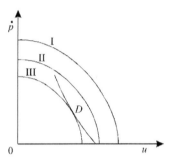

Figure 4.6

the SWF were 'bads' (such as unemployment, u, and inflation, $\dot{p}$) rather than 'goods' (such as Y_N and Y_S), the indifference curves would be represented differently.[1]

First, the preference order would differ: clearly, the lower the level of one 'bad' for a given level of the other, the higher the utility. Thus, curves closer to the origin represent higher levels of utility (figure 4.5). Second, the curves are concave rather than convex, indicating that the MRSs are increasing rather than decreasing.

However, here too the economic policy problem has a solution, which can be found by comparing the social indifference map with the transformation curve (figure 4.6). D is the point of highest social welfare.

For both goods and 'bads', the arguments of the SWF are the economic policy targets. However, unlike the fixed-target approach, in this case the targets are determined endogenously as the values that maximise social welfare, given the constraint. This is an 'optimising' approach, in contrast to the fixed-target approach.[2] The reason this method is called the **optimising approach** to planning should be clear: the values of the targets are not pre-determined; rather, they are defined by the optimisation process (by way of maximisation or minimisation) with the constraint given by the transformation curve or, more generally, by the model of the economy. By contrast, the values *assigned* to the objectives in the fixed-target approach, are simply satisfactory, not optimal. An

---

[1] Instead of a welfare function to maximise we would have a **loss function** to minimise. A specific case of a loss function is the misery index we will examine in subsection 4.3.4.

[2] The priority approach is an intermediate method.

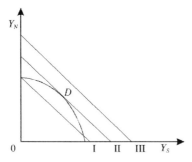

Figure 4.7

analytical treatment of the optimising approach to an economic policy problem is given in section 4.5.

4.3.4   Flexible targets: social welfare function with constant MRS

This case corresponds to a SWF that has been linearised for simplicity, and therefore has a constant MRS.[3]

Take our example of targets for regional income distribution. The SWF can be written as:

$$W = a\,Y_N + b\,Y_S$$

where a and b are the weights assigned to income in the two areas. These can take any value, reflecting the preferences of the person or group that defines the SWF.[4] In this case, a and b are constant for any value of Y_N and Y_S. Consequently, the MRS between Y_N and Y_S, given by b/a, is constant.[5] We can therefore represent the policy choice problem in terms of figure 4.7. Given the assigned weights, point D determines the optimal level of income in the two areas.

Let us now look at another example that offers an interesting connection with Okun's so-called *misery index*. If the arguments of the SWF with a constant MRS are $\dot{p}$ and u, we have the function:

$$W = a\dot{p} + bu$$

where a and b are negative constants. An increase in $\dot{p}$ or u means a decrease in welfare, or an increase in misery. If we choose to measure welfare on the scale of negative values,

---

[3] A SWF with a constant MRS is a good approximation to the true SWF only in the neighbourhood of the point at which the true SWF has a MRS equal to the one we have assumed as constant.

[4] For example, we could have $a = 1$ and $b = 2$, or $a = 1.5$ and $b = 1$.

[5] Assume $W = \overline{W}$ (i.e. choose an indifference curve); we therefore have $\overline{W} = a\,Y_N + b\,Y_S$, from which we can derive Y_N as a function of Y_S:

$$Y_N = \frac{\overline{W}}{a} - \frac{b}{a} Y_S$$

This is a linear function with a constant slope, $-b/a$. The MRS is equal to the absolute value of the slope of the indifference curve, i.e. b/a.

Table 4.1 *Misery indices in selected OECD countries, 1970–2003*[a]

	1970	1975	1980	1985	1990	1995	2000	2003
United States[b]	9.3	16.5	17.9	10.8	10.7	7.8	7.4	8.3
Canada	9.2	17.5	17.5	14.2	12.4	11.1	9.5	10.4
Japan	8.3	13.1	9.5	4.9	4.7	2.6	4.0	5.0
Germany	4.4	9.6	8.7	8.9	7.5	10.2	10	10.7
France	7.5	15.8	19.6	16.0	11.7	13.2	11.1	11.6
Italy	10.3	22.4	27.9	18.6	16.5	17.9	13	11.4
United Kingdom	8.9	28.0	22.6	16.5	12.4	11.3	7.4	6.4
Total OECD	**8.2**	**16.1**	**18.6**	**14.5**	**12.3**	**12.2**	**15.2**	**9.2**

Notes:
[a] The indices have been calculated by adding the unemployment rate (standardised for the purposes of comparison across countries) and the private consumption deflator.
[b] The methodology for calculating the CPI has changed considerably over the past years, lowering measured inflation substantially.
Sources: Our calculations on data from Maddison (1991) (until 1985) and OECD (2004) (for subsequent years).

and hence take misery (and not welfare) as our reference point, a and b are positive constants. In the special case where $a = b = 1$, we have **Okun's misery index**, which is the sum of the unemployment rate and the inflation rate.

This index is sometimes used to compare economic situations over time or in different places in order to obtain a summary view of economic conditions in one country or compare them across countries (see, for example, Bank for International Settlements, 1983; Coricelli, 1990). For example, table 4.1 gives the misery indices for the major industrial countries in various years, showing the considerable divergences between them even in restricted and relatively integrated areas such as the European Union. The disparity is a symptom of the considerable differences in structural conditions and their evolution. In all likelihood, however, the differences also depend on the broad diversity of preferences and policies, which calls into question the validity of the basic hypothesis used to construct the index – i.e. the equal weight assigned to the two 'bads' (in all countries, in our case).

This indicator of welfare has been criticised for a number of reasons, which we can summarise as follows.

(1) As mentioned, the misery index reflects preferences that might not be shared, since unemployment and inflation are given equal weights ($a = b = 1$). In other words, a 1 percentage-point increase in unemployment is assumed to have the same value for policymakers as a 1 percentage-point increase in inflation.

(2) One consequence of the preceding observation is that the decline in welfare associated with a 1-point increase in unemployment is always compensated by a 1-point fall in inflation, and vice versa, *whatever the starting point*. In terms of our discussion, this means that the MRS is constant (and equal to 1); this is difficult to accept, unless we remain in the neighbourhood of some given point. If the starting point for

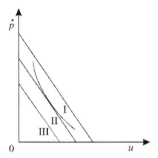

Figure 4.8

inflation and unemployment changes considerably, in general there is also a change in the ratio with which one is prepared to exchange increases in one variable for decreases in the other, leaving welfare unchanged. For example, if unemployment is 3 per cent and inflation is 20 per cent, we may be willing to accept a 1 per cent increase in unemployment in order to reduce inflation by 2 percentage points. However, if unemployment is 8 per cent and inflation is 6 per cent, we may be willing to accept an additional point of unemployment only if inflation falls more drastically, say by 4 percentage points.

Figure 4.8 shows the terms of the trade-off between unemployment and inflation when the SWF has a constant MRS.

4.4   The instruments of economic policy

4.4.1   *Definition*

A variable can be defined as a policy instrument if the following three conditions are satisfied:

(1) Policymakers can control the variable; that is, they can decide what value it should have and fix it directly with their own actions (**controllability**).
(2) The variable whose value has been fixed by policymakers has an influence on other variables, which are assigned the role of targets (**effectiveness**). In the simple case of one target and one instrument linked by a functional relation, effectiveness can be measured as the derivative of the target with respect to the instrument, dy/dx, where the target is y and the instrument x.
(3) It must be possible to distinguish the variable from other instruments in terms of its degree of controllability and, above all, effectiveness: two instruments with the same effects on all targets are not really two separate instruments (**separability** or **independence**).

As defined here, an instrument appears to be a variable whose sole function is to influence other variables, which are those relevant for policymakers' preferences. However, in the real world this is a rare occurrence, since some economic variables may also have an intrinsic value in addition to their instrumental value. In other words, the arguments of policymakers' preference functions can include target variables proper and other variables that normally have an instrumental role for the attainment of the target variables. For example, public expenditure is an instrumental variable, since it influences the level of numerous policy targets such as income, employment, the balance of payments, etc. However, policymakers may also assign an intrinsic value to the amount of public expenditure or the ratio between public spending and national income (the degree of government involvement in the economy).

The lack of a sharp distinction between targets and instruments does not create excessive difficulties for dealing with economic policy problems. Theil generalised the social welfare function to include the case in which its arguments include instrumental variables (see Theil, 1964).

On the other hand, difficulties may arise if there are constraints (floors or ceilings) on the use of instruments. These can be a consequence of institutional factors: i.e. the constitution, the laws or the customs (which can sometimes have the force of a law) that regulate the behaviour of the government or the central bank of a country (for example, a balanced-budget requirement or prohibition on the monetary financing of a deficit; see chapter 2) may inhibit the use of certain instruments or combinations of instruments.

When the causal relationship that links certain instruments to the (final) objectives is complex, it can be helpful to introduce the concepts of policy indicators, operative and intermediate targets. We will discuss these at length in chapter 11 in relation to monetary policy.

4.4.2 *The different types of instrument*

There are different ways of classifying policy instruments. One of these, suggested by Tinbergen (1956), distinguishes between quantitative, qualitative and reform policies. **Quantitative policies** are those that involve changing the value of an existing instrument (e.g. changing the level of government expenditure); **qualitative policies** involve the introduction of a new instrument, or the elimination of an existing one, without causing significant changes in the economic system (e.g. introducing a ceiling on bank lending or a new tax). **Reform policies** (or **reforms**) consist in the introduction of a new instrument or the elimination of an old one that does cause a significant change in the features of the economic system and the rules governing its operation. Reforms have a considerable institutional impact and include, in addition to the nationalisation (or privatisation) policies mentioned elsewhere: measures that define property rights, especially the degree of public or private involvement in firms and industries; the structure of the financial system (e.g. the 'separation' of short-term lending from medium and long-term lending); and the regulation of the economic structure or the conduct of firms in the marketplace (e.g. antitrust legislation). Reforms may have constitutional importance depending on the level at which they are implemented, which partly depends on historical and political factors.

We can also distinguish between *direct* and *indirect control measures*. **Direct control measures** aim to achieve certain objectives by imposing a given behaviour on certain categories of agents (for example, setting import quotas to reduce the trade deficit). **Indirect control measures** do not seek to achieve objectives by imposing a specific behaviour on agents, but rather by influencing the variables that guide agents' decisions (for example, in order to reduce the trade deficit, we could introduce a tariff on imports, which normally raises their prices, thus discouraging the consumption of foreign goods). There are many direct measures in addition to import quotas, including rationing consumption, lending ceilings, selective credit controls, wage and price controls, establishment of public sector enterprises and various forms of regulation (e.g. requiring scrubbers on coal-fired power stations, prohibiting the sale of meat from 'mad' cows, antitrust legislation, etc.).

The three main indirect measures are fiscal policy, monetary policy and exchange rate policy. **Fiscal policy** regards the level of government expenditure and/or taxation. **Monetary policy** operates on the liquidity of the economic system through changes in monetary base and/or the required reserve ratio. **Exchange rate policy** seeks to influence the **exchange rate**, i.e. the quantity of one currency needed to purchase one unit of another currency.

A further important distinction can be made between *discretionary measures* and *(automatic) rules*. Discretionary measures are policy instruments that can be adjusted at the policymaker's discretion in a case-by-case assessment of the situation. **Rules** are policy instruments that operate without the need to observe and decide on a case-by-case basis. One example of a rule is Milton Friedman's proposal to increase the money supply by a fixed annual percentage (the 'simple rule': see subsection 3.4.2), rather than assessing the situation periodically and deciding the measures to adopt.

A set of rules can act as a **monetary** or **fiscal constitution** if the breadth and range of the measures establishes the fundamental principles of government intervention in the two areas. Adopting a certain monetary regime (e.g. the Gold Standard) is an example of a monetary constitution (see chapter 16).

A specific class of rules is represented by **automatic** (or **built-in**) **stabilisers**, which help to smooth the cyclical fluctuations of the economy. Examples of these are unemployment benefits and progressive taxation. Both of these instruments, which were primarily introduced to reduce the inequality of personal income distribution, also counter the cyclical tendencies of the economy, limiting the decline in aggregate demand during recession and dampening the effect of an increase during expansion. The stabilising properties of progressive taxation will be examined in detail in chapter 12.

One advantage of automatic stabilisers, which were mainly introduced after the Second World War, is that they make government intervention more rapid, since they eliminate the *observation* (or *recognition*) *lag* and the *administrative* (or *decision*) *lag*, although the *effect lag* remains.[6]

---

[6] The **observation lag** is the time interval between the moment in which the event requiring action occurs and that when the need for intervention is recognised. It is essentially a statistical lag. The **administrative lag** is the interval between the recognition of the need for action and the moment the decision to act is taken. This lag is due to the time needed for policymakers to study and discuss the situation and select the most appropriate response. The time it takes to undertake a policy action – which includes both the observation and administrative lags – is called the **inside lag**. The **effect lag** is the interval separating the adoption of the measure and the emergence of its effects. It is also called the **outside lag**.

The superiority of automatic stabilisers over discretionary measures from the point of view of lags does not mean that the latter do not have an important role to play in countercyclical policy, mainly due to the extent of the adjustment that is necessary in certain situations. There are also many ways to reduce the lags associated with discretionary measures, ranging from increasing the speed of data gathering to the creation of a 'project fund' for extraordinary government spending to be drawn on if a rapid fiscal expansion is needed. Box 4.1 discusses time inconsistency issues in greater depth.

Box 4.1.   Time inconsistency: fixed rules and discretionary intervention

We have already discussed the meaning of rules and discretionary intervention (subsection 4.4.2) as well as some of the arguments in favour of rules (e.g. Friedman's 'simple rule' for which see subsection 3.4.2).[a] Essentially, three arguments are advanced in support of rules:

(a) the length and variability of the time lag with which the various policies (in particular, monetary policy) take effect means that it is possible that discretionary action could *exacerbate cyclical trends*
(b) expansionary discretionary measures are ineffective beyond the short run, producing only *inflation* in the long run
(c) simple rules are inexpensive in terms of the *administrative apparatus* required to implement them.

The idea that the performance of the economy should not depend on the will and the errors of policymakers and be freed of the cost of government administration has found expression in the search for automatic measures that are more complicated than Friedman's rule (i.e. rules acting at the level of market regime, such as perfect competition, and/or monetary systems, such as the Gold Standard) or more 'formal' systems (monetary and fiscal constitutions). The supposed merits of such regimes and systems will be examined at length later. Our concern here will be to analyse the implications of the choice between automatic rules and discretionary intervention in a multi-period decision environment. This will enable us to discuss some additional economic foundations of proposals for a monetary and fiscal constitution.

Let us first examine a situation in which there are no (automatic) rules. The time horizon is two periods and in each the government may choose the action that maximises its objective function.

Assume that the objective is the growth rate of output and policymakers wish to pursue this target through a policy designed to boost *innovation*. To stimulate technical progress, the government may initially promise inventors that they will be granted the right to the exclusive exploitation of their invention (patentability). However, once the inventions have been created (which we assume to occur by the end of period 1), the economy would benefit if everyone could use them freely, given the (allocative) inefficiency of monopoly. A policy of patent protection would therefore be *time inconsistent* – that is, it would be optimal in period 1 but no longer so in period 2, when private agents interested in producing inventions have already made their choices. Breaking the promise[b] to protect inventions, which is possible when government choices in period 2 are discretionary and not constrained by a rule, would generate a better outcome for the government. However, private agents are thus assumed to be *myopic* – i.e. they are induced to carry out research and development for their inventions, trusting that the patent protection promised at time 0 will be maintained in period 2. If, however, agents have rational expectations (more generally, forward-looking rather than backward-looking), discretion in government action does not ensure an optimal outcome: private agents, aware of the government's incentive to renege on its promise of patent protection, will not undertake any innovative activity.

This reasoning was initially advanced by Kydland and Prescott (1977) to argue that in the presence of rational expectations the optimal policy is not a time consistent one chosen discretionally in each period but rather an *a priori* rule that constrains future government action, inhibiting any change in that initial choice.[c]

The constraint on future government action (pre-commitment) may be based on *custom convention* or *law*,[d] adhered to by government in order to establish a *reputation* and strengthen its *credibility*. Thus, the daily practice of government activities that are consistent with previous commitments, repeated government affirmations of the inevitability of certain policies and the passage of laws with constitutional status or that delegate decisions to someone who does not suffer from the same temptation of opportunism (central banks, agencies) are different but not mutually exclusive ways of committing to a certain policy.

Although important, Kydland and Prescott's contribution does not demonstrate the superiority of fixed rules over discretionary policies. Discretionary policy is not simply that system in which policymakers have complete freedom of choice in the next period; the most general form of discretionary policy is the *flexible rule* (or strategy) that from the very beginning provides for the possibility of acting differently in period 2. It has been demonstrated that this sort of flexible rule is always superior to fixed rules under uncertainty (Buiter, 1981).

Returning to our patent protection example, a guarantee to protect the inventor based on a flexible rule that allows the duration of the protection to vary according to certain circumstances (e.g. the importance of the invention) produces better results than a fixed rule if there is uncertainty about the nature of the invention. Such a flexible rule would be time consistent, since the actual decisions will be taken (within the time limit set) in period 2 in the light of the information available at that time concerning the importance of the inventions realised. However, the rule does not give rise to credibility problems, or at least does not create larger credibility problems than those posed by fixed rules, which may in any case always be changed at some later time, since the terms of the future decision are set period 1 and are well known to private agents.

The literature in this area has identified other cases of time inconsistent policies. A particularly interesting example, discussed in Kydland and Prescott (1977) and later by other authors (e.g. Barro and Gordon, 1983) is choosing between *unemployment* and *inflation*. Assume two short-run expectations-augmented Phillips curves (f_1 and f_2 in figure 4B.1) and a long-run Phillips curve ($\bar{u}$, which according to the authors is vertical). The preferences of policymakers are also defined and are expressed as a map of indifference curves, W_1, W_2 and W_3.

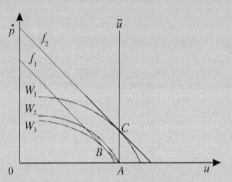

Figure 4B.1

Consider the choices of government[e] and workers in a two-period setting. In period 1 the government elects to choose point A, which is on indifference curve W_2, and announces that it will remain at A – i.e. will not introduce an expansionary and inflationary policy – in period 2 as well, after the unions have decided their wage policy. If the unions believed this promise, they would choose a policy of wage moderation (the relevant Phillips curve being f_1) that would allow the economy to remain at A. However, once the unions have chosen this strategy, the government would no longer have an incentive to remain at A in period 2, which is a second-best situation. Instead, the government could increase its utility by moving to the social indifference curve W_3, which is closer to the origin, at B (a first-best position) by adopting expansionary measures that reduce unemployment and raise the inflation rate. However, having rational expectations, the unions are aware of this possibility. Since they know the government will have an incentive to diverge from its announced non-inflationary policy, they will incorporate their inflation forecasts into their choices and seek large wage increases from the beginning of period 1. The relevant Phillips curve then becomes f_2. In this case, in period 2 the government should not expand the economy (i.e. let it move away from $u = \bar{u}$), which brings the economy of C, a third-best position. If the government adopted an expansionary policy, the economy would not move to C (where an indifference curve is tangent to the augmented Phillips curve) but rather to the left of that point along f_2, which would be suboptimal with respect to C.

Point C is therefore reached as the outcome of a time consistent policy, in which each agent chooses the best alternative in each period, taking previous decisions as given but forming rational expectations about the future. However, it is precisely these rational expectations that induce some agents (in our case, the unions) to take actions that limit the possible future choices of other agents (the government), leading to suboptimal results. Note that C provides less welfare than A, which is reached with a firm and credible commitment of the government to forgo expansionary policies of the kind mentioned earlier.

The problem of time consistency is certainly well founded, and the possibility that it will arise is a point in favour of rules. However, the constraint that such rules impose may be extremely burdensome if unexpected adverse events occur (e.g. a fall in world demand). In this case, the ability to react flexibly – through discretionary policies – may offer greater advantages than pre-commitment (Fischer, 1990; Bernanke and Mishkin, 1992). In other words, an initially desirable objective may lose its attraction with the passage of time. Time inconsistency is not necessarily an ill. Those who consider it so are perhaps influenced by the myth of Ulysses, who had himself bound to the mast in order not to succumb to the Sirens' song. Unfortunately, we lack a frame of reference to distinguish between good time inconsistency and bad time inconsistency and there is a risk that certain justified time inconsistency problems will be cited in support of irrevocable commitments (monetary and fiscal rules or constitutions), with hidden goals that are anything but neutral as regards the distribution of income and social impact.

Thus the question of the relative advantages of rules and discretion is not just an abstract quandary; rather, to a degree it reflects the different weight assigned to different policy objectives and different real-world circumstances. In particular, those who attribute considerable importance to monetary stability will try to rein in the competition that may give rise to inflation by means of rules that limit government action. Those who fear a fall in demand and employment will argue that rules limiting the freedom of government action make a recovery impossible and should thus be abandoned in favour of discretionary policies.

Notes:
a A survey of the debate on rules and discretionary intervention in recent years is given in Argy (1988).
b In the case of a threat the concept of *subgame perfection*, which is usually thought to be the same as time consistency, would be relevant (see Guiso and Terlizzese, 1990).
c Bear in mind that the rule must be fixed, i.e. a rule that provides for one action only and not one that determines the action on the basis of the prevailing circumstances or available information in the subsequent period. This sort of rule, known variously as a *non-contingent, non-causal, no-feedback* or *open-loop-rule*, contrasts with flexible rules (*contingent, causal, feedback* or *closed-loop*), which is the more general case of discretionary action.
d These terms represent the hierarchy of social institutions established by Max Weber (1922): custom (habits, etc.) is behaviour that has become habitual following protracted practice, conventions represent behaviour followed in order to avoid the disapproval of the social group to which one belongs; law is a behaviour followed in order to avoid specific punishments and penalties.
e Here, 'government' means any policymaker, which may be fiscal policy authorities or, as assumed in much of the literature, the monetary authorities.

4.5   The model

The pages that follow have an eminently technical purpose. They seek to clarify certain general aspects of the structure of an economic model and the modifications that a model must undergo in order to be used for policy purposes (a *policy* or *decision model*). In this context, the theoretical foundation of the models used (whether Keynesian, post-Keynesian, monetarist, etc.) is not important.

Let us briefly review the steps we took in the example in subsection 4.2.3. Once employment was identified as the objective, we considered an explanatory model of the variables that influence it (see (4.1)); this is an analytical *model in structural form*.

The structural form model was transformed through a series of mathematical steps in order to identify the variables on which employment ultimately depends, thus obtaining a *reduced form model* (4.2).

We then inverted the relationship between N and autonomous spending, thereby obtaining the *inverse reduced form* (see (4.3)); assigning a given value to N ($\overline{N}$) we solved the equation for G (4.4).

We will now examine each of these steps.

4.5.1   *The structural form of the model*

Recall that an analytical model is a set of relations, usually expressed in mathematical terms, that represents the economic process in an abstract and simplified form. A **structural form model** presents the relationships between variables as they are suggested by economic analysis.

The model is a simplified representation of reality and therefore captures only certain features of the actual economic system. Different policymakers may be interested in different aspects of reality. Therefore, for practical reasons it is necessary to construct a variety of models, each of which is intended to highlight specific features of economic life (see Tinbergen, 1956). Thus, we have microeconomic or macroeconomic models, static or dynamic models, deterministic or stochastic models, closed-economy and open-economy models, etc.

For the purposes of economic policy it is essential that the model be specified or modified in such a way that it can be used as a **decision model**: in other words, the variables that can be given the role of either fixed or flexible targets and those that can be used as instruments must be identified.

A model in structural form is composed of equations of various types:

(a) definitional equations
(b) behavioural equations
(c) technical equations
(d) equilibrium equations
(e) institutional equations.

Sometimes the same equation can be interpreted in a variety of ways.

The first equation in (4.1) is normally considered to be a **technical equation**, since it represents a special case of the production function $Y = f(K, N)$ – where K is the amount of capital goods available and N the supply of labour – when K is given (as is assumed in short-term analysis), so that income grows only when employment rises. In reality, since it is expressed in value terms rather than physical terms, the equation represents the behaviour of various agents (government, workers, firms, etc.), which is reflected in prices, and therefore is not a true technical equation.

The second equation in (4.1) is an **equilibrium equation** showing the relationship between output (supply) and the components of demand. With different specifications of the model, the equation could be considered a **definitional equation** of aggregate demand.

The last equation is a **behavioural equation**.

Institutional equations, which (4.1) does not have, express relationships and constraints deriving from the need to comply with laws or custom. An example of these is the prohibition on monetary financing of deficits in the Maastricht agreements, which regulate the process of EMU. This can be written as:

$$\Delta G = \Delta T + \Delta B$$

where G, T and B are, respectively, government expenditure, taxes and public debt. It expresses the rule according to which an increase in spending can be financed only with taxes or the issuing of government securities, not with monetary base.

Endogenous and exogenous variables

The variables in the structural form model can be classified as exogenous and endogenous.

Exogenous variables are those that determine other variables but are not in turn influenced by any variable; variables that fall into this category are data (in (4.1) they are c and $\bar{I}$)[7] and instruments (G, according to the hypothesis in the example).

Endogenous variables are those that can determine the value of some other variable but whose value in any case depends on other variables. Endogenous variables include

---

[7] A further distinction is sometimes drawn between *parameters* and *data* proper. In this case, **data** would be the exogenous variables that, although they can have different values in themselves (also as a result of public control), have a specific value in the model. **Parameters** are variables that indicate the sensitivity of certain variables to others in behavioural functions. These should be stable; i.e. they should be considered given (however, see the Lucas critique in section 4.7). When the model (i.e. the analytical perspective) changes, it sometimes becomes possible to explain such variables in terms of others; they therefore become endogenous variables.

For example, in model (4.1), as later amended by substituting $A = \bar{I} + G$, c is a parameter (while I is a datum). However, if we added the following equation to the simple consumption function in (4.1):

$$c = c_1 \frac{W}{Y} + c_2 \left(1 - \frac{W}{Y}\right)$$

where W denotes aggregate wages, c would become an endogenous variable, which can be influenced by income redistribution measures (e.g. an incomes policy).

The reader should note, however, that there is no consolidated terminology on the meaning of the term 'data' and 'parameter'. Sometimes, as we do in chapter 11, parameter is used with reference to constants that can be changed through government action.

objectives (in (4.1), N) and irrelevant variables (C and Y).[8] The reader can check that the variables indicated are endogenous variables: for example, C influences income but is also affected by it.

We can now say that the structural form of a model is the form in which endogenous variables are expressed as a function of other endogenous variables as well as exogenous variables. Indicating endogenous variables with y and exogenous variables with x, the structural form can be written as:

$$y = f(y, x)$$

4.5.2   The reduced form model

Fixed targets

Solving an economic policy problem expressed in terms of fixed targets requires that we first proceed from the structural form model to the reduced form, and then to the inverse reduced form.

The **reduced form model** is obtained from the structural model by eliminating through substitution all the irrelevant variables and expressing each residual endogenous variable (i.e. each target) in terms of exogenous variables only. There will therefore be as many reduced form equations as there are targets. This will prove helpful later in understanding the 'golden rule' of economic policy.

Equation (4.2) is the reduced form of the structural form model (4.1). Since there is only one target, the reduced form has only one equation. If the target is generically labelled y and the instrument x, (4.2) has the form $y = f(x)$.

With two targets, y_1 and y_2, and two instruments, x_1 and x_2, the reduced form model is:

$$y_1 = f_1(x_1, x_2)$$

$$y_2 = f_2(x_1, x_2)$$

(4.5)

The **inverse reduced form** is obtained by expressing the instruments as a function of the targets. In the case of a single target this means finding the inverse of $y = f(x)$, or expressing $y : x = f^{-1}(y)$; hence the name 'inverse reduced form'. In the case of two targets and two instruments the operation is similar, producing a system of the type:

$$x_1 = \phi_1(y_1, y_2)$$

$$x_2 = \phi_2(y_1, y_2)$$

(4.5')

Having expressed the instruments as a function of the targets, we need to assign a value to the latter in order to solve the policy problem, i.e. in order to determine the values

---

[8] The variables C and Y are irrelevant only with respect to the target of the decision model, N. This does not mean they are irrelevant in general.

of the instruments, which are unknowns. Thus, setting $y_1 = \bar{y}_1$ and $y_2 = \bar{y}_2$, we have:

$$x_1 = \phi_1(\bar{y}_1, \bar{y}_2)$$

$$x_2 = \phi_2(\bar{y}_1, \bar{y}_2)$$

(4.6)

However, to obtain the inverse reduced form a number of conditions must be met.

Recall that a necessary condition for solving a system of equations such as that given by (4.5) is that the number of unknowns be equal to the number of equations. Bearing in mind the fact that in an economic policy problem the unknowns are the instruments and the number of equations of the reduced form is equal to the number of targets, we can derive the **golden rule of economic policy**, which we owe to Tinbergen: in the case of fixed objectives, the solution of an economic policy problem requires that the number of instruments be at least equal to the number of targets.

If the number of (independent) instruments is exactly equal to the number of targets, the system is *determined*. If the number of instruments is greater (less) than the number of targets, the system is *underdetermined* (*overdetermined*), i.e. there are multiple solutions (no solutions).

Imagine that we have one target and two instruments: it is possible to assign an arbitrary value to one instrument and determine the value of the other by solving the inverse reduced form. There are, therefore, an infinite number of solutions, one for each of the values assigned to the first instrument; in general, if there are m targets and n instruments, with $m < n$, we say there are $n - m$ *degrees of freedom*.

If, however, there are two linearly independent targets, one instrument is not sufficient to ensure their attainment. In general, there are a number of possible responses where the number of instruments is less than the number of targets:

(a) *drop the excess targets*; if we have m targets and n instruments, we must drop $m - n$ targets
(b) find *new instruments with different effectiveness* than available instruments with respect to at least one target. The number of new instruments must be $m - n$
(c) abandon the attempt to set the policy problem in terms of fixed targets in favour of a *flexible-target approach*.

Before leaving the fixed-target example, two remarks are in order. The first concerns the reduced form (4.5). Note that the instrument x_1 influences both targets, as does the second instrument, x_2. In general terms, each instrument will influence both targets and it will not be possible to adjust a single instrument in order to influence a specific target without affecting other targets as well. Thus, as we mentioned at the beginning of section 4.2, in general it is necessary to determine the value of the instruments simultaneously, which tends to favour centralised policy control, thereby ensuring that decisions are coordinated. Nevertheless, there are situations where *decentralised solutions* (for example, independent management of monetary and fiscal policy) are possible or even desirable. We will return to this issue when we discuss the appropriate assignment of instruments to objectives in section 14.10.

Our second remark concerns the number of available instruments. The existence of numerous market failures may mean that the government will try to achieve multiple objectives. The possibility of attaining the objectives is linked to the availability of an equal number of instruments, if we wish to use fixed targets. Therefore, any inhibition on the use of certain instruments deriving from preconceived positions and political, social or ideological constraints does not facilitate the government's job.

Some such restraints are codified as laws or institutions, while others clearly go against both the letter and the spirit of laws or international treaties. In any case, they can create serious obstacles to the rational design and solution of economic policy problems. There are many situations in which these impediments occur: the willingness of a government to devalue or revalue its currency, resistance to direct controls, whether with reference to either domestic relationships (e.g. rationing or lending ceilings, price controls) or foreign ones (e.g. quotas, restrictions on capital movements) and so on.

Flexible targets

A flexible-objective problem is framed in terms of maximising or minimising a social welfare function subject to the constraints given by the relationships of the model, which represent the functioning of the economic system. With two generic targets, y_1 and y_2, we have:

$$\max[W = f(y_1, y_2)]$$

subject to

$$y_1 = f_1(x_1, x_2)$$
$$y_2 = f_2(x_1, x_2)$$

As we said earlier, this problem can be solved even if the number of instruments is less than the number of targets (for example, if we have only the instrument x_1 and not x_2). Clearly, in this case the value of the social welfare function that can be obtained will be lower. Gaining access to a larger number of instruments as a result of scientific progress or overcoming inhibitions and constraints will therefore have a positive effect on social welfare.

4.6   Limits and extensions of the classical approach

In the preceding pages we have set out the fundamental features of modern economic policy, whose founding fathers were Frisch, Tinbergen, Meade, Leontief, Hansen and Theil.

The key feature of this approach is its global vision of policy problems, which is reflected in the consideration of the diffuse effects of manoeuvring each instrument, i.e. effects that influence not one target only, but rather a number of targets, or even all of them. At the practical level, this conceptual apparatus enables us to approach real problems rationally, since we can calculate 'exact' solutions – i.e. the values of the instruments that will achieve certain objectives or maximise a social welfare function.

However, the reader must not be lulled into thinking that all problems can be solved in this way. The approach has a number of limitations; some (such as its static and certain nature) can be removed by specifying the model appropriately. We examine this aspect later in this section. Other criticisms are of a logical nature, but they can also have a crucial impact at the empirical level (e.g. the Lucas critique). We discuss these in section 4.7.

Still others concern: (a) the realism of characterising policymakers as 'representatives' of indistinct citizens; and (b) the problems associated with the cost and the political or administrative feasibility of the solutions generated by the models. These difficulties will be discussed in chapter 5.

Let us take a brief look at the problems associated with the static and deterministic nature of this approach.[9] These limitations can be overcome, although at the cost of reducing the tractability of the model.

Considering a dynamic model raises a number of specific problems that are worth mentioning. First, let us clarify some consequences of the 'golden rule' of economic policy. We saw that in the case of fixed objectives in a static context, the necessary condition for the existence of a solution is that the number of instruments should at least be equal to the number of targets. This condition does not hold in the case of a dynamic model where we seek, for example, to attain one or more fixed targets in the future.[10] Even if we have a smaller number of instruments than targets, under certain conditions it is possible to reach these objectives by extending the time necessary to achieve them. The 'golden rule' regains validity when we wish to maintain control of the target or targets over time – that is, when we desire to keep the economy moving along a given growth path.[11] A dynamic approach may also raise problems regarding the time consistency of decisions; we will not consider it in this book.

A different matter, which we mentioned earlier, concerns situations where a policy problem involving a number of targets and instruments can be solved separately, i.e. in a decentralised way, rather than simultaneously, i.e. in a centralised way. We will discuss this in section 14.10.

4.7 The Lucas critique

In decision models the behaviour of private agents (consumers, entrepreneurs, etc.) is assumed to be predictable on the basis of a given specification of the behavioural functions and the identification of the (fixed) parameters. Policy decisions are determined by setting certain objectives and taking into account the relationships between these

---

[9] In addition, we are dealing with a *linear model*. Overcoming this limitation requires advanced techniques that are not appropriate to our discussion here.

[10] This problem is known as a **target point controllability** problem and the target is also called a 'point target'.

[11] This is a problem of **perfect** or **target path controllability**. On this and target point controllability, see Preston and Pagan (1982).

objectives and policy instruments based on the behaviour of private agents. However, this approach ignores the feedback effect of government decisions on the behavioural *functions* of private agents.

We are not arguing that a decision model does not consider the reactions of private agents to government action at all. This would not be consistent with what we have said so far. If, for example, government influences national income (through government spending on consumption and investment) or disposable income (through taxes and transfers in addition to government consumption and investment), private consumption will be affected by fiscal policy: if $C = c(Y - T + Tr_h)$, where T are taxes and Tr_h are transfers to households, fiscal policy will affect C through G (which acts on Y), T and Tr_h, and therefore the model accounts for consumers' reactions to government action. Rather, we wish to argue that changes in policy regimes (or the rules governing policy choices) can influence the *parameters* of private behavioural functions (in our example, c), i.e. the sensitivity of private agents to government decisions, or the functional *form* of private agents' behaviour. This is the substance of the critique advanced by Lucas (1976) (the **Lucas critique**) against the classical model of economic policy.[12] Let us try to understand better the foundation and the nature of this critique.

The analytical models used as a basis for decision models are normally the product of econometric analysis that establishes the exact specification of the form of behavioural functions and the independent variables as well as the value of the parameters. Econometric tests are based on available data about the relevant variables in past situations (characterised by the presence of certain external shocks, certain types of policy, etc.). The tested model is then used to forecast the consequences of certain policies, e.g. an increase in government spending, and design an optimal policy. However, this is accomplished by taking as given and invariant the estimated values of the parameters and the form of the behavioural functions of private agents (e.g. the propensity to consume and the form of consumption function) in the new situation. This might not be the case. Suppose that government spending has not been adjusted in previous years or that any adjustment in the past involved different forms of spending, for example, investment rather than government consumption or transfers, or certain types of government expenditure (teachers' salaries) rather than others (student canteens). A change in the volume and/or content of public expenditure may give rise to new private behaviour. For example, a programme to increase the number of student canteens might change students' propensity to consume so that it differed from that estimated with econometric models based on data collected before the number of canteens was increased.

If the model parameters change, reflecting a change in the behaviour of the system, and the 'old' model is taken as a constraint in the government decision model, the ensuing policies will not be optimal at all: they would be so only if private behaviour

---

[12] Another limitation of the structure of the models we have examined goes beyond the hypothesis that private agents have behavioural functions that do not change in response to changes in government behaviour: it derives from the implicit hypothesis that private agents have no power and are unable to influence government behaviour with their actions, which is clearly unrealistic.

did not change. In other words, the constraint underlying the design of government action is not a real constraint, but rather *changes as government behaviour itself changes*.

The Lucas critique is undoubtedly well founded and raises both practical and theoretical problems. At the practical level, the amount by which parameters change in response to the change in economic policies is important: if the change is small, designing policy on the basis of previously estimated values will be broadly reliable. Obviously, reliability also depends on the data set used to estimate the parameters: the larger the set and the more it encompasses situations in which different policies are in use, the less the parameters will vary and the greater the reliability of the model's indication of optimal policies will be. In the 1970s many macroeconomic relationships broke down as a consequence of major changes in the policy regime, since agents adjusted their behaviour to the new environment (Chrystal and Price, 1994).

From a theoretical point of view, the Lucas critique underscores the presence of *reciprocal interactions* between the behaviour of private agents and government. In particular, the private sector plays an active rather than passive role, changing its behaviour as expectations about government behaviour change. The critique is a response to the fact that traditional analytical models do not admit this sort of interaction. In order to overcome these limitations, we need to change the type of model we use. For example, we might make use of **game theory**, since it is specifically structured to model strategic interactions between agents.

Questions raised by Lucas' critique have a specific relevance for the evolution of agents' conduct and market performance since the 1980s. The spread of economic knowledge, liberalisation and international opening of markets, the rising importance of financial markets and the speed of changes in those markets all imply the formation and spread of forward-looking expectations. By their nature, these features mean that sudden changes are possible, following rules that are difficult to detect.

There are at least two consequences relevant for economic policy:

(a) First, economic trends are more often the outcome of conventions and 'fads'; in this situation only *public policy* can move the economy out of liquidity traps, unemployment, and, more generally, undesired equilibria.
(b) Public policy must, however, take account of the active nature of private agents' conduct as well as the effects on the formation of their expectations. Hence, public action should not breed expectations that make it ineffective; on the contrary, it should create expectations that generate *desirable conduct*. These necessary features of public policy tend to limit the range of feasible policies.

In summary, the evolution of economic systems, while making public intervention more necessary, also seems to impose certain restrictions on the range of effective policies.

The importance of financial markets in these conclusions cannot be overstated. They are the main mechanism for channelling the influence of expectations and, then, the limits to the effectiveness of public policy. This is because expectations in financial markets change more rapidly than in other markets: since financial instruments are promises rather than physical objects, by their very nature they express evaluations of the future to a larger extent than physical assets, which, in any case, have a value in the present (see Gnesutta, 1999). At different points in the subsequent analysis we will underscore the interaction between public action and private agents' behaviour through the influence of public action on private agents' expectations.

4.8 Summary

1   The identification of numerous 'market failures' suggested the need for intervention by an agent that, having collective (public) motives and objectives, would be able to *transcend these failures*.

2   The normative theory of government intervention aims to provide the conceptual apparatus for the adoption of coordinated and consistent economic policy decisions (*planning*).

3   The need for coordination is a consequence of the *multiplicity* of instruments, each of which can influence all of the objectives (albeit each in a different way), and of the *interdependence* between decisions in different periods.

4   An *economic policy plan* (decision model) comprises objectives, an analytical model and instruments.

5   In a rational approach to economic policy, objectives are identified by policymakers and reflect the preferences of the public. They can be expressed as: fixed targets, priorities, flexible targets with a constant or variable MRS. In the case of the flexible-target approach, policymakers formulate a *SWF* whose arguments are the objectives and sometimes the instruments.

6   An *instrument* is a controllable, effective and separable (independent) variable.

7   We make a distinction between quantitative, qualitative and *reform policies*; direct and indirect *control measures*; *discretionary measures* and *automatic rules*.

8   *Structural form models* present the relationships between variables as suggested by economic analysis. They are composed of technical, definitional, behavioural, equilibrium and institutional equations. The variables in the models are exogenous (data, instruments) and endogenous (targets, irrelevant variables).

9   *Reduced form models* are obtained from structural form models and express targets as a function of exogenous variables alone.

10 In the case of fixed targets, the solution to the planning problem can be obtained with the *inverse reduced form model* (derived from the reduced form) by assigning the desired value to the targets and solving for the instrumental variables. A solution is possible if the 'golden rule' of economic policy is satisfied: the number of instruments must be at least equal to the number of targets. If this is not the case, we can: (a) increase the number of instruments; (b) reduce the number of targets; (c) change the design of the policy problem and express the objectives as flexible targets.

11 A *flexible-target problem* involves maximising a SWF, subject to the constraint imposed by the relations of the model.

12 The classical approach to rational economic policy has many limitations. One of the most important was identified by Lucas (the *Lucas critique*), who argued that it ignores the feedback effects of policy regimes on the behavioural functions of private agents, which are assumed to be invariant.

5 Government failures: elements of a positive theory of economic policy

5.1 Representing social groups

In section 4.6 we discussed the limitations of the normative or 'classical' theory of economic policy in general terms. In this chapter we will analyse the limitations associated with the *normative* character of the theory.

The *normative theory* of economic policy is a 'theory of the public interest' and ignores the problem of the realism of the hypotheses on which it is based, in particular with reference to the nature of individuals and the behaviour of policymakers. In this sense, it suffers from the same limitations that typify the conceptual apparatus of neoclassical theory, on which it draws extensively. Much of the neoclassical approach is constructed in axiomatic form: the behaviour of individuals is deduced from a set of postulates. The normative theory of economic policy postulates the existence of an agent (the policymaker) who acts in the interests of somewhat indistinct individuals, incorporating the 'will of the people' into a social welfare function (Downs, 1957).

This approach largely neglects the following aspects of reality:

(a) the economic system is not composed of *indistinct individuals*
(b) policymakers are not *anonymous*, as the theory assumes.

In this section, we address the first aspect before moving on to the second in section 5.2.

The normative theory of economic policy in its most extreme form assumes that individuals are virtually anonymous, albeit possessing specific (abstract) preferences and different initial endowments of resources. Within this framework, government action should seek to improve *efficiency* (and therefore the relatively undifferentiated position of 'individuals') and, possibly, the *personal distribution of income*, reflecting a view of the 'public interest' that is sustained by the idea of generic individuals. Such individuals ('the people') suggest their preferences to policymakers, who include them in the social welfare function (SWF).

The 'people', however, is not composed of indistinct members. We can aggregate these individuals into classes or groups with shared interests, needs or ideas, which tend to act jointly through their organisations – *interest groups, lobbies, cartels, unions, political parties*, etc. – in order to ensure that their preferences prevail over those of other groups.[1]

These classes or groups have different levels of power, which are expressed in both reciprocal economic relationships and the influence they can exert on the construction of the 'social welfare function' – i.e. in determining the weight to be assigned to the various policy objectives. From this point of view, the problem of the personal distribution of wealth, which was the only apparent difference between individuals in neoclassical theory, becomes a key point of conflict between different social groups. It is therefore of special importance to know how 'similar' individuals organise themselves to achieve common objectives within a society, including their use of 'public' action. What would otherwise be a largely 'anonymous' SWF thus begins to acquire texture and definition.

Economics, at least in the version given by the mainstream neoclassical school, does not provide appropriate conceptual categories to tackle some of the problems we have raised: for example, the concepts of *power* and *class* (or group) are missing or play a limited role, and *private institutions* other than the market are virtually non-existent.

By contrast, the concepts of power, class and institution are at the centre of other social sciences, especially political science (Alt and Chrystal, 1983). Since the 1980s this has given rise to a new approach to economic problems, called *political economy* or *political economics*, that gives greater importance to such concepts. The approach still lacks a clear and unifying conceptual structure but offers valuable guidelines for a more realistic treatment of economic policy problems[2] (see the work by Persson and Tabellini, 2000).

Keynesian macroeconomics, adopting in part the classical approach of Smith, Ricardo, Marx and others, innovated on the traditional neoclassical framework by introducing a systematic differentiation of individuals into different classes (capitalists–wage earners; savers–investors). Nevertheless, the implications of Keynesian economic policy broadly apply to society as a whole: especially in a model with fixed prices, in some situations achieving full employment can improve the situation of all of society's members, whether wage earners or capitalists, savers or investors. Similar results can be obtained if we consider other macroeconomic objectives such as the balance of payments or economic growth. Introducing inflation into this framework is more difficult. Inflation is the outcome of a competition between different categories of economic agents, and in fostering or dampening inflation government will probably fail to remain neutral between these groups.

An especially important contribution in this area has been made by **interest group theory** (or **capture theory**). This acknowledges the existence of groups of individuals

[1] In referring to *classes* or *groups* the existence of well-defined preferences shared by group members is usually assumed. However, it has recently been shown that, in practice, in many policy problems preferences can be unstable, uncertain and founded on inadequate information. This has important consequences for the role that can be played by institutions in debating and forming preferences (see Gerber and Jackson, 1993). On the other hand, Sen (1995) has noted that solving many vital problems of the contemporary world requires forming values through public discussion.

[2] In some cases it appears more the product of a fad. For a survey of the various strands of political economy, see Staniland (1985).

with shared interests (and/or values) and sees government action to some extent as a reflection of the pressure of such groups.[3] This theory, which has roots in the Marxian idea that capitalists control social institutions and in the work of political scientists at the beginning of the twentieth century, has been formulated in the post-war period by the **public choice school**, which was founded by Downs (1957), Olson (1965) and Buchanan and Tullock (1962). It also includes a number of other economists such as Becker, Niskanen, Peltzman, Stigler and Tollison, mainly affiliated with the universities of Chicago and Virginia. This school has a clear free market orientation.

The traditional figures of capitalists and wage earners have thus emerged in the role of social agents, no longer as individuals but as institutions representing them (unions, political parties, etc.). Even consumers, particular categories of firm (e.g. financial and non-financial enterprises, firms exposed to international competition and those sheltered from such competition) and workers (employed and unemployed, skilled and unskilled) have appeared in a different light when they have been represented as seeking to solicit government intervention in their favour through specific organisations.

The different social groups may wish to influence government action in a number of circumstances:

(a) in general *policy attitudes* such as the adoption of expansionary or restrictive poli-
     cies; the choice of some kinds of policy instruments that may have different conse-
     quences for various groups
(b) in more specific actions involving *selective intervention* (different tax rates, sectoral
     or regional incentives, protection of specific sectors, etc.).

Obviously, more general intervention is sought by larger groups capable of stimulating widespread support, while specific, 'sectional' actions are solicited by smaller groups (see Olson, 1982, p. 48). For example, a political party or confederation of industries or labour unions might advocate expansionary or restrictive policies; progressive or flat-rate taxation. By contrast, a company or local union might ask for support for individual firms or sectors, through tax exemptions, incentives or protection specific to a company or industry.

There are numerous ways in which groups exercise their influence on government authorities. They include: voting, personal connections, opinion campaigns of varying degrees of openness, corruption and promises to politicians and bureaucrats of a lucrative career when they leave government service (see Grossman and Helpman, 2001).

The new types of private agent that we have identified certainly make the concept of society richer than that obtained by considering a set of indistinct individuals alone. However, it is obviously not enough to crowd the stage with a variety of characters in order to achieve a better representation of the realities of social life and the way

---

[3] The term reflects the idea that politicians, who were initially seen by economists as promoting the public good, are in fact 'captured' by groups and induced to take positions and decisions that favour these particular groups.

public decisions are reached. What we really need at this point is a macroeconomic and macropolitical theory that incorporates hypotheses about the behaviour of social groups and their interactions.

The premises for such a theory exist and can be found, in our opinion, in the Keynesian methodology and in the growing body of work in other social sciences, especially political science. In addition, game theory seems to provide a powerful methodology, albeit not a robust one,[4] for analysing social interactions, especially under uncertainty and informational asymmetry.

5.2 Agency problems: the objectives of politicians and the political business cycle

The identity of policymakers is entirely ignored in the classical theory of economic policy. Much like firms in the theory of general equilibrium, policymakers in the classical theory could be replaced by a computer. They have no identity and their role as *agents* of the indistinct individuals or social groups that they should represent is not recognised. They have no personal ideas about the desirability of the various solutions and they have no personal or other interests to pursue apart from a generic 'public interest'. There is therefore no need for institutional constraints or incentives to induce them to pursue the public interest (or even the interest of a social group).

In addition, in pursuing the economic policies deemed appropriate, they do not have to overcome any obstacles either in the social context in which they work or in the executive apparatus. With specific reference to the latter, the people responsible for defining policy objectives in turn face no agency problem in implementing the policies needed to secure those objectives, even if implementation is necessarily overseen by others. Hence, the role of these people as 'agents' of those who have been charged with defining public objectives is not recognised either.

In order to underscore the anonymous character of the people to whom classical theory attributes the task of formulating objectives and taking the actual public policy measures, we have spoken generically of *policymakers* or 'public authorities'. From our discussion it is now clear that this indistinct government apparatus is composed of two categories of person, **politicians** and **bureaucrats**. The former, who are elected, define the objectives of government intervention. The latter, who are employees, translate the guidelines of the politicians into reality. For both politicians and bureaucrats an *incentive problem* arises.

On a stage no longer populated by amorphous 'actors' but rather by groups of individuals with specific features, it is natural that we also seek to characterise each category of policymaker. It is reasonable to think that each policymaker has specific values and interests and, in addition, interacts in different ways with the other social agents we have identified. In this section we will deal with politicians; in section 5.3, bureaucrats.

---

[4] We refer to the fact that the conclusions reached in using game theory are often very sensitive to the particular hypotheses adopted to model the games.

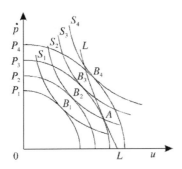

Figure 5.1

The mid-1970s saw the formulation of the so-called 'political business cycle' theory (Nordhaus, 1975, Lindbeck, 1976, MacRae, 1977 and others), which made specific reference to 'politicians' – i.e. elected representatives responsible for public decisions.

Actually, the first formulation of a **political business cycle theory** was offered by Kalecki (1943),[5] who argued that it was impossible for a capitalist system to pursue full employment in the long run: the elimination of the business cycle with expansionary demand policies and the creation of a *welfare state*[6] would reduce worker discipline owing to the removal of the threat of unemployment. Inflation and restrictive policies would result, which would thus give rise to a political business cycle.[7]

Nordhaus' political business cycle is not the secondary effect of policies with other goals (as it is in Kalecki and Robinson), but rather the result of the hypothesis that the decisions of politicians are an expression of their *own* preferences. In other words, Nordhaus' basic hypothesis is that politicians, like other people, can be characterised by their status and that they express preferences and interests accordingly. More precisely, the primary objective of politicians is to *remain in office*. They therefore attempt to steer the economy in such a way as to maximise the number of votes they can expect to receive.

Nordhaus' second hypothesis is that election results are significantly influenced by the current economic situation. In particular, he assumes that voters, as though affected by memory loss, give most weight to the performance of the economy in the period closest to the election and, by contrast, are short-sighted and unaware of the negative long-term consequences of the economic measures implemented during electoral periods.

A third hypothesis concerns the government's ability to expand the economy using monetary and fiscal instruments in the short run, even if the expansion is not sustainable in the long run except at the cost of higher inflation. This may occur since the inflationary consequences of expansion are delayed, thus giving politicians scope to increase their popularity at election time.

Nordhaus' model can be shown in fairly simple terms by figure 5.1.

---

[5] See also Robinson (1943).
[6] Both Kalecki's and Robinson's work emerged in relation to the preparation of the 1942 Beveridge Report, which set out the foundations of the welfare state.
[7] A similar sort of political business cycle was proposed by Glyn and Sutcliffe (1972).

S_1, S_2, S_3 and S_4 are short-run Phillips curves, while LL is a long-run Phillips curve (not completely vertical);[8] curves marked P represent the social preference function, with those furthest from the origin being associated with lower levels of welfare.[9] The equilibrium point for the politician who acts in the long-term public interest is A (the point of tangency between the long-run Phillips curve and a social preference curve). Assume the system is at A. The politician will be induced to choose the initially more popular solution B_2, which is on the short-run Phillips curve that passes through A. This, however, is not a sustainable position, since such a Phillips curve, if price expectations are incorrect, will shift upwards to S_3, then to S_4 and so on.[10] This means that in a subsequent election, feasible points will be on social indifference curves further away from the origin, with consequently lower social welfare. As a result, long-run inflation in democratic countries is higher than the socially optimal level. An additional consequence is that unemployment tends to decline during election periods.

Some of the hypotheses adopted by Nordhaus are plausible:

(a) the idea that politicians attribute considerable (if not primary) importance to being *re-elected*
(b) the dependence of *voter 'mood'* on the current economic situation.

Less convincing is the argument that politicians are always able to influence the short-run performance of the economy in the desired direction: for example, this is unlikely in a small country open to international trade in the midst of a global recession. Probably the strongest (implicit) hypothesis is that of the 'indistinct' politician seeking to orient equally 'indistinct' private agents. This hypothesis was discarded with the introduction of the **'partisan' politician** (from which comes the **partisan theory of the political business cycle**; see Hibbs, 1977, 1992; Madse, 1981; Alesina, 1987).

According to this theory, each political party assigns different weights to different economic objectives for ideological reasons and/or because it represents different interests and social groups. With respect to a given situation different solutions will be proposed by the various parties, even if they share the same information. The alternation of parties in government therefore implies different economic policies and gives rise to a business cycle that, given its political origins, can again be called a 'political' business cycle.

Taking the United States as an example, suppose that the Democrats give greater weight to reducing unemployment than to reducing inflation (as in fact they do); the opposite holds for the Republicans. A change of party at the helm of government will lead to a change in the direction of economic policy: the replacement of a Republican administration with a Democratic one will lead to an expansion of economic activity, a

---

[8] As with other economists, Nordhaus accepts the idea that the long-run Phillips curve is steeper than the short-run curve but, unlike the monetarists, argues that it does not become vertical.

[9] They are in fact '*iso-vote*' lines: each shows the combinations of inflation and unemployment that give rise to the same percentage of the vote for the incumbent. Voting can be considered as an indication of *social preference*.

[10] The reader will note that moving from A to B_2 and B_3 gives rise to a *business cycle* triggered by the actions of politicians.

reduction in unemployment and an increase in inflation; the return of the Republicans would reverse this trend.

The cyclical behaviour of the economy is suboptimal, but inefficiency can be eliminated if the parties commit to a common cooperative policy rule, which would make both the social groups they represent better off in the long run. Even without binding commitments, the parties can improve the outcome of discretionary policies with actions that enable them to acquire a reputation (for example, for anti–inflationary rigour, see Alesina, 1987).

The range of application of models that postulate some interaction between political dynamics and economic dynamics has broadened considerably in recent years (for an interesting review, see Hibbs, 2005). Rogoff and Sibert (1988) and others have sought to explain the apparent irrationality and suboptimality of voter behaviour in reaction to, for example, election-period tax cuts that are then followed by fiscal tightening or inflation after the elections. According to these authors, such behaviour is entirely understandable in a situation of asymmetric information, where the government has a privileged position and seeks to signal the positive performance of the economy by means of tax cuts.

Long-run problems have also been tackled, such as the growth in public deficits,[11] which some attribute to a divergence between the preferences of current voters and those of future voters or to the uncertainty of electoral outcomes;[12] others explain it as a function of the characteristics of the electoral and political system.[13] Consideration has also been given to the possible advantages of cooperation between governments with different preferences concerning employment and monetary stability (Acocella and Di Bartolomeo, 2003).

Finally, it has been suggested that competition between political parties not only leads to different economic policy proposals but also to different theories about the functioning of the economy. Such theories, which are usually attributed to the difference between the conservative and progressive ('liberal') visions, can emerge as a 'strategic' device to further the specific interests of different social groups or classes. For example,

---

[11] This is a different problem from the 'classic' problem of the rise in public expenditure, which has also been analysed by drawing on politics, sociology and the theory of organisation (theory of interest or pressure groups, theory of bureaucracy). A summary but complete survey of both problems is given by Mueller (2003, chapters 19 and 21).

[12] It is realistically assumed that the preferences of future voters are uncertain. This prevents current voters from knowing how public expenditure will be distributed in the future. They will then seek at least to direct current spending in their favour and thus to increase it, even if this gives rise to a budget deficit (Tabellini and Alesina, 1990). Alesina and Tabellini (1990) argue that public debt can be used strategically by a government to influence the decisions of future governments, as there is no incentive to internalise the burden of debt service (for interest and repayment of principal), given the high level of uncertainty regarding the identity of the politicians that will be elected in the near future and differences in political orientation.

[13] Roubini and Sachs (1989) find a clear tendency towards larger deficits in countries with short-lived governments and large numbers of parties in governing coalitions. Similar results were obtained by Grilli, Masciandaro and Tabellini (1991). McCubbins (1991) explains the US public debt in the 1980s as the product of the government being divided between a Republican president and a Democratic majority in Congress ('cohabitation'): the vetoes of each side over the spending plans of the other were overcome only through compromise solutions and log-rolling, which resulted in an increase in the public debt.

one can argue that the elasticity of the labour supply to the income tax rate is high (low) simply in order to obtain the votes of those in favour of low (high) tax rates and a correspondingly low (high) level of government expenditure (Roemer, 1994).

The available empirical evidence seems to give only partial support to the various political business cycle models, lending more weight to the 'partisan' version. In particular, there do not seem to be significant pre-electoral effects on economic variables of the sort predicted by Nordhaus (1975). Among other things, this may be the result of:

(a) the difficulty with which the government can influence economic variables, depending on external constraints
(b) the fact that, contrary to the central hypothesis of the Nordhaus approach, politicians do not attempt to win voter favour with expansionary policies.

Empirical studies show that the second hypothesis does not hold, since there is some evidence of a **political budget cycle**, i.e. expansionary fiscal (and monetary) policies in the run-up to elections (Alesina, Cohen and Roubini, 1992).[14]

The evidence gathered so far must be carefully studied and assessed in the light of more satisfactory models of the interactions between politics and the economy that leave room for the special characteristics of individual countries. The conditions in which opportunistic fiscal and monetary measures by the government can take place need further analysis. On the one hand, if the government feels certain to win the elections, it will have no reason to implement such measures. On the other, the probability of winning will depend on a variety of factors, including the 'naiveté' or 'myopia' of voters, which differs across countries and over time.

In conclusion, we should note that stressing the existence of politicians' own objectives – or in any case objectives that differ according to social group or class – weakens the emphasis on public (rather than private) interest as the defining feature of the government and accentuates the importance of another of its attributes: the power of *coercion* (see Holcombe, 1994).

5.3   Agency problems: bureaucracy

The **bureaucracy** is composed of the (unelected) individuals who implement the measures decided by politicians. Here, too, tasks are delegated by someone to someone else and agency problems arise, as they do in the relationships between voters and politicians.

---

[14] One embarrassing result of Alesina, Cohen and Roubini (1992) appears to emerge in relation to the presence of a **monetary policy cycle** in Germany. The embarrassment is linked to the fact that the Bundesbank even before EMU, was almost unanimously considered to be the central bank with the greatest independence from political authority. However, expansionary monetary policies implemented before elections would seem to counter this view, showing that the Bundesbank has an interest in favouring the government in power. An explanation for this could be the presence of representatives of states (*Länder*) in the governing body of the Bundesbank. In any case this would undermine the idea that the Bundesbank is highly independent of the government.

Various authors, including Tullock (1965), Downs (1967) and above all Niskanen (1971, 1975) have emphasised the fact that the behaviour of government officials can be explained if we assume that they seek to maximise their own utility. This behaviour can depend on a variety of factors, which certainly do not include only, or even mainly, the pursuit of the public interest. Rather, it includes the satisfaction of bureaucrats' personal aspirations for income, prestige, power, etc. According to Niskanen, many of these factors are linked to the size of the department, enterprise or agency in which the government officials work. The result is a bias in bureaucratic conduct towards increasing the size of government. This is made possible by the centralisation of bureaucratic functions and, therefore, the monopoly position of various departments with respect to both citizens (as suppliers of public goods and services) and politicians, who, in turn, have exclusive use of the departments themselves (*bilateral monopoly*). We know from economic theory that in this form of market the result (in our case, the level of government activity)[15] depends on the bargaining power of the two parties and cannot be said *a priori* to be in favour of one or the other. Nevertheless, in reality the situation favours the bureaucrats, owing to the incompleteness of the information on administrative activity available to politicians. The tendency towards a steady expansion of the public sector is thus fuelled by the personal interests of bureaucrats in addition to the factors we considered in section 5.1, which involve the interests of politicians.

Other authors have noted that bureaucracy tends to generate high costs owing to *operational inefficiencies*. This is largely attributable not only to the peculiarities of administrative work compared with normal productive activity, such as the relative scarcity of innovations,[16] but also to the difficulty of measuring results, the ambiguity of technologies and the multiplicity of objectives (which are typical characteristics of government activity). Moreover, government bureaucracy often places excessive emphasis on quality owing to the weight of the opinions of experts, who are not very interested in the production cost of the goods and services provided.

Although these analyses contain some elements of realism, they have also been criticised. In particular, it has been remarked that there is no positive correlation between the centralisation of departments and the growth of bureaucracy. Moreover, in the long run the possibility of creating multiple departments to carry out the same administrative work would undermine the situation of bilateral monopoly, replacing it with a monopsony of politicians. Migué and Bélanger (1974) have argued, contrary to Niskanen's position, that there are elements of conflict (substitutability) between the size of a department and the personal interests of bureaucrats: an expansion of the supply of government goods and services reduces the resources available to pay bureaucrats' salaries. Efficiency would still be a problem, since the level of bureaucrats'

---

[15] In Niskanen's original contribution, the preference functions of politicians and bureaucrats differ: the former tend to maximise the difference between benefits (in terms of the budget's size) and the production costs of public services; the latter seek to maximise the size of the budget subject to the constraint of covering costs. The result is a tendency for bureaucrats to increase the size of the budget beyond the level of maximum satisfaction for politicians, where cost is equal to marginal benefit. For a simple presentation of Niskanen's model, see Mueller (2003, chapter 16).

[16] These are common to both private and public sector bureaucracies.

pay could in a certain sense be too high, but this difficulty differs from that identified by Niskanen.

Apart from modifications of the emphasis placed on the various aspects of the behaviour of government bureaucracy, the real problem lies in the differences with the analogous behaviour of private sector bureaucracies. Certainly, empirical studies can contribute to identifying the existence and extent of the differences. However, studies conducted so far do not offer clear conclusions, although most indicate better results for the private sector (see, with different emphasis, Stiglitz, 1988 and Mueller, 2003). The feeling that government bureaucracy is inefficient is even more widespread than empirical results would suggest (Stiglitz, 1988).

Apart from differences with private sector bureaucracies, in a policy perspective it is important to identify the two fundamental problems that arise when one wants to improve the performance of government bureaucracies:

(a) specifying *individual tasks* in a way that is consistent with the information handling abilities of each bureaucrat
(b) ensuring that each bureaucrat conscientiously carries out the *tasks assigned* by politicians.

With regard to the second problem, the aims of politicians are to avoid *shirking*, the *corruption* of government employees by individuals who could benefit from the action of the bureaucrat[17] and the formation of *bureaucratic oligarchies* that favour the special preferences of government employees over those expressed through the democratic process. These goals can be achieved in two substantially different ways:

(1) through the establishment of sufficiently rigid *administrative procedures*: once the interests to be safeguarded have been identified, the actions of bureaucrats to satisfy those interests are guided by specifying the procedures to be followed, including the publicity of certain acts, and sanctions (i.e. a 'negative' incentive) for deviation from the prescribed procedures
(2) through the introduction of *explicit 'positive' incentives*[18], such as incentives linked to 'output', reliance on competition between bureaucrats or on consumer action.

The choice between the two approaches to obtaining the desired behaviour depends on many factors, especially uncertainty about the reactions of bureaucrats, which can limit the scope for explicit positive incentives. Nevertheless, in general it is widely acknowledged that control of the bureaucracy forms part of the larger framework of agency problems and that first best solutions – i.e. measures that guarantee perfect observance of the instructions of the principal without additional costs – do not exist.

More generally, the entire process of forming and implementing government decisions has been modelled in terms of *agency relationships* with the aid of game theory,

---

[17] There is an extensive literature on this issue (see, among others, Rose Ackerman 1975, 1986; Franzini, 1993; Shleifer and Vishny, 1993, 1998).

[18] The use of rules or incentives is one of the issues addressed by Pollitt and Bouckaert (2000), who discuss government reform from a variety of points of view.

and the most recent developments tend to identify a variety of 'ultimate' principals (for example, consumers and firms[19]) or 'second-order' principals (for example, in presidential systems, the president and the legislature). Spiller (1990) presents a game between consumers, industry, legislators and bureaucrats, in which consumers, thanks to their large number, tend to have greater influence over legislators, while industry influences bureaucracy by altering its system of incentives. Alt (1991) illustrates a different game in which the monetary authorities (the US Federal Reserve Board) are the 'agent' of three 'principals' (the President, Congress and the financial community).

Modelling agency relationships has served not only to analyse bureaucratic activity but also to suggest the most efficient solutions. This second line of research is still in its infancy but appears to promise interesting applications (Tirole, 1994; Martimort, 1996; Dixit, 1997).

5.4   Social groups, institutions and economic policy

Our analysis of the actual functioning of the government has revealed a decision process that differs from the ideal model presented by normative theory. We have seen that this process does not necessarily operate in the general interest but may instead serve the interests of politicians and bureaucrats (*moral hazard*). A more careful examination has revealed that politicians' and bureaucrats' actions can also reflect the interests of the largest or most powerful social groups. In any case, we must revise the view of government as an undifferentiated representative of the 'will of the people' (i.e. the preferences of citizens) that has underpinned much of the normative theory of economic policy.

Can we conclude that this theory is useless? There is no doubt that, as a normative theory, it retains its validity once we have postulated the desirability of government intervention. In some sense, the richer analysis of political economy that we have been discussing in this chapter tends to enhance that postulate, since this analysis shows that society is composed of groups of differing power: this may create a need for the government to intervene in order to prevent some distributive failure. The aspect of the classical theory of economic policy that seems to collapse here is the idea (which, in reality, only a few defend) that public action must and can tend towards a general improvement. Instead, we must accept the idea – which is much more consistent with the analysis of welfare economics[20] – that every public action has different effects on different social groups. For example, an employment policy has different effects from an anti-inflationary policy, not only on their explicit objectives (employment and inflation) but also on other objectives, especially income distribution in all of its many aspects. This fact is much clearer once we have diverse 'characters', i.e. different social groups, in our tale instead of undifferentiated individuals. In the end, the government is simply one of the institutions of a society and, while it reflects its history and the current

---

[19] The partisan model of the political business cycle is also based on the idea of *differentiated principals*.

[20] We have seen that no proposition about the desirability of a change can avoid value judgements, which represent ideals or interests.

economic and social structure, it tends either to sanction its preservation or shape its change. This occurs under the impulse of the various social forces, and in theory it is possible for all social groups to influence the formation and implementation of public choices through a system of controls and incentives for politicians and bureaucrats.

Depending on the degree of cohesion between social groups, public policy will be more or less inclusive. In other words, in a tightly knit society the social groups will act cooperatively and government policies will in fact be aimed at the public interest;[21] in a society with considerable conflict between its various groups, 'public' policies will be directed in favour of one or some groups in the struggle against others and every measure will be contested by one force or another.

The question we have to ask now is whether the government can be trusted as an instrument capable of implementing policies for efficiency and redistribution, or if it would be better to rely on markets and private institutions. Section 5.5 deals with this question.

5.5   Market and 'non-market' failures

The 1980s and early 1990s saw the emergence of widespread opposition to extensive government involvement in the economy in favour of a drastic reduction, or confinement with constitutional restraints, of its role. This shift was strongest in Great Britain and the United States, finding political expression with the election of Margaret Thatcher and Ronald Reagan. In practical terms, in these and other countries both the allocative and distributive functions of the government were reduced, sometimes drastically. In some cases, intervention has assumed new forms: for example, wider use has been made of instruments that mimic the market (such as the assignment of tradable rights, instead of taxes) or in any case require its presence (such as cash transfers instead of direct government provision of goods); public sector enterprises have also been privatised and some of their functions have been entrusted to regulation.

The origins of free market opinion movements are to be found both in the changes in the operation of the economy in the 1960s and in a number of influential theoretical contributions that in some cases were inspired by those changes. The poor performance of governments in some countries further explains such movements.

The main change in economic tendencies in the 1960s concerned the behaviour of economic agents, essentially as a consequence of the emergence of virtually full employment conditions in all the developed countries. The *expectations-augmented Phillips curve* conceived by Phelps and Milton Friedman can be seen as an expression of those behavioural changes. The altered operation of the economy gave rise to problems that were difficult to manage with existing institutions and often led to frequent but

---

[21] This does not mean that *every* policy measure must necessarily be to everyone's benefit or provide for compensation for those harmed by the measure. Government action effectively aiming at the public interest can result in a multiplicity of measures, which in all likelihood will benefit the various social groups in turn, ensuring 'such a division of benefits that most persons in every part of the country would be better off by reason of the program as a whole' (Hotelling, 1938, p. 259).

ineffective government intervention. An influential contribution that, unlike Phelps' and Friedman's, does not appear to have evolved in parallel with changes in economic reality but rather to have emerged autonomously, was made by Coase (1960).

In the view of some (Romani, 1984, pp. 30 ff.) another doctrinal contribution that played an important role in changing attitudes towards government involvement can be traced to the work of Simon. According to Romani, Simon (1976) shows the limitations of substantive (as opposed to procedural) rationality, thus reassessing positions such as Hayek's (see, for example, Hayek, 1945) that, within the framework of an evolutionary rather than Cartesian or Enlightenment approach, view the market as the most suitable institution for exploiting knowledge.[22] Without attempting to discuss the merits of such philosophical and epistemological problems,[23] it must be acknowledged that this approach has contributed (and in some cases rightly so) to the movement against government intervention.

A final cultural root of the free market movement is the 'public choice' school, which attempts to apply economic methodology to the process of forming and implementing policy decisions, in particular introducing the assumption that all agents, including politicians and bureaucrats, *pursue their own interests*. As we have seen, this school underscores the inefficiency and injustice that can accompany government action as a consequence of this behavioural assumption.[24]

Waste, erroneous calculations, the abuses of politicians and bureaucrats and the influence of sectional interests, together with the difficulty of reacting to new problems and to problems that we know about but which may appear in a different context, are a frequent occurrence and justify a significant reform, if not reduction, of government intervention. We have thus seen the emergence in reality and in the economic literature of **non-market failures** (or **government** or **State failures**). We have to ask whether these failures can be considered on the same plane as market failures, and whether they can be eliminated or not.

In order to tackle the first question, it is important to note that market failures are largely posed at a very high level of abstraction and constitute a logical as well as an empirical problem (consider, for example, externalities, public goods, merit goods, inequalities, adverse selection, insufficiently flexible prices).

At a lower level of analysis there are problems associated with moral hazard that lead to both market and non-market failures. This incentive problem is typical of all hierarchical organisations, both private and public. From this point of view – and at this level of analysis – it might be appropriate to make use of the *transaction costs approach* in future analysis for choosing between alternative governance structures (Dixit, 1996).

---

[22] Romani (1984, p. 37) considers 'presumptuous the attitude of the economist, and social scientist in general, who, when faced with an economic policy problem, thinks that the only way to solve it is to be given the desired ends by the politicians and to discover the most appropriate means to achieve them with the help of his personal substantive rationality'.

[23] Salvati (1985, pp. 142–3) notes, for example, that an evolutionary approach should be used with caution in relation to human societies. Moreover, according to the advocates of this approach themselves, the outcomes of the evolutionary process are usually 'satisficing', not optimal, which leaves the door open for improvement through external intervention.

[24] Despite the many contributions to this issue, there is still no satisfactory unified theory of public sector failures, apart from the attempts of Wolf (1979, 1988) (see Le Grand, 1991).

This approach has been used by Coase and other authors to explain the reasons for preferring hierarchic coordination to the coordination offered by the market.

The existing literature underscores three points in comparing the importance of moral hazard in private and public institutions: (a) the measurability of targets; (b) the extent and nature of agency situations; (c) the impact of complementary institutions in solving agency problems.

As to the first problem, it is usually argued that it is easier to monitor private managers because the target they are assigned, i.e. profit, is more easily measured than the targets assigned to policymakers. This is not true in a strict sense, since there are many measurable success indicators of government economic action, ranging from the literacy rate and average life expectancy to the employment rate, etc. However, it is also true that the multiplicity of government targets could cause some monitoring difficulties even if all the targets were measurable, simply because of the many facets involved.

With regard to the second question, the incentive problem is in fact more severe with government action because of the existence of multiple agency situations involving the electorate, politicians and bureaucrats (those at different levels, too: national, regional and local); in addition, there are often common agency relationships (e.g. politicians beholden to, or bureaucrats answerable to, multiple interest groups) (Dixit, 1996; 1997).

As to the impact of complementary institutions, it has often been asserted that incentive problems with private managers can be more easily solved because in addition to monitoring by (incumbent) owners, they are also subject to the discipline of the market, which may force the firm into bankruptcy or impose the replacement of the incumbent managers following a takeover, should the firm be poorly run. This point is not well founded, however. There is, in fact, an extensive literature on the limits of supervision and control that can be exerted by the stock market. Singh (1992), for example, shows that takeovers can involve profitable concerns as well as badly managed or unprofitable firms (see also Scherer, 1980). Stiglitz (1991) argues that the wave of takeover activity in the 1980s benefited managers – who exploited confidential information to reap enormous gains – rather than shareholders. In contrast, Dore (1992) points out the considerable influence and control exercised not by 'anonymous' stock markets but by other organisations (universal banks) in economies such as Japan and Germany. On the other hand, it must also be noted that effective monitoring of private managers depends on institutions that are conceived at the government level (e.g. trade law).

Summing up, moral hazard is a problem shared by both private and public governance structures. Not all the reasons for saying that the incentive problem is more acute for the latter are well founded, but two of them seem of particular importance: the larger number of layers where the agency problem arises and the multiplicity of goals – and, therefore, success indicators – for the government.

There are ways to tackle moral hazard in government action. Stiglitz suggests a number of reasons why public sector enterprises can provide their managers the same incentives as private enterprises with a broad shareholder base (Stiglitz, 1994, chapter 5). In chapter 6 we examine some incentive mechanisms that have been suggested for public sector enterprises.

The discretion of politicians and bureaucrats can be reduced by the introduction of appropriate *rules*. Some authors have suggested setting limits on budget deficits or making the central bank independent of the government, in both cases in order to limit inflationary impulses that might be imparted by politicians and bureaucrats. Such rules would also reduce the discretionary power of policymakers to counter unexpected negative shocks.[25] Setting such rules also involves a choice between different policy objectives. In principle, however, rules can be devised that reflect the values of anyone (or the majority of citizens). The need for a formal rule arises when there is deep social division. Unwritten rules or customs, often formed over decades or centuries as a part of a spontaneous process or the result of patient education, can be suitable in more cohesive societies. In any case, policymaking must be seen as a dynamic process that seeks to develop rules and organisations to cope with various limitations on partic-ipants' information and actions (North, 1990; Dixit, 1996). In this respect effective policymaking requires the participation of citizens and social groups in political life and administrative activity. The cooperation that they can offer and the control they can exercise are indeed difficult to replace with written rules and are often at the root of unwritten ones.

5.6   The process of defining government intervention

In the following we assume that moral hazard problems in the public sector can be tackled with the same degree of success as in the private sector.

Our objective is to construct a normative theory of government intervention that takes account of the existing alternatives and the multiple effects it produces in a varied social environment. The following are the three stages of defining a programme of public action:[26]

(1) *The origins of government action.* These are to be sought in politicians' awareness of the existence of a problem, either because of their own convictions or as a result of public debate or pressure from individuals and interest groups.
(2) *Analysing the operation of other institutions.* The existence of a problem does not necessarily mean that government intervention is required. It can be justified on the basis of the following conditions:
  (a) there is a failure of the market or other private institutions (e.g. private volun-tary organisations or firms, although a broader definition of the market would include the latter)
  (b) the government can obtain better results than other institutions in at least one respect (the result desired, e.g. employment; the cost of the intervention; or the different distributions of income generated by the various institutions), all other conditions being equal.

---

[25] The relative merits of rules and discretion have been the object of wide debate since the contributions of Kydland and Prescott (see Kydland, Prescott, 1977; Barro and Gordon, 1983 and, for a different position, Fischer, 1990; Bernanke and Mishkin, 1992). More recently the problem has been tacked by Laffont (2000) with specific reference to regulation.

[26] To a certain extent, we draw on Stiglitz (1988, chapter 9), generalising some of his arguments.

(3) *The choice between alternative measures.* In many cases government intervention can make use of a variety of instruments, which have different costs and results that must be carefully evaluated and compared. This operation precedes the choice of whether to intervene or not: satisfying condition 2(b) above implies that the most desirable type of intervention has already been identified.

The choice of the type of measures must take account of the following three key elements:

(a) political and bureaucratic *feasibility*[27]
(b) the *reactions* of the market and other institutions
(c) the nature of the *consequences*, both microeconomic (the various types of efficiency, personal distribution of income, satisfaction of merit wants) and macroeconomic (employment, inflation, balance of payments, development, functional or regional distribution of income).

Regardless of these considerations, it would appear necessary to pay special attention to strengthening *public institutions*. A World Bank report (see World Bank, 1997) recommends:

(a) the adoption of *effective rules and constraints* for the operation of public institutions at all levels
(b) use of greater *competitive pressure*
(c) more use of *democratic involvement and control.*

While some of the suggestions in the report are debatable, most are extremely important, not only for the developing countries but also for those developed countries in which the state apparatus does not have the tradition of good government seen in many other advanced nations.

Sections 5.7 and 5.8 will examine two specific issues in detail (federalism and independent authorities), which exemplify many other problems raised in the report and the topic of considerable debate in other fora. We will address other questions raised in this section elsewhere in the book. The questions of the assignment of instruments to targets (see section 14.10) and international coordination (see section 20.4) are part of this issue.

5.7 The decentralisation of central government functions and the federal state

The attribution of certain economic policy functions to separate entities or specific government bodies can be justified in terms of efficiency (and political democracy). Decentralisation can be either vertical or horizontal. In the first case, a function is performed by a separate public entity or given government body for the entire country: this occurs, for example, with the policies of an independent central bank (see chapter 11) or an *independent authority* (see section 5.8). In the second case, the functions of the

---

[27] Kanbur and Myles (1992) argue for political constraints to be integrated into the policy formulation process rather than being faced at the implementation stage.

various branches of government or other public entities are divided on a geographical basis. The economic justification for the latter form of state organisation is known as **fiscal federalism**, and the form of government it gives rise to is a '**federal state**'.

The argument underlying fiscal federalism (which we first encountered in section 2.9) is that public goods have different degrees of non-rivalry. Some actually benefit from economies of scale[28] at the level of the entire economy (pure public goods); for others, the economies of scale dissipate at a lower, more circumscribed level: problems of congestion arise,[29] there are no significant spillover effects between one area and another or there are differences in individual tastes. Achieving allocative efficiency requires that the responsibility for providing pure public goods (national defence, basic research, etc.) lies with central government, while responsibility for other sorts of public good (education, law enforcement, parks and recreation, health, etc.) should be borne by more local levels of government.[30]

The economic efficiency of a federal state was initially suggested by Tiebout (1956), who argued that if people can move freely throughout the territory of a country, they can decide to live in the jurisdiction (city, province, region or state, in the case of a federal system of government) that offers them the most attractive 'package' of taxes, services and laws (voting with one's feet). Any community that provides inefficient public services will lose part of its population and the accompanying tax revenues. As a result, it will be induced to improve its services in order to stem such flight.

While some argue that federalism creates an appropriate system of incentives, at least partially solving problems of moral hazard in public action (see Qian and Weingast, 1997), others emphasise the real-life obstacles that impede the effective mobility of people between jurisdictions that is supposed to ensure the efficient provision of public services. Mobility between jurisdictions is an unusual arrangement for achieving efficiency for political institutions, as it is essentially an 'exit' mechanism similar to that provided by the market.[31] As in the market, its successful operation depends on a number of conditions: in our case, perfect and timely information and perception by citizens of the effects of the policies adopted in each jurisdiction; the absence of restrictions on the mobility of individuals; the absence of costs in the definition or change of the geographical scope and functions of the jurisdictions; and the absence of collusion among inefficient jurisdictions. In addition, the outcomes of the mechanism also depend on the existing distribution. Where such distribution is considered unsatisfactory, the central government should be assigned a balancing function. From the distributive point of view, we could see the emergence of downward competition among

---

[28] Recall that this is due to the fact that the marginal cost of an additional individual's use of a public good is zero.
[29] Congestion reduces the benefit generated by the public good when it is used even by a relatively small number of people.
[30] A more complete analysis of fiscal federalism is given in Oates (1972).
[31] For Hirschman (1970) the disagreement of one person with the conditions posed for the 'cooperation' by another can manifest itself in two ways: '**exit**' (the decision to choose a different partner for cooperation) and '**voice**' (complaint, protest). The former mechanism corresponds to the operation of the *market*; the second to the operation of *political institutions*. See also Franzini (1997) for a generalisation of Hirschman's categories.

jurisdictions, which would tend to exclude the poorest segments of the population. In short, there are well-founded doubts that competition among jurisdictions as a mechanism for efficiency and participation in public life represents a superior alternative to competition within each jurisdiction to obtain the approval of its citizens, regardless of the existence of certain economic, social and political conditions (Donahue, 1997).

Since the 1970s a number of reforms have been adopted in various countries to introduce federalism or increase the degree of decentralisation. At the end of the 1990s, Italy witnessed a vigorous debate on the desirability of amending its Constitution along federalist lines. In early 2001, a federal reform law was approved. In 2003 a process of devolving new tasks to local authorities began in France, a country previously characterised by a high degree of centralisation of political and administrative structures.

5.8   Independent authorities[32]

Beginning in the early 1980s, all Europe witnessed the emergence and rapid spread of **independent authorities** – i.e. institutions that, while being part of government, had very specific features and enjoyed a much greater degree of independence than that normally accorded to government entities.

The growth of independent authorities can be associated with the trend towards the reduction or recasting of government's presence in the economy, in a process of externalisation and, at the same time, decentralisation of traditional government functions. As a result of the *privatisation process* (chapter 6), part of the functions that used to be performed by government are now carried out by the market under the supervision of a range of public bodies that, in the case of the authorities, have considerable autonomy from central government.

The United States has had independent authorities since the end of the nineteenth century; their number increased after 1900. In the United Kingdom, there are two types of institutions that can be defined as authorities. On the one hand we have the *quangos* (or quasi-governmental organisations), which have existed for quite some time and have traditionally enjoyed a certain measure of independence from political control. On the other, there are the agencies that have been established in more recent years to exercise public control over the companies created with the privatisation of public services (electricity, gas, telecommunications, transport).

France has had much less experience with public bodies charged with fostering the privatisation and liberalisation of public services. The only institution of this sort is the telecommunications authority, but its independence from the government is very limited. In Italy, the few authorities created before 1990 (to regulate the financial market, banks and insurance companies) were joined in the 1990s by many others responsible for regulating the conduct of companies and supervising the action of public and private entities.

---

[32] This section draws extensively on the treatment of the issue by Pezzoli and Schiattarella (1999), whom the author thanks.

Table 5.1 *Main independent authorities in selected Western hemisphere countries*

Country/Institution	Date established	Mission
USA		
Interstate Commerce Commission	1887	rail transport regulation
Federal Trade Commission	1914	safeguarding competition
Federal Communication Commission	1934	radio and television regulator
Securities and Exchange Commission	1970	financial market regulation
United Kingdom		
Quasi-governmental organisations (quangos)	Various	technical, scientific, cultural
Monitoring bodies for public utilities	1984–6	privatisation policies
Financial Services Authority	1997	regulation of financial markets and intermediaries
France		
Commission Nationale de l'Informatique e des Libertés	1978	safeguarding privacy
Commission des Operations de Bourse	1978	financial market regulation
Conseil de la Concurrence	1978	safeguarding competition
Commission d'Accès aux Documents Administratifs	1984	administrative transparency
Conseil de l'Audiovisuel	1989	guaranteeing freedom of information sources
Italy		
Banca d'Italia	1893	banking supervision and antitrust
Consob	1974	financial market regulation
Isvap	1982	insurance sector regulation
Autorità Garante della Concorrenza e del Mercato	1990	safeguarding competition
Autorità per l'Energia ed il Gas	1996	energy regulation
Autorità per le Garanzie nelle Comunicazioni	1997	telecommunications regulation and guaranteeing freedom of information sources
Garante per la privacy	1999	safeguarding privacy
Autorità per il volontariato	2001	supervising non-profit organisations

Table 5.1 shows the main authorities in the United States, Great Britain, France and Italy.

As we said, the emergence of these authorities is chiefly attributable to the rethinking of the *organisational structure* of government and the tendency to shift, where possible, from *direct to indirect forms of intervention*. The technical nature of these institutions, their status as bodies outside the traditional structure of government and their high degree of professionalism make authorities especially well suited to ensuring high levels of efficiency and administrative flexibility. In addition, as noted, the authorities owe their existence to a new view of the scope and methods of public intervention and the crisis of confidence in our political institutions.

They do present some risks, however. First and foremost, their very independence. The removal of some interests from the control of traditional political and administrative bodies must be rigorously justified and quantitatively limited. Among other things, we must not underestimate the risk that a majority might restrict future decisions by including among the segregated rights, positions and interests that do not meet the requirements for such independence.

Nor can we overlook the risk posed by the proliferation of 'independent' decision-making centres. Political decisions could increasingly be disguised in the 'impartial' clothes of technical decisions. In this case, the independent authorities could become a centre for the political mediation and negotiation of decisions that their establishment was supposed to remove from political control.

5.9 Summary

1 The *'normative' theory of economic policy* is a 'theory of the public interest', which does not address the problem of the realism of its basic hypotheses or the behaviour of the public authorities that they imply.

2 In reality, the economic system is not composed of anonymous agents but rather of *classes or groups of individuals* with shared characteristics or needs. They organise themselves into interest groups, cartels, unions, political parties, etc. in order to ensure that their preferences prevail over those of other groups, as highlighted by the 'political economy' approach.

3 The category of 'policymakers' can in fact be divided into politicians and bureaucrats. Both are faced with *agency* (and therefore incentive) problems.

4 With specific reference to the actual behaviour of politicians, a number of theories have been proposed that seek to explain the existence of expansionary and restrictive phases (in relation to elections or the alternation of different parties in government) and the growth of government expenditure and public deficits in terms of asymmetric information.

5 The problems of government bureaucracy have also been dealt with in similar terms. They do not differ greatly from those arising with private sector bureaucracies. Solutions to the problems of government bureaucracy may involve the introduction of *explicit positive incentives*, as in the private sector, or the establishment of *compulsory procedures*, including requiring that certain acts be public, with sanctions for those who do not comply.

6 The *positive theory of economic policy* rejects the idea that government action must and can tend towards a general improvement of everyone's position. It has contributed to inspiring political movements that have sought to underscore the failures of government action and, therefore, the need to reduce the influence of the

government or change its style of intervention. These failures differ from most market failures, sharing only the problems arising from moral hazard, albeit in different form and to a different extent.

7   In constructing a normative theory of government intervention that takes account of the *existing alternatives and the multiple effects of government action* in a varied society, special attention must be paid to:

(a) the interests involved and the reasons for government action, especially whether there is a market failure or not

(b) the superiority of the outcome of government intervention over the performance of other institutions

(c) the choice between different alternative programmes, with special regard to their feasibility and their expected outcomes.

8   In order to increase the efficiency of public intervention and enhance the structure of the decisionmaking process, recent years have seen a shift toward adopting a *federal form of government* (fiscal federalism) and/or creating *independent authorities*. These institutions, which often do increase efficiency and, in some cases, the spread of economic power, nevertheless present risks that cannot be overlooked.

III Microeconomic policies

6 Property rights, corporate governance and public enterprises

6.1 Introduction

Microeconomic policy consists of measures to:

(a) ensure the *existence and operation* of markets when they are able to produce the desired optimum
(b) correct the many *inefficiencies* of the actual operation of markets shown by microeconomic theory with reference to the different concepts of static and dynamic efficiency
(c) ensure an *equitable personal or household distribution* of wealth and guarantee the supply of merit goods.

Policies aimed at ensuring the existence and operation of markets (point (a)) represent the *minimal state*, or what the strongest advocates of the market feel are the (minimal) functions that should be performed by the government. An essential part of public policy to make the market work is *attributing property rights*. In capitalist systems, these are usually assigned to individuals, who tend to pursue profit (sometimes nonprofit) objectives. In some cases property rights are assigned to the state and other public bodies, giving rise – when they concern business organisations – to *public enterprises*. We discuss these policies in the remainder of this chapter.

Corrective policies (point (b)) are used to compensate for the existence of externalities, public goods, transaction costs and asymmetric information (even in a hypothetically perfect market), as well as for divergencies in actual markets from the ideal model of perfect competition (in particular, those caused by economies of scale, collusive agreements and entry and exit barriers). In all these cases the target is often – but not always – allocative efficiency. We discuss these policies in chapter 7. Policies designed to pursue dynamic efficiency – i.e. industrial, regional and trade policies – are dealt with in sections 8.1–8.4.

Redistributive policies and those aimed at ensuring the provision of merit goods (point (c)) are examined in section 8.5.

6.2   Making the market work: the minimal state and the attribution of property rights

The need for government intervention is often a source of disagreement among economists, not so much because the existence of market failures is denied but rather because of the possibility that government intervention might also fail, albeit for different reasons. There is, however, one area of government action that excites little controversy because it is considered necessary for civil society and even the very existence of the market itself.[1]

In this view, the minimal duties of government are assigning rights, protecting against force, theft and fraud, and enforcing contracts and rights. These are essential conditions for the existence and proper functioning of the market itself, for a variety of reasons. First, assigning rights (legislative activity), especially property rights, is the very foundation of the market. The way rights are assigned will also produce different results in terms of distribution and efficiency.[2] However, the mere assignment of abstract rights is not sufficient. *Respect for rights* must also be guaranteed. This requires that the same authority that assigns rights must take responsibility for interpreting them in relation to real-world situations (judicial activity) and ensuring that holders of rights are protected from others within or without the community who might threaten their enjoyment of such rights (police action).

Performing these functions requires the attribution of other subsidiary functions. For example, since legislation, justice and protection all involve expenditure, citizens must make some form of financial contribution, normally through taxation.

Section 6.3 deals with the attribution of *property rights*. Obviously, in a capitalist economy property rights are assigned to individuals,[3] even if collective and public ownership play some role. The distribution of income depends on the property rights that each of us possesses.

6.3   Property rights and corporate governance

The operation of the market requires that we identify the *owner of the property right*, without which all transactions would be discouraged: a person who wished to purchase a good would be reluctant to do so owing to the absence of any guarantee of possession and availability of the good, and the resulting need to obtain everyone else's consent to use the good itself.

---

[1] Certainly, the specific content of government action – e.g. the type of laws enacted – will differ in relation to the extent of the market; nevertheless, the performance of the functions that we will shortly list is in any case necessary.

[2] Recall Coase's theorem (see section 2.8).

[3] In historical terms, it is clear that as an incentive mechanism private property made it possible to achieve significant increases in efficiency. Obviously, all of the limitations of the market that we discussed in chapters 2 and 3 remain. In truth, a resource allocation regime should not be confused with a production and distribution regime. However, often in talking about the market (which is an allocation mechanism), as we have just done, implicit reference is made to a *capitalist production and distribution regime*, which is characterised by private ownership of the means of production and wage labour.

As we saw in section 2.8, the attribution of property rights can be done in such a way as to ensure efficiency. An important element of this framework is the issue of **corporate governance**,[4] namely the problem of what role to attribute to owners and controllers of firms – which, as we know, are separate in modern corporations – and to complementary institutions in order to ensure the static and dynamic efficiency of the economy.

The **ownership structure**, or 'who owns what', is an important factor in efficiency in the real world, where *transaction costs* exist. Take the realistic situation in which individuals have different levels of business skills, negotiations are costly and there is information asymmetry. An ownership structure will be efficient if, in shifting the bargaining power in the distribution of the returns of the production process to the owner, it increases the guarantees protecting the owner and encourages his contribution to that process more than it discourages the other participants in the production process.

In particular, *from a dynamic point of view*, what needs to be encouraged is innovation, a fundamental determinant of which is investment in **human capital** (see section 3.6) carried out in the production process to increase the specific skills of the various participants (learning and development of a procedure, technique or business skill). Accordingly, a dynamically efficient ownership structure is that which maximises the incentive to invest in human capital on the part of the persons to whom property rights have been assigned, net of the disincentive effect on investment in human capital by those excluded from ownership. In short, ownership should be attributed to the persons most 'suitable' in terms of talent, inclination and effort to invest in human capital (see Rajan and Zingales, 2000).[5]

Historically, the problem of allocating property rights has generally been solved with the *transmission of knowledge and financial resources* from one generation to the next. The slowness of this system and the existence of imperfections in financial markets (which limit access to credit by those who do not have their own capital) often prevent the allocation of property rights in such a way as to exploit the skills of the most 'suitable' persons. Public intervention of various sorts (redistribution of property and income, subsidised credit, especially for small firms) is therefore necessary.

A second problem arises in situations in which an individual – with or without skills to be exploited – does not have sufficient financial resources and can undertake an enterprise only with the risk capital (sharing of ownership) of other people or using debt capital. In this case there is a conflict of interest between the controlling owner (who wants to exercise control without interference) and other owners (who want to monitor the decisions of the controlling owner). A similar problem arises when a capitalist is

---

[4] According to Barca (1997), corporate governance is the set of rules and institutions used to ensure that control of firms is exercised by people with the skills to run those firms successfully, also using the capital of third parties, and that the attribution of control functions adjusts promptly to changes in technology, preferences and business skills.

[5] The arguments presented hereafter are drawn from the 'new theory of property rights' developed in the 1980s by Grossman, Hart and Moore, which pursues the analysis of Coase, Williamson and others (see Grossman and Hart, 1986 and Hart and Moore, 1990). See also Barca (1994) and Vives (2000).

not in the best position to run his firm (from the point of view of talent, education or working capacity) and therefore entrusts another person with the job.

Both of these cases (that of a capitalist owning a significant – but not full – share of the capital of a firm and that of a capitalist who does not run the firm personally) arise in the **managerial firm**, i.e. a firm run by non-owner managers. Since the controller (the manager) differs from the owner (the shareholders), we face the problem of how to govern the relationship between the two in order to achieve efficient outcomes, taking account of the *conflict of interest* (different incentives) between them. Essentially, it is a problem of reducing moral hazard (see Shleifer and Vishny, 1997).[6]

There are two needs that must be satisfied in both cases: first, the controller (whether the owner or a non-owner manager) must be encouraged to manage the firm in the interests of all the owners and pursue (maximum) profits rather than personal interests; second, the non-controlling owners must be encouraged to provide the capital required by the firm and hence need to be protected from possible misuse of those funds by the controllers. We therefore have a trade-off between the different interests involved, which need to be governed by *institutions complementary to property rights*.

These **complementary institutions** (or **non-ownership instruments of control**) include:

- *contractual instruments* (in addition to the contract between owners and managers with appropriate incentives[7] and penalties, these include bylaws or measures that limit the transferability of the property rights or voting rights of non-controlling owners)
- *shareholders' agreements* or other voting pacts
- *fiduciary relationships* (associated with family ties or other situations)
- *market discipline* over corporate control.

The role of the latter institution needs to be explained in more detail. An owner can change a firm's control structure, when the controller proves inefficient, by selling off his property rights to another owner, who gains control of the firm **(takeover)** and replaces the previous controller. This possibility can act as a deterrent to the abuse of power on the part of the controller. For this to happen, however, the non-controlling owners must have a large majority stake in the company so that it is possible to remove the controller against his will. In addition, non-controlling owners must be able to perceive the signs of poor management or abuse of power in time in order to intervene. Finally, the potential purchaser(s) must have the financial resources needed to acquire control.

---

[6] Kay and Silberston (1995) suggest an alternative to this shareholder–agency model of the corporation based on the recognition of existence of corporate personality: as trustees of the corporation, managers should further its purposes and not simply the financial interests of shareholders.

[7] These are highly varied and include various forms of remuneration tied to corporate performance. One form of incentive is stock options, i.e. the right granted to managers (or employees) to buy shares in their firm in order to increase their compensation. Managers and employees thereby have a more direct incentive to pursue strategies that raise the value of the shares of the company (at least in the short run) when they have been assigned stock options. The role of these financial instruments has been questioned (see Hall and Murphy, 2003).

All of this requires:

- an efficient system of rules governing the **market for corporate control**, in terms of the availability and circulation of information and mechanisms for the exchange of shares
- efficient *financial institutions* that can assess the reliability of potential owners of enterprises who do not have sufficient capital.

Obviously, some of the rules governing this market can also pursue objectives of equity (for example, protecting small investors), as we will see in section 6.4.[8]

The various models of corporate governance (box 6.1) can be distinguished by the different role of ownership control instruments and differences in the *complementary institutions*.

Box 6.1. Corporate governance and the role of financial markets; the function of takeovers

The role of takeovers

Takeovers play many roles:

(1) first and foremost, they can *discipline the actions of managers* who might otherwise pursue their own objectives
(2) second, they can be used as a tool in managers' efforts to create *business 'empires'*
(3) third, they can unleash *synergies* associated with the presence of externalities and joint costs
(4) finally, they can *reduce competition and increase market power*.

To the extent that they perform functions (1) and (3), takeovers should, at least in theory, increase allocative efficiency. Again in theory, allocative efficiency is reduced in roles (2) and (4).

Any positive assessment of a takeover must necessarily consider the *post-operation consequences*. For example, a takeover motivated by the desire to exploit synergies, thus increasing allocative efficiency, could be hampered by difficulties in getting the two organisations to mesh, which would reduce efficiency. This is a fairly common outcome of concentrations, and on average mergers tend to reduce returns (see Ravenscraft and Scherer, 1987; Franks, Harris and Mayer, 1988; Caves, 1989).

---

[8] The problem of the conflict (and the composition of interests) between owners and managers is part of a broader problem. The modern firm is conceived by some as hosting the interests of **stakeholders**, namely agents with specific interests in its activity (its employees, suppliers, the community where it operates, etc.). Some even speak of a **corporate social responsibility**, i.e. a responsibility of firms towards society at large. This new way of thinking has caught on and influences the mission statements adopted by some big firms. For an introduction to the concept of stakeholder see Donaldson and Preston (1995), Kelly, Kelly and Gamble (1997). Blair (1995) offers an important contribution. Driver and Thompson (2002) tackle the issue of practical implementation. For a critique of the view of corporate commitment see Gregg (2001) and Henderson (2001).

Conversely, a reduction in the number of competitors does not always harm competition: the disappearance of small competitors, some of which merge among themselves, may even strengthen competition if it gives rise to larger and more efficient producers that can play an active rather than passive role in their industry.

The overall assessment of the role of takeovers is uncertain not only as regards allocative efficiency but also *dynamic efficiency*. Apart from the uncertainty of the specific effects of takeovers on technical progress, the very issue of the relationship between monopoly and innovation is not clear-cut (see section 2.14).

The market for corporate control

Given the many functions of takeovers, it is important to know if experience confirms or rejects the arguments of those who view the market for corporate control as an efficient instrument for monitoring the actions of managers and, more generally, owners. Let us therefore examine the actual operation of this market.

Singh (1971, 1975) was the first to analyse closely the selection and control functions of takeovers, using empirical studies of the financial market in the United Kingdom. Singh compared the economic and financial characteristics of: (1) the 'survivor' companies and the 'non-survivors' in takeovers and (2) the 'predator' companies and their 'victims'.

The types of companies that become survivors and non-survivors tend to be part of different groups, in periods of both normal operations and, to an even greater degree, in periods of considerable takeover activity. *Profitability* and *size* are the main discriminating factors, although not so characteristic as to distinguish the two groups clearly. The probability of being taken over is higher than average for low-profitability firms, but for the third to the tenth decile it is virtually the same. As regards size, small firms are not usually the targets of takeover bids, probably because they are often family-run. Medium-sized enterprises are more likely to be taken over, while the probability for large firms declines significantly.

Predator companies, which are normally very dynamic, tend to be large, while their prey is usually smaller. Although this characteristic has become less marked following the wave of takeovers that began in the 1980s – which were financed with a wide range of instruments, including junk bonds[a] – it has remained, leaving an asymmetry that is difficult to reconcile with the claimed efficiency of the financial market as a governance mechanism. Contrary to the expectations of its advocates, the evidence suggests that a relatively inefficient large firm is less likely to be acquired than a relatively more efficient smaller firm.

As a result, rather than forcing firms to improve profitability, the threat of takeover may in fact prompt them to increase their size further. This result can be reinforced by the takeover mechanism itself, given that it can be used by unprofitable firms to expand by acquiring more profitable companies and virtually immunise themselves against hostile takeovers.

These features, noted by Singh in the 1970s, have been confirmed by subsequent research for the United States as well as for the United Kingdom (see, for example, Warshawsky, 1987 and Hughes, 1993, respectively; see also Jenkinson and Mayer, 1994; Singh, 1992, offers a review of research on the topic). Stiglitz (1991) argues that the wave of takeovers in the 1980s benefited managers – who exploited inside information to make enormous gains – rather than shareholders.

A more positive reading of the role played by the US market for corporate control was advanced by Holmstrom and Kaplan (2001). The authors, who do not test their arguments with statistical or econometric analysis, suggest that the wave of hostile takeovers employing leveraged buyouts financed by junk bonds in the 1980s was in fact a response to new circumstances. The new situation that had emerged in that period was the result of *deregulation* – which created scope to improve corporate performance and raise share prices – and the advent of new and less costly ICT. The stock market reacted more swiftly than managers to these developments and, drawing on increased support from institutional investors as well as external financing, punished examples of mismanagement such as unprofitable diversification, the creation of excess capacity or inefficiencies generated by managers' preference for safeguarding the interests of **stakeholders**[b] other than owners. Thanks to the experience of takeovers in the 1980s and the consequent productive and organisational restructuring, there has been an evolution in incentive schemes for managers (stock options are one example) and a change in the attitude of managers that have reduced the number of hostile takeovers.

Notes:
a   *Junk bonds* are high-risk securities that, however, are popular because they offer high yields. They are often issued to finance **leveraged buyouts** (i.e. an acquisition of equity holdings financed with borrowed funds secured by the company's assets) in order to realise the difference between market capitalisation and the real value of the target's assets.
b   *Stakeholders* are those who have an interest of some sort in a company. In addition to owners, these include management, employees, customers, creditors, the inhabitants of the area where the company is located, etc. The concept has more recently been extended to cover non-governmental organisations (NGOs) and, even more generally, all of 'civil society', towards which – it is argued – companies have a form of corporate social responsibility.

In some cases, the onus of corporate governance is placed almost entirely on *ownership instruments*, strengthened by complementary institutions that limit the transferability of rights or that in any case guarantee the trust of controlling owners. Ownership and fiduciary relationships are the main ingredients of corporate governance in economies such as Germany and Japan (the so-called **German–Japanese model**): ownership of firms is controlled by institutions such as other firms or banks that closely monitor the strategy of the company. **Firms with large shareholders** are an example of this form of corporate governance, with ownership characterised by the concentration of shareholdings in the hands of a few shareholders. *Banks* play a major role in this model, since in order to accentuate the control of some shareholders, there is a tendency to limit the overall amount of share capital. Bank financing therefore becomes the predominant source of financial resources and banks exert at least an informal influence over company strategy. The stability of ownership permits the development of long-term strategies, especially as regards technological innovation. The weakness of the model is that it fails to protect the interests of minority shareholders, concentrates financial wealth and opens a breach for the formation of dangerous combinations of economic and political power.[9]

The **Anglo-American model** of corporate governance is different. The development of strategy and the monitoring of its implementation are, of course, entrusted to a controlling owner, but an important complementary role is played by the *financial market*, which can remove the controller when he proves to be inefficient: decisions made by managers that do not pursue the objective of profit maximisation prompt owners to sell their shares. This reduces the value of the firm and encourages other capitalists to buy it (through takeovers) when they see scope for raising that value by removing current management (see Holmstrom and Kaplan, 2001). The **public company**, i.e. a company with a large shareholder base (which enables the transfer of control from one owner to another even with a small share of capital) is a manifestation of this form of corporate governance. The ownership structure of this kind of firm can have a major, and not always positive, impact on its decisions and performance. For example, if the only constraint on the action of managers is the distribution of dividends, there is a risk that decisions that may strengthen the long-term profitability of the firm (such as technological research or professional training) but are expensive in the short term may be inhibited (see Shleifer and Vishny, 1997). Conversely, this model reduces the concentration of financial wealth and power.

France and Italy have models similar to the German–Japanese system, albeit with certain differences arising out of historical circumstances: the control and supervision of many firms of all sizes was, and continues to be, in the hands of families, which are frequently directly involved in management. A cause and consequence of the German–Japanese model is the small size of the stock market, although this has been expanding in recent years, thanks in part to the privatisation of public enterprises (see section 6.4).

Corporate governance rules pursue two partially conflicting aims, namely protecting minorities and ensuring the efficiency of the securities market and the contestability of ownership through the equity market.

Protecting minority interests and shareholders in general is normally pursued through:

- *Direct protective mechanisms* (reduction of minimum shareholdings required by law for the calling of shareholders' meetings; reservation of the appointment of one or more members of the board of auditors to minority shareholders, giving auditors stronger control powers, etc.).

---

[9] For a description and defence of the German–Japanese model, see Aoki and Dore (1994), Dore (2000), Edwards and Nibler (2002), and Hoshi and Kashyap (2004).

- Harsher penalties for **insider trading**, i.e. transactions in shares by employees or managers with access to confidential information about their company.

Ensuring the contestability of ownership through the stock market is pursued with:

- *Ceilings on cross-shareholdings* (for example, 2 per cent in Italy, 10 per cent in France; 25 per cent in Germany), with possible departures from this rule in bylaws or resolved by shareholders' meetings in order to permit the formation of industrial alliances.
- Requirements to disclose to financial market regulators any *equity investments* that exceed a given percentage threshold of a company's equity and to ensure the transparency of control through shareholders' agreements by setting rules on disclosure, duration and the possibility of withdrawal.
- Requirements for *mandatory takeover bids* for the transfer of control of a listed company in order to protect minority shareholders.

6.4   Public enterprises and privatisation

In previous sections we saw that assigning property rights to different agents can play an important role in achieving static and dynamic efficiency. This is also true with regard to the public or private nature of the subject of the property right.

The **public sector** (or **state-owned**) **enterprise** (SOE) has traditionally been considered in European countries and in many developing nations an effective instrument for achieving a variety of specific objectives (allocative efficiency, full employment, sectoral, regional and general development, etc.) and increasing the general consistency of corporate behaviour with policy objectives (for example, promoting exports, abstaining from activities that replicate private sector behaviour). In the United States and Japan, public enterprises have traditionally been assigned a smaller role.

The large number of privatisations in various countries since the mid-1980s is a tangible sign that, at least from a practical and contingent point of view, governments have lost confidence in public enterprises.[10] Table 6.1 gives some idea of the importance of the public sector in a selection of European countries at the beginning of the 1980s and the 1990s. The figures reflect the first wave of privatisations in France in 1986 and most of the privatisations in the United Kingdom. They do not show some large-scale privatisations in Italy (which began in 1993) or the second wave of privatisations in France in 1993 as well as privatisations in Spain and Germany. Table 6.2 gives an idea of the size of privatisations in these countries in the 1990s.

Between 1979 and 1999 the largest revenues from privatisation were generated in the United Kingdom ($165 million). Italy ($122 million), France ($71 million), Germany ($63 million) and Spain ($62 million) followed (see IRI, 2001).[11] Privatisation has also

---

[10] We ignore here the pressing budget concerns that have prompted many governments to dispose of public property. On privatisation see Bös (1991).

[11] In some cases before selling shares in public enterprises governments inserted special clauses into the bylaws of the companies involved (the so-called **golden share**). These usually limit the cases in which the company may be dissolved, restrict the transfer abroad of the company headquarters and place limitations on changes in the corporate purpose, mergers and splits. They may even require state approval of actions, agreements or taking significant equity stakes in other companies.

Table 6.1 *Public enterprises: employment, value-added and gross capital investment as a percentage of the non-agricultural market sector, 1991*

	Employment	Value added	Gross capital investment	Average of the three indicators			
				1991	1988	1985	1982
France	13.4	15.1	24.2	17.6	18.3	24.0	22.8
Germany[a]	8.3	10.0	14.9	11.1	11.6	12.4	14.0
Italy	13.5	20.0	23.5	19.0	19.6	20.3	20.0
United Kingdom	4.3	4.0	6.0	4.5	7.4	12.7	16.2
Spain	6.0	8.0	12.8	9.0	10.0	12.0	12.0
Portugal	10.6	21.5	30.0	20.7	24.0	22.7	23.9
Belgium	9.8	7.5	8.4	8.6	10.3	11.1	12.1
The Netherlands	6.1	8.0	9.2	7.5	9.6	9.0	9.0
Greece	14.7	17.0	30.0	20.6	20.8	23.2	22.3
Denmark	8.2	8.7	17.6	11.5	11.9	11.4	12.0
Ireland	8.7	11.5	16.9	12.4	14.4	15.3	15.1
Luxembourg	3.2	5.2	4.6	4.4	4.9	4.5	5.0
Europe[b]	8.9	10.9	15.6	11.8	13.3	15.3	16.4

Notes:
[a] Provisional estimates excluding the former East Germany.
[b] The former East Germany not included.
Source: CEEP (1993).

Table 6.2 *Privatisation receipts in selected European countries, 1992 and 2000 (billion dollars and percentage shares)*

	Public offerings	%[a]	%[b]	Private sales	%[a]	%[b]	*Total*
Italy	98.3	87.3	35.3	14.3	12.7	12.0	*112.6*
Spain	52.9	59.6	19.0	35.8	40.4	30.1	*88.7*
Germany	49.5	58.0	17.8	35.8	42.0	30.1	*85.3*
France	53.4	84.6	19.2	9.7	15.4	8.2	*63.1*
United Kingdom	24.5	51.3	8.8	23.3	48.7	19.6	*47.8*
Total EUR–5	**278.6**	**67.1**		**118.9**	**32.9**		**397.5**

Notes:
[a] Percentage of total receipts of the country.
[b] Percentage of total public offerings and private sales in the five European countries.
Source: IRI (2001).

been accompanied by a shift in the attitudes of many experts with regard to the ability of public enterprises to achieve the objectives they have been assigned. The changes in the real-world situation and theoretical views are the product of a variety of factors. These include: the ideological and political changes of the period, which saw the triumph of 'Thatcherism' and 'Reaganism', the economic crisis and the associated fiscal crisis of recent years, and unsolved problems with controlling public enterprises; technological changes that have eliminated some positions of natural monopoly.

As regards the latter, there have been important innovations in telecommunications, transportation equipment, energy production and distribution. In particular, new information technology makes it possible to restrict natural monopoly positions to one or a few stages of the production process (usually the ownership and operation of the network), allowing a multiplicity of operators to have access to earlier or subsequent stages.

Let us, then, try to understand the economic arguments for and against using public sector enterprises as an instrument of economic policy.

For our purposes in this section, public enterprises should replace private sector firms operating under natural monopoly conditions or operate alongside private firms under oligopoly[12] in order to increase allocative efficiency. In both cases the public enterprise should not aim to make a profit, and in the first situation could even operate at a loss.[13] Losses under such conditions should not be interpreted negatively, since they would be closely tied to the objective assigned to the public enterprise. It is often argued – especially in the current economic policy debate – that losses create distortions in the allocation of resources. From what has been said, we can infer that this is not true *per se*.

Since the time of Marshall we have known that profit maximisation is a barrier to increasing output to the socially efficient level in industries facing decreasing costs. Public intervention and the associated losses (under the assumed conditions) make it possible to achieve an efficient allocation of resources, which the market is unable to guarantee. By contrast, setting higher prices in order to avoid losses, whether by a public or private firm, would lead to allocative inefficiency.[14]

Many public enterprises operate, or should operate, in industries facing decreasing costs. In fact, some of the critics that underscore losses by public enterprises contradict themselves by arguing that such firms should be present in (or perhaps confined to) innovative industries, which normally have (dynamic) economies of scale. The widespread conviction that operating at a loss by public enterprises is inefficient is therefore regrettable and incomprehensible in rational terms.

---

[12] In the former case, we would have the nationalisation of the firm (or industry); in the second, we would shift from private oligopoly to **mixed oligopoly**. The latter has only fairly recently been modelled (see De Fraja and Delbono, 1989).

[13] This would be the case of a public enterprise operating under the conditions shown in figure 2.3. The firm should set price equal to marginal cost; fixed costs (or the loss that the firm would incur with such price-setting behaviour) would have to be covered by a lump-sum tax to ensure allocative efficiency (see Hotelling, 1938).

[14] In the case of a single-product firm facing decreasing costs, the prices that ensure allocative efficiency, subject to the constraint of equating costs and revenues, are those equal to *average costs*. In the case of a multi-product firm, prices will still exceed marginal cost, but will be set in an inverse relation to the elasticity of demand of the different goods. These are called **Ramsey–Boiteux prices** (see Ramsey, 1927; Boiteux, 1956). However, these prices ensure efficiency subject to a constraint (breaking even), and are therefore suboptimal. They should thus be used by public enterprises only when the latter are subject to budget limits (e.g. when the public debt is large) and must be self-sufficient.

In truth, this view may be the product of the idea that losses are not the result of conscious decisions to increase allocative efficiency but are rather the result of management inefficiency (e.g. 'X-inefficiency'), inefficiency caused by 'constraints' imposed by policymakers, improper relationships between public managers and politicians or even corruption. The fact is, however, that these sorts of problems can also arise with private firms, where they are concealed by setting monopoly prices: in other words, the exploitation of monopoly power has often allowed private firms to offset the high costs of their inefficient management with high revenues (even allowing a net profit).[15]

Inefficiency in public enterprises has also been attributed to the lack of incentives for public managers in the presence of a 'soft budget' constraint and a multiple agency relationship and without the discipline exerted by the financial market on management. Such problems certainly afflict public enterprises, but the difference with private sector firms seems one of degree rather than kind. In order to limit the discretion of managers, both private and public enterprise should implement incentive schemes. These should have a different content for the two types of firms. Simple profit-sharing arrangements would be enough for the managers of private firms whereas the incentive schemes for the managers of public enterprises should consider other indicators as well: for example, their pay could vary as a direct function of profits and an inverse function of prices (see Finsinger and Vogelsang, 1985).[16]

Claims of the relative efficiency of private firms compared with public enterprises often do not stand up to scrutiny. Comparisons between the two are frequently made with regard to costs or operating profits. The latter has a bias, since it focuses on a variable, profit, that is the prime objective of private firms but an irrelevant or secondary consideration for public enterprises. Cost comparisons can also be biased for similar reasons. In any case, such assessments do not lead to unambiguous conclusions: in some cases the prevailing view of the inefficiency of public enterprises is vindicated, while in others there are no significant differences, as in the case of state-owned and private railways in Canada or public and private hospitals in the United States. In still other instances, public enterprises are clearly more efficient than private firms: although public social security systems are being threatened with dismantlement, it is not widely known that the administrative costs of these systems amount to less than 2 per cent of

[15] Obviously, this does not excuse the conduct of economic policymakers. They have not guaranteed the efficient operation of either public enterprises, by means of adequate supervision, or private enterprises, with the adoption, and implementation, of antitrust legislation or the proper use of price controls. The causes of this *non-market failure* are complex, having roots in historical, social and political conditions.

[16] An important difference is the constraint imposed on public enterprises by equity considerations. For example, the pay of a public manager in the United States cannot be much higher than that of the country's president (Stiglitz, 1988, p. 201). Less important is the argument that only private firms are concerned with bankruptcy. Difficulties at large firms, whether public or private, often prompt efforts to avoid insolvency and, at least in theory, there is nothing to prevent a public enterprise from going bankrupt. The same effect on managers could also be achieved with the threat of privatisation. In the end, if a public enterprise is not able to carry out its assigned task, it is appropriate that it should be removed from the public sector or cease to exist altogether.

benefits paid, compared with 30–40 per cent for private insurance companies (Millward and Parker, 1987; Stiglitz, 1988; Martin and Parker, 1997).

Assessing comparative studies of the performance of public and private enterprises nevertheless requires caution. Among other things, a systematic difference with regard to operating results is the tendency of private firms to abandon less profitable sectors: the fact is that some 'firms are government enterprises because they were running at a loss; they are not running at a loss because they are government enterprises' (Stiglitz, 1988, p. 197).

There are few assessments of the performance of privatised firms. Galal *et al.* (1994), Megginson, Nash and Van Randenborgh (1994) and D'Souza and Megginson (1999) note an increase in profitability and operational efficiency following privatisation, but the higher profitability is largely attributable to the pricing strategies adopted by the privatised firms. Moreover, it is often difficult to distinguish the impact of privatisation from that of other changes, such as macroeconomic conditions, the behaviour of the prices of inputs and outputs, liberalisation and regulation. Findings have differed in the few cases where this effect has been isolated. A positive impact was found in Boubakri and Cosset (1998) and in La Porta and Lopez-de-Silanes (1999). By contrast, little contribution to the increase in allocative efficiency is discerned in Florio (2004) in the case of British privatisation: any positive effects are mainly ascribable to factors other than the change in ownership (see box 6.2).

Box 6.2. The welfare impact on consumers of British privatisations

Price trends before and after privatisation

The comparison between the trends in nominal prices 'before' and 'after' privatisations in the United Kingdom does not show a clear structural break (see table 6B.1). This could be interpreted as meaning that privatisation had no effect on allocative efficiency.

In addition, in a very few cases table 6B.1 shows a fall in prices. This could mean that in those cases privatisations have had a positive effect. Both this and the previous conclusion are, however, unwarranted, as other factors were operating at the same time as privatisation. We will deal with such factors in a fairly systematic way and then take account of them in assessing the likely impact of privatisation on allocative efficiency.

Absolute and relative prices

Considering the trend in absolute prices can only be misleading if we want to detect the nature of the impact of privatisation. In fact, we must first consider the trend of the price of a specific good in relation to some measure of the *general price level*, as the latter tends to increase continuously. This is of specific importance in periods of high inflation or inflationary change as was the case in the 1970s and the 1980s: privatisation could be successful from the point of view

Table 6B.1 *Price indexes, 1974–1999*

	Phone	Rail	Bus	Electricity	Gas	Water	Coal
1974				21.9	25.0		19.4
1975							
1976							
1977				45.1	41.2		37.3
1978				49.7	42.5		41.4
1979	46.4	48.5	49.5	54.0	44.1		48.4
1980	62.2	60.3	62.7	68.7	51.4		61.9
1981	76.9	69.0	69.4	82.6	64.8		72.8
1982	85.6	79.1	80.0	91.5	80.7		78.5
1983	84.7	83.4	84.6	94.1	90.4		83.0
1984	87.4	84.2	86.5	95.3	93.7		89.4
1985	93.2	89.6	90.1	98.3	97.5		95.2
1986	98.2	95.7	97.7	100.5	99.4		97.9
1987	100.3	100.6	103.4	100.0	98.4	104.5	98.8
1988	101.2	107.6	110.6	105.4	99.7	113.6	100.2
1989	102.4	117.4	119.3	113.1	103.3	127.3	101.4
1990	108.3	127.7	125.9	122.2	110.4	144.2	105.1
1991	117.5	141.0	143.6	134.5	118.1	167.7	111.9
1992	120.7	151.3	153.6	141.5	118.0	187.4	116.2
1993	121.4	161.9	160.4	141.0	113.3	203.7	116.8
1994	113.9	169.1	164.6	145.7	120.1	218.9	124.3
1995	109.5	176.6	170.7	147.7	124.2	232.0	126.4
1996	106.9	183.7	177.1	147.1	124.3	244.2	127.6
1997	104.0	187.5	183.4	140.0	123.1	255.2	128.7
1998	102.6	195.2	189.4	133.6	118.9	269.4	129.9
1999	100.1	202.3	196.1	132.0	118.2	281.9	132.5

Source: Based on National Economic Development Office (1976), Office for National Statistics (n.d.).

of allocative efficiency, even if absolute prices continued to rise, but at a slower pace than the general price level. On the other hand, even if prices began to fall after privatisation we could still have a failure in allocative efficiency if there was a significant slowdown in inflation.

The role of regulation

For regulated utilities an important factor is simply the signal given by the *price cap* (a ceiling imposed on price increases: see chapter 7). Thus in the case of water, UK prices rose after privatisation (1989). This can be interpreted as the almost complete transfer to consumers of the cost of investments made compulsory by regulation by setting a high ceiling, even when the benefits of investment – for example, in terms of the environment – affected taxpayers in general. In the case of gas, the reductions in both absolute and relative prices after UK privatisation (1986) were fostered by a fairly stringent price cap in the face of a prolonged conflict between the regulator and the privatised monopolist. In the case of telephony services, the price cap mechanism allowed for the rebalancing of tariffs within a basket of services, enabling British Telecom to raise tariffs for some services (domestic use, which is less exposed to competition and has more inelastic demand) and to reduce them for others (international calls, business users). It is clear that all of this has less to do with the change in ownership than with the advent of different approaches to the *public management of the prices* of certain services.

The role of exogenous changes in costs

In some sectors, the empirical evidence shows that movements in *factor costs* explain a large part of the change in prices after privatisation. In the case of electricity and gas, there was a spectacular crash in the cost of input both before and after privatisation. In the case of telephony, a cycle of technological innovation generated a sizeable increase in productivity. In other sectors the change in costs was due to changes in environmental or health regulations (water).

The different sectors experienced different phases of their *technological cycles* and only a detailed case-by-case analysis can unbundle the effect of the new regulations from that of the new technologies or other exogenous factors.

The case of electricity is particularly illuminating. The key elements for comprehending the restructuring of the industry after privatisation (but not necessarily connected with it) were the abolition of the obligation for the Central Electricity Generating Board (CEGB) to use British Coal as a supplier; the end to EU restrictions as to the use of gas as a fuel in the sector; and the more restrictive EU rules regarding sulphur emissions. At the time of privatisation (1990) the CEGB used the following mix of fuels: coal 92 per cent; oil 7 per cent; gas 1 per cent. In 1998, the sector as a whole used this mix: oil 5 per cent; coal (and others) 63 per cent; gas 32 per cent. For some years, nuclear generation enjoyed a substantial levy on consumers' bills. There was also a large increase in imports (especially from France). It is therefore evident that a large part of the reduction in generation costs was due to three simultaneous changes in public policy. At the time of the coal miners' strike in 1984 there were 250,000 miners; in 1994 there were just 7,000. One can speculate as to whether the continuation of a nationalised CEGB would have allowed a restructuring on this scale. Newbery and Pollitt (1997) think it unlikely.

The restructuring process might have been delayed, but – as in the case of coal, steel and other sectors – in the end it would have happened under public ownership as well, partly in response to EU environmental regulations and in any case to help the public finances. The same can perhaps be said for the reduction in employment at the CEGB: it could have been delayed, but not put off indefinitely.

On the other hand, as Newbery and Pollitt themselves observe, until 1997 very little of the cost savings had been transferred to consumers through prices. The case of electricity is perhaps an extreme one, but it is not isolated (and it is in itself important).

The impact of market structure

British privatisations were not uniformly characterised by extensive liberalisation. The monopoly of British Gas remained intact for over a decade after privatisation. In electricity, the process preserved an oligopoly in production, regional monopolies in distribution, a 'corporatist' solution for the control of the National Grid and a spot market in the pool that probably led to collusive practices. With the exception of some profitable routes, the deregulation of bus services did not lead to a competitive system, giving rise instead to a multitude of small local monopolies or duopolies (although in some cities there was chaotic 'on-the-road' competition, particularly in Oxford and Manchester). British Airways was allowed to take over its only private competitor, British Caledonian, while for many years British Telecom was granted a monopoly in some services and a duopoly in others, etc.

However, there were also opposite trends – e.g. in international telephone calls, in electricity supply to major customers and elsewhere. The degree of competition varies from sector to sector, and in the more than twenty years examined these conditions changed, there has been greater liberalisation and obviously the mark-up on the costs charged by the companies may in part have changed in response to liberalisation (or lack of it).

The UK Monopolies and Merger Commission (MMC), regulators and ministries intervened so frequently in the market structures that it is virtually impossible to discern a price trend that is independent from policy changes. When comparing price interference by government in the nationalised industries and by the regulators in the privatised industries, it is perhaps fair to say that in the latter case companies were in a stronger position.

Conclusions

In the case of electricity (privatised between 1989 and 1995), prices had been falling as a ratio to the general price level for over a decade under public ownership. They rose in preparation for privatisation and in the years that followed, especially prices for residential users, despite the removal of the obligation to use coal and the consequent possibility of making use of cheaper inputs. Prices subsequently began to fall again in a manner not too different from the long-term trend.

Privatisation thus seems to have had no significant positive effect, if any, on allocative efficiency.

In the case of gas, there was a net drop in relative prices after privatisation, but they were falling sharply even when British Gas was a nationalised industry.

As for water, tariffs rose considerably after privatisation; they also increased in the case of buses and railways (1995–7). One reason was the implementation of EU legislation on environmental standards and the adoption of a price cap formula that allowed the regulated firms to pass their capital costs on to consumers.

In telecommunications, the construction of a price index is particularly difficult. The figures suggest that after privatisation there was a reduction in the unit cost for business users and, for a number of years, an increase in the unit cost for domestic users, followed by a generalised reduction after a change in regulatory constraints and increased competition.

One could also find fairly contradictory evidence for various other sectors not discussed here. In any case, it does not seem tenable to argue that, in itself, privatisation in the United Kingdom generally produced an improvement in allocative efficiency and a reduction in prices, understood as a structural break in the time series.

Source: Adapted from Florio (2004).

Public enterprises are often viewed negatively, not because public intervention is considered inappropriate or ineffective but because it is felt that there exist more effective control instruments. Some suggest using regulation rather than public enterprises because it does not give rise to incentive problems. Regulation in the form of antitrust legislation or price controls would prevent the extraction of monopoly profits by private firms, thus ensuring, if not Pareto efficiency, at least that efficiency constrained by the need to balance costs and revenues that guarantees a normal profit. We will consider this issue in the next chapter.

6.5 Non-profit institutions

Most of the economic policy debates that we have examined so far concern the merits and limitations (failures) of the market and the state. However, the market and the state (in the broad sense of the definitions we gave them in section 2.1) do not represent the full range of operators in an economic system. There are also actors who pursue collective interests, similar to those of the state, which differ from this both in their legal form and their lack of the authority typical of the state.

This category includes **non-profit institutions**, which are variously defined but generally comprise all bodies that do not distribute profits to their members or the persons who control them (Hansmann, 1980). In particular, they are enterprises that do not distribute profits to those who have invested capital in them (Gui, 1993).

According to some economists, non-profit institutions remedy market failures, offering a valid alternative to public intervention. On this view, the absence of the objective of distributing profits (although not that of earning them) contributes to creating a reputation for the quality of the goods produced by the enterprise and their attractiveness for consumers, thus strengthening its position with respect to the 'market'.

However, the range of non-profit institutions is not limited to those that operate in the goods market. Other non-profit groups do not operate in the market at all. For example, some are active in charity. The explanation for the existence and success of such organisations must therefore be sought elsewhere. In some cases, it can be attributed to non-economic or altruistic motivations. This requires us to go beyond economics' normal assumption of egotistical behaviour and to examine certain phenomena from a different standpoint than the pursuit of efficiency.

Non-profit institutions could also offer a solution to *failures of the state*. The prevalence of non-egotistical motives solves the incentive problem. At the same time, however, we must also verify that such motivations do in fact underpin the action of non-profit groups. If they do, then such institutions might not only complement public action in the economic and social field, but even provide a stimulus to and maintain a dialogue with public institutions. In reality, non-profit groups often operate successfully thanks to public help, while the action of such groups in turn awakens the state to significant problems and provides an indication of how to solve them. Two areas in which cooperation between the non-profit and public sectors appears to be especially interesting is the traditional redistributive functions of the welfare state (see section 8.5) and international cooperation.

The governance mechanisms of these institutions differ. They are weaker and more complex than those of firms and public institutions: their governing bodies are not accountable to shareholders and rarely are they elected. The scrutiny typical of the stock market does not exist even in the abstract. Such bodies often lack control and incentive mechanisms and they are frequently 'captured' by the people who work in them (see Glaeser, 2003).

6.6   Summary

1   Microeconomic policy seeks to:
    (a) ensure the *optimal operation* of the market
    (b) correct the *market failures* identified by microeconomic theory, which give rise to inefficiency and inequality.
2   The operation of the market is 'guaranteed' by charging the government with the functions of *assigning, enforcing and protecting rights*. Carrying out these tasks involves additional functions, such as taxation.
3   *Assigning property rights* is important from the point of view of both efficiency and equity. Corporate governance involves the attribution of property rights and complementary institutions, such as trust relationships and the working of the market for corporate control. There are two main models of corporate governance: the

German–Japanese model and the Anglo-American model: in the former monitoring is performed mainly through the active exercise of property rights, whereas in the latter an essential role is played by the financial market.

4 Public enterprises have traditionally been considered an effective tool for achieving a variety of specific objectives as well as ensuring greater generic consistency between corporate decisions and public objectives. Pursuing allocative efficiency when facing scale economies means that the public enterprise will operate at a loss. Hence, losses do not in themselves imply inefficiency.

Incentive problems for public sector managers are similar to those faced by private sector firms.

Evaluating the performance of public enterprises does not present systematic differences with evaluating that of private firms. However, in the last two decades a large-scale process of privatisation has taken place, prompted by a variety of factors.

5 *Non-profit institutions* can solve failures of the market and the state, especially in the areas of redistribution and international cooperation.

7 Competition policies; policies for externalities and public goods

7.1 Competition policy instruments: market liberalisation and international opening

The pursuit of *Pareto efficiency* is one of the foundations of competition policies. Competition policy can be implemented by liberalising markets and opening the economy to the rest of the world, introducing various forms of regulation and establishing public enterprises.

Some countries have used liberalisation and international opening as instruments of competition policy, although *protectionism* against foreign competition has been a more frequent occurrence for reasons of industrial policy or, as the political economy literature has often underscored, to effect a redistribution of income in favour of certain domestic industries or firms (and to the detriment, at least temporarily, of domestic consumers).

International opening can be a valid instrument to reduce the market power of firms in sectors that are effectively exposed to international competition and in the short term.

However, not all industries are exposed to international competition, even when there are no government-imposed barriers. While agricultural and non-agricultural raw materials and manufactures are normally traded internationally (**tradables**), most services are not (for example, hair cuts or aerobics lessons). International opening thus cannot work effectively to reduce market power in these sectors.

Even in tradable goods, the capacity of international opening to affect market power is often limited to the short term. The impact of international opening on competitive performance is almost always positive, but the passage of time often gives rise to the formation of oligopolies or even monopolies at the international level. One example is the international air transport industry. After fierce competition in the 1980s and 1990s, we now have a situation in which some busy national and international routes are dominated by a small number of airlines. A similar example is offered by the music industry, where the world market is now concentrated in the hands of just a few firms.

7.2   Regulation

In a strict sense the term **regulation** indicates the direct control measure with which central government or some other public body governs in abstract (legislation) or in substance (executive action) the conduct of private agents in a given economic sector or under certain circumstances. More generally, regulation is the legislative or administrative activity with which a public body governs various economic and social activities. Unless otherwise indicated, we will discuss regulation in the first sense.

Regulatory activity can have multiple objectives that fall under headings (b) and (c) at the start of section 6.1, such as encouraging innovation, safeguarding and governing competition, containing negative externalities and stimulating positive externalities, and redistribution.

There are many forms of regulation:[1]

(1) **Regulation of entry and effective competition**: for example, requiring authorisation for entry for reasons of hygiene, professional qualifications, protecting a minimum income, extracting monopolistic rents (when the licence or concession is dependent on payment of a fee) or establishing a minimum number of producers, with the possible obligation to break up monopolistic entities.

(2) **Regulation of the structural elements of the market or the conduct of firms** (competition legislation).[2]

(3) **Tariff and price controls**, with the aim of achieving static or dynamic efficiency or pursuing redistribution.

(4) **Environmental regulation**, which seeks to specify property rights in activities that have an impact on the environment, so as to encourage the creation of external economies and deter the production of external diseconomies.

(5) **Regulation of intellectual property**: in order to stimulate innovation, and with it dynamic efficiency, intellectual property rights (IPRs) are defined and protected (copyright, patents, trademarks, etc.).

(6) **Financial regulation**: to guarantee the efficient allocation of resources (and good corporate governance) as well as financial stability, rules are introduced to ensure the transparency of firms' conduct and good management of financial intermediaries.

(7) **Quality and disclosure regulations** in order to protect consumers when there are safety issues associated with the use of a product (especially industrial products) or significant information asymmetries (as in the case of chemical or pharmaceutical products).

Sections 7.3 and 7.4 address the issues raised in points (1) and (2) above. Section 7.5 deals with price control policies. Section 7.6 focuses on environmental regulation, while regulation for innovation is discussed briefly in chapter 8. Box 11.1 (p. 255) deals with

---

[1] In this as in other points of this section, we follow in part Bentivogli and Trento (1995).
[2] Note, however, that in some antitrust legislation (such as that in Europe in general and Italy in particular) the dominant feature is its **penalising** nature rather than the **prescriptive** character inherent to regulation.

financial regulation. We do not address the quality or information policies mentioned under point.

Before concluding this section, we should emphasise that there is a risk that regulation can be used not for collective but for 'sectional' purposes, i.e. to pursue the interests of well-defined sections, parties or groups of the community which lobby economic policy authorities to obtain favourable regulatory action.[3] Thus, legislating longer protection for copyright or patents may have little positive impact on innovation and, conversely, significantly hinder the spread of knowledge, giving rights' holders 'unjustified' benefits. In some cases mandating filters or other devices may have little effect on pollution while increasing the profits of manufacturers of pollution abatement devices. Requiring authorisation to engage in a profession may not guarantee a practitioner's skills while at the same time constituting a major obstacle to the entry of new agents and increasing the income of those already in the sector. Rather than boosting allocative efficiency and protecting consumers, price controls may simply create extra profits for firms in the regulated industry. Finally, imposing safety standards may discriminate in favour of certain producers.

7.3   Regulation and deregulation of entry; regulation of effective competition

We said that regulation of entry in a given market can be used for a variety of purposes, ranging from supporting the income of **incumbents** (existing firms) to protecting consumer safety or guaranteeing quality, again to the benefit of consumers. The pursuit of any of these objectives may prompt policymakers to limit entry to a market by establishing various restrictions (such as requiring a certain level of educational attainment or passing a qualifying examination or the possession of other qualifications, health requirements and so on).

From the point of view of achieving static efficiency, instead of restricting access to a certain activity, policymakers may encourage as many as possible to enter the sector by reducing or eliminating natural entry barriers, those created by the strategic behaviour of the incumbents and those created by regulation itself (**deregulation**).[4]

As we said in subsection 2.6.2, increasing **contestability** (greater potential competition) certainly contributes to increasing the efficiency of the market (although not necessarily its allocative efficiency) and can be achieved by removing government barriers

---

[3] The reader will recall from chapter 5 that this is the essence of the capture theory advanced by the *public choice school*.

[4] An example of 'natural' barriers to entry that public action can lower are the absolute cost advantages (i.e. advantages enjoyed by firms already in the market in terms of access to financing, human capital, etc.). Examples of **strategic barriers to entry** (i.e. action by incumbent firms aimed at discouraging new entrants to their market) are sunk costs (excess productive capacity, advertising expenditure, etc.), product differentiation, the expansion of the areas and markets in which the firm is present (market pre-emption), and the predatory fixing of abnormally low prices compared with competitors (especially new entrants). Regulatory (or administrative) barriers include authorisations to engage in a business (in many countries, despite the abolition of some restrictions, many service sectors, such as retail trade and banking, still require authorisations or licences of some sort).

to entry and exit[5] (when they are not sufficiently justified for other reasons, such as the need to ensure specific skill levels, health requirements, etc.) and by controlling the strategic behaviour of firms, which can be accomplished through regulation. Nevertheless, contestability will never be perfect simply because some entry and exit barriers cannot be eliminated. As we mentioned earlier, these are associated with *sunk costs*, which make it impossible for potential competitors to 'hit and run'.

We might also argue that the government should or must seek to create **effective competition** in addition to or in place of potential competition. Let us consider two measures that can be used for this purpose.

First, assume the existence of natural monopoly, with production and demand conditions similar to those shown in figures 2.2 and 2.3. Without government intervention there would be only one firm, with unit costs equal to $0P$. Let us now assume that the government compels the monopoly to split itself into a number of smaller firms, as was done with ATT in the United States in 1982. In the place of the single monopolist we now have a number of independent firms, which could create effective competition between them.[6] This would both reduce firms' ability to exploit market power and increase their internal efficiency. However, each of the new companies would produce some fraction of $0Q$ at a unit cost higher than $0P$, with the additional cost rising as the number of firms increases. Since the rise in unit costs is virtually certain (thus generating production inefficiency), this alternative cannot be considered except in cases where the economies of scale are not very strong compared with the extent of the market, or for those specific production tasks in which there are no appreciable economies of scale.

The second possibility for increasing effective competition even in the presence of scale economies consists in auctioning the exclusive right of access to the market (**'competition for the market'** or **'competition for monopoly'**). The underlying reasoning is as follows. Although producing at the minimum average cost compatible with demand in the presence of scale economies implies the existence of a single firm, the monopoly profits generated by this firm could be appropriated by the government by auctioning the right to produce the good to potential market entrants (a form of *franchising* suggested by Demsetz, 1968). Effective competition would thus be increased not at the stage of production, but rather at the previous stage of the attribution of the right to produce the good.

The price set by the monopolist would still be higher than marginal cost, meaning that the conditions of *allocative efficiency* are not met. The auction would allow only the appropriation of the monopolist's surplus profit. There is, however, an alternative approach to the auction that would both secure allocative efficiency and appropriate

---

[5] This can also include the liberalisation of foreign trade and capital movements. However, the long-run outcome of liberalisation is not necessarily greater (effective) competition but rather, in some circumstances at least, less competition.

[6] In fact, in the ATT case, competition was low and was limited to long-distance telephony since the so-called 'Baby Bells' (i.e. the smaller firms resulting from the splitting up of the Bell Communications Co.) operated in different regions. However, it was thought that independent local telephone companies in this segment of the industry would reduce the incentive to favour one long-distance carrier over another.

the monopoly profit. First, regulation can be used to force the firm to set its price equal to *marginal cost*. This would give rise to a loss, since in a natural monopoly marginal cost is lower than average cost, but the loss could be offset by the government with a subsidy. An auction could then be used to ensure that the subsidy is not excessive: the right to produce the good in a natural monopoly – but with price equal to marginal cost – would be assigned to the firm bidding the lowest subsidy.

The auction mechanism, which increases effective competition not in the exercise of the activity itself but rather in access to the market, can also be viewed as an instrument for simulating contestability (and hence the existence of potential competition) through the periodic award of the right to engage in the activity.

The advantage of the auction mechanism described is that it can extract monopoly profits or achieve efficiency without placing an undue burden on the regulatory authorities. However, the characteristics of most industries are such that competition for monopoly cannot work, for many reasons. We shall examine two:

(a) There is a risk that the participants in the auction might *collude*; the risk increases as the number of firms in the auction decreases.
(b) It is possible that one firm has a *strategic advantage* over the others. For example, a firm might already have experience in the field; knowledge thus acquired would allow it to offer a higher price, perhaps even dissuading others from competing for the franchise (in greater detail, see Vickers and Yarrow, 1988, pp. 111 ff.). Such conditions are highly likely in industries with large static and dynamic (learning) economies of scale.

We can therefore conclude that the scope for increasing potential competition is limited by the existence of *irremovable entry and exit barriers*. Strengthening effective competition is also difficult to achieve, owing to the impracticability of auctions aimed at appropriating monopoly profits, and may not necessarily be desirable, since it means giving up the low costs tied to scale economies.

Rather than aiming at the impossible, ineffective or damaging goal of increasing potential or effective competition, antimonopoly policy could instead seek to ensure that the market power associated with scale economies and entry and exit barriers (or any other factor)[7] is not exploited. The instruments available are essentially the following:

(a) regulation of *private sector monopolies*, which can take the form of:
  • competition legislation
  • price controls
(b) *public enterprises*.

We examine alternatives under (a) in sections 7.4 and 7.5. We analysed public enterprises in section 6.4.

---

[7] The presence of many firms in an industry does not guarantee competitive results; for example, the firms could still *collude* to raise their price.

7.4   Competition legislation

7.4.1   *Foundations and nature*

Regulating the market power of private sector firms[8] with *competition* (or *antitrust or antimonopoly*) *legislation* has at least three objectives:

(a) *safeguarding economic liberty*, especially that of small firms to enter the market and survive, thus allowing the exercise of free enterprise
(b) controlling the economic and political power associated with *economic concentrations*, which may be used in a variety of ways to jeopardise economic and political democracy
(c) increasing *allocative efficiency*.

We will pay particular attention to the last objective. We know that the allocative inefficiency of a particular market structure is caused by:

(1) agreements to *limit competition* (collusive price-fixing, market quotas, etc.)[9]
(2) abuse of a *dominant position* (setting low purchase prices or high selling prices, price discrimination, adoption of strategic barriers to entry)
(3) *mergers or takeovers* that adversely affect potential and effective competition.

These practices either pave the way for creating 'monopolistic' conditions (the practices mentioned under points (1) and (3)) or represent the exploitation of such conditions (point (2)). Some argue that firms can use these practices to obtain increases in production efficiency (through static and dynamic scale economies) that offset the loss of allocative efficiency. Obviously, this argument does not exclude the need for competition legislation, partly because greater allocative efficiency could itself give rise to greater production efficiency (by means of 'X'-efficiency). However, it does strengthen the argument for examining the effects of these practices on a case-by-case basis.

Competition legislation can thus seek to affect the *structure of the economy* (economic concentration in a market) or the *conduct of firms* (abuse of dominant position, collusive agreements). As regards market structure, one possible course for competition legislation is to force firms that have achieved a large market share to divest part of their business.

Those who do not believe there is a mechanical relationship between structural elements (for example, the degree of market concentration) and conduct (monopolistic behaviour) prefer to focus their intervention not so much on the dominant position itself as on any possible exploitation (or abuse) of that position.

A *dominant position* of one or more firms is the ability to set prices in a given market that are above long-term marginal costs on the basis of the power acquired in that market. The key element for the purposes of competition legislation would be the unlawfulness of the method used to obtain a dominant position (for example, the

---

[8] This can also be applied to public enterprises if for some reason it is feared they will imitate private sector firms.
[9] Small and medium-sized enterprises (SMEs) can also enter into collusive agreements.

erection of strategic barriers to entry by creating excess capacity) or the unlawfulness of the use made of a dominant position (for example, anticompetitive practices such as the direct or indirect imposition of unjustifiably onerous prices or other contractual terms, such as tied sales[10]) or the use of discriminatory practices (in addition to tied sales or discriminatory prices[11]). In the case of agreements between firms, elements of conduct again are significant, but we can also consider performance to attenuate the scope of disapproval (where one can show that the agreement improves the performance of the firms in some other way than simply increasing market power).

It is sometimes objected that the behaviour outlined under points (1)–(3) allows firms to increase their *innovative efficiency*. Competition legislation in a number of countries (notably certain European countries before the entry into force of Community regulations) was relatively tolerant of economic concentrations precisely because of the argument that the improvements in innovative efficiency that could be achieved would offset the loss of allocative efficiency. Obviously, this reasoning is not sufficient to rule out the need for competition legislation, but rather emphasises the wisdom of assessing the impact of such practices on a case-by-case basis. Normally, the task of identifying violations of competition law is entrusted to quasi-judicial bodies established as *authorities* independent of executive power.

7.4.2   Antitrust legislation in the United States

Some countries, like the United States, have used instruments other than opening their economies to international competition, such as antitrust legislation, since the end of the nineteenth century. The reason for this preference for antitrust law was twofold: first, even if international openness was guaranteed, structural factors (the sheer size of the economy) would have impeded any significant increase in competition; second, the very size of the country allowed the development of the national productive system and the growth of large firms associated with static and dynamic economies of scale without major government intervention, especially in the form of public enterprises. However, the emergence of large private sector companies on a continental scale called for some system of regulation and sanctions, such as that provided by antitrust legislation.

In 1890 the United States Congress passed the *Sherman Act*. The first two sections of the Act contain substantive regulations. The first section states: 'Every contract, combination in the form of trust[12] or otherwise, or conspiracy, in restraint of trade or commerce . . . is . . . declared to be illegal.'

The second section deems any 'monopolization' or 'attempt to monopolize' trade a felony. The meaning of these terms is fairly vague: they appear to seek to punish

---

[10] *Tied sales contracts* subordinate the sale of a product (or more generally, any contractual performance) to the sale of another product (or performance).

[11] *Price discrimination* is the practice of charging different prices to different customers for the same product or service.

[12] This term indicates the combination of the activity of many firms in an institution that ensures *joint control and action*. In terms of market behaviour, trusts ensure perfect collusion among the participants.

not only abuse of a dominant position but also the acquisition of such a position.[13] The task of identifying specific violations of antitrust law is assigned to the judicial system.[14]

The emergence of problems of interpretation as well as the need to lend antitrust legislation a broader sweep prompted the enactment of many later laws, including the Clayton Act and the Federal Trade Commission Act, both passed in 1914, and the Celler–Kefauver Amendment of 1950.

Under the 1914 law, the Federal Trade Commission (FTC) was established and assigned an important triple role:

(a) to provide general assistance to the *definition* of the many questions of law that may arise in relation to the scope of the legislative text
(b) to prevent and repress *unfair competition*
(c) to investigate suspected instances of *restraint of trade*, taking action to obtain voluntary compliance with the law (note, however, that the rulings of lawfulness for a given trade practice obtained by petitioners to the Commission do not guarantee their acceptance by the courts, who have ultimate jurisdiction).

7.4.3   EU competition legislation

Some European countries had no competition legislation whatsoever until recently (this was the case in France, which introduced legislation in 1986, and Italy, which enacted such laws only in 1990). In some cases of both older law (United Kingdom) and newer law (France), industrial policy concerns tempered the goals of competition policy, leaving scope for concentrations or even fostering the creation of *national champions*, which were often public enterprises (see Bianchi, 1988; Bentivogli and Trento, 1995).

Such industrial policy considerations did not bypass the European Economic Community (EEC). Especially in the 1960s and 1970s it was often claimed that the practical implementation of competition law had weakened the ability of Europe's economy to fend off the competition of foreign rivals.[15] European competition law is broadly based on US legislation[16] and is founded in articles 81, 82 and 88 (formerly articles 85, 86 and 92) of the Treaty of Rome and Community Regulation 4064 of 21 December 1989. This gives executive power to the European Commission. One of the commissioners is responsible for competition policy and runs the Competition Directorate General (DG IV). The Commission's decisions can be appealed to the European Court of Justice.

---

[13] See Petersen (1989) for the intellectual and political roots of the US legislation and its consequences. The paradox of the impulse given to concentration by the generic formulation of section 2 of the Sherman Act was underscored by Machlup (1952).

[14] As is well known, in common law countries, court interpretations of the law in their sentences are a key part of the law itself. In the case of US antitrust law, this has followed divergent lines of development over the years. Hovenkamp (1999) and Sullivan and Grimes (2000) discuss the application of US antitrust law.

[15] The European Commission itself expressed an explicitly favourable view of concentration. See European Commission (1970).

[16] For a comparison of the two, see Neumann (2001).

Article 81(1) establishes that:

> The following shall be prohibited as incompatible with the common market: all agreements between undertakings, decisions by associations of undertakings and concerted practices which may affect trade between Member States and which have as their object or effect the prevention, restriction or distortion of competition within the common market.

It forbids, considering them void, agreements to fix prices, share markets, limit production, apply dissimilar conditions to equivalent transactions and tie contracts to other obligations.

Paragraph 3 of article 81 (1) declares the inapplicability of paragraph 1 to agreements and decisions that:

(a) contribute, for example, through the specialisation of productive skills, to an improvement in the production or distribution of goods or promoting technical or economic progress
(b) allow consumers a fair share of the resulting benefits (for example, through the establishment of common standards)
(c) while imposing restrictions indispensable to the attainment of these objectives, do not enable firms to reduce competition significantly in the goods market.

In order to ensure regulatory certainty, the European Commission introduced the practice of issuing **block exemptions** for categories of agreements and decisions. In any case, agreements,[17] except for some, such as those with little impact, must be notified to the European Commission, which can approve or bar them.[18] The Commission may initiate proceedings following a complaint or if it notes signs of *collusive behaviour* in a given sector. If such behaviour is proven, the Commission may suspend the agreement and impose penalties on the firms involved or it can informally request that the accord be dissolved or amended in such a way that it does not harm competition.

Article 82 establishes that:

> Any abuse by one or more undertakings of a dominant position within the common market or in a substantial part of it shall be prohibited as incompatible with the common market insofar as it may affect trade between Member States.

Article 82 also provides examples of abuse, such as directly or indirectly imposing unfair purchase or selling prices, limiting production or technical development, applying dissimilar conditions to equivalent transactions or tying contracts to other obligations.

---

[17] *Implicit agreements*, such as a series of equal prices changes in the same direction by different companies, have been considered in the same manner as explicit agreements: the Commission does not appear to have accepted the defence that the oligopolistic structure of the market generates a context similar to a repeated non-cooperative game, in which agreements are not necessary to produce a collusive equilibrium (Bentivogli and Trento, 1995).

[18] Insignificant agreements are those in which a firm has a market share of no more than 5 per cent or the turnover of the firms involved does not exceed 15 million euros. In November 2002 the rules requiring notification of agreements were reviewed.

Three steps are needed to sanction the conduct of one or more firms under Article 82:

(1) First, define the *relevant market*
(2) Identify a *dominant position* in the market
(3) Clarify the concept of *abuse*

The relevant market

The **relevant market** or reference market (*marché en cause*) is defined in relation to numerous product, geographical and economic factors. First, a market is defined by the *characteristics of the product* involved: for example, the market for short-range aircrafts. It is also defined in terms of its *geographical scope*, which in the case of short-range aircrafts is global but could be European or even national for other goods. Nevertheless, a dominant position (however defined) in the aircraft market may not distort competition not only when the firm does not abuse its position but also when the product in question has many close substitutes: in our case, aircraft could be substituted by land or sea transport. **Substitutability on the demand side** (as measured by cross-elasticity) is an essential factor in determining the relevant market. In our example, therefore, the relevant market may not be short-range aircraft but rather short-range transport equipment, since there is a high cross-elasticity of demand for these products.[19] The dominant position of one or more firms must therefore be assessed in relation to this market (box 7.1).

> **Box 7.1.   Defining the relevant market: imports and recycled products and the 'cellophane fallacy'**
>
> How do we define a relevant market in the presence of imports and recycled goods? Both of these were central to the 1945 US court case to determine whether Alcoa had a monopoly in the aluminium market. Alcoa had an especially strong domestic position in the manufacture of virgin aluminium (90 per cent of domestic output) and, obviously, the existence of a monopoly depended on the definition of the relevant market. Taking a narrow definition (that the relevant market excluded imports and recycled aluminium), Alcoa would have had a dominant position. If, however, a broader definition of relevant market were used, Alcoa might not have been dominant. The court ruled that imports formed part of the relevant market but recycled metal did not. This second part of the ruling is controversial. Recycled aluminium is a substitute for virgin metal and, therefore, the existence of a secondary market represents a constraint on the action of the leading firm in the sale of virgin aluminium. However, some scholars (Gaskins, 1974) argue that the decision to exclude recycled metal from the relevant market was correct because rising demand for recycled aluminium associated with economic growth

---

[19] However, beware of the 'cellophane fallacy' (see box 7.1).

would reduce its importance over time. Others (see Fischer, 1974) insist that it was wrong to exclude recycled aluminium from the relevant market: such exclusion can be justified only in relation to the values of the different variables in play (in particular, the rate of demand growth and the initial shares of the two markets held by the firm involved) on a case-by-case basis.

As we remarked on p. 167, the degree of *substitutability* among various goods is an important factor in determining the relevant market. A high degree of substitutability indicates that the relevant market should encompass both products. Any firm with a dominant position in only one of the two markets will have a smaller market share in the combined relevant market. However, we must be alert for the *cellophane fallacy*, as noted in the following example. In 1947, the US Justice Department charged Du Pont with having monopolised the US market for cellophane. The court ruled in favour of Du Pont, arguing that the relevant market was that for 'flexible packaging materials' (wax paper, aluminium foil, etc.), given the high degree of substitutability among them. Du Pont had only a 20 per cent share of this broader market, and therefore could not be held to control the market.

This decision is known as the 'cellophane fallacy' ruling. It essentially stated that there was one market for flexible packaging materials on the basis of the high cross-elasticity of demand among the various products, which was a consequence of the high price of cellophane: this stimulated strong demand for substitute products even if these were not always suitable for all uses.

The dominant position

The **dominant position** must not be assessed on the sole basis of the market share held (unless this is extremely large), but rather in relation to the effective *capacity* of a firm to *engage in anticompetitive behaviour*, which must consider many *structural elements* such as the number of market participants, barriers to entry and exit, degree of vertical integration, etc.

Abuse of a dominant position

Abuse of a dominant position is the conduct of a firm that puts it in the position to *significantly reduce competition* in the market, adopting practices that go beyond *normal* competitive behaviour. According to the Court of Justice, all external growth aimed at increasing market share by firms in a dominant position constitutes abuse of that position.[20] This interpretation has enabled regulatory intervention in the case of mergers and takeovers. The field was in any case clarified with the adoption of Regulation 4064 of 1989.

The reason a dominant position is subject to sanctions only in the event of actual abuse of that position can be expressed as follows: a dominant position achieved either

---

[20] Conversely, internal growth does not constitute abuse of a dominant position.

through internal or external growth may involve gains in productive efficiency and, at the same time, an increase in market power and hence a possible deterioration in allocative efficiency (see box 7.2). Economies of scale do not always materialise, although they have often been assumed. Accordingly, there has been a tendency to frown upon dominant positions mainly when there is a clear erosion of allocative efficiency.

Box 7.2.   The antitrust paradox

Let us take a business combination, considering figure 7B.1.[a] The effects that the operation have on productive and allocative efficiency are the following:

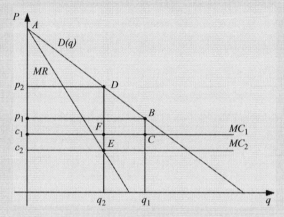

Figure 7B.1

(1) First, we have a *rationalisation of production and organisation*, with the simplification of tasks, the elimination of duplicate activities and more extensive exploitation of economies of scale. This should lead to a *reduction in the average production cost* (which for simplicity is assumed to be constant – and hence equal to marginal cost, MC – before and after the combination),[b] as shown in figure 7B.1, where it declines from c_1 to c_2.

(2) We then have an *increase in market power*: before merging the two or more firms could only apply a small mark-up, setting their price, for example, at p_1, corresponding to the quantity for which marginal cost (assumed to be equal to average cost), MC_1, and marginal revenues, MR, are equal; following the combination, the mark-up that can be charged increases and, at the limit, if the company emerging from the merger has a monopoly, the price charged will be the monopoly price, which will be equal to the point where the new marginal cost (assumed to be equal to average cost), MC_2, and marginal revenues, MR, are equal – i.e. the new price will be p_2.

Productive efficiency is measured by the level of costs, and from this point of view there is a gain resulting from the combination, equal to the reduction in the unit cost multiplied by the (new) quantity produced, which is equal to the area

$c_1 FEc_2$ in figure 7B.1. As we know from basic economic principles, allocative efficiency is traditionally measured by the sum of the producer and consumer surpluses. Accordingly, there is a reduction in allocative efficiency in this case, which is equal to $DBCF$. If the gain in productive efficiency is greater than the loss of allocative efficiency, that is if the area $c_1 FEc_2$ is larger than the area $DBCF$, the combination can be judged positively (the **antitrust paradox**).[c]

Notes:
a   The example is drawn from Martini (1998).
b   Note that this is not always true. In fact, in many cases the costs of the company produced by the merger will be higher than those of the individual firms before the operation owing to 'cultural' differences, the inability to manage the changes required, organisational shortcomings and so on. See Scherer (1980).
c   The reasons for and against considering the possible positive effects in antitrust authorities' scrutiny of mergers and takeovers are analysed in theoretical terms and in the light of US, Canadian and European legislation by Ilzkovitz and Meiklejohn (2001).

Mergers and takeovers effected through the purchase of shares or other means (such as shareholders' agreements, joint management by a number of companies) that fall within the scope of the regulation are those that have a Community dimension, namely concentrations involving firms with an aggregate turnover of more than 5 billion euros and Community-wide turnover of more than 250 million euros. National authorities are responsible for other operations or those involving firms that generate at least two-thirds of their turnover in a single member state.[21] Concentrations must be notified beforehand to the Commission, which may refuse to allow the operation to go ahead. Decisions taken to date are addressed briefly in box 7.3.

Box 7.3.   A case study: the General Electric–Honeywell merger

Between 1990 and 31 March 2001, a total of 1,672 mergers were notified to the European Commission with an acceleration in more recent years. In the 1,593 cases for which a final decision was reached, the Commission granted 1,366 unconditional authorisations and 127 authorisations with remedies. Only fourteen mergers were barred. Of these, the most important were the acquisition of De Havilland (Boeing) by Aerospatiale and Selenia (in 1991) and the acquisition of First Choice by Airtours in 1999.

In July 2001 the European Commission declared the proposed merger between US companies General Electric (GE) and Honeywell incompatible with the common market, as it would create a dominant position in various relevant markets in which the companies are active.

GE is a diversified corporation operating in aircraft engines, appliances, information services, industrial systems, financial services, transportation systems

---

[21]   Regulation 1310 of 1997 introduced additional criteria to identify concentrations with a European dimension even when they do not breach these thresholds.

and many others. Honeywell is another conglomerate firm, active in advanced technology, aerospace products and services, automotive products, electronic materials, transportation systems and others. The merger affected aerospace products (jet engines, avionics, non-avionics[a] and engine starters) and industrial systems (small marine gas turbines).

The Commission examined three categories of jet engines markets (those for large commercial, regional aircraft and corporate aircraft – the last two with different submarkets), and the related markets for maintenance, repair and overhaul. The investigation showed that the concentration would create no horizontal overlap in the market for jet engines for large commercial aircraft, whereas it would do so in the markets for jet engines for large regional aircraft and for medium-sized corporate aircraft. In order to assess market shares, the Commission considered both the installed base of jet engines and the order backlog of engine suppliers, as indicators of, respectively, current and future incumbency positions.

On the market for large commercial aircraft engines, GE held the largest position in both cases. GE and Honeywell accounted for the totality of the market for large regional aircraft engines. As to the medium-sized corporate jet aircraft engines, Honeywell was the leading firm, well ahead of GE and others, so that the merger would strengthen its position.

GE's dominant position in the first two submarkets for engines resulted from the combination of a series of factors – besides its market share, its integration into aircraft purchasing, financing and leasing and its financial strength. As to financial strength, not only had GE the world's largest market capitalisation, it was a leading industrial conglomerate and had a major financial organisation through GE Capital. This contributed around half of the consolidated revenues of the whole corporation, could offer enormous financial means and enabled GE to undertake riskier projects than its competitors. GE's financial strength gave it an advantage through the use of heavy discounts on the initial sale of engines. GE was thus in a position to increase rivals' funding cost, by delaying their inception of cash flows, increasing their need for external financing and raising their financial costs. GE was found to exploit this advantage in order to make its competitors more vulnerable to adverse cycles or strategic mistake. In addition, it had financially supported airframe manufacturers in order to obtain exclusivity for its products, thus reducing its competitors' access to such airframes.

In avionics and non-avionics products Honeywell accounted for a majority of the world-wide sales and held particularly strong positions on a number of 'key' products.

The rejection of the proposed merger was to a large extent determined by the combination of GE's financial strength and vertical integration into aircraft purchasing, financing and leasing with Honeywell's leading position on the markets for jet engines, avionics and non-avionics products. For these reasons, the merger would have led to either the creation or strengthening of dominant positions in several markets.[b] The wide range of complementary products sold by the firm resulting from the merger and its financial strength would have enabled it to foreclose competition through bundling/tying[c] and other anticompetitive means.

The rejection of the merger triggered protests not only from the firms involved but also from US policymakers. In the past, among mergers between US firms only that between Worldcom and Sprint had been barred by the European Commission, but on that occasion the decision did not give rise to bad feelings or accusations of excessive rigour and fears of strategic decisions with little regard for consumer interests because the merger had also been rejected by the US courts. By contrast, the GE–Honeywell merger had been approved by US antitrust authorities.

In reality, the difference in the positions of Europe and the United States that emerged with the GE–Honeywell merger is linked to differences in the approaches of their respective competition authorities. The United States has long held that mergers between *conglomerates* do not restrict competition and in fact considers diversification to be a source of innovation and competitive stimulus. In addition, low prices are seen as an expression of competition and as such are to be encouraged as long as they do not constitute predatory pricing. Finally, tying contracts are not judged negatively at the time of a merger but are rather tackled later by competition authorities.

The negative stance of Europe is largely based on consideration of the so-called 'portfolio effect', namely the strategic advantages of multiple significant positions in related businesses (such as aircraft engines and other aircraft components), which facilitates bundling or tying sales. Since such practices are difficult to control through the *ex post* intervention of the competition authorities, preference is given to countering them on a preventative basis.

GE and Honeywell have appealed the ruling to the European Court of Justice.

Notes:
a   Avionics products include equipment used for the control of the aircraft, navigation and communication, assessment of flying conditions. Non-avionics products include auxiliary power units, environmental control systems, electric power, wheels, brakes, landing gear and aircraft lighting.
b   Nearly all of this first part is drawn from Giotakos *et al.* (2001).
c   These consist in selling two or more goods in a package deal (*bundling*) or in conditioning the sale of one good to purchase of an associated one (*tying contract*). For example, GE could have forced its customers for engines to buy other components as well, extending its dominant position in the first market to the market for other aircraft components.

These regulations concern *firms*. Article 87 of the Treaty establishes that 'any aid granted by a Member State or through State resources in any form whatsoever which distorts or threatens to distort competition by favouring certain undertakings or the production of certain goods shall, in so far as it affects trade between Member States, be incompatible with the common market'. Such aid comprises that granted for exports and investment.

By contrast, the following categories of aid are not considered to distort competition and hence are compatible with the common market:

(a) *regional* **aid**, namely that to promote the economic development of areas where the standard of living is abnormally low or where there is serious underemployment (such areas are those with *per capita* GDP of less than 75 per cent of the Community average or an unemployment rate above the Community norm; see section 18.7)
(b) *horizontal* **aid**, such as aid for R&D, the environment, energy conservation, and promoting non-EU exports
(c) *sectoral* **aid** regulated by the Commission (especially in steel and shipbuilding, synthetic fibres and, more recently, automobiles) or other categories of aid specified with a decision of the Council, which decides with a qualified majority on proposals from the Commission.

7.4.4 *Competition legislation in EU member states*

The laws of individual member states normally complement EU legislation, fully incorporating its underlying principles. This is especially true in the case of Germany and Italy, less so for France and the United Kingdom, whose basic position is that competition is essentially *neutral*, generating positive or negative effects according to the circumstances. The main difference between EU rules and French law regards the control of concentrations, with France placing considerable emphasis on what it perceives as a need to strengthen its national productive system. The United Kingdom also gives weight to forms of efficiency other than allocative efficiency. The differences between the criteria adopted in these countries and those at the EU level have, then, a number of foundations, ranging from the pre-eminent role assigned to non-allocative efficiency (and the partial acceptance of the Schumpeterian argument regarding the advantages of monopoly) to only partly economic considerations (the need for 'national champions' to ensure the independence of the economy from the domination of foreign capital).

Obviously, in the case of a conflict EU rules prevail over national legislation. However, EU legislation and national legislation have some relatively distinct and non-conflicting areas of application, leaving room for laws based on different criteria. In fact, European rules prohibit only restrictive agreements and abuses of dominant positions that affect trade between member states, which excludes almost all such practices in the services sector and many in agriculture and industry. Moreover, the existence of a *minimum threshold* for economic concentrations to be considered at the European level introduces an even sharper separation between the two spheres than the rules governing collusive agreements and dominant positions.

7.4.5 *International coordination of national legislation*

The national scope of most competition legislation hinders its effectiveness when dealing with firms whose operations cross national borders. International economic relations and international trade suffer as a result (see Tizzano, 2000). Competition legislation, as with any economic policy measure taken at the national (or regional) level, may differ from or conflict with similar measures taken in other countries. This is all the more likely the greater the level of globalisation and the determination of a government to regulate anticompetitive behaviour not only within its national frontiers but also abroad. This is the case of the United States, which seeks to control the action of firms abroad that has an impact on competition at home. However, even simple differences between national laws or the orientation of competition authorities in different countries can cause problems. Take, for example, a cross-border merger (i.e. a merger involving firms that operate in various countries). Such an operation could be assessed differently by the competition authorities in the countries involved.[22]

This may be so even between EU member states. In order to head off such a risk, arrive at a unitary assessment and reduce the difficulty of identifying the appropriate procedures to invoke, four EU countries in 2001 submitted a case of concentration to the Commission that did not fall under its authority. This was made possible by the creation of an association of EU competition authorities, which established an information channel among the authorities and enhanced cooperation between them and with the European Commission.

In recent years, we have seen the emergence of *agreed or bilateral competition action* between the United States and the European Union or the United States and Canada.

On a multilateral plane, at the Doha intergovernmental conference in November 2001 the World Trade Organisation (WTO) decided to initiate multilateral negotiations to achieve cooperation among national competition authorities. In October 2001 the International Competition Network (ICN) was established to bring together all countries with competition regimes, of which fifty are currently participating. The network seeks to foster a collaborative environment for solving the substantive problems of combating anticompetitive behaviour (Autorità garante della concorrenza e del mercato, 2002).

It is to be hoped that this will evolve into the drafting of a multilateral competition code applied by international organisations. The ICN has begun to work along these lines, drafting eight guidelines at its Naples meeting in September 2002 aimed at preventing divergent or conflicting decisions on the part of national competition authorities (for more on the internationalisation of antitrust policy, see Dabbah, 2003).

7.5   Other competition policy instruments; price controls and public enterprises

7.5.1   *Price controls*

Price controls are another form of regulation (and are therefore a direct control measure). They involve setting *maximum* or *minimum prices*, depending on the objective. If the aim is to guarantee a given income to the supplier of a good or service, the

---

[22] An example of divergent decisions is the merger between GE and Honeywell, which was approved by US authorities and rejected by European authorities in 2001. The divergence was the source of considerable friction between policymakers in the two areas. Box 7.3 is devoted to the analysis of this case.

government will set a minimum price.[23] For antimonopoly purposes, a maximum selling price will be set.[24] Price controls are an instrument (which is not alternative to antimonopoly legislation or public enterprises) to increase allocative efficiency (and/or 'X'-efficiency and, in some cases, dynamic efficiency).

Direct[25] control of prices can be accomplished in a number of ways:

(1) establishing a *maximum profit margin*
(2) fixing a *rate of return* (profit) on invested capital
(3) setting a *maximum price* (price cap).

Maximum profit margin

The first technique involves setting a *maximum percentage of profit over unit costs*. This should restrain prices and, therefore, the exploitation of market power. However, since the regulatory authorities do not control unit costs, they do not actually control prices. In fact, the regulated firm will have an incentive to let unit costs rise, thus earning a larger total profit, given the margin fixed by the regulator.

Fixing a rate of return

Given capital and costs, *fixing a limit on the rate of return on capital* will determine the maximum unit price and thereby ensure allocative efficiency. However, the regulated firm will have an incentive to choose capital-intensive techniques rather than the technique that ensures production efficiency as a way to increase total profits (the *Averch–Johnson effect*; see Averch and Johnson, 1962).

Setting a maximum price

Given costs, setting a *price cap* implies a certain profit margin for each level of demand and, given capital and demand, a certain rate of return or profit. With this technique, the regulator aims to induce the firm to seek allocative efficiency (since the maximum price is fixed) and static and dynamic internal efficiency (since, given the price, the firm has an incentive to reduce costs). A dynamic version of this price control mechanism is the **RPI–X method**, where RPI is the annual rate of change in the retail price index and X is a percentage decided by the regulator. If, for example, annual inflation is 5 per cent and X is set at 3 per cent, the price set by the regulated firm[26] can increase by a maximum of 2 per cent per year. This means that the price of the regulated good

---

[23] Price controls are often used for this purpose in agriculture. The European Union's Common Agricultural Policy (CAP) still guarantees minimum prices to support farm incomes (although the level was reduced in a 1992 reform).

[24] Fixing maximum prices can also serve a macroeconomic purpose, such as ensuring price stability. We discuss this in chapter 13.

[25] Indirect control can be exerted by imposing a tax whose amount is inversely related to the volume of output. This raises allocative efficiency by encouraging the firm to increase production, which will lower the price for a given demand curve. Alternatively, the government could grant a subsidy directly linked to the level of output. The subsidy could be financed by auctioning the right to produce the good (the *franchising mechanism* we spoke of earlier).

[26] In the case of a firm producing more than one good, the constraint is normally placed on the increase in the price of a *basket* of the goods rather than each individual good. The formula referred to here was developed by Littlechild (1983) and has been widely used in the United Kingdom for privatised public utilities.

must decline by 3 per cent annually in real terms, which the firm can accomplish *by increasing productivity* (the reason the formula was introduced). Given the level of costs that can be reached by increasing productivity, the regulator implicitly fixes a rate of return or profit in setting the size of X. Nevertheless, the regulated firm may still have an incentive to let costs rise in order to induce the authority to lower the value of X.

As a direct control measure, price regulation is potentially very effective. It is certainly effective in the short run in emergency situations if the administrative apparatus is efficient enough to ensure that it is implemented properly. In the longer run, its effectiveness greatly depends on solving a number of information problems. Let us see why.

The objective of regulating a private firm is to constrain its behaviour in some way (in our case, limiting the firm's ability to set prices) while allowing it to stay in business in the long run. To achieve this, the firm must be able to cover all its costs and earn a minimum rate of profit sufficient to ensure survival and, possibly, growth,[27] whatever price control method is used. On the other hand, the rate of profit must not be too high, since this would undermine the purpose of regulation. Regulation with price controls must therefore pass between the twin perils of Scylla and Charybdis: on the one side there is the risk that the firm will earn *excessive profits*; on the other, there is the danger that investment will be *discouraged* by a low rate of return or uncertainty about the price level to be set by the regulator. In order to avoid both risks, the regulator should know the firm's production costs. However, this is not always an easy task, even if the regulator has access to the firm's accounts, for many reasons: first, monitoring has costs itself; second, the firm could alter its production costs to subvert regulation by increasing them during the price revision period.[28]

Price controls, which with full information might contribute to increasing efficiency, thus encounter difficulties when there is asymmetric information between regulator and firm, owing to the scope this gives the firm for strategic behaviour. For control to be effective, it is therefore essential to reduce the regulator's information disadvantage as much as possible (Baron and Besanko, 1984). If there are many firms in the market, the costs of each can be compared and under certain conditions it will even be possible to set prices efficiently with the maximum profit margin method by linking the price set by firm A to the costs of firm B and vice versa, in the simple case of two firms (**yardstick competition**; see Shleifer, 1985).[29] The incentive effect of yardstick competition is discussed in box 7.4.

Even if there is only one firm it is occasionally possible to obtain at least some information by comparing the same cost item among the various divisions of the firm. In a

---

[27] In a time perspective we should also consider that, since it is possible that firms may be uncertain about the future rate of return allowed by regulators, there is a danger that investment will be below the socially efficient level (Vickers and Yarrow, 1988, especially pp. 427–8).

[28] This sort of regulation does appear to have had positive effects on efficiency and has given rise to an improvement in the accounts of regulated firms in the United Kingdom (see Veljanovski, 1991).

[29] However, this requires that at least some basic cost data be available to the regulator.

Box 7.4.   Yardstick competition as an instrument for dealing with information asymmetry

Yardstick competition has an *incentive effect*. As on p. 176, let us consider a duopoly. The price that each firm can set is unlinked from its production costs and, therefore, each firm has an incentive to contain those costs. In doing so, it reduces the price applicable for the other firm. If the latter mimics the first, it will also seek to reduce its costs and, in doing so, lower the price applicable to the other firm. In general, this form of regulation makes the firms compete on costs, which ultimately reduces prices.

One difficulty with this criterion is related to the fact that certain cost components are exogenous for some firms and their amount is justified by factors specific to those firms. Thus, they cannot be used as a basis for the maximum price applicable by another firm. A second problem may emerge from the possibility of collusion between the firms in a given industry. This danger increases as the number of firms in the industry decreases. While the criterion is often not applicable in determining the entire base cost for setting the price of a firm, it can serve for comparing cost components among firms, adopting – where justified – the lowest value as the basis for determining the price ceiling.

dynamic context, the regulator can try to learn about the firm's cost conditions gradually and choose the appropriate price-fixing mechanism in the light of this knowledge.

Price regulation has developed considerably since the mid-1980s years, often as a result of privatisation programmes. In the United States the most common method has been to set a rate of return on invested capital, whereas dynamic price caps have been the most frequently used method in the United Kingdom (for example, in the privatisation of British Telecom), Italy and other countries.

7.5.2   *Public enterprises and competition policies*

Public enterprises have been used as a competition policy instrument on numerous occasions. In Italy, ENI was used for antitrust purposes in the 1950s and 1960s, helping to reduce the market power of the dominant international oil companies at the time (the 'seven sisters'). Other areas in which public enterprises have been employed for competitive purposes in Europe and the developing countries include the steel industry, cement and chemicals (see Shonfield, 1965).

More recently, the active role of public enterprises has gradually declined in some countries while there has been a rise in the number of cases of collusion (in sectors characterised by **mixed oligopoly** – i.e. those with private sector and public sector firms, such as cement and chemicals) or conduct that imitates (in sectors with dominant or total public control, such as telecommunications and energy) that of private sectors firms, with patently 'monopolistic' conduct.

The process of formal or substantive liberalisation and privatisation involving most public enterprises in the 1990s has not yet had an appreciable impact on such conduct, and in some cases has accentuated it. In certain situations, the rapid liberalisation of sectors with the demerger of businesses that had formerly been carried out by a single firm (often public) increased costs (owing to the loss of economies of scale) and created *local monopolies*, with an adverse impact on prices.

7.6   Externalities, public goods and public policies

We said that externalities create an inequality between private and social cost (or product), if we are dealing with production externalities, or between marginal private and social utility in the case of consumption externalities. These divergences cause inefficiencies that can be eliminated by removing the divergences themselves – i.e. by internalising the social cost or benefit with the originating agent.

This can be accomplished in a number of ways. In particular, we can:

(1) *tax (subsidise)* activities that give rise to external diseconomies (economies)
(2) provide *incentives* to eliminate external diseconomies
(3) introduce *tradable rights* (permits) to create external diseconomies
(4) regulate the behaviour of *economic agents*.

We will deal with these in order, referring primarily to external diseconomies. However, much of our discussion holds equally well for external economies (with the appropriate adaptations, i.e. subsidies instead of taxes, etc.).

7.6.1   *Taxation*

It is intuitively clear that if a productive activity creates external diseconomies (economies), the difference between marginal private cost (benefit) and marginal social cost (benefit) can be removed by introducing a positive (negative) tax.[30] Thus, in the case of an external diseconomy if a tax equal to the value of the externality were added to the original marginal private cost, the firm would bear a new, higher marginal private cost equal to the marginal social cost, and would be induced to take its production decisions in relation to the latter. If the taxes are set as a fixed amount per unit of product, a tax a would be added to the marginal private cost, MC, of firm i generating the externality. The firm would then set output where $MC + a = p$, with p being the price of the good.

---

[30] In the case of a diseconomy, we have a true tax; a 'negative tax' is a subsidy. These taxes are called *Pigovian taxes*.

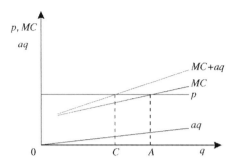

Figure 7.1

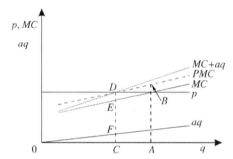

Figure 7.2

Referring to figure 7.1, let us now imagine a competitive firm that generates external diseconomies of $a \cdot q$ *per additional unit of product*.[31] Without government intervention, the firm would produce $0A$. If the externality were internalised by imposing a tax of $a \cdot q$ per additional unit, marginal private cost (including the tax) would equal marginal social cost and output would decline to $0C$.[32] If a firm generating an external economy is subsidised, it will raise its output. The reader is invited to present this in diagram form.[33]

7.6.2 *Incentives for eliminating external diseconomies*

Now look at figure 7.2, which is simply figure 7.1 with a number of additions. The firm produces $0A$, whereas the socially efficient level is $0C$. Rather than setting a tax of $a \cdot q$ per additional unit of output, it would be possible to induce the firm to produce the socially efficient level by granting it a subsidy, equal to DE (which is the value of the

---

[31] More simply, the diseconomy could be fixed, equal to a for each unit of product, as in the previous example. We have chosen this other hypothesis to elucidate a number of differences between various policies for correcting externalities.

[32] The reader can imagine situations in which the externality increases more or less than proportionally with respect to output and, correspondingly, the unit tax varies with the variation in output.

[33] Pigovian taxes or subsidies could be extended to consumers if they were to generate externalities.

diseconomy at the social optimum) for each unit of output reduction. The marginal cost of production for the firm would therefore rise by *DE* for each unit of output. If the firm continued to produce 0*A*, its cost would be *AB*, equal to the effective cost of production plus *DE*, which is the subsidy forgone by continuing to produce at the previous level. The same can be said for each lower level of output. The marginal private cost curve is therefore *PMC* with a fixed subsidy equal to *DE* for the reduction in output. The result in the short run is the same as that obtained with a tax per unit of output: the firm will position itself at *D* and produce 0*C*. In the long term, the external diseconomy produced by the industry under this policy could be even greater, owing to the entrance of new firms and the subsequent increase in output (see Baumol and Oates, 1975; Pearce and Turner, 1990).

Note that the incentive to reduce output is different from the incentive to use plant, materials and so on in such a way as to eliminate or reduce the external diseconomy. Suppose the diseconomy is pollution. It is true that using cleaner technology, made possible by the subsidy, would eliminate or reduce the external diseconomy. However, output would still be greater than the socially efficient level because the firm has its production cost reduced by the subsidy. The firm uses the pollution-reducing technology but will keep output above the socially efficient level, i.e. where marginal social cost equals price (see Stiglitz, 1988).

7.6.3   *Tradable permits to produce diseconomies*

Tradable discharge permits were first introduced in the 1980s as a response to pollution. They work as follows. The 'optimal' level of the external diseconomies created by different industries in a given environment is first determined. For each industry, this corresponds to the level of output 0*C* in figure 7.1. 'Pollution rights' are then assigned (for example, by auction) up to the established level. All firms (as well as conservationists) can participate in the auction. They can use the rights themselves or can stop polluting (if an appropriate technology becomes available) and sell their pollution permits to others.[34] Firms will pay a maximum price equal to the value of the right, which is the value of pollution that corresponds to output 0*C*, i.e. *DE* (or *CF*). The firms' marginal cost curve will therefore rise by *DE*, as in the case of the subsidy for reducing output (See figure 7.2), and each firm will produce 0*C*. In the long run the level of diseconomy may be higher because of the entry of new firms.

One effect of a system of pollution rights – like taxes – may be to stimulate investment in pollution abatement technology, since under this system pollution is costly. Another shared advantage of tradable rights and taxes over subsidies is that they are a source of revenue for the government. The magnitude of the effect on the level of pollution

---

[34] For details, see Dales (1968).

is more predictable with rights than with taxes, since in the former case the level is specifically predetermined rather than estimated, as in the case of taxes.[35]

7.6.4 Regulation

An alternative to taxes is regulation, a *direct control measure* that normally imposes certain obligations or prohibitions on economic agents: for example, requiring firms to use pollution abatement equipment or certain production methods, or forcing home-owners to keep the sidewalk in front of their house clear of snow, etc. As we will see, regulation can be aimed at eliminating *external diseconomies* (the most frequent case) or creating *external economies*.[36]

The results of regulation can differ from those produced by taxation. They are not greatly different in static terms, since they are aimed at eliminating external diseconomies and, therefore, increasing efficiency. In fact, the results are quite similar only if the same information is available for the two policy options and administrative costs are assumed to be the same.

In reality, however, information is always incomplete and any policy measure will be ineffective if founded on inaccurate data or erroneous calculations. Nevertheless, regulation and pollution permits seem preferable to taxes and subsidies for pollution abatement if the reaction of firms is uncertain. Administrative costs are probably lower for (uniform) regulation than for taxes (or subsidies) and permits.

A 'dynamic' advantage of taxes and tradable rights is that all firms have an incentive to reduce pollution in order to reduce the costs associated with taxes or the purchase of rights. In the case of regulation, the incentive exists only for those firms that are not in compliance with the established standards when they are introduced. The measures also have different effects on the distribution of income. For firms, regulation is less costly than taxation. If subsidies for reducing output or for investing in pollution abatement techniques are used instead of taxes or pollution permits, the cost to the firm is reduced even further.

The range of applications of the various policy instruments for increasing allocative efficiency in the presence of externalities is extremely varied. In the United States, a core of legislative measures (for example, the Clean Air Act from the early 1970s) has been supplemented with a system of pollution permits created by the Environmental Protection Agency (EPA) to ensure that the standards are reached. The agreement reached at Kyoto in 1997 at the conclusion of the third session of the UN conference on climate change (**Kyoto protocol**) envisages a system of *tradable permits* to reduce

[35] Taxation acts on the price imputed to the external diseconomy, leaving it to the firm to decide the quantity. With the 'pollution right' system, however, the level of the diseconomy is set and the market fixes its price. Obviously, this holds if the administrative apparatus used to set and monitor pollution levels is efficient.
[36] We will see later that regulation can also be used for other purposes. The objectives, techniques and substitutes for regulation are considered in Waterson (1988), Spulber (1989) and Kay and Vickers (1990), among others. An interesting reformulation of the 'capture' theory of government decisionmaking – with specific applications to regulation – is given by Laffont and Tirole (1991).

pollution. The proposal to introduce a *carbon tax*, advanced by the European Union in 1991 as a tool for countering the greenhouse effect, met with fierce opposition from the United States and Japan, as well as industry.[37]

The problem of protecting *transnational commons* is of special importance. It requires the international coordination of individual country policies and the creation of suitable institutions, which can be of the same type as those operating at the national level (pollution permits, regulatory agencies, etc.). We will deal with the problems encountered in coordinating national policies in more detail later (see chapter 20). However, we can say now that the difficulties of coordinating environmental policies can be reduced or eliminated if countries negotiate not only in terms of pollution levels but also use some other instrument (e.g. trade policy, foreign debt, development aid) to induce other countries to cooperate.

7.6.5   *Financing and producing public goods*

The problem of supplying a public good is threefold and involves:

(a) determining the *socially efficient* amount of the good
(b) *financing* the good
(c) *producing* the good.

The first two aspects are closely linked. In fact, the reason for determining the socially efficient amount of the good (which is not done by the market) is that private agents are reluctant to finance it, preferring to engage in free riding behaviour. The third aspect can be dealt with separately. Let us refer briefly to the first two problems.

We can determine the amount of the public good to produce and, at the same time, the division of the related cost with a number of mechanisms, including voting. However, each raises some kind of difficulty with asymmetric information (see Cornes and Sandler, 1996, part III).

In practice, the methods used to measure demand for public goods make use of both market and non-market data. With the former, we gain indirect information on individuals' willingness to pay for the public good or its close substitutes (e.g. spending on trips to less-polluted areas). Methods based on non-market data make use of interviews or experiments. Needless to say, we cannot insist on scientific precision with such methods, but we can obtain responses that provide reasonable approximations of the optimal amount of the public good. Once output has been determined, some government body will provide for its financing using funds from its budget and/or specific contributions from private consumers.

The third aspect of the problem of public goods regards the actual production of the good. The fact that the government must take responsibility for determining the

---

[37] On the effects of this tax see Carraro and Siniscalco (1993). More generally, on the role played by economic institutions for the effectiveness of environmental policy see Franzini and Nicita (2002).

optimal level of output and financing production does not mean that it must also produce the good itself. There may be reasons why the private sector can produce the good more efficiently: once the problems of financing and optimal output have been solved, the problem of production can be tackled separately.[38] Since some of the discussion of public sector firms in section 6.4 is relevant to this issue, the reader is invited to consider our analysis there.

7.7 Summary

1 *Market power* has uncertain effects on dynamic efficiency and negative effects on (Pareto) allocative efficiency. To counter the latter a number of competition policy tools can be used. Liberalising markets and opening economies to international competition normally have a positive impact on allocative efficiency in the short term. The long-term effects are less certain.

2 *Regulation* consists of obligations (to do or not do) aimed at governing the behaviour of private agents. It may have multiple objectives and take various forms. *Competition policy* may involve deregulating entry or regulating effective competition, market structure, firms' conduct or prices.

3 *Reducing barriers to entry and exit* fosters potential competition. Effective competition can be increased by using regulation to break up monopolies or auctioning the right of access to the market.

4 Given the limitations of increasing potential or effective competition, steps can be taken to ensure that the market power associated with scale economies or entry and exit barriers is not exploited. This can be done with various forms of *regulation* (antitrust laws, price controls) and the *nationalisation* of monopoly firms.

5 *Competition legislation* seeks to safeguard economic liberty and control the economic and political power of concentrations. It also aims to increase allocative efficiency by forbidding agreements that restrict competition and the formation and abuse of dominant positions (including those formed through mergers or other forms of concentration). Nearly all competition legislation adopted by countries is based in some way on the Sherman Act in the United States. In recent years, various attempts to coordinate national competition action at the international level have met with success.

6 *Price controls* are a form of regulation that can involve:
   (a) setting a *profit margin*
   (b) setting a *rate of return* on invested capital
   (c) introducing a *price cap*.

   The importance of regulation has increased in recent decades in conjunction with privatisation.

---

[38] However, bear in mind that if the value of the public good has been set equal to its cost, the problem of production should be solved *before* determining the optimal level of output, which depends on its value and, therefore, its cost.

7 Policies for correcting *inefficiencies produced by externalities* include:
   (a) taxing (subsidising) activities that generate external diseconomies (economies)
   (b) providing incentives for eliminating external diseconomies
   (c) introducing tradable rights to produce diseconomies
   (d) introducing regulations to prevent external diseconomies and generate external economies.

   Taxation and regulation are the traditional tools for correcting externalities. The importance of pollution permits has increased in recent years.

8 The production of public goods requires that we decide:
   (a) the *socially efficient level* of the good
   (b) the procedures for *financing* its production
   (c) the *agent* that should actually produce the good.

The first and second elements of the decision process can be dealt with various, not entirely satisfactory, mechanisms. Public goods do not necessarily have to be produced by the government.

8 Industrial and regional policies; redistributive policies

8.1 Dynamic efficiency and industrial policies

The principal, and almost exclusive, criterion of the economic policy options outlined in chapters 6 and 7 has been (static) *allocative efficiency*.

Other important microeconomic problems arise when the objective is to increase *dynamic efficiency*. Here, too, we can speak of market failures that call for some form of public intervention (see sections 2.14 and 3.6).

As we know, dynamic efficiency is the ability to manage change and/or react to change introduced by others, making it possible to secure higher profits and faster growth. The ability to do this is linked to many important features of the **productive structure** of an economy – i.e. the lasting rather than transitory aspects of an economic system. In addition to certain *macroeconomic characteristics* (such as the size of the economy, the degree of international openness, etc.), this includes *microeconomic features* (sectoral composition and regional division of production; technical, economic and financial concentration; production technologies used and the innovative content of products; entry and exit barriers; productive organisation; integration among firms; the available factors of production – i.e. 'natural capital', physical and human capital). Note that some of the microeconomic features also have an impact on allocative efficiency.

We briefly discussed the effects of monopoly on innovation in section 2.15. Other microeconomic features of the productive structure appear to have a clearer impact on dynamic efficiency. An economy's capacity for growth and employment seems to depend directly on the *sectoral composition of production*: if an economy specialises in sectors in which world demand is growing more quickly at a given time, it will have greater scope for output growth and employment, *ceteris paribus*. Similarly, introducing innovative technologies (**process innovation**) can increase the rate of output growth, although in the short term it may accentuate employment problems. On the other hand, **product innovation** should have a positive impact on both objectives. The relationships between firms and between productive sectors can play a key role in determining innovative capacity (and even static efficiency). Technology-sharing agreements, or even merely being located in the same area (for example, in an industrial district), in the same sector or in sectors linked by trade relationships, can help to increase static and dynamic efficiency.

As we saw in chapters 2 and 3, the operation of market forces alone often does not guarantee the most efficient productive structure. This creates scope for public intervention. Policies aimed at modifying the productive structure and, therefore, increasing allocative and dynamic efficiency are called **industrial policies**. They may be aimed at altering the sectoral composition of production, and/or inducing other changes in the productive structure, such as a change in technology, in the degree of integration, etc. (**restructuring**).

Many of the policies we have discussed in chapters 6 and 7 can be considered as specific kinds of *industrial policy*. Public enterprises can be an effective instrument of industrial policy; in the thirty years after the Second World War they were in fact conceived for this very purpose in various European countries (see Vernon, 1974). Regulation in the form of *antitrust legislation* or *price controls* can often be a powerful stimulus to allocative and dynamic efficiency if it aims at both introducing innovations and eliminating the burden that monopolies in key sectors can impose on related industries. Even some policies for dealing with externalities and public goods can have a significant impact on industrial structure. Subsidies and tax incentives for investment, public procurement policies and trade policy are additional instruments. We will not consider positive and negative taxes. We will deal with procurement policies in section 8.3 after having briefly sketched the evolution of post-war industrial policy in the next section. Trade policy is discussed in chapter 15.

8.2   The evolution and the tools of post-war industrial policy

Post-war industrial policy can be divided into three stages: the first was that of selective industrial policy; the second was that of general industrial policy targeted at sustaining the market; the third was that of general industrial policy aimed at setting the rules of the game.

The first stage ran from reconstruction through the 1970s. Europe, Japan and the United States sought to strengthen their productive systems, especially in what they considered to be strategic sectors, not only for military purposes but also because of the importance of the growth of global demand and, above all, strong interdependence with other sectors and the ability to generate dynamic external economies on the supply side.

This approach adopted a variety of instruments, including customs protection, public demand management (especially in Japan and the United States), tax and credit incentives and public enterprises (in Europe). The public enterprise was the vehicle of choice for the creation of **national champions** in the industries (steel, chemicals, energy, telecommunications, transport, radio and television, etc.) that the European countries considered to be strategic.

This stage came to a close in the early 1980s, both in the Anglo-American world, owing to the change in general economic policy wrought by Margaret Thatcher and Ronald Reagan, and elsewhere. In continental Europe, that period saw a shift from 'sectoral policies' to 'factor policies' – i.e. 'horizontal' or 'general' policies.

The period of general industrial policy aimed at sustaining the market lasted for a decade, from the early 1980s until the early 1990s. In Europe, it was imposed by supranational organisations (above all by the European Community, with the publication of the White Paper on the completion of the internal market in 1985 envisaging the creation of a **European Single Market**, i.e. dismantling non-tariff barriers (NTBs) to intra-Community trade; see chapter 18). As part of this strategy, Europe approved the Community Regulation on concentrations in 1989, while various European countries adopted antitrust legislation modelled on Community law, policies to promote scientific research and innovation as well as many liberalisation measures.

The third stage of industrial policy, that aimed at ensuring a 'level playing field' for participants, began in 1993, which saw three events marking the change of orientation at the international level: the start of the European Single Market, the creation of the North American Free Trade Area (NAFTA) and the conclusion of the Uruguay Round of trade negotiations (see the fuller discussion in chapters 17 and 18). All three of these events modified the framework of industrial and trade policy, which became increasingly less discriminatory against foreign competitors (box 8.1).

This shift in approach is tied to the **globalisation** of markets and production – i.e. the global expansion of international trade and production (see chapter 19): on the one hand, the liberalisation of trade and capital movements stimulated globalisation, while on the other the growth of this globalisation stimulated further liberalisation measures, mainly owing to the fear of sanctions and the reduced effectiveness of national economic policies (chapters 19 and 20). Many countries thus decided to focus public action to improve their productive systems on so-called '**system externalities**', which involves setting rules and property rights tailored to enhance the price and quality competitiveness of the entire economic system. In terms of both industrial and trade policy, the new rules have a clear *pro-market orientation*.

The second and third stages were marked by interventions of a *horizontal nature*, which facilitated reconversion and restructuring only indirectly, namely **social shock absorbers** (above all, unemployment benefits, early retirement and other public assistance programmes). Some initiatives to provide specific support to sectors in crisis also continued, however.

The type of industrial policy that has prevailed since the 1980s, with its focus on general measures and the competitiveness of the economic system (rather than on individual firms or industries), has a clear justification. One limitation of general industrial policies is that policymakers must still make *sectoral choices* that cannot be left to the whims of the market. The market can conceal opportunities for specialisation of a given country consistent with its long-term comparative advantage for a number of reasons (e.g. the existence of established positions in other countries, which have developed dynamic economies of scale; the existence of competitors abroad exploiting their market power). An application of this concept to protection of infant industries is the subject of section 15.4 (box 8.2)[1].

---

[1] For an analysis of industrial policy in European countries in the last century see Foreman-Peck and Federico (1999). The experiences of France and Japan are dealt with briefly in box 8.3.

Box 8.1.   Tools of selective and horizontal industrial policy

Selective industrial policy

(a) *Financial incentives* (for example, capital grants or interest subsidies; consolidation or transformation of company debt; financing of specific functions, such as research; loan guarantees)

(b) *Fiscal incentives* (for example, tax relief, accelerated depreciation, charging social security contributions to the budget)

(c) *Direct public intervention*:
   • equity investment in private firms in specific sectors
   • public enterprises

(d) *Administrative intervention*:
   • licensing to engage in a business
   • selective management of public sector demand.

Horizontal industrial policy

(a) measures to foster *labour mobility*:
   • easing of administrative and regulatory barriers concerning health care benefits and the transferability of pension rights
   • publicising information on job vacancies
   • increasing labour market flexibility (e.g. part-time and fixed-term contracts; temporary labour; job sharing; 'jobs-on-call')
   • increasing flexibility of exit from labour market (easing of restrictions on redundancies)
   • increasing social shock absorbers such as unemployment benefits and reducing the duration of such benefits

(b) measures to foster the *mobility of firms and capital* at the national and international levels, for example, with the liberalisation of capital and goods movements (see chapter 16) or the recognition of authorisations to engage in a business issued by other countries (see subsection 18.4.4)

(c) reform of the *goods market*:
   • regulations to safeguard competition and market openness
   • reduction of legal barriers to entry

(d) *innovation policy*:
   • public research initiatives
   • incentives for private research

(e) provision of *substantive public services* (e.g. information, technical assistance, vocational training, public research)

(f) public provision of *infrastructure* (e.g. roads, ports, urban infrastructure, telex networks).

Box 8.2. Automatic and discretionary incentives

The distinction between automatic and discretionary incentives concerns the way in which they are granted. **Automatic industrial and regional policy incentives** are granted on the basis of *eligibility requirements* laid down by law. The administrative bodies that authorise their disbursement merely check that the requirements of the operations carried out (normally investments) meet those specified in the relevant legislation. At the most basic, all that is required to receive the subsidy is to make the proposed investment, possibly with certain requirements concerning its characteristics (if it is an industrial policy incentive) or the area in which it will be made (for regional policy incentives), without limitations regarding the industry involved or other features (e.g. innovative content) of the initiative. One approach to granting automatic incentives that reduces administrative complications is to set off subsidies against firms' tax liabilities.

By contrast, **discretionary incentives** are granted only after an administrative body has ascertained the eligibility of the applicant (or proposed action) under the general requirements laid down in the relevant industrial or regional policy legislation (sector, characteristics of the investment, etc.).

Each of these types of subsidy has advantages and disadvantages, which must be carefully weighed in relation to the purpose of the intervention, the funds available and the characteristics of efficiency and correctness of the public administration.

Automatic incentives have the advantage of being more rapid and less vulnerable to abuse and improper conduct in government action. Expanding the scope of the incentives to a broader pool of applicants is not without costs, however. It means fewer funds are available for each of the beneficiaries and produces less focused intervention, which may be diverted towards irrelevant or distorted objectives.

The most aggressive and pro-active (rather than passive) industrial and regional policies tend to be those implemented through *discretionary schemes*.

8.3 Public demand management policies

Public sector demand for goods and services can be used to achieve a number of objectives:

(1) ensure the operation of *government administration and the provision of public services*
(2) support various branches of *economic activity* (industrial policy)
(3) govern *effective demand* (countercyclical policy).

The first purpose is fundamental to the existence of government itself and is created with it. The others have followed later.

As regards objective (1), while Parliament is responsible for identifying, quantifying and distributing over time the needs of the community, it is the government that must effectively provide public services, seeking to employ efficiently the available human and physical resources and those that become necessary over time. *Efficiency* implies opting for the least expensive solution for any given level of results (or the solution which provides the best result for any given price).

As for (2), over the centuries in nearly all the countries that have found themselves at one time or another as latecomers in industrial development, the birth and growth of strategic sectors have been stimulated with a range of instruments, such as government contracts (e.g. steel and shipbuilding) and customs protection (e.g. in maritime transport as well as the sectors we just mentioned (box 8.3); see section 15.3).

Box 8.3.   Industrial policy in France and Japan

Objectives and Instruments

Post-war growth in France and Japan has relied on a particularly active industrial policy. Its objectives were the development of a large manufacturing base in the emerging industries of the 1950s and 1960s – steel, auto, and chemicals, the typical sectors of 'Fordist' production – and, since the 1970s, the development of new activities in electronics, aircraft and biotechnology. At the same time, industrial policy has aimed at assuring efficient telecommunications and transport networks, a crucial infrastructure for modern economies, and a stable supply of energy, which is essential in industrial countries with few energy resources.

From the perspective of microeconomic policies, therefore, the aims included:

(a) *achieving static efficiency* by addressing market failures
(b) *achieving dynamic efficiency*, favouring the growth of industries with strong learning and productivity growth, able to sustain international competitiveness and permanent high wage employment.

A wide range of *policy instruments* has been adopted, and can be summarised as follows:

(a) *Subsidies for private firms*, support for their R&D and investment, creation of the necessary infrastructure in order to ensure that a large share of the demand in growing industries was met by domestic producers.
(b) Trade *protection* in infant industries (including voluntary export restraints, such as car exports from Japan to Europe) and use of managed trade and negotiations to open selected export markets, in order to foster the growth of new industries (for the meaning of trade policies, see chapter 15).
(c) Public *procurement* of high-technology goods, providing an early 'demand pull' to the development of new industries; examples include advanced trains, telecommunications, military equipment, aerospace, biotechnology and health.
(d) Policy agreements with large oligopolistic private firms in order to plan the *state-sponsored development of new sectors and activities* (typical of Japan).

(e) Creation or expansion of state-owned firms in strategic industries (typical of France).

(f) Development of *large state-owned firms* in natural monopolies.

(g) Development of a large-scale system of *public education*, R&D with close links between public research, public services (such as in the health sector) and public and private firms.

(h) Creation of institutions in charge of setting *standards and regulations* for fostering the development of new industries.

France

France has a long tradition of state involvement in the economy as a key promoter of new economic activities and growth, dating back to the time of Colbert during the first industrial revolution. In the post-war period, state-owned firms in France were established in electricity (EDF), telecommunications (France Télécom), cars (Renault), aerospace (Aérospatiale, now merged in the European group EADS, which manufactures the Airbus) and several other industries. Even in the 1990s, which were dominated by pressure to privatise and open markets, French state industries maintained their role, and the sale of shares to private investors was limited.

At the same time, the extensive role of state industries has represented an answer to the classic market failure problems of natural monopolies, and a strategy for achieving dynamic efficiency through technological change and development of new industries. A major strength of this approach has been the integration, within the public policy sphere, of the range of activities from basic and applied research to original product and system development, to large-scale industrial production, with public procurement playing the key role of ensuring market outlets for pioneering industries.

This strategy has been highly successful in some fields; French high-speed trains have been a model for all countries; in 2003 the French-initiated Airbus overtook Boeing as the world largest producer of civilian aircraft; in health sciences (including AIDS) French research, drugs and services are highly advanced. However, the modest size of the national economy and restricted public resources have limited the possibility of success in a wide range of fields. In information technology (IT), France has shared the failure of all European countries to create and sustain firms with the skills and products needed to face the competition from the United States and Japan; the result is now a major trade deficit in ICT (see Chesnais, 1993).

The main actors in French industrial policy have been ministries, sectoral agencies and state-owned companies, often managed by graduates of the élite National Schools, who also play key roles in the public administration and in private firms.

In a European context dominated by privatisation and deregulation, the tradition of French '*dirigisme*' still provides some direction to the country's development, a direction which is now lacking in all other European countries and in the European Union as a whole. Since the mid-1980s France has attempted to introduce new responses to the power of US and Japanese industries and technologies in European policy, starting with the Eureka technology programme. The challenge for the future of French industrial policy is perhaps transferring its approach – with a long-term vision and a coherent use of a variety of complementary policy tools – to the scale of the European Union, where much larger resources, markets and policy leverage in the global economy can be wielded.

Japan

Japan has conducted an industrial policy based on the systematic development of dynamic industries as engines of the country's specialisation and growth. With post-war economic growth based on export markets, the 1960s were marked by the replacement of traditional activities in textile and shipbuilding with the steel, auto and consumer electronics industries. The emergence of ICT has now largely replaced previous specialisations, making Japan the largest exporter of ICT goods and giving it the largest trade surplus with the United States.

Currency policy has also played a role in this strategy. For a long time, the low value of the yen supported the country's export strategy. Since 1985 the managed rise of the yen against the dollar opened a period marked by the shift from export to direct investment, both in the United States (and to a limited extent, Europe) and in the East Asian countries, where cheaper labour and high skills are available. Industrial policy has therefore emphasised the controlled transfer, without major employment disruptions, of low-value-added production to export platforms in East Asia or closer to final markets, while domestic capabilities have been concentrated on higher-value activities in fast-growing industries and on the research, innovation, financial and strategic functions of the increasingly global networks organised by Japanese multinational firms. The concentration of Japanese industry in a small number of large diversified private groups has made it possible to carry out key industrial policy decisions through concertation and cooperation between government and these groups, involving the unions in the process. Trade policy, subsidies, infrastructure and public procurement have all played a role in this strategy. The key policymaker in this field has been the Ministry of International Trade and Industry (MITI) which has directed most of Japan's industrial transformation, acting through a range of agencies (the Council on Science and Technology, the Science and Technology Agency, National Research Institutes, etc.) (see Odagiri and Goto, 1993).

This approach to industrial policy was highly successful in the fast-growth decades up to the 1990s, first in catching up with Western technologies and later in developing selected fields of world excellence. Japan now has huge trade surpluses in high-technology products and demonstrated strong skills in innovation, as measured for instance by growth in international patenting. In recent years – a period that has also been marked by a substantial slowdown in macroeconomic growth – the country has shown a weakness in its limited ability to expand in the US-dominated fields of software, media, business and financial services. Current challenges for Japan's industrial policy include institutional change in a deeply traditional environment, advancing its university–industry links, and reorganising its ailing industrial conglomerates and large but fragile financial institutions.

Source: Mario Pianta.

The pursuit of industrial policy objectives involves directing public sector demand towards certain goods, especially those incorporating *innovation*. When allowed, demand for each good can also be directed at specific categories of firms, such as domestic producers or firms located in areas where development is desired, or SMEs. Among other things, a government procurement programme aimed at achieving industrial policy goals presupposes a high ratio between public demand and output; an emphasis on discretionary decisionmaking criteria; government skill in evaluating the technical and economic conditions and repercussions of public purchases as well as the persistence of the reasons for such support; a reduction in the time lags of planning, decision and settlement of transactions; and the constant exchange of information between users and producers. The pursuit of industrial policy objectives may require divergence (at least in the short run) from the principles of efficiency that should be observed in producing public services. For example, this happens if support to some firms means paying a higher price to purchase a good.

A public procurement policy designed to govern aggregate demand must emphasise *timing over content*. At the extreme, the latter is irrelevant, but given the primary function of the government agency to provide public services, appropriate planning and design of government purchases – perhaps through the establishment of a 'project fund' – can ensure the consistency of the two objectives.

8.4 Regional policy

Regional policy is essentially industrial policy targeted at a specific part of a country's territory. It seeks to stimulate the growth and development of a given geographical segment of an economic system through the use of industrial policy instruments aimed at encouraging existing firms to stay in a region, fostering the creation of new firms by local entrepreneurs and attracting firms from outside the area. Regional policy is, in short, focused on improving the *regional distribution* of income.

The main economic obstacle to the location of firms in a backward area is the high cost of producing in that area. Although wages are normally lower, the total cost of production is higher for a number of reasons, which are reflected in lower labour productivity, as well as the higher costs of procuring raw materials and capital and, not infrequently, the existence of significant 'rent from illegal activity'. Low productivity can be attributed to more poorly trained workers, possibly lower-quality management (if we consider local resources only) and the inefficiency of infrastructure and services in the area.

The operation of the market does not produce the spontaneous convergence of conditions in a backward area towards those in more advanced regions, as we saw, in particular, in our discussion of endogenous growth theories (see section 3.6): the initial disadvantage tends to remain or increase. In the presence of a vicious circle (or **'cumulative causation'**), government intervention may be needed to spark local development. Regional policy can seek to reduce backwardness through financial and fiscal incentives, direct intervention by central government and other public bodies, and administrative measures.

Many of these instruments have been used to stimulate growth in Southern Italy, which offers an important case study (see box 8.4), and in other countries.

Box 8.4.   Regional development policy in Italy

Italian regional development policy from the end of the Second World War up to the end of the 1980s was essentially identifiable with the decision to provide extraordinary public aid to the regions of southern Italy, abandoning the liberal non-interventionist approach of former policy towards the South (Graziani, 2000):

(1) Extraordinary intervention began in 1950, with agricultural reform and the establishment of a fund for extraordinary works of public interest for the South (the Southern Italy Development Fund – *Cassa per il Mezzogiorno*), whose initial task was to design and build infrastructure. The intervention did not stem the large-scale abandonment of the countryside and massive internal and external migration, which was in part stimulated by the strong demand for labour in the North and in many countries in Europe and elsewhere around the globe.

(2) In a second stage, which began in the second half of the 1950s and continued until the first half of the 1970s, intervention sought to foster industrialisation through **capital investment incentives** (capital grants and interest subsidies) and, beginning at the end of the 1960s, **labour incentives**, with the **charging of social security contributions to the state budget** and income support schemes. The Southern Italy Development Fund financed and subsidised business activity, before closing down in 1986. In the second half of the 1950s, government departments were required to reserve a specified share of their expenditure on procurement (30 per cent) and investment (40 per cent) for southern firms. A similar obligation was imposed for

state-controlled companies (60 per cent of new plant and no less than 40 per cent of total investment to be directed to southern Italy).

The capital investment incentive stage led to the establishment of many highly *capital-intensive* (and often public) enterprises, which did not make a significant impact on southern Italy's historical problem, namely open and hidden unemployment. Labour market incentives encouraged northern Italy's large private sector companies to set up establishments in the South. This second stage of public intervention, albeit marked by major defects, sparked a process of *industrialisation* that significantly narrowed the gap with the rest of the country as measured by the main economic indicators (employment, investment, *per capita* income). Continuing the effort could have launched a process of self-sustaining development and solved the problem of regional disparities once and for all.

(3) However, the process came to a halt with the emergence in the second half of the 1970s of a new public policy orientation. The new approach sought to expand the share of ordinary public expenditure directed at supporting household and corporate incomes. In many cases, support was provided within the framework of a policy aimed at ensuring *social control*, providing fertile soil for corruption and hindering the operation of the labour market. It is perhaps no coincidence that from 1975 onwards the convergence between the South and the rest of the country essentially came to a halt (see Costabile and Giannola, 1996).

(4) The fourth stage of public intervention in the South began in the early 1990s. It came in the wake of the closure of the Southern Italy Development Fund, which had been charged with managing incentives for this area of the country. The effort to subsidise southern development weakened significantly – as regional policy was extended to cover other areas of Italy – and its methodology was changed. Law 488 of December 1992 – by far the most important piece of industrial and regional policy legislation of the 1990s – envisages:

(a) the end of extraordinary government intervention in Southern Italy and the assignment of regional development policy to the ordinary administrative mechanisms of the state

(b) the extension of public intervention to 'disadvantaged areas' throughout the country, which includes parts of the Centre and North that are home to 30 per cent of the total population of those areas

(c) the implementation of public intervention in close collaboration with the European Union, which has frequently warned against diverting the location of production in a manner that distorts competition

(d) the implementation of initiatives within the framework of cooperation between public bodies (central and local government) and firms, this is known as *negotiated development planning*, which has been implemented with measures subsequent to Law 488 and is discussed below (Graziani, 2000).

In the 1990s, it was increasingly acknowledged that underdevelopment in the South was the cumulative result of numerous causes (economic factors, external diseconomies, lack of business skills), which also comprise dysfunctional public policies (crime, corruption and inefficiency in government;[a] excessively centralised decisionmaking;[b] a lack of long-term planning and financial certainty of intervention programmes[c]) and the shortage of **social capital** – i.e. the set of fiduciary relationships that facilitates cooperation and exchange.[d]

This awareness prompted a change of course, with the implementation of **negotiated development planning**, which is essentially a form of 'regulation' agreed between public entities or between the competent public entities and private parties for the implementation of initiatives targeted at a single development objective, which call for an overall assessment of the related activities. The end result of negotiated planning is a series of agreements on the various aspects involved.

These instruments are intended to foster cooperation at the local level among government bodies, firms and unions to finance and realise productive investment and infrastructure. They also seek to ensure that the actions of the contracting parties are consistent with and conducive to this aim. Specifically, in addition to granting financial incentives, the government bodies involved also undertake to coordinate their activities, create special offices to accelerate administrative procedures, streamline bureaucracy, set definitive deadlines for the assignment of areas for industrial development, etc.; the unions agree to wage reductions, flexible working hours, etc.; and trade associations commit to generating a specified volume of investment and employment, vocational training and so on.

Negotiated planning got off to a rocky start, but implementation has been more satisfactory in recent years. It has had to overcome numerous risks and obstacles (first and foremost, the bureaucratisation of procedures, which initially slowed the entire process). However, the most significant question is whether a simple negotiated process, without direct public intervention in the economy and with merely more efficient public administration, is capable of leading the economy of southern Italy out of underdevelopment with sufficient speed (Zazzaro, 2001).[e] Negotiated planning does have the merit of seeking to attack the causes of underdevelopment and to spur the simultaneous effort of private institutions (especially firms and unions) and public institutions (the state and local authorities), whose failures lie at the root of underdevelopment itself.

Notes:
a On organised crime in Southern Italy, see SVIMEZ (2002); on corruption see Costabile and Giannola (1996); Del Monte (1996); Marselli and Vannini (1996).

b However, Franzini (1999) underscores the risk that solutions based on a high degree of local participation can also be tainted by strong private or local interests.
c This requires long-term measures, which envisage the use of simple and certain (automatic) procedures for the granting of incentives or, in any case, the intervention of public bodies. On the drawbacks of automatic incentives compared with discretionary intervention, see box 8.2
d Coleman (1990); Putnam (2002).
e In any case, overall *per capita* public expenditure (i.e. spending by the state, regions, local health authorities, provinces and municipalities) in the South began to fall below that in the Centre and North in 1998, and in 2000 was about 9 per cent less (SVIMEZ, 2002).

8.5 Redistribution policies and the welfare state

Redistribution policies are implemented using the entire range of economic policy measures. For example, while competition legislation seeks to achieve efficiency, it also has redistributive effects. Industrial policies, which we discussed earlier, tend to produce a redistributive impact, improving the position of some industries and agents while making other industries and agents worse off. Macroeconomic measures, such as monetary, fiscal or incomes policy, generally have redistributive effects, as we will see later.

The sheer number of ways to affect the income distribution and the fact that redistributive objectives are often disguised make it advisable in adopting any economic policy measure to make the distributive consequences of the measure as explicit as possible so that even non-economist citizens can grasp their implications (Stiglitz, 1989). Bringing all redistributive actions into the light of day is a necessary condition for distinguishing between desirable and undesirable interventions in terms of justice and equity (Bös, 1989). Such an exercise also makes it possible to identify any unintended perverse effects the measures might have (Baumol, 1986, chapter 1). Finally, it also makes it possible to adopt the redistributive measures that distort efficiency the least (Stiglitz, 1989).

While there are many redistributive measures, *budget policy* is the main instrument for achieving equity objectives. We will discuss the macroeconomic aspects of budgetary policy later (see chapter 12). Here, we focus on its impact on the distribution of income, first and foremost from a personal (or household) perspective, but also from a functional, territorial and sectoral standpoint. The effects are linked not so much to the overall volume of expenditure and revenues as to their composition and structure. For example, it is not so much (or only) the overall amount of taxes[2] that is important for the purposes of redistribution, as it is (or is also) their *composition* (for example, direct and indirect taxes by their very nature present different degree of *progressivity*)[3] and their structure (for example, for any given direct tax, we need to know the tax schedule, i.e. the tax rate established for each level of income).

---

[2] Obviously, this does have an impact on distribution. For example, it depends, *ceteris paribus*, on the level of employment and hence various aspects of the income distribution.
[3] **Progressivity (regressivity)** regards the ability of taxes to change more (less) than proportionally with respect to income.

In addition to taxes, redistribution through budgetary policy can also be carried out with cash and in-kind transfers. **Cash transfers** involve the transfer by government of cash or other instruments (coupons and vouchers that can be spent freely by individuals). **In-kind** transfers involve the direct provision of goods and services that government wants to make available to the needy (health services, education, food provision) or the distribution of non-transferable coupons and vouchers that can be used for specific purposes.[4]

The complex of government activities comprising cash transfers, health, education, food provision, housing and other essential services goes under the name of **welfare state** (see Lampman, 1984). The definition of welfare state is not entirely unambiguous, however. It is sometimes extended to include progressive taxation, government action to maintain full employment and even the collective bargaining system (see Freeman, 1995). The birth of the welfare state can be traced to the Beveridge Report (see Beveridge, 1942), the essential elements of which were implemented in the United Kingdom and, with variations, in other countries. The term was first introduced in 1914 to distinguish between the British wartime government and the imperialist German 'warfare' state, but came into common usage after Beveridge[5]. In the following pages we will generally focus on the redistributive aspects of the welfare state. Nevertheless, its contributions to efficiency can be anything but negligible and we will deal with them later, in box 8.6.

Real welfare states differ as to the types and levels of intervention and the methods for financing them.[6] These differences can be attributed to differences in the systems of values prevailing in each country. There are basically four models of welfare state:

(a) the *conservative–corporatist* model
(b) the *liberal model*, which can be divided into:
- the pure liberal model
- the reform liberal model
(c) the *social democratic* model
(d) the catholic model.

The conservative–corporatist model, which was adopted in Austria, Germany and Italy until the Second World War,[7] grants the right to benefit from the welfare state to those who are (or have been) employed. Redistribution is primarily carried out through the family and, in any case, the private sector (charity in particular). Government intervenes only in residual cases of need. The system tends to maintain distributive differences created by the market while attenuating the most extreme inequalities.

---

[4] The use of distributive mechanisms that mimic the market – such as cash transfers – should be preferred since they increase the freedom of beneficiaries and the efficiency of the system. However, in-kind transfers prevent false expressions of need in the presence of information asymmetry, thus contributing to the achievement of an efficient redistribution (Blackorby and Donaldson, 1988), and aiming at objectives with social rather than private value (Guesnerie, 1995). On school vouchers see the opposite positions taken by Ladd (2002) and Neal (2002).

[5] On the intellectual roots of the welfare state, see Sandmo (1991).

[6] The following survey of the various welfare state regimes draws extensively on Mishra (1993).

[7] For a comparative historical discussion of the welfare state, see Barr (1992) and, more extensively, Barr (1993).

The liberal model, which has been adopted in the United States, Canada and Australia, also provides for government intervention at the margin: 'The state encourages the market, either passively, by guaranteeing only a minimum, or actively, by subsidising private welfare schemes' (Esping-Andersen, 1990). Assistance may be subject to **means testing**, which implies that transfers may not necessarily be universal. In the reform version of this model, of which the Beveridge Report is an example, redistributive measures are closely linked to other market failures.[8]

The social democratic model is exemplified by the welfare state in the Scandinavian countries, which seeks to promote equality not only between workers but between all citizens. The market and the family play only a marginal role.

The catholic model is a more recent addition. It differs from the conservative–corporatist model in that government intervenes only when the individual, the family and, finally, the local community (which includes the church, other voluntary organisations and non-profit institutions) fail to provide support.

The post-war expansion of the welfare state that has occurred in almost all countries, regardless of the model adopted, is attributable to a variety of factors. In addition to those associated with the developments of welfare economics and those that explain the increase in government spending as a result of the specific interests of politicians and bureaucrats (see sections 5.2 and 5.3), other possible factors highlighted by some economists are:

(a) The asymmetry between the *costs and benefits of redistributive policies*: costs are often divided among many people (e.g. the employed, the healthy) and therefore constitute a relatively small burden for each individual, meaning that they are not seen as excessive and therefore do not elicit opposition. At the same time benefits often accrue to smaller groups (the unemployed, the disabled), which, since they expect high benefits, have a strong incentive to ask the government for them. This would explain why interest groups can form and are successful in inducing subsequent additions to the welfare state's tasks.

(b) The interaction between *egalitarian policies, individual preferences and political attitudes*. Redistributive policies induce changes in individual preferences (in the sense of both fostering greater egalitarianism and reducing incentives to work or take risks).[9] In both cases the government is induced to increase its redistributive role and broaden the sphere and reach of the welfare state (see, for example, Persson, 1995; Lindbeck, 1995b).

The redistributive activity of the government has been severely criticised, not only because the value judgements that support it are open to debate but also because it is often considered to be ineffective. The results of analyses reported in box 8.5 reject these conclusions. It is true, however, that in some cases government action has been effective but insufficient.

---

[8] According to Beveridge, poverty is a consequence of 'accidents' (such as illness or unemployment) and, therefore, can be insured against. Since people tend to underestimate risk for various reasons, eliminating poverty requires that the government intervene to compel individuals to obtain insurance.

[9] The reader should weigh this argument against the other suggested above, according to which a welfare state is a device for stimulating *risk-taking*. Which one prevails in reality is a matter of empirical investigation.

Box 8.5. Empirical studies of the effectiveness of the welfare state

The redistribution effected through progressive taxation and the welfare state reduces income and wealth differentials and poverty. The effects of redistributive action on poverty and **primary income distribution** (i.e. the distribution before government redistributive policy) vary according to the country and the instruments.

Table 8B.1 shows the moderate incidence of different redistributive tools in the United States,[a] which in 1984 increased the disposable income share of the poorest 20 per cent of the population by a total of 2.5 percentage points above the 4.7 per cent share of primary income (equivalent to a 53 per cent increase), while lowering that of the richest quintile by 4.2 percentage points (i.e. a 10 per cent decrease in primary income).

Note:
a In addition to progressive taxation, these include programmes such as Medicare and Medicaid (which are health care schemes for the poor) and food stamps (i.e. food relief for poor families).

Table 8B.1 *Corrected family income distribution, United States, 1984 (per cent)*

	Share of income received by each quintile of families				
	Ist (poorest)	2nd	3rd	4th	5th (richest)
Current population survey definition (pre-tax, cash only)	4.7	11.0	17.0	24.4	42.9
Current population survey definition *less* taxes	5.8	12.3	17.8	24.1	40.0
Current population survey definition *less* taxes plus Medicare, Medicaid and food stamps	7.2	12.2	17.7	24.3	38.7

Source: Levy (1987, p. 195).

A pattern of redistribution similar to that in the United States seems to have existed in Australia and the United Kingdom in roughly the same period. In other countries, such as Belgium and Italy, in the same period, there was less redistribution, probably because of the reduced skewness of the primary distribution. By contrast, in Finland and Sweden the share of disposable income of the lowest quintile increased over that of primary income by 7.5 and 6.2 percentage points to 10.8 per cent and 9.5 per cent, respectively (Mueller, 2003, p. 60).

For more recent years, Kenworthy (1998) shows the considerable reduction in **relative poverty** (defined as the percentage of individuals in households with incomes – adjusted for household size – below 40 per cent of the median

Table 8B.2 *Relative poverty rates, c. 1991 (per cent)*

	Relative poverty after tax and transfer	Relative poverty before tax and transfer
Australia	6.4	21.3
Belgium	2.2	23.9
Canada	5.6	21.6
Denmark	3.5	23.9
Finland	2.3	9.8
France	4.8	27.5
Germany	2.4	14.1
Ireland	4.7	25.8
Italy	5.0	21.8
Netherlands	4.3	20.5
Norway	1.7	9.3
Sweden	3.8	20.6
Switzerland	4.3	12.8
United Kingdom	5.3	25.7
United States	11.7	21.0

Source: Kenworthy (1998).

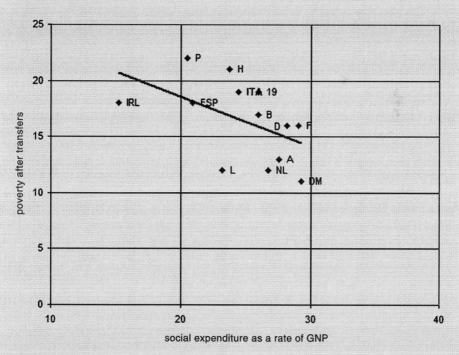

Figure 8B.1
Source: Adapted from Brandolini, Granaglia and Scicchitano (2002).

within each country) attributable to the welfare state (see table 8B.2). Brandolini, Granaglia and Scicchitano (2002) find a clear negative correlation between the extent of poverty and social benefits in the EU countries, as shown in figure 8B.1

In addition, under pressure from individuals and interest groups, the coercive power of the government has sometimes been used to 'take from the poor and give to the rich', disguising redistribution under forms of government activity other than the welfare state or progressive taxation (Stiglitz, 1989): in the redistributive struggle, the powers of the government have been used by the better-off to increase inequality.[10] Increasing equity would in this case mean changing spending procedures (more generally, the ways in which government action is decided), as well as the political relationships between social classes and groups. As to the former, the procedures of government intervention, which probably do not show the public the redistributive pressures exerted by wealthier groups or classes, should be amended. As to the latter, the balance of power between social groups must change to ensure that the interests of the neediest individuals prevail.

It is difficult to prevent the government from being captured by the rich without altering conditions, such as in education, that block less fortunate groups' access to power. Some studies suggest that the welfare state should be considered in a broad, systemic sense, and that its various components (progressive taxation, cash and in-kind transfers, collective bargaining) are closely linked and produce positive results only if all the elements are present (Freeman, 1995).[11]

While aware of the many policies with distributive effects and the fact that implementing one of these alone is not sufficient to have a decisive effect on equity, one important area of further study would be to identify the *minimum conditions* that must be satisfied by government action to guarantee individuals the possibility of enjoying a reasonable standard of living and, therefore, positive liberty (Helm, 1989).[12]

Criticism of redistribution in general and the welfare state in particular has also focused on their negative consequences for *efficiency*, specifically through the possible disincentives to the supply of labour and saving. This topic is dealt with in both abstract and empirical terms in box 8.6.

Recent criticism of the welfare state has also underscored a variety of factors, such as the emergence of adverse demographic profiles (ageing of the population) and economic situations (the crisis of the public finances) as well as the increased drive to reduce labour costs under the impulse of globalisation. Forceful arguments have been advanced to reduce or at least restructure the welfare state. The debate has thrown up numerous possible refinements or changes of varying degrees of feasibility, efficiency and consistency with the underlying principles of the welfare state. A brief sample of these includes:

[10] The importance of **rent seeking** is underscored by Krueger (1974). For a survey of the literature, see Mueller (2003, chapter 15). According to Le Grand (1987) the welfare state has been captured by the middle class, which has had mixed consequences: these are negative from the point of view of the dispersion of transfers, which should be primarily or exclusively directed at the poor; at the same time, there has been a positive effect in terms of the pressure exerted to maintain high-quality standards. This second point, together with the desirability of fostering social integration, is in reality a strong argument in favour of universal direct provision of services such as education, health and social security.

[11] Both the positive and negative aspects of dynamic interaction between the various elements of the welfare state and the entire system of individual preferences were noted earlier.

[12] Recall Sen's (1987) arguments for ensuring human 'capabilities'.

Box 8.6.   The impact of the welfare state on efficiency

Traditional objections to the welfare state focused on the risk of heteronomy, passivity, corruption of individual autonomy, reduction of 'agent subjectivity' or the constriction of the sphere of personal liberties underscored by the great liberal thinkers from de Tocqueville to von Hayek and Einaudi. This thinking also underpins more recent positions, such as that of Lindbeck (1995a, 1995b), which we will discuss shortly, even if they are presented in an apparently modern guise.

The more specifically economic adverse consequences of the welfare state have mainly been associated with the related *administrative costs* and the *disincentive effects on the labour supply and saving*, which emerge when the presence of information asymmetry prevents the use of non-distortionary taxation. Their existence has also been admitted by some liberal economists willing to accept the trade-off between efficiency and equity exemplified by the parable of the leaky bucket offered by Okun (1975): redistribution is like moving water in a leaky bucket, delivering a smaller amount of water (to the less well-off) than that drawn at the source (from the better-off).

Let us examine in more detail why redistribution might reduce efficiency. The critics of the welfare state – while not denying that its crisis is in part attributable to the impact of exogenous shocks – tend to emphasise the *endogenous nature* of the reduction in employment and income (or its rate of growth), attributing this to the negative effects of the welfare state. The disutility of work in conjunction with the availability of the various forms of benefits offered by the welfare state (unemployment benefits, other forms of assistance, pensions) may prompt individuals to reduce the supply of labour in terms of hours worked and participation in the labour force.

The second traditional argument against the welfare state regards its disincentive effects on *saving*: public pensions, generic assistance programmes and specific benefits for various adverse life events (unemployment, illness, etc.) induce individuals to reduce their saving to an extent that varies in relation to the level of the benefits provided by the welfare state, the credibility of the promise to provide such benefits and any eligibility requirements to receive the benefits (means or asset testing).

The problem of the incentive to engage in behaviour that undermines redistributive action tends to worsen in the long term. This occurs when the social mores that stigmatise such behaviour no longer operate, either because of steady erosion of those mores, which once it has achieved a critical mass triggers major, irreversible effects (**ketchup effects**), or because of the impact of large macroeconomic shocks that reduce income to such an extent as to encourage tax avoidance and transfer seeking behaviour, which thereby accelerates the erosion of the social stigma associated with receiving aid. The 'corruption' of individuals is reflected in and supported by the behaviour of politicians, who in the long term tend to adapt to the 'lax' preferences of the public. Unemployment ceases to perform its disciplinary function, public budget deficits and debt mount, interest rates rise and, as a consequence, uncertainty increases (Lindbeck, 1995a, 1995b). According to this reformulation of an older argument, the crisis of the welfare state emerged not immediately but rather decades after its creation for these very reasons.

These disincentive effects and the lure of moral hazard should cause growth rates to slow. The negative impact of the welfare state on growth would thus explain the rise in the ratio of social spending to income simply as a result of the fact that at a certain volume (or growth rate) of social expenditure, the volume (or growth rate) of income diminishes, as a consequence of social spending itself.

However, the adverse effects on income attributed to the welfare state vary substantially across programs (e.g. they are low where assistance goes to populations having no capacity to change their behaviour or combine behavioural mandates along with transfer payments; see Blank, 2002). In addition, they should be assessed together with the efficiency effects that have traditionally been cited in its support. We will mention only a few. The fact that consumers usually have seriously deficient information about the prices and quality of some goods and services may make it necessary for the government to produce them directly, thus ensuring some minimal quality standard at a reasonable cost, as in the case of health services. Asymmetric information, which gives rise to adverse selection and moral hazard, makes it advisable to restrict individuals' *freedom of choice* by, for example, imposing compulsory (and therefore general) insurance against adverse events, such as illness, accidents, disability, old age or unemployment, with only small distortionary effects on preferences and probably large efficiency gains.[a] The possibility that an individual may be faced with an *uninsurable risk* (for example, chronic illness or unemployment), thus creating a situation of incomplete markets, may induce the government to step in and offer insurance services (Barr, 1992, 2001). The difficulty that low-income countries and people have in maintaining health and hygiene gives rise to externalities and public goods that require recourse to the welfare state in order to eliminate or reduce the threat of epidemics.[b] In addition, redistribution and the welfare state enable people to overcome indivisibilities, budget constraints, capital market imperfections, social stratification and segregation, investing in human capital and stimulating risk-taking, thereby liberating productive forces and increasing aggregate income (Bénassy, 1992; Ledebur and Barnes, 1992; Atkinson, 1993; Galor and Zeira, 1993; Rusk, 1993; Sinn, 1995; Aghion, Caroli and Garcia-Peñalosa, 1999).

Atkinson (1995) showed that the existence of a general public pension system reduces private saving, but the replacement of such a system with one providing targeted benefits for the poor (means-tested assistance, assistance pensions) does not necessarily improve the result because it can create a 'savings trap'. The conditional provision of pensions introduces a binary, either-or choice: people either save enough to be independent or they do not save at all and rely on the public pension scheme. The net effect of conditionality on private saving is therefore uncertain.

More generally, any institutional system provides a range of incentives and disincentives, meaning that in recommending a change from one system to another it is not enough to assess only the benefits (for example, in terms of more incentives). It is also necessary to take account of the costs (for example, in terms of greater disincentives). Thus, when a public pension system is replaced by a compulsory private pension system, we must consider all (or at least the main) differences between the two institutions. In a private system, the presence of active institutional investors may, for example, produce major changes in the operation of the market for ownership rights, imposing constraints on the desired rate of growth in managerial firms (Atkinson, 1995).

In view of the favourable and critical arguments regarding the impact of the welfare state on efficiency, empirical studies are especially important. While they often produce divergent results, existing studies nevertheless appear to show that the welfare state generates few *work disincentives* (Atkinson, 1993). With specific regard to unemployment benefits, it does not appear that the amount of the benefits has a significant effect, although the duration of benefits probably has a larger impact (Layard, 1996). The weakness of the negative effects of the welfare state on work incentives is due to the fact that they do not affect the main component of the labour supply (adult males), reserving their greatest impact to secondary (marginal) components, especially mothers with pre-school-age children (Dilnot, 1995). The effects are in any case limited (Moffitt, 1992), and can be reduced even further with appropriate adjustments. Some argue, however, that such measures are expensive and, at least in the Swedish experience, have generated appreciable efficiency losses (Rosen, 1997).

As regards the *saving disincentive*, there is little empirical evidence of a problem, although some (Dilnot, 1995) argue that the effect increases in line with the size of the expected value of the benefit and the stringency of eligibility requirements.

One empirical study (Perotti, 1996) regarding *inequality and growth* for a sample of forty-nine countries (conducted with safeguards to avoid interpretations based on inverse causal relationships) shows among other things that the *marginal income tax rate* has a significant positive effect on the growth rate. Similarly, other distributive variables, such as public expenditure for social and welfare benefits, health care and housing, have a significant and positive impact on economic growth.

Other empirical investigations have produced results similar to Perotti's work. For example, Bird (2001) finds that in countries in which risk indicators (in terms of the variability of income) are higher spend a larger proportion of GDP in social benefits. This is interpreted as evidence that the welfare state encourages risk-taking and, through this, economic growth. Brandolini and Rossi (1997) find that productivity growth is increased rather than diminished in the presence of institutions that ensure greater distributive equality. Similar results emerge from a comparative survey of the findings obtained from the various models of welfare state that are discussed in section 8.5: the models that pursue redistributive objectives in a more incisive and generalised manner (i.e. the social democratic model and, subordinately, the corporatist model) not only obtain better results in this area but also record faster *per capita* income growth (Goodin *et al.*, 1999).

Notes:
a Orszag and Stiglitz (2001) report that private pension schemes can have *transaction costs* (for attracting customers, administration, profits) on the order of 40 per cent, compared with virtually negligible costs for public systems.
b According to some Chinese health officials, the difficulty they had in tackling the SARS epidemic that exploded in 2003 in China before spreading to other countries was also attributable to the high costs – virtually unaffordable for private citizens – of medical treatment following liberalisation of the sector there. People tended not to seek treatment and hid their illnesses rather than use money they could not afford to spend. This happened for all pathologies (and even for the victims of traffic accidents, who could be turned away from emergency rooms if they could not pay), but in the case of SARS this complicated the work of health authorities.

(1) the replacement of social security contributions with *income or value-added taxes*
(2) the introduction or strengthening of the link between *benefits and work status* (i.e. the adoption of **workfare** systems, which make receipt of transfers conditional on the existence or acceptance of a job) (see Freeman, Topel and Swedenborg, 1997)
(3) the reduction of the *duration of unemployment benefits* and transforming such benefits into an *employment subsidy* after a certain period of time (Layard, 1996)
(4) the expansion of the use of **means-testing**, which has been suggested as a way to reduce the overall amount of social security expenditure by giving benefits only to those in (extreme) need
(5) **earmarking (hypothecation)**, or allocating the receipts from certain taxes or contributions to specific expenditure items (Hills, 1995)
(6) **opting out**, or allowing citizens to forgo access to one or more welfare services in exchange for reimbursement of a portion (to be determined) of their cost, with the aim of fostering competition between the welfare state and private sector providers of the same services (Snower, 1994).

Some of the proposals appear feasible and consistent with the purposes and principles of the welfare state. These include the transformation of social security contributions into value-added taxes and the calibrated introduction of some sort of workfare requirements for some benefits. Even the reduction of the duration of unemployment benefits, if accompanied by the maintenance of other measures that ensure a social protection network for the needy (perhaps means-tested) could be feasible, effective and consistent.

The linking of eligibility for benefits to income or wealth, suggested to reduce the overall amount of social security spending, could raise questions among those who believe that the benefits of the welfare state are the fruit of enjoying a very right of citizenship, as the founders of the welfare state intended. Under a comprehensive welfare system, however, what appears to be a limitation when taken individually can be overcome.

Similarly, earmarking could dangerously fragment the welfare state as it weakens the community elements of the system. This is perhaps the main criticism of the proposal, rather than the technical difficulties of matching revenues and expenditure needs noted by others. However, it could overcome the 'distrust of politics' (see Franzini and Pizzuti, 1994) that some have cited as the cause of the problems raised by government action. If earmarking were seen as a temporary test bed for the nurturing of greater trust between citizens and government in countries where this trust has been seriously undermined, it could be accepted with the spirit that inspired the creation of the welfare state.

Opting out appears to be able to reduce the cost of the welfare state and/or improve the quantity and quality of services available, as it provides appropriate incentives to the government officials in charge of programmes. However, it has feasibility problems similar to those facing earmarking, which are not just technical but strike at the very foundations of the welfare state as an instrument of social cohesion, equity and human dignity.

Note that trimming the welfare state does not mean that the community will pay less for benefits. On the contrary, in certain respects expenditure tends to increase when such benefits are provided in the private sector because the welfare state is far more efficient than the market in meeting certain needs, as we have seen. The only opportunity to reduce expenditure when the provision of certain goods and services is transferred to the private sector is to offset the resulting higher costs by narrowing the universal scope of benefits: some citizens (probably the poorest) will be expelled from the market as they do not have the necessary purchasing power and will reduce their social consumption. *Reducing the reach of the welfare state is*, above all, a way of redistributing the costs and the benefits of the functions it performs.

8.6 Summary

1 The *dynamic efficiency* of an economic system is linked to the structural elements of the system itself. Industrial policy impacts these elements using numerous instruments. Unlike the past (in which the main instruments were public enterprises and sectoral intervention), since the 1980s industrial policy has acted through *horizontal measures*, carrying out extensive privatisations practically in all countries.

2 *Public demand management* seeks to provide efficient public services, stimulate the development of industries and govern the economic cycle.

3   *Regional policy* is essentially industrial policy targeted at a specific geographical area of a country. It makes particular use of infrastructure policy and tax and credit incentives.

4   There are many *redistributive instruments* but the most important is budget policy, which uses taxation and cash or in-kind transfers.

5   The welfare state has both *efficiency and redistributive aims*. More recently, various factors have generated problems for which a range of proposals to cut back or modify the welfare state have been advanced. Some of these appear feasible and consistent with the principles underlying the system. Others seem clearly to conflict with those principles.

9   Social choice and cost-benefit analysis

9.1   Choice criteria in private and public projects

Welfare economics has other important practical applications in current public choices, in addition to those we discussed in previous chapters. In particular, the government can use it to assess whether to undertake a project or programme or not and to choose among mutually exclusive projects or programmes. Evaluating a project for constructing public works, establishing staff training projects, subsidising private investment and regulating pollution are some of the areas in which welfare economics can make a major contribution. With reference to the evaluation of public sector projects, we can define a **public project** as a change in the net supplies of commodities from the public sector. *Mutually exclusive* projects are those that serve (approximately) the same purpose, through alternative solutions (such as building a dam with different techniques). We will consider only *small* projects, which involve small changes in output and demand. When a project is large, measuring the change in welfare caused by the project requires us to take account of a large number of variables and introduces analytical complexities (see Starrett, 1988; Hammond, 1990). In assessing the effects of any project and selecting one of various alternative solutions, a government agency will measure the costs and benefits of each and will reject those that are the least attractive, much the same as a private investor would do.

As a basis for an investment decision, a private entrepreneur prepares a list of *costs and revenues* for each alternative investment project. The procedure involves the following steps:

(1) to identify the *alternatives*, which include the *status quo* (no action)
(2) to identify the *consequences* of each alternative in physical terms (i.e. the quantity of inputs and outputs each project entails) in each period of the time horizon
(3) to estimate the *costs and revenues* in each period on the basis of these quantities and the market prices of the inputs and outputs
(4) to refer the costs and the revenues to the same time period (*discounting*)
(5) to *add up the discounted costs and revenues* and to calculate the expected rate of return (profit) for each project, so as to be able to choose the most profitable one.

The government can proceed in a similar manner to evaluate a project. However, in steps (2) and (3) government economic calculations differ from firms' evaluations. A firm carries out only a **financial analysis** of the project, which is limited to the *monetary consequences* of the project relevant to the firm itself. The government, in addition to the financial analysis, also considers all the direct and indirect consequences (**economic analysis**). Economic analysis serves to assess the validity of the project. Financial analysis can serve the purpose of indicating the need of financial resources for the firm or agency or body that will administer the project.[1] To underscore the difference between the private and government assessment of a project, when we discuss government action we speak of *costs and benefits*, rather than costs and revenues; assessing the costs and benefits of a project from a social point of view is therefore known as **cost-benefit analysis** (CBA).

Before examining the differences, let us first take a look at the similarities, with reference to steps (4) and (5).

Assume that steps (1), (2) and (3) have been completed. For each project m, we have a set of benefits, b_t^m, and costs, c_t^m, at time t. As we know from economic and financial analysis, a good (or quantity of money or asset) available in different time periods can be considered as a different good. Nevertheless, the values of an asset in different times can be compared if they are adjusted to refer to the same time period (for example, the initial period).[2] This process is known as **discounting**. In the case of CBA, we discount costs and benefits.

The sum of the present values of the benefits of project m can be given as:

$$B^m = \sum_{t=0}^{n} b_t^m (1+i)^{-t}$$

where i is the interest (discount) rate and $(1+i)^{-1}$ is the discount factor.
Similarly for costs:

$$C^m = \sum_{t=0}^{n} c_t^m (1+i)^{-t}$$

In this way the effects of project m can be summarised by the (absolute) **net present value**, NPV (or present discounted value), of its costs and benefits:

$$NPV^m = B^m - C^m$$

---

[1] The government can also carry out a **fiscal analysis** of a project (to assess its contribution to the budget) and a **political analysis**, to assess its impact on the probability of re-election or the aims of the political party or social group the government wants to serve; see chapter 5.

[2] An asset worth 100 at the beginning of the second period (or at the end of the first) is financially equivalent to an asset worth $100(1+i)^{-1}$ at the beginning of the first period (time zero). The amount $100(1+i)^{-1}$, invested for 1 year at interest rate i, earns $100(1+i)^{-1} \cdot i$ in interest; adding up the interest and principal, the amount available at the end of the year is $100(1+i)^{-1} + 100(1+i)^{-1} \cdot i = 100(1+i)^{-1}(1+i) = 100$. Similarly, an asset worth 100 at the end of the second period is equal to one worth $100(1+i)^{-1}$ at the end of the first period and $[100(1+i)^{-1}](1+i)^{-1} = 100(1+i)^{-2}$ at the beginning of the first.

The NPV can be used as a yardstick for judging the *desirability* of a project: any project with a positive NPV at a given discount rate is viable and therefore *eligible* for support; we then choose the project with the highest NPV, among a number of mutually exclusive projects. CBA can be applied with some difficulty to choice of projects that are not mutually exclusive – e.g. a project for the reduction of pollution and a project for the construction of a dam. This would require a detailed specification of the *SWF*.

Nevertheless, this criterion is clearly inadequate for *ranking projects*, since it does not take account of *project size*, on which the absolute value of the costs and benefits depends: large-scale projects may have large net benefits in absolute terms but small net benefits in relation to invested capital. In order to take this factor into account, we normalise the absolute NPV to obtain the 'relative' NPV (NPV$_r$), which is equal to the NPV divided by the discounted costs:

$$NPV_r^m = \frac{B^m - C^m}{C^m} = \frac{B^m}{C^m} - 1^3$$

We then choose the project with the highest NPV$_r$.[4]

This is our second possible criterion.[5] Shifting from NPV to NPV$_r$ does not affect the eligibility of a project, since the relative NPV is greater than zero if and only if the absolute NPV is positive. However, the projects' ranking may differ.

We must emphasise that with both rules the final choice is crucially dependent on the *discount rate, i*. The economic attractiveness of projects with immediate (or nearly immediate) social costs and deferred social benefits increases as the discount rate declines, since the lower discount rate has a smaller negative influence on benefits (because of discounting). Since different projects have a different time distribution of costs and benefits, changing the discount rate may change their relative attractiveness. Figure 9.1 shows the importance of the discount rate in choosing among different projects.

For discount rates lower than i_0, project *m* is more attractive than project *p* in terms of NPV, but for $i > i_0$, the opposite holds; for $i > i_1$, project *m* has a negative NPV, as does project *p* for $i > i_2$.

---

[3] This relation makes it clear why this criterion is also referred to as the 'benefit-cost ratio' (BCR) criterion.

[4] In reality, if the social costs are calculated properly – i.e. if they include the 'opportunity costs' associated with the scarcity of financial resources – there should be no reason to favour small-scale projects; the absolute NPV would reflect the different use of financial resources by projects of any dimension. Small projects have low financial costs, which, other circumstances being equal, tends to increase the absolute NPV; conversely, large projects have high financial costs, which tends to reduce the absolute NPV, *ceteris paribus*. However, using the relative NPV can be justified when the scarcity of financial resources results in their being rationed: with a given quantity of resources it may be worth our while to classify projects by their NPV$_r$, choosing among them so as to maximise total net benefits and use all the available resources.

[5] Note that for a private sector firm the NPV$_r$ is none other than the expected rate of profit corresponding to the market interest rate. $B^m - C^m$ represents the discounted expected profits. C^m, the discounted value of the costs, is financially equivalent to the firm's capital: it is the sum available today that can be invested at the market interest rate i to obtain future payment flows that exactly match the costs to be borne at future dates.

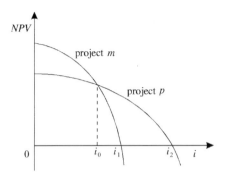

Figure 9.1

A third decision criterion is the **internal rate of return** (IRR), which is the discount rate at which the *sum of discounted benefits equals the sum of discounted costs*. In other words the IRR is the discount rate at which the NPV is equal to zero. The IRR of project m is the discount rate i implicitly determined by the following equation:

$$\sum_{t=0}^{n} b_t^m(1+i)^{-t} - \sum_{t=0}^{n} c_t^m(1+i)^{-t} = 0 \qquad (9.1)$$

or

$$B^m - C^m = 0^6 \qquad (9.2)$$

Referring to figure 9.1, the IRR of project m is equal to i_1 and the IRR of project p is equal to i_2. These are the discount rates at which the projects' respective NPVs are equal to zero. If we use the IRR as a criterion, a project will be considered eligible if its IRR is higher than the social discount rate, which for the moment we will assume to be equal to the market interest rate. In choosing among more than one project, that with the highest IRR will be selected. In the example given in figure 9.1, this would be project p.

At first glance, this third criterion seems the most attractive since it does not require any prior selection of a discount rate in order to discount costs and benefits and calculate the net return of a project. However, problems can arise that may counsel against its use. We limit our comments here to the problem of multiple IRRs for a given project. Equation (9.1) is a polynomial equation of degree n in i, which in general admits n distinct roots,[7] as shown in figure 9.2, where there are three (positive) IRRs, i_0, i_1 and i_2.

---

[6] The reader may have already encountered something similar to the IRR in Keynesian investment theory, where the marginal efficiency of capital is defined as the interest rate at which the sum of the discounted flows of net expected yields equals the cost of the investment. There are a number of differences between the two concepts that we cannot deal with here.

[7] As we know, the root is unique if there is only one change in the sign of the flow of net benefits (benefits net of costs) in the various periods (*Descartes' rule of signs*). This usually occurs if costs prevail in the initial periods and benefits prevail in later periods. Even if there is more than one sign inversion, it is possible to solve the problem of evaluating the IRR of the project if certain conditions hold (see, for example, Theichroew, Robichek and Montalbano, 1965; Gronchi, 1984).

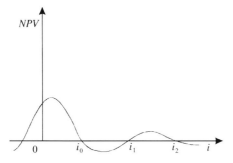

Figure 9.2

In this case it is difficult to compare the IRRs of the different projects, or even assess the value of a single project.

Although the existence of multiple rates of return for a single project can be conceptually inconvenient, as long as all the roots are higher (lower) than the social discount rate we can still determine whether a project is (is not) eligible for consideration. Similarly, if project a has multiple rates of return that are all higher (lower) than those of project b, we can say that the former is (is not) preferable to the latter. However, there is no guarantee that this will happen, and we may even face paradoxical situations where, if the social discount rate lies between the minimum and maximum roots of the project, the project is simultaneously not eligible if we compare the social discount rate with the minimum rate of return (the minimum root) and eligible if we compare the social discount rate with the maximum rate of return. Similarly, the superiority of one project over another is uncertain if its rates of return are not all higher than those of the other.[8]

---

[8] A second problem is pointed out by Boadway and Bruce (1984, pp. 295–7). We said that if the decision criterion is the IRR, we will choose the project with the highest IRR, regardless of the social interest rate (assumed to be equal to the market rate) and assuming that this is lower than the IRR. However, if at the market interest rate the NPV criterion orders the projects differently, it is possible to carry out a series of transactions on the capital market at this interest rate to obtain better results that those of the project selected using the IRR criterion. To this end let us suppose that the assessments of financial and economic analysis coincide and refer to figure 9.1. If we use the IRR criterion, we will choose project p; if we employ NPV, however, at an interest rate $i < i_0$, we will choose m. At this rate, the net benefit flow of project m can be converted into a larger flow of net benefits than project p through appropriate financial transactions.

This can be shown with a simple example. The two projects have the following costs (−) and benefits (+):

	Year 0	Year 1	Year 2
Project m	−1,000	550	634
Project p	−1,000	1,150	0

From this we can deduce that $IRR^m = 0.12 < IRR^p = 0.15$. But, if $i = 0.05$, $NPV^m > NPV^p$. At this interest rate, it would be possible to exchange project m in the financial market for another project that is

9.2   Identifying the effects of a project

We said earlier that the typical problems of calculating the social benefits of a project concern:

(a) identifying the *quantitative effects* of each project
(b) assigning a *value* to those effects.

We will discuss these in order.

Forecasting the *effects of a project* is an extremely difficult operation that must be carried out with care. In particular, we must consider:

(1) the direct and indirect effects of the project in terms of *inputs and outputs of goods and services*
(2) the effects of the project on *incommensurable and intangible goods.*

First, the relevant (direct or indirect) costs and benefits are those produced by the project in the economy as a whole. *Direct* effects are those generated by changes caused directly by the project in the demand for (input) or supply of (output) goods. *Indirect* effects are those that cause changes in the input or output of other, distorted, markets.

For example, the construction of a new underground line has direct effects in the form of purchases of cement, steel, labour and other goods and services, as well as the increased supply of underground transportation services. The indirect effects are a consequence of the fact that underground transportation is a substitute for congested road transportation. The reduction in road traffic induced by the increase in underground transportation services eases this congestion – i.e. *it reduces the external diseconomies of road traffic.*[9] Considering *indirect effects* is therefore the first difference between the social and private calculations of costs and benefits.

A second difference is the consideration of incommensurable and intangible costs and benefits, which have no market prices (for example, effects on life, health, free time

identical except that it involves borrowing 600 in year 1 (repaying 630 the following year). Call this project *m'*. It will have the following structure of costs and benefits:

	Year 0	Year 1	Year 2
Project *m'*	−1,000	1,150	4

This project is clearly superior to project *p*, which should have been preferred on the basis of the IRR criterion. The inconsistency is a consequence of the fact that the IRR criterion postulates the reinvestment of benefits within the cash-flow of the project at the same IRR, even if the market interest rate is different (in our case, it is lower than the IRR). The IRR approach thus neglects the *financial aspects* of the problem.

[9] This description accurately fits real-world cases, such as the well-known example of the construction of the Victoria line of the London Underground. The indirect effects were in fact the largest benefits of the project, as the line was designed to replace travel by road and thus reduce negative externalities. Note that the indirect effect is large and gives rise to a social benefit if and only if there is a large distortion in the affected market that is eliminated as an effect of the project: if the price in this market is not significantly distorted, there should not be any socially significant indirect effect since by hypothesis the social benefit (represented by the price of the good in the market considered) would be approximately equal to the social cost for each additional unit produced and sold (the marginal cost of producing the good).

and the environment). The fact that these effects do not have a market price makes them irrelevant to the private calculation but does not mean we can ignore them in our social computation. We return to indirect and incommensurable/intangible effects in discussing the assessment of costs and benefits.

9.3 Evaluating the effects

Evaluating the effects of a project is an equally (or even more) complex operation in CBA. There are two specific questions to examine. The first regards choosing a numéraire for expressing benefits and costs. The second concerns the criterion for the valuation of the effects of the project.

As to the first question, instead of national currency, a foreign currency or consumption goods or investment goods can be taken as the numéraire. The choice among these different units of account is to be made according to the country's specific situation and policy objectives. If, for example, an underdeveloped country has a shortage of foreign currency, it can assess the benefits and costs of the project in terms of a foreign currency (e.g. dollars).

With reference to the second question, as a general criterion the society will find it advantageous to devote some of the available resources to a project if the benefits it derives from this project are larger than the benefits it could obtain from alternative uses of the same resources. The benefits of the project are measured by its beneficiaries' aggregate **willingness to pay (WTP)**. The benefits of alternative projects that are forgone when resources are employed in the project in question represent what a society is *willing to pay* to have those resources diverted to alternative projects and are measured by the **opportunity cost** of these resources.[10]

To measure WTP for benefits and opportunity costs we could use market prices in a competitive economy. As we know, if real markets were perfectly competitive, prices would represent both the benefits of a project, as valued by consumers, and its costs in terms of the goods society uses in that project, thereby forgoing the chance to use them in some other activity.[11] (Recall that under perfect competition the price of *every good* is equal to its marginal cost.) However this is not the case in reality.

Indeed, there are several reasons why prices in actual markets cannot be taken as an appropriate measure of the willingness to pay and opportunity cost:

(a) The project under consideration is large enough to have an influence on the *prices of outputs and/or inputs*.
(b) Some markets are *distorted* by monopoly, taxes, quotas, etc.; in addition, markets are incomplete; there are incomplete markets due to externalities, public goods, transaction costs and asymmetric information; there are also intangibles (i.e. immaterial benefits and costs that cannot be measured since they have no market price).

---

[10] There is a problem in the assessment of willingness in the time horizon of the project: in fact, willingness may change through time.
[11] A problem may arise owing to the fact that WTP can change as the time horizon of the project changes.

(c) The *distribution of income and wealth* can have distortionary effects on individual valuations (and so on the prices) of goods;[12] in addition, **preferences** are **endogenous** (i.e. they are shaped by the working of the economic system and social forces through such things as advertising) or some consumers' preferences are not shared by policymakers (merit wants).

For reasons of brevity we do not deal with points (a) and (c) in this book, referring the reader to Acocella (1998). We will deal with 'distortions' deriving from the distribution of income and wealth in section 9.4 and with missing markets in section 9.5.

9.4   Shadow prices

The need to use shadow prices arises when *market prices do not reflect social values*. As we said, in competitive markets the market price is also an indicator of the *cost* to society of using a good as an input in the project. By contrast, in non-competitive markets, the market price no longer reflects the cost to society since it is higher than marginal cost. It must then be replaced with a more accurate indicator of social value: the **shadow** (or **social**) **price**. This can be defined as the gain in the value of the (social) objective function from increasing expenditure on a given project by one unit. As the objective in CBA is net social benefits, the shadow price of an output or input is the value of the marginal willingness to pay (for an output) or the production forgone in alternative projects – i.e. the opportunity cost (for an input). In general, shadow prices correspond to the prices that would prevail in an economy with complete markets where all markets were competitive. To calculate shadow prices, actual prices should be 'purged' of the surplus profit earned by firms as a result of their market power as well as of market failures and the existence of taxes or subsidies in the absence of market failures (see chapter 2).

However, we must consider that the difficulty of calculating shadow prices, which always involves approximations, means that it is advisable to use market prices where the distortions are not significant.[13]

As it is a measure of the opportunity cost, in principle the shadow price should be zero for resources that would otherwise remain unused; the opportunity cost of their use is, in fact, nil. However, we need to bear in mind the fact that in the real world there are situations where physical or human resources that would otherwise remain unused are used in conjunction with other *scarce* resources. This means that we must use different prices for each that reflect the different situations.

We can apply the concepts introduced here to a number of questions:

(a) determining the shadow prices of goods produced in *non-competitive* markets
(b) determining the shadow prices of labour in the presence of *involuntary unemployment*
(c) choosing the *social discount rate*.

---

[12] There is also the problem that prices reflect *endogenous preferences* or, in any case, preferences that are not shared by the government (as in the case of merit goods).

[13] The very difficulties associated with calculating shadow prices generate costs and inaccuracies that reduce the net benefit of using them in the first place.

9.4.1 Shadow prices in non-competitive markets

The market prices of goods used as inputs in a project will not reflect the social cost of using them if the market in which the prices are formed is not competitive. In CBA, we should consider the price corrected for the effects of market power. If we do not, our calculation of social value will be distorted. This would penalise projects that make use of goods whose prices are high due to the market power of their producers (even if using these goods does not excessively drain resources from alternative uses) rather than projects that make intensive use of scarce goods.

9.4.2 Shadow wages

A second important application of the concept of shadow prices is when we have *involuntary or hidden unemployment*.[14] The unemployed labour used in projects subjected to CBA cannot be evaluated at the market price of labour, i.e. the prevailing wage. Since it is a good that is not fully used, its shadow price would be zero if we did not take account of the special features associated with the fact that labour is a cause of disutility.[15] Even if this is taken into account, the shadow wage may be lower than the current wage, since the latter may be the product of unions' monopoly power.

If we decide to take account of the disutility of labour in determining its shadow price in the presence of involuntary unemployment, the shadow price will be equal to the supply price of labour, which is equal to or less than the (net) market wage. However, if we did not accept, at least under these conditions, the neoclassical value judgements and hypotheses regarding the disutility of work, the shadow price of labour with involuntary unemployment would tend to be zero.[16]

Everything said so far holds if we assume that all of the jobs created by the project are filled by drawing from the ranks of the involuntary unemployed and that hiring them does not involve specific costs, such as moving expenses. If, however, the jobs created are filled by people who are already employed and decide to change their jobs, the shadow price of labour for these workers will be equal to the (pre-tax) market wage paid in their original job or even higher if this causes a reduction in output (e.g. agricultural production) with negative economic and social effects (see Harris and Todaro, 1970).

Since a real-world project will use both types of labour, the imputed shadow wage will be a weighted average of the wages of the two categories of worker: the current market – or even higher – wage for workers drawn from other jobs; zero or, at most, the supply price of labour for those drawn from the involuntary unemployed.

---

[14] Recall that *involuntary unemployment* was defined as that occurring when the wage at which workers are willing to offer their services (the labour supply price) is less than or equal to the market wage of employed workers. *Hidden unemployment* is that which arises when the marginal product of labour is zero (see, for example, Lewis, 1954).

[15] The emphasis placed on the disutility of labour in the presence of total involuntary unemployment (i.e. zero hours of work) of part of the labour force is excessive considering the various costs (including psychological costs) of forced idleness.

[16] Note that this is an especially controversial point. Among those in favour of imputing a shadow wage close to zero in the case of involuntary unemployment, see Haveman (1977).

9.4.3   Choosing the social discount rate

Choosing the social discount rate is a very important step in CBA, and its impact increases the further costs and benefits are deferred into the future.[17] As in the other cases, we can start with the market price, i.e. the market interest rate.[18] However, there are at least two reasons to choose a different rate.[19] The first regards the market power of financial intermediaries and other distortions (e.g. those induced by taxation, credit rationing) that cause the interest rate to differ from its hypothetical level under perfect competition. The second concerns future generations, which might not be adequately safeguarded even if capital markets are perfect: since future generations are unrepresented, the markets may express a large time preference for the present.

This latter issue is controversial, even outside the confines of CBA. Some argue that current generations take the interests of future generations into account in making their consumption decisions, if only because future generations are the descendants of current generations. However, this link is not always present. Childless individuals may express a greater time preference for the present since emotional considerations linking them directly to future generations are virtually absent and other considerations may be lacking. In addition, the current generation is influenced by factors (advertising, demonstration or imitation effects) that tend to increase current consumption. Note that such considerations are one-sided, since future generations, which would presumably choose to increase future consumption and reduce current consumption, cannot express their preferences.[20] Thus, markets tend to underestimate the value of the goods that, having deferred returns, enable such preferences to be satisfied (i.e. capital goods). From this point of view, future consumption can be considered as a form of *merit good*, which should be valued regardless of the preferences expressed by (current) consumers.

Some authors are critical of using a below-market rate for the social discount rate for a variety of reasons, including the fact that without total government control of investment the rate of return of public and private investments will not be equal, which causes *production inefficiency*. This is an important point that can be overcome in practice within the framework of a project analysis (see Acocella 1998), but it nonetheless gives us an idea of the theoretical difficulties that CBA can encounter.

---

[17] Consider, for example, that the present value of 1 pound is equal to 0.5 pounds if the pound will be available in 23–24 years and the discount rate is 3 per cent; however, if the discount rate is 7 per cent, the present value falls by half in 10–11 years. If the pound were to become available in 23–24 years, its present value would be about 0.2 pounds, a fall of 80 per cent rather than 50 per cent.

[18] This section is very general. We therefore ignore certain aspects of reality, such as the fact that there are multiple market interest rates for different maturities or that consumer interest rates differ from producers'. This might lead us to adopt different interest rates, one for each 'maturity' (i.e. period) of the project. Market interest rates are also different for various risk prospects.

[19] We must emphasise that the choice of the social discount rate depends on the choice of the numéraire, since the **discount rate** is nothing other than 'the rate of fall in the value of the numéraire against which goods are valued each year' (Drèze and Stern, 1987, p. 967).

[20] According to Pigou (1920, pp. 28–9) there is a 'natural tendency of people to devote too much of their resources to present service and too little to future service' (*irrational discounting*). Underlying this may be the 'limited generosity' of the human soul remarked on by Hume (1739).

9.5 Valuing non-marketed goods

Non-marketed goods include both *tangible* (i.e. material) and *intangible* (i.e. immaterial) goods.

Examples of tangible goods whose use is not traded in a market are motorways, bridges or other infrastructure that government could theoretically charge a price to use but, in the absence of congestion, generally supplies free – i.e. at a price equal to the marginal cost, which is zero if there is unused capacity. However, the fact that a public good is provided free does not exempt us from calculating its value (i.e. its benefit to society) with reference to the WTP for that good, in the same way we do for marketed goods.

The problem of intangible goods is usually more difficult to solve because these goods are often even further removed from the market since they involve non-economic values. In particular, how do we place a value on human life, the environment or time?

9.5.1 *Valuing life*

Nearly every public project has considerable consequences in terms of costs and/or benefits for human life. Different versions of a basic project can be designed to provide different levels of safety. Choosing between these versions (or alternative projects) depends on the expected costs and benefits of each. We therefore need to assign a value to life precisely in order to safeguard it (as we might reasonably want to do), even if it is an incommensurable good in principle.

There are many techniques for valuing life. We will discuss only two: the **direct** or 'constructive' **method** and the indirect or **'hedonic price index'** method.

With the first method, we measure the value of a life as the *net discounted earnings* of an individual over his expected life span. Only net earnings are considered; we therefore exclude those used to meet the costs of generating the earnings themselves. A problem with this method is that it identifies the value of a human life with the *value of earnings*, so that the value attributed to the lives of retired people or the disabled would be close to zero, which seems unjust and immoral.[21]

The **indirect** or **'hedonic price index' method** makes use of the preferences revealed[22] by individuals with regard to alternatives with different probabilities of death. Those who place a greater value on living longer will choose less dangerous lines of work or goods and services (e.g. food, transportation), forgoing higher earnings or bearing higher costs in exchange. Wage or price differentials should be used with caution, however (see Viscusi, 1983), since they may be due to other unrelated factors (different disutility or social status of professions; different taste of foods; convenience of different types of transportation); there is also often a lack of information about the true probability of death associated with different jobs. 'Life preferences' revealed in the choice of work

---

[21] The direct method also raises technical problems, since the result is very sensitive to the discount rate adopted (Stiglitz, 1988).

[22] We can also consider declared rather than revealed preferences (see, for example, Jones-Lee, 1976).

and goods and services are also influenced by individuals' state of need and, therefore, the income distribution. Consequently, the indirect method measures not only WTP, but also ability to pay. Adopting this method, we will be forced to assign a lower value to the life of a pauper, who is more willing to accept a very risky job, than to that of a rich person, who will avoid risk like the plague. This considerably reduces the attractiveness of this method to those who consider that immaterial factors alone should be taken into account in valuing human life.

However controversial the methods used to measure it, the value of life is still a necessary element of CBA. Taking it into account favours projects with a lower probability of causing death, while ignoring it would have the opposite effect.

Even if a project does not place human life at risk, it may still affect the *physical integrity or health of individuals*. In other words, it may reduce or increase the probability of injuries causing temporary or permanent disabilities, or adversely affecting people's health in some way. To value this, we can use the same methods employed in valuing human life, supplementing them with a consideration of the additional costs to society of disability or illness.

9.5.2   *Valuing the environment*

The first step in identifying and valuing the effects of a project on the environment is the difficult task of *defining the environment itself*. We can rather vaguely define it as the set of conditions, objects and external circumstances on which the existence, health, satisfaction and ability of people to carry out certain functions depend.

There are direct and indirect methods for valuing the WTP of people for using the environment. Recall that as a public good the value of the environment is equal to the sum of the values attributed to it by the various individuals.

Direct methods attempt to recreate the conditions in which the value of the environment would be expressed in the market. They use subjective evaluations obtained by field surveys (interviews). The most widely adopted method is **contingent valuation**, which uses a set of techniques (referendums, simulated markets, interviews) to identify the monetary value of the change in welfare associated with a change in the quantity of a public good, which in our case is a change in the environment. Let us consider the case of *environmental damage*. We can envisage two hypotheses:

(1) the change in the environment is considered to have already happened and people are asked what **compensating variation** they require – i.e. the minimum amount that would return the individual to the original position
(2) the change in the environment is considered not to have already occurred and people are asked to specify the **equivalent variation** they require – i.e. the maximum amount they would be willing to pay to prevent the change.

If an action improves (rather than damages) the environment, as we have supposed, so far, the contingent valuation would identify the maximum amount that people would be willing to pay to return to their positions before the action or the minimum amount they would pay to have the action carried out.

Special care must be exercised in using contingent valuation techniques in order to avoid systematically distorted results (see Mitchell and Carson, 1986; Cummings, Brookshire and Schulze 1989). An application of contingent valuation techniques in the case of a work of art, the Fès Medina, is illustrated in box 9.1.

Box 9.1. Valuing the benefits of conservation of the Fès Medina

The project

Like the rest of Morocco's Medinas,[a] the Fès Medina has been largely overlooked for much of the twentieth century as investment concentrated in areas outside the traditional urban centres. The result has been a serious deterioration of the historic building stock, of the urban infrastructure, and of the urban environment ...
A 1995 survey found that 36 per cent of the Medina's 150,000 inhabitants are below the poverty threshold, a proportion far exceeding the national average for both urban (10.4 per cent) and rural (28.7 per cent) populations. Moreover, half of the housing stock is seriously decayed and housing occupancy levels surpass acceptable levels. Many small-scale polluting industries have concentrated in the Medina, resulting in poor air and water quality and important negative health impacts including cholera. Most infrastructure is in need of replacement or modernisation, particularly water supply, sewerage and solid waste disposal, telecommunications, and transport ...

In 1980 UNESCO launched an international safeguarding campaign, which raised awareness of the site's importance but did not succeed in generating the financial support needed to carry out significant rehabilitation works. Most conservation activity to date has concentrated on individual monuments, with little attention to the remaining built environment.

The ... World Bank-financed project will assist in the conservation and rehabilitation of the Fès Medina, with particular attention to the historic housing stock and the quality of the urban environment. It will do so with direct interventions as well as efforts to increase private conservation efforts. Priority rehabilitation activities will upgrade the historic housing stock. Tourism offerings will be expanded. Access for emergency public services will be improved and extended to the centre of the Medina, facilitating logistical activities for residents and businesses and creating more favourable conditions for urban development and private sector investment. Solid waste collection and pollution reductions for small-scale industries programs will be instituted. The capacity of the municipality and responsible local agencies to plan and carry out proposed improvements will be strengthened. A labor-intensive public works program linked with the rehabilitation process will create employment and hence contribute to poverty reduction.

Analysis of benefits

Five major groups can be identified as benefiting from the planned activities in the Fès Medina:

(1) Residents of the Fès Medina and of Fès generally
(2) Moroccans who are not residents of Fès
(3) Foreign visitors to Fès, including:
  • tourists; about 160,000 adult foreign tourists remain overnight at Fès hotels annually
  • Islamic pilgrims
(4) Foreign visitors to Morocco who do not visit Fès during their current trip, about 1,5000,000 adult foreign tourists visit Morocco annually
(5) Non-Moroccans who do not visit Morocco.

A full analysis would require the benefits received by each of these groups to be investigated.

The residents of Fès will benefit directly from the improvements carried out to the Medina's infrastructure. Analysis of likely increases in property values resulting from improved accessibility, for example, shows a rate of return of 17 percent to expenditures on this component. In addition to benefiting from the physical improvements, residents will also benefit from the conservation and revitalisation of the Medina's cultural heritage. Other Moroccans will likewise benefit from the same improvements, albeit to a smaller extent than residents.

Although Moroccans, and particularly residents, are likely to benefit significantly from the preservation of the Medina's cultural heritage, time and resource constraints meant efforts to quantify the cultural heritage benefits of the proposed project had to be targeted on tourists and foreign residents. Tourists represent a significant source of potential income which could help finance the required improvements but which is only partially captured at present. In addition, research was also undertaken on the benefits to be received by non-Moroccans who do not visit Morocco, to get a sense of the global value of the existence of the Fès Medina.

Contingent valuation of tourist WTP for conservation of Fès

To estimate the benefits that foreign visitors to the Fès Medina would receive, a contingent valuation survey was carried out with World Bank financing during the summer of 1997. The survey distinguished the WTP for improvements of visitors of the site itself from those of other visitors to Morocco.

A multi-stage sample of 600 adult visitors was designed to represent visitors (including both tourists and those visiting for business or other purposes) to Morocco who visited the country during June–July 1997. Of the total of 600 interviews, 400 interviews were undertaken in Fès. Of the remaining interviews,

120 were carried out in Casablanca and 80 in Tangier, on the basis of their respective visitor flows.

The first section of the survey consisted of 16 questions requesting information about the respondent's visit to Morocco and to Fès. In the second section, the situation at Fès was presented to respondents using a short narrative supplemented by showcards featuring coloured photographs of the Medina. This presentation provided respondents with a standardised set of information about the character and condition of the Fès Medina today. It concluded by saying that without a major rehabilitation effort the Medina will continue to decline. The third section of the instrument presented a plan to rehabilitate the Fès Medina, which was described as having been developed by 'the Moroccan Government in collaboration with experts from international agencies.' Respondents were told the plan would accomplish three things:

- it would improve the Medina's appearance; buildings, streets, sewers, public spaces, and monuments would be repaired and cleaned up
- it would preserve the Medina's traditional character and cultural heritage for future generations
- it would ensure that the Medina would continue to be a productive and vibrant living city.

These prospective accomplishments represent the public goods that the proposed rehabilitation plan will provide.

Respondents were then told that 'one way to help pay for' the proposed activities would be to charge visitors such as themselves a special fee. Fès visitors were asked whether they would have included Fès in their itinerary if they had had to pay a Fès preservation fee of a specified amount when they registered at their hotel. For non-visitors to Fès, the fee was presented as a departure fee. Respondents were randomly assigned to one of six price-point sub-samples which varied between 25 and 2,000 dirhams (between $25 and $200). The amounts were chosen to bracket the anticipated range of median willingness to pay. It was assumed that visitors to Fès would be willing to pay more than tourists who were not visiting Fès. The upper ranges for these two groups were thus fixed at the equivalents of $200 and $100, respectively.

Interviewing began in Fès on June 16, 1997 and continued until July 3. The Casablanca and Tangier interviews were conducted between July 15 and July 25.

Benefits received by visitors

Visitors have a demonstrated preference for the site, since they have taken the trouble to come and visit. Since they are on-site, they will also experience directly the results of any improvements. They are likely, therefore, to have a high WTP for improvements. The survey found that visitors to the site itself would be willing, on average, to pay as much as US$70 each for improvements aimed at preserving and improving conditions in the Medina. Given the number of visitors each year, this is equivalent to a total annual benefit to visitors of about US$11milion. This figure would increase if the number of visitors increased.

Benefits received by non-visitors

Other visitors to Morocco may share an overall appreciation for this kind of site, but since they are not physically present at the site they will not receive any use benefits; their willingness to pay for preservation is based on the value they place on the site's existence, and to some extent on the possibility that they might visit it in the future (known as option value). The survey found that such visitors would be willing to pay about US$30 each. Given the number of tourists visiting Morocco each year, this is equivalent to a total annual benefit to visitors of about US$47 million.

To further investigate the benefits received by non-visitors, a Delphi survey was conducted among European CVM [contingent valuation method] experts to determine what, in their opinion, the mean and median WTP for the rehabilitation of the Fès Medina would be among the European population in general. A Delphi survey involves solicitation of the opinions of experts rather than consumers. When funding or time are not available for the collection of original data, such a survey may be the only way to develop an estimate of the value. The Delphi exercise was conducted using a stratified random sample of 30 attendees at the June 1997 meeting of the European Association of Environmental and Resource Economists (EAERE) in Tilburg, Netherlands. This meeting was chosen because it was likely to contain the largest concentration of European economists familiar with contingent valuation.

The results of the Delphi survey indicated that the household WTP for preservation of Fès ranged from $12.1 (mean WTP) to $2.15 (median WTP). To be as conservative as possible, the lowest estimated value ($2.15), was used. This estimate was applied to the 144,342,000 households in Europe, giving an estimate for the total value of Fès Medina to European households of about US$310 million. The best use of this number is to indicate that European households place a relatively high value on restoration of the Fès Medina.

Even if only a fraction of the amount of benefits received by visitors (US$11 million to Fès visitors and US$47 million to other visitors, for an annual total of about US$58 million) could be captured in Morocco – for example, by increasing the tourist tax – it would generate a substantial annual income flow which could be used to finance the required conservation investments.

Note:
a   The term 'Medina' means the ancient city.
Source: World Bank (1998).

Indirect methods use available information that implicitly reflects the value attributed to the environment by different people. Three methods are especially widely used: the defensive spending method, the hedonic price method and the travel cost method.

Under the **defensive expenditures method**, the value of the environment can be inferred from the amount that society is forced to spend to *limit the impact of environmental degradation*. Thus, an increase in air pollution causes an increase in the number of cases of respiratory disease, whose treatment carries a cost: this is the value of defensive spending and hence the value of the environment.

The **hedonic price method** values the environment through the expenditure borne by individuals to enjoy those aspects of the environment *that give them pleasure*: the value of clean air and the countryside is given by the spending of individuals to enjoy them in the places where they can still be found, as given by a rise in price of housing.

The **travel cost method** values the environment through the amount of money people are willing to spend to *visit places where it is protected*.

To eliminate the many uncertainties surrounding the evaluation of the effects of a project on the environment, recourse has been made to the ambitiously named **'environmental impact assessment' (EIA)**, which simply involves the determination of the qualitative or quantitative effects (in physical terms) of a project on the environment. This technique has come into widespread use in Europe in recent years, primarily under the impulse of EU legislation, and seeks to establish a basis for negotiation between the government and those intending to carry out a project with a significant environmental impact. Since 2001 a simplified version of EIA, the **'strategic environmental assessment'**, has been required to obtain funding from the Union through its structural funds (see section 18.7).

9.5.3 *Valuing time*

The impact of a project on individuals' leisure time must also be considered, since it can affect their *utility level*. For example, reducing workers' travel time by building a new underground line produces a social benefit.

Once again, however, the problem is one of *measurement*. We can use a variety of criteria, in particular WTP. In the case we are dealing with, this is revealed by choosing faster, albeit more expensive, means of transport, such as taxis, private automobiles and so on. Obviously, this choice may also be influenced by other characteristics of alternative means of transport (comfort, safety), which must be taken into account in valuing the increased leisure time resulting from the project.

9.5.4 *Cost-effectiveness*

If the effects on life, physical integrity or health (or other similar effects) are the main (rather than accessory) elements of alternative projects, as is the case in the field of health and safety, it may be appropriate to adopt a technique derived from CBA known as *cost-effectiveness analysis*. The objective of the project is taken as given (for example, a specific reduction in the number of fatal accidents due to some cause) and we focus on measuring the cost of *alternative ways to achieve it*. The advantage of this technique is that it avoids attributing a value to the benefits, which are identified only in *qualitative* and *physical* terms.

This technique can also be used for projects with objectives that are not identical but can be compared in physical terms. For example, Stiglitz (1988) cites a study in the United States to estimate the number of additional workers that would be protected against hearing loss by alternative noise reduction programmes. The study found that giving hearing protectors (ear plugs!) to workers would provide almost all the benefits of a general engineering-only noise standard (with the consequent drastic modifications of plant and equipment) at a much lower cost.[23]

9.6   Summary

1   An important practical application of welfare economics is *cost-benefit analysis* (CBA). This involves evaluating the costs and benefits of alternative government projects, much the same as private sector firms do.
2   Choosing the *best project* can be carried out on the basis of:
    (a) the net present value (NPV) of the costs and benefits
    (b) the internal rate of return (IRR).
3   The main differences between CBA and the estimations of a private firm concern:
    (a) the approaches to *valuing costs and benefits*
    (b) the consideration of the *positive and negative external effects* of the project, as well as 'incommensurable' costs and benefits.
4   The general rule for the evaluation of costs and benefits is agents' *willingness to pay* (WTP). In particular, the valuation of the goods and services produced by the project and that of its inputs can be based on *market prices* (perhaps corrected by the change in the social surplus if the market prices are affected by the project) when markets are competitive; if this is not the case, the valuation of the costs and benefits must make use of *shadow prices*, which represent the true marginal social benefit or cost.
5   The *shadow price* corresponds to the price that would prevail under perfect competition with complete markets. Therefore, where the goods and services used in the project are produced in non-competitive markets, their prices must be purged of the extra profits attributable to market power.
6   Determining the shadow wage is especially important and particularly difficult when the project draws on *unemployed workers*.
7   Deciding which *social discount rate* to use is also important, since it influences the choice between projects whose returns are spread over different lengths of time. The reasons for not using the market interest rate concern the market power of

---

[23] Similar studies have been conducted for various disease-screening programmes (see Drummond, 1980).

financial intermediaries, as well as the existence of other distortions, and a desire to safeguard the interests of future generations.

8 Among non-marketed goods and services, valuing human life and environment is particularly difficult. There are many methods for placing a value on life and environment, although none is entirely satisfactory. However, the difficulty of determining such a value does not mean that we can do without it, precisely because we wish to protect them more effectively.

IV Macroeconomic policies

10 Macroeconomic schemes of analysis in an open economy

10.1 The balance of payments, the foreign exchange market and the exchange rate

10.1.1 The balance of payments and the exchange rate

For simplicity we will initially refer to a world with only two countries, the home country and the 'Rest of the World'.

The balance of payments was introduced in section 3.7: all economic transactions that normally give rise to payments and receipts in foreign currency are usually recorded. The residents of the home country that need to make payments to non-residents will demand foreign currency; conversely, residents that receive payments in foreign currency will supply it. This is the **foreign exchange market** where, like all other markets, a price, called the *exchange rate* or, more precisely, the **nominal bilateral exchange rate**, is determined.

The nominal bilateral exchange rate is the *price of a currency in terms of another currency*. There are two ways to express this price. With the first, the reference unit is the foreign currency and its price is expressed in terms of the domestic currency: this is the **price-quotation system**, which indicates the variable price in terms of the domestic currency for one unit of foreign currency. The second method, known as the **volume-quotation system**, expresses the variable quantity of foreign currency that can be purchased with a unit of domestic currency. Unless otherwise indicated, we will adopt the price-quotation system, which is used by most countries (the United Kingdom and the euro area being the major exceptions). Thus, a rise in the exchange rate in Japan (e.g. from ¥100/\$1 to ¥110/\$1, assuming the Rest of the World uses the US dollar as its currency) indicates a fall in the value (**depreciation**) of the yen with respect to that of the dollar (i.e. a depreciation of the yen). If the ¥/\$ exchange rate rises, the \$/¥ exchange rate, which gives the number of dollars needed to purchase ¥1, falls, i.e. the dollar **appreciates**.

Obviously there are more than two countries in the real world and it may therefore be useful to calculate an average of nominal bilateral exchange rates (e.g. ¥/\$, ¥/€) in order to produce a synthetic indicator. If n is the total number of countries, the **nominal effective exchange rate** is a weighted average of the $n - 1$ nominal bilateral exchange rates with the home country's currency. The weights can reflect the level of international trade between the country under consideration and the other $n - 1$ countries.

Returning to our initial hypothesis of two countries, we now need to have at least an approximate understanding of the forces that determine the level and changes in the nominal exchange rate and what variables the exchange rate is capable of influencing.

We said that the exchange rate is determined in the *foreign exchange market*, which reflects the balance of payments. Referring to our previous example, the depreciation of the yen that occurs when the exchange rate rises from ¥100/$1 to ¥110/$1 is a consequence of the worsening of the balance of payments of Japan. Assume that the initial exchange rate of 100 corresponds to balance of payments equilibrium (which means that demand for foreign currency equals supply). If the demand for foreign currency subsequently increases relative to supply, the exchange rate cannot remain at its initial level. It must increase instead. Note that any deterioration in the balance of payments (even if we do not begin in equilibrium) leads to a depreciation of the currency. Similarly, improvements will lead to an appreciation. In addition, the worsening (or improvement) in the balance of payments influences the exchange rate independently of the composition of the overall balance – i.e. the relative size of the goods movements and capital movements balances.

Although the changes in the *exchange rate* are triggered by variations in all the items of the balance of payments, they influence only some transactions, more specifically foreign trade, having an effect on the competitiveness of domestic goods and services.[1] The role of the *exchange rate* in this is easily understood. Assume that the price of a good or basket of goods produced in the home country (Japan) is ¥100, and the price of the same good produced in the Rest of the World is $1. If the exchange rate were exactly ¥100/$1, in the absence of any barriers to international trade it would make no difference whether we bought the good produced in Japan or that produced abroad. If, however, the exchange rate were higher (say ¥120/$1), both Japan's residents and non-residents would benefit by buying Japanese goods, thus increasing Japanese exports. A lower exchange rate would reverse the situation in favour of goods produced abroad, generating Japanese imports.

From this simple example, we can deduce that the exchange rate influences competitiveness if prices are given in the two countries. Let us now assume that the exchange rate remains at ¥100/$1. If the price level in Japan falls below ¥100 and/or the price level abroad rises above $1, consumers will gain by purchasing from Japan, which will boost its exports and reduce imports, thus increasing net Japanese exports.[2] We therefore need an indicator that simultaneously takes account of the nominal exchange rate

---

[1] We will see later that this statement is valid only as a first approximation: actual changes in the exchange rate may have an influence on expected changes in the same variable and, thus, on capital movements (see section 10.2) and also goods movements, if they induce agents to adopt leads and lags in the payments of goods.

[2] We will see later that this statement, too, is valid under some conditions. In addition, in the real world, imperfections, differences in the quality of domestic and foreign goods, etc. introduce friction that makes it possible for some imports to persist even in the presence of a currency depreciation and for the increase in exports to lag behind.

and domestic and foreign prices. Such an indicator is in fact easy to devise: we take the price of foreign goods expressed in the domestic currency (yen), which is given by the price of foreign goods in foreign currency (dollars), p_w, multiplied by the nominal exchange rate (¥/$), e, and divide it by the yen price of domestic goods, p. This gives us the **real bilateral exchange rate**, e_r:

$$e_r = \frac{p_w \cdot e}{p} \tag{10.1}$$

The price level in the two countries is usually measured in terms of wholesale or producer price indices.[3]

More realistically, if there are numerous foreign countries rather than the single country we have assumed here, e will be the effective exchange rate rather than the bilateral exchange rate. In this case, e_r will represent the **real effective exchange rate**.

From (10.1) we can derive that the change in the real bilateral exchange rate[4] is approximately:

$$\dot{e}_r = \dot{p}_w + \dot{e} - \dot{p} = \dot{e} - (\dot{p} - \dot{p}_w) \tag{10.2}$$

where a dot above the variable indicates its rate of change per unit of time.

The terms in parentheses denote **relative inflation**. It is clear that if relative inflation is lower than the change in the nominal exchange rate, there will be an increase in the home country's competitiveness; in this case the real exchange rate will increase.[5] This represents a 'depreciation' in the real exchange rate, which will have the same effect as a 'depreciation' in the nominal exchange rate (i.e. an increase in the rate) when prices are constant: i.e. the competitiveness of the home country's goods will increase.

Our discussion so far has focused on the causes and effects of changes in the nominal exchange rate, assuming that there are no limits to such changes. If there are in fact no limits, we generally speak of **floating exchange rates**; if there are limits (or no variations at all), we speak of **fixed exchange rates**. To understand the operation of the foreign

---

[3] The index of unit labour costs is sometimes used in order to underscore some of the factors that cause changes in competitiveness. This precludes consideration of factors that are not included in the labour cost index. Differences between the real exchange rate constructed with the labour cost index and the rate based on producer prices reflect the behaviour of these other variables. For example, in France the real exchange rate measured in terms of unit labour costs rose by 5 percentage points between 1987 and 1991, denoting a moderate increase in that country's competitiveness; the increase in terms of producer prices was much smaller, about 2 points, indicating small gains in competitiveness. Over the same period, in Italy the real effective exchange rate measured in terms of unit labour costs fell by 11.3 per cent, indicating a sharp decline in competitiveness; the fall was only 4.3 per cent if measured on the basis of producer prices, signalling a smaller loss of competitiveness. Canada recorded results similar to Italy's. The difference between the two indices in the three countries could first be attributed to differences in the behaviour of other variable costs not included in the index of unit labour costs. This is unlikely, since it is difficult to imagine that the costs of raw materials and energy in the three countries behaved differently from those of their main trading partners. It is more likely that the differences in the behaviour of the two indicators of competitiveness were produced by the behaviour of *profit margins* (increasing in France, decreasing in Italy and Canada).

[4] If we want to calculate the change in the real effective exchange rate, the change in the nominal bilateral exchange rate ($\dot{e}$ in (10.2)) should be substituted with the change in the nominal effective exchange rate.

[5] Suppose that prices increase by 5 per cent in the home country and by 2 per cent abroad. This means that relative inflation is 3 per cent. If the nominal exchange rate depreciates by more than 3 per cent (say, 4 per cent) the home country increases its competitiveness.

exchange market, with specific reference to the conditions that may limit exchange rate fluctuations, we need to specify the nature and operation of the different monetary systems. We will examine this in chapter 16. For the moment, we can say that the fixed rate is maintained either through the intervention of the monetary authorities or other mechanisms. In a floating-rate regime, intervention by the monetary authorities can curb exchange rate fluctuations (**dirty** or **managed float**).

A system that falls somewhere between fixed and floating-rate regimes is the **target zone regime** proposed by John Williamson (see J. Williamson, 1985), which is an attempt to combine the advantages of both. It essentially calls for relatively large fluctuation bands around a fundamental equilibrium exchange rate,[6] which is recalculated period-ically. The fluctuation bands would also be 'soft', i.e. the monetary authorities would not be required to intervene in order to prevent the exchange rate from breaching the fluctuation limits. In certain respects the system resembles the target zone of the Euro-pean Monetary System (EMS) established after 2 August 1993, when the fluctuation bands around the central rate – which were binding, however – were raised to ±15 per cent (see chapter 16).

Let us consider a fixed-rate regime. In this case, the exchange rate fluctuates between set limits around a value called **parity** or the **central rate**. If the exchange rate is stated using the price-quotation system (the variable number of units of the domestic cur-rency for one unit of foreign currency), then the parity or central rate must be defined consistently (units of domestic currency for one unit of foreign currency). The parity or central rate are normally constant over a relatively long period but they can change.

When the parity or central rate (defined consistently under the price-quotation sys-tem) decline, we have a **revaluation** of the domestic currency (or devaluation of the foreign currency). When the parity or central rate increases, then we have a **devaluation** of the domestic currency.

If the exchange rate is quoted using the volume-quotation system, then the central parity or rate must also be expressed consistently (units of foreign currency for one unit of domestic currency). In this case, a revaluation (devaluation) of the domestic currency indicates an increase (decrease) in the parity or central rate.

Let us now examine the relationship between changes in the parity (revaluation or devaluation) and changes in the exchange rate (appreciation or depreciation). A revaluation normally implies an *appreciation*, while a devaluation normally produces a *depreciation*. Take an example using the price-quotation system. In this case, a reval-uation means a decrease in the parity and a corresponding decrease in the exchange rate. A devaluation means an increase in the parity and an increase in the exchange rate.[7] Since a devaluation is normally associated with a depreciation in the currency, unless otherwise indicated we will use both terms without distinction, as we do with

---

[6] See section 16.3 for the definition of fundamental disequilibrium.

[7] By way of example (and distorting current reality, which is dominated by floating-rate regimes), suppose that Europe and the United States have fixed-rate systems, with a parity of 1.1 (i.e. €1 is worth $1.1) with a fluctuation band of ±3 per cent. The \$/€ exchange rate can therefore change from $(1.1 - 0.03 \cdot 1.1 = 1.067)$ to $(1.1 + 0.03 \cdot 1.1 = 1.133)$. Suppose that on a given day the actual exchange rate is 1.080, that the euro is devalued by 5 per cent and that the fluctuation band remains at ±3 per cent of the parity. The new

revaluation and appreciation. Obviously, when using the volume-quotation system the same correspondence is preserved. The only difference is that under the latter system, a devaluation (revaluation) implies a decrease (increase) in the parity or central rate and a corresponding decrease (increase) in the exchange rate.

10.1.2 Foreign exchange transactions

First, we need to clarify that the market essentially includes:

- *firms* (as exporters and importers or entities carrying out direct investment or other capital movements)
- *consumers* (for the export and import of goods and services and capital movements)
- *banks and other financial intermediaries* (for bank and non-bank capital movements or as parties acting with others in the purchase or sale of foreign currency)
- *central banks*, for both the purchase and sale of foreign currency with banks and direct intervention to govern the exchange rate.

Progress in communications technology has made national markets highly interdependent and makes it impossible for currencies to have different exchange rates at the same time in those markets. Such differences would offer opportunities for **arbitrage**, i.e. a series of simultaneous transactions with which a trader seeks to benefit from price differences in two submarkets. This would give rise to changes in the supply and demand on such markets that would eliminate the temporary price differences.[8] Given the exchange rates of a currency with two other currencies, the equilibrium exchange rate between the latter is also implicitly given (the **cross-rate**).[9]

Like the markets for some goods and financial assets, the foreign exchange markets can be either spot markets or forward markets.

Spot markets are used for the immediate exchange of currencies at the prices formed on them. These markets are normally used for trade operations and non-speculative capital movements or for arbitrage and hedging (to be defined shortly).

Forward markets are used to negotiate today the price of a currency that will be available in the future (in one, two or more months): for example, we can buy $1,000

central rate will be 1.045, with a lower fluctuation limit of $(1.045 - 0.03 \cdot 1.045 = 1.01365)$ and an upper limit of $(1.045 + 003 \cdot 1.045 = 1.07635)$. In our example, the exchange rate cannot stay at its former level, which lies outside the fluctuation band allowed under the new central rate, and will have to rise, which indicates a depreciation.

[8] Suppose the $/€ exchange rate is 1.170 in Frankfurt and 1.171 in New York. By purchasing €1 in Frankfurt and selling it in New York, i.e. by buying euros where the euro costs less in dollar terms (which causes the exchange rate to rise) and reselling them where the exchange rate of the euro in dollar terms is higher (which causes the exchange rate to decrease), the two exchange rates tend to converge. Note that the equality holds when the Frankfurt market was under the volume-quotation system and the New York market was on the price-quotation system. If both markets quoted the currencies under the same system, arbitrage would mean that the exchange rate on one market was equal to the inverse of the rate on the other.

[9] Suppose that the ¥/$ exchange rate is ¥128.7/$1 and the €/$ rate is 1.17. In the presence of perfect information on the value of these exchange rates and in the absence of transaction costs and risk, the equilibrium value (i.e. the value that does not give rise to arbitrage opportunities) of the euro in terms of yen (that is, the number of yen needed to purchase €1) would be equal to $128.7 \cdot 1.17 = 150.58$.

today that will be available in one month at a price that will be paid in one month but is established today. Forward transactions are used to **hedge** exchange rate risk – i.e. to purchase foreign currency at a set price (and thus avoid the risk of exchange rate fluctuations), as well as for speculative purposes, as we will see shortly.

In some circumstances it may be advantageous to enter into contracts on the spot and forward markets at the same time. For example, a firm that currently has excess funds in a given currency (say dollars) can invest them for six months in another currency (say yen) by selling dollars and buying yen spot, if the yield on the investment in yen is higher. At the same time, the firm will repurchase dollars and sell yen on the forward market at 6 months if it wants to have the funds available at the end of the period. This is called a **swap**. It reduces transaction costs since rather than carrying out two separate transactions (a spot purchase of yen and a forward sale of yen) the same result can be obtained with one transaction.

Swaps can involve not only currencies but also interest flows (**interest rate swap**). For example, one of the two parties agrees to pay to the other at periodic intervals (e.g. once a year) a fixed rate of interest on a notional principal, while the other undertakes to pay a floating rate (for example, every six months at 6-month Libor[10]). The advantages of an interest rate swap are linked to the differing *expectations* and different levels of *risk aversion* of market participants as well as the different *loan terms* that the various parties can obtain in different markets.

As with goods and financial assets, there are also foreign currency futures. **Futures contracts** are *standardised forward contracts*, i.e. they have standard clauses common to all such contracts. They can easily be traded on the futures market without having to execute the contract at maturity. A futures contract can be used whenever a party wants to set a **future price** (that is, the price agreed with the contract but paid at maturity) different from the expected spot price for the maturity date of the contract.

Foreign currency options are standardised forward contracts[11] in which one of the parties pays a premium (the option price) for the right to purchase or sell a certain quantity of a foreign currency at a set price at a given future date or within a set period of time.

The right to purchase (sell) currency is called a **call (put) option**. In addition to arbitrage and hedging, options and futures can also (and above all) be used for speculative purposes.[12] Foreign currency **speculation** involves the purchase (sale) of a foreign

---

[10] **Libor** (London Interbank Offered Rate) is the short-term interest rate used for the main currencies on the London interbank market (i.e. loans of funds between banks).

[11] Like futures, options are **derivatives contracts**, in that the price of these financial instruments depends on (is derived from) the price of another underlying financial instrument (in this case, a foreign currency).

[12] Let us see how speculation works with a call option. Let e_o be the exchange rate established in the contract at which the currency can be purchased and e be the current exchange rate of the currency at maturity. The purchaser of a call option will exercise the option and purchase the foreign currency if $e_o < e$; otherwise it is better for him to write off the premium and not purchase the currency.

The premium paid has no role in determining whether the option right should be exercised. It is paid at the moment the contract is made and as such at expiry is a sunk cost that cannot be recovered whatever one does. However, the premium is important at the time the contract is made, since the option could be profitable if the premium is less than the difference between the exchange rate set in the contract, at which the call option can be exercised, and the spot rate at exercise. With p_r as the premium and using the other symbols introduced earlier, an option will be profitable if $e_o + p_r < e$.

currency with the intention of carrying out a subsequent sale (purchase) for the main purpose of gaining on a change in the exchange rate (and not on the use of the currency, its transformation or movement between different markets) (see Kaldor, 1939).

By essentially reducing the amount of capital required to the payment of the difference between the agreed exchange rate and the spot rate at maturity, futures and options enable parties to enter into a large number of transactions with a given amount of capital, which can have a major impact on current prices. While the price of futures and options depends on the spot price of the underlying instrument, it also has a *feedback effect* on the exchange rate itself. The movement of the price in the futures and options markets is indicative of future exchange rate trends based on the forecasts of the various market participants and thus has signalling value. The key point is that spot exchange rate developments are affected by changes in the forward rate and that this can also be influenced by participants with relatively limited amounts of capital using futures and options. In order to understand the determinants of spot exchange rates, it is important to examine the factors that affect expectations of operators and, therefore, their behaviour in forward markets. We return to this point elsewhere (see section 20.2).

10.2   Theory of the balance of payments

In section 3.7 we saw that the balance of payments is composed of three accounts: the current account, the capital account and the financial account. In the coming pages we analyse the determinants of the first two accounts jointly and then those of capital movements, which are a part of the financial account (indeed, the total financial account with the exclusion of changes in official reserves), before turning to the determinants of the balance of payments as a whole.

10.2.1   The current and capital account (movements of goods)

Excluding unrequited transfers, which often involve non-economic considerations, the current and the capital account are made up of imports and exports of goods.

Let us take a world consisting of two 'countries', say Switzerland (the home country, which uses the Swiss franc) and the Rest of the World (the foreign country, which uses the dollar); we refer to the imports and exports of the home country.

Imports are normally made to depend on the level of demand (**demand factors**). In its simplest form, we have $M = mY$, where M denotes imports in real terms, m is the propensity to import and Y is the level of domestic real income. The variable m is considered given in a first approximation, but in reality it depends on **structural factors**, which change only in the long run,[13] and on **factors of competitiveness**, i.e. the quality and other similar characteristics of goods (**non-price competitiveness**)[14] and the prices of domestic goods compared with those of foreign goods (**price competitiveness**).

---

[13] For example, other things being equal, a 'small' country or one lacking raw materials such as Switzerland will have a higher propensity to import.

[14] For example, the technology incorporated in a product, which affects its quality and its image, as well as the quantity and type of associated services offered, payment terms, etc.

Structural factors and most factors of price and non-price competitiveness are influenced by industrial policies, antitrust legislation, etc., which normally do not change in the short run. Price and demand factors are normally affected by short-run macroeconomic policies.[15] Let us focus on price factors, which can be represented by the general price level (measured, for example, by the producer price index) in the home country, p, and that in the Rest of the World expressed in dollars, p_w, as well as the nominal exchange rate, e. Given the exchange rate, the quantity imported will rise if p rises and decline if p_w rises. If p and p_w are given, we can assume that imports will fall as e rises.[16]

We can therefore write $m = m(\overset{+}{p}, \overset{-}{p_w}, \overset{-}{e})$ and then

$$M = m(\overset{+}{p}, \overset{-}{p_w}, \overset{-}{e})\,Y \tag{10.3}$$

where the signs of the partial derivatives are shown above the independent variables: for example, $(\partial m/\partial p > 0)$.[17] If we wish to introduce the real exchange rate e_r defined in section 10.1, we can write $M = m'(\overset{-}{e_r})\,Y$.

We can also write a similar expression for exports, bearing in mind that the exports of Switzerland, X, are simply the imports of the Rest of the World, M_w, which we can treat as we did with the imports of Switzerland:

$$X = M_w = m_w(\overset{-}{p}, \overset{+}{p_w}, \overset{+}{e})\,Y_w \tag{10.4}$$

where M_w, m_w and Y_w are the imports, propensity to import and aggregate demand of the Rest of the World; the arguments of this propensity to import are again marked with the signs of the partial derivatives. Obviously, the signs of prices and the exchange rate are reversed in (10.4) with respect to those in (10.3), since the position of the Rest of the World is symmetric to that of the domestic country.

Introducing the real exchange rate, e_r, we would have:

$$X = m'_w(\overset{+}{e_r})\,Y_w$$

In introductory macroeconomics textbooks a simple specification of the functions (10.3) and (10.4) is given: as to imports, $M = mY$, where m is constant; as to exports, $X = \overline{X}$. We want now to show how these simpler specifications can be related to ours. In the case of the import function there is no problem: the specification is the same; the only difference is that m is taken as constant by introductory textbooks. With reference to (10.3), the demand of the Rest of the World must be considered given, at least in a first approximation, since it cannot be influenced by a small country such as Switzerland by means of changes in its domestic income and, therefore, its imports. If m_w is also considered constant, as is done in the first approximation for m in the import function

---

[15] Prices are also influenced by the policies cited earlier for non-price factors of competitiveness.

[16] As explained later in this chapter this is a shaky assumption. It is true that a higher exchange rate – i.e. a higher number of Swiss francs for one unit of the foreign currency – has to be paid to buy foreign goods. A reduction in the physical quantity of imports will ensue. However, the value of imports denominated in the domestic currency will decline only if the proportionate decline in the physical quantity is higher than the proportionate increase in the domestic price of imports (see section 14.8).

[17] For readers who have not studied calculus, this simply means that an increase in domestic prices causes a rise in imports, *ceteris paribus*: a positive derivative means that the dependent and the independent variable we are considering move in the same direction – e.g. as p rises, m and, then, M rise.

when *it is assumed that structural and competitiveness factors are substantially constant*, (10.4) reduces to $X = \overline{m}_w \cdot \overline{Y}_w = \overline{X}$, where $\overline{m}_w$ and $\overline{Y}_w$ are the given values of the two variables. The apparent asymmetry between the functional form of exports ($X = \overline{X}$) and that of imports used in introductory textbooks ($M = mY$, with m constant) is thus explained. In reality, both depend on *income*, but in the case of exports the relevant income is that of the Rest of the World, which, for our small exporting country, is given. Exports can therefore be considered exogenous. The reader should bear in mind the fact that in the simpler specification of the import and export functions (i.e. $M = mY$, where m is constant, and $X = \overline{X}$), all possible causes of change in the propensity to import, both long and short-run, including competitiveness factors, are ignored.

If we return to (10.3) and (10.4) the goods balance in real terms of Switzerland can be expressed as:

$$CA = X - M = f(\overset{-}{p}, \overset{+}{p}_w, \overset{+}{e}, \overset{-}{Y}, \overset{+}{Y}_w) \tag{10.5}$$

or $\qquad CA = f'(\overset{+}{e}_r, \overset{-}{Y}, \overset{+}{Y}_w)$

It therefore depends on competitiveness factors (p, p_w, e) and demand factors (Y, Y_w).[18] In particular, a rise in the exchange rate always improves the goods balance. In what follows we will usually assume that p, p_w, Y_w are given; we could then express CA as a function of the nominal exchange rate and the domestic income only, i.e. $CA = g(\overset{+}{e}, \overset{-}{Y})$.

10.2.2 Capital movements

Capital movements depend on long-term interest rate differentials (portfolio investment, long-term loans and credits), short term interest rate differentials (short-term loans and speculative flows), as well as expected changes in exchange rates (especially, but not solely, for short term and speculative flows).[19] Direct investment is influenced by other variables and circumstances that are more difficult to represent in aggregate terms: differences in profit rates, the position of firms in their markets and related

---

[18] However, recall the influence of *structural and non-price competitiveness factors*, which are not made explicit in (10.5) and in the expressions from which it is derived.

[19] The so-called **uncovered** (i.e. without cover on the forward market) **interest rate parity** of capital movements can be written as: $i = i_w + \dot{e}^e$. It assumes *perfect substitutability* between domestic and foreign financial assets with the same yield in a given unit of account (currency); see Gandolfo (2001).
  We can easily demonstrate the validity of the indicated equilibrium condition. Take two financial liabilities issued by the same debtor but denominated in two different currencies, Swiss francs and dollars. Over a certain time span (1 year, for example) they should pay the same return in a given currency. If the nominal values of the two liabilities in Swiss francs and dollars are shown by K_{SF} and K_{US}, respectively, and e^e is the expected exchange rate at the end of the year, (K_{SF}/e^e) gives the equivalent in dollars of the capital value of the liability in Swiss francs. Indicating the rate of change in a variable over the time period with a dot, $\dot{K}_{US}$ gives the rate of return in dollars of the liability denominated in dollars and $(\dot{K}_{SF}/e^e)$ gives the rate of return in dollars of the Swiss franc-denominated liability. The indifference condition between the two liabilities can therefore be written as $(\dot{K}_{US} = \dot{K}_{SF}/e^e)$. However, the rate of return in dollars of the dollar-denominated liability is given by the prevailing interest rate in the United States, i_{US}, while $(K_{SF}/e^e) \cong \dot{K}_{SF} - \dot{e}^e$ where the rate of return in Swiss francs of the Swiss franc-denominated liability is equal to the rate of interest in Switzerland, i. Thus, the indifference condition between the two liabilities can be written as $i_{US} = i - \dot{e}^e$, or $i = i_{US} + \dot{e}^e$.

strategic matters, the size and rate of growth of the countries in question, etc. (Acocella, 1992a, 1992b).

If for simplicity we overlook direct investment and assume that in each country long-term rates are closely linked to short-term rates and their relationship does not change over time,[20] the balance of capital movements, KA, will depend only on interest rates (short *or* long-term) in the two countries and expected changes in the exchange rate:

$$KA = g(\overset{+}{i}, \overset{-}{i_w}, \overset{-}{\dot{e}^e}) \tag{10.6}$$

where i and i_w are interest rates in Switzerland and the Rest of the World, respectively, and $\dot{e}^e$ is the expected rate of change in the exchange rate of the guilder; the signs of the partial derivatives are shown above the variables. In what follows we will usually consider i_w and $\dot{e}^e$ as given. In this case we could express the balance of capital movements as $KA = \dot{g}(i)$.

10.2.3   The balance of payments

The overall balance of payments is the sum of the balances on goods and capital movements. It can be written as:

$$BP = CA + KA = \psi(\overset{-}{p}, \overset{+}{p_w}, \overset{+}{e}, \overset{-}{Y}, \overset{+}{Y_w}, \overset{+}{i}, \overset{-}{i_w}, \overset{-}{\dot{e}^e}) \tag{10.7}$$

The balance of payments thus depends on:

(a) the *balance of goods movements*, which is a function of:
   • price competitiveness factors (p, p_w, e), i.e. the real exchange rate, e_r
   • demand factors (Y, Y_w)
(b) the *balance of capital movements*, which depends on interest rate differentials and the expected change in the exchange rate (i, i_w, $\dot{e}^e$).

If we consider p, p_w, Y_w, i_w, $\dot{e}^e$ as given, we have: $BP = h(e, Y, i)$.

These elements of the theory of the balance of payments will be helpful in understanding the possibilities for automatic adjustment of the balance and the factors that economic policymakers can act on to redress imbalances.

10.3   International openness, analytical frameworks and economic policy

The international openness of an economic system has a significant impact on the performance of the system and the scope for public intervention.

International openness introduces a new objective (or constraint) for government action over and above those that can be set in a closed system: balance of payments equilibrium. On the other hand, an open economy also offers additional instruments,

---

[20] We also assume that the expected change in the exchange rate is constant (in particular, equal to zero) over time, so that it affects short- and long-term capital movements in the same way.

such as the exchange rate. In addition, international openness influences the effectiveness of the other policy instruments that a national government can use, in terms of both (usually) weakening that influence and changing the relative effectiveness of the various instruments.

In order to understand the effects of international openness on macroeconomic equilibrium and the scope for government intervention in an open economy, we must adjust the closed-economy analytical framework. In doing so, we will use the *Mundell–Fleming model*.

10.4   The Mundell–Fleming model

The Mundell–Fleming model (see Mundell, 1963 and Fleming, 1962) goes beyond the initial Keynesian hypothesis of a closed economic system and generalises the *IS-LM* analytical framework. This is done by introducing:

(a) *net exports* (i.e. exports net of imports, $X - M$) as an additional positive component of aggregate demand. The export and import functions are those given in section 10.2
(b) an *external-payments 'market'* in addition to the goods and money markets.

Let us first examine the changes that occur to the *IS-LM* framework when we introduce net exports. In the simplest case, where $X = \overline{X}$ and $M = mY$ (where m is the country's propensity to import), adding these components of demand to the usual elements (also expressed in their simplest form) transforms the equilibrium of the goods market as follows:

$$Y = C + I + G + X - M \tag{10.8}$$
$$C = cY$$
$$I = I(i)$$
$$G = \overline{G}$$
$$X = \overline{X}$$
$$M = mY$$

From this we obtain by substitution:

$$Y = \frac{1}{1 - c + m}[I(i) + \overline{G} + \overline{X}] \tag{10.9}$$

From (10.9) we can obtain a relationship between i and Y of the same form as the normal *IS* curve in a closed economy.[21] However, the *IS* schedule in an open economy has the following notable features:

---

[21] Since the *IS-LM* model assumes constant prices, the real interest rate is equal to the nominal interest rate; we can therefore use either. Prices variability poses problems that, for simplicity's sake, we will not examine. No basic macroeconomics texts (of which at least partial knowledge is assumed here) deal with the problem. From here on, we will therefore refer to the two interest rates indifferently even in the few cases in which we introduce price changes into our discussion.

(a) for a given I and $\overline{G}$, the curve tends to shift to the right with the increase in $\overline{X}$, which is an additional exogenous component of demand

(b) it is steeper than the IS curve for a closed economy, since the multiplier is reduced by the diversion of some demand towards foreign goods; this is reflected in a positive propensity to import.

If we take *price competitiveness* factors into account, we have $M = m\,(p, p_w, e)\,Y$ and $X = m_w\,(p, p_w, e)\,Y_w$, instead of the simple forms of the import and export functions used in (10.8). IS then becomes sensitive to domestic and foreign prices (although the latter are largely beyond the control of the home country) and the exchange rate. A rise in domestic prices tends to shift the IS schedule to the left, owing both to the real balance effect and the adverse impact the rise would have on exports. It also causes IS to become steeper by increasing the propensity to import. A rise in the exchange rate and/or foreign prices would have the opposite effect. International openness does not cause changes in the money market, which means that the LM schedule can be drawn in the usual way.

Let us now consider the third market, external payments, which is characteristic of an open economy.

First, recall the theory of the balance of payments outlined in section 10.2. We know that the following relation holds:

$$BP = \psi(p, p_w, e, Y, Y_w, i, i_w, \dot{e}^e) \qquad (10.10)$$

As we have already said, this representation of the factors on which the balance of payments depends can be simplified for the purposes of the present analysis. Some variables are entirely (p_w, Y_w, i_w) or largely ($\dot{e}^e$) outside the control of policymakers in the home country and must therefore be considered given.[22] Domestic prices can change, but we will initially assume that they are also given, as is normally done with the IS-LM model. The balance of payments can therefore be written as:

$$BP = h(Y, i, e) \qquad (10.11)$$

Balance of payments equilibrium in the light of (10.11) can be shown diagrammatically on the (Y, i) plane used for the IS and LM schedules (figure 10.1), setting $BP = 0$ in (10.11) and considering e as given.

The BP curve in this figure represents the combinations of Y and i that ensure balance of payments equilibrium, or external balance ($BP = 0$). We can intuitively construct the curve as follows. Let A be a combination of Y and i, Y_0 and i_0, that ensures equilibrium in the balance of payments for a given e ($e = \overline{e}$). If Y rises above Y_0, imports rise and the goods balance deteriorates, all the more so the higher the propensity to import. To keep the balance of payments in equilibrium the domestic interest rate, i, must rise in order to attract larger net inflows of capital. BP will therefore have a positive slope,

---

[22] It would be possible to examine the consequences for BP of alternative values for the variables. In this case, we say that we are analysing *parametric variations* in the variables considered. We will briefly discuss this issue later on.

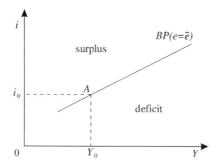

Figure 10.1

with the curve being flatter the lower the propensity to import and the more sensitive capital flows are to the interest rate. With perfect capital mobility – i.e. when domestic and foreign financial assets are perfect substitutes and there are no obstacles to the international movement of funds – the curve will be horizontal at a domestic interest rate exactly equal to the world interest rate. In other words, with perfect capital mobility there is only one interest rate that ensures a balance of payments equilibrium for any level of income. In this case, the conditions for balance of payments equilibrium are completely dominated by the rate of interest and capital movements (Dernburg, 1989, p. 109). If the domestic interest rate exceeds the world rate (even by an infinitesimal amount), there will be unlimited capital inflows, causing a balance of payments surplus whatever the goods balance. The opposite will occur if the domestic rate is lower than the world rate.

By contrast, BP is vertical if there is no capital mobility. In this case, balance of payments equilibrium is independent of i and corresponds to a single value for Y. This can easily be shown if we consider the simple specification of the export and import functions given by the last two relations of (10.8). We have $X - M = \overline{M} - mY$, where m is given. There is one and only one level of Y that ensures $\overline{X} - mY = 0$.

Returning to figure 10.1, points above and to the left of BP represent a balance of payments surplus: for each level of income there is an interest rate above that for which $BP = 0$ (or, for each given interest rate, the level of income is less than that which insures $BP = 0$) and therefore $BP > 0$. Points below and to the right of BP correspond to a balance of payments deficit.

This discussion holds for a given exchange rate. If the exchange rate were to rise (following depreciation or devaluation), and the Marshall–Lerner conditions are satisfied, balance of payments equilibrium would occur at a lower interest rate (for a given income level) or a higher income (for a given interest rate); BP would therefore shift downwards and become flatter. The downwards shift is due to the fact that – if the appropriate conditions, called Marshall–Lerner conditions, which will be stated in section 14.8 hold – a devaluation increases exports while decreasing imports (for a given level of income), thus generating a balance of payments surplus: a higher income level is then needed to ensure higher imports and, therefore, balance of payments equilibrium

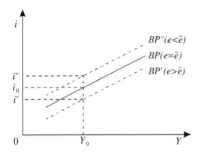

Figure 10.2

for any given level of the interest rate. The reduction in the slope of the curve corresponds to a reduction in the propensity to import. By contrast, BP would be higher and steeper if the currency were to appreciate or to be revalued. (The diagrams that follow ignore changes in the slope of BP brought about by variations in the exchange rate or other prices.)

In figure 10.2 the curve BP'' corresponds to an exchange rate lower than $\bar{e}$ and BP' to a higher rate. For a given income level Y_0 and an exchange rate $\bar{e}$, external balance would require $i = i_0$; with an exchange rate higher than $\bar{e}$ (which reduces imports and boosts exports) and an unchanged level of income Y_0, equilibrium would require a lower net inflow (or larger net outflow) of capital and hence $i' < i_0$. The opposite occurs if $e < \bar{e}$.

More generally, recall that the position and slope of BP in the (Y, i) plane also depend on the other variables of (10.7) as well as the structural factors discussed earlier. Thus, for example, a fall in domestic prices[23] tends:

(a) to *lower BP* by raising exports
(b) to *flatten BP* by reducing the propensity to import.

A similar effect is produced by a rise in foreign prices, while an export subsidy has the same effect as (a) and the imposition of a tariff has the same effect as (b). An increase in foreign income also lowers BP. For countries that produce and export goods with high income elasticity and import goods with low income elasticity, the BP curve shifts gradually downwards in a world with rising income.

The crucial point concerns the effect of domestic prices on the real rate of interest. As we have seen, when prices are constant, $i = r$; when prices can vary, the nominal rate of interest normally varies as well. This makes it difficult to use the *IS-LM* framework in a context of changing prices since the effects on goods market equilibrium are transmitted through the real interest rate, while those on money market equilibrium operate through changes in the nominal interest rate.

Let us now consider the goods market, the money market and the balance of payments together. Point A in figure 10.3 shows the simultaneous equilibrium of the three

---

[23] A decline might be the result of an increase in productivity and/or a reduction in wage rates or profit margins.

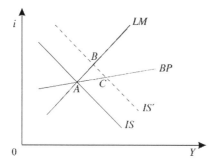

Figure 10.3

markets.[24] In general, starting in such equilibrium, a change in the equilibrium conditions in one of the three markets (which implies a shift in one of the three curves) causes at least one of the other two to move into imbalance. For example, if *IS* shifts upwards following an increase in government spending, we move to point *B*, at *B* the money market would be in equilibrium but not the balance of payments; at *C* the opposite would be the case.

The imbalance thus created can essentially be eliminated in one of the following ways:

(a) the system may tend to revert (to some extent) to its *original position*; or
(b) it may move[25] towards a *new equilibrium position*.

Which alternative will actually occur depends on both the type of *imbalance created* (monetary, real or external) and the *exchange rate* regime (fixed or floating). We will discuss this aspect more fully in our examination of fiscal and monetary policy. For the moment we will examine shifts in *BP* caused by changes in the exchange rate.[26]

We have seen that a devaluation (or depreciation) normally causes *BP* to shift downwards. This is not the only effect, however, since the rise in the exchange rate also produces an increase in autonomous spending (higher exports) and therefore causes *IS* to shift as well.

Referring to figure 10.4, let us assume that we are in a fixed-exchange rate regime and the initial simultaneous equilibrium position is at *A*. If the appropriate conditions are met, a currency devaluation improves the balance of payments, thus causing *BP* to move to *BP'*. At the same time, the increase in exports following the devaluation increases aggregate demand, thus shifting the curve for goods market equilibrium to *IS'*. With the money supply unchanged, we move along *LM* to *B*. But even under the previous

---

[24] The steeper slope of *LM* with respect to *BP* reflects the hypothesis (which does not always hold in the real world) of considerable international capital mobility.
[25] The reader must bear in mind that although we use expressions that in a strict sense should only be used with regard to dynamic analysis, ours is a purely comparative statics analysis.
[26] More generally, such shifts can be caused by all the other factors that determine the position of *BP* in the (*Y*, *i*) plane, including changes in the structure of the economic system. In the case here, we assume that variations in the exchange rate do not cause domestic prices to vary in order to avoid the difficulties that may emerge in the Mundell–Fleming model when prices are not held constant.

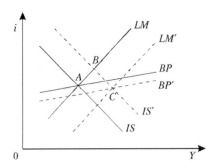

Figure 10.4

exchange rate there was a balance of payments surplus at *B* and the imbalance increases further at the new exchange rate. Holding other conditions unchanged and assuming there is no sterilisation, this will expand monetary base and therefore the money supply, since the increase in foreign reserves is converted into *domestic currency*. This lowers the equilibrium interest rate corresponding to the new, higher level of demand. Hence, *LM* will also shift right until the balance of payments surplus is eliminated, which happens at the new equilibrium point *C*. However, adjustment takes time and may encounter numerous obstacles, as we will see in chapter 14. The reader can try to diagram the consequences of a devaluation (or depreciation) beginning in a situation of balance of payments disequilibrium.

10.5   The limitations of the Mundell–Fleming model and ways to overcome them

The Mundell–Fleming model suffers from a number of limitations that must be borne in mind to avoid unwarranted conclusions. There are essentially four types of limitation:

(1) the model assumes that *both domestic and foreign prices* are given
(2) only *credit and debit flows with the rest of the world* are considered, independently of their relationships with stocks
(3) the model considers the *overall equilibrium of the balance of payments*, not its full equilibrium
(4) expectations of *exchange rate variations* are not considered.

We comment on each of these points in turn:

(1) We have briefly dealt with this limitation in section 10.4. The interested reader is referred to Acocella (1998) for further analysis of this issue.
(2) In our discussion of the effects of domestic interest rate variations on capital movements we implicitly used a *flow rather than stock model*. Foreign investment was considered as a flow that lasts as long as there is a positive differential between domestic and world interest rates.[27] However, foreign investment can be considered

---

[27] We are assuming no change in the expected exchange rate. If we drop this assumption, the flow will arise or persist when the differential net of the expected variation in the exchange rate is positive.

as the effect of the adjustment of the stock of financial capital invested at home and abroad. Take an initial situation of equilibrium in the portfolio of domestic and foreign investors. For simplicity, we can assume that the domestic interest rate is equal to the world rate. A decline in the domestic interest rate will trigger a portfolio adjustment with an increase in holdings of foreign assets and a reduction in domestic assets, giving rise to net capital outflows. However, this impact effect may not continue for the entire period in which the interest rate differential persists. In other words, such capital flows represent a temporary process of *stock adjustment* rather than a permanent equilibrium flow.

Considering the riskiness as well as the rate of return of various assets may reduce the elasticity of capital movements: the fact that assets are denominated in different currencies reduces their substitutability owing to the specific risks associated with the individual currencies, making demand less sensitive to variations in interest rates. The outcome of these considerations is that *BP* tends to become steeper.

In this context, higher and higher domestic rates are required to sustain a permanent net inflow of capital, given the world interest rate: the effect of changes in the interest rate on capital movements therefore tends to be temporary; an increase in the rate results in a temporary improvement in the balance of payments through capital movements.

When we consider stocks, changes in interest rates may also have an impact on goods movements owing to variations in interest payments abroad, which are included under the 'investment income' item. These effects run in the opposite direction to those on capital movements and are lasting: the rise in the interest rate attracts foreign capital for a period, thus increasing total outstanding foreign debt, on which it will be necessary to pay interest at a higher rate until the debt is redeemed. These effects imply a (gradual) shift to the left in the *BP* curve.

(3) The latter considerations introduce the third limitation of the Mundell–Fleming model: the fact that it considers the overall equilibrium of the balance of payments rather than full equilibrium. Overall equilibrium can be attained with various combinations of balances:
   (a) a goods movements surplus and a capital movements deficit
   (b) a goods movements deficit and a capital movements surplus
   (c) balance for both goods and capital movements (**full equilibrium of the balance of payments**).
The sustainability and the domestic effects of (a) and (b) differ significantly. We discussed sustainability under point (2) to some extent. Domestic income and employment are usually lower in (a) than in (b).

(4) The final limitation of the standard Mundell–Fleming model concerns the hypothesis that investors do not expect changes in the exchange rate. Some argue that this assumption should be dropped because it is inconsistent with many real-life situations, especially concerning the policies we have discussed, such as monetary policy. In section 10.4, in fact, we saw that exchange rate expectations can play a role.

10.6   Summary

1   The foreign currency payments and receipts recorded in the balance of payments fuel the foreign currency market, which in a two-country world forms a price called the *nominal bilateral exchange rate*. In a world with more than two countries, the nominal effective exchange rate can be defined as the weighted average of the different bilateral rates.

2   The *real exchange rate* is an indicator of the competitiveness of domestic goods that takes account of the nominal exchange rate and domestic and foreign prices.

3   In a fixed-rate regime the exchange rate can fluctuate within a *narrow, well-defined band* around a parity or central rate. In a floating-rate regime, the exchange rate can fluctuate *freely without restrictions*.

4   The *foreign exchange market* can be used to carry out spot and forward transactions for the purposes of arbitrage, hedging and speculation. Major forward transactions include foreign currency futures and options, which are mainly used for speculative purposes.

5   The *balance of goods movements* in real terms depends on various factors, including price competitiveness (indicated by the real exchange rate) and income factors. The *balance of capital movements* depends on interest rate differentials and expectations of exchange rate variations.

6   The Mundell–Fleming model extends the *IS-LM* analytical apparatus to the case of an open economy, introducing:
    (a) *net exports* as an additional component of aggregate demand
    (b) an *external payments market* in addition to the goods market and money market.

7   The *BP curve* represents the combinations of income and interest rates that ensure external equilibrium when the exchange rate, foreign prices and domestic prices are given. The curve shifts as these variables change. In particular, beginning in a situation of unemployment, a devaluation can ease the balance of payments constraint, making expansionary monetary and fiscal policies possible.

8   The limitations of the Mundell–Fleming model concern:
    (a) the assumption of *given prices*
    (b) its reference to *flows* rather than stocks
    (c) its focus on the *overall equilibrium of the balance of payments* only
    (d) the neglect of *expectations of exchange rate variations*.
    These limitations can be overcome with varying degrees of difficulty.

11 Macroeconomic objectives and monetary policy

11.1 Objectives, instruments and models of macroeconomic policy

Macroeconomic policy seeks to achieve objectives defined in terms of *aggregate economic variables*: full employment, price stability, balance of payments equilibrium, growth.

Since market failures in achieving these objectives are largely identified through macroeconomic theories, the latter underlie the analytical model that:

(a) enables us to identify variables that can be used as instruments
(b) indicates the links between targets and instruments, thus permitting us to set instrument values at the optimal level.

We have seen that there have been attempts to undertake a microeconomic analysis of at least some of the problems considered here: unemployment is one example. This is the approach taken by many theories belonging to the 'classical' strand of economic thought. Some of these give no explanation for involuntary unemployment; others explain it, but only as the product of 'imperfections' (e.g. imperfectly flexible prices). Theories of this sort tend to suggest microeconomic solutions, such as reducing or eliminating the causes of price stickiness, rather than policies based on the *adjustment of aggregate variables*, such as government expenditure, tax revenue, liquidity, etc.

While the search for macroeconomic models constructed on microeconomic foundations is a worthy task, it must be said that currently available models of this kind are inadequate. Their shortcomings are such that Keynesian macroeconomic models still seem to offer more satisfactory explanations of reality. We will therefore rely primarily on such theories in identifying the most appropriate solutions to the macroeconomic aspects of market failure.

The macroeconomic instruments are: monetary policy, fiscal policy, price and incomes policy and exchange rate policy. Although these instruments are aimed at macroeconomic targets, their effects are not necessarily spread equally over the entire economic system. On the contrary, they are often *selective*.

For example, this is the case with a restrictive monetary policy, which has a greater negative impact on small firms; these usually pay higher interest rates, are **credit rationed** and can make only limited use of self-financing and cross-subsidisation.[1] Similarly, a revaluation or appreciation of the exchange rate will reduce exports more for firms producing high price elasticity goods than those producing innovative or high-quality goods, for which the price elasticity of demand is lower.

These selective effects are important and must be considered in formulating policy choices. However, for reasons of brevity we will not discuss them here, although the reader is invited to pursue the study of these issues.

11.2   The monetary economy

In chapter 3, we discussed the importance of money in the operation of the economy and argued that in order to understand the reasons for and nature of the instability of a capitalist system it is absolutely necessary to introduce the hypothesis of a **monetary economy**. Let us briefly review the characteristics of money before examining financial intermediaries.

It is well known that the first and most important function of money is its role as a **medium of exchange** or **means of payment**: compared with a barter economy money reduces *transaction costs* (the time and effort spent searching for a suitable counterpart).

A second function of money is its role as a **unit of account**: it is the 'good' in which all prices are calculated and values are stated. Note that the good used as a means of payment may not necessarily be the same as that used as a unit of account.[2]

Money's third function is to serve as a **store of value** – i.e. a means for transferring purchasing power in time, in association with or as an alternative to other financial and real assets.

Money has an essentially *fiduciary* nature. Throughout history, the attribution of a monetary function to one or another means has always been of a conventional and fiduciary nature:[3] 'the necessary condition for the performance of this exchange function is general acceptability in settlement of debt' and this 'falls within that perplexing but fascinating group of phenomena which is affected by self-justifying beliefs' (Newlyn, 1962, p. 2).

---

[1] We have **cross-subsidisation** when profits in one sector are used to finance investment in another sector in order to sustain the growth of the firm in this second area. The term is also used when profits from one line of business are used to cover losses in other activities resulting from, for example, aggressive pricing policies (*predatory pricing practices*) aimed at eliminating competition. Cross-subsidisation and self-financing can be used by large firms, especially when they are part of financial groups.

[2] With reference to modern economies, for example, accounts might be kept in dollars or gold while transactions are settled in yen, pounds sterling or euros. The existence of different 'goods' for different monetary functions can cause problems if the ratio between them is not constant. An example of a pure accounting currency is the guinea, an English gold coin that has not been minted since 1813 but remained in use as a unit of account in Great Britain until the 1970s. Some prices were expressed in guineas, even though payment could be made only in the existing currency (pounds sterling and coins), at a ratio of 1.05 pounds to the guinea. The euro, too, was a mere unit of account until 2002 (see chapter 16).

[3] This is the case even when the use of a currency is imposed by an outside authority, such as the state or when this authority recognises some currency as **legal tender** for the settlement of debts. Such status may help a particular means of payment gain acceptance, although this is not fully guaranteed (or welcomed) in all circumstances.

Once agents have come to trust some means, it is accepted as a medium of exchange and as a store of value, and transactions are stipulated in terms of it. The form of money has changed over time. The earliest forms were **commodities** (cattle, shells, etc.), followed by metal coins and then by paper money (banknotes) and bank money. In order to understand the evolution of money, and especially the emergence of modern money (which is primarily bank money), we will introduce the concept of *financial intermediation* (see section 11.3). Acceptance of bank money is in fact prompted by the rise of institutions able to *generate trust*, such as financial intermediaries.

11.3 Financial intermediaries

In an economy the moment incomes are received and the moment they are spent do not coincide; if the division of labour is well developed, the agents who own goods do not coincide with the agents who demand those goods either. In a monetary economy, 'the participants in the production process' receive a quantity of money[4] granting them *purchasing power* over goods. Some participants (typically, households) demand only part of the goods they are entitled to buy (consumption) while other agents (typically, firms and often the government) demand more than they have been assigned in the distribution of income, in order to expand their productive capacity (investment). We thus have some agents with a *savings surplus* and others with a *savings deficit* (or excess spending). Satisfying both the saving plans of one group and the spending plans of the other depends on the existence of financial instruments, primarily **direct credit**, through which agents with a surplus can temporarily transfer purchasing power to those in deficit.

Direct credit is traded in the **financial markets** or **capital markets**, and financial systems in which they are the dominant form are called **market-centred**. Financial markets can be divided into **primary markets** (those for new issues of securities), **secondary markets** (where existing securities are traded) and **derivatives markets** (markets in financial assets whose value is specifically linked to that of other assets; we discussed derivatives traded on international markets in subsection 10.1.2).

However, direct credit, in the form of loans, bonds or shares (issued by firms and subscribed by households) has a limited range of action if, as happens in the real world, there is a considerable difference between the terms (interest rates and/or maturities) requested by the two groups or if there are market imperfections. This is especially so if information costs are high, since agents do not have full information in a broad and differentiated market.

More specifically, the two sides will desire different *loan maturities*. Creditors will seek to shorten them as much as possible in order to reduce their exposure to insolvency risk, which rises as maturities lengthen. By contrast, borrowers will prefer to lengthen maturities until they match the time needed for the investment to produce the desired

---

[4] The actual type of money is irrelevant here. It may simply be some commodity to which monetary functions have been attributed.

gains, in order to avoid the risk of not being re-financed when the initial shorter-term credit matures. Obviously, this fundamental divergence can be bridged by increasing the price paid by borrowers (i.e. raising the interest rate), which will incorporate a premium for the risk associated with a longer maturity. However, this solution would be very costly for debtors.

Financial intermediaries[5] – and with them **indirect credit** from holders of surplus savings to financial intermediaries and then to those with a savings deficit[6] – can lower the cost of credit for essentially three reasons:

(1) There are **economies of scale** and **economies of scope** in acquiring savings from surplus agents and channelling them to deficit agents. Economies of scale are linked not only to the reduction of management costs permitted by specialisation and standardisation of operations, but also to the existence of fixed costs for information on the *ex ante* riskiness of firms and specific investment projects as well as on the *ex post* risk associated with the actual use that has been made of the loan funds. This means that financial intermediaries are in some way involved in *certifying borrower quality*. Economies of scope are connected with the benefits (externalities) produced by lending in one field (e.g. short-term credit) for lending in another (e.g. long-term credit): this is clear from the fact that, for example, information costs are not only fixed (which gives rise to *economies of scale*) but are also joint costs for the different types of credit (*scope economies*).

(2) Intermediaries also have scope for **maturity transformation** thanks to the economies of scale associated with the law of large numbers: since not all suppliers of funds will demand repayment on maturity,[7] intermediaries can lend money for a longer period of time, keeping only a small precautionary reserve (*excess* or *free reserves*). Moreover, the insolvency risk of some borrowers can also be negatively correlated with that of others, thus lowering the overall level of risk.

(3) The presence of financial intermediaries makes it easier **to diversify the risk** of individual portfolios. Owing to the relatively small size of their wealth, most surplus agents could at most lend to only a few borrowers. This would increase the insolvency risk they face compared with that of a more diversified portfolio, prompting surplus agents to demand a higher interest rate. Intermediaries make it possible to pool small individual savings and thereby diversify lending, reducing overall risk and, therefore, the interest rate.

The direct and indirect credit granted in a given economy constitutes the **financial liabilities** of that economy. For a closed economy, total financial assets must equal total

---

[5] Among the initial contributions to the concept of financial intermediary was the Radcliffe Report (see the Committee on the Working of the Monetary System, 1959).

[6] Economic systems in which the role of financial intermediaries is especially well developed are known as **credit-centred**. The importance of financial intermediaries is greatest in Germany, which as we will see is dominated by the universal bank (although its role is declining). Anglo-American financial systems are market-centred, and specialised banks prevail there (see p. 253).

[7] Or immediately, if the funds must be repaid on demand.

financial liabilities. This remains true for an open economy if we include 'the Rest of the World' as an institutional sector.

Financial intermediaries, financial assets (or liabilities) and the related markets form the **financial system** or the **financial structure** of an economy. Albeit in different ways, direct credit (financial markets) and indirect credit (financial intermediaries) perform the task of spreading information and channelling purchasing power. They are, therefore, instruments for allocating and controlling credit.

The presence of financial intermediaries thus enriches not only the set of economic agents but also the ways financing can be provided. It generates a variety of financial instruments that differ in form,[8] maturity or other terms, as well as by issuer, i.e. the agent that assumes the liability either directly (if the agent operates in the deficit sector) or indirectly (if the agent is a financial intermediary).

The specialisation of financial intermediaries varies according to national characteristics and historical circumstances. *Specialisation* may take place according to borrowers' branch of activity (lending to agriculture, real estate, film companies, etc.), the maturity of the loans granted or received (short, medium or long-term credit) or the form of credit usually granted (in some countries, such as the United Kingdom, this led to the emergence of commercial banks, discount houses, accepting houses, etc.).

Of particular importance is the specialisation or *separation* between short-term credit and medium and long-term credit that characterises **English-type banks**, in contrast to **universal** or **German-type banks**, in which there is no such separation. The universal bank was partly blamed for the financial instability of the 1920s, which saw the collapse of a number of such institutions. More recently, however, the universal bank model has been adopted in the European Union.

11.4   Money as a liability of financial intermediaries

In the evolution from money with an *intrinsic value* (various forms of **commodity** money and specie in particular) to token money, money has become nothing more than a *liability* (with or without paper form) issued by a financial intermediary. Historical circumstances, often (but not always) associated with the shared belief in the reliability and solvency of a particular financial intermediary, have led to the acceptance of its *sight* or *short-term liabilities* as a means of payment.

There are two types of money and two corresponding types of financial intermediary: *banknotes*, which are created by central banks, and *deposits*, which are created by banks.

Banknotes are *legal tender*. After a period in which numerous issuing institutions coexisted, banknotes are now issued under a monopoly (originally as a government concession, now by law). Until 1914, and in some countries even after the First World War for a certain period, it was possible to convert banknotes into specie or bullion (see

---

[8] This may or may not be represented by a marketable security. If it is, we can speak of **securitisation**.

chapter 16). With the end of convertibility, the acceptance of banknotes was imposed by law (**fiat money**).[9]

Bank deposits are the second type of financial liability used as money. In this case, their acceptance as money is still based on an entirely fiduciary relationship that has not been imposed by an outside authority. The circulation of bank deposits, necessary to their monetary role, takes place through cheques and giro transfers.

In recent years, banks have introduced new liabilities that have assumed an important role thanks to their considerable liquidity and can therefore be included in the definition of money: bank fund-raising through repurchase agreements; bank certificates of deposit and banker's acceptances.

Financial innovation is partly the result of private agents' attempt to elude credit regulations, such as compulsory reserve requirements and lending ceilings, which we will discuss later. In other cases, it involves creating new liquidity instruments to improve the performance of the financial system by meeting agents' needs more appropriately.

Repurchase agreements are temporary operations in securities consisting in the spot sale of government securities by one party to another and the simultaneous forward repurchase of the same securities by the original seller at a stated price. Banks can use repurchase agreements with their customers to raise funds.

Certificates of deposit are negotiable securities issued by banks representing time deposits.

Banker's acceptances, or bills drawn on a bank by a customer, are not a new instrument. However, since the mid-1970s they have been fairly widely used in some countries as a substitute for other forms of bank credit in order to avoid regulations limiting lending growth.

The existence of numerous liquidity instruments makes it necessary to introduce a variety of empirical definitions of money (*monetary aggregates*). The latter are often redefined to take account of financial innovation. We currently use a number of monetary aggregates, although definitions vary from country to country.

At the beginning of the 1990s, in the United States the aggregate M1 included current account deposits and traveller's cheques in addition to currency (i.e. banknotes and coins); M2 comprised M1 plus other chequeable assets, small-denomination certificates of deposit, overnight repurchase agreements and overnight Eurodollar funds; M3 comprised M2 plus other less liquid assets such as large-denomination certificates of deposit, long-term repurchase agreements and Eurodollar term deposits. In 2004, three monetary aggregates are used under EMU: M1, defined as currency in circulation and current account deposits; M2, which includes M1, deposits with an agreed maturity of up to two years and deposits redeemable at notice of up to three months; and M3, which includes M2, repurchase agreements, money market fund shares/units and money market paper and debt securities up to two years.

---

[9] The term 'fiat money' indicates that, without the original fiduciary relationships, something becomes money as a result of *government imposition*; literally, it is 'created out of nothing'. Nevertheless, its acceptance and the spread of its use still depend to some degree on individuals' willingness to accept the currency on a fiduciary basis.

11.5   The central bank and monetary base

Banks to which the government privilege of issuing banknotes had been granted initially continued to perform ordinary banking activities. Subsequently, this privilege, the close relationship with government and the centralisation of metal reserves gave the banks of issue a special position compared with other banks. Nevertheless, they often continued to act as commercial enterprises and maintained their private-sector legal status (Goodhart, 1988).

For reasons that we will elaborate on later (see section 11.7), the evolution of financial systems mentioned in section 11.4 can give rise to increased risk of instability. In particular, there is a danger that banks' reserves might not be sufficient to cope with unexpected withdrawals. Insolvency can be avoided if the issuing institution provides banks with *liquidity*, acting as a **lender of last resort** or **banker's bank**. Central banks in the leading countries (e.g. the United States and the United Kingdom) perform this function. A major exception was Germany, where the Bundesbank had a totally discretionary attitude towards granting credit of last resort. This is because it was felt that preserving the stability of the financial system conflicted with the Bundesbank's primary objective of regulating the money supply, i.e. ensuring a stable value for the Deutsche Mark. The European Central Bank (ECB) is largely based on the Bundesbank model, but provides overnight lender of last resort services through the 'marginal lending facility' (see section 18.4).

Central bank functions also include bank regulation and supervision to ensure compliance with sound management rules and thereby guarantee the stability of the financial system; bank regulation is part of the regulation of the financial system (box 11.1).

Box 11.1.   Financial regulation: why and how?

We address two questions here:

(a) Why does the financial system require public intervention at the microeconomic and macroeconomic level?
(b) Why does the financial system in particular require regulation, and what sort of regulation is needed?

The justification of government intervention

Regulation of the financial market and financial intermediaries is driven by two characteristics of the market:

(1) The vulnerability of the financial system to *microeconomic failures* in terms of inefficient resource allocation and inequitable outcomes
(2) The vulnerability of the system to *instability*, which gives regulation a role at the macroeconomic level as well.

The *microeconomic justification* for public intervention in the financial system is represented by the need to compensate for the informational asymmetry between the various parties involved in financial transactions. In general, the less well-informed party is the creditor, who therefore must to some extent be protected from the debtor. Operators such as financial intermediaries who are both debtors and creditors have more information than savers.

Such asymmetry may:

(a) permit fraud or, in any case, harm the interests of the counterparty, who may not receive full information on, for example, the terms of a contract

(b) lead to failures in identifying the true scope of the risks involved, which are all the greater the more the effects of such failures can be shifted to others.

These outcomes of *information asymmetry* can make it difficult to engage in finance in an efficient manner and may undermine the role of the financial market and financial intermediaries (such as banks) as instruments of corporate governance.

From the *macroeconomic standpoint*, the 'failure' of markets and financial intermediaries is associated with the possibility of *systemic crises* triggered by the insolvency of financial and non-financial operators. Systemic crises are situations in which losses accumulate following an event (normally default or insolvency) originating on one part of the economic system that triggers, as in a chain reaction of falling dominoes, a series of successive losses within the financial system (Kaufman, 2000). Systemic crises are made possible by three characteristics of the financial system:

(1) First and foremost, the high degree of *financial integration* among contemporary economies, which can be measured by the ratio of financial liabilities in an economy to GDP: economic agents have a large number of reciprocal debtor and creditor relationships.

(2) One part of the financial system – *banking* – is inherently vulnerable owing to the mismatch between the maturity of its liabilities (mainly demand liabilities) and that of its assets (normally long term). This can lead to *liquidity shortages* that may prompt a run on banks to withdraw deposits, as we saw in Argentina in 2001.

(3) The *information asymmetry* that dominates in the financial system prevents depositors from discriminating between illiquid but solvent debtors and liquid but insolvent ones, thereby amplifying systemic crises.

Financial crises can give rise to instability in the economy, which leads to unemployment and a decline in economic activity.

The scope for and limitations of self-regulation

Before we can claim a need for public intervention (in particular, regulation) to prevent the microeconomic and macroeconomic failures we have discussed, we must examine the possibility that the market can equip itself with some form of self-regulation that can *prevent failures*, or at least cure their effects.

The necessity of maintaining a *good reputation* in the market is often a strong antidote to the abuses and distortions that information asymmetry can engender. Reputation is especially important when companies are rated by specialised agencies, such as Standard & Poor's or Moody's.[a] In addition, individual financial intermediaries or associations of intermediaries could adopt explicit or implicit codes of conduct and self-regulation, following the economic logic of the quality seals used in other industries.

The scope of the positive effects of reputation and self-regulation is, however, necessarily limited. First, building a reputation or self-regulating is voluntary.[b] Second, the individual players in a self-regulatory regime tend to consider only some of the consequences of their behaviour, ignoring others, such as the risk of systemic instability. Moreover, the temptation to pursue short-run profitability or to act as a free rider with respect to self-regulatory codes is high – especially at times when competition is fierce – for weaker operators or those who have a strong preference for short-term gains or, simply, pursue gains using dishonest means (as testified to by myriad examples, with Enron and Parmalat among the most recent cases[c]). Finally, self-regulatory codes adopted by companies governed by shareholders' agreements or majority shareholders with more than 50 per cent control tend to offer only mild or illusory protection for minority interests.

Why regulate and what sort of regulation?

Now that we have examined microeconomic and macroeconomic market failures and determined the inadequacy of private-sector solutions, we need to clarify the reasons for specific intervention such as regulation. Alternatives to regulation include the establishment of public enterprises, in the banking and insurance sectors. The reasons for and against regulation were discussed at length in chapter 7. The particular features of the issue we are dealing with here add two elements to the analysis conducted in that chapter. Specifically, they involve rules aimed at:

(a) Ensuring the *transparency* of the position of firms that turn to the financial market for funds and guaranteeing the proper functioning of the financial markets. These rules emphasise preserving the allocative function of financial markets and protecting the weaker counterparties in transactions.
(b) Guaranteeing the *proper functioning* of banks and other financial intermediaries. In addition to safeguarding the allocative function of the market, regulation of financial intermediaries seeks to ensure the stability of the financial system, which can easily be jeopardised by poor management at intermediaries.

As regards point (a), we must first specify that the proper functioning of financial institutions and markets requires that *information asymmetry* be reduced. As noted before, this can be done in various ways, which differ in relation to the system of corporate governance in place.

In the German–Japanese model, it is the direct commitment of the financial intermediary (bank) or other agents holding the controlling interest that dominates. In countries such as Germany, which, beginning in the second half of the 1990s saw the emergence of broader share ownership, the need for greater guarantees in corporate management to protect all investors began to be felt more acutely, with the aim of increasing transparency. In February 2002 a public corporate governance code was issued, although its adoption was left voluntary on a **comply-or-explain** basis.[d]

In the Anglo-American system, where control by single shareholders (especially financial intermediaries) is less common, it is essential that the allocation of savings be guided by accurate information available to the public in general. This requires *transparent and reliable accounting*. Clever accounting tricks or outright fraud not only have an adverse impact on the position of individual financial intermediaries (or, more generally, other investors) by inducing them to invest in firms that they erroneously believe to be sound, they also undermine confidence and the stability of the entire financial system.

The need for greater transparency has emerged with force in recent years in the United States: the US financial market registered heavy losses following the collapse in confidence in the wake of a series of scandals and frauds at a string of major corporations. The managers of these firms engaged in fraudulent accounting, which was either tolerated or missed by internal control bodies and external auditors, as in the case of Enron. The concern that the information held by the market for other companies might also prove false helped drive down share prices on Wall Street and, in consequence, on the main exchanges in other countries as well. US policymakers reacted with the introduction in 2002 of new, more stringent accounting standards, more severe penalties for accounting fraud by company directors and new powers for supervisors such as the Securities and Exchange Commission (SEC).

At the same time, however, transparency is necessary even where the financial markets have a less prominent role than in the Anglo-American system. The aim is to safeguard all those who have relationships with a company, such as creditors, employees and suppliers, as underscored in the upheavals at the largely family-controlled Italian firm Parmalat.

The desire to enhance transparency in order to increase the efficiency of financial markets lies behind the European Union's enactment of a regulation in 2002 requiring all listed companies to adopt the International Accounting Standards (IAS) by 2005 in drafting their consolidated financial statements. The member states may extend the new rules to cover the individual accounts of listed firms and those of unlisted firms. However, the laws governing accounting fraud in the member states differ.

In addition to the need for transparency regarding the activity of borrowers, it is also necessary to ensure the proper functioning of markets, such as the stock market, where financial assets are traded and a variety of persons operate, many of whom are often poorly informed. Regulation governs the way in which information is provided by borrowers,[e] the ways in which new investors can take controlling interests in companies (public tender offers) and the price formation mechanisms for the assets involved in transactions.

As regards point (b), banks, insurance companies and other financial intermediaries must be managed in such a manner as to safeguard the efficiency and stability of the financial system and foster the growth of the economy.

Beginning in the mid-1980s, Europe and other countries around the world shifted from **structural supervision** (controlling the structure of the banking system through rules governing the degree of concentration, ownership structures, etc.) to **prudential supervision** (based on minimum capital requirements for banks). At the Bank for International Settlements (BIS), in 1975 the Group of Ten (G10), i.e. the ten leading industrial countries, drew up rules governing capital requirements for banks. Known as the **Basle Capital Accord**, the original rules are now being revised, with the new requirements due to come into force at the end of 2006. The aims of the new regulations are to foster the stability of banks, to establish capital requirements on the basis of the more accurate and comprehensive measurement of the risks taken on by banks, to create a level competitive playing field and extend the adoption of the rules to banks outside the restricted group of large international banks of the G10 countries. The Accord defines the various types of risk faced by banks, establishes solvency ratios and supplements the quantitative capital adequacy requirements (the first 'pillar' of the regime) with prudential controls (the second pillar) and disclosure requirements (the third pillar).

Given the specific nature of non-bank financial intermediation, the regulatory approach to this sector has special features that, for the sake of brevity, we do not address here.

Notes:

a There is, however, a possible contradiction between the desire for an *efficient allocation of resources* (which would encourage rating activities) and that of *macroeconomic stability* (the downgrading of financial intermediaries or securities as a result of a deterioration in economic conditions) could in fact accentuate the crisis; see Ferri, Liu and Stiglitz, 1999).

b This does not necessarily mean that enforcement is less strict. Severity depends, on the one hand, on the relative strength of the pressure of other operators or associations and, on the other, the efficiency with which public regulations are applied (Padoa Schioppa, 2002).

c Enron is a major US energy firm that used elaborate accounting schemes and complex financial structures to mislead investors about the profitability and financial soundness of the company. It also used its money to buy influence and power, forge US energy policy and elude regulation. Parmalat is a family-controlled Italian multinational that over the years engaged in fraudulent accounting and siphoned off company funds to owners and managers.

d Under this principle, anyone who does not adopt the code must explain why.

e In addition to ensuring transparency, the rules also have to prevent the improper use of confidential information (*insider trading*).

Responsibility for banking supervision can be assigned to the central bank (as in the United States) or to another body. These bodies often conduct supervision of non-bank financial intermediaries (NBFIs), such as insurance companies and pension funds. This is the arrangement adopted in many countries, such as the United Kingdom and Japan[10] (see box 11.2).

Box 11.2.   Supervising financial activity: how many regulators should there be?

Financial activity needs to be regulated because of *information asymmetry*. The fact that one party knows more than the other makes it possible to hide fraudulent activity or disguise the true extent of the risks taken on by a financial intermediary. It may also mask the risks associated with the operation of financial markets, with a potentially damaging impact on *macroeconomic stability* (financial instability) and the *efficient allocation of resources*. In particular, it may impede the efficient operation of the corporate governance functions performed by financial intermediaries and markets themselves. The need for regulation has grown stronger in the wake of the many recent cases of fraudulent corporate conduct, such as the Enron affair in the United States in 2001 and the Parmalat case in Italy in 2003.

The tools of *financial regulation* consist of rules designed to ensure the transparency of the position of firms that tap the financial markets for capital and to guarantee the proper operation of banks and other financial intermediaries. Compliance with these rules is normally monitored by specific independent regulatory authorities.

The issue we address here regards the number of bodies to which responsibility for such supervision is assigned. Countries have taken a wide variety of approaches, ranging from the (rare) extreme of complete centralisation with a single regulator to the other (less rare) extreme of extensive decentralisation, with the middle ground occupied by the most frequent case of a limited number of regulatory bodies.

The United States boasts a large number of regulators (with different, and multiple, bodies overseeing banks, insurance companies, pension funds and markets), in addition to the self-regulatory bodies of the larger financial markets themselves. The functional overlap is a deliberate policy choice, the idea being to stimulate *beneficial competition* among regulators. At the opposite extreme, since 1997 the United Kingdom has concentrated all responsibility – with the exception of protecting systemic stability, which remains in the hands of the Bank of England – in a single new body, the Financial Services Authority (FSA). Japan and Germany have followed similar approaches. Other European countries have arrangements

---

[10] The need for regulation and supervision of the financial system by an external entity is examined by Goodhart (1988) in both analytical and historical terms. All the issues we address in this chapter closely involve the institutional sphere, which is undergoing far-reaching change.

that lie between these extremes. In Italy, various authorities – although not as many as in the United States – oversee the banking system, the insurance industry, pension funds, companies and financial markets, but the model adopted is likely to be changed as a consequence of the Parmalat affair.

In the European Union, member states supervision remains the preserve of *national authorities*, with no coordination at the European level (although national authorities can establish forms of bilateral or multilateral cooperation), and is separate from monetary policy functions, which are carried out by the ECB (see section 18.4). The European Union has moved to establish minimum harmonisation of the basic rules of prudential supervision, in line with the standards of the Basle Committee on Banking Supervision, and in coming years it is likely that the scope of *harmonisation* will be expanded.

Both extreme solutions of complete centralisation and extensive decentralisation have their merits and shortcomings. There are essentially two arguments in favour of *centralisation*:

(1) A single regulator has a *global view* of the financial market, reaping economies of scale, which are reflected in lower costs for the entities and markets subject to supervision.
(2) The mobility of the operational and geographical confines between intermediaries, markets and financial instruments reduces the effectiveness of *segmenting regulators*.

The arguments in favour of *decentralising* regulatory functions include:

(1) Supervision of the various activities that are conducted in the financial market involves *specialised functions* despite the fuzziness of borders within finance. For example, the business of banking retains specific features that differ from those that characterise the operations of insurance companies or pension funds, and so monitoring the sector calls for different skills and rules;
(2) Having a variety of regulatory bodies reduces the risk of the *concentration of administrative power*, thereby preventing abuse and politicisation.

No solution comes without costs: both centralisation and decentralisation have advantages and disadvantages. The most appropriate solution will differ, depending on actual financial structures and the way policymakers want those structures to evolve. In any case, regulatory responsibility for safeguarding the stability of the financial system – or at least banks – should be assigned to the body in charge of monetary policy, given the complementarity of the two functions with regard to understanding monetary, banking and financial operations and the link between the stability of individual intermediaries and the stability of the system as a whole.

Less clear-cut is the connection between supervisory action and antimonopoly functions. Some argue that there is no trade-off between the two, since competition is a necessary (although not sufficient) condition for ensuring the soundness of the banking industry and financial stability. However, in some countries, Italy included, for many years there was virtually no competition among banks, a condition that was evidently felt to be helpful for managing monetary policy by the Bank of Italy, which was assigned the role of antimonopoly supervision for banking. This situation might have been assessed differently had safeguarding competition been assigned, as it has for industries other than banking, to the Competition Authority.

In the event, the concomitant existence of numerous financial regulators requires that their activities be coordinated, which, at the very least, calls for the exchange of information and policy views.

The regulatory function can complement the central bank's lender of last resort role. The existence of such a lender could create a form of moral hazard because the banks, feeling themselves protected ('insured') by the central bank, might engage in excessively risky transactions. Regulation and supervision by the central bank can reduce this risk. The regulatory function often includes requiring banks to maintain minimum *compulsory reserves* in addition to their excess reserves. The original aim of this regulation was to protect depositors, but compulsory reserves now have only the function of regulating money supply. The financial assets that can be used to constitute these reserves make up **monetary base** (or **high-powered money**). It includes all sight liabilities issued by the monetary authorities as well as others that can be readily converted into such liabilities.

Monetary base meets the need of the banks to maintain excess reserves as well as comply with the reserve requirement (see section 13.7). Moreover, since monetary base includes legal tender, it serves the public (i.e. the non-bank sector) as a stock of *circulating currency*. The *uses* of monetary base (which represent the demand for monetary base) are the free and compulsory reserves of banks (**monetary base held by banks**) and the **currency in circulation** (or **monetary base held by the public**).

The *sources* of monetary base creation – which determine its supply – correspond to the institutional sectors that act as counterparties in central bank lending operations, mainly, the foreign sector, the Treasury, open market operations and bank refinancing:

(1) The central bank creates (destroys) monetary base through the foreign sector when it acquires (sells) reserves (mainly gold and foreign reserve currencies), which constitute a loan to that sector or an asset (gold) that can be used in transactions with it. This always happens independently of the will of the central bank when there is a balance of payments surplus (deficit) in a fixed-exchange rate regime. It does so to maintain a fixed exchange rate. When there is an excess supply of (demand for) foreign exchange, the exchange rate would appreciate (depreciate). To satisfy that excess supply (demand) the central bank must demand (supply) foreign exchange and supply (demand) monetary base.

With totally flexible exchange rates the central bank does not intervene to ensure a fixed exchange rate and again it does not control the monetary base.

(2) Monetary base can be created by the Treasury, since the Treasury itself can issue coins (and/or notes) and the central bank may grant it credit by purchasing government securities on the *primary market* (i.e. at issue) or in other ways (e.g. special loans). The EU agreements signed in Maastricht (1992) prohibit central banks from financing the Treasury (see chapter 16).

(3) The central bank can create or destroy monetary base with purchases or sales of government securities on the secondary market (**open market operations**, OMOs): if it purchases government securities on the secondary market it creates monetary base; if it sells, it destroys monetary base. OMOs can be outright sales or purchases (when the effect of the change in monetary base lasts until the security matures). They can also be **temporary operations**[11] (such as repurchase agreements).

(4) In its capacity as the 'banker's bank', the central bank creates monetary base through refinancing – i.e. providing finance to the credit system by rediscounting bills or providing advances against securities. The central bank can regulate access to credit of last resort by altering the terms on which it will supply this credit, primarily by changing the *minimum lending rate* (or *official discount rate*) and the rate on advances (the rate on the marginal lending facility in EMU). The central bank sets the terms of the credit it provides but the initiative in drawing on that credit is taken by the banks, which can decide whether or not to use the facility, depending on its terms and external circumstances. Consequently, the central bank's role in monetary base control emerges most clearly during moments of market tension, when the banks are forced to draw on central bank credit.

The total supply of monetary base through different sources should equal its total demand, i.e. its *total uses*. Obviously, changes in supply and demand should also be equal. They give the balance of monetary base, which can be expressed as follows: $BP_m + TFIN + OMOs + BR = \Delta PMB + \Delta BMB$, where the symbols indicate, respectively, the change in gold and foreign reserve currencies (in monetary terms), change in Treasury financing, OMOs, change in bank refinancing, change in the monetary base held by the public, change in the monetary base (i.e. reserves) held by banks.

11.6   Banks and deposits

11.6.1   *Banks' balance sheet and the deposit multiplier*

As mentioned earlier, bank liabilities (**deposits**) are another means of payment (in addition to legal tender and, more generally, monetary base) and are conventionally assigned a pre-eminent role among the liabilities of financial intermediaries. However, this form of money is not independent of monetary base. To see this more clearly, let us first take a look at a simplified bank balance sheet.

---

[11] These are also called **reverse transactions**, as opposed to **permanent** or **outright transactions**.

Table 11.1 *The balance sheet of a bank*

Assets	Liabilities
BMB	*D*
CR	

In table 11.1 *BMB* is the stock of monetary base held by banks in the form of excess and compulsory reserves (bank monetary base or bank reserves); *CR* are loans to customers; *D* are deposits.[12] For simplicity, the balance sheet does not show other potentially significant items, such as securities and debts with the central bank (bank refinancing).

Let us now see how, under certain conditions, deposits depend on the amount of monetary base held by banks.[13]

First, we assume the following strict behavioural rules:

(1) The public wants to maintain a fixed ratio between its holdings of monetary base (or currency in circulation), *PMB*, and deposits, *D*; let this ratio be *h*, such that:

$$PMB = h \cdot D \qquad 0 \leq h \tag{11.1}$$

(2) Banks maintain a fixed ratio between monetary base held as excess and compulsory reserves, *BMB*, and deposits; let this ratio be *j*, such that:

$$BMB = j \cdot D \qquad 0 < j < 1 \tag{11.2}$$

Let us now state the equilibrium condition between monetary base demand (i.e. its uses) and supply (the total of all its sources, *MB*):

$$MB = PMB + BMB \tag{11.3}$$

Substituting (11.1) and (11.2) into (11.3) we have:

$$MB = hD + jD = D(h + j) \tag{11.4}$$

from which:

$$D = \frac{1}{h + j} MB \tag{11.5}$$

Under the assumed conditions, there is a fixed ratio between monetary base and deposits – and, in fact, if the total of *h* and *j* is (as it is in reality) less than 1, we can say

---

[12] These include current account, or demand, deposits (checking accounts or sight deposits in the United States) and time deposits (savings deposits in the United States).

[13] In what follows we will refer to the banking system as a whole; alternatively we assume that only one bank operates.

that deposits are a multiple of monetary base. The ratio $1/(h+j)$ is therefore called the **deposit multiplier**.

If we define the money supply as currency in circulation (i.e. monetary base held by the public) plus deposits, we can express the money supply as a function of monetary base, thus enriching the usual *IS-LM* framework. If:

$$L_S = PMB + D \qquad (11.6)$$

where L_S is the total money supply, recalling from (11.1) that $PMB = hD$, we obtain:

$$L_S = hD + D = D(1 + h) \qquad (11.7)$$

But, since

$$D = \frac{1}{h+j}MB$$

we have:

$$L_S = \frac{1+h}{h+j}MB \qquad (11.8)$$

where $(1 + h)/(h + j)$ is the **money multiplier**, which is larger the smaller are h and j.[14]

We can easily supplement the *IS-LM* model by introducing an additional relation such as (11.8). L_S is thus no longer an exogenous variable (possibly an instrument), but becomes an endogenous, 'irrelevant' variable. However, new variables are introduced that can be used as instruments: in particular, MB and j. Even h might be used as such, since the monetary authorities can influence it by, for example, introducing changes in the payment system, which, obviously, operate over the long run.[15]

The relationship between monetary base and deposits, which we have now derived in a mechanical way, can easily be grasped more intuitively. We continue to assume the second behavioural rule expressed by (11.2) and assume $h = 0$, i.e. that the public holds no monetary base, all of which instead goes to the banking system. In other words, the public uses bank money only.

Now suppose that a quantity MB of monetary base is created.[16] Since the public does not want to hold cash, the monetary base is deposited in a bank (the **primary deposit**, $D_1 = MB$). The bank must comply with the reserve requirement and in any case follows behavioural rule (2) above, and therefore retains $BMB_1 = j \cdot D_1 = j \cdot MB$, while lending $CR_1 = (1 - j) \cdot MB$. The loan to the public is transformed into another deposit, D_2, of the same amount, i.e. $(1 - j) \cdot MB$, since the public does not want to hold any monetary base, by assumption. The new deposit is called a **derived deposit**, since it is generated by a loan granted by the bank.

Having received an additional deposit and continuing to follow rule (2), the bank will hold monetary base equal to $BMB_2 = j \cdot D_2 = j \cdot (1 - j) \cdot MB$ and make a loan

---

[14] In the case of j, the inverse relation is clear. Readers familiar with calculus can also verify that the derivative of the multiplier with respect to h is positive.

[15] An example of developments that would lower h is the spread of bank branches and credit cards.

[16] MB can either be the absolute amount of or the change in monetary base.

Table 11.2 *Stages of the deposit multiplication process*

Stages of the process	Liabilities	Assets	
	Deposits	Monetary base	Loans
1	$D_1 = MB$	$BMB_1 = jMB$	$CR_1 = (1-j)MB$
2	$D_2 = (1-j)MB$	$BMB_2 = j(1-j)MB$	$CR_2 = (1-j)^2 MB$
3	$D_3 = (1-j)^2 MB$	$BMB_3 = j(1-j)^2 MB$	$CR_3 = (1-j)^3 MB$
n	$D_n = (1-j)^{n-1} MB$	$BMBn = j(1-j)^{n-1} MB$	$CR_n = (1-j)^n MB$

equal to $CR_2 = (1-j) \cdot D_2 = (1-j)^2 \cdot MB$. The loan is again transformed into a deposit, $D_3, = (1-j)^2 \cdot MB$, of which the bank holds $BMB_3 = j \cdot D_3 = j \cdot (1-j)^2 \cdot MB$ and lends $CR_3 = (1-j) \cdot D_3 = (1-j)^3 \cdot MB$, and so on. In the nth round the bank will receive a deposit equal to $D_n = (1-j)^{n-1} \cdot MB$, retain $BMB_n = j \cdot (1-j)^{n-1} \cdot MB$ and lend $CR_n = (1-j)^n \cdot MB$. Its balance sheet will appear as shown in table 11.2.[17]

Each item in the balance sheet is given by the sum of a geometric progression with a ratio of $(1-j)$. Total deposits, D, are equal to:

$$D = D_1 + D_2 + D_3 + \cdots + D_n =$$
$$= MB + (1-j)MB + (1-j)^2 MB + \cdots + (1-j)^{n-1} MB$$

Recalling that the sum of such a progression is equal to

$$S_n = a_1 \frac{1-q^n}{1-q}$$

where a_1 is the first term and q is the ratio, in our example we have:

$$D = MB \frac{1-(1-j)^n}{1-(1-j)}$$

For $n \to \infty$, $(1-j)^n \to 0$, since $(1-j) < 1$, and thus $D = MB/j$.

Similarly, we can show that $BMB = MB$ and $CR = MB(1-j)/j = MB/j - MB = D - MB$.

Suppose that $MB = 1,000$ and $j = 0.20$. We therefore have $D = 1,000 \cdot 1/0.20 = 5,000$; $CR = 5,000 - 1,000 = 4,000$. The bank's balance sheet will appear as in table 11.3.

If we abandon the hypothesis of $h = 0$ and assume more realistically that $h > 0$, it is easily seen that the potential for creating derived deposits is reduced, since the amounts lent by the bank do not return entirely to the bank (or the banking system) in the form of deposits: a part, h, of the monetary base given by the bank to the borrower is retained by the latter.

---

[17] Unlike real balance sheets, liabilities are shown before assets in order to highlight the sequence of bank transactions.

Table 11.3 *The balance sheet of a bank: II*

Assets		Liabilities	
BMB	1,000	D	5,000
CR	4,000		

The deposit multiplier given by (11.5), i.e. $1/(h + j)$, is larger the smaller are h and j. If h is small, this means that for a given increase in monetary base a larger share flows to the banks; that is, the larger is the percentage of monetary base on which the loan (and deposit) pyramid is constructed.[18] Similarly, a low j means a higher multiplier effect, since the banks recycle a larger percentage of the monetary base at their disposal through loans, which will again return to them in the form of deposits.

If $h = 0.1$, $j = 0.15$ and $MB = 100$, we have $D = [1/(0.1 + 0.15)] \cdot 100 = 4 \cdot 100 = 400$; $PBM = 0.1 \cdot 400 = 40$; $BMB = 0.15 \cdot 400 = 60$; $CR = D - BMB = 400 - 60 = 340$.

This last relation gives the condition for the accounting balance between bank assets and liabilities.

The reader will note that the public made an initial deposit $D_1 = [1/(1 + h)] \cdot MB$ (i.e. $D_1 = [1/(1 + 0.1)] \cdot 100 = [1/1.1] \cdot 100$)[19] and that the bank subsequently made a series of loans well in excess of the amount of this initial deposit (a total of 340). The bank received further deposits after the initial deposit as a *direct consequence of its lending*. This occurred because the public preferred to hold part of its assets as bank liabilities rather than cash.

In short, the ability to lend a larger amount than the initial deposit depends on the fact that each time the bank makes a loan the resulting loss of reserves is small, since a large part of the monetary base transferred to the borrower returns sooner or later to the bank itself, given the public's propensity to use bank money (i.e. deposits) as a means of payment.[20] Granting credit and creating money are two closely related activities in the economy of a bank: *lending* leads to the creation of bank money, i.e. *deposits*, because the public accepts these bank liabilities as a means of payment.

Note that the value of the deposit multiplier shown in (11.5) – where j is the reserve ratio desired by the bank, at a given lending interest rate – is the largest possible. In other words, it is a **potential multiplier** and not necessarily the **actual multiplier**. The

[18] This explains why the monetary instruments available to banks for excess and compulsory reserves are called 'monetary base'.
[19] The public thereby maintains a ratio of h between monetary base and deposits. If the public deposits $[1/(1 + h)] \cdot MB$, it will retain $[h/(1 + h)] \cdot MB$; the ratio between retained monetary base and deposits is equal to h, as can easily be verified.
[20] The situation of non-bank financial intermediaries (NBFIs) differs because they generally do not issue liabilities that can be used as a means of payment. Note that deposits are not necessarily preferred to cash because they yield a return. Often, for example, banks in the English-speaking countries do not pay interest and in fact charge fees for demand deposits, which are those that perform a primary monetary function. Demand deposits are mainly preferred for their convenience and safety.

entire process of (derived) deposit creation begins only as a result of bank lending. In addition, for the process to take place the willingness of banks to grant credit must be matched by the willingness of the public to borrow, as we have implicitly assumed. However, this does not always hold in reality. The demand for credit is a function of the terms on which it is offered, first and foremost the interest rate. If demand falls short of supply at the given interest rate, actual j will be higher than the desired j and the actual multiplier will be lower than the potential one.

On the other hand, the supply of credit is not automatically given either, as is assumed in (11.2). Since the reserve coefficient j includes not only the compulsory reserves, but also a percentage of excess reserves, it must depend on the interest rate on loans, which represents the opportunity cost to banks of holding free reserves. Supply and demand functions for credit should then be introduced.

Similar considerations hold for deposits: in the place of the rigid behaviour implicitly or explicitly assumed in our description of the multiplier process, we need to introduce demand and supply functions for deposits that depend on various factors, including any interest rate paid.

Dealing with this more complex situation does not fall within the scope of this book. Nevertheless, our discussion so far enables us to conclude the following:

(1) The two main forms of money, monetary base and deposits, are linked because the monetary base available to banks is the basis of a *process of credit and deposit creation*.

(2) In the analysis of the deposit multiplier presented here, the relation between monetary base and deposits is constant, but this hypothesis is acceptable only as an initial approximation. In reality, the link exists but is *variable*, since the coefficients in the multiplier can change as a function of the numerous factors underlying the demand and supply functions for credit and deposits.

11.7   Controlling monetary base and the money supply

In section 11.6 we identified the variables on which the money supply, L_S, depends.

We saw in chapter 3 that the money supply plays an important role in determining the level of economic activity and/or prices according to Keynesians and first-generation monetarists. In particular, we know that in Keynes much of the instability of capitalism is linked to the existence of a *monetary economy*. Some authors argue that this is truer the greater the fiduciary nature of the monetary regime. They claim that in the case of a commodity money, crises of confidence could not occur because the value of money was guaranteed by the intrinsic value of the commodity used as a medium of exchange. However, with the introduction of specie it became possible for the ratio between the nominal value of the coin and its intrinsic value to change, which introduced an element of arbitrariness and, hence, confidence. This change was accentuated by the introduction first of banknotes convertible into metal coins, then fiat money and, above all, bank money.

By increasing the *fiduciary character* of money, the developments in monetary systems we have discussed – prompted by the need for greater flexibility in money creation – undoubtedly increase the risk of *instability*. However, it is not true that systems based on commodity or metal money are immune from such instability. In the past, waves of inflation have been caused by events (for example, the discovery of America) that increased the supply of precious metals used as money. The opposite dangers – deflation and reduced economic activity – were avoided only because the growth of output and trade was accompanied by a parallel but incidental increase in the output of precious metals.[21]

We can conclude that, far from professing confidence in automatic monetary systems, policymakers should supervise the financial structure and, in particular, the money supply, contracting or expanding it according to circumstances.[22] In order to do so, however, it is essential to know which of the variables underlying the money supply can be *controlled* by the monetary authorities. We saw in section 11.6 that the quantity of money is an *endogenous variable*, since it depends on monetary base, the ratio between currency in circulation and deposits and the bank reserve ratio. In order for the monetary authorities to control the money supply, they must be able to affect at least one of these variables. Those that seem most open to control in the short run are: (1) monetary base; and (2) the compulsory reserve ratio.

The controllability of these two variables and the consequences for the controllability of the money supply must be discussed in greater detail:

(1) Let us first examine the *controllability of monetary base*. We can provisionally say that monetary base is controllable in principle if policymakers control at least one source of monetary base creation, so as to be able to offset any undesired creation or destruction of monetary base through other channels.

The foreign source is not directly controllable if the exchange rate is rigidly pegged or if it fluctuates freely (as we have seen in section 11.5)[23] unless direct control measures such as administrative constraints on the movement of goods or capital are used.

By contrast, the Treasury source is controllable if there are no special requirements imposed on monetary authorities (as, for example, in Italy until November 1993, where the central bank was obliged to advance the Treasury up to 14 per cent of budget expenditure). Without such obligations, central bank purchases of government securities on the secondary market (OMOs) or even the primary market

---

[21] We refer in particular to the surprising stability of money during the Gold Standard era (from the second half of the 1800s to 1914), when banknotes were convertible into gold on the basis of the fixed gold content of the monetary unit.

[22] An important example of the need to adapt monetary action to circumstances is the expansionary action taken by the Federal Reserve in October 1987, which headed off a liquidity crisis in the presence of capital losses by banks and firms following an unexpected fall in share prices.

[23] Obviously, the channel can be controlled through changes in the exchange rate. Those induced by variations in the parity are attributable to decisions of the government, which is normally responsible for such choices. Changes within the fluctuation bands (in the case of fixed rates) and those under a dirty float are influenced by the central bank.

can be independently decided by the bank. Obviously, in managing such operations, the central bank will try to avoid any failure to place government securities, excessive falls in government securities prices or crises of confidence that undermine the soundness of the financial structure. If, however, the bank must purchase Treasury securities that fail to find buyers or must grant some form of advance to the Treasury, the central bank's only instrument for controlling the Treasury source would be OMOs (i.e. transactions on the secondary market).[24] However, it would be difficult to carry out OMOs under these conditions. Take, for example, the case where a new issue of government securities fails to be fully taken up. If the central bank is required to purchase these securities, it will be forced to issue monetary base. In theory, it could sterilise this creation either by selling the securities purchased or selling other securities in the financial market. However, the first option would be difficult to carry out in reality since the securities were not placed on the primary market, while the second could unbalance the securities market since the central bank has increased demand for an unpopular security (the partially unplaced issue) and, at the same time, decreased demand for an attractive security.

The central bank controls bank refinancing through changes in the interest rates charged on credit of last resort when and within the limits in which it is granted. It thereby influences the availability of *reserves* (i.e. monetary base) for banks. However, changing the official discount rate or that on advances (when these operations are conducted by the central bank) is not always effective, especially for *expansionary* purposes: even if the monetary authorities lower these rates considerably,[25] the banks might not increase their recourse to central bank credit significantly if they already hold excess reserves of liquidity owing to modest credit demand. In this case, demand for refinancing is inelastic to its price, i.e. the interest rate. The degree of controllability of this source of monetary base in a *restrictive* monetary policy is greater: the central bank can always raise the cost of refinancing (or set quantitative restrictions) to reduce monetary base creation to the desired level.[26] However, in this case lack of refinancing raises problems for the equilibrium of banks, and indirectly for other financial intermediaries, which could give rise to liquidity crises and thus undermine the confidence of depositors.

To sum up, in a fixed-exchange regime the monetary authorities do not control the foreign sector unless they use direct controls, they substantially control the Treasury source if there are no requirements to finance the Treasury's borrowing requirement and they control bank refinancing, albeit with some difficulty when they wish to provide an expansionary boost.

---

[24] It was said earlier that open market operations (OMOs) are often considered a separate source of monetary base. In this case, and in the absence of any requirement for the central bank to finance the Treasury, the Treasury source would be controllable only in one way: the *possibility* that the bank could purchase government securities on the primary market.

[25] In any case, nominal rates are normally not negative. Although possible in theory, applying negative rates would amount to subsidising the banks. The only possible justification for negative nominal rates would be high administrative costs for deposit accounts, as happened in Japan toward the end of the 1990s.

[26] This is an example of the **asymmetry of the effects** of expansionary and restrictive monetary policies. This phenomenon has many other interesting features, as we will see shortly.

The controllability of at least one source of monetary base creation should allow overall control, unless the uncontrolled sources are affected by very strong disturbances, in which case the controlled sources might prove insufficiently flexible in the short run.

In particular, under fixed exchange rates, the foreign sector can destroy (or create) any amount of monetary base created (or destroyed) by other sectors under certain conditions. For example, suppose that monetary base is created through OMOs. Interest rates will fall, prompting a *capital outflow* if capital is sufficiently sensitive to interest rates. The balance of payments will deteriorate, causing a reduction in official reserves and destruction of monetary base (see section 11.9).[27]

Control of monetary base does not guarantee control over the money supply. Such control is possible only if the deposit multiplier is constant (i.e. if h and j are given), or if any change in their values is predictable. In reality, however, this is not necessarily so, for the following reasons:

(a) As we said earlier, both h and j (for the part constituted by excess reserves) are sensitive to interest rates on deposits and loans, respectively, which represent the opportunity cost to savers and banks of holding monetary base; the values of h and j will also be influenced by interest rate expectations and will be higher when interest rates are expected to rise, which induces the public and banks to increase liquidity. As a result, an expansionary monetary policy may not be able to increase the money supply if the markets and banks are convinced of its ineffectiveness, since in that case an increase in monetary base induced by the central bank would be offset by an increase in the liquidity preference of the public and the banks. This is an example of the interaction between *public intervention and the behaviour of private agents* through the influence of the former on expectations (see section 4.7).

(b) The coefficient j (again for excess reserves) is also determined by the demand for credit at a given interest rate. We saw that the multiplier mechanism for deposits requires that the public's demand for credit equal the banks' supply of credit. Only in this case will the actual multiplier be equal to the potential multiplier. This is less likely to occur when monetary base is expanded than when it is contracted. In the latter case, deposits must be reduced, by curbing lending, if the bank was operating at the limit in creating deposits – i.e. with an effective j equal to the desired value. In the former case, however, the increase in deposits cannot be taken for granted, since it must be accompanied by an increase in credit demand, which the bank does not control (even reducing its lending rate may not be effective).

(2) Let us now examine the possibility of controlling the money supply through the *compulsory reserve ratio*. This is certainly controllable, since it can be subject to specific regulation. It is therefore a direct control measure prescribing a specific behaviour on the part of banks.

---

[27] This may take time, however, especially if capital is relatively immobile.

The impact of changing the reserve ratio on the money supply, analogously to adjusting monetary base, is highly influenced by a wide variety of circumstances. First, it has a greater effect in restrictive policies than in expansionary policies. In the former, it is much more likely that the effective deposit multiplier will be close to its potential, while in the latter it tends to be lower in the presence of inadequate credit demand.

Let us now see what can happen if the reserve ratio is increased, with monetary base unchanged. An increase means that, with the volume of deposits initially given, the banks must increase their holdings of monetary base in the form of compulsory reserves. If the banks do not have large excess reserves (as is likely in an expanding economy)[28] or other forms of liquidity, they will be forced to reduce their lending and thereby reduce the volume of deposits. This leads to a contraction in the monetary base required to be set aside as compulsory reserves, thus offsetting the effect of the increase in the reserve ratio. In this case the monetary restriction will be fully effective. Similarly, as we have already seen, a reduction in the banks' monetary base with no change in the reserve ratio leads to a reduction in lending and, therefore, in deposits. Once again, the effect will necessarily occur if banks do not have excess liquid reserves.

Now suppose that banks, while not holding large amounts of monetary base, do have other liquidity instruments that can be disposed of in the market or otherwise converted into monetary base (e.g. very short-term securities that the banks can decide not to renew at maturity). They may therefore decide not to reduce their lending, at least in the short run and with their 'best' customers, sacrificing short-run profits for long-run considerations (and profits). In these circumstances, changing the reserve ratio may be relatively ineffective and operate only with a considerable lag; regulating deposits (and the money supply) can be achieved only with other direct control instruments, such as **credit ceilings**, whereby banks are required to keep lending growth within certain limits, which may differ according to loan type (e.g. consumer credit, corporate lending, export credit) or borrowing sector (financial and commercial firms, industry, etc.). Banks that exceed the limits incur penalties.

11.8   (Final) objectives and agents of monetary policy

Monetary policy shares the same possible objectives as other macroeconomic policy instruments: price stability, balance of payments equilibrium, employment and growth. The existence of complementarities between objectives facilitates monetary policy choices, as it does for other instruments. From this point of view, by maintaining the competitiveness of national goods and services, the pursuit of price stability (i.e. containing inflation) also tends to ensure balance of payments equilibrium and therefore exchange rate stability. Similarly, a certain degree of price stability may help

---

[28] It is in such circumstances that a tightening of the monetary policy stance may be needed.

to stimulate the formation of financial savings, facilitating long-term growth if this has been slowed by insufficient saving.

However, there may be problems of *substitutability* between objectives, at least in the short run. Pursuing one may preclude, or make difficult, the achievement of another. The clearest case of substitutability concerns price stability and balance of payments equilibrium, on the one hand, and employment, on the other. Substitutability creates problems for all instruments, but they may be especially serious for monetary policy, as we will see.

In general, substitutability means that we must make choices, and every choice involves some sort of sacrifice. Making a rational choice means defining the preference functions of policymakers and, therefore, the weights assigned to each objective, or their order of priority. This becomes more pressing when economic policy decisions are decentralised. We then must tackle the problem – which we briefly mentioned earlier and which will be examined in more detail in section 14.10 – of the appropriate assignment of instruments to targets; that is, deciding the specific objective that each instrument must seek to achieve exclusively or on a priority basis. There are now only a few cases in contemporary economies in which the body responsible for fiscal policy (the government and, in particular, the Treasury) is also responsible for monetary policy, giving instructions and orders to a central bank whose functions are essentially executive. More frequently, the central bank is entrusted with almost complete and independent responsibility[29] for monetary policy. In this context, the identification of the objectives of each authority (monetary and fiscal) is of special theoretical and practical importance.

Tradition[30] and much of economic theory assign the task of pursuing price stability and balance of payments equilibrium to the monetary authorities. Many economists agree on the ability to achieve equilibrium in the balance of payments. There is also an agreement that a restrictive monetary stance has powerful effects on the level (and rate of change) of prices, as well as on the level of income and employment, but, as we will shortly see, monetary policy is less powerful when it aims to stimulate an *increase* in income and employment beginning with an underemployment equilibrium.[31] By

---

[29] On the degree of **political** or **goal independence** (i.e. independence in choosing objectives) and **economic** or **instrument independence** (i.e. ability to choose instruments) of various central banks at the beginning of the 1990s consult Grilli, Masciandaro and Tabellini (1991). To meet the requirement for a monetary policy autonomous from fiscal policy imposed by the 1992 Maastricht agreements for EMU, all European central banks – including the Bank of Italy and the Bank of France, which have traditionally been less independent of the government – increased their independence; however, the Bank of England has been granted economic independence only to further objectives decided by the government. On the other hand the Statute of the ECB (see chapter 18) has been modelled on that of the Bundesbank and guarantees a very high level of independence for this institution. The problem of the political accountability of independent 'bodies' in a democratic system remains.

[30] Note, however, that many central banks were created 'out of the desire of the executive power to free itself of the tight control exercised by Parliament over its spending powers . . . for declared or disguised inflationary purposes' (De Cecco, 1995). The emphasis on monetary stability arises with the emergence of a broad social class of creditors (De Cecco, 1995, p. 26).

[31] Even if less powerful for expansionary purpose, monetary policy is usually thought to be non-neutral with respect to real variables – i.e. to have real effects – at least in the short run (see Walsh, 2003). Conditions for non-neutrality of monetary policy in policy games are stated in Acocella and Di Bartolomeo (2004).

contrast, monetary policy may play some role in long-term growth. This can be done in two quite different ways: (a) by ensuring monetary stability and thus providing an incentive for the formation of financial savings; (b) by using some degree of monetary instability to govern income distribution so as to foster investment and, consequently, growth. The choice between the two alternatives depends on the nature of expectations (rational, regressive, inelastic) and some features of the economic and social system. The emphasis given by some authors and in political debates to monetary stability as an absolutely necessary condition for growth seems therefore to be excessive.[32]

11.9   Monetary policy under fixed and floating exchange rates

The effects of monetary policy on income and employment under the two exchange rate regimes differ profoundly.

In brief, with fixed exchange rates (and high international capital mobility) monetary policy will be relatively ineffective over aggregate demand, all the more so the greater is the mobility of capital. The opposite is the case if exchange rates float. To understand why this is so, we must first make clear that in a fixed-exchange rate regime, balance of payments surpluses or deficits caused by monetary policy cannot cause changes in the exchange rate, causing variations in the monetary base instead, if no sterilisation is carried out:[33]

(1) Let us consider an *increase* in *monetary base*, which causes the money supply to expand and, therefore, interest rates to fall. The consequent stimulus to investment would be large if the reduction in the interest rate were lasting. This does not happen, however, since the effect is only temporary. On the one hand, the lower interest rate will cause a deterioration in the capital movements balance while, on the other, any increase in income deriving from the increase in investment will worsen the goods balance. Upward pressure will be exerted on the exchange rate. However, under a fixed-exchange rate regime the exchange rate cannot rise. To stop the exchange rate from rising above its fluctuation limit the monetary authorities normally have to intervene in the foreign exchange market, selling foreign currency and buying domestic currency, which gives rise to a progressive reabsorption of the liquidity created initially.[34] This is the reason it was argued that the exchange rate regime can influence the ability to control the creation of monetary base (see section 11.7). In the present example of fixed exchange rates, monetary base creation tends to be endogenous rather than exogenous – since it is created by the operation of the economy itself – and therefore cannot be controlled by the monetary authorities. Controllability declines as the sensitivity of capital movements to the interest rate increases. The size of the balance of payments deficit associated with a given action to reduce the interest rate is in fact larger (and the larger and more rapid will be

---

[32] This is consistent with the finding of an association between central bank independence and lower inflation and the lack of any systematic impact of that independence on real output growth (Grilli, Masciandaro and Tabellini, 1991).

[33] *Sterilisation* basically consists in OMOs that offset changes in monetary base through the foreign sector.

[34] Nevertheless, large capital outflows would not be sustainable, owing to the limited size of reserves.

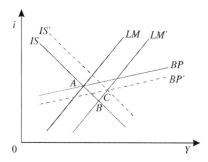

Figure 11.1

the related contraction of monetary base) the greater the mobility of capital.[35] The situation is shown in figure 11.2.

The *LM* curve initially shifts to the right to *LM'*. At *B* income is higher and the interest rate is lower. Nevertheless, owing to these effects, at *B* there would be a balance of payments deficit and a consequent tendency towards the depreciation of the currency. Intervention by the monetary authorities to avoid the depreciation would return *LM* to its original position.

(2) With floating exchange rates and capital mobility, monetary policy can be effective in controlling the level of aggregate demand.

In order to understand the operation of monetary policy in a flexible-exchange rate environment, we must bear in mind that the incipient balance of payments surplus or deficit[36] that they can produce leads to a change in the exchange rate rather than a change in monetary base, as it does under fixed exchange rates, as a result of central bank intervention to keep the exchange rate within fluctuation limits. Thus, an incipient worsening of the balance of payments, far from causing monetary base destruction (with restrictive effects), gives rise to a depreciation

[35] The relationship between the money market and the balance of payments has been studied by the advocates of the so-called '**monetary theory of the balance of payments**'. According to this strand of economic thought, for a country with a fixed-exchange rate system, a balance of payments surplus (deficit) reflects excess demand for (supply of) domestic money. Agents will get rid of (say) an excess supply of money by increasing aggregate demand, which will generate a balance of payments deficit. In the absence of sterilisation, changes in foreign reserves associated with balance of payments disequilibrium – which, as we have said, is a reflection of a disequilibrium in the money market – tend to be self-eliminating. Let us take the case of a balance of payments deficit, which is a symptom of excess money supply. This deficit will reduce international reserves and destroy monetary base, thus reducing the excess money supply. Under flexible exchange rates, the adjustment of the money market occurs through changes in the exchange rate rather than flows of foreign reserves. On this view, real factors (changes in preferences, increases in income, trade policy measures, etc.) would influence the balance of payments and/or the exchange rate only to the extent that they have an effect on the money market. The literature of the monetary approach emphasises that in the long run in a small economy with fixed exchange rates the money supply tends to take on the characteristics of an endogenous variable: the monetary authorities do not control the overall size of monetary base but rather only its division into domestic and external components. A number of the most important contributions to the vast literature of the monetary theory of the balance of payments and the exchange rate are contained in Frenkel and Johnson (1976, 1978).

[36] We refer to an 'incipient' imbalance since, at least in theory, in the regime we are dealing with now exchange rate variations automatically produce external balance. Economists sometimes refer to an *ex ante* imbalance – i.e. to the imbalance that would tend to be created *before* changes in the exchange rate produce the adjustment of the balance of payments (see Dernburg, 1989, pp. 117–18).

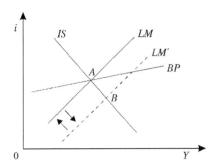

Figure 11.2

(with expansionary effects). The opposite occurs if the balance of payments tends to improve.

The effectiveness of monetary policy in a flexible-exchange rate system stems from its tendency to cause a balance of payments disequilibrium that is not followed by central bank intervention to peg the exchange rate (as in the fixed-exchange rate system, which gives rise to changes in monetary base in the opposite direction from that of the monetary policy stance). Since the exchange rate is free to fluctuate, the tendency towards an imbalance will only modify the exchange rate itself, with effects that operate in the same direction as monetary policy. A monetary expansion will cause interest rates to fall and, therefore, tend to worsen both the goods balance (owing to the expansionary effect on income) and the capital movements balance. The result will be a *depreciation of the currency*, which will also have an expansionary effect. The expansionary impact of monetary policy on income in a flexible rate regime is greatest when capital is perfectly mobile: any monetary base creation places downward pressure on the interest rate; in this case, even a small fall in the interest rate will give rise to capital outflows large enough to cause the currency to depreciate significantly and, therefore, shift *IS* considerably.

We can summarise the effects of monetary policy by referring to figure 11.2. The increase in the money supply shifts *LM* to *LM′* and the system moves from *A* to *B*, where there is an incipient balance of payments deficit that causes the currency to depreciate. The depreciation causes *IS* to shift to *IS′* and *BP* to move to *BP′*. Point *C* is the final equilibrium point for the three markets.

Table 11.4 summarises the effects of monetary policy, respectively, in the two exchange rate systems and with differing degrees of capital mobility. For reasons of clarity, we refer to an expansionary policy only.

The claim that a country gains independence under a flexible-exchange rate regime (see section 16.7) means it can separate its monetary policy stance from balance of payments objectives – which are now achieved through exchange rate variations – and assign it to domestic goals. However, the greater effectiveness of monetary policy is counterbalanced by the reduced effectiveness of fiscal policy, at least when capital is sufficiently mobile, as we will see in section 12.4.

Table 11.4 *Effectiveness of expansionary monetary policy on income under different exchange rate regimes and different degrees of capital mobility*

Fixed exchange rates		Floating exchange rates	
Capital mobility	No capital mobility	Capital mobility	No capital mobility
Completely ineffective: capital mobility causes capital outflows and considerable destruction of monetary base	*Limited and temporary effectiveness*: the impact of the monetary action on the balance of payments is limited to the current account	*Very effective*: capital mobility causes the currency to depreciate, providing an expansionary stimulus to autonomous spending as well	*Effective*: the depreciation is relatively small, being largely due to the impact on the current account

11.10   The operation of monetary policy; indicators, operative and intermediate targets

Assume that all the sectors of the economy are initially in equilibrium. An increase in monetary base following open market purchases from banks has the immediate effect of increasing both the banks' excess reserves and securities prices, which reduces the latter's yield. Excess reserves and lower yields induce a substitution process in banks' portfolios, producing an increase in the supply of credit and a reduction in the lending rate. This may stimulate overall demand, causing an increase in deposits, which enables banks to balance their assets and liabilities. The increase in deposits and credit demand will be part of a more general process of change in the composition of the portfolios of households and firms. The final effect is usually an increase in demand and employment.

Depending on the economic situation, the increase in demand may or may not lead to an increase in prices. The change in the interest rate will also have an impact on the balance of payments, especially capital movements.

Tightening the monetary stance will have the opposite effect. However, in both cases (and especially in a restriction) monetary policy will affect real variables not only through changes in the *cost* of credit but also, or primarily, through changes in the *availability* of credit, for a number of reasons.

(1) The increase in the market interest rate induced by the monetary tightening causes a fall in the prices of securities held by banks; they will therefore find it less attractive to raise funds through the sale of securities for their lending activities, which will have become more profitable owing to the rise in interest rates: selling securities would lead to capital losses. This disincentive effect on the supply of credit is called the **Roosa effect** (see Roosa, 1951) or the **lock-in effect** and helps explain the particular effectiveness of a restrictive monetary policy, which influences not only the *demand* for credit but also its *supply*.

(2) The monetary restriction may increase uncertainty about the future and increase the demand for liquidity (see Kareken, 1975).

(3) Faced with borrower insolvency risk and asymmetric information, **endogenous rationing** (rather than the exogenous rationing of the two previous examples) may take place: this occurs independently of external events such as a restrictive monetary policy. Whenever a bank faces excess credit demand, it will react not by raising interest rates but by offering credit to some and denying it to others. Under the assumed conditions, raising rates could have a negative effect on the bank's profitability, since:

(a) it leads to *adverse selection of riskier customers*; and

(b) it encourages some customers to undertake *riskier projects* (moral hazard).[37]

Our discussion so far shows the complexity of the operation of monetary policy. Before it can affect ultimate objectives (employment, the price level, balance of payments, growth), monetary policy requires time. It may also encounter obstacles and its effectiveness may not be easily discerned. In short, monetary policy is conducted in a highly uncertain environment, where it is important to follow the evolution of market conditions and continually adjust actual target values to the desired level. This has prompted the monetary authorities to direct their attention to variables that are intermediate between instruments and the ultimate targets of monetary policy.

It can be helpful to track the behaviour of variables that are either closely linked to instruments, in order to evaluate the magnitude of the stimulus or restriction, or closely tied to the ultimate targets, in order to assess the likely impact of the monetary action on the ultimate targets themselves, possibly in advance.

The former are known as **monetary policy indicators**. These are variables, such as money supply growth and the interest rate, that provide a summary assessment of the magnitude of the monetary expansion or restriction,[38] even when the policy action involves the use of numerous instruments.

Nevertheless, it may be difficult to find a reliable indicator that measures *only* the magnitude of the monetary policy action. The problem arises because, as we have seen, aggregates that reflect monetary measures alone do not exist. For example, the money supply is determined endogenously to some extent through the demand for credit, which also reflects the current state of economic activity and the outlook for the future. On the other hand, there are a variety of aggregates that enable us to measure the indicated variables (M1, M2, M3, etc.). Interest rates are also determined endogenously and there are many of them. In fact, we speak of the *term structure of interest rates*. The

---

[37] We have been discussing *equilibrium rationing*, not **dynamic rationing**, which is associated with delays in the adjustment of bank interest rates to changing conditions in the money market. The importance of credit rationing can scarcely be overemphasised: it casts a very different light on the working of an economic system from that deriving from the traditional neoclassical theory (specifically, monetarist theory), in which there are hardly any binding constraints on the actions of individuals.

[38] However, the reader should bear in mind that monetary policy action is much more varied and may not be narrowly confined to restriction and expansion, especially as it reflects long-term objectives. For example, reform of the payment system or compulsory reserve regulations can have a restrictive or expansionary effect in the short run but are introduced for long-run purposes.

interest rates that serve as monetary policy indicators are normally short-term rates, for example rates on 6-month Treasury bills or the overnight interbank rate (i.e. the rate on loans between banks maturing the first business day following the transaction). Note that in the presence of *credit rationing*, bank interest rates no longer function as a signal in the allocation of credit or as an indicator of the restrictiveness of the monetary policy stance.

In order to anticipate the effects of monetary measures on the ultimate targets it is helpful to aim at **intermediate targets** – i.e. variables that have an influence on the ultimate targets and are either affected by the monetary measures before the latter or can at least be learned before them, enabling the monetary authorities to regulate monetary policy promptly in subsequent periods.[39] For this reason, intermediate targets are frequently monetary or credit aggregates, which have both of these characteristics.[40]

One possible intermediate target is **domestic credit expansion** (DCE). The DCE aggregate is also called 'monetary credit', since it is equal to the monetary financing (i.e. financing with monetary base) of the Treasury plus bank lending to the private sector which, as we know, also translates into changes in the money supply through the creation of *derived deposits*. Other widely used intermediate targets are the money supply (M2, M3 or other monetary aggregates), interest rates, credit targets (including various forms of credit and not only bank credit, as does DCE) and the exchange rate.

The choice of one or another intermediate target depends on numerous factors, each of which must be carefully assessed. There are three issues to consider in the various steps that link adjustment of the instruments to hitting the targets:

(a) the *controllability* of the aggregate being considered for use as an intermediate target
(b) the *stability* of behavioural functions
(c) the links between *intermediate and ultimate targets*.

The specification of intermediate targets involves the formulation of **two-step intervention** approaches, which means the indirect pursuit of the final target through the direct achievement of an intermediate target. In recent years, monetary authorities in some countries have opted for **one-step intervention**, which involves announcing and directly pursuing their final target, which has generally been price stability (**inflation targeting**) (see Svensson, 1999). This is the approach taken by the ECB, which has adopted inflation targeting, although not exclusively, as the bank also seeks to control M3 (see section 18.4). The change in orientation can be attributed to:

---

[39] In the case of a fixed intermediate target, the monetary authorities should in principle act as if this target were in fact the true final target. In practice, however, not only do authorities monitor a variety of intermediate targets, they also monitor shifts away from the target values of both intermediate and final targets. For example, in April 1994 the Bundesbank lowered the discount rate despite the fact that its intermediate aggregate (M3) had expanded considerably more rapidly than the target rate because at the same time inflation (the ultimate target) had fallen significantly. The reason why in practice monetary authorities monitor a number of variables is that the relations between the different variables are uncertain and unstable.

[40] Monetary and credit statistics are normally available more quickly than data on the real economy.

(a) The reduced stability of the velocity of circulation and the diminished control that can be exercised over the money supply. This is associated with the increase in the range of financial assets available and the international mobility of capital, all of which has made it difficult to use monetary targets.

(b) The increase in exchange rate volatility in 1992–3, which made the pursuit of an intermediate nominal exchange rate target less feasible.

However, the return to one-step intervention policies is not problem-free owing to the persistence of lags and uncertainty in the impact of monetary policy on final targets. In particular, the use of inflation targeting can present problems when inflation depends on non-monetary factors. This is acknowledged by the ECB and underlies its interpretation of the approach (with the specification of an operative target, which we now turn to).

The last type of intermediate variable is given by *operative* or *reference targets*, which are variables standing between instruments and intermediate objectives that can be observed without a lag and directly affected by monetary authorities. As we have said, the ECB has announced an inflation target but has also indicated a reference target for M3 growth.

11.11   Considerations on the effectiveness of monetary policy

In concluding this chapter, we briefly consider the effectiveness of monetary policy. Effectiveness has a *quantitative* dimension (which we discussed in theoretical terms in section 9.4) and a *temporal* dimension. We first examine the latter.

Monetary policy is affected by much the same observation lag as other discretionary instruments but its administrative and effect lags are different. The *administrative lag* of monetary policy is normally much shorter than that of other policy measures, especially all those that require some sort of political mediation in a representative democracy, fiscal policy first and foremost. The shortness of the administrative lag is therefore an advantage deriving from the independence of many central banks from political bodies, although there are also significant limitations and risks involved in such independence.[41]

By contrast, the *effect lag* of monetary policy can be long and variable, at least for some targets. We have already noted the complexity of substitutability relations and the portfolio readjustment processes of banks and other agents. This means that with targets such as income, employment and price stability the effects of monetary policy

---

[41] It is worth underscoring this point at a moment in time when the freeing of central banks from political interference is practically complete and has often received uncritical agreement. There are three especially important points to bear in mind when judging the advisability of separating monetary and fiscal authorities. The first concerns the fact that the monetary authorities are *not elected* (by citizens or their representatives); we mentioned this in section 11.8. The second point concerns the possibility that a non-cooperative game between the two authorities might lead to *worse results* than a cooperative game, in both theory and in the real situations in which the preference functions of the authorities are expressed. This point must be related to the issue of the decentralisation of economic policy and appropriate assignment (see section 14.10). The third point is related to the issue of *time inconsistency*, which would require central bank independence (see Acocella, 1998). On the question of central bank independence see Eijffinger and Schaling (1993), De Cecco (1995) and Piga (2000).

may emerge quite slowly. By contrast, the time lag between the policy action and the emergence of its impact on targets such as the balance of payments can be shorter under certain conditions. For example, if the monetary authorities are able to influence interest rates, they can quickly eliminate a balance of payments deficit if capital is sufficiently mobile and there are no perverse effects on expected exchange rates (see chapter 14).

In any case monetary policy is ill-suited to **fine-tuning**. It instead requires large, if not massive, intervention[42] in order to be effective, especially if the financial markets are not deep or broad. In particular, massive intervention may have positive *announcement effects* that shorten the lag.

As we noted earlier, the effectiveness of monetary policy action depends on whether it is used for *expansionary* or *restrictive* purposes (**asymmetry of effects**), tending to be greater when a restrictive stance is adopted, for a number of reasons:

(1) We have already remarked that the *actual deposit multiplier* tends to be higher for a reduction, rather than an increase, in monetary base.

(2) The existence of a 'floor' on the nominal interest rate has the same effect, since the interest rate is usually not negative and might not even be able to fall below some positive value if we find ourselves in a Keynesian *liquidity trap*. By contrast, there is no limit on the upward movement of the interest rate following a monetary tightening.

(3) *Credit demand* may be inelastic with respect to the interest rate. This is not a very satisfactory explanation of the asymmetry of the effects of monetary policy action, since inelasticity should emerge for expansionary and restrictive policies alike. The matter is somewhat more complex in reality. It is not so much inelasticity that gives rise to asymmetric effects as the possibility of *credit rationing*: in this case, a restrictive monetary policy does not cause an appreciable rise in the interest rate on bank credit (and therefore the elasticity of demand aspect seems irrelevant), but rather induces a reduction in the *supply* of credit to certain customers, who are rationed. Total supply is therefore reduced with certainty (even if demand does not fall). By contrast, an expansionary monetary policy action does not so much cause a fall in lending rates (and therefore once again the elasticity of credit demand is irrelevant) but rather prompts an increase in the supply of credit, perhaps to a level where it exceeds demand.

The monetary action thus has *asymmetric results*: it undoubtedly reduces the supply of credit (and with it the volume of credit actually granted) when policy is restrictive; it increases supply when policy is expansionary, but demand does not necessarily match the higher supply (and so credit actually granted does not necessarily increase). Take the typical course of the business cycle: in order to slow demand expansion, the monetary authorities may reduce monetary base, which leads to credit rationing in a situation in

---

[42] The need for massive intervention may conflict with the continuous action required to maintain intermediate targets at the desired level.

which demand for credit is high. With the onset of recession, the monetary authorities induce banks to increase the supply of credit but at this point credit demand is probably no longer rationed owing to the negative impact of the recession on the outlook for profitability.

11.12   Summary

1   *Macroeconomic policy* aims at ensuring the 'stability' of a market economy by adjusting aggregate variables. The main instruments of this policy are monetary policy, fiscal policy, incomes policy and exchange rate policy.

2   *Money* serves three essential functions: (a) means of payment or medium of exchange; (b) unit of account; (c) store of value.

3   In a monetary economy, agents with a surplus of financial savings finance agents with a deficit through direct and indirect credit. *Direct credit* is granted to a deficit agent directly by the surplus agent. *Indirect credit* is channelled through financial intermediaries.

4   In modern economies, money is a *liability* issued by a financial intermediary and accepted on a fiduciary basis as a medium of exchange and store of value. The constant process of monetary innovation is driven by a variety of factors (above all, reducing costs and avoiding constraints).

5   *Central banks*, which are granted the privilege of issuing legal tender, also act as lenders of last resort (banker's bank) and supervisors of banking activity.

6   The *monetary base* is composed of the financial assets that banks can use to meet reserve requirements. Its sources comprise the 'foreign' sector, the 'Treasury' sector, 'open market operations (OMOs)' and the 'bank refinancing' sector. Monetary base is held by the public and the banks.

7   The main operations for *monetary base creation* with the banks are the rediscounting of bills and advances backed by securities.

8   *Deposits* are a liability issued by banks and function as money (bank money). The quantity of deposits created within the banking system is a multiple of the monetary base held by the banks and depends on the behaviour of the banks themselves in addition to the behaviour of the public: banks supply credit that will be partially converted into deposits, owing to the public's willingness to hold bank liabilities in addition to currency.

9   The monetary authorities can affect the *volume of bank money* and the *money supply* through its control of monetary base and the compulsory reserve ratio. The money supply can also be regulated by setting a *lending ceiling*. A restrictive policy is more effective than an expansionary one and the actual deposit multiplier tends to be higher in the former case than in the latter.

10   Under *fixed exchange rates* monetary policy is completely ineffective in the presence of high capital mobility. Conversely, in a *floating-exchange rate system* monetary policy is very effective, all the more so the greater is capital mobility.

11 *Monetary policy* can be directed at achieving a number of ultimate objectives: price stability, balance of payments equilibrium, employment and growth. Recent monetary theory and practice assign monetary authorities with the task of pursuing the first two objectives.

12 *Monetary measures* can have expansionary or restrictive effects by triggering changes in the cost and availability of credit (rationing).

13 The monetary authorities usually pay attention to *variables* that stand between instruments and ultimate targets (indicators, operative and intermediate targets) because of the complexity of monetary policy actions and their impact on ultimate targets.

14 The choice of the *intermediate target* depends on:
   (a) the controllability of the aggregate being considered for use as an intermediate target
   (b) the stability of behavioural functions
   (c) the links between intermediate and ultimate targets.

15 Monetary policy is to be preferred to other instruments for its very short *administrative time lag*. However its effect lag is long and variable.

12 Macroeconomic objectives and fiscal policy

The term **fiscal policy** refers to the government budget measures aimed primarily at changing income and employment in the short run. Since debate on fiscal policy is often obscured by improper reference to the institutions governing it, it can be helpful to first state the meaning of certain terms denoting the agents of fiscal policy. The *general government sector* consists of the following group of resident institutional units: (a) all units of central, state or local government; (b) all social security funds at each level of government; (c) all non-market non-profit institutions that are controlled and mainly financed by government units. The sector does not include public corporations owned by government units. However, *unincorporated enterprises* owned by government are included. Individual countries may be organised in such a way that some of the units indicated will be absent – e.g. states for countries that do not have a federal constitution (see Commission of the European Communities *et al.*, 1993). Our analysis will generally refer to the general government sector as a whole. This means that relationships within the sector (e.g. transfers from the central to local governments) will not be examined.

12.1 The budget and its components

Let us now provide a number of definitions. The **fundamental budget accounting** identity is:[1]

$$T - C_g - Tr_c - INT - I_g - Tr_k = B_t \tag{12.1}$$

The symbols stand for:

T = current revenues
C_g = government consumption
Tr_c = current transfers (transfer payments), excluding interest payments

---

[1] Note that the identity given in (12.1) can be expressed in any unit of account, as long as the same unit is used for all the terms: we can use current pounds sterling, pounds sterling at 1950 prices, dollars or some other unit. In order to reduce the number of symbols employed, we prefer to express all the values for the various budget items in real terms – i.e. in terms of quantities of goods and services that the corresponding monetary values would enable us to purchase.

INT = interest payments on the public debt
I_g = government investment, net of disinvestment
Tr_k = capital account transfers (transfer payments)
B_t = budget balance

We need to clarify the relationships between these variables and those that we have used so far, which we will continue to adopt in certain contexts: government spending on goods, G, and total transfers, Tr:[2]

$$G = C_g + I_g \tag{12.2}$$

$$Tr = Tr_c + INT + Tr_k \tag{12.3}$$

Let us give a more precise definition of a number of terms, beginning with **government revenues**, which include current revenues and those on capital account.

Current revenues are largely generated by direct and indirect taxes and social security contributions, with a small amount coming from other sources (e.g. profits from public sector enterprises). The general use of these funds is fairly clear: apart from the obvious use of financing expenditure, the level of current revenues can be adjusted for counter-cyclical purposes. The composition of revenues (and expenditure) can be adjusted to pursue redistributive goals.

Capital account revenues come from the sale of government property and public sector enterprises and the repayment of loans. For simplicity we have subtracted them from the investment expenditures indicated below.

Let us now look at government expenditure:

(1) Government expenditure on goods and services is composed of two parts:
   (a) **Government consumption**, which includes wages and salaries plus spending on current purchases of goods and services; it is used for the current operation of the public sector.
   (b) **Government investment**, aimed at increasing the stock of publicly owned capital (buildings, schools, roads, etc.).
(2) **Current transfers** proper include:
   (a) **Transfers to households**, for redistributive purposes and to supply merit goods (e.g. benefits to certain categories of person, such as the disabled or veterans; covering social security expenditure in excess of contributions from firms and workers).
   (b) **Transfers to firms**, which consist of production subsidies (e.g. exchange rate guarantees, subsidies to firms that undertake to provide certain transport services, etc.) for various purposes: improving the balance of payments, redistribution, increasing demand, etc.
   (c) **Official transfers**, especially in the form of contributions to international organisations and aid to developing countries; in the first case, the transfers are

---

[2] In chapter 4 we referred to current transfers to households, denoted by Tr_h. These are part of current transfers, including interest.

part of membership in such organisations; in the second, they are a form of redistribution.

(3) **Interest** is paid on government debt; it is a special component of current transfers that is best considered separately, as we will see. Interest transfers can have a *redistributive effect* if the distribution of taxes financing interest transfers among different income earners differs from that of public debt holders.

(4) **Capital account transfers**: these consist of payments normally made to firms to boost private investment (for example, grants for regional development programmes).

The **overall budgetary balance** is the sum of the current and capital account balances. The **current balance** is analogous to private saving, as it is the excess of current revenues over current outlays, which can be used for expenditure on capital account.[3] For this reason, a current surplus denotes (positive) **public saving**. Public saving is often negative, however, since in many cases governments run *current deficits*.[4]

By subtracting interest outlays from *total* expenditure (which we indicate with $G_t = G + Tr$), we have **primary government expenditure** (G_p). Considering (12.2) and (12.3), we have:

$$G_p = C_g + I_g + Tr_c + Tr_k \qquad (12.4)$$

If we subtract interest outlays from the current balance or the total balance – thus considering primary expenditure only – we have the **primary current balance** or the **total primary balance**, respectively. The primary current balance is therefore equal to $T - C_g - Tr_c$, while the total primary balance is $T - G_p = T - C_g - I_g - Tr_c - Tr_k$.

12.2   Income, employment and taxes

In this section we examine the effects of taxation on income and employment. First note that in a Keynesian model, taxation, T (net of transfers to households), enters the income circuit only indirectly, through its influence on consumption and/or investment:

$$C = f(Y, T) \qquad I = g(i, T)$$

For simplicity, we will ignore its effects on investment. We can distinguish between:

(a) lump-sum taxation
(b) proportional taxation
(c) progressive taxation.

[3] For households, *current revenues* are current income; current expenditures are consumption of non-durables and services; capital account spending comprises the purchase of consumer durables. (However, consumer durables, such as automobiles, furniture, appliances and so on, for which it is difficult to calculate the value of current services provided, are included under current spending. Spending on housing, for which it is easier to estimate the services provided, is included under capital spending.)
[4] The trend in the 1990s in many European countries has been towards a return to positive public saving.

12.2.1   Lump-sum taxation

With a **lump-sum tax** affecting consumption only, in a simple Keynesian model of the real economy we have:

$$Y = C + I + G$$
$$C = c(Y - T) \tag{12.5}$$
$$I = \bar{I}$$

from which we obtain:

$$Y = \frac{1}{1-c}(\bar{I} + G - cT) \tag{12.6}$$

The lump-sum tax multiplier is therefore $-c/(1-c)$, which is smaller (even in absolute value terms) than that for government expenditure, G, which is equal to $1/(1-c)$. This means that a £1 increase in taxes leads to a reduction in income that is smaller than the increase in income produced by a £1 increase in government expenditure. This will be important in understanding the balanced-budget theorem (see subsection 12.3.1).

The smaller effect of taxation is due to the fact that the £1 tax does not enter the income circuit directly. It therefore translates into (less) demand only to the extent that it influences consumption (which is a direct component of total demand), i.e. for an amount equal to c.

12.2.2   Proportional taxation

If, in addition to the three equations of (12.5), we assume that $T = tY$, where the tax rate, t, is constant (i.e. **proportional taxation**), we have:

$$Y = \frac{1}{1 - c(1-t)}(\bar{I} + G) \tag{12.7}$$

The effect on income of an increase in the tax rate is, obviously, always negative, since it increases the denominator of the multiplier $1/[1 - c(1 - t)]$.[5]

We can use the proportional taxation framework to analyse a problem that was much debated at the beginning of the 1960s and again in the 1980s: the effects on total tax revenues (or the government budget) of a reduction in the average tax rate. In the early 1960s the issue was tackled within the framework of the *potential output concept* and the expansionary policies adopted in the United States by the Kennedy administration. The question re-emerged in the 1980s, albeit in a considerably different context, in connection with the Reagan administration's attempts to stimulate income growth and

---

[5] The reader will note that all of the multipliers we have seen so far have been derived from a model that assumes that there is no money (or, better, the money supply changes so as to leave the interest rate unchanged as income varies) and a closed economy. If we drop these hypotheses (the first will be abandoned in this chapter), the expenditure and tax multipliers are lowered as a result of two factors: the first is linked to the change in the interest rate following a change in income; the second is related to the fact that part of domestic demand can be met by foreign production.

reduce the federal budget deficit with tax cuts, counting on the expansionary **supply-side effects** on saving and labour, rather than the demand-side effects on consumption and investment.[6]

While the 1960s policy was successful, the more recent attempt failed, as the supply response to the tax cut proved to be much smaller than estimated, given the initial level of taxation. The failure of the supply-side policies of 1981–2 prompted the Reagan administration to take a more orthodox approach in subsequent years, adopting Keynesian measures based on increasing government spending. This produced considerable income and employment growth after 1982, despite a restrictive monetary policy. The consequence of the latter for the balance of payments was a large capital inflow and the accumulation of a massive foreign debt.

12.2.3 Progressive taxation

With **progressive taxation**, the average tax rate is no longer constant but is instead an increasing function of the taxpayer's income. The variability of the average tax rate implies that tax revenue depends on both the structure of taxation and personal income distribution. Despite the greater complexity of the analytical treatment of this case, we can continue to use expression (12.7), albeit with a number of caveats, to examine the effects of progressive taxation on income.

First, we interpret t in (12.7) as the average effective tax rate – i.e. the *average tax burden*. In addition, for simplicity, we consider average (or *per capita*) income as the only relevant aspect of income distribution. If there are variations in autonomous spending that give rise to a change only in the number of income earners, leaving *per capita* income unchanged, the average rate will not change. By contrast, changes in autonomous spending that are also reflected in variations in the same direction in *per capita* income tend to alter the average tax rate, t, raising it if autonomous spending rises and vice versa, all other conditions being equal. The multiplier will therefore fall or rise, respectively, in line with the rise or fall in autonomous spending. The final effect on income of a change in autonomous spending will therefore be less than that under proportional taxation.

It follows that progressive taxation is an important *automatic stabiliser*: the effects on real income of fluctuations in the value of the autonomous components of aggregate demand are dampened by changes in the opposite direction of the multiplier caused by changes in the average tax rate.

Note that the stabilising effect may be amplified if we consider price changes, which we have so far left out of our analysis. We have in effect considered real variables only. Let us now examine the case of pure price movements.

Assume that we have a '*classical*' *business cycle* in which an increase (decrease) in the price level corresponds to a positive (negative) shock to the level of autonomous expenditure. Starting for simplicity from a situation of full employment,[7] an increase in

---

[6] An essential reference for these policies is Fink (1982).
[7] As with other assumptions, this is not necessary but it helps us make our point.

Table 12.1 *Effects of an increase in prices and income in the presence of progressive taxation*

Time (1)	Nominal gross income (2)	Price level (3)	Real gross income (4) = (2)/(3)	Tax (5)	Nominal net income (6) = (2) − (5)	Real net income (7) = (6) / (3)
t_0	1,000	100	10	200	800	8
t_1	2,000	200	10	200 + 300 = 500	1,500	7.5

demand will lead to a rise in prices and thus an increase in the nominal income of each taxpayer (if the income distribution does not change). Since progressive tax rates are set in relation to nominal income, which has increased for each taxpayer, the average tax rate will rise. Real disposable income will fall and consumption will decline, lowering overall demand.

The increase in taxes in real terms that results from the combination of a rise in prices and a progressive tax schedule is called **fiscal drag**. Let us take a look at a simple example to clarify the problem further. Assume a nominal gross income of 1,000 and a price level of 100 at time t_0. Further assume that the tax rate is 20 per cent for incomes between 0 and 1,000 and 30 per cent on the portion of incomes between 1,001 and 2,000 (**tax bracket progressivity**). A doubling of prices and nominal income at time t_1 leaves real income unchanged but will move income tax payers into higher tax brackets (**tax bracket creep**) and will increase nominal tax revenues by a factor of 2.5, thus reducing net real income (or real disposable income) from 8 to 7.5 (table 12.1).

Conversely, a reduction in nominal income (caused by or associated with a reduction in prices) will lower the tax burden, strengthening demand.

Fiscal drag also occurs outside the framework of a classical business cycle, but in this case does not act as an automatic stabiliser. Take a situation of **stagflation** such as that experienced in a number of countries after 1973, when prices rose despite slack demand and steady or even rising unemployment. The price rise increased the tax burden, thereby accentuating the slowdown.

This depressive effect and pressure from the taxpayers who bear most of the burden may prompt policymakers to adopt a variety of relief measures: for example, tax refunds or indexation of tax brackets. In the former case, fiscal drag is offset by granting taxpayers a *tax credit* of comparable value. Indexing tax brackets is not a compensatory measure but rather an attempt to avoid fiscal drag in the first place. For example, let us suppose that there is initially a 15 per cent tax rate for incomes of between £10,000 and £20,000 and that the extreme values of the brackets rise at a rate equal to the rate of inflation. If inflation is 10 per cent, the subsequent year the 15 per cent rate will apply to incomes of between £11,000 and £21,000. Obviously, partial indexation schemes are also possible.[8] Indexation has been introduced in various countries, such as the United Kingdom (in 1976), the United States (1986) and Italy (1989). In Italy, tax credits had previously been used.

12.3   Expenditure financing

From a short-term aggregate perspective, according to Keynes, the economic impact of government expenditure does not depend on its precise content. However, this does not imply either that we must accept inefficiency and patronage or that in a capitalist system any type of expenditure is feasible. Spending can be financed with taxes – with a balanced budget – or in deficit (**deficit spending** or **financing**). In the latter case, spending can be financed either by issuing government bonds (holding monetary base unchanged) or creating additional monetary base. The effects of the various options are different.

12.3.1   Balancing the budget

If expenditure is tax-financed, an increase in spending still has an expansionary effect, since it acts directly on national income, while the simultaneous increase in taxes affects disposable income, and hence consumption, and only through this national income (see section 12.2). An increase of £1 in government spending gives rise to an immediate increase of £1 in income; an increase of £1 in taxes gives rise to an immediate decrease of £c of consumption and, therefore, income. Since c, the marginal propensity to consume, is usually less than 1, there is an immediate net increase in income, which will be followed by additional increases thanks to the multiplier process. In short, the spending multiplier is larger than the tax multiplier, as shown by (12.6) (repeated here for convenience):

$$Y = \frac{1}{1-c}(\bar{I} + G - cT) \tag{12.6}$$

where the expenditure multiplier is $1/(1 - c)$ and the tax multiplier is $-c/(1 - c)$.

If we assume a change in government spending *and* taxation, the corresponding change in income will be:

$$\Delta Y = \frac{1}{1-c}(\Delta G - c\Delta T) \tag{12.8}$$

If the increase in spending is entirely financed by taxes, i.e. if $\Delta G = \Delta T$, from (12.8) we have:

$$\Delta Y = \frac{1-c}{1-c}\Delta G$$

---

[8] In abstract terms, the fiscal drag that occurs in a given situation is the excess taxation in this situation over the hypothetical case in which real gross income increases by the same amount as the effective change and the general price level remains unchanged.

from which we derive:

$$\frac{\Delta Y}{\Delta G} = 1$$

So, a £1 increase in government spending financed by an equal increase in taxation raises income by £1. This result, known as the **balanced budget theorem** or the **Haavelmo theorem**, shows that any income target can be achieved without adding to the budget deficit, but only with a change in the level of government expenditure equal to the desired change in income; in other words, all the additional demand would come from the public sector. Ideological opposition to such a prospect helps explain why deficit spending is used at least on a temporary basis in market economies, even those which have mandated a balanced budget rule.

12.3.2   Deficit financing

Expenditure normally provides a larger boost to income and employment if it is not financed with taxes. This is the reason Keynes favoured deficit spending over tax-financed spending to escape from the Great Depression of the 1930s.

In the 1970s and 1980s many countries used deficit financing of government expenditure for a wide variety of reasons. In some cases it was difficult to control spending on the one hand and increase taxation on the other, owing to obstacles associated with the structure of modern societies, such as the existence of a multitude of interest groups wielding considerable economic and political power. This is the reason for the **asymmetry of fiscal policy**, which is related to the decisionmaking process: an expansionary policy (reduction of tax revenues, increase in spending) is easier to adopt than a restrictive policy.[9] In addition, the institutions that emerged after the Second World War provided for *automatic stabilisers*, such that the first real recessionary impulse (which came in the wake of the 1973–4 oil crisis) generated large budget deficits. The increase in budget deficits that occurred in the 1970s and 1980s was not only a consequence of structural factors or automatic stabilisers. The oil crisis itself and the ineffectiveness of other policies (such as the supply-side measures in the United States) prompted the adoption of discretionary measures that also increased deficits. An additional influence was the restrictive monetary policy stance taken in the United States and, at the same time, in Germany beginning at the end of the 1970s, which increased the interest that had to be paid on the public debt.

A final factor in the increase in public deficits is tax evasion, avoidance and erosion. *Tax evasion* refers to illegal actions to reduce one's tax obligations. *Tax avoidance* involves reducing one's tax obligations by taking full advantage of the provisions of the tax code, through such devices as: (a) income shifting to lower-income taxpayers, if the tax system is progressive; (b) tax deferral (in particular, payment of taxes on

---

[9] This sort of asymmetry is different from monetary policy asymmetry (see chapter 11) and that associated with exchange rate policy (see chapter 14): here the asymmetry involves the greater ease with which expansionary policy measures can be *adopted* compared with restrictive ones, not differences in their effectiveness, as in the case of the other two policies.

capital gains can be deferred in a number of ways); (c) tax arbitrage, i.e. exploiting differences in tax rates on different kinds of income, individuals or countries.[10] The provisions of the tax code that give rise to tax avoidance are often 'technical' in nature and the consequences may well be unintended. There are other provisions, however, which purposely grant tax exemptions in order to encourage the development of an industry, a region or certain social groups (e.g. the poor or the disabled). Such tax provisions are called *tax expenditures*, since they are a substitute for direct government expenditure or subsidies.[11] In this case we speak of *erosion of the tax base*. Tax evasion and tax avoidance have tended to increase in connection with the globalisation of markets and production (see UNCTAD, 1994). Tax expenditures have also risen in recent years for a number of reasons, ranging from the decline in growth rates and the rise in unemployment rates in many countries to the increased pressure of interest groups.

Government expenditure, revenues and deficits in the G7 countries in a selection of years since 1970 are shown in table 12.2.

Let us now return to (12.1). If the budget is balanced we have $B_s = 0$. If total expenditure exceeds revenues – i.e. there is a budget deficit – $B_s < 0$. As we said, the deficit can be financed in two ways: through the creation of monetary base, ΔMB, or by issuing government debt, ΔB. Taking account of the possibility of deficit financing, the following budget identity can be derived from (12.1) and (12.4):

$$T - G_p - INT + \frac{\Delta MB}{p} + \frac{\Delta B}{p} = 0 \qquad (12.9)$$

where ΔMB and/or ΔB are positive values.

Note that the additional monetary base and the new government debt have been deflated (remember that we decided to express the budget identity in terms of real variables in section 12.1).

We will examine the two methods of deficit financing separately, since they have significantly different natures and effects.

12.3.3 *Monetary base financing*

The first difference between the two methods is their *cost to the government*. Debt financing is obviously expensive. Monetary base financing, on the other hand, is often

---

[10] For some of the tax avoidance devices mentioned in the text, see Stiglitz (1988). Special mention should be made of **transfer pricing**, a tax avoidance (and in some case, a tax evasion) method that exploits differences in tax treatment in different countries. Transfer prices are those applied to transfers of goods or services within a financial group. For example, if the parent company of the group sells a semifinished product (or the right to use a patent) to a foreign subsidiary in a country where taxes are lower, it will set a lower price on the transfer in order to reduce its profit (taxed at a higher rate) and increase the profit of the subsidiary (taxed at a lower rate in the foreign country), thus minimising its tax liability.

[11] Provisions may also be designed to help other people in special positions (e.g. the head of state, MPs, etc.) or powerful lobbies. A special form of tax expenditure is the partial or total exemption of interest on certain categories of bonds (usually government securities).

Table 12.2 *Total expenditure, current revenues and overall general government budget balances as a percentage of GDP in the seven leading industrial countries, 1970–2003*

	1970[a]	1975[a]	1980[a]	1985	1990	1995	2000	2003
United States								
Total expenditure	31.6	34.6	31.4	32.9	33.6	32.9	29.9	35.9
Current revenues	28.9	28.8	30.0	29.7	29.3	29.8	31.6	31.0
Budget balance	−1.1	−4.1	−1.4	−3.2	−4.3	−3.1	1.7	−4.9
Japan								
Total expenditure	19.4	27.3	32.0	31.6	30.5	34.4	36.8	38.3
Current revenues	20.6	24.0	27.6	30.8	32.4	30.2	29.4	30.9
Budget balance	+1.7	−2.8	−4.4	−0.8	1.9	−4.2	−7.4	−7.4
Germany								
Total expenditure	38.6	48.9	47.9	47.0	43.8	46.3	43.3	49.4
Current revenues	38.3	42.7	45.0	45.8	41.8	43.0	44.4	45.3
Budget balance	+0.2	−5.6	−2.9	−1.2	−2.0	−3.3	1.2	−4.1
France								
Total expenditure	38.5	43.4	46.1	52.1	47.5	51.4	48.7	54.4
Current revenues	38.5	39.7	46.1	49.3	45.4	45.9	47.4	50.4
Budget balance	+1.1	−2.2	0	−2.9	−2.1	−5.5	−1.4	−4.0
Italy								
Total expenditure	34.2	43.2	41.9	50.9	52.9	51.1	44.8	48.5
Current revenues	30.4	31.2	33.3	38.3	41.2	43.5	44.2	45.8
Budget balance	−4.0	−12.9	−8.6	−12.6	−11.8	−7.6	−0.6	−2.7
United Kingdom								
Total expenditure	38.8	46.6	43.0	44.0	39.1	42.2	37.3	42.8
Current revenues	40.2	40.5	39.6	41.2	37.5	36.5	38.9	39.9
Budget balance	+2.9	−4.6	−3.4	−2.8	−1.6	−5.8	1.6	−2.9
Canada								
Total expenditure	34.8	40.1	38.8	45.3	45.7	45.0	37.7	40.1
Current revenues	34.2	36.1	36.1	38.5	39.9	39.7	40.9	41.2
Budget balance	+0.8	−2.5	−2.8	−6.8	−5.8	−5.3	3.2	1.0
Average								
Total expenditure	32.3	37.7	36.2	38.2	41.9	43.3	39.7	37.1
Current revenues	30.8	32.2	33.4	34.8	38.2	38.4	39.5	40.6
Budget balance	0	−4.4	−2.7	−3.4	−3.7	−4.9	−0.2	−3.6

Note:
[a] The figures for 2003 year are not strictly comparable with those for 1985 onwards owing to different definitions of the government sector and some aggregates.
Sources: OECD (1990, 2004).

less expensive or even without costs.[12] It generates no costs if it is carried out by directly printing money (ignoring printing costs), while it involves minimal costs if effected by means of credit agreements between the government and the central bank, which set

[12] A differential cost to consumers could arise from monetary base financing if this stimulates demand to such an extent as to cause inflation (or higher inflation than debt financing).

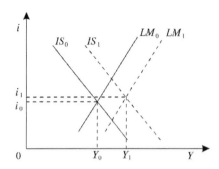

Figure 12.1

a below-market interest rate, thus generating a hidden revenue equal to the difference between the cost of funds raised through government securities issues and the cost of central bank financing. This hidden revenue is called **seigniorage**.[13]

The term is also used to mean the creation of monetary base in excess of that needed to keep the purchasing power of the currency stable. This creates a sort of **inflation tax**, which benefits the government (as it does any other debtor), since inflation reduces the real value of debt if, being unexpected, it does not lead to an increase in nominal interest rates.

The second difference between monetary and debt financing is in the magnitude of their *expansionary effect on income*. In terms of the *IS-LM* framework, monetary financing of expenditure would shift both the *IS* and *LM* curves to the right (figure 12.1). Note that while an increase in income is certain, the effect on the interest rate is ambiguous.

We will provide a formal derivation of the condition for the invariance of the interest rate in a note to subsection 12.3.4. However, we can say right now that this condition is generally difficult to meet. The change in monetary base needed to keep the interest rate constant can be larger or smaller than the additional expenditure to be financed. A monetary policy that seeks to maintain a constant interest rate is called an **accommodating monetary policy**. If such a policy is adopted, an expansionary fiscal policy has full effect and the pre-eminent role assigned to it by Keynes is justified. From this point of view, close coordination of fiscal and monetary policy is vital for obtaining higher income and employment. By contrast, an independent central bank that did not adequately expand the money supply in the presence of an increase in government spending could be harmful, since this would trigger a rise in the interest rate, with adverse effects that we will examine in greater detail in subsection 12.3.4.

---

[13] The term was originally used to indicate the privilege connected with the minting of metal coins with a face value greater than their (positive) intrinsic value. Subsequently, it indicated the profit earned by the central bank as a result of its ability to issue paper money (with no intrinsic value at all) in exchange for financing the government. Seigniorage is also used to indicate the benefits accruing to a reserve currency country (see Chapter 16).

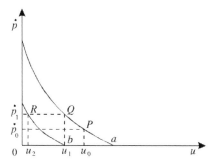

Figure 12.2

Monetary financing can lead to inflation in the presence of full employment or sectoral bottlenecks, or if wage rates, profit margins and other income are an increasing function of the level of economic activity. The inflationary effect, emphasised by the monetarists, is a real possibility in these conditions. If present, policymakers' short-run options would be higher income and employment together with inflation or lower income and employment together with greater monetary stability.

This trade-off is partly a consequence of the fact that the structure of the economic system should be considered given in the short run. In addition to implementing appropriate short-term measures, effective policymaking will be directed towards changing the economic structure, so as to reduce the constraints that bear on short-term decisions.

Consider the following example, which uses the concept of a 'transformation' curve between objectives (see section 4.3), with unemployment and inflation rates as our policy objectives. Referring to figure 12.2, policymakers must choose a point on the Phillips curve a.

Beginning at P, for example, where the unemployment rate is u_0 and the inflation rate is $\dot{p}_0$, policymakers must decide if an expansionary fiscal policy (e.g. an increase in expenditure financed with monetary base) is advisable, being aware that this may cause inflation to increase. This possibility prompts a measure of caution and leads them to choose point Q, where the unemployment rate is u_1, only slightly less than u_0 and inflation is $\dot{p}_1$. Unemployment lower than u_1 would mean higher inflation, which is judged to be unacceptable. If, however, policymakers were able to shift the Phillips curve from a to b, it would still be possible to have an inflation rate of $\dot{p}_1$ with unemployment of $u_2 < u_1$ with an expansionary fiscal policy.

Policymakers can shift the 'transformation' curve[14] downwards with:

- *professional training policies* (obviously, in sectors and jobs where bottlenecks exist)

---

[14] Shifting the curve downwards gives policymakers a wider range of choice, since the objectives are expressed as 'bads' to be minimised. If the objectives were formulated in terms of 'goods', widening the range of choice would mean shifting the transformation curve upwards.

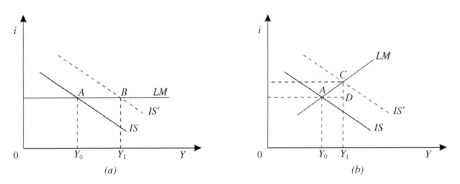

Figure 12.3

- *labour flexibility policies* (in addition to those regarding employment conditions, this includes measures to improve transportation and communications, develop the housing market, etc.)
- *policies to increase productivity* (reorganisation of production, innovation policies) and *output* (incentives to supply, directives to public enterprises) in certain sectors (those affected by bottlenecks, which can cause prices to rise, or those whose products are widely used as inputs by other sectors).

12.3.4 Debt financing

The Keynesian arguments for deficit spending have been criticised, especially by monetarists. The latter have raised the possibility that deficit spending may have no expansionary effect. In their view, monetary financing of public expenditure would only create inflation (see subsection 3.4.3), while government spending would crowd out private investment if it were financed with government debt.

To understand the monetarist critique, let us first examine what would happen if the increase in debt-financed government spending occurred in the presence of a horizontal LM curve – i.e. if the increase was matched by an accommodating monetary policy, expanding the money supply enough to keep the interest rate unchanged. In this case, an increase in spending equal to ΔG would produce an increase in income $\Delta Y = AB$ (figure 12.3a, where LM is horizontal). In other words, we would have an increase in income equal to the increase we would obtain in a Keynesian model that considered only the real economy.

If monetary policy is not accommodating (figure 12.3b, where LM is not horizontal), the increase in income generated by the increase in spending will be smaller, equal to AD; i.e. the multiplier $\Delta Y/\Delta G$ is lower owing to the **crowding-out effect** of the unchanged money supply. Here, the increase in income leads in sequence[15] to a rise in the transaction demand for money, an excess of money demand over money supply, a

---

[15] Note that the reference to a sequence is for illustrative purposes only. In reality, the Keynesian reference model is a static one.

rise in the interest rate, a decline in investment and, therefore, a brake on the increase in income itself.

The *braking effect* can be identified in an analytical framework with reference to a simple Keynesian model:

$$Y = C + I + G$$
$$C = cY$$
$$I = I_0 - ai$$
$$\frac{L_s}{p} = L_d \tag{12.10}$$
$$L_d = L_d^1 + L_d^2$$
$$L_d^1 = kY$$
$$L_d^2 = L_0 - vi$$

where the symbols have the usual meaning (the reader can consult the list of symbols on p. xix).

Solving with respect to Y,[16] we have:

$$Y = \frac{1}{1 - c + ak/v} \left[I_0 + G + \frac{a}{v} \left(\frac{L_s}{p} - L_0 \right) \right] \tag{12.11}$$

The *crowding-out effect* is expressed by the positive term ak/v, which increases the denominator of the multiplier, reducing its value. The reader can verify that the value of the multiplier will be smaller the more sensitive is transaction demand for money to income (the coefficient k), the less sensitive is speculative demand to the interest rate (v) and the more sensitive is investment to the interest rate (a).[17]

The substitution of private investment with government spending is a case of **financial crowding-out**,[18] associated with the increase in the interest rate as a result of the non-monetary financing of government spending (or, more generally, a non-accommodating monetary policy).

Empirical studies have not lent much support to the hypothesis of financial crowding-out. The **crowding-out ratio**[19] has often proved very small or even nil, as in France (0),

---

[16] Substitute the sixth and seventh equation in (12.10) into the fifth, and the fifth into the fourth; then solve the fourth for i and substitute its value into the third; substituting the latter together with the second into the first, we obtain expression (12.11).

[17] Note that the crowding-out effect is always operative, even when government spending is partially or entirely financed with monetary base. The effect would not operate if only the money supply changed so as to keep the interest rate constant.

[18] This differs from **real crowding-out**, which may be caused by a number of factors: proximity to the full employment barrier or the existence of sectoral bottlenecks; substitution of government consumption for private consumption; depressive effects on investment due to a possible increase in uncertainty as a result of government spending; a reduction in exports and an increase in imports under flexible exchange rates and capital mobility (see section 12.4). One possible substitution of public consumption (more generally, government spending) for private consumption (generally, private spending) will be examined in this section.

[19] This is defined as $(l^* - l)/l^*$, where l^* is the government spending multiplier with an accommodating monetary policy and l is the same multiplier with a non-accommodating monetary policy.

and the United States and Canada (0.12). One exception is Japan, where it has been estimated at 0.63 (see Price and Chouraqui, 1983, p. 29, table 8). These issues have been at the heart of a wide-ranging and complex debate, on which we will offer only a few brief remarks to give an idea of the complexity of the issues involved.

According to the new classical macroeconomists, an increase in government spending financed by issuing debt would give rise to full *real* crowding-out, since individuals – predicting that the government will have to raise future taxes to repay the debt – prepare for this by reducing current consumption. Current income will not be affected by government expenditure. To state this position in other terms, government securities do not constitute net wealth: an increase in government debt in private individuals' portfolios will be offset by the perception of an equivalent increase in the present value of their debts owing to expectations of higher future taxes. This assumption of consumer 'ultrarationality', which is already debatable on theoretical grounds, does not appear to find sufficient support in the real world either. In any case the proposition it has generated is known as **Ricardian equivalence** or **Barro–Ricardo equivalence**,[20] meaning that debt financing of government spending is equivalent to tax financing.

The most interesting element of this hypothesis is the consideration of the effects of public action on the formation of expectations (see section 4.7). Nevertheless, the hypothesis fails to convince because individual behaviour is not strictly bound to expectations: expectations that future taxes will have to exceed expenditure does not automatically dictate the need to increase savings on the part of an individual, who may believe that 'others' will pay the excess taxation.

In contrast to the hypothesis of ultrarationality, others argue that the effectiveness of debt financing could be enhanced by the interest-bearing nature of government debt, which would increase disposable income, thus helping to boost the expansionary effects of government spending (Blinder and Solow, 1973). This effect would disappear as soon as a deficit reduction policy were adopted, because the higher taxes would offset the increase in disposable income resulting from interest payments to holders of government securities.[21]

12.4   Fiscal policy under fixed and floating exchange rates

The effects of fiscal policy on income and employment under the two exchange rate systems – similarly to what happens for monetary policy – differ profoundly.

In brief, with fixed exchange rates fiscal policy has full control over aggregate demand, all the more so the greater is the mobility of capital. The opposite is the case if exchange rates float. We will try to understand why this is so by referring first to fixed and then to floating exchange rates:

[20] It was first formulated by David Ricardo and restated by Barro (1974). In a more recent paper Barro admits that the way public expenditure is financed can affect the level of income through labour supply effects (see Barro, 1989).

[21] An excellent survey of the various positions in the debate on debt financing of government spending is given by Stevenson, Muscatelli and Gregory (1988, section 6.3).

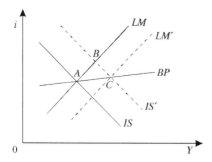

Figure 12.4

(1) It may be useful to recall that under fixed exchange rates balance of payments surpluses or deficits cannot cause changes in the exchange rate, producing variations in monetary base instead if sterilisation is not used. Let us consider an expansionary *fiscal policy* – for example, an increase in government spending that is not financed with the monetary base. This measure will have two effects on the balance of payments: first, the goods balance will worsen, owing to the resulting rise in income; second, there will be an improvement in the capital movements balance, owing to the rise in the interest rate following the increase in income with no expansion of the money supply. The net effect will depend on the responsiveness of the different markets.

We initially consider the case of an improvement in the balance of payments resulting from a situation in which the international financial market is more responsive than the international goods market. There will therefore be an increase in monetary base to facilitate the expansion triggered by government spending. This is shown in figure 12.4.

The initial point of simultaneous equilibrium is *A*. *BP* is flatter than *LM* owing to the considerable responsiveness of international capital movements to changes in the interest rate. The increase in government expenditure will shift *IS* to the right, moving its intersection with *LM* to *B*, which, since it is above *BP*, denotes a balance of payments surplus. The surplus gives rise to an increase in the monetary base and thus shifts *LM* to the right, to *C*, where the surplus is eliminated and general macroeconomic equilibrium is restored, although at a higher level of income.

If the negative effect on the balance of payments of the deterioration in the goods balance should predominate, owing to a lack of capital mobility, *BP* would be steeper than *LM* and the situation would be that shown in figure 12.5.

Point *B* now denotes a balance of payments deficit. The deficit causes a contraction in the monetary base and, therefore, shifts *LM* upwards to *C*, where there is a new equilibrium for all markets at a higher income level, despite the crowding-out effect deriving from the contraction in the money supply.

A shared feature of these two situations is the positive effect on income of an expansionary fiscal policy under a fixed-exchange rate system, which is reinforced by high capital mobility and dampened by low capital mobility.

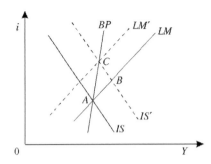

Figure 12.5

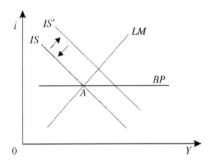

Figure 12.6

(2) Let us now refer to fiscal policy under floating exchange rates. We should remind ourselves that in a flexible-exchange rate environment the incipient balance of payments surplus or deficit[22] that fiscal policy can produce leads to a change in the *exchange rate* rather than a change in monetary base, as it does under fixed exchange rates.

An increase in debt-financed government spending will cause both income and interest rates to rise. This will worsen the goods movements balance and improve the capital movements balance, respectively. If capital movements are sufficiently responsive to cause an incipient improvement in the overall balance of payments, the currency will appreciate, as it is no longer constrained within the limits of the fixed exchange rate system. The resulting loss of competitiveness will reduce net exports and income. The pressure on the currency to appreciate will be stronger the greater is capital mobility (i.e. the inflow of capital induced by a given change in the interest rate) and the greater is the tendency of the interest rate to change following the initial increase in autonomous spending.

Figure 12.6 shows the impact of fiscal policy in the case of perfect capital mobility. In this case, fiscal measures are entirely ineffective. The pressure to appreciate

---

[22] We refer to an 'incipient' imbalance since, at least in theory, in the regime we are dealing with now exchange rate variations automatically produce external balance. Economists sometimes refer to an *ex ante* imbalance – i.e. to the imbalance that would tend to be created *before* changes in the exchange rate produce the adjustment of the balance of payments (see Dernburg, 1989, pp. 117–8).

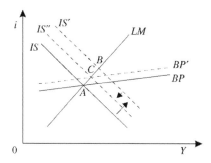

Figure 12.7

is so strong that only a reduction in net exports equal to the initial increase in autonomous spending will restore equilibrium at *A* (complete crowding-out). Only then will the demand pressure that gave rise to the initial increase in interest rates disappear. Note that if capital is highly mobile, even if the final equilibrium is almost exactly equal to the initial equilibrium in terms of the income level and interest rates, the composition of demand and the balance of payments has changed: the government expenditure component of demand has increased, while foreign demand has fallen, and the net balance on goods movements has declined, while that on capital movements has increased.

If capital is not perfectly mobile, fiscal policy may be effective to some degree: the less mobile is capital, the greater the effectiveness. Examine figure 12.7, which shows a fairly flat *BP*, indicating high but not perfect capital mobility. With an expansionary fiscal policy, *IS* shifts to *IS'* and the system moves from *A* to *B*. At *B*, there is an incipient balance of payments surplus owing to the high interest rate, and the surplus will cause the currency to appreciate.

Given the increase in the interest rate, the size of the net inflow of capital will depend on the *mobility of capital*. The less mobile is capital, the smaller the inflow and consequently the smaller the appreciation of the currency. The appreciation will cause a reduction in net exports and therefore in aggregate demand (*IS'* will therefore move backwards to *IS''*) and shift the equilibrium conditions for the balance of payments: at a given interest rate, the appreciation of the currency will make equilibrium possible only at lower levels of income. *BP* will therefore move upwards to *BP'*. The final point of simultaneous equilibrium in the three markets will be *C*, with a lower income level than *B* (owing to the fall in net exports) but higher than the initial level at *A*.

If capital mobility is so low that *BP* is steeper than *LM*, fiscal policy can be quite effective. Examine figure 12.8. An expansionary fiscal policy will shift *IS* towards *IS'* and the system will move from *A* to *B*, where *B* denotes a balance of payments deficit owing to the dominance of the adverse effects of the expansion of demand (which have a direct impact on net exports) over the beneficial effects of the expansion (which operate on capital movements through the interest rate). The beneficial effects are small owing to the limited mobility of capital. The trend towards

Table 12.3 *Effectiveness of expansionary fiscal policy on income under different exchange rate regimes and different degrees of capital mobility*

Fixed exchange rates		Floating exchange rates	
Capital mobility	No capital mobility	Capital mobility	No capital mobility
Highly effective: capital mobility also causes monetary expansion	*Effective*, albeit less so than under capital mobility	*Not very effective*: capital mobility causes the currency to appreciate; with perfect mobility, there is complete crowding-out of foreign demand	*Effective*: the depreciation of the currency reinforces the fiscal stimulus

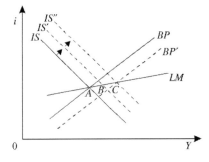

Figure 12.8

a balance of payments deficit causes the currency to depreciate, which boosts net exports, shifting *IS'* to *IS''* and *BP* to *BP'*. The final equilibrium will be in *C*.

Table 12.3 summarises the effects of fiscal policy in the two exchange rate systems and with differing degrees of capital mobility. For reasons of clarity, we refer to an expansionary policy only.

12.5   Public debt

12.5.1   Historical developments in selected countries

Public debt will grow over time if budget deficits persist. This has occurred in many countries in the post-war period, as shown by table 12.4.

12.5.2   The determinants of the growth in public debt

Let us take a look at the reasons for the rise in the ratio between nominal public debt, B, and nominal GDP, pY, first from an abstract point of view and then in more concrete terms.

Table 12.4 *The public debt in various European countries, 1970–2003 (percentage of GDP)*

	1970	1975	1980	1985	1990	1995	2000[b]	2003[b]
Austria	18.9	23.3	36.2	49.2	57.2	69.2	66.8	65.0
Belgium	65.3	59.5	78.6	122.3	129.2	134.0	109.6	100.5
Denmark	–	6.5	36.5	70.0	57.8	69.3	47.3	45.0
Finland	11.7	6.6	11.5	16.2	14.3	57.2	44.5	45.3
France	–	–	19.8	30.8	35.1	54.6	57.2	63.0
Germany[a]	18.6	24.8	31.7	41.7	43.5	57.0	60.2	54.2
Greece	19.8	20.2	25.0	53.6	79.6	108.7	106.2	103.0
Ireland	53.6	63.6	75.2	109.6	101.5	82.7	39.3	32.0
Italy	37.9	57.2	58.2	81.9	97.2	123.2	110.6	106.2
Luxembourg	19.0	12.3	9.3	9.7	4.4	5.6	5.5	4.9
The Netherlands	–	40.8	46.0	70.1	77.0	77.2	55.8	54.8
Portugal	–	22.2	32.3	61.5	58.3	64.3	53.3	59.4
United Kingdom	78.7	61.2	53.2	52.7	34.0	51.8	42.1	39.9
Spain	15.0	12.3	16.8	42.3	43.6	63.9	60.6	50.8
Sweden	27.4	26.6	40.3	62.4	42.3	76.2	52.8	51.9
EU–15	–	–	**38.0**	**53.2**	**54.4**	**70.2**	**64.3**	**64.2**

Notes:
[a] Prior to 1990 data refers to Western Germany.
[b] Data from 1970 to 1995 are not comparable with the rest.
Source: European Commission (2004).

The ratio $B/(pY)$ increases over time if the numerator increases more rapidly than the denominator, i.e. if, approximately:

$$\dot{B} - \dot{p} - \dot{Y} > 0 \tag{12.12}$$

where a dot over a variable indicates its rate of change per unit of time. Thus, $\dot{B} \equiv (\Delta B/\Delta t)/B$. If we always refer to changes over the unit of time considered, we can write $\dot{B} \equiv \Delta B/B$.[23]

On what does ΔB depend?

(1) Assume that we start with a *primary balance equal to zero*, i.e. $G_p - T = 0$. In this case public debt can increase only as a result of interest payments (equal to iB) on the existing stock of debt, if there is no monetary financing. The rate of increase in public debt will then be iB/B, or i. Expression (12.12) can be rewritten as:

$$i - \dot{p} - \dot{Y} > 0 \tag{12.12'}$$

---

[23] Let us denote $B/(pY)$ with z, i.e. we have $z = B/(pY)$. Taking the log of this expression and differentiating with respect to time, we obtain $\dot{z} = \dot{B} - \dot{p} - \dot{Y}$. We can state that $\dot{z} > 0$ if $\dot{B} - \dot{p} - \dot{Y} > 0$; but if $\dot{z} > 0$, the ratio of debt to nominal GDP increases. Hence, the condition for an increase in the ratio is $\dot{B} - \dot{p} - \dot{Y} > 0$. This condition holds for continuous changes in the variables, but is only approximately valid for discrete changes.

But $i - \dot{p}$ is the real (*ex post*) interest rate. We can therefore say that with no primary deficit (or surplus) and no monetary financing the ratio of public debt to GDP increases if the real interest rate is higher than the GDP growth rate.[24]

(2) Suppose instead that we have a *primary deficit*. If it were entirely financed with the monetary base, public debt would not be increased by the primary deficit and the conclusion under point 1 would still hold. If the primary deficit were only partly financed with the monetary base, there would be an additional source of debt growth: the debt could in fact increase even if the real interest rate were equal to, rather than higher than, the rate of GDP growth. By contrast, the existence of a primary surplus would slow the growth in the debt, even eliminating it if appropriate real interest rates and GDP growth rates prevailed.

This brief analysis can help us understand the sharp increase in the ratio of public debt to GDP in the 1980s and in the early 1990s. During this period the real interest rate was well above the rate of GDP growth, for at least two reasons:

(a) the monetary tightening in the United States at the end of the 1970s caused world interest rates to rise

(b) the rate of GDP growth slowed down in Europe as a result of a tight monetary policy and participation in the Exchange Rate Mechanism (ERM) (see chapter 16).

12.5.3   *Limits to debt growth*

Are there limits to the growth of public debt? Obviously, the problem must be stated in relative, rather than absolute, terms. We therefore need to identify the most suitable yardstick. In our earlier discussion, we compared the size of public debt with GDP at current prices. This was done simply for '**normalising**' purposes. Since each new issue of securities is denominated in money at current purchasing power, the nominal value of the debt tends to increase over time; we can see if the debt is growing in real terms by dividing this value by the current price level. Dividing the real value of the public debt by real GDP, we can determine the relative increase in the two variables – the same as we would, say, in comparing the growth rate of consumption and investment with income.

Beyond this, we cannot attribute any other economic meaning to the ratio of public debt to GDP. The question about limits to the growth of public debt is relevant insofar as that growth has economic repercussions, such as insolvency risk. From this point of view, a more significant ratio would be that between *public debt and the total assets (or liabilities) of the economy*. The concentration of debtors, of which an increase in this ratio would be an indicator, is in fact dangerous in itself.

Nevertheless, the ratio of public debt to total assets is not used for a variety of reasons, including greater calculation difficulty. Instead, we use the ratio of public debt

---

[24] Note that, alternatively, the condition can be expressed in terms of the nominal interest rate and the rate of GDP growth at current prices (approximately equal to the rate of GDP growth at constant prices increased by the rate of inflation): the ratio increases if $i > \dot{Y} + \dot{p}$.

to income in order to have at least a rough idea of current trends and the risk of default. The underlying issue can be stated as follows: if a high debt/GDP ratio rises continuously rather than stabilising or falling, there are two possible outcomes. One is the insolvency of the debtor (the government); the other is credit rationing (or complete denial of credit) by the creditor (i.e. the market).[25] There have been real-life instances of both, although they have been associated with 'revolutions' or 'breakdown' in the countries concerned.

12.5.4   Debt-reduction policies

Apart from debt repudiation, a variety of instruments can be used to influence the variables on which the dynamics of the debt/GDP ratio depend, as discussed in subsection 12.5.2.

In general, debt reduction objectives expressed in terms of a ceiling on the ratio between the deficit and GDP and the ratio between public debt and GDP were established in the 1990s in Europe with the Maastricht agreements, which set out the eligibility requirements for admission to EMU. Participation in EMU imposed a similar restriction on the deficit/GDP ratio under the Stability and Growth Pact (SGP) (see subsection 16.6.3 and section 18.6).

Income growth policies

Measures designed to promote *income growth* (the growth of the denominator of the debt/GDP ratio) may be difficult to implement because under our assumption of a large public debt we cannot use traditional fiscal tools to stimulate global demand (increasing expenditure and reducing taxes), since this would increase the deficit. Growth can be fostered by restructuring government spending and taxes (without increasing the deficit). Government spending can be made more efficient and a growth-oriented industrial policy can be implemented. Taxation can be directed to enhancing incentives for private economic activity. Growth can also be enhanced by using other policy tools, both microeconomic, such as regulation (or deregulation)[26], and macroeconomic, such as an easy monetary policy, an incomes policy (see chapter 13) and devaluation or depreciation of the domestic currency (see chapter 14).

Policies for the primary balance

Although not strictly necessary, a primary surplus certainly facilitates the reduction of the debt/GDP ratio. Improving the primary balance is an explicit objective of any policy aimed at stabilising this ratio. In order to generate a primary surplus, policymakers can either *reduce primary spending* or *increase revenues*:

---

[25] Insolvency can take a number of forms: the government may **repudiate** the debt, **fund** it (i.e. convert maturities from short-term into long-term, or even perpetual ones) or introduce some other change in the terms of the loan (e.g. the interest rate). Credit rationing may occur in the form of only partial placement of new issues or as attempts by the public to **monetise** existing public debt.

[26] International opening and liberalisation were the main instruments used by Ireland to reduce the debt/GDP ratio.

(1) *Expenditure policies.* Reducing spending is one theoretically possible step, but this can produce a considerable welfare loss for the public as well as undermine the growth potential of the economy unless the quality of public services can be significantly improved.

(2) *Revenue policies.* Increasing revenues would also help increase the primary surplus and so help reduce the debt/GDP ratio. However, raising tax revenue has an adverse impact on income, thus reducing the denominator of the ratio. As with expenditure, the most appropriate solution seems to be the reorganisation and improved operation of the administrative machinery of government, which should reduce tax evasion, avoidance and erosion. A role in this can be played by closer international coordination.

Privatisation of public sector enterprises is seen as a possible source of revenues to reduce the borrowing requirement and a way to increase the efficiency of the productive system, with a beneficial effect on income growth. However, this second aspect of privatisation is controversial since it is debatable whether the efficiency of the private sector is clearly superior to that of the public sector, as we saw in section 6.4. In Italy, privatisation made a significant contribution to policies first for admission to EMU and then to compliance with the SGP.

Interest rate policies

Lowering the real interest rate paid on public debt may contribute to lowering the debt/GDP ratio. This can be accomplished in at least two ways:

(1) The public debt can be managed in such a way as to reduce the *real cost of the debt*, especially by adjusting the terms applied to debt issues or improving issuing techniques and the functioning of the secondary government securities market.

(2) A more general solution to lowering the real interest rate involves the relationship with *world financial markets*. With a fixed (or managed) exchange rate, a country's interest rates, apart from the exchange rate risk, are more closely linked to those abroad the greater is the international capital mobility. There are then two possible solutions:

   (a) One can think of *reducing capital mobility* in order to make it feasible to undertake policies aimed at keeping domestic rates lower than those abroad, without triggering undesired increases in the exchange rate (depreciations). This can be done by imposing constraints on capital movements or a tax on capital invested abroad, as suggested by Tobin. We will return to this question in section 20.2.

   (b) A very different solution is to enhance *exchange rate stability* and induce similar expectations, in order to reduce or eliminate the exchange rate depreciation premium demanded by agents buying liabilities denominated in the home currency (see subsection 10.2.2).

The former solution has not been implemented by any country so far. The latter has been followed by some countries: e.g. Italy decided first to renew its participation in fixed exchange agreements (the EMS, see section 16.6) in 1996, after having suspended their application in 1992, and then to participate in EMU (see section 18.4) having an eye also to the possibility offered by this participation to reduce home interest rates.

12.6   Summary

1   *Fiscal policy* involves tax and expenditure measures. It is normally aimed at achieving income and employment objectives.

2   *Taxation* can come in the form of lump-sum taxation, proportional taxation or progressive taxation. The latter serves as an *automatic stabiliser*. Tax revenue increases if prices rise in the presence of progressive taxation (fiscal drag). The stabilising effect of progressive taxation can be amplified by pro-cyclical price movements. Fiscal drag has perverse effects in the presence of stagflation.

3   In the 1970s and 1980s *growth in government expenditure* in the industrial countries was often more rapid than the increase in tax revenue, for a number of reasons. In recent years, this has primarily been due to interest payments on public debt.

4   *Expenditure* can be financed with taxes (balanced budget) or by a deficit. The balanced budget theorem stresses the possibility of achieving any income objective without adding to the budget deficit.

5   According to Keynes, *deficit spending* has a larger impact on income. Deficit spending can be financed either with the monetary base or government bonds.

6   *Monetary base financing* is less expensive (seigniorage) and has a larger impact on income, since it gives rise to a simultaneous rightward shift of the *IS* and *LM* curves. Close to the full employment level, the effect on income may also be associated with inflationary tensions.

7   *Debt financing* leaves the quantity of monetary base unchanged and causes interest rates to rise; consequently, government expenditure crowds-out private investment (financial crowding-out).

8   Real *crowding-out* mainly takes place: when the economy is close to full employment; when government spending replaces private spending, which could occur if the 'ultrarationality' hypothesis holds (Barro–Ricardo equivalence); and when public spending is a substitute for exports under flexible exchange rates and capital mobility.

9   Fiscal policy is very effective with *fixed-rate regimes*, all the more so the higher the mobility of capital, which causes a change in money supply. More precisely, an expansionary fiscal policy increases the money supply, thus reinforcing the expansionary effect.

10   The *ratio of public debt to GDP* increases when the real interest rate is higher than the rate of GDP growth in the presence of a primary balance or deficit.

11   There are no definite limits to the increase in the debt/GDP ratio, which is not, however, the best indicator of a government's insolvency risk. Policies aimed at *reducing this ratio* comprise measures for income growth, reduction of primary expenditure and interest rates and increasing revenues.

13 Incomes and price policies

13.1 Introduction

In chapter 3, inflation was characterised as the outcome of a competition in which agents seek to increase their share of income by increasing the price of the good they sell. The connection between the distribution of income and the price level should therefore be clear.

The objective of **incomes policy** is to contain increases in the general price level by controlling *distributive variables*, which are essentially the wage rate and/or the profit margin. Take the wage rate, for example. It represents *income* for a worker and a *cost* for a firm. An incomes policy may seek to limit wage increases in order to keep labour costs – and costs in general – low and thus reduce the possibility of price increases. In section 13.2 we develop this simple concept in an abstract context, referring to a closed economic system in which there is one good and only two categories of income: *wages* and *profits*. We then distinguish between different types of incomes policy on the basis of their degree of *coerciveness* (section 13.3). Section 13.4 analyses the many problems that arise with the direct *control* of wages and/or other incomes (statist policies), while section 13.5 examines the possibilities and limitations of 'market-based' incomes policies. Section 13.6 is devoted to 'institutional' incomes policies and section 13.7 analyses the role of productivity-boosting measures in relation to incomes policies. Section 13.8 offers a brief survey of incomes policy experiments in the real world.

13.2 Income distribution, full cost and incomes policy

For simplicity, we consider a closed economy producing only one good; there is no fixed capital and there are only two types of income recipient: workers and capitalists. The total value of output will therefore be equal to:

$$pY = W + R \tag{13.1}$$

where p and Y are the price and quantity of the good, W is total wages and R total profits, both expressed in money terms.

Total wages are obtained by multiplying the nominal wage rate, w, by the number of employed workers, N. If we take this relation into account and divide both sides of the previous expression by Y, we have:

$$p = \frac{wN}{Y} + \frac{R}{Y} \tag{13.2}$$

Now consider that *total profits* can be expressed in a variety of ways. For example, they can be given as the **rate of profit** (i.e. profits as a ratio to the capital employed) times capital employed or the *mark-up rate* times prime costs. In the second case, since costs are represented by wages only, if we indicate the profit margin with g we have $R \equiv wNg$. Equation 13.2 can therefore be rewritten as:

$$p = \frac{wN}{Y} + \frac{wNg}{Y} = \frac{wN}{Y}(1+g) \tag{13.3}$$

Equation (13.3) is simply a mark-up equation, expressing the *full cost principle*. Considering that *average labour productivity* is $\pi = Y/N$, by substitution we have:

$$p = \frac{w}{\pi}(1+g) \tag{13.4}$$

Deriving this simple relation from the identity between output and distributed income underscores the link between *price-setting* and *income distribution*. We will consider additional aspects later.

Let us now examine (13.4). In dynamic terms price changes can be expressed as:

$$\dot{p} = \dot{w} - \dot{\pi} + (1 \dotplus g) \tag{13.5}$$

Sufficient conditions for no inflation (i.e. $\dot{p} = 0$) are that $\dot{w} = \dot{\pi}$ and $(1 \dotplus g) = 0$. In other words, there will be no rise in prices if the percentage change in the nominal wage rate is equal to that in productivity *and* the profit margin does not change. A change in the wage rate equal to that in labour productivity is on its own neither a necessary nor a sufficient condition.

If both sufficient conditions for no inflation held, distributive shares would not change. The share of wages in income is equal to $W/pY = wN/pY = w/p\pi$. This does not change if $\dot{w} - \dot{p} - \dot{\pi} = 0$. If $\dot{w} = \dot{\pi}$ and $\dot{p} = 0$, this condition is met and the ratio remains constant. The invariance of the share of wages in total income means that the share of profits is also unchanged, since these are the only categories of income.

To sum up, *price invariance* requires certain forms of behaviour on the part of both categories of income recipient. If the change in the wage rate is equal to that in productivity and the profit margin does not change, distributive shares do not change. Obviously, constant prices are not inconsistent with a change in distributive shares. We said that $\dot{w} = \dot{\pi}$ and $(1 \dotplus g) = 0$ are only sufficient conditions: prices can still be constant if the change in the wage rate is different from that in productivity (thus permitting changes in distributive shares) as long as the profit margin changes in the opposite direction by an amount equal to the difference between wage and productivity growth. For example, there will be no change in prices if $\dot{w} = 10$ per cent, $\dot{\pi} = 6$ per cent and $(1 + g) = -4$ per cent.

This reconfirms our depiction of inflation as the product of a *competition to increase one's share of total income*. Inflation ceases if this competition ends and the various classes of income recipient maintain (or are induced or forced to maintain) their share of income, or if they agree on how shares should change, offsetting an increase for one group with a decline for the other group.

Before examining the ways incomes policy can be implemented, we should emphasise the limitations of the simple framework we have adopted so far. First and foremost, note that we have assumed a one-good (or one-industry) economy without fixed capital where productivity is the same for all firms. In a many-industry world, productivity changes differ across industries, which gives rise to the problem of which change in productivity should be used as a benchmark for changes in nominal wage rates. We address this question in section 13.4. In addition, the multiplicity of goods forces us to consider other variable costs, such as those of *raw materials*, in the mark-up formula.[1]

The existence of fixed capital in real life means that we must interpret the profit margin, g, as a *gross* margin, so as to cover the depreciation costs of capital itself. Changes in the gross margin do not necessarily indicate equal changes in the net margin; nor does a constant gross margin imply a constant net margin and therefore a constant share of profits in income. Moreover, in reality there is at least one other class of income recipients in addition to workers and capitalists: recipients of rent, or *rentiers*. The form and importance of rent can change over time, so prices may change even when the shares of wages and profits are unchanged. Part of income (more precisely, part of GDP at market prices) is also appropriated by the government in the form of direct and indirect taxes (net of subsidies). Changes in *taxation* can therefore also give rise to changes in the prices of goods. The theory of *tax shifting* can help us predict these effects (see Stiglitz, 1988, chapter 17).

Finally, an *open economy* poses an additional problem, since price changes in the domestic currency of imported raw materials and semifinished goods also give rise to price changes in the final product.

We can conclude by recalling that many conditions (or rules) must be satisfied for prices to remain constant. The most frequently used rules (or **guidelines**) of incomes policy are those that require wage rates to increase at the same rate as average labour productivity and no change in the profit margin. These are not the only possible rules, however, nor do they guarantee no inflation if other conditions are not met (e.g. if there is a change in taxation or the share of rent in national income or in the prices of imported raw materials).

---

[1] Moreover, logical difficulties arise in using the mark-up formula to explain price setting by a firm that produces more than one good. These are a consequence of the fact that the price of each product is made to depend on labour productivity, but this cannot be calculated if we do not know the prices of the various goods.

13.3   Coercion and incomes policies

Incomes policies can be distinguished according to their relative coerciveness into three
basic types: statist, market and institutional.

Statist incomes policies impose specific behaviour – by way of regulation, moral
suasion or mere jawboning – on workers and/or capitalists with regard to changes in
wages or profit margins: for example, a *wage freeze* ($\dot{w} = 0$) is a statist policy where
government rules replace the free decisions of workers and capitalists. They are therefore
direct control measures.

By contrast, **market incomes policies** involve the government's use of a system of *incentives or disincentives* (rather than prescriptive rules) to steer the autonomous choices of
income recipients in an anti-inflationary direction. For example, an agreement between
workers and capitalists to hold prices steady might be rewarded with tax concessions.

Institutional policies seek to instil cooperative industrial relations, by establishing a
structure of appropriate *institutional mechanisms* such as arbitration procedures, 'social
agreements', etc. Institutional policies are essentially reforms that aim to change the
nature of the competition (or game) between the various income recipients.

13.4   Statist policies

Since they consist of direct control measures, statist policies should offer the advantage
of immediacy and effectiveness. In practice, however, many problems can arise. We will
distinguish such difficulties according to whether the policies affect wages only or also
comprise other forms of income.

Wage policies, which have the advantage of being easier to implement, do not guarantee an anti-inflationary outcome. We know from (13.5) that any rule governing wages
(e.g. limiting growth in the wage rate to productivity growth) may not ensure price
stability as long as profit margins can still be widened. In fact, the latter can be set arbitrarily in the absence of government or market constraints (e.g. strong international
competitive pressures, which might force a narrowing of margins).

The possibility of price increases occurring even with constraints on wage rises may
be increased by the conditions in which the incomes policy rules must actually be
formulated, especially by the presence of different industries with differing levels and
rates of growth of productivity. In this case, two different rules are possible:

(a) the *wage rate in each industry* should change by the same percentage as productivity
in that industry; or
(b) the *wage rate in all industries* should change by the same percentage as the change
in the *average* productivity of the economy as a whole.

Rule (a) is better suited to avoiding changes in the general price level: if profit margins
remained unchanged, prices would not rise in any industry. However, a labour union
sensitive to problems of equity among workers would find it difficult to accept such
a rule. The more equitable rule (b) has greater problems of effectiveness. In industries

with slower productivity growth, the wage rate would rise faster than productivity, since its growth would be linked to the rise in average productivity for all industries. With no change in profit margins, prices would rise. This increase would result in a *general* increase in the price level unless it was offset by a reduction in prices in industries with faster productivity growth. Such a reduction would be possible in theory, as long as profit margins did not change in these industries, since the wage rate would be increasing less rapidly than industry productivity. However, it is unlikely that the required conditions can be met as there are strong *inertial factors* inhibiting any reduction in prices.[2] The likely consequence of rule (b) is therefore an increase in the general price level associated with an increase in prices in industries with a low rate of productivity growth and no change in prices in more dynamic industries.

It must also be noted that a coercive incomes policy limited to wages only may not have significant and immediate effects if its announcement provokes a reaction from workers supported by a highly combative and powerful union. In addition to the coercive nature of the policy, the union may object to its partial nature, which offers the prospect not so much of a frozen distribution (which might in any case be considered unsatisfactory) but rather a worsening of wage earners' share of income, if average profit margins are increased.

Let us now examine the problems that arise in relation to more complete (or general) forms of incomes policy.

The usual reason cited for limiting policy measures to wage income is the simplicity of measuring wages compared with the difficulty of ascertaining profits, which is often only possible after a detailed examination of jealously guarded company information. This problem has prompted efforts to supplement wage policies with price control measures: while it is difficult to determine profit margins, prices are 'visible and measurable'. However, there are also a multitude of different prices, the types of good sold change and classifications are more difficult and uncertain than for wages. There is also a difference between the position of wage earners and entrepreneurs: the former are paid on the basis of prices *agreed* during wage bargaining; the latter obtain their income from prices *set* in a relatively free manner, albeit with certain limitations imposed by the existence of actual or potential competitors. Changes in wages are thus slower, more difficult and transparent, while changes in profits are more rapid, freer and difficult to observe (partly due to qualitative and quantitative differences in products). This explains the difficulties of price control policies as a substitute for controlling profit margins, but these should not be overstressed. In fact it is possible to identify a relatively limited number of goods whose prices play a key role in the overall price structure, such that exercising close control over them would ensure control over the general price level (Rothschild, 1973).

Given the difference in the ability of wage earners and entrepreneurs to set the price of the good they supply, effective price control can play an important role in persuading workers to accept wage control policies.

---

[2] In addition to the factors determining *price stickiness* (e.g. menu costs), this is due to the resistance of oligopolistic firms to price reductions for fear of triggering a price war with competitors, who might interpret the cut as a sign of aggression.

It is often argued that another obstacle to a *general* incomes policy is that price controls reduce the efficiency of the economy by constraining 'market forces'. In particular, constant profit margins do not provide an incentive to increase productivity. More generally, 'freezing' distributive shares conflicts with the motivations and the operation of a market economy. There is some element of truth in this argument. However, the problem is largely an abstract one. In the real world of non-competitive markets, *administered prices* are the norm and they are quite different from those of Walrasian equilibrium, which would reflect scarcity and guarantee allocative efficiency. In this reality, directives and intervention in the price sector are not necessarily more problematic than intervention in the wage sector, even though there may be substantial differences in their implementation (Rothschild, 1973). In fact, a *government* price policy might at least act as a counterweight to the market power of large oligopolistic firms.

13.5 Market-based policies

There are two types of market-based incomes policies:

(1) One is founded on the idea that inflation is an *external diseconomy*, like pollution. The government can therefore set a total amount of the diseconomy that can be produced and assign rights to produce the diseconomy to individual firms up to that point, leaving them free to choose between exercising the right directly or selling it to someone else. In other words, **tradable price increase permits** can be created. If, for example, the limit on price increases is 1 per cent and a firm does not raise its prices at all, it can sell the right to other firms. This mechanism can also be used to restrain that special kind of price which is the wage rate, thus creating tradable wage increase permits.

Proposals of this sort, which have been advanced by leading scholars (see Weitzacker, 1975; Lerner, 1978; Lerner and Colander, 1980), seek to reconcile the macroeconomic objective of price stability with microeconomic flexibility for firms, introducing rewards for virtuous behaviour and penalising inflationary conduct. Nevertheless, if productivity growth differs across industries and is largely independent of firm behaviour, this sort of policy may excessively punish industries that are already disadvantaged by a low rate of productivity growth. Moreover, the difficulties of implementing such proposals are at least as formidable as those facing statist policies. This may help explain the absence of any practical attempts to implement them.

(2) The second type of market-based policy seeks to create incentives for not increasing prices and disincentives for increasing them through the tax system. Such measures are called **tax-tied incomes policies** or **tax-based incomes policies** (TIPs) (Wallich and Weintraub, 1971).

If incentives are granted to firms or workers that do not increase their prices (or do not raise them above some threshold), we have so-called **reward TIPs**. If, instead, sanctions are imposed for excessive price increases, we have **penalty TIPs**.

The objections to this sort of policy are similar to those for price increase permits (for more on this, see Seidman, 1978).

13.6   Institutional policies

We can try to avoid the inflationary consequences of the distributive conflict by establishing certain rules of the game, i.e. we can introduce regulations or practices that *foster cooperative behaviour*. We have already said that institutional policies seek to transform the nature of the distributive game from non-cooperative to cooperative. This can be done in three ways:

(1) First, the government can introduce an explicit requirement for cooperation or in any case impose a 'last-resort' cooperative solution, such as *arbitration*.
(2) An alternative solution would be to engage in an **economic exchange** that, for example, ensures certain levels of taxes, subsidies, various measures with regard to incomes, labour and industrial policies for employers and workers that reach a non-inflationary agreement on wages and/or behave in a non-inflationary way. Another possibility would simply be to announce different government policies in response to different behaviour by employers and workers. More generally, an *institutional incomes policy* could be applied within the framework of a planned economy. For example, the plan could forecast some level of private investment, set the level of government investment and the rate of wage increase that, ensuring a flow of savings equal to investment, would avoid both cost-push and demand-pull inflation. The content of such an incomes policy would be significantly different from that normally attributed to it. It would be a much more complex mechanism, ensuring both the desired level of investment and monetary stability.
(3) A third approach involves a **political exchange** consisting in the government's promise to act in certain ways in areas that are not strictly economic (e.g. civil rights) or that involve the general political programme of the government itself, or even in drafting a '**social pact**' (or *social agreement*) that sets out lines of action in economic and social matters agreed to by the social partners.

The feasibility of implementing the various forms of institutional policy depends on a wide variety of economic, social and political circumstances. We have indicated the policies in increasing order of difficulty of implementation. Some argue that a key element in instituting effective institutional incomes policies is **neo-corporatism**, which is a situation characterised by centralisation of bargaining, a general attitude of consensus between labour and employers and government involvement in wage negotiations. The findings of some econometric studies reveal the existence of a negative relationship between the degree of neo-corporatism and the Okun misery index (Tarantelli, 1983): this means that a high level of neo-corporatism is successful in lowering the inflation rate (given the unemployment rate) or the unemployment rate (given the inflation rate). Later studies have been contradictory, both confirming and rejecting these findings (Calmfors, 1993; Acocella and Ciccarone, 1995; Acocella and Di Bartolomeo, 2001).

13.7 Incomes policy and productivity policies

Except in some of its versions, such as the economic and political exchange models, incomes policy does not seek to change many aspects of the existing situation, in particular the rate of *productivity growth*. This variable has an important role in determining the consistency of wage growth with price stability. For example, if productivity increases by 2 per cent, an equal rise in the wage rate and an unchanged profit margin will ensure price stability. If productivity rose by 4 per cent, it would be possible to increase the wage rate by more than 2 per cent and/or increase the profit margin without inflationary consequences.

Accordingly, we can broaden the choice set of incomes policy to comprise measures aimed at increasing the rate of productivity growth. In order to identify these measures we must first examine the factors on which productivity depends. These can be factors *internal* and *external* to the firm.

Among the internal factors, some are controlled by workers, others by the firm. The former include the level of *work effort* and any preparation and professional training undertaken at the worker's initiative. The latter include professional training provided by the firm, work organisation, capital and technology. Some of these factors can then be the object of negotiations over incomes policy between workers and employers, since such factors are under their control. More specifically, a union may accept a temporary ceiling on wage increases, taking the productivity gains obtainable in the short term as given, but at the same time it may ask for a commitment from firms to introduce organisational and technological innovations that will ease the productivity constraint on wage rises in the future.

Among the external factors that influence labour productivity are those associated with *interfirm* and *intersectoral relationships*. For example, the availability of inputs of goods as well as the terms of their supply (e.g. quality and cost) can be important factors. The overall productivity of, say, the manufacturing sector thus depends on the availability of cheap and efficient transportation and communications networks, schools and universities, research centres, information services, financial services, etc. Since it is not possible for the market to guarantee all the conditions necessary for the optimal development of these activities, government intervention – in particular, through industrial policy – may be necessary, as we argued in section 8.1. This form of intervention can play an ancillary role to incomes policy.

13.8 Incomes policy in the real world

The various forms of incomes policy we have discussed here have been implemented on numerous occasions in the post-war period (see box 13.1). Above all, governments have established non-coercive guidelines backed up by *moral suasion* as well as the threat of some form of retaliation (restrictive measures, as in Sweden, or exclusion from government procurement contracts, as in Austria or the United States). There have also been examples of negotiation and more-or-less formal exchanges between wage moderation and expansionary policies, such as in the United Kingdom in the 1960s and 1970s and France in the 1960s.

Incomes policies were implemented intermittently up to the early 1980s in many countries. The Netherlands' experiment in incomes policy was exceptional, since it lasted from 1948 to the 1960s. The number of countries resorting to such policies has fallen in the 1980s. Let us take a closer look at some of the more interesting cases.

Box 13.1.   Wage bargaining in Europe *since the 1980*s

Since the 1940s, *multi-employer* bargaining had been the dominant type of wage setting in Western Europe, with late and incomplete adjustments in Southern Europe, but in all cases (including the United Kingdom) with bargaining patterns that are quite distinct from the single-company bargaining patterns found in the United States and post-war Japan. *Sectoral bargaining* is still the dominant pattern in Europe today, though it is rare that all bargaining occurs at one level. Instead, most bargaining systems are characterised by *multi-level* negotiations.

The 1980s were marked by a general and powerful thrust towards *decentralisation*, which was especially evident in the United Kingdom, but also in Sweden, the country that had long given primacy to centralised wage bargaining in pursuit of wage solidarity policies. France, Italy and Britain returned to decentralised bargaining after unsuccessful experiments with concerted policies in the 1970s. Other countries where central level bargaining was ended in the 1980s included Denmark (1983), Ireland (1981) and Spain (1986). Nor did countries in which central level negotiations or consultations continued in one way or another (Austria, Belgium, Norway, Finland, the Netherlands) seem immune to the decentralisation process.

At first sight, the 1990s seem to have brought a reversal of trends as a result of the increasing occurrence of *national agreements and tripartite social pacts*, formally, as in Finland, Greece, Ireland, Italy, Norway, Portugal, and Spain, or informally and on a more continuous basis, as in Austria and the Netherlands. Failed attempts include Belgium, France, and Germany, whereas it is not easy to classify the attempt to forge an 'Alliance for Jobs, Training and Competitiveness' in Germany after the change in government in 1998. These agreements and pacts often involve the government and are typically intended to promote wage moderation and labour market and social policy reforms for the purpose of restoring competitiveness to the national economy and securing participation in a 'hard currency' regime. Many of the successful pacts were negotiated in the 'peripheral' EU member states, outside the D-mark zone (Countries seeking a fixed-exchange rate with the Deutsche mark), in order to ensure membership of EMU in 1999.

The social pacts of the 1990s differ from the incomes policies of the 1970s and early 1980s. Rather than a 'political exchange', in which unions forgo wage increases in exchange for increased public sector expenditure, compensating social policies and increased employment protection rights (the typical content of the social contracts of the 1970s), the more recent pacts aim at less wage growth, less public sector growth, less costly social policies, and less employment protection, for some greater good in the future, such as membership of EMU and macroeconomic stability as a condition for investment and employment growth, or a more employment-friendly welfare state. The incomes policies of the 1970s were without exception centralising, relocating decisionmaking power within labour market actors to higher levels, and usually brought in the state. This happened everywhere except in Austria, Germany, Sweden and Switzerland, the four main countries where state intervention in collective pay bargaining is anathema. Incomes policies broke down because they overrated the taste for or capacity of centralisation in unions or employers' associations, and the capacity of states to foot the bill of increasingly expensive social or industrial policies.

The current pacts are attempts to improve coordination, both among labour market actors and between private (wage, productivity) and public (monetary, fiscal) policies. In order to do so successfully, and continue doing so, central organisations need to have the cooperation and resources from their members (individuals, companies, member-organisations), and they must learn to trust each other. When successful, social pacts establish or influence *mutual expectations and norms* concerning the bargaining conduct of unions and firms, or the budgetary and fiscal policies of governments. In so doing, they do not normally constrain industry- or company-level negotiations, nor do they prevent firms from designing different pay systems and incentive structures. In this sense, the Belgian incomes policies of the 1990s and the Irish pacts beginning in 1987 (five pacts between 1987 and 2002) appear exceptional, though the two most recent pacts in Ireland have become more loosely defined. The Finnish and Norwegian agreements on incomes policies are also exceptional insofar as they define the *boundaries of legal industrial action* in lower-level bargaining. This has no counterpart in the central agreements or accords that have been concluded between confederations in the Netherlands, since these do not constitute any legally binding text or commitment.

Beginning with the Wassenaar agreement of 1982, the Dutch central agreements may be typical of the new trend in social pacts. They substitute informal consensual norms, moral suasion and inter-agency trust-building for *formal centralisation of wage bargaining*, in a situation where the general development towards lower-level bargaining has made centralisation unlikely. Through their impact or norms and expectations, these pacts exert influence on overall wage dynamics (moderation, long-term stability), while leaving the task of determining relative wage levels to decentralised negotiations. In the Dutch case, the successive central agreements increased the confidence of unions and employers in each other, increased their autonomy in wage-setting against the interference of the state, and encouraged unions and employers to take further steps in decentralisation, below the level of industry bargaining. Traxler (1995) has called this development – examples of which are also found in Austria and Denmark – as 'organised decentralisation', contrasting it with the 'unorganised decentralisation' of collective bargaining found in Britain, New Zealand or the United States.

Thus, what at first sight appeared a 'reversal of trends' is in fact a continuation of decentralisation, but with an important supplement: the realisation that, firstly, a certain measure of *coordination* is necessary to ensure that decentralisation is efficient; and, secondly, that bargaining outcomes and processes can improve when embedded in a process of *social dialogue*. The first point is related to the 'hold-up' problem in bargaining, the second point to the dilemma faced by negotiators who must decide on a superior course of action and the distribution of costs and benefits.

Renegotiating contracts is costly, because it undermines incentives for investment. Bargaining over the returns on investment after the investment is made places the investor in a disadvantaged position. If individual workers and firms delegate bargaining to outside institutions and cannot influence the result, this hold-up problem is minimised. The delegation of the right to adjust wage increases (not levels) to external agents breaks the linkage between the level of specific investments and bargaining power. The empirical correlate is that non-market-conforming wage differentials related to sector, firm size or tenure, which do not contribute to efficiency, tend to be larger under decentralised bargaining. Company bargaining under control of the external union tends to suppress local rent-sharing whereas unrestrained local unions eat it. They 'are drawn into this strategy as a moth towards the flame that would burn it' (Teulings and Hartog, 1998: 303).

Social dialogue, involving public and private actors, can be defined as a process in which actors inform each other of their intentions and capacities, elaborate and exchange information provided to them, and clarify and explain their assumptions and expectations. This is not the same as bargaining, but provides a setting for *more efficient bargaining* by helping to separate the analysis of facts, problems and possible solutions from negotiating feasible courses of action and the distribution of costs and benefits.

Source: Adapted from Visser (2002).

In the United States, the Kennedy administration introduced voluntary wage and price guidelines in 1962. The government hoped to obtain the cooperation of unions and firms, in part encouraged by moral suasion. Kennedy got the steel industry unions to comply with the limit on wage increases by assuring them (after a three-month-long strike) that the steel companies would not raise prices. Nevertheless, after the agreement with the union was reached, the steel companies raised their prices significantly, prompting the government to threaten severe retaliatory measures (enforcement of antitrust legislation, exclusion from military procurement contracts). The clash continued the following year, until the president's assassination, with Kennedy's (vain) attempt to swing public opinion against the companies. The guidelines remained in force until 1968 and the Johnson administration proved more effective in exerting informal pressure on the industries involved, especially aluminium producers in 1965.

Australia has a federal arbitration commission and regional commissions that can take binding decisions on wage matters. The federal commission is in fact a court. Australia has also experimented with more complex forms of incomes policy, developing a kind of 'social agreement'.

Austria has a centralised bargaining structure, the Parity Commission for Wages and Prices, in which the government, unions and firms participate on equal footing. The Commission operates on the basis of two guiding principles: first, wage increases must be related to productivity growth; second, for goods not directly subject to government price controls (certain essential goods), firms whose costs have risen more rapidly than productivity can request a price increase. After verifying the validity of the request, the Commission can recommend full or partial acceptance, or reject it altogether. Firms are free to increase prices even if the Commission rejects their request, but they may be subject to government retaliation in the form of taxes or other punitive measures (e.g. exclusion from government procurement contracts).

In France, as part of the 'V plan' in 1964, it was decided to consider wage and price problems explicitly. The prospect of a high rate of growth in national income was offered in return for wage moderation. The government and firms also drafted 'programme agreements', which gave particular attention to the pricing policies of firms. Incomes policies have become less and less incisive since the end of 1960s.

In the United Kingdom between 1948 and 1950 the Labour government negotiated a voluntary policy of wage restraint with the trade unions. Later, between 1974 and 1979, an attempt was made to draft a 'social contract' between trade unions and the Labour government. The unions were granted a role in the formulation of economic policy – especially industrial relations legislation – in exchange for wage moderation. The failure of the contract for economic and political reasons contributed to Labour's defeat in the 1979 elections.

In Italy, the scope of price policy gradually narrowed over time until the second half of the 1990s, when it was given new impetus as a form of regulation of privatised firms. From 1992 greater recourse was made to wage containment policies. The automatic mechanism for indexing wages to prices was eliminated, the period between collective bargaining rounds was lengthened and it was agreed that wage increases should be consistent with the government's target rate of inflation, with some possibility, however, of later recouping the difference between actual and target inflation in order to safeguard the purchasing power of wages.[3]

---

[3] More information on incomes policy in the United States, Australia and the European countries can be found, respectively, in Pencavel (1981), Burrell and Stutchbury (1994) and Dore, Boyer and Mars (1994). Flanagan, Soskice and Ulman (1983) is also a good reference for European experience with incomes policy in the 1960s and 1970s.

13.9 Summary

1 The objective of incomes (and price) policy is to avoid any increase in the general price level by controlling *distributive variables*. These are essentially the wage rate and/or the profit margin.

2 The most frequently adopted *incomes policy rules* provide for growth in the wage rate equal to that in average labour productivity and no change in profit margins.

3 Depending on the degree of coercion involved, incomes policies can be described as *statist*, *market* or *institutional*.

4 *Statist policies* involve direct control measures and, as such, should have large and immediate effects. In practice, there are many problems regarding the variables to be controlled and the specific rules governing wage growth in the presence of sectoral productivity differences.

5 One type of *market-based incomes policy* consists in assigning firms a tradable permit to raise their prices. A second type attempts to create incentives not to raise prices using fiscal measures.

6 *Institutional policies* seek to place industrial relations on a cooperative basis by establishing rules to regulate them (e.g. arbitration, economic exchange, political exchange).

7 The range of incomes policies can be extended by including measures aimed at increasing the rate of *productivity growth*, which depends on factors internal and external to the firm.

8 The many real-world examples of attempts to implement incomes policies have not always produced satisfactory results with regard to *controlling inflation*.

14 Balance of payments policies

14.1 Balance of payments: equilibrium and disequilibrium

By *balance of payments equilibrium* we mean a situation in which the sum of the goods balance and the capital movements balance is equal to zero. We have a surplus (deficit) when official reserves increase (decrease). Equilibrium of the balance of payments is a long-run economic policy objective, in the sense that a country must seek on average to offset deficits it may run in some periods with surpluses from other periods. The pursuit of continuous surpluses is feasible in appearance, while persistent deficits are not, since they would eventually exhaust the country's foreign reserves and make further net payments abroad impossible. An exception to this is when the country is itself the issuer of a reserve currency that is accepted without limits by the other country (for instance, under a Gold Exchange Standard in which the convertibility of the reserve currency is, for whatever reason, always credible).

Upon closer analysis, however, running a constant surplus is not feasible either, since it implies a persistent deficit for the other country, which is not technically possible in general, as we have said. Therefore, when we speak of 'persistent surpluses', we mean a country that runs a balance of payments surplus for a long but not infinite period.

A surplus is certainly preferable to a deficit, but it may be awkward for two reasons:

(a) it implies *deficits for other countries*, which may be important when a country's international stance is markedly cooperative (although this is quite rare)
(b) it may give rise to *domestic inflationary pressures*; recall that a balance of payments surplus is a source of monetary base: if it proves difficult to sterilise through other sources, monetary base may expand fast enough to generate inflation.

A country may also seek to limit, if not eliminate, balance of payments surpluses for another reason. In reality, if it wants to increase the world market shares of national firms it can try, on the one hand, to achieve a surplus on goods movements and, on the other, to pursue a deficit on capital movements (especially in terms of direct investment).[1] The deficit on capital movements will thus at least in part offset positive goods movements balances.

We said that balance of payments equilibrium is a long-run objective. In the short term, the aim may be different. Depending on the circumstances, the variety of objectives can include: reducing the deficit, balancing international transactions or running a surplus. We will therefore analyse the following problems: assuming there is a balance of payments disequilibrium (surplus or deficit):

(a) Are there forces working for *automatic adjustment*?
(b) If not, or if they are not sufficiently strong, what *adjustment policies* are possible?

We examine the first problem in section 14.2 and the second problem in the sections that follow.

14.2   Automatic adjustment mechanisms

Automatic adjustment mechanisms can operate for both the goods movements account and the capital movements account. These mechanisms are normally analysed separately, with the former usually receiving more attention, a practice we will follow here.

The capital movements account can adjust if capital movements are sufficiently mobile. Given exchange rate expectations, the net inflow of capital induced when domestic interest rates are higher than foreign rates will cause domestic rates to fall and foreign rates to rise, eliminating the initial differential. In reality, this has a simultaneous effect on the goods movements account, and we should therefore examine the overall process of balance of payments adjustment. Somewhat greater detail of this process can be obtained from the analysis of a model of flow disequilibria of the sort suggested by Fleming and Mundell, which was presented in section 10.4.

Under *floating exchange rates*, adjustment of the goods account is assured by the flexibility of the exchange rate, which affects competitiveness. Under a fixed-exchange rate regime, two adjustment mechanisms operate, both of which affect the goods account. The first is based on *price changes*, which – like exchange rate movements – cause variations in the competitiveness of domestic and foreign goods; the second is based on *income changes*. We will examine these in order.

14.2.1   *Price changes*

Price changes were emphasised by the classics with reference to actual situations (such as the Gold Standard and the relative flexibility of prices) and theories (such

---

[1] Note that a surplus on capital movements corresponds to *borrowing* by the country. The debt will have to be repaid at maturity and interest must be paid in the meantime. This requires the country to have access to sufficient resources in the future, which must translate into positive net exports. The resources could come from the investment of foreign capital. However, servicing the debt (interest and principal) introduces a rigidity into the balance of payments that may make it difficult to achieve balance in the presence, for example, of a fall in world demand.

as the quantity theory of money) with which they were familiar. The hypothesis of a Gold Standard system is not essential to the operation of the mechanism;[2] however, the other hypotheses – those underlying the quantity theory of money – are.

Assume there are only two countries, A and B. Beginning in equilibrium, country A for some reason accumulates a balance of payments deficit. Conversely, country B will run a surplus. A's loss of gold will reduce its money supply and, if the conditions for the validity of the quantity theory (constant velocity of circulation, full employment, price flexibility) are met, prices will decline. The exact opposite will occur in country B. Consequently, the prices of goods produced by country A will decline with respect to those produced by country B. Other things being equal, this change in relative prices will generally improve the goods movements account of A (see (10.2)). This process will continue until the balance of payments equilibrates.

This mechanism could also operate in monetary systems other than the Gold Standard, as long as they ensure that the price changes we have described occur in at least one of the two countries. Since price flexibility in modern economies is asymmetric – i.e. prices rise more easily than they fall – it would be sufficient for prices to rise at an adequate rate and by an adequate amount in the country running a surplus – i.e. for there to be an appropriate inflation differential between the two countries (in our example, prices in A must rise less rapidly than in B).

However, bear in mind that the problems facing the operation of this mechanism are not simply a consequence of the specific features of modern economies. Adjustment has never occurred without difficulties and social costs, even when economies did not have the technological, financial and institutional rigidities they do today. Moreover, adjustment takes time. For these reasons, even when policymakers had confidence in the mechanism and some of the conditions for its operation were satisfied, adjustment *policies* were nonetheless undertaken. Faced with a decline in gold reserves (or even the mere expectation that they would decline), central banks usually reacted by raising the discount rate in order to attract foreign funds immediately. In due course, this policy measure also had a dampening effect on domestic economic activity, thus reducing imports. Such a policy action seems to have been even more effective than the automatic adjustment mechanism we have described. Nevertheless, it also has *social costs*, in that it depresses domestic demand (and employment).

14.2.2   *Income changes*

A different automatic mechanism relies on changes in income associated with balance of payment disequilibria.

Let us again consider two countries, A and B. Assume that the balance of payments is initially in equilibrium and that there is an exogenous increase in A's exports. This will cause B's goods movements balance to deteriorate and will improve A's, if demand

---

[2] There must be a link between balance of payments disequilibria and changes in the domestic money supply. A Gold Standard is a sufficient but not necessary condition for the existence of such a link.

in A remains unchanged. However, this occurs only in part. Let us examine the reasons for this. The increase in A's exports will cause A's income to rise, since exports are a positive component of aggregate demand.[3] The increase in income will cause imports to rise in turn (according to (10.3)). The country thus moves from equilibrium to surplus (owing to the increase in exports) and then to a decline in the surplus (owing to the increase in imports). The opposite happens in country B, where the rise in A's exports causes an initial balance of payments deficit. If the level of autonomous expenditure on domestic output in B decreases simultaneously by the same amount, there will be a decline in income that will produce a fall in imports, while exports will rise as an effect of the higher imports by A, where demand has increased.

This mechanism probably acts more rapidly than that based on price movements (since downward price flexibility usually takes a long time), but it does not guarantee perfect adjustment under the conditions normally assumed in Keynesian models (see Acocella, 1998) – and, above all, it generates social costs associated with the variations (especially reductions) in income and employment caused by its operation. In the previous example, country B experiences a reduction in employment owing to the increase in import demand until the adjustment is complete. If there is underadjustment, the reduction in employment will never be fully absorbed.

14.3 Adjustment policies and the causes of disequilibrium

Both automatic adjustment mechanisms of the goods movements account described above with reference to fixed exchange rate regimes can operate in the real world. Indeed, they may do so *at the same time*. We have separated them for analytical reasons only and will continue to do so in this section.

In the light of our discussion, the Keynesian mechanism has the advantage of probably being more rapid, but it may not allow full readjustment and, above all, it imposes relatively high social costs. The price movement mechanism is hindered by the imperfect (downward) flexibility of prices – which takes time – and the absence of the conditions on which the quantity theory is based.

Accordingly, achieving balance of payments equilibrium under fixed exchange rates requires specific government intervention. However, the form of such intervention must be tailored to the causes of the imbalance. We first examine those regarding capital movements (section 14.4) and subsequently move on to those involving goods movements (section 14.5 for imbalances caused by the level of demand and section 14.6 for those relating to competitiveness).

---

[3] In an open economy, we have: $Y = C + I + G + X - M$; taking account of the relevant behavioural functions in a simple Keynesian model that considers only the real economy and ignores price factors ($C = cY; I = \bar{I}; M = mY$) we have the following reduced form:

$$Y = \frac{1}{1 - c + m}(\bar{I} + G + X)$$

In chapter 10 we saw that the more complicated versions of the Keynesian model do not ignore price factors. Nevertheless, the direct relationship between exports and income remains valid.

Before beginning this discussion, it is helpful to consider that, in general, understanding the factors on which the balance of payments depends would enable policymakers to adjust any imbalance whatsoever (for example, one caused by poor competitiveness) with measures aimed at any of the variables on which the balance depends (for example, increasing the differential between domestic and foreign interest rates). In this case they could offset the deficit on goods movements caused by poor competitiveness with a surplus on capital movements.[4] Nevertheless, in the long run it is always advisable to target the same factors that caused the imbalance in the first place: in our example, we should take steps to redress the competitiveness problems.

14.4   Policies for adjustment of capital movements

In the absence both of barriers to capital movements and differences in the riskiness of debtors, equilibrium on the foreign exchange market is achieved when the domestic interest rate is equal to the foreign interest rate, increased by the expected rate of change in the exchange rate. The latter represents the specific risk[5] faced by an agent who purchases an asset denominated in the foreign currency:

$$i = i_w + \dot{e}^e \tag{14.1}$$

If the exchange rate is expected to remain stable, this condition reduces to the elimination of interest rate differentials.[6]

Given the foreign interest rate, simple monetary policy operations will allow the capital movements account to improve: in the case of a deficit, for instance, policymakers can reduce the quantity of the monetary base and thus the money supply in order to obtain an increase in the domestic interest rate and an improvement in capital movements; they should do the opposite if they want to reduce the capital movements balance. However, we have already noted the drawbacks of this measure, which causes income in the deficit country to fall as the interest rate rises. Under certain circumstances, or if there are no alternatives to a restrictive monetary policy stance, these drawbacks cannot be avoided. In other circumstances, they can be avoided by resorting to other instruments, such as controls on capital movements, which we will discuss shortly. Of course, the latter policy instrument has negative effects as well. Accordingly, the choice of one or the other policy option cannot be decided *a priori* by rejecting direct controls out of hand, although this is often done. Instead, a variety of circumstances need to be assessed, such as the severity of unemployment, the sensitivity of investment

---

[4] However, there are limits to the effectiveness of certain policies in certain situations. We will see later that policies to increase competitiveness through changes in the exchange rate are ineffective if there is excess demand.

[5] The risk is 'specific' in that it is not related to different degrees of creditworthiness of debtors in the two countries (assumed equal) but simply to the possibility of variations in the exchange rate. The agent is assumed to be risk neutral, so as not to seek forward cover.

[6] Obviously, as with our previous conclusions, this is strictly dependent on the hypotheses we have made (generally, absence of barriers to capital movements and equal riskiness of debtors, in addition to expectations of a stable exchange rate for the specific condition just introduced in the text).

to the interest rate, the degree to which capital movements are speculative in nature, the effectiveness of capital controls, etc.

The most interesting aspects of adjustment policies for capital movements come into play in the presence of expectations of a change in the exchange rate. If these were entirely exogenous to the behaviour of policymakers, no specific issues would arise. In the real world, however, this hypothesis does not hold. There are many links between public policy and expectations of exchange rate variations. First, monetary policy itself, with which policymakers can influence domestic interest rates, also has an impact on exchange rate expectations. Take a situation where the foreign interest rate is equal to the domestic rate and investors expect the domestic currency to depreciate. In this case, there would be an outflow of capital, which could be stemmed by adopting a more restrictive monetary policy stance. Now, the restriction should raise domestic interest rates by less than the size of the initial expected depreciation, since it is likely that the restriction itself will influence expectations, reducing them. Similarly, other government policies can affect exchange rate expectations (if the expected change is not especially large and is not considered very likely) and facilitate the adjustment of capital movements.

Nevertheless, these considerations hold only within certain limits. First, they are valid only if the expected exchange rate variations are small; when they are large, corrective monetary action is practically impossible. For example, consider a situation where a 10 per cent devaluation of a currency within at most 10 days is expected with near certainty. Buying foreign currency today and repurchasing the domestic currency after the devaluation will generate an expected capital gain of 10 per cent within 10 days, which is equal to an annualised gain of at least $(365/10) \cdot 10$ per cent $= 365$ per cent! In order to counter such expectations and the consequent investment behaviour, the monetary authorities would have to raise interest rates to a level close to the expected (annualised) return generated by the devaluation.[7] However, such action will probably be ineffective[8] if the expected devaluation is large. It may even be counterproductive: the abnormality of the measure may create alarm or at the very least confirm investors' expectations. If these investors include powerful financial intermediaries, or even other types of firms with large cash holdings, they may be encouraged to bet on a 'sure thing' by investing their capital abroad for speculative purposes.

Another limit on using a tight monetary policy to reduce expectations of devaluation consists in the possible repercussions on the budget: a rise in interest rates increases interest payments on the public debt.[9]

Let us now consider the effects of the adoption of fixed exchange rates on a country with a large public debt and high (cost-push) inflation. Some argue that fixed exchange rates would increase the 'credibility' of the country, in particular reducing expectations

---

[7] This is exactly what the Swedish central bank did during the exchange rate crisis of September 1992, raising interest rates to an annualised 500 per cent.

[8] In fact, the Swedish krona had to be devalued.

[9] Moreover, high interest rates that even produce capital movements surpluses (and therefore foreign debt) may have an adverse impact on the goods balance as a result of the increased outlays of foreign currency for payment of interest on that debt.

of a devaluation. Nevertheless, financial markets do not believe in agreements and treaties if these are not backed up by daily action and, in any case, good balance of payments performance. Assuming that the government does not use fiscal policy to reduce the (primary) budget deficit and incomes policy to lower labour costs – policies that would also produce an improvement in the goods movements balance – the credibility of its commitment to maintaining its parity depends on a restrictive monetary policy stance. However, raising interest rates, which may in itself enhance credibility, has a negative impact on the budget, thus possibly undermining credibility on that side. The effect on the public finances of a restrictive monetary policy is therefore uncertain.[10]

The more general problem is that international capital movements:

(a) have become excessively sensitive, especially to expectations of exchange rate variations
(b) have a major impact on expectations of further exchange rate changes and, through these, the actual behaviour of exchange rates, interest rates and real variables
(c) are now so large that they can themselves ensure that the expected event occurs, whether the forecast is well founded or not, as long as agents have sufficient financial resources, as is the case with large multinational firms.

These observations are the basis of fairly widespread proposals to limit the freedom of international capital movements with *direct controls* (such as administrative rules imposing information requirements, limits on foreign exchange outflows, etc.) or indirect controls (imposing an explicit tax – called the **Tobin tax**[11] – or an implicit tax by requiring a non-interest-bearing deposit equal to the entire capital outflow or some fraction of it[12]). The effect of these limitations – initially suggested by Tobin (1978) and more recently proposed again by other authors, such as Eichengreen and Wyplosz (1993) – would create a diaphragm or wedge between domestic interest rates and foreign interest rates, enabling policymakers to keep the former lower than the latter without triggering capital outflows. Nevertheless, much attention must be paid to the possibility that agents will find ways to circumvent the controls (for example, through the **overinvoicing** or **underinvoicing** of exports of goods).[13] To be effective in the long term, such controls must be pervasive and in some cases require the cooperation of foreign countries. They would nonetheless be effective in the short term, helping to

---

[10] Such situations have in fact occurred in the real world. The case that most closely fits the assumed conditions was that of Italy in 1992, but the same sort of problem arose in France and in other countries in 1992–3.

[11] Tobin sought to throw 'sand in the wheels' of international financial markets.

[12] This would reduce the return on investment abroad. Such a control, which can also be viewed as a form of prudential supervision, was adopted in Italy in the 1970s and in Spain in 1992. On the Tobin tax see ul Haq, Kaul and Grunberg (1996).

[13] It is possible to export capital by overinvoicing imports and/or underinvoicing exports. In the case of multinational firms, these transactions are simple indeed, since transfers of goods and services are not at arm's length – i.e. they do not take place between independent trading partners but rather between different units of the same company: it is therefore easier to adjust the prices of internal transfers (as the reader will recall, these are called *transfer prices*).

avoid unexpected speculative crises: arranging evasion and avoidance of controls takes time, enabling policymakers to adopt appropriate corrective measures.

14.5   Adjustment policies for excess or insufficient demand

Recall from (10.5) that the balance of goods movements is an inverse function of the level of domestic demand and a direct function of foreign demand.

The home country's policymakers cannot affect *foreign demand*, if not through appeals to the Rest of the World (in practice, the leading foreign countries) to expand its economy, acting as a *locomotive* for the home economy.[14]

On the other hand, policymakers can take measures to affect the level of *domestic demand*, restricting (expanding) it to reduce a goods movement deficit (surplus) if the imbalance is the result of excess (insufficient) domestic demand with respect to productive capacity.

The instruments for implementing such variations in domestic demand are those we have examined at length in previous chapters, fiscal and monetary policy in particular. The only difference with regard to the problems now under examination is that whereas earlier we viewed increases in demand as desirable *per se*, we have now considered them as an intermediate target with respect to the final objective of adjusting the goods movements balance.

In reality, increases in demand and goods balance adjustment can both be final objectives. In this case, they may conflict (or be inconsistent). For example, in the presence of unemployment, the use of demand-restricting measures to adjust a goods movement deficit would worsen the employment problem; similarly, measures aiming at raising aggregate demand, thereby reducing unemployment, would cause a worsening of the goods movement balance. The situation is difficult to solve with short-run, aggregate policies: structural measures for unemployment and/or the balance of payments are needed.

14.6   Policies for competitiveness

From (10.5) we know that, apart from demand factors, disequilibria in goods movements can also depend on excessive or insufficient competitiveness. Let us examine the matter in more detail. Take a homogeneous good produced in both Switzerland and the Rest of the World, limiting our examination to competitiveness factors only. If we consider competitiveness factors only and assume away any kind of transportation costs or market 'imperfection', and no capacity constraints to meeting demand, international arbitrage implies

$$p = p_w \cdot e \tag{14.2}$$

i.e. there is no advantage to exporting or importing if the price of the domestic good in Swiss francs is equal to the price of the foreign good in dollars times the exchange rate

---

[14] We are assuming fixed exchange rates or flexible exchange rates when these are not completely isolating.

(which corresponds to the price of the foreign good in Swiss francs).[15] If the first term of (14.2) is greater than the second, Swiss goods are less competitive; if it is smaller, they are more competitive. Therefore, an imbalance in goods movements due to excess or insufficient competitiveness (meaning that (14.2) is not satisfied) can be eliminated, thus re-establishing the equality in (14.2), by adjusting each of the three variables in the equation or their underlying factors:

(a) p – or, better, the factors on which this variable depends (essentially wages, productivity and profit margins) – can be adjusted
(b) e (i.e. the nominal exchange rate) can be adjusted: under a fixed-exchange rate regime, this can be done by devaluing (setting a higher parity or central rate) or revaluing (setting a lower parity or central rate) in the case of insufficient or excessive competitiveness, respectively; in a system of managed floating rates it is done by letting the currency depreciate or appreciate
(c) it would appear impossible to affect p_w, since the factors underlying the dollar price of the foreign good are beyond the reach of Swiss policymakers; however, the same effect can be attained through protectionist policies (such as levying a tariff) that increase the price of the foreign good, rather than acting directly on the exchange rate.[16]

We discussed the policies regarding point (a) in chapter 13. Those in point (c) are examined in chapter 15. More space is devoted to the adjustment of the exchange rate in section 14.7, where we discuss its controllability, and sections 14.8 and 14.9, where we examine the effectiveness of exchange rate adjustments.

14.7 The controllability of the exchange rate

As with any other variable, the scope for using the exchange rate as a policy instrument depends on a number of conditions. We consider the problems of controlling the exchange rate and the effectiveness of adjusting it.

Controllability is related to the *exchange rate regime*. First we examine the case of fixed exchange rates. In all fixed-exchange rate systems (Gold Standard, Gold Exchange Standard, EMS), if the exchange rate is actually fixed (i.e. if the fluctuation limits are close to the parity or central rate), in what sense is the exchange rate a controllable variable and therefore a practicable policy instrument? In other words, does not the fixity of the exchange rate conflict with its controllability? The problem appears substantive but is in fact only semantic. In this case, control is exercised through the variable to which the exchange rate is linked, i.e. the parity or the central rate[17]: policymakers

---

[15] Obviously, these conditions are not met in reality and only for simplicity do we assume that they are. The true significance of condition (14.2) is to highlight some factors which have an influence on the goods balance: a fall in p or a rise in p_w and e will all tend to stimulate exports and depress imports.
[16] Instead of acting on the underlying variables of price competitiveness *in absolute terms*, we can take measures to affect *changes* in the variables if we are interested in *changes* in the goods balance.
[17] It is also possible to influence the level of the exchange rate to some degree within the allowed fluctuation margins by appropriate intervention in the foreign exchange market.

change the exchange rate (or rather, the band within which it can fluctuate) by altering the parity or central rate (with a devaluation or revaluation).

A similar problem arises with floating-exchange rate regimes. In theory, in such systems the exchange rate is completely free to move in both directions (free floating). If the exchange rate is free floating, how can it be an instrumental variable? Flexibility and controllability would seem irreconcilable. Nevertheless, controllability (or effective control) implies that the exchange rate is not entirely free floating – or, rather it does not react only to market forces but also reflects government intervention. In the real world, floating-exchange rate regimes have never been entirely free (or 'clean') floating; they have instead tended to be managed regimes, as we will see.

14.8 The effectiveness of exchange rate adjustment

14.8.1 Demand elasticity conditions

Effectiveness means that changes in the exchange rate induced by government action[18] have an effect on some variable, specifically the level of income and/or the variables making up the balance of payments, notably the balance of goods movements. In what follows we will refer specifically to the balance of payments, setting aside the effects of changes in the exchange rate on aggregate demand. The reader will note, however, the link between the two targets from what we will say later. Let us refer to the balance on goods movements in nominal terms, which can be expressed as:

$$CA_m = p_x q_x - (p_m e) q_m \tag{14.3}$$

where p_x and p_m are the prices of imports and exports in the currency of the country of origin (p_x in domestic currency, p_m in foreign currency); e is the quantity of domestic currency per unit of foreign currency; q_x and q_m are physical quantities of exports and imports, respectively.[19] Recall that the depreciation of the currency (i.e. an increase in the price-quotation exchange rate) does not necessarily produce a rise in the *value* of exports and the balance of goods movements. Obviously, it will increase q_x and reduce q_m, but at the same time it will also tend to increase the value of imports in the domestic currency owing to the rise in e.

For an intuitive grasp of some of the conditions (**elasticity conditions**) that must be met for a rise in the exchange rate (depreciation) to improve the balance of goods

---

[18] In what follows we will refer to the effects of such action simply as *depreciation* or *appreciation* of the currency. This may be the effect of government intervention in the foreign exchange market, in a floating regime, or of a devaluation or revaluation, in a fixed exchange rate regime.

[19] It is implicitly assumed that the reference currency is the domestic currency. Using the foreign currency as the reference would not alter our conclusions. The reader may ask what the relationship between q_x and X, and q_m and M is. We have said that q_x and q_m are physical quantities of exports and imports. X and M are values, expressed in terms of the common unit of all the components of aggregate demand, which usually is the GDP price deflator, p.

In other terms, $X = p_x \, q_x/p$; $M = p_m \, e \, q_m/p$. (In the special but often assumed case $p_x = p$ and $p_m = p_w$, we would have $X = q_x$; $M = \dfrac{p_w \cdot e}{p} q_m$.)

The reader should note that $CA = CA_m/p$. Since p is assumed to be constant (or to vary parametrically), if a depreciation improves the balance of goods movements in monetary terms, then it improves the goods balance in real terms as well.

movements in nominal terms, let us begin with a situation where goods movements are in equilibrium ($CA_m = 0$) and p_x and p_m are given and constant even after changes in the exchange rate. We will later discuss the justification of the latter assumption.

Setting the right-hand side of (14.3) equal to zero, we can write the initial balance of good movements as:

$$\frac{p_x q_x}{p_m e q_m} = 1 \tag{14.4}$$

or

$$\frac{p_x}{p_m e} \cdot \frac{q_x}{q_m} = 1 \tag{14.5}$$

Equation (14.5) gives us the terms of the problem exactly.

An increase in e will normally cause q_x to rise and q_m to fall, but it will also simultaneously reduce the price of domestic goods with respect to the price of foreign goods expressed in the domestic currency. That is, it will worsen the terms of trade, $TT = p_x/(p_m e)$,[20] since e has increased while p_x and p_m have been assumed to remain constant.

From (14.5) we can state that if exports, q_x, did not react to the depreciation (i.e. if the elasticity of foreign demand with respect to the price of the domestic good, ε_x, were zero), the entire burden of improving goods movements would be borne by the denominator and q_m would have to fall by a larger percentage than that by which e increases; that is, the elasticity of imports would have to be greater than 1 ($\varepsilon_m > 1$) for it to improve the balance of goods movements.[21] If, however, the volume of imports did not change at all with respect to changes in the exchange rate ($\varepsilon_m = 0$), the burden of balancing the increase in e in the denominator of (14.5) would fall entirely on q_x, which would have to increase by a greater percentage (i.e. $\varepsilon_x > 1$).[22] However, if we allow for a positive elasticity of both exports and imports, the condition for the improvement of the goods balance following a depreciation or devaluation is obviously that

---

[20] The terms of trade are defined differently from the real exchange rate, despite their apparent formal similarity to the inverse of the latter. The variables p_x and p_m indicate the prices (or unit values) of exports and imports rather than the general price level (as measured by producer or wholesale prices or other indices of tradable goods), as is the case with the real exchange rate. The difference reflects the different analytical purposes of the two indicators: the real exchange rate is an indicator of *potential competitiveness* and the prices it refers to are prices that can be applied in international trade, if profit margins in the domestic and foreign market are the same. The terms of trade are a relative price, and the prices whose ratio determines the terms of trade are those used in actual (as opposed to potential) international trade. They are therefore in some sense an *ex post* indicator of competitiveness. (In both cases the ratios are not used in terms of the absolute values of the variables but rather in terms of their index numbers, i.e. to express changes in competitiveness.)

[21] We can refer indifferently to the elasticity of imports to the exchange rate or to prices in the domestic currency, since it is assumed that the price of foreign goods in foreign currency, p_m, is constant. In this case the price of these goods in domestic currency changes by the same percentage as the exchange rate.

[22] We can speak indifferently in terms of the elasticity of exports with respect to the exchange rate or to prices in foreign currency, since the increase in the exchange rate enables domestic producers to lower the foreign currency price of exports by an amount equal to the depreciation of the currency, leaving the domestic currency price of exports unchanged, as we have assumed. In other words, we assume that the export price in domestic currency, p_x, remains unchanged while the exchange rate increases, which means that the foreign currency price of exports will fall by the same proportion. Thus, speaking of the elasticity of exports to the exchange rate or prices is the same thing.

$\varepsilon_m + \varepsilon_x > 1.$[23] This is known as the **Marshall–Lerner condition** for the effectiveness of a depreciation (devaluation).

We have so far either implicitly or explicitly introduced a variety of assumptions that we should examine closely:

(a) p_x and p_m are given
(b) there are no constraints on the supply of export goods (as well as the supply of foreign goods for import)
(c) prices and quantities exported and imported adjust instantly
(d) there are no effects on expectations regarding future exchange rate variations.

Let us examine the problems raised by these assumptions in order.

14.8.2   The pass-through of exchange rate variations to prices

The hypothesis that p_x and p_m are given is meant to express the idea that the prices of internationally traded goods are constant in domestic currencies and, as exchange rates change, prices on foreign markets change accordingly. If our home country is Switzerland, as in the previous example, a given increase in the exchange rate of the Swiss franc would lower the dollar prices of Swiss goods by the same amount as the rise in the exchange rate; similarly, it would leave the dollar prices of foreign goods unchanged and increase their prices in Swiss francs. This can happen only if we make certain assumptions about the features of the different markets. For example, the dollar price of Swiss goods will fall in exactly the same proportion as the depreciation if there is perfect competition among the Swiss producers of each exported good that represent a significant part of the world supply of the good.[24] By contrast, the dollar prices

---

[23] The formal demonstration is fairly simple. With $CA_m = 0$ initially, we can write:

$$\frac{p_x q_x}{p_m e q_m} = 1 \tag{14.6}$$

If p_x and p_m remain constant and e increases, the improvement in the balance means that:

$$\dot{q}_x - \dot{e} - \dot{q}_m > 0 \tag{14.7}$$

where the dots over the variables indicate the rate of increase per unit of time. Divide (14.7) by $\dot{e}$. We then have:

$$\frac{\dot{q}_x}{\dot{e}} - \frac{\dot{q}_m}{\dot{e}} > 1$$

but

$$\frac{\dot{q}_x}{\dot{e}} = \frac{dq_x}{q_x} \Big/ \frac{de}{e} = \varepsilon_x$$

and

$$\frac{\dot{q}_m}{\dot{e}} = \frac{dq_m}{q_m} \Big/ \frac{de}{e} = -\varepsilon_m$$

Therefore, we must have $\varepsilon_m + \varepsilon_x > 1$. For a generalisation of the problem and some reservations about the significance of these conditions for an improvement in the goods balance, see Gandolfo (2001).

[24] The requirement that the good represents a large part of the total world supply can be thought of as being met for such goods as tulips (for the Netherlands), whisky (for the United Kingdom), champagne (for France), olive oil and pasta (for Italy), etc.

of goods imported into Switzerland will remain unchanged if the domestic market accounts for only a small fraction of the world market for these goods. Obviously, if these assumptions do not hold, then the depreciation may not be entirely **passed through** to the foreign currency prices of exports or the Swiss francs prices of imports.

It is entirely possible that these conditions do not hold in the real world. Given that markets are usually not perfectly competitive, firms have the power to pass the depreciation through to foreign currency prices on the basis of a number of factors.

Let us take a more detailed look at some elements that must be considered in the process of deciding how much of the depreciation to pass through.

For example, take a Swiss firm that sells its product in the United States at a unit price of $100. At the initial exchange rate of SF 2/$1, this will generate a unit revenue of SF 200. If the Swiss franc depreciates by 10 per cent, the firm must decide how much of the depreciation it must (and can) pass through to the dollar price, lowering it so as to increase foreign demand. This decision will be dictated by company objectives (e.g. maximising profits). The firm will consider the fact that the larger the pass-through, the lower the unit revenues in Swiss francs and the lower the *unit* profit, other things being equal. On the other hand, a larger pass-through will increase foreign demand. The greater the elasticity the lower the need to have a larger pass-through to boost demand. The firm must therefore weigh both effects, which have an opposite impact on profits.

Graphically, the effect of the devaluation can be shown with a shift to the right in the supply curve of the good: the same quantity can be supplied at a lower foreign currency price. Note that the pass-through is smaller the higher the elasticity of demand.

The pattern of production costs introduces a further element. If there are scale economies, a larger pass-through will not necessarily lower unit profit, since the increase in demand – and therefore production – caused by the pass-through will lower average costs, which will increase unit profit. In this case, even the complete pass-through of the depreciation to the foreign currency price could increase the unit profit and therefore benefit the firm, prompting it to alter the allocation of resources between goods produced for the domestic market and those produced for export in favour of the latter.

There may also be cases in which the complete pass-through of the depreciation may prove advantageous even if it does not increase unit profits, since it increases the demand for the domestic firm's good. Assume that the firm has excess capacity owing to weak domestic and foreign demand and is therefore 'rationed' on the demand side. The depreciation offers an opportunity to increase foreign demand, which will rise as a direct function of the size of the pass-through. It is likely that unit profits will also rise owing to the scope for lowering the unit incidence of fixed costs (since productive capacity is being more completely used). But even if this does not occur, the increase in foreign demand, by eliminating rationing, may still be beneficial since it will increase total profits, even with unchanged unit profits. This is the case in a depression, when the problem is to use the available resources as completely as possible and not change their allocation, making it more attractive to sell abroad than on the domestic market.

We can therefore conclude that the pass-through is larger the greater are the scale economies and the lower are the price elasticity of foreign demand and the level of domestic and foreign demand in individual sectors and in the economy as a whole.

14.8.3   The elasticity of supply

Let us now consider the implicit assumption that there are no supply-side constraints on exports (or imports), i.e. that supply elasticity is infinite in both countries. This means that if demand is sufficiently elastic (i.e. the Marshall–Lerner condition is met), *supply will always adjust to it* – without any change in supply prices, which are assumed to be constant – and the balance on goods movements will improve.

In order for the increase in demand generated by the devaluation to be fully met, supply must be elastic in all relevant sectors (or markets). High supply elasticity at the aggregate level and not just in individual markets presupposes the only partial use of physical resources and labour; otherwise, supply may not be able to adjust sufficiently to the increase in demand, making the depreciation ineffective.

To examine the consequences of insufficient supply elasticity, we must abandon our assumption that p_x and p_m and the general price level in the two countries are constant. An increase in the exchange rate gives rise to an increase in demand, which in full employment will lead exclusively to an increase in all prices, including those of exports. In a situation of demand-pull inflation (either already under way or incipient), adjusting the exchange rate will therefore be ineffective. In other words, devaluing the currency or letting (making) it depreciate will not improve the balance of goods movements for an economy with full employment. On the contrary, in such a situation the deficit may be at least partly due to the pressure of domestic demand, which a depreciation would only increase, accentuating demand-pull inflation. Policymakers must therefore use depreciation or devaluation with care. The incentive to recoup competitiveness lost as a result of domestic inflation is strong. However, if this was caused by the pressure of demand, depreciation would be an inappropriate response, as it would trigger a vicious circle of inflation–depreciation–inflation.

The adverse effect of an increase in the exchange rate on domestic prices can be channelled through costs as well as demand. The increase in the exchange rate is reflected in a rise in the prices of imported goods, and if these are used in the production of domestic goods – as in the case of raw materials – the production cost of domestic goods will rise. This effect will be accentuated (dampened) by excess (insufficient) domestic demand with respect to the country's productive capacity. The experience of two European countries, the United Kingdom and Italy, is exemplary. Both saw their currencies depreciate sharply from September 1992 onwards. Despite a depreciation of the pound of more than 12 per cent in terms of the effective exchange rate, inflation in the United Kingdom fell from 6.5 per cent to 3.4 per cent between 1991 and 1993; similarly, despite an effective depreciation of the lira of 18 per cent, inflation fell from 7.75 per cent to 4.3 per cent over the same period.

Apart from other specific circumstances of each of these countries, the reduction of inflation was made possible by the low level of domestic and foreign demand. This hindered a complete pass-through of the depreciation to the prices of imported goods in both the United Kingdom and Italy and led to a narrowing of profit margins on domestic goods in domestic markets, which was compensated by an increase in profit margins in foreign markets owing to a partial pass-through.

14.8.4   *The effect lag: the j-curve*

In addition to the size of the effects, an increase in the exchange rate raises the problem of the time needed for these effects to operate. The initial impact of a depreciation on the balance of payments can be 'perverse', since the reaction of export and import quantities to the change in competitiveness emerges with a lag (for various reasons: time needed to recalculate prices, contracts with pre-established terms, etc.), whereas the terms of trade worsen immediately owing to the increase in the exchange rate, if p_m and p_x remain constant. For a better understanding of these effects, consider (14.5). An increase in e causes the first ratio to increase immediately, i.e. worsens the terms of trade (if all agents keep prices in their domestic currencies, p_x and p_m, constant), and leaves q_x and q_m unchanged. If we begin with equilibrium in goods movements, as is assumed in (14.5), after the devaluation we will have $(p_x/p_m e)q_x/q_m < 1$, or $p_x q_x < p_m e q_m$.[25]

Only after a certain period of time will the beneficial effects on quantities emerge and – if the conditions outlined in the previous sections are met – more than offset the adverse effects on the terms of trade. If we wished to show the balance of payments over time in diagram form, the curve would initially be decreasing and then increasing, giving rise to a j-shaped curve (hence the term **'j-curve'** or **'j-effect'**).[26]

14.8.5   *The effect on capital movements*

We have so far considered the effects of exchange rate changes with exclusive reference to the balance of goods movements. However, such effects are not limited to exports and imports of goods and services: changes in the actual exchange rate can influence the expected exchange rate and hence capital movements. *Under certain circumstances,* a depreciation may induce expectations of further depreciation and therefore cause a capital outflow;[27] in other circumstances, the opposite can occur: a depreciation considered sufficiently large or excessive might give rise to expectations of a future appreciation.

The main conclusion we can draw is that adjusting the exchange rate is effective only in certain situations of *balance of payment disequilibrium*: depreciation is appropriate

---

[25] Obviously, if we begin with a deficit in goods movements, the immediate effect of the devaluation will be a worsening of the deficit.

[26] For empirical evidence on the *j*-curve see Wood (1991).

[27] We will apply these considerations in section 15.7.

when competitiveness is being lost owing, for example, to changes in unit labour costs and/or other costs and profit margins that are higher at home than abroad. In the case of a deficit on goods movements caused by excess demand, the proper response would be the adoption of restrictive fiscal and monetary policies. If policymakers wished to devalue under such circumstances, this would have to be accompanied by restrictive fiscal and monetary measures freeing resources for production to meet increased foreign demand. Similarly, depreciation is not an appropriate response to a deficit caused by capital movements and may actually have undesired adverse effects on the balance of capital movements.

The analysis of the effects of a depreciation on goods movements can be used to assess the consequences for other policy objectives. We have already briefly mentioned the positive effects on income of an increase in net exports. At the same time, there may be adverse inflationary effects owing to the impulse imparted to demand and the increase in the cost of imported goods.

14.9   The asymmetric effects of a variation in the exchange rate

The effects of a change in the exchange rate have so far implicitly been assumed to be *symmetric*. This is only a rough initial approximation, however. Consider the entry and exit decisions of an individual agent with regard to the foreign market as the exchange rate changes (figure 14.1).

We can assume that entering the foreign market is worthwhile only for exchange rates $e \geq e_0$, given production costs and demand prospects in term of foreign currency prices. As the exchange rate rises exports will increase, as shown by the solid line, which therefore represents the *potential* pattern of exports, i.e. that before entering the foreign market.

Once the agent has entered the foreign market, the pattern may change and, if the exchange rate falls below e_0 but remains above, say, e_1, it may still be worthwhile to remain in the market in the short run, albeit supplying fewer goods (hysteresis). If the exchange rate falls below e_1 it may be more profitable to abandon the market, even in the short run. The agent's decision to remain in the market if $e_1 \leq e < e_0$ depends on the existence of *sunk costs* (for example, tangible and intangible fixed costs incurred to first enter the foreign market) that would have to be written off if the firm abandoned the market.[28] Having incurred sunk costs to penetrate a foreign market a firm can establish a kind of **beachhead** in that market. The firm will not find it profitable to leave the market since it will lose its initial investment (Baldwin, 1988).

In this case the behaviour of the firm will be shown by the broken line in figure 14.1. The firm would remain in the foreign market in the short run, in the hope that a depreciation will bring the exchange rate back above e_0, which would allow it to stay in the market in the long run. Studies have shown that under certain conditions the exit

---

[28] Obviously, these costs are specific to the firm (plant or other fixed capital suitable for certain purposes; advertising). Often only a very small part of these costs can be recovered by transferring the related rights to other firms.

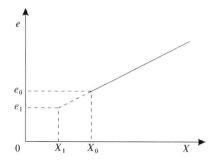

Figure 14.1

value of e_1 (i.e. the value of e below which firms decide to exit the foreign market) may be much lower than that predicted by traditional Marshallian theory, since firms may be induced to stay in the market by high variability in the exchange rate as well as the prospect of facing very high new sunk costs to re-enter the market (Dixit, 1989, 1992).

14.10   Internal and external equilibrium: decentralisation and the appropriate assignment of instruments to targets

In our discussion of the reduced form decision model (subsection 4.5.2) we saw that each instrument influences all the targets. Therefore, in general we cannot assign *individual instruments exclusively to individual targets*. This means, for example, that the exchange rate lever cannot be used to reach balance of payments equilibrium alone, since in addition to exports and imports it affects other target variables, such as inflation. Failing to consider these additional effects when setting the value of the exchange rate would mean ignoring its full impact, concentrating on one aspect only (perhaps the main element but certainly not the only one). As we can see from the inverse reduced form (4.6), the value of each instrument should be chosen by taking account of both objectives simultaneously. A simultaneous solution is clearly a centralised solution, at least as far as *decision* is concerned. Execution can nevertheless be delegated to separate bodies responsible for the various policies (exchange rate policy, fiscal policy, monetary policy, etc.).

However, we must consider the fact that we often know only approximately the parameter values of the model describing the economy, so that we can only determine the order of magnitude of the effects of each instrument. In other words, we may only know that one instrument is more effective than another in achieving a given objective, without being able to calculate its exact effects. In this situation, a simultaneous solution of the policy problem is difficult to formulate and even in a centralised context policymakers must proceed by trial and error, by adjusting one instrument at a time.

In addition, in the real world, each of several institutions may be charged with independently *choosing* the level of one instrument in order to achieve its target: for instance, the central bank decides the quantity of monetary base to create in order to hit its target (e.g. price stability), while Parliament establishes the amount of public expenditure or the level of taxation needed to achieve its objective (e.g. employment).

There are two aspects to this problem:

(a) first, we must determine the conditions in which such decentralisation of economic policy decisions can be considered *rational* in economic terms
(b) second, we need to determine which *objective* to assign to each of the bodies that control the various instruments of government action.

A decentralised approach, if feasible, could offer the advantages of lower costs associated with specialised functions of policy management. We will shortly show that in the Mundell–Fleming setting the decentralised solution is possible and that, in theory, it gives the same result as the centralised approach if:

(a) the instruments have different degrees of effectiveness on the objectives – i.e. if one instrument is more effective than another for one objective and less effective for others
(b) each instrument is adjusted by the relevant authority in relation to the objective for which it is relatively more effective (**appropriate assignment** of instruments to objectives[29]).

For example, let there be two objectives (full employment income, or internal balance, and balance of payments equilibrium or external balance) and two instruments (government expenditure and liquidity). If the effectiveness of monetary policy in impacting income, compared with the effectiveness of fiscal policy, is less than its effectiveness over the balance of payments (again relative to that of fiscal policy), then monetary policy should be assigned to the balance of payments objective (i.e. it should be adjusted with a view to reaching the desired value for the external balance) and fiscal policy should be assigned the income objective.

Let us examine the problem in more detail in intuitive terms. Assume that the desired target values are $Y = \overline{Y}$ and $BP = 0$, where the symbols have the usual meanings and $\overline{Y}$ denotes full employment income. At time t_0, $BP = 0$ and $Y < \overline{Y}$. The monetary authority (say, the central bank), appropriately assigned to ensuring external balance, has no reason to take action. By contrast, the Treasury, which has been assigned responsibility for fiscal policy in pursuing internal balance, should adopt expansionary measures, increasing government spending. Assume that this policy is fully effective and produces $Y = \overline{Y}$ at time t_1.

The increase in income leads to a worsening of the balance of goods movements, however; if capital is not highly mobile (as we assume in order to replicate the original

[29] This is also known as the **Mundell principle** (or the **effective-market classification principle**), as it was introduced by Mundell (1962). The sufficient conditions for the appropriate assignment of instruments to targets within the framework of dynamic models are analysed in Aoki and Canzoneri (1979). For a clear statement of the conditions for the validity of the principle and, more generally, for an analysis of problems of centralisation and decentralisation see Johansen (1978, chapter 7) and Vandenbroucke (1985).

Mundell analysis), a balance of payments deficit will result ($BP < 0$). At this point it is the central bank's turn to intervene by restricting liquidity so as to foster an inflow of foreign capital. But the monetary squeeze also has a depressive effect on income. The fall in imports associated with the reduction in income, together with a larger inflow of foreign capital, will return the balance of payments to equilibrium ($BP = 0$). Nevertheless, as a result of the restrictive monetary stance, income at t_2 will be below the desired level ($Y < \overline{Y}$).

At t_2 we are therefore in a situation that resembles that where we began at t_0. In the periods after t_2, each of the two policy authorities will continue to act in the same manner. The question we must ask is whether there will be convergence towards the desired position (where we have $Y = \overline{Y}$ and $BP = 0$ simultaneously); that is, whether the corrective interventions of the authorities gradually become smaller.

The answer is 'yes', given that the instruments – as posited – have been assigned appropriately: to correct an imbalance (in income or balance of payments) the relatively more effective instrument has been used for the unmet target. We know that each instrument influences both targets; nevertheless, since using the liquidity instrument to correct a balance of payments deficit had a larger impact (compared with the fiscal instrument) on that target than for the income target, the (negative) effect of the liquidity squeeze on income was less than the beneficial impact on the balance of payments. Liquidity thus has the maximum positive impact on the balance of payments, with the smallest disturbance effect on income (assuming we begin with income in equilibrium), precisely because liquidity is relatively less effective in influencing income.

Conversely, if use were made of the relatively less effective instrument for the balance of payments – i.e. fiscal measures – in the presence of a balance of payments deficit, the positive effect on this target would be smaller, while the negative effect on the other target (income) would be larger.

The validity of this reasoning is strictly dependent on our hypotheses about the functioning of the economy; that is, on the model. In particular, it is assumed that the exchange rate is fixed. With this hypothesis, fiscal policy is more effective than monetary policy for domestic equilibrium, as was argued in sections 11.9 and 12.4.[30] It is also assumed that interest rate differentials generate lasting outflows of capital, rather than temporary flows associated with stock adjustment.[31] In addition, the position of policymakers in the Rest of the World is taken as given, not depending on the choices made by domestic policymakers. This is a reasonable assumption only if the economy in question is very small. Actually, when a country of some size changes its policy stance, especially monetary policy, it may have an effect on interest rates in the Rest of the World, which normally responds by adjusting its own policy. More generally, if

---

[30] This makes it easier to satisfy the required condition that fiscal policy is more effective than monetary policy for internal balance as compared with their relative effectiveness for external balance.

The assumption of fixed exchange rates can create problems in defining monetary base as a policy instrument since we know that this regime tends to make monetary base an endogenous variable (also through sterilisation), all the more so the higher is capital mobility. The assumption of low capital mobility hence serves the purpose of strengthening the control of monetary authorities over monetary base.

[31] This was discussed in detail in section 10.5.

the reference model were to change, the conclusions regarding the *type* of appropriate assignment could change as well. For example, this is the case of the New Cambridge School, which adopts a different model of the economy and reaches opposite conclusions to the foregoing regarding the pairing of monetary and fiscal policy with internal and external balance targets (see Cripps and Godley, 1976; Fetherston and Godley, 1978).

A second limitation of our previous argument is the assumption that there are no costs or barriers to the use of the various instruments. In particular, they must be completely flexible and available for immediate use (effect lags must not be excessive).

A further limitation stems from our assumption that there are only overall internal and external balance targets, whereas in the real world the composition of both aggregate demand and the balance of payments is not irrelevant. For example, with reference to the latter, we have already seen that an overall balance deriving from a capital movements surplus and a goods movements deficit can raise problems for policymakers, since the surplus may represent additional debt for the country. As to internal balance, it can make a difference (especially in terms of the economy's capacity to grow) whether an income target is obtained with a larger or smaller investment component.

A final limitation regards the possibility of overshooting in the use of the instruments. Consider the case where the two instruments available for achieving the same targets indicated earlier, namely internal and external equilibrium, are government spending and the exchange rate.

Let us assign government spending to the income target and the exchange rate to external equilibrium. We assume that internal equilibrium is initially satisfied and we have a balance of payments surplus. In order to achieve external equilibrium the currency must be revalued, but this will cause exports to decline and imports to increase, with a negative impact on income. The fall in income prompts an increase in government spending. Once the desired income level is achieved, the external balance deteriorates, which requires a *devaluation*. An appropriate devaluation gives us balance of payments equilibrium, but stimulates excess demand and possible inflationary pressures that force a reduction in government spending. This could bring income to the desired level, but it causes a balance of payments surplus. This apparently returns the economy to a situation similar to its starting point. If, however, the instruments were assigned appropriately to the targets – namely, if public spending is relatively more effective than exchange rate policy in achieving internal equilibrium rather than external equilibrium – the balance of payments imbalance after the stages outlined above will be smaller than the initial imbalance and, by repeating the measures, it is eventually possible to attain simultaneous balance in the two markets.

The reader will have noted, however, that although decentralisation of policymaking enables convergence on final equilibrium, in this case it succeeds only after numerous rounds of intervention, each of which produces some degree of **overshooting**, in the sense that the adjustment of the instruments in each round is excessive, thereby requiring a corrective adjustment in the opposite direction. For example, we saw the currency must first be revalued then devalued, while government expenditure must first increase then decrease. Since overshooting has costs (for implementing the many interventions and the uncertainty of private agents induced by the multiple changes of course in public action), this is one reason to favour centralising economic policy decisions.

14.11 Summary

1 *Balance of payments disequilibrium* is represented by either a deficit or a surplus. Capital mobility can contribute to automatically equilibrating the balance of payments.

2 *Imbalances in goods movements* tend to be eliminated automatically by exchange rate variations under a floating rate regime. Under fixed exchange rates, equilibrium is attained through price movements (which are slow, however) or changes in income (with possible depression in the deficit country).

3 The slowness of *automatic adjustment mechanisms* for goods movements or the existence of a collateral depressive effect on income under fixed exchange rates are an incentive to search for appropriate discretionary adjustment measures.

4 In the presence of excess or insufficient demand, *discretionary adjustment measures* consist of, respectively, restrictive or expansionary monetary and fiscal policies.

5 *Insufficient or excessive competitiveness* can be eliminated by acting on domestic prices (or the factors on which they depend) or the nominal exchange rate (with depreciations or appreciations, respectively), or by imposing a tariff on foreign goods.

6 If capital is *insufficiently mobile*, restrictive or expansionary monetary action may be needed to increase or reduce the domestic interest rate in order to compensate a deficit or a surplus in capital movements. Expectations of exchange rate variations and associated speculative movements can undermine discretionary policy measures.

7 The impact of *exchange rate variations* on goods movements in nominal terms depends on the elasticity of demand for exports and imports (the Marshall–Lerner condition), the degree of 'pass-through', the elasticity of supply and the speed of the variations. Exchange rate changes can have an impact on capital movements, influencing expectations of future changes. These effects are uncertain.

8 *Exchange rate variations* can have asymmetric effects. In particular, entry by firms into foreign markets may occur at a high exchange rate, while exit can occur at a low rate, owing to the presence of sunk costs.

9 The basis of *planning* lies in the consistent use of the different instruments in attaining the desired objectives, given that each instrument influences all objectives. The need to search for the values of instruments that simultaneously ensure the achievement of all objectives clearly justifies a centralised solution. However, in the real world the choice of different policy instruments is often entrusted to different bodies, each of which aims at a specific target. The decentralisation of policy responsibility is possible and in principle will produce the same result obtained with centralised policy control, even if obtained by trial and error, if the effectiveness of instruments

differs in relation to the various instruments and if each instrument is assigned to the objective for which it is relatively most effective.

10   In certain cases of *decentralisation*, overshooting may occur even if there is convergence towards the final simultaneous solution. In other words, the correction adopted by each policy authority may be excessive in relation to that required in the case of a simultaneous solution.

15 Trade policies: free trade and protectionism

15.1 Trade policies and the foundation of free trade

Trade policy can be defined as the attitude of a country's economic policymakers towards foreign trade. Putting it very briefly, they can take a liberal attitude, meaning that they do not raise barriers to exports and, above all, imports, or they can assume a **protectionist** stance, meaning that they attempt to safeguard domestic firms against foreign competition. A third position is **autarky**, which seeks to close the domestic economy to the rest of the world.

Liberal policies consist simply in the elimination of all barriers to foreign trade. In this section we give a brief sketch of the fortunes of protectionism and free trade in the modern era and lay out the foundation of free trade; in section 15.2 we discuss protectionist instruments and in section 15.3 we examine their effects. Sections 15.4–15.8 analyse the various justifications of protectionism. Section 15.8 discusses the relationships between trade policy and industrial policies. We do not examine autarkic policies.

As a *trade policy* alternative to free trade, protectionism has been both the subject of an extensive theoretical debate that marked the very birth of economic science and the focus of a variety of government actions over the ages.

To limit ourselves to the modern era, examples of such policy measures include the Navigation Act of 1651, with which Oliver Cromwell made use of vessels of the English merchant marine mandatory for all the country's imports and exports. This was a powerful instrument for advancing English economic power against the superior might of the Dutch. Once it had established its hegemony, Britain adopted and promoted free trade. Especially important moments of this policy were the abolition of the Corn Laws restricting trade in grain in 1846 (although Ricardo had advocated their repeal many years earlier) and the Franco-English trade agreement of 1860, which had a liberal orientation, partly owing to the inclusion of a **most-favoured-nation (MFN) clause**.[1]

A constant feature of the history of economic development would seem to be that countries become industrial powers thanks (in part) to protectionism. In addition to

---

[1] This guarantees the automatic extension of any preferential trade conditions granted to one country to all other signatories.

Table 15.1 *Comparative costs*

	Wine	Cloth
United Kingdom	20	40
Portugal	10	30

England, similar situations can be found in France (with the mercantilist policies of Colbert), Germany, Italy and the United States in the last quarter of the nineteenth century, and in Japan after 1945. The newly industrialising economies (NIEs) of East Asia are a striking exception, having enjoyed rapid growth since the end of the 1970s thanks to markedly free trade policies.[2]

The scientific foundation of free trade lies in the advantages of *specialisation* at the international level, advantages that were underscored by David Ricardo with the **comparative-cost principle**: if two countries have different relative abilities to produce two goods (which is reflected in their comparative costs of production), both countries will be better off if each specialises in producing the good whose cost is *comparatively* lower and trades the quantity of that good in excess of domestic demand to secure the other good from the other country. Take the production costs in table 15.1 (expressed in labour units, according to the labour theory of value adopted by the classical economists) for the two goods, wine and cloth, in the two countries, the United Kingdom and Portugal.

The comparative costs can be defined as $20/40 = 1/2$ (which implies that 2 units of wine exchange for 1 unit of cloth) in the United Kingdom and $10/30 = 1/3$ in Portugal. Wine costs relatively less in Portugal than in the United Kingdom and therefore Portugal could profit from specialising in that good. The United Kingdom, on the other hand, should specialise in cloth. Although cloth costs more in the United Kingdom than in Portugal in absolute terms, it costs only twice the cost of wine in the United Kingdom, whereas it costs three times the cost of wine in Portugal. It can be demonstrated that despite the fact that costs for both goods are higher in the United Kingdom than in Portugal, both countries will benefit by specialising as long as the international terms of trade between the two goods lie between the domestic terms of trade in each of the two countries under autarky (see Gandolfo, 1998).

All subsequent theories substantially incorporate the Ricardian principle. The most recent also adopt more realistic hypotheses of scale economics and imperfect competition (see Helpman and Krugman, 1985).

Nevertheless, the Ricardian principle suffers from many implicit and explicit limitations mainly associated with the static nature of the analysis and the assumption of full employment.[3]

The economic arguments in favour of protectionism are largely based on these limitations. We discuss them in sections 15.4–15.7. The non-economic arguments that

[2] However, this growth has been sustained in most cases by clearly statist domestic policies. See Lall (1994).
[3] These have been partly overcome by later work, although these theories in turn have their own limitations.

are usually advanced in support of protectionism hark back to Adam Smith. In fact, the founder of modern economics and father of liberalism argued that 'defence is of more importance than opulence'. On this argument, we can justify the protection of certain 'industries' (agriculture, basic industries, some services) despite the fact that their production may be unprofitable from a strictly economic point of view. The positive effects of protectionism for the country that adopts it can in reality be smaller than the theoretical benefits when other countries react with countervailing measures. This is an argument in favour of international cooperation, which we will address in chapter 20.

15.2 Protectionist instruments

Protectionists have a wide range of tools at their disposal. One form of **protection** is **tariff** protection, which involves the imposition of duties on imported goods. Duties are simply indirect taxes, which normally increase the prices of foreign goods. As taxes, they are a source of tax revenues, but they are rarely used for this purpose (**fiscal duties**). Normally, they are intended to protect domestic goods from their foreign competitors (hence **protective duties**).[4]

In recent decades, a multitude of sophisticated **non-tariff instruments (non-tariff barriers, NTBs)**, have been used (see Gandolfo, 1998) in addition to or in replacement of tariff protection, such as:

(1) **quotas**, which involve the setting of quantity or value limits on imports
(2) restrictions on the purchase of *foreign goods* (for example, requirements for a minimum level of domestic content or import deposits)
(3) regulations purportedly imposed for other purposes (health, safety, environmental protection) but which effectively create obstacles and bureaucratic delays that *raise costs for foreign producers*; a variety of administrative ploys such as channelling certain imports (perhaps perishable goods) through a single or small number of customs offices or other techniques for lengthening the time needed for customs inspection
(4) restrictions in calls for *tenders, concessions, government procurement* (see section 8.3)
(5) *subsidies* (see section 15.2) and other forms of export incentives, such as devaluation (see section 14.8).[5]

---

[4] The *set* of duties is known as the **customs tariff**. 'Duty' and 'tariff' are often used interchangeably.
[5] In chapter 14, we saw that the exchange rate influences the terms of trade of the goods and services of one country with respect to the Rest of the World. The same effects of a depreciation of the exchange rate – i.e. a simultaneous incentive to exports and a disincentive to imports – can be obtained through the use of subsidies and general tariffs, respectively. However, note that the effects of the simultaneous application of subsidies and general duties are the same as those of a devaluation only for goods movements (or income). In addition to the effects on goods movements, exchange rate changes can also impact capital movements by influencing expectations of further exchange rate variations (see subsection 14.8.5). In addition, subsidies and duties are often selective rather than general, being applied to individual goods.

The remainder of this section deals with the instruments in points (1) and (2), while for the others the reader is referred to Gandolfo (1998) or to the other parts of this book where indicated.

Import quotas are normally implemented by granting *licences* to persons or firms: in order to import a given foreign good, importers must apply for licences, which are issued in a total amount equal to the overall quota.

Quotas can be applied by exporting countries as well as importing countries. In this case we have what are called **voluntary export restraints** (VERs), which have often been used by Japan in its trade with the United States, France and Italy (automobiles are a case in point). **Orderly market agreements** (OMAs) are similar as they consist of voluntary restrictions on exports involving a number of countries. The Multifibre Agreement (MFA)[6] is a sort of OMA. Although introduced by the exporting country, VERs and OMAs are in fact requested by the *importing nation*, which threatens to adopt other types of restriction if the exporting country does not do so.

Another form of trade restriction is the **minimum national content requirement**. It establishes that a foreign good must contain a minimum level of *domestic content*, in either physical or value terms, in order for it to be eligible for import. This type of restriction is often introduced by developing countries in an attempt to increase the share of local value-added in imported goods: rather than just importing components for assembly in the country, they seek to stimulate the *local manufacture* of some components.

Disputes involving minimum national content requirements have arisen between various developed countries (including the United States and France) and Japan with regard to the practice of many Japanese manufacturers of directly investing abroad in **screwdriver plants**[7] to avoid other import restrictions (such as VERs). In the early 1990s, France argued that the Bluebird (a Nissan car made in the United Kingdom) should be considered a Japanese rather than Community product and therefore subject to the VER imposed by the Japanese government. The dispute was resolved after Nissan agreed to increase the local content of operations carried out in the United Kingdom.

Import deposits consist in the obligation to deposit an amount equal to the value of the goods imported in a non-interest-bearing account with the central bank for a set period of time. This instrument was adopted in Italy for a short period in the 1970s.

15.3   The effects of tariff and non-tariff protection

Let us first examine the impact of the introduction of tariffs graphically, assuming the international price is fixed. Curves VW and YZ (see figure 15.1) are, respectively, domestic demand and supply in the country.

---

[6] Since 1973 this has restricted imports of textiles from twenty-seven developing countries to sixteen advanced countries. The Uruguay Round of trade negotiations provided for its gradual elimination over a ten-year period ending 1 January 2005 (see chapter 17).

[7] This colourful term regards the establishment of local affiliates whose only task is assembly of components produced elsewhere.

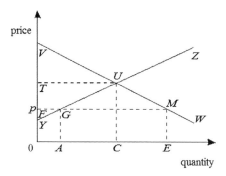

Figure 15.1

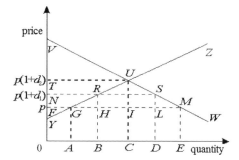

Figure 15.2

If the domestic price were $p = 0F$ and equal to the international price, with demand exceeding supply it would be necessary to import enough goods to meet the excess demand, i.e. in an amount equal to AE.

Let us now look at figure 15.2 to examine the effect of the introduction of a duty with a rate of d_1. If the international price remains unchanged, the new domestic price will be $0N = p(1 + d_1)$. At this new price, the excess demand to be met with imports will be smaller, equal to RS.

If the duty were equal to $d_2 = 0T/0F - 1 = UC/IC - 1$, it would in fact eliminate the excess demand altogether.

Figure 15.2 shows the various effects of the duty:

- *consumption effect* (equal to DE): the duty causes the price to rise, thereby reducing domestic demand
- *output* (or *protection*) *effect* (AB): the duty causes the price to rise, which makes domestic output increase; if the country does not have full employment, this effect can be large
- *import effect* ($AB + DE$): as a consequence of the two previous effects, imports decline
- *tax revenue effect* ($HLSR$): tax revenues increase by the tariff rate multiplied by the (new) quantity imported

- *redistribution effect* (*FLSN*): consumers pay a higher price to domestic manufacturers and the duty to the government.

Quotas have partly similar effects. Looking again at figure 15.2, we can see that the effects of a quota tending to reduce imports from *GM* to *RS* < *GM* consist in an increase in the domestic price of the good from $p = 0F$ to $p' = 0N$. Unlike in the case of a duty, however, the government does not receive any of this in the form of tax revenues. Quotas redistribute income to the detriment of consumers and to the benefit of importers, who enjoy quota rents.

The range of trade policy instruments also includes export subsidies. Subsidies, which can take various forms (credit, insurance subsidies, generic monetary transfers and tax allowances[8]), normally supplement profits for exporters: the unit profit net of taxes is increased by at least part of the amount of the subsidy, thereby directing resources towards export-oriented production. The effects of subsidies on prices are symmetric to those of duties and can be analysed with the help of a figure similar to figure 15.2, but considering an international price that is higher than the domestic equilibrium price. First and foremost, export subsidies raise the price of the good in the exporting country because producers will not be willing to sell in the domestic market at a price that is lower than the price obtained from exports – equal to the international price – increased by the subsidy. In addition, when the country that introduces subsidies is large – as in the case of the European Union[9] – the world price of the subsidised good declines as a result of the increased supply on the world market. This means that price within the European Union will not increase by the full amount of the subsidy.

15.4   Protecting 'infant industries'

The need to nurture **infant industries** has been cited as a reason for protection at least since John Stuart Mill, who argued that the temporary imposition of a protective tariff was justified by the attempt to naturalise 'a foreign industry in itself perfectly suitable to the circumstances of the country. The superiority of one country over another in a branch of production often arises only from having begun it sooner', consisting of 'a present superiority of acquired skill and experience' (Mill, 1848, p. 918). A country that protects an infant industry may acquire the same skills and experience over time, thus enabling it to compete on an equal footing (or even gain an edge).

This is especially the case when there are **dynamic economies of scale** to be gained as producers *learn by doing*: their special importance lies in the fact that they are not linked to the quantity produced per unit of time, but rather to cumulative output over time.

---

[8] As regards the first, the subsidy can involve a reduction in the interest rate (interest rate subsides) or an increase in the amount of credit available under credit rationing. Insurance incentives consist in free or reduced rate insurance coverage of foreign exchange risk, default risk and political risks. These are specific kinds of transfers from a government body that can also take a generic monetary form. Tax allowances normally include exemptions or reductions in tax rates.

[9] Export subsidies are now used most frequently in the European Union as a support measure for farmers in the place of **intervention prices** (i.e. guaranteed prices for producers), which had made it necessary to warehouse enormous surpluses of certain agricultural products (see chapter 18).

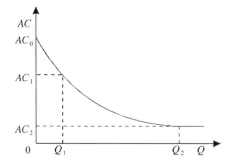

Figure 15.3

Their presence produces a **learning curve** of the sort shown in figure 15.3. It indicates average cost, AC as a function of *total output since production began, Q.*[10]

Country 1, which has yet to begin production of the good in question, could produce at cost AC_0, which is higher than that in countries 2 and 3, which have lower costs thanks to the time they have spent producing the good (and, perhaps, to the size of their market). The advantage of protection is that the scope for foreign producers to expand their share of the domestic market is curbed, allowing domestic producers to increase their market share and raise their total output more rapidly. Even if after a certain number of years country 1's production costs fell only to the level in country 3 and no more, protection would still have been advantageous if the presence of the industry generated positive spillover effects for country 1's economy. Such effects are associated with close inter-industry linkages that can help spread knowledge, stimulate innovations and determine their orientation through the relationships arising between innovators and the users of innovations.

Country 1 may derive further benefit from protection if its production costs are lower than those in other countries – due, for example, to lower wages or rents, or narrower profit margins. In this case, the learning curve of country 1 may be below that shown in figure 15.3 (which earlier was assumed to hold for both country 1 and the other countries). In this case, country 1 could produce the good at a lower cost than abroad even before having achieved a cumulative output of $0Q_2$.

Die-hard free traders have argued that at least where there are no spillover effects, the prospect of profits deriving from the gradual reduction of production costs as producers learn their craft should be enough on its own to induce new firms to enter the market, making any protectionist incentives unnecessary. However, in addition to ignoring spillover effects, which may cause a divergence between private and social returns, this position also fails to take account of: (a) the risky outlook for sufficiently large profits, which in any case would be deferred in time; (b) the imperfections of financial markets, by raising the cost of capital or rationing credit, especially for riskier activities, often

[10] This curve was initially introduced for the aeroplane industry. It was noticed that the number of hours of labour – which was taken as a measure of average costs – fell drastically as production passed from the construction of prototypes to mass production and then as the *total* number of planes increased. Cumulative production thus assumed the role of a proxy for accumulated experience.

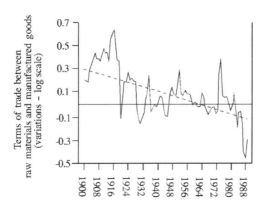

Figure 15.4

discourage innovation and/or the entrance of goods that are not immediately profitable into the market.

The difficulty of identifying infant industries that will become viable in the future or produce positive spillover effects and the possibility that firms may sit comfortably behind the protective tariff barrier well beyond the time necessary for the new industry to take off should be borne in mind. However, this does not lessen the importance of this argument in favour of protection, whose scope has actually been broadened, with reference not to specific industries but to manufacturing in general in underdeveloped countries, where the problem is not individual infant industries but rather entire infant economies, to cite Myrdal (1956, 1957). The problem in developing countries is to install manufacturing industries as soon as the production of primary goods has developed sufficiently to meet the country's basic needs.

The latter seems a necessary but not sufficient condition for economic development, which must be completed by the growth of industry. One reason for this is that as soon as the country moves from production of subsistence commodities to primary production for the market, it risks specialising in an activity where the terms of trade with respect to manufactured goods worsen continuously, as was argued by Prebisch (1950) and Singer (1950) and verified by numerous studies (most recently, Ardeni and Wright, 1992, from which figure 15.4 is drawn). In addition, manufacturing is the area where the greatest productivity gains are to be made.[11]

Nevertheless, recent studies have shown that the considerable change in the composition of developing countries' exports (towards a greater proportion of manufactured goods) has only attenuated the worsening of the terms of trade between primary products and manufactures: between 1970 and 1987, there was an annual decline of 1 per cent in the terms of trade between the manufactures of developing countries and

---

[11] This statement does not contradict our earlier statement regarding the worsening of the terms of trade to the detriment of agriculture and the benefit of manufacturing. The main reason for this is the different market regime for the two types of good (Kaldor, 1971). Manufactured goods are normally traded under oligopolistic conditions and productivity gains usually lead to increases in the incomes of 'factors' (wages and profits) rather than lower prices (Sylos Labini, 1962).

similar products of the developed world, while the terms of trade between primary products and manufactures fell by more than 2 per cent annually (Sarkar and Singer, 1991). This occurred despite the more rapid productivity growth in the developed countries, which, *ceteris paribus*, could have led to a fall in the prices of their goods. This means that (a) the remuneration of factors in the developing countries declined with respect to that in the advanced nations and (b) the problem of the sectoral structure of production was only one of the difficulties facing the developing economies. Other equally important problems concerned the structure of trade, finance and services, the size of economic activities and market regimes.

15.5   Protection as a tool for improving the terms of trade

A second economic argument in favour of protection is the possibility for a country to improve its terms of trade if certain demand and supply conditions are met.

We said that a duty (tariff) is an indirect tax and, as such, may be shifted onto the price of goods. The more elastic is demand, the less likely the shift is. A low elasticity of supply also tends to reduce the shifting of the duty onto the price. If the price does not rise, the tax is borne by the foreign supplier. Let us now examine the conditions for the shifting of the tariff onto the foreign supplier in more detail. The influence of demand elasticity seems to be clear. Consider instead the meaning of *supply elasticity*. First, this should be taken with reference to the price net of the duty, which represents the net unit revenue for the exporting firm. Inelastic supply thus means that the firm does not change its supply despite the reduction in price: after a duty is introduced, the firm is willing to sell the same quantity at a lower price. This may be due to the importance of the market for the exporting firm[12] and the fact that the good is produced under significant economies of scale.

If the foreign exporter keeps the price unchanged after the introduction of the tariff, the tariff-imposing country's terms of trade improve. Recall that the terms of trade are $TT = p_x/(p_m \cdot e)$. Both p_x and the price (in domestic currency) of imports, $p_m e$, remain unchanged, but the latter is inclusive of the duty, which is collected by the importing country. From the point of view of the country as a whole, we must consider the price of imports *net of the duty*, which has fallen. The tariff improves the terms of trade even in the more frequent situation when it is partially shifted onto prices.

Let us examine figure 15.5 to understand the scope for improving the terms of trade more clearly. If the country that imposes the duty is not small, the world price will tend to fall, say to p', owing to the decline in demand in the country induced by the duty.

In this case, the new domestic price within the country will be $p'(1 + d_1) < p(1 + d_1)$ and the tariff-imposing country will improve its terms of trade, since it pays a price (net of the tariff) for imports, p', which is lower than the earlier price, p, with no change in the price (not considered here) of its exports.

---

[12] J. S. Mill made this argument, as he did with infant industries.

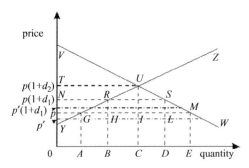

Figure 15.5

15.6   Protection from cheap labour and social dumping

This issue is often presented as an argument in favour of protectionism. It is frequently used in the developed countries to argue for the general protection of industry or protection of certain sectors (mainly labour-intensive industries) threatened by cheap foreign labour, which makes inadequately protected industries uncompetitive.[13] The argument has also been advanced recently with regard to the problem of **social dumping** – i.e. 'unfair' competition from many countries, often developing nations, where labour costs are kept low by giving workers little social protection.[14]

In reality, this position fails to take account of the fact that the lower labour costs of less-developed countries largely correspond to lower productivity, so that labour costs per unit of output are often not much different and in any case not as dramatically low as the labour costs *per se*. It is thus a justification that is not always founded on reality and is often advanced only to promote purely sectoral interests.[15] Although it is understandable that these are defended at the government level in the short run to avoid dangerous and painful falls in employment, it is less justifiable to do so in the long run. The task of avoiding this situation must be entrusted to a full employment macroeconomic policy and an industrial policy to ensure rapid productive reconversion and restructuring in response to changes in the international division of labour.

---

[13] A comparison of wages in large cities in different countries is given in World Bank (1995, p. 11). The differences are such that, for example, the ratio of the salary of an engineer in Germany to that of one in Keyna (calculated not at market exchange rates, but on a **purchasing power parity (PPP)** basis, i.e. at exchange rates that ensure equal purchasing power in the countries involved) is equal to 7, while the same ratio for a female textile worker is 18. The differences are even greater for workers outside of large urban areas or in the informal sector (underground labour).

[14] **Dumping** is a form of competition often considered unfair that consists in selling abroad at lower prices than those charged on domestic markets. *Social dumping* is similar to traditional dumping but is based on the argument that low prices (both domestic and abroad) can be applied by some countries only because of their low level of social protection.

[15] Caffè (1990, p. 265) rightly does not consider this to be an economic argument in favour of protectionism, classifying it as a non-economic argument. More recently, there have been proposals to adopt social protection standards, to be imposed through trade policy (see section 17.4). This approach, a debatable one within the framework of trade policy, could be well founded in relation to problems of FDI and the shifting of segments of the production process abroad.

15.7   Protection as an employment policy

If an economy suffers from unemployment, protection can help push it back to full employment.

Looking at the reduced form of any Keynesian model for an open economy, we can see that the value of the multiplier rises if the propensity to import declines, a result that can be obtained through protectionist policies. If there is unemployment, the same initial level of autonomous spending will give rise to a *higher level of aggregate demand and employment* because of the increase in the multiplier.

Protection and the reduction of the propensity to import lower (raise) the level of the country's imports if the consequent increase in income is proportionately smaller (larger) than the reduction in the propensity to import. But the imports of one country are the exports of the Rest of the World. Protection can thus cause a decline (or a rise) in the autonomous spending of the Rest of the World and, therefore, in its income and employment. If the imports of the domestic country (the Rest of the World's exports) decline, we have a **beggar-thy-neighbour policy**. This is the substance of many protectionist positions, beginning with mercantilism. They can be criticised because they expose the country that adopts protectionist measures to justified reprisals by other countries. Such a result is less likely if protection is undertaken together with expansionary policies in the domestic country. Keynes examined the matter with reference to the United Kingdom in the years 1918–39. Although initially arguing from a free trade position, Keynes came to suggest some form of protection, such as import duties, as a way to ease the balance of payments constraint that would have arisen owing to expansionary fiscal and monetary policies. In his view, lowering the propensity to import would prevent an increase in imports – and the worsening of the current account balance – in the presence of an increase in government spending and aggregate demand. The level of imports could remain constant owing to the effect of the reduction in the propensity to import and the simultaneous increase in domestic demand, thus leaving other countries unaffected. Protection in conjunction with expansionary monetary or fiscal policies would *simultaneously* achieve full employment and balance of payments equilibrium.

The possibility that a devaluation of the currency (or, where this is not possible, other forms of protectionism)[16] associated with an expansionary policy will not shift internal problems onto the country's neighbours can be examined in graphical terms using the Mundell–Fleming model. Assume there are no international capital movements, which allows us to focus on movements of goods and to capture the effects of a devaluation on the income of both the country involved and the rest of the world as well as on the balance of payments. Under this assumption, the BP schedule is vertical, as in figure 15.6. The system is initially in equilibrium at A. If Y_A does not correspond to full employment, the monetary or fiscal authorities could attempt to boost income to its full employment level, $\overline{Y}$, with measures aimed at shifting LM or IS. If monetary

---

[16] Recall that devaluation can help protect domestic industry.

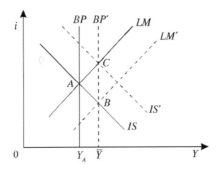

Figure 15.6

or fiscal measures alone are adopted, the economy would then be at *B* or *C*, respectively. However, in both cases government action would produce a balance of payments deficit: the increase in income would cause imports to rise, while exports would remain unchanged. The resulting deficit is not sustainable in the long run in the presence of limited foreign reserves.

The only way to sustain such an expansionary policy in the long run is to *'ease' the balance of payments constraint*. This can be accomplished by either a devaluation or other protectionist measures, which reduce the propensity to import of the country involved and/or raise it in the rest of the world in the case of a devaluation. Suppose that the government adopts an expansionary fiscal policy that shifts *IS* to *IS'*. If the currency is simultaneously devalued, *BP* will move to *BP'*.[17] The new equilibrium between imports and exports is now reached at a higher level of the two quantities, which means that not only is the country exporting more than before, it is also importing a larger quantity of foreign goods. In this case, the devaluation (or other protectionist measures) would not shift domestic problems (the elimination of unemployment) onto trading partners. In some circumstances it could even help to increase income and employment in other countries.

This is the substance of Keynes' position. It matured slowly and unwillingly over the years, but it was strenuously defended in the end. In particular, he came out in favour of subsidies and tariffs as an alternative to devaluation, taking account of Britain's special position as an international financial centre: a devaluation would have weakened or undermined that position, thus reducing net foreign capital inflows.[18]

15.8   Industrial policies and trade policies

Trade policies have a direct impact on the flows of imports and exports, given certain demand and supply functions for the various goods. Industrial policies, which we

---

[17] For the sake of simplicity, we ignore the effects of the devaluation on *IS*, which we can consider to be included in the rightward shift of the curve.

[18] Consider the fact that devaluation can induce expectations of future devaluation and therefore give rise to net outflows (or smaller inflows) of capital (section 14.8). It is therefore absolutely necessary for a country that is a financial centre and wishes to continue to operate as such to ensure the stability of its exchange rate. For Keynes' argument in favour of protection see Milone (1993).

discussed in chapter 8, tend to influence the factors that determine supply functions (and to some degree demand functions as well): production techniques, types of products, the degree of concentration, relationships between firms and between industries and the shifting of production abroad.

Industrial policy clearly contributes to creating the conditions for the trade success of a country. In particular, industrial policy can seek to improve the competitive position of a country through:

(1) the *appropriate positioning of a country's industry* in the sectors in which world demand is growing fastest
(2) the *strengthening of strategic sectors* (for the creation of dynamic external economies)
(3) the reinforcement of the conditions that help reduce the *price elasticity* of foreign demand (product innovation, economic concentration)
(4) ensuring suitable relations *between firms as well as industries* at the domestic and international levels (in particular, foreign direct investment (FDI) operations, for which, see chapter 19; appropriate relations between firms and markets and financial intermediaries).

However, this does not mean that industrial policies are at the exclusive service of trade policy. The opposite may well be the case: trade policy actions can help strengthen the *productive structure* of a country, contributing to the achievement of dynamic economies of scale (e.g. by protecting infant industries) or channelling investment to certain sectors that can increase the economy's overall growth rate (this, for example, is one of the functions of the '**hard exchange rate policy**' adopted by some countries, such as Italy in the EMS and, earlier, by others such as Germany).[19]

15.9 Summary

1 *Free trade and protectionism* are alternative trade policies. The scientific foundation of free trade lies with advantages of specialisation identified by Ricardo with the comparative-cost principle.
2 There are many *protectionist measures*. Tariffs, subsidies, devaluation, and quotas are some of the instruments available to a protectionist policy for domestic goods.
3 Protectionist measures usually imply an increase in the *price of the protected good* and can have a variety of effects on consumption, production, imports, income distribution and tax revenues.

---

[19] With regard to Italy, this policy essentially involved not devaluing the currency even in the presence of relatively higher inflation than in the other European countries, thus imposing a degree of discipline on public and private agents. This would produce a loss of *price competitiveness*, thus worsening the country's position in sectors in which it had a relatively strong presence (traditional industries), but leaving relatively unchanged its position in sectors with low price elasticity (e.g. innovative industries), in which competitiveness is more closely linked to non-price factors. Over time, a strong currency policy would have increased the country's competitiveness since it would stimulate technological innovation in both processes (reducing costs and thus prices) and products (with quality improvements that would enhance non-price competitiveness). In addition, it would induce wage moderation, as we will see in subsection 16.6.2. The exchange rate policy followed by Germany in the 1970s had similar objectives.

4   The *Ricardian principle* suffers from numerous limitations associated with the existence of infant industries, with the possibility of improving the terms of trade, with the need to protect domestic workers (in the short run) against cheap foreign labour and with the need to ensure full employment and balance of payments equilibrium simultaneously.

5   *Industrial policies* work through numerous channels to strengthen the competitiveness of the country. In turn, trade policies can help strengthen an economy's productive structure.

V   Public institutions in an international setting

16 Monetary systems and exchange rate regimes

16.1 Monetary systems

By the **monetary system** we mean the set of rules that govern the monetary aspects of the operation of an economic system and/or its relationship with other economies. More specifically, a monetary system is a specification of rules that:

(a) define the *monetary unit*, i.e. the instrument used as legal tender, which is (usually) also the unit of account
(b) regulate the issue of *money*
(c) define the *currency's relationships with foreign currencies* in terms of its value, circulation and convertibility.

Points (a) and (b) concern the domestic aspects of a monetary system. Point (c) concerns its international aspects. When we speak of an 'international monetary system', we refer to the set of rules concerning the international aspects (which are usually fairly independent of those governing domestic aspects) adopted by some group of countries.

In the following sections we will examine the main monetary systems, with specific reference to their international aspects. We will generally describe the structure and operation of each system in abstract terms and then examine real-life systems based on these models. Bear in mind that a real monetary system may often have features that do not exactly fit one of the abstract reference systems described here. In other words, there may not necessarily be a one-to-one correspondence between abstract and real-life systems. This is understandable given the fact that the content of the rules underlying each system is the product of a mix of ideas and interests whose shape is largely determined by the vicissitudes of history. Identifying types of monetary system is to a certain degree an *ex post* rationalisation of highly diverse realities.

16.2 The Gold Standard

The value of a monetary unit can be linked to that of a commodity, especially a precious metal, if the monetary unit is defined in terms of that good and certain additional conditions are met. Linking a currency's value to a commodity is one attempt to ensure the *stability* of that value and to remove control of money creation from the arbitrary decisions of some authority.[1] This does not mean, however, that the attempt is always successful or that a monetary unit not linked to a commodity cannot be stable, as we will see in greater detail later.

The basic elements of the **Gold Standard** are the following:

(a) in a country that adopts the Gold Standard, banknotes are issued by the central bank and can be exchanged for goods (whether they are called dollars, yen, pounds, francs, etc.), therefore constituting that country's *currency*

(b) the gold *'content'* (i.e. equivalence) of the monetary unit is defined (for example, a yen 'contains' 0.5 grams of gold, a dollar is equivalent to 1 gram of gold, etc.)

(c) the central bank holds a *gold reserve*, either coins or bars, that is some proportion of the quantity of currency issued; legal tender can be converted into gold on request – or, vice versa, the central bank can exchange banknotes for gold on the basis of the gold content of the currency

(d) gold can be freely *imported or exported*.

As mentioned, our focus here is the *international dimension* of monetary systems. If a number of countries simultaneously adopts the Gold Standard, these international aspects can be immediately identified as follows.

Since the monetary units of each country are all defined in terms of a homogeneous common base, gold, the relative value of these units can be determined by dividing their respective gold contents. For example, using our earlier example of the yen and the dollar, the relative value of these currencies is equal to $0.5/1 = 0.5$: a dollar has twice the gold content of a yen and therefore has twice its value. This ratio, called the **mint parity**, is an abstract relative price, i.e. a relative reference price. The actual price of the yen in terms of dollars – which is the nominal bilateral exchange rate of the yen in terms of dollars – may move away from the parity depending on the actual supply of and demand for yen against dollars.

However, a special feature of the Gold Standard is that the fluctuations around the parity are *objectively* limited, for the following reasons. A Japanese who needs to make a payment in dollars will always be able to do so by purchasing gold and sending it to the United States, where it can be converted into dollars, rather than purchasing dollars in Japan and sending them abroad. This means that the exchange rate (in our example, the price of a dollar in terms of yen) cannot exceed what is called the **gold-export point**, which is equal to parity plus the cost of shipping the gold (transport, insurance and forgone interest[2]): above this value, it is profitable to convert yen into gold (given the gold 'content' of the yen), ship the gold abroad and have it converted into dollars instead of purchasing dollars on the foreign exchange market. Conversely,

---

[1] Precious metals, and gold in particular, are preferred not only because of their chemical and physical properties but above all because of the *relative* stability of their value.

[2] The loss of interest is due to the fact that the capital represented by the gold sent abroad does not bear interest while it is in transit.

if the exchange rate falls below the **gold-import point**, which is equal to parity minus the gold shipment costs, it becomes more profitable for a Japanese to accept gold in payment from abroad rather than foreign currency (in our case, dollars). Since the shipping costs of gold are usually small with respect to the value of the goods shipped, the Gold Standard is essentially a *fixed*-exchange rate system.

In such a system, equilibrating goods movements in the balance of payments is entrusted to *price movements* (in addition to variations in income, as we will see) within the countries affected by the imbalance, rather than changes in the nominal exchange rate as happens in monetary systems where the nominal exchange rate can vary significantly. Without changes in the nominal exchange rate, it is price changes that ensure the variation of the real exchange rate that may be needed to adjust the balance of goods movements.

Note that a variation in the exchange rate will produce a simultaneous change of the same magnitude in the relative prices of all goods in the two countries (the price of bread in country *A* compared with its price in country *B*, as well as the relative price of iron in the same countries, etc.). By contrast, the changes in relative prices that occur under Gold Standard or any other fixed-exchange rate system following the variation in the price level in each country may differ, since in the real world the prices of some goods (e.g. bread) vary more easily and rapidly than prices of other goods (e.g. iron).

The Gold Standard is largely of historical interest. Gold has had a monetary role since ancient times, but the foundations of a true Gold Standard were laid in the United Kingdom only in 1821, when the Bank of England was legally required to redeem its notes in gold and restrictions on the melting of coins and gold shipments were lifted. The Gold Standard later acquired an international role between 1870 and 1880, when it was adopted by a sufficiently large number of countries. With the increase in monetarily financed government spending at the outbreak of the First World War in 1914, and the consequent difficulty of maintaining convertibility, nearly all countries abandoned the Gold Standard, only to reintroduce it for a few years during the inter-war period (see Bordo and Schwartz, 1984; Grubel, 1984).

The United Kingdom's attempt to return to the Gold Standard in the mid-1920s would probably have met with greater success without the mistake that was made in setting the gold 'content' of the pound too high and the effects of other external circumstances. The decision to adopt the pre-war gold content despite the increase in currency in circulation and a higher price level, implied a monetary restriction and a general fall in prices (and wages). Such a fall in prices and wages is always a threat to economic activity and is in any case difficult to achieve when faced by powerful labour unions and the resistance of firms. Under these conditions, the most likely outcome was a *fall in output and employment*, which is what actually happened, as predicted by Keynes, who considered the Gold Standard a 'barbarous relic' (see Keynes, 1924, p. 138). When the impact of adverse external circumstances was added, including the consequences of the world depression that began in 1929, keeping the Gold Standard in the United Kingdom became impossible and the devaluation of the pound in September 1931 marked its demise.[3]

Some economists and politicians still admire the Gold Standard today. They underscore its stability and automatic nature, which they credit for the economic growth achieved before 1914. In reality, these presumed merits are attributable to a series of fortunate circumstances as well as the careful monetary policy of the central banks and the trade policy of the period.

16.3   The Gold Exchange Standard and the International Monetary Fund

Under the **Gold Exchange Standard**, at least one country adopts the Gold Standard while the others:

(a) set the gold '*content*' of their currencies
(b) *hold the currency* of the Gold Standard country (rather than gold or in addition to it) as the reserve backing for their national currency[4]
(c) permit the *conversion of the national currency into the reserve currency* at a constant, fixed value, which represents the *parity* between the two currencies – i.e. the ratio between their respective gold contents (similar parities can be defined between the currency of the country under consideration and those of other Gold Standard countries).

If the Gold Standard country were the United States (as it was), the dollar would serve as the reserve currency for other countries (e.g. France) and, in a pure gold exchange system, the French franc could be converted into gold by virtue of its convertibility into dollars, since this could in turn be converted directly into gold. In practice, conversion of national currency into gold may be limited to central banks only. Conversion of the national currency into foreign currency can also be subject to restrictions. For example, rather than circulating freely, use of reserve currencies may be limited to settling foreign transactions (*non-resident convertibility*).

The Gold Exchange Standard can economise on the use of gold, which proves useful if this is scarce. It also has the advantage of allowing countries that adopt it to hold interest-bearing reserves, as (unlike gold) the foreign currency assets held as reserves normally earn interest. However, the system may become unstable if the countries adopting this system want to keep gold among their reserves when the solvency of the Gold Standard country becomes uncertain, as we will see later in this section. In this case the countries that have adopted the Gold Exchange Standard could convert their reserves of foreign currency into gold, triggering a sort of 'run' on the central bank of the Gold Standard country.

---

[3] Actually, some argue that the Gold Standard had a leading role in causing the Great Depression (see Eichengreen, 1992).
[4] The currency of the first country is called the **reserve currency** since it can be used for the net foreign payments needed in the event of a balance of payments deficit.

If a gold exchange system allows all agents to convert domestic currency into gold, it works in exactly the same way as the Gold Standard. In particular, the exchange rate between the currencies of two countries that adopt the Gold Exchange Standard is set around their parity. However, the **parity** in this case is an **adjustable peg** rather than an unchangeable value: it can be *devalued* or *revalued*. Changes in the parity are usually accompanied by significant variations in the exchange rate, producing changes in the trade balance (see chapter 10).

If convertibility is restricted in some way, the fluctuations of the exchange rate around its parity can be quite large and can be avoided only through the active intervention of the monetary authorities to absorb the excess demand or supply of foreign currency causing the fluctuations: if the exchange rate rises above a given upper limit as an effect of excess demand for the foreign currency, the monetary authorities will supply that foreign currency; vice versa, they will buy foreign currency if the exchange rate falls below a given lower limit.

This was the situation with the **International Monetary Fund** (IMF) system, established in 1944 at Bretton Woods (United States), which operated as a Gold Exchange Standard until 1971. Only central banks were allowed to convert dollars into gold and in many countries private agents could buy foreign currency (in particular, dollars) only to make payments to non-residents (**convertibility for non-residents**).[5]

Participating countries committed themselves to: (a) setting the gold content of their currency; (b) intervening to limit fluctuations in the exchange rate to a maximum of 1 per cent above or below parity; (c) paying a quota to the Fund that could be used for loans in case of need; (d) complying with other rules designed to avoid frequent and widespread changes in parities.

Changing parities was allowed only to overcome a **fundamental disequilibrium** (i.e. a severe and persistent imbalance). In the absence of such a situation, each country had to tackle balance of payments difficulties with other economic policies (as we saw in chapter 14).[6] While waiting for the effects of these **adjustment** policies to operate, it was nevertheless possible for deficit countries to obtain loans – i.e. to be **financed**.[7]

[5] This ensured the **multilateralism** of trade, which we can define in this context (but more generally see section 17.1) as the possibility of offsetting any deficit that a country might have with respect to another with its surplus *vis-à-vis* a third country, thus overcoming the tendency towards **bilateralism** (i.e. balancing trade country by country) that had distinguished the 1918–39 period, which reduced allocative efficiency.
  Although the dollar has not been convertible into gold since 1971, the convertibility for non-residents of other currencies into dollars has remained and, in fact, most countries have expanded the convertibility of their currencies into all foreign countries for all transactions.
[6] The burden of the structural adjustment should in principle be borne both by debtor countries (those with balance of payment deficits) and creditor countries (the others). This was done to avoid the deflationary effects that would have resulted from placing the burden on debtor countries only, which might have meant adopting deflationary policies as an instrument to re-establish equilibrium. It was Keynes, fearing a repetition of the depression of the 1930s, who insisted on the necessity of a *symmetric adjustment* that nevertheless found little application: in reality, it was the debtor countries that made the greatest adjustments.
[7] Loans could (and still can) be granted by the IMF to meet temporary balance of payments imbalances by drawing on the members' quotas or by borrowing from a member. In addition, there were (and still are) long-term loans available for specific projects, usually on normal bank terms, from the International Bank for Reconstruction and Development (IBRD). This institution, more commonly known as the World Bank, is the second of the institutions created at Bretton Woods (see chapter 17).

The IMF also **monitored** the appropriateness of member countries' macroeconomic policies with an impact on exchange rates and international monetary relationships (for the developments regarding these functions of the IMF, see section 6.5).

This system had a greater basis in convention than the Gold Standard, and conventions need a durable preliminary agreement. It is again clear, in this as in other areas, why no institutions are perfectly suited to all occasions. For example, the Gold Exchange Standard, which did not work well between the wars, was quite successful after the Second World War until 1971.

One problem with the Gold Exchange Standard is that the constancy of the gold content of the reserve currency underpins confidence in the system. This creates a conflict since, if the gold content is kept constant, there is a risk of an *international liquidity shortage* as international transactions grow. If sufficient liquidity is provided, however, it may prove difficult to maintain the gold content of the reserve currency (**Triffin's dilemma**). In general, there is no guarantee whatsoever that the quantity of the reserve currency issued by the Gold Standard country and circulating in the rest of the world will match other countries' demand for reserves, i.e. the demand for reserve currency related to international transactions (Triffin, 1960). If the Gold Standard country decides to regulate the money supply to adjust it to the level of international transactions, it loses a further degree of freedom (in addition to that of altering the gold content of its currency) in the use of its economic policy instruments. Bear in mind that the reserve currency enters circulation in the rest of the world only if the Gold Standard country runs balance of payments deficits.[8] Such deficits may or may not occur. Even if they do, they may not be sufficiently large if difficulties arise in regulating the balance of payments or the Gold Standard country's economic interests or other policy aims take precedence. However, if the balance of payments deficit over a certain span of time is sufficiently large to ensure adequate international liquidity, confidence in the stability of the value of the reserve currency *may* be undermined. This occurs precisely because the amount of reserve currency held by the central banks of the rest of the world is too large in relation to the gold reserves of the Gold Standard country, creating concern about its ability to redeem banknotes for gold upon request. Conversely, if the amount of reserve currency supplied through balance of payments deficits is regulated so as to avoid these risks, it might be insufficient to ensure steady trade growth.

The former situation did in fact occur in the post-war period. After a span in which there was a dollar shortage, the opposite situation emerged during the 1960s in connection with large US balance of payments deficits. While these solved the international liquidity problem much more effectively than the creation of Special Drawing Rights

---

[8] For this reason some speak of the *seigniorage* of the Gold Standard country, by analogy with the situation inside a country when it issues money whose nominal value exceeds its intrinsic value or when non-interest bearing (rather than interest-bearing) liabilities are issued in exchange for goods and services. The analogy is justified by the fact that the reserve currency country can exchange non-interest-bearing liabilities (banknotes) or low-interest-bearing liabilities for an excess of imported goods and services (for more on this see Grubel, 1984). However, this and other benefits are offset by disadvantages, some of which we mentioned in the text (the impossibility of changing the currency's parity to secure the desired balance of payments equilibrium, the necessity of subordinating domestic economic policy to the objective of maintaining adequate international liquidity).

(SDRs, see section 16.4), it also generated growing worries about dollar convertibility. On 15 August 1971, President Nixon was forced to suspend the convertibility of the dollar into gold, thus bringing an end to the gold exchange system embodied by the IMF.[9]

The IMF continues to operate, but there are floating rates between the main regional areas. The IMF's current functions are to provide financing and monitor economic policies in member countries (see section 16.5).

16.4 Centrally created reserves

An alternative to the monetary systems we have examined so far would be to establish an international monetary organisation to act as a *central banker for the world*, much the same as the national central banks. This organisation would be responsible for creating the international liquidity it judged necessary to achieve some world-level objective (e.g. global income growth) as a true fiat money.

In a world of independent nation states, such a supranational central bank could be established only cooperatively. Even if an agreement were reached, however, the lack of effective executive powers would make such a system difficult to design and implement. Since states tend to reserve the right to regulate domestic liquidity directly or to determine the level of the exchange rate (as well as other non-monetary economic variables), an international central bank would only be able to create international money used exclusively by national central banks to settle debts between themselves. The quantity of domestic currency would continue to be regulated by each national central bank.

Any international agreement would have to clarify:

(a) the alternative methods for distributing international money among the various countries (the distribution of *seigniorage*)
(b) the criteria for deciding *how much reserves to create* and their possible uses, in order to maintain the value of the fiat money stable and ensure balance of payments adjustment (Grubel, 1984).

This system, which would represent an advanced stage of the transformation of the international monetary system towards the centralisation and discretionary regulation of the currency, has found only partial application.

At the IMF's 1967 meeting in Rio de Janeiro – i.e. still within the framework of the IMF system – it was decided to create a special unit of account known as **Special Drawing Rights** (SDRs), whose initial value was equal to that of the dollar.[10] SDRs, which are still in use, have no paper form, existing only as accounting credits. Countries

---

[9] For the working of the IMF until 1971 see De Vries and Horsefield (1969), Horsefield (1969a, 1969b), De Vries (1976, 1985), James (1996).

[10] In 1974, after two devaluations of the dollar and the switch to a floating rate regime, SDRs were transformed into a **basket currency** whose value depended (and still depends) on the *weighted value of a selection of major currencies*. The weight and the amount of the currencies included in the valuation basket of the SDR as of 30 April 2003 are indicated in box 16.1.

with balance of payment deficits can make payments or intervene in foreign exchange markets by exchanging SDRs for other members' currencies. The countries accepting SDRs (normally those in surplus) can use them to settle any future deficits (earning interest in any case) in the meantime. Therefore, SDRs are real money (box 16.1).

Box 16.1. SDR valuation, 30 April 2003

Table 16B.1 *SDR valuation, April 2003*

Currency	Amount of currency units	Exchange rate[a]	US dollar equivalent
Euro	0.4260	1.11290	0.474095
Japanese yen	21.0000	119.48000	0.175762
Pound sterling	0.0984	1.59610	0.157056
US dollar	0.5770	1.00000	0.577000
			1.383913

Memorandum:
SDR 1 = US$1.383913
US$1 = SDR 0.722589
Notes:
[a] Exchange rates in terms of US dollars per currency unit except for the Japanese yen, which is in currency units per US dollar.

Source: IMF (2003), p. 76.

Many obstacles had to be overcome to reach the stage of issuing SDRs. The obstacles were a sign of the resistance to the centralised creation of international liquidity as fiat money, resistance that still exists today (see Salin, 1990; Schröder, 1990). The hostility to such a system derives from fears that at both the international and national levels creating non-convertible money produces inflationary pressures. The surprising feature of this resistance to a true international means of payment is that it emerged in a period in which the various countries continued to make widespread use of the dollar, whose creation was inevitably linked to the trend in the balance of payments of the United States and thus its domestic economic policy and general political orientation.[11]

16.5 Floating exchange rates and the evolution of the IMF

Systems in which the value of a currency is allowed to float like other market prices differ completely from those we have seen so far (**floating exchange rate**). As with any other price, fluctuations in the exchange rate should be able to ensure equilibrium in the relevant market (the foreign exchange market in our case): if demand for foreign currency (e.g. dollars) exceeds supply, the exchange rate (i.e. the price of the dollar in the

---

[11] For the problems associated with SDRs, see Van Ypersele (1977).

domestic currency) will rise, thus curbing demand and expanding the supply of dollars (*depreciation* of the currency); if demand for foreign currency falls short of supply, the exchange rate will fall (*appreciation*).

Under a floating-exchange rate system (or fixed-rate systems that allow parity adjustments), international adjustment is partly or mainly entrusted to fluctuations in the exchange rate: a balance of payments surplus (deficit) will cause the currency to appreciate (depreciate). This will affect goods movements in such a way as to return the overall balance of payments to equilibrium (whatever the balance on capital movements).

The advantage of such a floating-rate system is that it streamlines the duties of policymakers who, being freed of the burden of equilibrating the balance of payments, do not have to undertake specific interventions or accumulate reserves to finance future deficits. Nevertheless, leaving exchange rate movements entirely to market forces has a number of drawbacks. For this reason, real-life floating exchange rate regimes have tended to be **dirty** (or **managed**), i.e. not fully free.

One of the arguments in favour of floating (or *flexible* or *fluctuating*) exchange rates is that fixed exchange rates encourage speculators by 'guaranteeing' them large profits (M. Friedman, 1953). When a change in a parity is thought to be highly likely (and the extent of the speculation itself may contribute to this), the fixed level of the exchange rate becomes a sort of bonus for speculators (the narrower the fluctuation band, the larger the bonus). They can acquire the foreign currency at a (low) fixed price – i.e. one that is independent of the demand for the currency – and then sell it at a higher price, after the devaluation. This would not happen in a flexible-exchange rate system, where the exchange rate is not (officially) kept fixed.

For example, let us take a historical perspective beginning with the situation in the 1960s, a period in which nearly all countries had fixed exchange rates, and examine the question of the relative benefits of fixed- and floating-rate regimes with regard to discouraging speculation. (Remember that nearly all countries, with the main exception of the United Kingdom, used the price-quotation system.)

The lira/dollar parity in the IMF system was Lit 625/$1, with a fluctuation band of ± 1 per cent; dollars could be bought in Italy at a maximum price of 631.25 lire, a price that would not rise in reaction to the increase in speculative purchases. If a 5 per cent devaluation of the lira against the dollar were forecast, the expected gain to speculators would have been 4 per cent, excluding transaction costs. If the fluctuation band had been 3 per cent, the expected maximum gain to speculators forecasting a 5 per cent devaluation would have been 2 per cent, since the exchange rate would have increased to $625 + 0.03(625) = 643.75$ as an effect of speculative purchases of dollars.

Widening the fluctuation band would not have been sufficient to fend off large-scale speculative movements triggered, for example, by expectations of an even larger devaluation. In this case, only a freely floating exchange rate would have enabled the lira to depreciate sufficiently to reduce the profitability of speculation, in parallel with speculative activity. However, in a flexible-exchange rate system another factor may also encourage speculation. As a currency depreciates under the pressure of speculative purchases of the foreign currency, the initial forecast of the future exchange rate does not remain unchanged – i.e. the expected exchange rate for a given date (e.g. two months hence) is not independent of the current exchange rate and its most recent fluctuations.

Floating exchange rates present clear disadvantages in terms of the uncertainty of the price of foreign currencies, potentially hindering trade and medium and long-term capital movements, which are not speculation-induced, as well as non-speculative short-term flows.[12] However, it should be noted that exchange rate uncertainty is often a reflection of other factors and that, if the underlying tensions were not smoothly channelled into the current exchange rate, they might build up and explode, causing sharp and possibly traumatic fluctuations in the parity.

A further issue is the degree of discipline that the different exchange rate regimes exert over the conduct of private and public agents. Some economists argue that fixed rates should be favoured, since they act as a tighter constraint on the agents of a country than floating exchange rates. To understand this argument, first consider the position of private agents such as firms. If the exchange rate is fixed, they will find it difficult to increase their prices by more than their competitors in both domestic and international markets. They will therefore have an incentive to contain costs, resisting pressure for wage increases and improving their static and dynamic efficiency. Policymakers will also be encouraged to implement policies to increase the competitiveness of domestic goods, since they will otherwise risk a deterioration in the balance of payments. The country will thus be forced to adjust its domestic situation to that prevailing abroad. Fixed exchange rates are therefore a powerful tool of (implicit) *international coordination* and should therefore be favoured. By contrast, other economists favour a floating-rate regime because it gives a country greater autonomy: balance of payments adjustment under floating rates occurs directly in the external transactions market and does not lead to appreciable changes in domestic prices or incomes, as would happen in the case of a fixed-exchange rate regime.

Two aspects of this debate should be singled out. One concerns the *disciplinary role* to assign to external rules. We will deal with this in sections 16.6 and 16.7. The other concerns the actual ability of floating rates to confine the adjustment to the *external transactions market*, which can be limited by the links between exchange rates, on one hand, and prices and incomes, on the other. We discussed this issue in section 14.8. As we can see, the picture is highly varied and there are no clearly superior solutions except in relation to the objectives posed and the specific situation.

A floating-exchange rate system is now in place world-wide and was accepted by the IMF in the 1970s[13] after the suspension of dollar convertibility and after an attempt to maintain a system of fixed exchange rates (albeit not linked to gold) with wider

---

[12] Uncertainty can be eliminated by appropriate hedging on the forward exchange rate market. Anyone who wants to ensure that a future purchase (or sale) of a given currency is executed at a certain exchange rate will turn to the forward market. This can be expensive, however. Frankel (1992) considers the different factors that affect the volume of foreign trade and argues that the negative effect of exchange rate uncertainty is very small.

[13] The IMF amended its bylaws in 1978 to allow countries to choose the exchange rate regime they consider most appropriate. For the working of the international monetary system since 1971 see De Vries (1985), James (1996) and Boughton (2001).

fluctuation bands. Some countries had sought to introduce floating rates for international capital movements only,[14] keeping fixed rates for current transactions. However, this **dual** (or **two-tier) foreign exchange market** did not last long owing to the lack of a sharp distinction between current transactions and capital movements.[15]

Box 16.2. The IMF's regular financing activities

The IMF conducts its regular lending activity through the *General Resources Account* (GRA), which holds the quota subscriptions of members. The bulk of the financing is provided under Stand-By Arrangements, which address members' balance of payments difficulties of a short-term, cyclical nature, and under the *Extended Fund Facility* (EFF), which focuses on external payments difficulties arising from longer-term structural problems. Loans under Stand-By and Extended Arrangements can be supplemented with short-term resources from the *Supplemental Reserve Facility* (SRF) to assist members experiencing a sudden and disruptive loss of capital market access. All loans incur interest charges and can be subject to surcharges based on the type and duration of the loan and the amount of IMF credit outstanding. Repayment periods also vary by facility.

Source: IMF (2002), p. 57.

In recent years the duties of the IMF have expanded considerably. Its role as a source of financing (box 16.2) has grown to encompass long-term funding in order to cope with a lengthy series of financial crises in the developing world (see section 20.1). Concession of credit by the IMF is usually **conditional**, i.e. conditional on the agreement of the borrower country to undertake domestic policy actions in accordance with the Fund's recommendations (box 16.3). This has prompted wide criticism (see section 20.3).

The surveillance function of the IMF has also broadened over the years, and now comprises nearly all policy measures and not just macroeconomic policies with a direct impact on exchange rate stability and international monetary relations (see Mussa, 1997). The Fund's functions have developed in reaction to the increased interdependence among economies in the wake of globalisation (see chapter 19), which has blurred the distinction between economic policies with solely domestic relevance (**domestic policies**, which include most microeconomic policies) and those with an impact in the international monetary arena (**international policies** proper, which primarily include exchange rate policy and traditional trade policies as well as internal macroeconomic policies: monetary policy, fiscal policy and incomes policy).

---

[14] It was thought that floating rates would discourage speculative capital flows and excessive currency depreciation, for the reasons set out earlier in this section.

[15] Capital can be transferred by anticipating or delaying current payments (leads and lags) and overinvoicing or underinvoicing of international trade transactions.

Box 16.3.   The IMF's financing mechanism

The IMF's lending is financed from the *paid-in capital* subscribed by member countries. Each country is assigned a *quota* that determines its maximum financial commitment to the IMF. A portion of the quota is provided in the form of *reserve assets* (foreign currencies acceptable to the IMF or SDRs) and the remainder in the *member's own currency*. The IMF extends financing by providing *reserve assets* to the borrower from the reserve asset subscriptions of members or by calling on countries that are considered financially strong to exchange their currency subscriptions for reserve assets.

The loan is disbursed or drawn by the borrower 'purchasing' the reserve assets from the IMF with its own currency. Repayment of the loan is achieved by the borrower 'repurchasing' its currency from the IMF with reserve assets. The IMF levies a basic rate of interest (charges) on loans based on the SDR interest rate and imposes surcharges depending on the type and duration of the loan and the level of credit outstanding.

A country that provides reserve assets to the IMF as part of its quota subscription or through the use of its currency receives a *liquid claim* on the IMF (reserve position) that can be encashed on demand to obtain reserve assets to meet a balance of payments financing need. These claims earn interest (remuneration) based on the SDR interest rate and are considered by members as part of their international reserve assets. As IMF loans are repaid (repurchased), the amount of SDRs and the currencies of creditor members is restored and the creditor claim on the IMF is extinguished.

The 'purchase/repurchase' approach of IMF lending affects the composition, but not the overall size, of the IMF's resources. An increase in loans outstanding will reduce the IMF's holdings of reserve assets and the currencies of members that are financially strong and, at the same time, increase the IMF's holdings of the currencies of countries that are borrowing from the IMF. The amount of the IMF's holdings of reserve assets and the currencies of financially strong countries determines the IMF's lending capacity (liquidity).

Source: IMF (2002), p. 57.

The Fund's activities have been criticised by many scholars and institutions (for a recent review, see Vines and Gilbert, 2003). The Meltzer Report recommended that the Fund should perform a sort of lender-of-last-resort role for the emerging economies, restricting its operations, however, to supplying *liquidity* (i.e. short-term funds) at penalty rates only to financially sound countries but without imposing detailed conditions (US Congress, 2000).

16.6 The European Monetary System

16.6.1 Objectives

In April 1972 a number of European countries had reacted to the widening of exchange rate fluctuation bands around the world by narrowing the bands between their currencies (the *snake*). In 1979, they decided to strengthen and extend this agreement, which had proved to be more difficult to implement with the emergence of an international system of floating rates, by establishing a fully-fledged European Monetary System (EMS) of fixed exchange rates.

In addition to their shared desire to create an area of monetary stability, and therefore economic and political stability within the EEC, the countries had independent motives that nonetheless converged on a system of fixed exchange rates: low-inflation countries (i.e. those in the German mark area) wanted to use the system to prevent *competitive devaluations* (or *depreciations*) by high-inflation countries. On their part, the latter sought to introduce an external element of discipline on the behaviour of unions[16] or to increase the credibility of their anti-inflation policies.[17]

The final structure of the system was the result of a compromise between the various interests and largely reflects political considerations (Coffey, 1984, p. 17; Van Ypersele, 1984, p. 16).

The EMS was essentially composed of two elements:

(a) the European Exchange Rate Mechanism (ERM), which was intended to *reduce fluctuations in the exchange rates* between EU currencies. Not all the members of the then EEC (now European Union) participated in the ERM

(b) a mechanism for providing *credit to countries with balance of payments difficulties*. All EU members participated in this.

According to the ERM a 'grid' of bilateral parities was first established; that is, a central rate was set for each pair of currencies.[18] Central rates could be changed ('realigned') but participating countries were supposed to tend to keep them stable. The system initially called for a fluctuation band of only ± 2.25 per cent (± 6 per cent for a few currencies).[19] On 2 August 1993, the band was widened to ± 15 per cent for all countries in order to counter increased speculative attacks.

The mechanism to ensure that exchange rates remained fixed operated asymmetrically in practice. Interventions were more costly for countries with a balance of payments deficit than for those with a surplus, since the former might use up their reserves and find it difficult to borrow, while the latter faced only the possibility of an

---

[16] The game was in fact more complex. Firms, and often the central bank, also had the objective of preventing the government and Parliament from running up budget deficits.

[17] These higher-order 'objectives' will be discussed later.

[18] Since the EMS was not based on gold, it is more appropriate to speak of *central rates* rather than parities, as these are defined as the ratio between the gold contents of two currencies.

[19] With discrete variations in the exchange rates the margins were not perfectly symmetrical, with the lower being narrower than the upper (Gandolfo, 2001).

unwanted increase in the domestic money supply, which they could in any case offset with sterilisation.

A basis for a more symmetric fluctuation mechanism had also been devised. This was the ECU, which was created as a 'basket currency' containing the currencies of the EEC member states. This mechanism should have ensured greater symmetry than that based on the parity grid in signalling tensions and allocating the burden of adjustment, thus constituting a more balanced instrument for initiating co-ordination of the economic policies of the ERM countries. However it did not work in practice for a variety of reasons, the most important of which being the absence of a firm obligation to intervene with monetary and fiscal *adjustment* policies in the case of divergences of the actual value of the ECU from its value at central rates.

16.6.2   Objectives and achievements

To what extent were the various goals set by EMS participants achieved? The answer depends on the objective.

If we consider the aim of extending and strengthening *currency coordination* and we take the variability of exchange rates as an indicator of coordination, such variability was reduced more among ERM participants than among other OECD countries. This was especially true after 1983, when the high frequency of realignments declined with respect to that in the initial period, at least until 1992–3 (when there were five realignments).

As regards *eliminating the asymmetry of the 'snake'*, we previously noted that this objective was generally not achieved. Only Germany was in a position to decide its monetary policy independently, while the others normally adjusted their own policies accordingly, if they were not at least temporarily insulated by controls on capital movements (Giavazzi and Giovannini, 1989, p. 75).

Nevertheless, the asymmetric operation of the EMS seems to have laid the foundation for reaching the objective set by some countries of exerting external discipline on the behaviour of certain agents. Since monetary policy in the EMS was essentially dictated by Germany, which set price stability as its primary objective, the domestic behaviour of agents in the other countries had to fall into line. This explains the reminders that repeatedly came from policymakers (especially central banks) in high-inflation countries of the obligations imposed by EMS membership; these reminders were sometimes a powerful tool in arguing against domestic wage settlements or fiscal policies that were felt to be inflationary (*hard exchange rate policy*; see section 15.8). The question of how successful this external discipline was (especially between 1987 and 1992) in influencing union and government action – and, conversely, to what extent it imposed an excessive sacrifice in terms of high interest rates and, therefore, a worsening of public debt problems – still needs to be addressed in a dispassionate fashion, especially in the light of the devaluations that subsequently occurred in 1992–3.[20]

---

[20] The costs of this policy choice have been considered in detail by a 'neutral' observer in Dornbusch (1988).

Some have argued (Giavazzi and Pagano, 1988) that membership in the EMS lent *credibility* to the anti-inflationary policies of certain countries, acting as a guarantee of high-inflation countries' commitment to implementing such policies by tying the hands of their policymakers and lowering the public's inflationary expectations. Whether this actually occurred is not at all clear[21]: the frequency of *parity realignments* until 1983 is itself indicative of the fact that the commitment was not so credible after all. The situation may have changed to some extent after 1987.[22]

The EMS may have served to reduce the magnitude of the *devaluations* that high-inflation countries might have resorted to in order to maintain their competitiveness. Two facts support this hypothesis: the progressive reduction in the variability of exchange rates; and the growth in the trade surpluses of Germany and other low-inflation countries with the other ERM countries.

Fratianni and von Hagen (1990, 1991) argue that the EMS also helped to absorb external shocks (a **shock-absorber**), especially those originating in the United States, by inducing the European countries to coordinate their economic policies.

16.6.3   *European Economic and Monetary Union*

The Single European Act (SEA) of 1986 sealed the intention of the European countries to forge ahead along the path of economic and monetary integration. It was decided to complete the creation of the **Single European Market** (SEM), beginning in 1993, with the elimination of the remaining non-tariff barriers (NTBs) to the movement of goods and services and obstacles to the movement of capital and people (Cecchini, 1988).[23] At the same time, the mechanisms for credit and the coordination of intervention among the central banks were strengthened. Finally, in 1989 the **Delors Report** (named after the chairman of the committee that drafted it) was issued, setting out the stages for the achievement of European Economic and Monetary Union (EMU).

The Report established three stages for monetary union. The first began in 1990 and, among other things, provided for the elimination of restrictions on capital movements between the member states. Stage 2 began in 1994 with the creation of the European Monetary Institute (EMI), which has been charged with strengthening the coordination of monetary policies and preparing for the final stage. Stage 3 began on 1 January 1999 and involved:

(a) the full and irreversible convertibility of currencies
(b) the absence of any restrictions on capital transactions and the full integration of EU money and financial markets

---

[21] Weber (1991) made an attempt at measuring credibility, obtaining largely negative results.

[22] The hypothesis of the EMS as an instrument of credibility is linked to the complex issue of the *time inconsistency* of government action, for which we refer to Acocella (1998).

[23] These barriers – together with other factors such as transport costs and differing consumption behaviour – were responsible for the persistent segmentation of markets in the different countries noted in, among others, Caselli (1993). For more on the SEM, see section 18.8.

(c) the elimination of fluctuation margins and the irrevocable locking of exchange rates between the EU currencies and between these and the euro, the new European currency.

In addition:

(d) the ECU ceased to exist as an official basket currency, replaced by the euro as a unit of account at par
(e) monetary policy is decided by a European System of Central Banks (ESCB), composed of the national central banks and the European Central Bank (ECB), whose mandate is to ensure price stability (see section 18.4).[24]

The euro entered circulation on 1 January 2002 and replaced national currencies by 1 March 2002.

Stage 3 has involved only those countries that have met the *convergence standards* laid down at the Intergovernmental Conference (IGC) in Maastricht (the Netherlands) in December 1991 (which produced the Treaty on European Union (TEU), the so-called **Maastricht Treaty**),[25] which concerned:

(1) price stability
(2) the convergence of long-term interest rates
(3) the sustainability of governments' financial position, in terms of the ratio of the stock of government debt to GDP and the ratio of the government budget deficit to GDP
(4) exchange rate behaviour consistent with the aim of exchange rate stability.

The **Stability and Growth Pact** (SGP), reached at the Dublin European Council in December 1996, established that countries participating in EMU should tend to have surplus or balanced budgets. The maximum deficit/GDP ratio allowed is 3 per cent. Countries that do not observe this limit are subject to heavy penalties (see section 18.6).

16.6.4 *Nominal and real exchange rates in the European Monetary System*

Over the entire period in which the EMS was in operation, especially the period in which exchange rates were virtually fixed (between January 1987 and September 1992), the small variation (or even no change) in nominal exchange rates led to a real appreciation of the currency in countries (for example, Italy, Ireland and, for a certain period, France) where inflation was above the European average and a depreciation in other countries, such as Germany, where relative inflation was negative. This generated large deficits

[24] It was agreed that a system of fixed exchange rates (the so-called EMS 2) will continue to link the currencies of the participants in monetary union and those initially excluded from participation.
[25] The Maastricht agreements amended the Treaty of Rome, which established the EEC. The countries taking part in EMU in January 2004 are: Austria, Belgium, Finland, France, Germany, Ireland, Italy, Luxembourg, the Netherlands, Portugal and Spain. Greece was admitted to the EMU on 1 January 2001.

on the balance of goods movements for the high-inflation countries and equally large surpluses for the low-inflation countries.

In the deficit countries, overall equilibrium in the balance of payments was achieved thanks to high interest rates that attracted net capital inflows. The consequent expansion of foreign debt was reflected in an increase in payments abroad for investment income and, hence, the deficit in goods movements.

The policy of fostering an appreciation in the real exchange rate – i.e. the *hard exchange rate* policy, was aimed at imposing discipline on the behaviour of public and private agents (see subsection 16.6.2), in addition to giving an innovative stimulus to industry (see section 15.8). Policymakers expected that achieving this goal would reduce relative inflation and, therefore, lead to the stabilisation of the real exchange rate over time.

The real appreciation of weak currencies has, however, lasted for a long period. The unexpected persistence of the appreciation can be explained in a number of ways. Some argue (Miller and Sutherland, 1991; see also Giavazzi and Spaventa, 1990) that it was due to the long lags in the effects of the hard exchange rate policy, which is more effective and rapid in the financial markets than the labour market, owing to the different ways expectations are formed in the two markets or to the *hysteresis effects* of inflation (e.g. owing to indexation of nominal wages). However, considering the fact that nominal interest rate differentials with Germany remained large in countries with current account deficits, such as Italy, it seems difficult to imagine that even before the realignments of 1992–3 the financial markets believed the commitment to fixed nominal exchange rates and/or the possibility of maintaining them.

Both the fact that inflation differentials with Germany did not narrow significantly for a number of countries, such as Italy, and the reduction that other countries, such as France, were able to achieve can account for the increase in unemployment in ERM countries between 1986 and 1992, in contrast to the decline (at least until 1990) recorded in other OECD countries.

In countries such as Italy, the appreciation in the real exchange rate explains at least part of the weakening of demand growth and, therefore, the increase in unemployment. On the other hand, countries, such as France, that were able to reduce their inflation rate to a level even below that in Germany, could do so only by adopting severe *domestic deflationary measures*, which again explains the rise in unemployment. Meanwhile, Germany adopted consistently restrictive measures. This illustrates the generally deflationary situation in the ERM economies. This is testified to above all by the considerable reduction in inflation, which from a starting point above levels in other OECD countries fell to virtually the same level in more recent years. Deflation is even more evident in real terms, with a much sharper increase in unemployment in the ERM countries than in the other OECD countries.

A rise in the natural rate of unemployment owing to greater labour market rigidity in Europe has been cited (De Grauwe, 1990) to explain the increase in unemployment in the EMS countries. In the light of our discussion here, we can legitimately cast doubt on the importance of this line of reasoning, which at most may help explain the hysteresis in the rate of unemployment in terms of the deflationary effects of the hard exchange rate policy.

16.7   Fixed versus flexible exchange rates: reflections from experience

In many countries, the change to a floating-exchange rate regime was made necessary by the practical impossibility of keeping exchange rates within their fluctuation limits as official reserves were used up. The experience gained in these years can help assess the relative merits of the two systems and the validity of a number of hypotheses about the determinants of exchange rate fluctuations. Nevertheless, the fact that exchange rate movements have never been completely free means that we must exercise a certain degree of caution in reaching our conclusions.[26] By the same token, in at least part of the period in which floating rates prevailed (the 1970s), international economic relationships were considerably influenced by such a complex variety of factors that it is difficult to identify their respective individual influences.

First and foremost, it does not seem that floating rates had a significant negative impact on the volume of international trade and capital movements, despite the possible indirect consequences of incentives to adopt protectionist measures in reaction to the sharp depreciation of some currencies.

If kept for too long, fixed parities (and, hence, exchange rates) can have severe adverse consequences for some economies. This was the case of the EMS (which we examined earlier in this chapter) and of some less-developed economies. In some cases fixed exchange rates took the extreme form of a **currency board** (where – as in Argentina from 1991 to 2001 – the fixed exchange rate is guaranteed by a strict monetary policy which permits creation of the monetary base only in step with the growth of foreign exchange reserves) or the adoption of a foreign currency (usually, the dollar, hence the term **dollarisation**), as in the case of Liberia, Panama and other small countries (see Edwards, 2001). Notwithstanding the disadvantages of fixed exchange rates, Robert Mundell has suggested the adoption of a single world currency.

On the other hand, the greater autonomy lent to countries' economic policies by floating rates did not manifest itself – or, in any case, did not guarantee higher levels of income and employment. According to some, the trade-off between employment and inflation proved illusory, at least during the 1970s, for reasons unrelated to the exchange rate system. Others argue that many governments were simply not willing to exchange lower unemployment rates for higher inflation, at least after the second oil crisis of 1979. In any case, whether or not the domestic constraints were objective or subjective, any greater autonomy did not translate into an incentive to pursue expansionary policies.

The point of disagreement between the opposing advocates of fixed and floating exchange rates on which the experience since the 1980s shines most light is the

---

[26] In other words, we are not comparing fixed exchange rates with floating exchange rates but rather *fixed rates and managed floating rates*. According to Milton Friedman, this sort of fluctuation may turn out to be the worst of all possible worlds, since speculators must predict not only the underlying behaviour of equilibrium exchange rates but also the policy stance of monetary authorities.

presumed ability of floating rates to discourage speculative capital movements. In fact, this has not always been the case and, on the contrary, speculation has often been fuelled by the variation in the exchange rate that it helped trigger in the first place. There were therefore many cases of persistent exchange rate *overshooting*, giving rise to **currency cycles**.[27] For example, both the nominal and real effective exchange rates of the dollar appreciated by one-third in the five years following 1980. Over the same period the real DM (German mark)/$ exchange rate rose by about 60 per cent. Currency cycles may be caused by economic policy choices or autonomous shocks, or even be produced by the self-fulfilling expectations of private agents (**bootstraps**): some forecasts may prove true only because they induce the behaviour needed for the expectation to be realised. The size of the transactions is essential: if major traders expect the dollar to appreciate, their large purchases of dollars will fulfil those expectations. Self-fulfilling behaviour may even be spurred by the prospect of breaching what are viewed as 'key' exchange rate levels. In any case, in the short-to-medium term the existence of currency cycles appears to conflict sharply with the **purchasing power parity (PPP) theory**, according to which movements in (nominal) exchange rates reflect **relative inflation** – i.e. inflation differentials between the different countries.[28]

16.8   Summary

1   The behaviour of exchange rates is influenced by the type of *monetary system* adopted. With regard to international aspects, the most important monetary systems are: the Gold Standard; the Gold Exchange Standard; systems of centrally created reserves; floating or flexible exchange rate systems; the EMS.

2   The *Gold Standard* is a fixed-exchange rate system; more precisely, it allows only small movements around the parity.

3   The Gold Exchange Standard – which economises on the use of gold – is also a fixed-exchange rate system under certain conditions, but it admits adjustable parities. It is more heavily reliant on convention than the Gold Standard.

4   A system of *centrally created reserves* requires an international monetary organisation to act as a central bank for the world, operating in a similar manner to a national central bank in a single country.

5   A *floating-exchange rate regime* ensures balance of payments adjustment through exchange rate movements. Among the merits attributed to this system is that the flexibility of exchange rates discourages speculation. Drawbacks include the adverse impact on trade of uncertainty about the price of foreign currencies.

6   The final objectives of the members of the EMS appear to have been to: (a) ensure an area of *economic and political stability*; (b) reduce the opportunities for *competitive devaluations* by high-inflation countries; (c) *exert external discipline* over these countries. The EMS was composed of the ERM, which was intended to

---

[27] On the dollar cycle, see Gerlach and Petri (1990).
[28] This theory, which was originally formulated by Cassel (1918), implies that variations in real exchange rates are zero.

reduce exchange rate fluctuations, and credit facilities for countries with balance of payments difficulties.

7 The system had two mechanisms to ensure the stability of exchange rates. The first was a *bilateral parity grid* in which exchange rate fluctuations might occur within a band. The second, based on the *ECU* (a basket currency), was intended to ensure greater symmetry and provided for divergence thresholds for exchange rates.

8 *EMU* began on 1 January 1999 with the participation of the eleven member countries of the EMS that initially satisfied the convergence criteria of the Maastricht Agreements, and Greece which joined the eleven countries on 1 January 2001. The *euro* is the new currency introduced with EMU and it fully replaced national currencies as a means of exchange on 1 March 2002.

9 Experience since the 1980s shines light on the debate between the advocates of fixed and floating exchange rates: exchange rate flexibility has not been able to discourage speculation, giving rise instead to *currency cycles*. The increased autonomy of countries has proved illusory. On the other hand, it does not appear that floating rates have had a significant negative effect on the volume of international trade.

17 Development and trade organisations

17.1 The system of cooperative institutions created in the post-war period

The public institutions created after the Second World War to govern international economic relations are founded on *cooperation*. The key principle inspiring their action is **multilateralism**,[1] i.e. cooperating at the world level and tackling issues regarding economic relations among countries within the international institutions created for this purpose.

Under the principle of multilateralism, any favourable terms in agreements between two countries are automatically extended to the other countries, giving international agreements a **non-discriminatory** character. Multilateralism thus stands in contrast to **bilateralism**, which involves the resolution of international economic problems through bilateral agreements with individual foreign countries. Special cases of bilateralism include general or sectoral agreements to balance trade or limit imports by one country from the other. Bilateralism was the mainstay of international economic relations in the period between the two world wars. Multilateralism can also be compared with **regionalism** – i.e. cooperation between a few (geographically close) countries. For more on this, see section 20.6.

Although founded at different times and in different circumstances, nearly all international economic institutions existing today can be considered members of the 'family' of the United Nations Organisation, established at the San Francisco Conference of 1945. More specifically, the public international economic organisations are *subsidiary bodies* of the United Nations or *independent specialised institutions* (created under separate international agreements) linked to the United Nations through agreements to harmonise activities and objectives.

The United Nations is involved in the economic sphere either directly (by providing technical assistance to developing countries) or through its subsidiary bodies, which include the United Nations Conference on Trade and Development (UNCTAD), the United Nations Development Programme (UNDP) – especially for issues involving developing countries – and the United Nations Environment Programme (UNEP).

---

[1] This definition of multilateralism is more general than that offered in section 16.3, which concerns the specific stance of countries with regard to balancing international trade.

The main specialised economic institutions are the International Monetary Fund (IMF), the World Bank and the World Trade Organisation (WTO). Coordination between them and the United Nations is not entirely effective, for a variety of reasons. These include differences in voting procedures which, unlike the unweighted system used by the United Nations, for the IMF and the World Bank are based on members' share of the capital and reflect the economic importance of the countries involved, thus penalising the less developed countries. The WTO, the IMF and the World Bank are linked by collaboration agreements that have been given a more formalised structure in recent years. They envisage the exchange of documents and information, institutional consultation and reciprocal recognition of observer status in their decisionmaking bodies in areas of common interest.

We examined the activity of the IMF in chapter 16. We will discuss the others here.

17.2   The World Bank

The International Bank for Reconstruction and Development (IBRD), more commonly known as the World Bank, was born, like the IMF, out of the Bretton Woods agreements of 1944. It is charged with fostering public and private investment in the less-developed countries and regions in order to raise living standards in those areas. The Bank pursues this mission by financing investment and providing *technical assistance* for the design and implementation of projects and, more generally, planning public action.

Projects that receive World Bank funding include both infrastructure and directly productive initiatives. More recently, its emphasis has shifted towards projects in the fields of education, social infrastructure, food production and environmental protection. In the latter area, since 1990 the World Bank has operated the **Global Environmental Facility** (GEF), which provides assistance, including funding, to developing countries for the realisation of environmental improvement projects with transnational scope.

The resources available to the Bank include its own capital (which is formed by contributions that reflect the economic weight of its members) and, to a larger degree, external financing from public and private sources. Since the Bank does not take on exchange rate risk, it raises funds in the currencies in which the financing is denominated. Loans are granted at market rates only to member countries or those with member country guarantees.

The World Bank also operates through three affiliate organisations: the International Finance Corporation (IFC), the International Development Association (IDA) and the Multilateral Investment Guarantee Agency (MIGA). Unlike the World Bank, the IFC grants loans only to private companies in the developing countries and seeks to act as a *catalyst* for other financial resources and business initiatives.

The IDA grants *interest-free or subsidised loans* to the poorest countries. Since its capital suffers significant erosion as a result of borrower default, it is periodically replenished by the donor countries. The MIGA, which was founded in 1988, insures the political risk faced by direct investors in the developing countries and provides *country marketing services* for investment and legal advice to governments that want to attract foreign investment.

The World Bank's financing priorities and the terms of its funding have changed over the years. It initially preferred to finance *infrastructure* projects, partly to meet the needs of post-war reconstruction. In the 1970s its focus shifted to financing investment to help specific social groups living in poverty, with the aim of simulating economic growth. In doing so, the World Bank rejected the theory of **trickle down development**, according to which the growth of an economic system implies, but does not require, an increase in the incomes of the poorest members of society.

In the 1980s, the causal relationship between poverty and growth was stood on its head again: liberal policies aimed at expanding the role of the market were adopted to alleviate poverty. The theoretical underpinnings of this approach also produced debatable interpretations of the growth and development of certain countries,[2] which attributed, with little evidence, their progress to liberal policies. The countries that received financing were required to 'adjust' their economies by:

- *removing constraints and 'distortions'* in goods markets, the labour market and domestic financial markets
- *privatising* large segments of the public sector and drastically cutting budget deficits
- *liberalising* movements of goods and capital.

A special emphasis was placed on bringing domestic market conditions into line with those in international markets; in other words, on integrating the economy into the international system.[3]

Some economists have argued that the policies recommended or imposed by the World Bank (and the IMF) on various countries, including Chile, Mexico, Turkey, the Eastern European countries and South Korea, frequently turned out to be highly costly, not only in terms of equity but also in terms of the excessive and prolonged reduction in the growth of income and employment (see Patnaik and Chandrasekhar, 1998; Pieper and Taylor, 1998). Privatisation and liberalisation, which were often carried out in the absence of real markets (notably in Eastern Europe), and the often abrupt exposure of vulnerable economies to the impact and shocks of international markets – especially financial markets – triggered major economic crises, thus raising the costs of adjustment (see Stiglitz, 2002). In recent years, the World Bank's privatisation and liberalisation policies have been questioned by its own senior officials.[4]

---

[2] This is the case of the report on the 'economic miracle' of the South-East Asian countries (World Bank, 1993), which offered a markedly liberal interpretation of the factors underlying development in those countries. The validity of this interpretation has been questioned (see Lall, 1994).

[3] This set of measures required of borrowing countries goes under the name of the **Washington Consensus**, to mean an identity of positions between the US Treasury, the World Bank and the IMF, all located in Washington. It implies a complete change of attitude with respect to the former Keynesian orientation of the international organisations created at Bretton Woods (see Stiglitz, 2002).

[4] On the structure and the policies of the World Bank, see Gilbert and Vines (2000).

17.3   Multilateral governance of trade: GATT and the WTO

The Bretton Woods agreements reached at the end of the Second World War envisaged the establishment of three institutions to ensure international economic cooperation: the IMF, the World Bank and the International Trade Organisation (ITO). The third body, which was to have been a forum for cooperation in trade policy, should have been a UN agency but was never established owing to the refusal of the United States and other countries to sign the founding agreement (the Havana Charter).

17.3.1   GATT

Instead of the ITO, trade relations were governed within the framework of the General Agreement on Tariffs and Trade (GATT), an initially temporary international agreement (it eventually ran until 1 January 1995) signed in Geneva in 1947. GATT essentially sought to increase the *social welfare* of signatories through:

(a) The *elimination of trade discrimination* such as preferential tariff agreements. Achievement of this objective was entrusted in large part to what was known as the **most favoured nation (MFN) clause**, which guaranteed the automatic extension to all the other signatories of a treaty of any preferential trade conditions subsequently granted by one country to another.[5]

(b) The *stabilisation and gradual reduction of tariffs*, primarily achieved through eight successive rounds of multilateral negotiations, the most recent being the Kennedy Round, the Tokyo Round and the Uruguay Round (which ended in December 1993 but whose decisions were formally ratified in Marrakech in April 1994).

(c) The *elimination of quantitative restriction* (QRs), such as quotas, and the reduction or regulation of other measures with protectionist uses, albeit with exceptions and safeguard clauses (Van Meerhaeghe, 1992, pp. 111 ff.).

Over the years, GATT's focus shifted from tariff to non-tariff barriers to trade. Such measures were banned if they were not in conformity with GATT principles, which allowed them, subject to restrictions, when they were used for domestic policy purposes. The sectors covered by GATT were gradually expanded. Further new issues were introduced during the Uruguay Round.

GATT found it difficult to pursue its objectives owing to the need to obtain unanimous approval of the countries involved – for example, in a dispute over the introduction of trade barriers by a country. Nevertheless, the overall balance of its work is positive, since it enabled the gradual restoration of multilateralism after the spread of discriminatory trade practices through bilateral agreements in the period 1918–39.[6]

---

[5] To understand how this clause works, let us suppose a case in which two countries, A and B, in the absence of multilateral treaties, agree to reduce duties to 10 per cent, including an MFN clause in their accord. Subsequently, B enters into another bilateral treaty with country C that sets the duty on trade between them at 5 per cent. This reduction would also apply to country A under the terms of the MFN clause of their bilateral agreement.

[6] On the technical and institutional arrangements of the GATT, see Dam (1970).

17.3.2 *The Uruguay Round*

The Uruguay Round was the last session of the multilateral trade negotiations organised under the auspices of GATT. The round was initiated in 1986, mainly under pressure from the United States and Japan. The United States was especially insistent on starting a new round of talks to counter the adverse consequences of the appreciation of the dollar and improve its competitive position in world markets (especially in South-East Asia, for manufactured goods and services, and Europe, for agricultural products).

The main results of the negotiations were the product of a compromise reached among the many diverse negotiating positions. They involved:

(1) a further reduction of duties on *manufactured goods*
(2) a ban on other *protectionist barriers*
(3) the inclusion of *new sectors* within the multilateral cooperation framework
(4) the introduction of new rules to reduce non-tariff barriers (NTBs) and govern trade disputes more effectively in situations involving, for example, antidumping measures.[7]

We shall now examine each of these in more detail:

(1) Tariffs on *manufactured goods* were reduced by an average of 40 per cent, lowering the average duty from 6 per cent to 4 per cent. They were eliminated altogether in ten major sectors, increasing the proportion of duty-free goods from 20 per cent to 43 per cent.
(2) NTBs such as voluntary export restraints (VERs) and orderly market agreements (see chapter 15) were essentially banned, although a transition period for their elimination was established.
(3) The *new sectors* brought under the wing of the international trade institutions are:
    (a) *Agriculture*; trade in agricultural products was brought into the multilateral trade framework and will gradually be liberalised. With few exceptions, all NTBs were converted into tariff barriers (**tariffication**), which were reduced by 36 per cent by the developed countries over a period of six years. Export subsidies were also reduced. Tariff reductions for developing countries were smaller and were to be introduced over ten years. The agreement also included the adoption of the so-called **peace clause**, which forbids the use of unilateral action and countervailing duties.
    (b) *Textiles and clothing*, which are subject to the multilateral monitoring of the WTO, with trade in about half of all products to be liberalised over ten years. Accordingly, the *Multifibre Arrangement* (MFA), which regulated trade in textiles for more than thirty years, will gradually be eliminated (it will expire on 1 January 2005), thus removing the main barrier to developing countries' exports of manufactured goods to the developed world.
    (c) *Services*, with the adoption of the **General Agreement on Trade in Services** (GATS), which includes use of MFN status and establishes the transparency

---

[7] The texts of the various agreements resulting from the Uruguay Round negotiations are available on the WTO web site (www.wto.org).

of trade restrictions in this area. Negotiations for certain areas (financial and insurance services, movement of persons, maritime transport, basic telecommunications) were or will be concluded under the WTO, as we discuss later.

(d) *Intellectual property*, with the **Trade-Related Aspects of Intellectual Property Rights** (TRIPS) agreement, which establishes standards for the protection of rights and instruments for the application and enforcement of agreements through national legislation and for dispute settlement. In particular, patent protection in all technology areas shall not end before twenty years.

(e) The regulation of *foreign investment*, with the **Trade-Related Investment Measures** (TRIMs) agreement. The agreement forbids any regulation of foreign direct investment (FDI) (for example, by introducing minimum local content requirements) that interferes with the principles of free trade. Developing countries have more time to implement the new rules.

(f) Domestic regulation of the *environment and competition*, in relation to the distortive effects this can have on international trade. Work in this area is currently at the preparatory stage.

(4) The Uruguay Round also introduced new rules to ensure that technical regulations (for example, rules governing the characteristics and operation of a machine for safety, energy savings or other purposes) and certifications of quality, origin or other features do not create barriers to international trade by favouring domestic producers. While recognising the validity of the rationale for technical regulations and certification, the aim is to encourage the adoption of *minimum international standards* without preventing individual countries from adopting stricter, non-discriminatory standards.

In the area of *government procurement*, especially public works and purchasing, which are often skewed in favour of domestic firms (see section 8.3), agreements have been reached to limit protectionist practices. Subsequent developments in the telecommunications sector will be discussed shortly in our examination of the WTO.

A precise definition of *subsidies* has also been developed, making a distinction between acceptable subsidies (for example, incentives for research and regional development), those against which countermeasures can be taken by the affected countries to offset harmful effects and prohibited subsidies. Developing countries benefit from a number of exemptions.

New rules and codes of conduct have been established for *antidumping measures*. Antidumping measures shall expire five years after the date of imposition.

The instances in which a country may introduce safeguards and the procedures for doing so have also been specified. Finally, neither these measures nor antidumping measures can be imposed if the dumping does not cause injury. This happens when the volume of dumped imports is negligible – i.e. when the volume of the imported good for which action is taken is less than 3 per cent of the total imports of that product into the country taking action against dumping.[8]

---

[8] For more on the results of the Uruguay Round, and the tasks of the GATT and the WTO, which we discuss shortly, see IMF (1994) and Martin and Winters (1995). See also WTO's *Annual Reports*.

17.3.3   The WTO

On 1 January 1995, the World Trade Organisation (WTO) began operations. Created with the Marrakech agreement in 1994, it is the forum for multilateral trade negotiations and discussion between countries on issues involving the *implementation of trade agreements*. It therefore performs the role of the trade organisation originally conceived at Bretton Woods. The WTO has replaced the GATT, but preserves its principles and many of its rules. It seeks to ensure the application of existing multilateral regulations governing trade in goods and services, to promote free trade in sectors that remain protected (notably agriculture, textiles and services) and to remove barriers to trade created by policies in member countries in trade-linked areas (for more, see Lal Das, 1999).

The WTO has a stronger institutional identity than the GATT, as it has a permanent structure and provides for the virtually automatic settlement of trade disputes among members through its Dispute Settlement Body (DSB) (see box 17.1). The instruments available include conciliation and arbitration procedures and the option of imposing trade sanctions on violators who refuse to abide by WTO rulings.

Box 17.1.   The European Union, the WTO and the 'banana war'

In May 1996 the WTO established a Panel to consider complaints by Ecuador, Guatemala, Honduras, Mexico and the United States regarding the European Union's regime for importation, sale and distribution of bananas. The European Union was claimed to grant preferential treatment to EU and African, Caribbean and Pacific (ACP) bananas at the expense of other countries. The regime's allocation of *import quotas* and *licensing procedures* were alleged to be inconsistent with a number of provisions of the Uruguay Round (GATT, GATS, FATS, TRIMS Agreement, Agreement on Agriculture, Import Licensing Agreement).

The European Union's common market organisation for bananas, instituted in 1993, had different import regimes depending on the origin of the bananas: EU bananas – like all other EU goods – could circulate freely; ACP bananas entered duty-free up to a maximum quota and beyond that were subject to an out-of-quota tariff. Imports from third countries entered the EU subject to a low in-quota tariff and a much higher out-of-quota tariff. Licenses were allocated to importers in accordance with the types of bananas (whether EU, ACP or third-country) they had marketed during the previous three years.

The banana regime was subject to a *GATT waiver* – the Lomé waiver – since it involved preferential trade with ACP countries which are signatories of the Fourth Lomé Convention (1989)[a]: until February 2000 the waiver allowed derogations from GATT most favoured nation (MFN) treatment in order to accommodate the preferential treatment that the EU is required to give to ACP states under the Convention.

One year after its establishment, the Panel found that the EU's banana import regime was inconsistent with GATT and GATS rules. As an example of such inconsistency the Panel found that import quotas were allocated to certain countries without a substantial interest in supplying bananas to the EU (e.g. Nicaragua and certain ACP countries) but not to other similarly situated countries (e.g. Guatemala). However, the Panel found that the Lomé waiver permitted the inconsistency of the EU's position with MFN treatment.

In September 1997 the Appellate Body upheld the Panel's principal findings, but reversed the Panel's decision that the inconsistency with the GATT regime was permitted by the Lomé waiver.

In the same month the GATT's Dispute Settlement Body (DSB) adopted the Appellate Body report and the Panel report, as modified by the Appellate Body. A binding arbitrator was then appointed, who determined the 'reasonable period of time' for implementation to be fifteen months from the date of adoption by the DSB.

In 1998 the EU enacted a revised banana import regime which Ecuador and the United States argued was still inconsistent with its WTO obligations. Both countries requested authorisation from the DSB to suspend concessions to the Union equivalent to the level of nullification and impairment suffered. In 1999, following arbitration, the appropriate level for the suspension was determined by the DSB, which reduced the initial requests by the complainants.

In 2001 the EU adopted a Regulation establishing three different tariffs for all imports irrespective of their origin: for the first quota of 2,200,000 tonnes a tariff rate of 75 euros/tonne bound under the WTO was established; for a second autonomous quota of 353,000 tonnes the tariff rate was also 75 euros/tonne; for the third autonomous quota of 850,000 tonnes the rate was of 300 euros/tonne. The tariff quotas were conceived as a transitional measure leading ultimately to a tariff-only regime, to be implemented by 1 January 2006. Imports from ACP countries would enter duty-free.

Following understandings between the EU and the United States and the EU and Ecuador, quotas would be allocated among the different countries on the basis of historical licenses. The United States and Ecuador would suspend the application of increased duties or terminate the right to suspend concessions or other obligations.

After a number of threats and counterthreats among the countries involved, the transitional regime agreed upon was implemented by the Union in December 2001 with effect as from 1 January 2002. The DSB will monitor implementation of the adopted ruling.[b]

Notes:
a The first Lomé Convention was signed in 1975 between the European Union and forty-six LDCs in Africa, the Caribbean and the Pacific. It exempted ACP products from EU tariffs and established various forms of technical and financial assistance. On the system of the EU preferences see section 18.8.
b For more on the legal aspects of the dispute and the welfare effects of the EU banana import regime, see Breuss, Griller and Vranes (2003).
Source: WTO, Annual Report, various years, Geneva.

In its first few years of activity, the WTO continued the work of GATT, strengthening action in the new areas addressed by GATT during the Uruguay Round. At the first WTO ministerial conference in Singapore in December 1996, agreement was reached on the full liberalisation of trade in pharmaceuticals and information technology (IT) products. A framework agreement was also reached on basic telecommunications, an area in which limited commitments had been made under the GATS. The agreement was formalised in February 1997.

The Singapore conference also made important progress on labour standards and regional trade agreements. We address labour standards in section 17.4. As regards regional trade agreements for the establishment of free trade areas (FTAs), economic unions, etc., which proliferated in the 1990s (see section 20.6), the conference agreed that they are not necessarily inimical to multilateralism, representing a potentially complementary form of international agreement that facilitates the integration of the developing countries and the former socialist countries in the world economy.

Within the GATS framework, in December 1997 seventy members of the WTO (including all of the leading developed nations) agreed to liberalise financial services in the banking and insurance sectors, securities and financial information. The liberalisation, which came into force on 1 March 1999, concerned in particular the lowering of tariff barriers and the use of MFN treatment.

A new round (the Development Round) of liberalisation negotiations was launched at the fourth WTO Ministerial Conference (Doha–Qatar, November 2001), focusing especially on agricultural products and textiles as well as services. Negotiations are also planned for direct investment, government procurement and intellectual property rights (IPRs). Negotiations should end by 1 January 2005. A Declaration was also passed on the TRIPS agreement and public health, introducing some flexibility in its interpretation. Under some circumstances it allows member countries to authorise production of patented drugs without the approval of the patent owner (**compulsory licensing**). This will be of help for some developing countries in their struggle against HIV and other contagious diseases.

17.4   The impact of domestic economic policies and international cooperation on trade

In recent years special attention (first under the GATT, then the WTO) has been paid to the impact on international trade of domestic economic policies that do not refer directly to trade but can be *trade-related*, such as:

(a) foreign investment policies
(b) environmental policies
(c) antitrust policies
(d) labour protection policies.

In some cases operational conclusions have been reached on the issues involved, while in others work is still at the discussion and study phase, but in any event they are likely to receive closer scrutiny from the WTO. This interest on the part of the institutions involved in promoting cooperation in international trade emerged in parallel with the evolution of the IMF's role in granting long-term loans and monitoring *domestic policies* (see section 16.5). The common roots of these developments lie in the process of liberalisation and globalisation (see chapter 19).

17.4.1 Foreign investment and multinational companies

Most of the economic literature concurs that regulating foreign investment can distort international trade, as in the case of *local content rules* or *import restrictions*. Such policies were frequently used by both developed countries (notably Australia and Canada) and underdeveloped countries in the 1960s and 1970s to increase inward foreign investment to boost domestic development. The TRIMS agreement in the Uruguay Round essentially banned such measures, requiring members to eliminate them by a specified deadline (for the LDCs, the time limit is seven years from the date of the agreement).

Some question the appropriateness of the remaining instruments available to the developing countries for controlling the activities of powerful multinational companies (MNCs).

17.4.2 Environmental policy

The impact of environmental policy on trade was initially discussed during the Uruguay Round, at the end of which it was decided to establish a working group to study the issues involved and report to the WTO. Environmental policies can influence international trade in three main ways:

- a country can protect a domestic industry with laws that discourage the use of products that do not meet certain *technical requirements* (for example, energy consumption, pollution levels)
- a country can try to increase its share of world trade by lowering environmental protection rules (**ecodumping**); the reduced protection would (at least in the short term) lower production costs of domestic goods and encourage investment in the country
- a country can protect a domestic industry by restricting imports from countries that do not adopt adequate environmental standards (a sort of **anti-ecodumping measure**).

17.4.3 Competition policies

Competition policies raise two issues:

- *uncoordinated national policies* may not be sufficient to counter monopoly strategies or situations, eroding the beneficial effects that international trade might otherwise generate(see subsection 7.4.5)
- *divergences between national policies* may lead to discrimination in trade and international investment, giving some countries an advantage and **diverting trade** from more restrictive countries.

Here, too, the Uruguay Round established a working group to study the issue and report to the WTO.

17.4.4 Social dumping

Early on, the WTO addressed the issues involved in social dumping (see section 15.6), which has raised concern among the advanced countries and generated pressure to introduce a 'social clause' requiring minimum **labour standards**[9] and allowing the imposition of import restrictions on countries that do not meet those standards. The developing countries were firmly opposed to any such social clause, arguing that their economic backwardness justified a lower level of protection and that raising that level would merely satisfy the protectionist interests of the developed world.

The opposition of the developing countries prevented approval of the social clause at the Singapore ministerial conference in December 1996. The conference did approve a declaration of intent on internationally recognised labour standards, which while recognising the importance of compliance with certain minimum levels of labour protection confirmed the International Labour Office (ILO, or Bureau International du Travail, BIT) as the competent forum in this area, sanctioning opposition to the use of labour standards for protectionist purposes and to attempts to require compliance with such standards through trade policies.[10]

17.5 Inequality of starting points among countries and permissive and distortive policies

In a world in which (as we will see later) competitive pressures have mounted as a result of progress in transport and communications and international efforts to eliminate classic tariff barriers and NTBs have met with considerable success, a country can seek to strengthen its competitive position by adopting more permissive rules regarding the environment, antitrust issues, FDI and multinationals and social protection. More generally, it is possible to take such an approach in all areas of regulation. The incentives to take such a stance may be strengthened by the backwardness of the country involved.

---

[9] Labour standards include:

- safeguarding *workers' rights* to associate, bargain and strike
- protecting *vulnerable groups* (ban on forced labour, child labour, establishing wage equality and equal opportunities, protecting female labour)
- establishing *minimum compensation* (minimum wage, non-wage compensation, such as paid holidays, and overtime pay)
- warranting *workplace safety*, setting health rules and establishing a maximum working day
- ensuring *social protection* (health, pensions, unemployment)
- banning *unjustified redundancies*.

For more on the reasons for such labour market measures and the formal and effective levels of protection available in the various countries for each of these areas, see World Bank (1995). For a discussion on the impact of labour standards legislation see Brosnan (2003), De Martino (2003), Heintz (2003), Singh and Zammit (2003).

[10] On this see Maskus (1997).

Such permissive policies enable a country to gain a short-term advantage, albeit at the potential cost of disadvantages for itself and others in the long term.

There are thus two factors underlying policy choices that have received special scrutiny from international trade organisations:

- competitive pressure
- the backwardness of the starting points of countries that adopt such policies.

Obviously, the adoption of permissive policies by some countries can prompt similar policy action by the others in order to re-establish initial conditions. Such a 'race to the bottom' (see section 20.4) between governments not only does not solve the problems of the most backward countries, it also threatens to reduce public intervention to levels that would jeopardise effective control of markets.

The need for *international coordination* is clear (we address the issue more fully in chapter 20). However, we must also be aware of the limitations of international coordination of domestic economic policies that does not take adequate account of considerations of equity and inequality in the international distribution of income and wealth, not only as a source of possible 'distortive' or permissive policies but also as *distortions* to be removed.

The safeguard clauses and exceptions in the application of international rules to the developing countries acknowledge the special status of these nations. Whether they are sufficient to allow these countries to remove the distortions that afflict them is a problem that requires further reflection.

Certainly, in some cases free access to the markets of the developed countries would be enough to enable them to raise output. However, this may be a necessary but not sufficient condition if those countries lack the information and the management and marketing skills needed to break into open markets. The efforts of the various international organisations should therefore be focused in this direction.

A timid start has been made with the complementary projects to strengthen the export capacity of the developing countries involving UNCTAD, the UNDP, the World Bank, the IMF, the WTO and other international institutions in recent years. These institutions have also provided technical assistance to develop management skills.[11]

17.6 Summary

1 The *public institutions* created in the aftermath of the Second World War to govern international economic relations are guided by the principles of cooperation. They are linked in a variety of ways to the United Nations, which acts in the economic field directly through subsidiary bodies and specialised institutions, the IMF, the World Bank and the WTO.

2 The *World Bank group* (which also includes three affiliated organisations) funds public and private investment in infrastructure and directly productive activities

---

[11] See Finger and Nogués (2002) for a critique of the role played by the WTO with respect to the problems of developing countries.

using its own capital and external financing. The Bank's preferences in select-ing projects for funding have evolved over the years. In the 1980s and 1990s, the Bank preferred those consistent with a liberal government policy orientation. Some economists have argued that this exposed often fragile economies to the influences and shocks of international markets, thus increasing the cost of adjustment.

3   In the post-war period, international cooperation in trade policy was conducted under the auspices of the GATT, which sought to reduce trade discrimination, reduce tariffs and eliminate or at least regulate quantitative restrictions and other NTBs. In the last round of international trade negotiations (the Uruguay Round) under the GATT, new areas were brought within the scope of the international institutions responsible for governing international trade.

4   In 1995, GATT was replaced by the *World Trade Organisation* (WTO), which has a stronger institutional identity, as it has a permanent structure and mechanisms for the settlement of trade disputes. The WTO has continued the GATT's work, strengthening action in the new areas addressed during the Uruguay Round.

5   Among the issues that received particular attention during the Uruguay Round and from the WTO, special mention must be made of *domestic policies* – such as those governing foreign investment, the environment, antitrust policy and labour standards – that have an impact on international trade.

6   The importance of the repercussions of these policies on international trade has increased as a result of mounting competitive pressures and the backwardness of many developing countries. This clearly poses problems of *international coordination* and safeguarding the interests of the backward countries.

18 Regional public institutions: the European Union

18.1 European integration

The foundations of European integration were laid immediately after the end of the Second World War. Economic, military and political interests lay behind the US aid programme for European countries (the Marshall Plan), which made the aid conditional on effective cooperation between European governments and the gradual liberalisation of trade and payments in Europe.

European economic cooperation, originally sparked by US action, strengthened with the establishment of the European Coal and Steel Community (ECSC) in 1951 and expanded further with the Treaty of Rome of 1957, which established the European Common Market and the European Atomic Energy Community (Euratom) between Italy, France, Germany and the Benelux countries (Belgium, the Netherlands, Luxembourg).

The Common Market was more (but not much more) than a customs union. It provided for the lowering of internal duties and the setting of a single customs tariff for countries outside the Market (the **common external tariff**, CET), a set of common policies, notably in agriculture and transport, and competition legislation. In addition to the pragmatic need to introduce European-wide policy coordination gradually, the limited scope of the initial approach to integration was prompted by the liberal extraction of the founding fathers of Europe. The concept of microeconomic market failures had not penetrated the political sphere, while the years in which the Common Market was born were also years of rapid growth, with falling unemployment against a background of price stability and balance of payments surpluses for nearly all European countries.

After a pause in the 1970s, European cooperation was revived in the monetary arena with the creation of the European Monetary System (EMS; see section 16.6). This was followed by another pause in the early 1980s that lasted until 1985, when European integration accelerated with the publication of the White Paper on completing the Internal Market. The recommendations of the White Paper were incorporated in the European Act, which was signed in February 1986 and entered into force in July 1987. The Single European Act (SEA) amended and completed the Treaty of Rome. Its main aim was to eliminate any remaining non-tariff barriers (NTBs) with a view to completing the European Single Market by 1992 (see section 18.8). It also set out new objectives for European action in the areas of the environment, technological research, economic and social cohesion, and health and safety in the workplace. Numerous long-term objectives were confirmed, such as continuing progress towards economic and monetary union. Finally, the SEA envisaged institutional changes, including a shift from unanimous to qualified majority voting (QMV) in the Council of Ministers.[1]

In 1992 the Maastricht accords amended the Treaty of Rome and heralded the birth of the European Union (EU). The agreements also established the creation of the monetary union, which we will address again in sections 18.3 and 18.4. In addition, the Maastricht Treaty envisaged common policies for education, vocational training, culture and health. The euro was introduced in 1999 and euro notes and coins entered circulation in 2002 (see section 16.6).

Apart from the introduction of the euro, the main development in the twenty-first century has been the enlargement of membership in the Union to ten other European countries since May 2004.[2] This itself is a prelude to further enlargements. The implications of the change are significant at both the economic and institutional levels. From an institutional point of view, the enlargement will require myriad changes and the adoption of a true constitution.

18.2   The institutions of the European Union

The eight main institutions of the European Union are:

- The *European Council*, made up of the heads of state or government of the Member States and the President of the European Commission. It meets at least once a year and establishes general policy.
- The *Council of Ministers* or Council of the Union or simply the Council. It is made up of the ministers of the member states responsible for the areas addressed on the agenda of a given meeting. For our purposes, the Council of Economic and Finance Ministers (Ecofin) is of special importance. The Council of Ministers legislates on the basis of proposals advanced by the European Commission and performs a control and policy role. Depending on the matters being examined, it adopts measures by majority, qualified majority or unanimous vote.
- The *European Commission*, composed of thirty (twenty-five as from November 2004) independent members designated by the President in common accord with national governments. They serve five-year terms. The Commission is a collegial body and,

---

[1] A detailed historical review of the process of European integration is given in Tsoukalis (1997). McCormick (2002) provides a valuable discussion of numerous aspects of European policies.

[2] Following the 2004 enlargement, the European Union is composed of Austria, Belgium, Cyprus, the Czech Republic, Denmark, Estonia, Finland, France, Germany, Greece, Ireland, Italy, Hungary, Latvia, Lithuania, Luxembourg, Malta, the Netherlands, Poland, Portugal, the Slovak Republic, Slovenia, Spain, Sweden and the United Kingdom. The candidate countries next in line for accession are Bulgaria and Romania.

acting under the political guidance of the President,[3] has powers of initiative, execution, management and oversight.

- The *European Parliament* (EP), which approves the budget, votes its approval of the Commission (under the Treaty of Amsterdam) and monitors its activity.
- The *Court of Justice*.
- The *Court of Auditors*.
- The *European Investment Bank* (EIB).
- The *European Central Bank* (ECB).

We will examine the ECB, which strictly speaking is not a Community institution as it has independent legal personality, in section 18.4.

18.3   The operation of a monetary area

We have already examined the process that led to European monetary union (EMU). This section briefly addresses a number of issues regarding the single currency.[4]

The replacement of the various currencies of the member states with a single currency has major implications, generating both benefits and costs for the group of countries as a whole and individually.

The *benefits* are both direct and indirect. The direct benefits essentially consist in lower transaction costs since it is no longer necessary to exchange currency in order to carry out commercial or financial transactions between countries within the monetary union.

The *indirect* benefits are linked first and foremost to the reduction of uncertainty (due to potential exchange rate fluctuations) regarding the prices of goods or financial instruments denominated in the currencies of the other area countries. In addition, having the prices of the same good stated in a single currency in different countries reveals possible divergences, which fosters competition and the formation of a common market.

The direct and indirect benefits are all the greater the closer is the integration among the countries that adopt the single currency. These benefits in turn increase integration further. Monetary union has *costs*, however, in the presence of asymmetric demand shocks, differences in labour market institutions and other differential factors.

Asymmetric demand shocks are changes in demand that involve one country in a monetary union while not affecting the others. For example, imagine that the demand for Italian goods falls off in a certain period (with respect to the previous period) in favour of demand for German goods. The impact of this shock can be viewed in terms of aggregate supply and demand curves (see chapter 3). The aggregate demand curve in Italy will shift to the left, while that in Germany will move right (the aggregate supply

---

[3] This is one of the changes to the Treaty of Rome introduced by the Treaty of Amsterdam of October 1997, which entered into force on 1 May 1999.

[4] See De Grauwe (1998). The original contribution on monetary areas was made by Mundell (see Mundell, 1961).

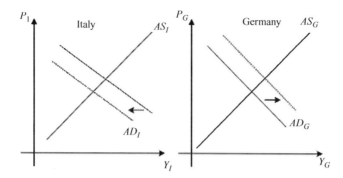

Figure 18.1

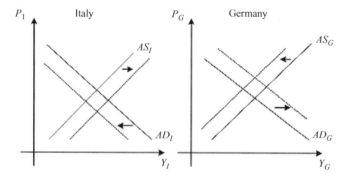

Figure 18.2

curve remains unchanged in both countries). As shown in figure 18.1, this will lead to a downward shift in the aggregate demand curve in Italy and an upward shift in the aggregate demand curve in Germany, with the supply curves being unchanged in both countries. This prompts a reduction in output in Italy and an increase in Germany and, if domestic spending in Italy does not decline by the same amount,[5] a deterioration in Italy's net exports to Germany. The opposite will occur in Germany.

Both countries will face *adjustment problems*, since Italy will experience recessionary pressures (with an increase in unemployment) while Germany will expand (with possible inflationary pressures). These problems could be managed with *automatic adjustment mechanisms*, given wage flexibility and labour mobility. A reduction in wages in Italy and an increase in Germany would shift the aggregate supply curve to the right in Italy and to the left in Germany, restoring the original level of output in the two countries (with prices lower than their pre-shock level in Italy and higher in Germany), as can be seen in figure 18.2.

However, the automatic adjustment mechanisms may not work smoothly: especially in European labour markets, wages are sticky and labour mobility is very limited.

---

[5] This can be the effect of the support given to disposable income by unemployment benefits.

Germany could seek to curb aggregate demand. Doing so, however, might solve the inflation problem but not the surplus on goods movements (and Italy's goods deficit).

The short-run solution[6] to both problems would be to revalue the mark (the German currency) against the lira (the Italian currency), which would increase demand for Italian products, reduce that for German goods and thus return the aggregate demand curve in both countries to its original position. However, this option is not available in a monetary union, which is the main limitation of monetary unions in the presence of inflexible wages and low labour mobility.

An alternative solution to the problem of adjusting to asymmetric shocks would be for Germany to raise taxes, the revenues from which could be used to increase public spending in Italy. However, the euro area is only a monetary union, with no centralisation of fiscal policy at the European level, which remains in the hands of the individual member states.

Differences in *labour market institutions* between countries can also cause problems in a monetary union. For example, take a supply shock (such as that generated by the oil crises) that affects all of the countries in the union. If labour market institutions differ from country to country, the reaction of wages and prices to the shock will also differ, causing the aggregate supply curve to move differently as well, thereby producing situations similar to those seen with asymmetric demand shocks. Once again, the scope for adjustment is reduced since exchange rate adjustments are not possible in a monetary union.

Additional difficulties can be caused by differences in *growth rates* or in policymakers' preferences for *inflation and unemployment*: this can give rise to imbalances in goods movements of the sort discussed earlier.

The balance between the benefits and costs of monetary union depends on numerous circumstances, such as the extent of real and monetary integration, the degree of differentiation between the factors indicated above and the size and type of any shocks. Monetary union raises tricky problems in a variety of areas, such as the labour market and fiscal policy, that need to be tackled in order to prevent the emergence of imbalances.

18.4 Monetary policy

18.4.1 Institutions and organs[7]

European monetary policy is conducted by the European System of Central Banks (ESCB), which is composed of the European Central Bank (ECB) and the National Central Banks (NCBs) of the EU member states. The ESCB differs from the 'Eurosystem', which comprises the ECB and the NCBs of the countries that have adopted the euro.

---

[6] In the long run the devaluation of the lira would tend to increase prices and costs in Italy, while the opposite would happen in Germany. This could lead to the situation preceding the devaluation of the lira.

[7] The institutional aspects of the operation of the ESCB are described in detail in ECB (2001), from which much of the following discussion has been drawn.

The operation of the ESCB is regulated by the Maastricht Treaty and the Statutes of the ESCB and the ECB. It is governed by the decisionmaking bodies of the ECB, namely the President, the Executive Board and the Governing Council. The President represents the ECB and is appointed by common accord by the Governments of the EU Member States. The duration of the term of office, eight years, insures independence from national governments. The Executive Board is responsible for implementing monetary policy as established by the Governing Council, which is also responsible for choosing the instruments to be adopted and the terms, the criteria and the procedures for implementing monetary policy. The Governing Council is composed of the members of the Executive Board and the governors of the NCBs.

The NCBs are responsible for the execution of ESCB decisions.

18.4.2   Tasks, functions and status of the ESCB

Pursuant to Article 105(2) of the Treaty, the ESCB shall perform the following basic tasks:

(1) to define and implement the *monetary policy* of the Community; in particular, the ECB has the exclusive right to authorise the issue of banknotes within the Community[8] and thus to perform the operations we examine below
(2) to conduct *foreign exchange operations* to influence the exchange rate of the euro and counter excessive or erratic fluctuations in that rate
(3) to hold and manage the *official foreign reserves* of the member states
(4) to promote the smooth operation of *payment systems*.

The duties assigned to the ECB reflect a restrictive interpretation of the tasks of a central bank. We will see that the ECB does not perform a *lender-of-last-resort* function (except in the limited framework of marginal lending facilities) nor does it have a regulatory or supervisory role in the financial system, as these tasks are carried out by the NCBs or other bodies under domestic legislation in the member states.

In performing its functions, especially defining and implementing monetary policy, the primary objective of the ESCB is to maintain *price stability*. The Governing Council defined price stability as an annual average medium-term rise of below 2 per cent in the harmonised index of consumer prices in the euro area countries. *Without prejudice to that objective*, the ESCB shall support the general economic policies in the Community, acting in accordance with the principle of an open market economy with free competition, favouring an efficient allocation of resources.

In assigning duties to the ECB, a very specific political decision was made to assign a pre-eminent role to the objective of price stability with respect to other objectives. The

---

[8] From 1 January 1999 to 31 December 2001 the euro did not circulate as a physical currency. It existed solely as a *unit of account*. The national currencies, which were technically subunits of the euro, continued to circulate in its place. As from 1 March 2002, after a period of dual circulation of national currencies and the euro, the latter became the sole legal tender in the countries participating in monetary union.

model for this arrangement was the Bundesbank, rather than the US Federal Reserve, which is charged with seeking full employment as well as price stability.

In addition to the length of the term of office of members of the Executive Board, the *political independence* of the ECB is also safeguarded by Article 7 of its Statute, which forbids it to seek or take instructions from governments.

The *operational independence* of the ECB is sanctioned by articles 18, 19 and 21 of the Statute. In particular, the latter prohibits the ECB from providing credit facilities to Community or national public institutions. It may acquire government securities only in the secondary market (i.e. as part of open market operations or OMOs).

The only possible outside influence on the ECB could come from the provision of the Maastricht Treaty that gives the Council of Ministers responsibility for establishing the exchange rate of the euro. Since the ECB has operational responsibility in this area (see point (2) above), it could be required to intervene to cause a depreciation of the euro and, therefore, to create the monetary base in an amount that could conflict with the price stability objective (Cottarelli, 1994).

However, two aspects must be considered in this regard.

First, the creation of the monetary base does not necessarily imply a reduction in the *internal value* of the currency. This will not occur if there are unemployed factors of production and no pressures in the market for labour and other factors.

Second, although it is true that the depreciation of a currency (in our case, the euro) can generate *inflationary pressures* owing to the rise in the prices of imported goods, in Europe's case this effect is small since the ratio of imports to GDP is relatively minor.

The ESCB is the monetary policy authority of the euro area, enjoying political and operational independence. Its political independence is ensured by its power to decide the inflation rate that constitutes the price stability objective. Operational independence is safeguarded by its authority to select what it deems are the most appropriate means for achieving price stability without interference from other institutions.

The ESCB's political independence has been criticised by some, not only because there are unresolved issues concerning the *political accountability* of the bodies of the system itself (as with every independent central bank: see chapter 11), but also because of the European *institutional context* in which it operates, where there is little political representation of other institutions (first and foremost the EP), and other economic policy authorities (especially those in charge of fiscal policy, as we will see shortly) are institutionally weaker.

18.4.3   *Modes of intervention and monetary policy instruments of the ESCB*

In choosing between two-step or one-step intervention (see chapter 11), it was decided to take the latter approach, setting a final target directly (inflation targeting) with no specification of intermediate targets. However, this approach has been interpreted in a rather loose way, as no fixed horizon for the inflation target is stated and other information is also relevant for deciding monetary policy.

Some weight is indeed given to a number of intermediate variables lying between the instruments and the final target. An *operational target* is used, normally the short-term interest rate. This target is announced periodically in order to eliminate any uncertainty about the stance of monetary policy.

Monetary aggregates also played a central role in the first four years of operation of the ECB. In fact, the Governing Council also decided to announce a reference rate for M3 growth.[9] However, this aggregate was not a true intermediate objective, since the interest rates set by the ESCB did not change in any 'mechanical' way to deviations in actual monetary growth from the reference value (ECB, 2001, p. 47). In addition to this first 'pillar' of monetary policy given by the reference rate for M3 growth information from other indicators was also used (various indices of prices, costs and economic activity, inflation forecasts). These other indicators constituted the second pillar of the ECB strategy.

The rationale for this **two-pillar strategy** lay in the fact that the ECB maintained that in the long run inflation is a *monetary phenomenon* and controlling it must be effected through the control of money. However, in the short-to-medium run it can be generated by variables other than the quantity of money, such as shifts in the relationship between supply and demand and/or cost pressure on prices in the goods, services and labour markets.

In May 2003 the ECB Governing Council decided:

(1) To maintain the previous target of price stability giving a less ambiguous definition of it ('below but close to 2 per cent').
(2) To reduce the prominence of the first pillar (the monetary one), and exchange the order of the two pillars: the monetary pillar (relabelled 'monetary analysis') is now mainly a means of 'cross-checking' the assessment deriving from the other indicators (which previously constituted the second pillar) (ECB, 2003c). These decisions represent a move towards adopting an explicit and exclusive strategy of *(flexible) inflation targeting* (Svensson, 2003).

The monetary policy instruments available to the ESCB are essentially drawn from those discussed in chapter 11, with a few important exceptions. The main instruments are OMOs and the reserve requirement, which are **operations conducted at the initiative of the ECB**. Other operations are carried out at the initiative of counterparties.

---

[9] The components of this aggregate were given in section 11.4. In order to understand how the reference value for M3 is calculated, we consider the assumptions used in December 1998 and reconfirmed in subsequent years to set the growth rate at 4.5 per cent:

- a maximum rise in the consumer price index of less than 2 per cent was assumed (or rather, a target value was set)
- it was assumed that the trend rate of GDP growth was between 2 and 2.5 per cent
- it was assumed that over the medium term the velocity of circulation of M3 declines by about 0.5–1 per cent per year (see ECB, 2001, p. 50).

If one takes the central values of the bands indicated for GDP growth and velocity of circulation, setting the reference value for M3 growth at 4.5 per cent implies that the target inflation rate was set at 1.5 per cent, using Fisher's equation of exchange.

The ECB's **open market operations** can be divided into four categories:

(1) **Main refinancing operations**, which are temporary liquidity-providing operations (reverse transactions) conducted on a weekly basis with a maturity of two weeks. They are executed by the NCBs through tenders conducted within twenty-four hours of their announcement (**standard tenders**). These operations have a key role in achieving monetary policy objectives and provide most refinancing needed by the financial sector. The interest rate on these operations is the key interest rate used by the ECB to influence market rates.

(2) **Longer-term refinancing operations**, which are temporary refinancing operations conducted on a monthly basis with a maturity of three months. They are conducted by the NCBs through standard tenders. These operations are used to provide longer-term liquidity but are not intended to signal the market and, consequently, are normally carried out in a way that does not influence interest rates;

(3) **Fine-tuning operations**, which are conducted on an ad hoc basis (i.e. they do not follow a standardised calendar) to regulate market liquidity and steer interest rates, mainly to reduce the impact on interest rates of unexpected liquidity fluctuations in the money market. They may involve reverse or outright transactions, currency swaps or the collection of fixed-term deposits, depending on the objective. They are carried out by the NCBs, or directly by the ECB in exceptional circumstances, using quick tenders or bilateral procedures.[10]

(4) **Structural operations** may involve the issuance of debt certificates, reverse and outright transactions to modify the structural position of the ESCB *vis-à-vis* the financial system. Reverse transactions and the issuance of debt certificates are carried out by the NCBs through standard tenders, while the others are conducted using bilateral procedures.

The rates applied in OMOs are the most significant indicator of the stance of monetary policy.

Operations carried out at the initiative of counterparties (standing facilities) are used to provide or absorb overnight liquidity, signal general monetary policy intentions and set a limit to fluctuations in overnight interest rates. There are two types of facility:

(1) The **marginal lending facility**. In an illiquid market counterparties can use this to obtain unlimited overnight liquidity from the NCBs against deposit of sufficient **collateral** (see box 18.1). The interest rate on the facility sets a ceiling on the overnight rate. The ECB can use these very-short-term operations to perform a highly limited lender-of-last-resort role, one similar to that performed by the Bundesbank[11] and unlike that carried out by the Bank of Italy and the other European (before the euro) and non-European central banks.

---

[10] **Quick tenders** are conducted within an hour of their announcement. **Bilateral procedures** are operations carried out with a single counterparty without a tender.

[11] Before January 1999, in Germany the lender of last resort was not the Bundesbank but rather a Bank Liquidity Consortium, in which the Bundesbank had a minority interest.

Box 18.1.   Collateral in financial transactions and credit in the ESCB

Article 18.1 of the Statute of the ESCB allows the ECB and the NCBs to transact in financial markets by buying and selling underlying assets outright or under repurchase agreements and requires all Eurosystem credit operations to be based on adequate collateral. This requirement is designed to protect the Eurosystem against financial risk. Consequently, all Eurosystem liquidity-providing operations are based on underlying assets provided by the counterparties.

In order to protect the Eurosystem from incurring losses, ensure the equal treatment of counterparties and enhance operational efficiency, underlying assets have to fulfil certain criteria in order to be eligible for use in Eurosystem monetary policy operations. The Eurosystem accepts instruments issued by both private and public debtors as collateral in order to respect the principle of equal treatment.

Owing to the differences in financial structure across Member States, a distinction is made – essentially for purposes internal to the Eurosystem – between two categories of assets eligible for monetary policy operations. These two asset categories are referred to as 'tier one' and 'tier two'. Tier one consists of marketable debt instruments which fulfil uniform euro area-wide eligibility criteria specified by the ECB. Tier two consists of additional assets – marketable and non-marketable – which are of particular importance for national financial markets and banking systems. The eligibility criteria for these assets are set by the NCBs, subject to the minimum eligibility criteria established by the ECB.

Eurosystem counterparties may use eligible assets on a cross-border basis, i.e. they may obtain funds from the NCB of the Member State in which they are established by making use of assets located in another Member State. This cross-border mechanism ensures that institutions all over the euro area can use the complete lists of ECB tier one and national tier two assets. Finally, all eligible assets are subject to specific risk control measures which are defined in such a way that account is taken of market practices.

Source: ECB (2001, pp. 63–4).

(2) The **deposit facility** at the NCBs. In a highly liquid market counterparties can deposit excess liquidity, with the interest rate on the facility effectively setting a floor on the overnight rate.

The rates on the ECB's marginal lending and deposit facilities constitute the upper and lower limits of a **'corridor'** for the overnight market rate (EONIA).[12] The fluctuations of EONIA within the corridor and its proximity to the rate of the main refinancing operations are shown in figure 18.3.

---

[12] The Euro Overnight Index Average (EONIA) is the weighted average of any uncollateralised overnight loans made by a panel of the banks most active in the money market.

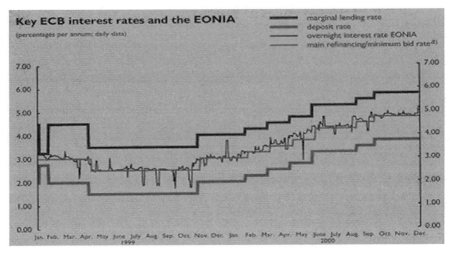

Key ECB interest rates and the EONIA

(percentages per annum; daily data)

─── marginal lending rate
─── deposit rate
─── overnight interest rate EONIA
─── main refinancing/minimum bid rate[a])

Note:

a) On 8 June 2000 to ECB announced that starting from the operation to be settled on 28 June 2000 the main refinancing operations would be conducted as variable rate tenders. The minimum bid rate refers to the minimum interest rate at which counterparties may place their bids. Before 28 June 2000, the main refinancing operations were conducted as fixed rate tenders.

Figure 18.3
Source: ECB (2001).

The choice of counterparties is very important for the efficiency of monetary policy operations. In the Eurosystem, it was decided to make a large number of counterparties eligible for OMOs and those that counterparties can undertake at their initiative in order to increase the efficiency of monetary policy action, ensure equal competitive conditions, decentralise ESCB monetary policy operations and enhance the operation of the payment system. This principle prompted the decision to impose no restrictions on the range of eligible counterparties for outright transactions. For others, however, counterparties normally must be financial intermediaries subject to the reserve requirement, which we discuss shortly. In order to ensure swift action, fine-tuning operations may be carried out with selected counterparties. In any case, counterparties must be financially sound, above all to ensure successful conclusion of reverse transactions. 'Financial soundness' is assured by the fact that counterparties must be subject to at least one form of EU/EEA harmonised supervision by national authorities envisaged under the second European Banking Coordination Directive (89/646/EEC), although institutions subject to comparable non-harmonised national supervision may also be accepted.

After some initial hesitation, the ESCB also adopted a *compulsory reserve* system: the creation of a structural liquidity shortage for financial intermediaries enables the monetary authorities to influence money market rates by varying the quantity of money. At the same time, the option available to intermediaries to mobilise their reserves – i.e. to change the quantity of monetary base held as reserves from day to day while ensuring compliance with the *average* requirement over the reserve maintenance period – helps stabilise interest rates, since it encourages credit institutions to smooth the effects of temporary liquidity fluctuations: an unexpected but temporary increase in the demand for money can be met by temporarily reducing the monetary base held for reserve purposes. The opposite action can be taken to cope with a temporary decline in the demand for money (ECB, 2001).

Credit institutions established in the member states are subject to a reserve requirement. The reserve base on which the requirement is calculated comprises their liabilities excluding interbank liabilities and those *vis-à-vis* the ECB and the NCBs. However, deposits and **debt securities**[13] with a maturity of over two years and repurchase agreements are subject to a zero reserve ratio, while deposits and debt securities with a maturity of up to two years are subject to a positive reserve ratio (equal to 2 per cent in December 2003). The ECB can change the reserve ratio at any time. The minimum reserves are remunerated at the average marginal rate on main refinancing operations carried out by the ESCB over the reserve maintenance period.

As we saw in chapter 11, monetary policy can have a different impact on different operators. The differential effects should be more pronounced in Europe, where productive structures and behaviour are more varied. For more on this issue, see Guiso *et al.* (1999).

18.4.4 The structure of the financial sector

The financial sector has been significantly affected by the creation of the single market, bearing the brunt of the elimination of numerous NTBs, which also and perhaps primarily affect international trade in services even more than trade in goods.

In addition to foreign exchange controls, NTBs were represented (and to some extent still are) first and foremost by the various regulatory systems adopted in the member states. The regulations, which were justified on the basis of the need to safeguard the stability of their financial systems, imposed different restrictions and rules from country to country, thereby segmenting the individual national markets.

The European Community first sought to reduce existing barriers between the various financial markets with a series of interventions:

(1) the **liberalisation of capital movements**, which was begun in 1990, having been envisaged in the Delors Report of 1989
(2) the **harmonisation** of certain key financial legislation, which involved the adoption of the universal bank model and the establishment of minimum capital requirements and ratios of own funds to assets (solvency ratios)[14]

---

[13] This term refers to securities (other than those issued on the money market and shares) that are normally marketable, such as *certificates of deposit*.

[14] The introduction of *minimum capital requirements* in place of controls over credit structures (degree of concentration, ownership structures, etc.) marked the shift from **structural supervision** to **prudential supervision**. This began in the second half of the 1980s.

(3) the application in this field (as in others, see section 18.8) of the **principle of mutual recognition**, under which any financial institution (bank or investment company) authorised to operate by the competent authorities of an EU member state may engage in that business in the other countries without further authorisation **(the single banking licence)**

(4) the introduction of the principle of **preventive home country supervision** over all the activities of a bank, including foreign branches; this preventive control is associated with the supervision of liquidity by the host country authorities

(5) an attempt to harmonise the tax treatment of investment income. This effort has failed so far (but see section 18.8).

While the benefits of eliminating NTBs in the financial sector were considerably overstated in the *White Paper on Completing the Internal Market* of 1985 and in the Commission study on the *Costs of Non-Europe* (Tsoukalis, 1997), the solutions developed to overcome those barriers, although dictated by obligatory pragmatism, raise numerous questions. These regard not only the complete liberalisation of capital movements but also the complete lack of any European-level regulatory or supervisory power over the financial system on the part of the Commission, the ECB or any other authority (see subsection 18.4.5).

The Report of the Group of Wise Men on the regulation of European securities markets (the **Lamfalussy Report**) presented in February 2001 emphasised the difficulties that hinder the development of a single market. Among others, these include: the lack of common rules in many areas (prospectuses, cross-border collateral, etc.); inefficient regulation; differences in application of rules from country to country; multiple trading, clearing and payment systems; different tax regimes. The Committee offered recommendations – accepted by the European Council – to reduce the time needed to approve regulations and directives aimed at ensuring greater integration of supervisory systems and fully integrated financial markets by 2005 (see European Commission, 2001a).

The integration of the European money market is facilitated by the introduction of a *specific payment infrastructure*: interbank funds transfers between EU countries are made through a system that handles euro payments between European countries as easily as domestic payments, thereby optimising cost savings, security and speed. The TARGET system (the acronym stands for *Trans-European Automated Real-time Gross Settlement Express Transfer*) links the domestic gross settlement systems that the NCBs agreed to set up in their respective countries (for more detail, see EMI, 1997; European Central Bank, 2003b).

18.4.5   Considerations on the monetary policy arrangements of European Monetary Union

As we saw briefly above, the institutional arrangements for the conduct of European monetary policy offer a number of points for discussion. We do not intend to re-examine the issues concerning the political independence of the ECB and the imbalance between the weight accorded to monetary policy authorities and that of other economic policymakers. Retaining our focus on monetary policy, we intend to assess the institutions envisaged to handle *financial crises*, which raise issues concerning supervision and oversight, and bank refinancing.

As we have remarked, there are no provisions for European-level *prudential supervision* of financial intermediaries. This task remains the province of the national legislation of the member states, with obvious consequences in terms of:

- differences in *regulatory treatment*
- *administrative complications* for financial intermediaries that operate in more than one country
- a lack of *price transparency* on the part of financial intermediaries
- possible *conflicts* between regulatory systems.

There would appear to be a need to centralise regulatory and supervisory functions, or at least to adopt common rules or encourage ad hoc cooperation among national authorities.

The limited scope of the bank refinancing operations that the ECB can conduct is indicative of the choice to adopt a pure bank-of-issue model that does not mix the functions of monetary policy with those of lender of last resort. The reasons for this decision lie first and foremost in the old but recently revived arguments (with regard to the IMF) that performing lender-of-last-resort functions increases the probability of negligent behaviour on the part of financial intermediaries (*moral hazard*) – i.e. that it prompts intermediaries to reduce the precautions they take in lending: financial intermediaries, knowing that they have access to credit of last resort in an emergency, could enter into riskier transactions and pay less attention to creditworthiness than they would otherwise do. Our discussion of international monetary issues has already shown that this argument is not well founded.

A different rationale for the decision to not give the ECB lender-of-last-resort functions is associated with the demands of *monetary stability*. Since the ECB is charged with ensuring price stability, it was felt that the need to prevent financial crises through bank refinancing could conflict with this objective, since refinancing is a source of monetary base creation (see chapter 11): financing banks in difficulty could lead to the creation of enough monetary base to jeopardise price stability. If one accepts the premise of the argument (namely, the pre-eminence of the ECB's price stability objective), that is a forgone conclusion. However, this does not mean that credit of last resort should not be provided at all; rather, the function should be separated from the monetary authority. In fact, as noted earlier, Germany had an institution relatively independent of the Bundesbank that supplied short-term liquidity to financial intermediaries.

On the other hand, the merger of regulatory and supervisory functions with that of lender of last resort could reduce moral hazard (see section 11.5) and justify the performance of this function by the ECB. We reach a similar conclusion if less weight is given to the importance of price stability as the ECB's objective.

The excessive emphasis placed on monetary stability as the objective of European monetary policy threatens to undermine the stability of the financial system, clashing with the goal of fostering the creation of a complex financial system closer to the Anglo-American model than the German approach (see section 11.3), which is necessarily at greater risk of financial instability.

18.5   Exchange rate policy

Having eliminated (or more precisely, *irrevocably fixed*) the exchange rates among the currencies of the countries participating in European monetary union, the euro area's exchange rate policy is aimed at regulating the exchange rate of the euro with the currencies outside the area, including those of other EU members and non-EU countries.

At the start of Stage 3 of monetary union, the EMS was replaced by a new exchange rate mechanism, informally called **EMS II**, which is based on the voluntary linkage of non-euro European currencies to the euro (as of May 2004, only the Danish krone was tied to the euro, but the new EU members that intend to participate in monetary union will also do so). The euro is completely free to float against non-EU currencies, since there are no provisions for a target zone system (suggested by some), never mind a fixed-rate regime. In the months before the start of monetary union, many policymakers and economic commentators insisted on the need for a **strong (or hard) euro** – that, is a euro with a high value against other currencies – in order to ensure the credibility of the ECB. One might ask whether this credibility is better served by a high external value of the new currency or rather a stable internal value. In fact, a higher external value is not a necessary index of the high credibility of a country's monetary policy but rather of a set of factors that, first and foremost, involve the monetary policies of other countries and, second, depend on factors other than credibility.

In some circumstances, an expansionary monetary policy could cause the euro to depreciate;[15] but this does not necessarily imply the end of internal price stability if there are unemployed factors of production.

At the start of 1999 the various NCBs contributed part of their reserves, totalling 39.5 billion euros, to the ECB. Some 15 per cent of the reserves consist of gold, while the remainder is in convertible currencies. The management of the reserves still controlled by the NCBs must not interfere with the ECB's conduct of monetary and exchange rate policy.[16] The ESCB uses the reserves for the key task of *intervening in*

---

[15] In section 18.4 we noted that if the European Council were to attempt to induce a depreciation of the euro, it could weaken the independence of the ECB.

[16] In 1998 a lively debate arose in some member countries regarding the possibility of using their excess reserves to stimulate employment. The proposal, which is technically sound, did not go anywhere despite the fact that economic conditions were such that inflation would not have been a concern (it was, in fact, falling).

foreign exchange markets as part of possible agreements concerning non-European currencies and to pursue the general exchange rate policy established by the Council of Ministers.

18.6   Fiscal policy

Fiscal policy in the European Union remains largely the responsibility of national governments, within the constraints imposed by the SGP. Member states are supposed to have budgets in surplus or balance. The maximum permissible budget deficit as a percentage of GDP is the same as that envisaged in the Maastricht Treaty for admission to monetary union (3 per cent). In order to ensure compliance with this ceiling, each member state must submit a *medium-term public finance programme* that specifies its adjustment path and the main measures that will be adopted to achieve the goal. The Ecofin Council and the European Commission monitor the process. If the limit is breached, the *excessive deficit procedure* is activated, which can lead to the imposition of large fines for offenders. The procedure is not activated only in exceptional circumstances (for example, in the event of natural disasters or a recession in which GDP contracts by more than 2 per cent). Where GDP contracts by between 0.75 per cent and 2 per cent, the Council, taking account of the circumstances, may rule that the Member State does not have an excessive deficit.[17]

In a situation of slow growth in global demand such as that prevailing at the turn of the Millennium, the restrictive nature of the Pact prompted scholars, politicians and EU officials to call for the strictures to be eased or the adoption of measures to attenuate their impact (see box 18.2): some suggested that the calculation of the deficit should exclude public investment expenditure, while others recommended measuring the **deficit in structural terms** – i.e. adjusting the actual deficit to take account of its cyclical components, which as we know tend to increase the deficit in recession and decrease it in expansion as a consequence of the operation of *automatic stabilisers* independently of other discretionary fiscal measures (see chapter 12).

---

[17] The procedure was activated for Portugal in November 2002 as a result of the deficit recorded the previous year; the country reduced it below the 3 per cent ceiling in 2002 before a sanction was imposed. In 2003 the Council failed to apply the procedure with respect to France and Germany, whose budgets showed a similar deficit.

For a critique of a number of technical aspects of the system, see Balassone and Monacelli (2000), and Rossi and Sorge (2000). The role of the Stability Pact and the problem of coordinating fiscal policies are addressed in Buti and Sapir (1998). Balassone and Franco (2001) underscore the moral hazard problems associated with the decentralised structure of European fiscal policy as key determinants of the stringent rules of the Pact. Artis and Buti (2000) note the need for an initial position of budget balance or surplus in order to be able to adopt countercyclical policies. There would be no contradiction between fiscal discipline and fiscal flexibility and, in fact, the Pact could be interpreted as the commitment necessary for regaining room for countercyclical budgetary measures. Some scholars (Sutherland, 1997) argue that with an expansionary deficit-financed budget, the fear of the unsustainability of the debt could increase the risk premium on the interest rate paid on the public debt, crowding-out private investment. Private consumption could also be adversely affected by an increase in the public debt if its initial level is high, as it could more easily give rise to the belief that the current generation will have to pay for that debt.

Box 18.2.   The Stability and Growth Pact: proposals for reinterpretation or amendment[a]

The Stability and Growth Pact and, before it, the fiscal rules for admission to EMU, which inspired some of the provisions of the Pact, have attracted considerable criticism. Attention has focused on: the definition of the aggregates used in establishing the requirements; the arbitrariness of the ceilings imposed (3 per cent for the deficit/GDP ratio and 60 per cent for the debt/GDP ratio for participation in monetary union; 3 per cent for the deficit/GDP ratio under the Pact); the difficulties the rules create for stabilisation policies during recession; the inadequate incentive for fiscal restraint during expansions; and the increased pressure that fines for violating the Pact would place on the public finances. Some of these criticisms have been answered by arguing that there is always a trade-off between the theoretical optimality of the rules and the simplicity of formulation and enforcement.

Any change must preserve the *credibility of the rules* by not creating the impression that they are easily revised to suit the contingent needs of this or that country. When, however, a sizeable number of countries – not just one or a few – simultaneously bump up against the Pact's ceilings,[b] it is advisable to revise the rule (or interpret it in a more flexible manner) in order to prevent a general deterioration in macroeconomic conditions.

The proposed reinterpretations or amendments include:

(1) interpreting the *deficit ceiling* as referring to the cyclically adjusted budget balance

(2) excluding *investment expenditure* from the deficit calculation, allowing it to be financed with borrowing (the 'golden rule')

(3) setting *different ceilings for each country* based on their debt/GDP ratios

(4) maintaining the 3 per cent ceiling for the deficit, but permitting the use of *extra-budgetary stabilisation funds* during downturns.

We shall consider each of these in turn:

(1) As discussed elsewhere (see sections 4.4 and 11.4), the public finances can act as an *automatic stabiliser*: during recessions, government expenditure increases and revenues decrease, while the opposite occurs during expansions. Take a downturn, for example. The increase in expenditure and the contraction of revenues cause the budget balance to worsen and may push the deficit beyond the ceiling established in the SGP. Considering the structural balance (that is, the balance adjusted for cyclical factors) rather than the actual deficit would facilitate compliance with the deficit rule.

The cyclically adjusted budget balance as a percentage of GDP, b_a, can be expressed as a function of the actual balance (as a percentage of GDP),

b_s, and the gap between actual and equilibrium GDP (again as a ratio of GDP), g:

$$b_a = b_s - \alpha g$$

where α is the effect on the actual budget balance of a change in the output gap. The average value of α has been estimated at 0.5 for Europe. An actual deficit of 4 per cent – above the Pact ceiling – in the presence of a negative gap of 2 per cent gives a cyclically adjusted deficit of 3 per cent, in line with the Pact rules.

The greatest difficulty in calculating the cyclically adjusted budget balance is estimating the output gap. There is no universally accepted method of doing this. One approach is purely statistical and consists in smoothing the actual GDP series by applying the so-called *Hodrick–Prescott filter*. However, the estimates of equilibrium GDP are also influenced by actual GDP developments when there are persistent deviations from equilibrium – for example, because of prolonged demand disturbances. An alternative method to estimating potential GDP is the production function approach, based on assessments of equilibrium levels of inputs of capital and labour, and trends in total factor productivity (TFP). In this case, the main problem is determining the *equilibrium unemployment rate*. The most frequently used method is to adopt a Phillips curve approach, estimating the unemployment rate consistent with a constant rate of inflation (**NAIRU**).

The fact that there are different approaches to estimating the structural budget balance complicates the use of this interpretation of the rules, since levying fines on violators could be controversial.

(2) The *'golden rule'* is enshrined in the constitutions of some countries (for example, Germany) or adopted in practice in others (the United Kingdom). Borrowing to fund investment would be permitted in situations in which public capital expenditure would generate an increase in future incomes such as to give rise (with an unchanged fiscal structure) to tax revenues whose present value is at least equal to financing costs. Many have called for the adoption of the rule by arguing that since public investment mainly increases future productivity, it has been severely penalised by the application of the Maastricht criteria and the SGP rules, falling below efficient levels.

Applying the rule, which is already complicated by the difficulty of distinguishing between current spending and investment, would also require identifying which investment expenditure complies with its requirements and which does not. However, this would still penalise investment that, while productive, does not generate sufficient future increases in tax revenues, the calculation of which is in any case an arduous task.

(3) In 2002 the European Commission proposed a reinterpretation of the SGP that did not establish different deficit/GDP limits for different countries but rather sets different medium-term budget targets in relation to the debt/GDP ratio of each country: lower deficit ceilings for countries with large public debt ratios and higher ceilings for those with smaller debt ratios. This would require changes in the Maastricht Treaty. Nevertheless, this approach also presents implementation problems, such as how to graduate *deficit limits in relation to the outstanding debt*.

(4) Under the 2002 proposal, the current 3 per cent deficit ceiling would be retained but countries would be allowed to use *extra-budgetary stabilisation funds* (so-called 'rainy-day funds'). These exist in many US states and some Canadian provinces. They could be constituted in inverse proportion to the debt/GDP ratio. The implementation difficulties of this approach are similar to those for proposal (3).

Notes:
a This box is based on EEAG (2003).
b In 2002 both Germany and Portugal breached the 3 per cent limit on the deficit/GDP ratio; France and Italy have come close to the ceiling and the performance of other countries has deteriorated sharply from the forecasts and commitments made a few years earlier.

Such solutions would be helpful, but their adoption is complicated by the letter (and with regard to the former, also the spirit) of the SGP. It would nevertheless be possible to increase coordination between the fiscal policy authorities in the member states (through Ecofin), preserving compliance with the Pact, in order to achieve higher demand and employment. The member states' high propensity to import (about 25 per cent on average) together with the large volume of intra-European trade (about two-thirds of the member states' foreign trade) means that an increase in public expenditure in one country, for example, would trigger:

(a) a small *increase in income* in the country and, therefore, a small increase in tax revenues, thereby increasing the budget deficit
(b) an *increase in demand and income* of the other European countries as a result of the increase in imports from those countries by the original country
(c) a *deterioration in the balance of goods movements* in the original country with respect to the others.

If, however, all the euro area countries acted together to boost demand by raising public spending, mutually reinforcing expansionary effects would occur (we discuss these in more detail in section 20.4), which should increase income in all countries without any appreciable increase in budget deficits or deterioration of the balance of payments.

18.7   The structural funds and redistributive policies

The European Union has established a number of 'structural funds' to help reduce the social and economic imbalances between the various regions of the Union. The funds account for about one-third of the EU budget and can act as an important complement to the efforts of the individual Member States:

(1) The **European Regional Development Fund** (ERDF), which is intended to reduce regional inequalities through investment in infrastructure, research and development, educational and healthcare facilities and trans-European networks.
(2) The **European Social Fund** (ESF), which seeks to increase employment by financing training and adjustment programmes for workers affected by industrial transformations.
(3) The **European Agricultural Guidance and Guarantee Fund** (EAGGF), guidance section, which contributes to the cofinancing of national aid schemes for agriculture and actions involving agricultural structures as well as promoting the environmentally compatible development of rural areas in a variety of ways, including the diversification of agricultural activities.
(4) The **Financial Instrument for Fisheries Guidance** (FIFG), which is intended to support restructuring in the fishing sector, including processing of final products and aquaculture.

The priority objectives of the structural funds are:

(1) promoting the structural adjustment of regions whose development is lagging behind (so-called **Objective 1** regions), which are those where *per capita* GDP is less than 75 per cent of the European average; these regions are concentrated in Greece, Portugal, part of Spain, Northern Ireland and most of Southern Italy
(2) converting regions or parts of regions seriously affected by industrial decline (**Objective 2** regions), which are those with an unemployment rate above the European average or which are experiencing a steady decline in employment
(3) combating long-term unemployment and facilitating the integration into working life of young people and of persons threatened by exclusion from the labour market (**Objective 3**)
(4) facilitating the adaptation of workers to industrial changes and to changes in production systems (**Objective 4**)
(5) promoting rural development by speeding up the adjustment of agricultural structures in the framework of the reform of the Common Agricultural Policy (CAP) (**Objective 5a**), or facilitating the development and structural adjustment of rural areas (**Objective 5b**)
(6) promoting the development of sparsely populated regions of the Nordic countries (**Objective 6**).

For the programming period from 2000 to 2006, the number of objectives was reduced from 6 to 3, incorporating Objective 6 into Objective 1, Objectives 2, 5a and 5b into a new Objective 2 and Objectives 3 and 4 into a new Objective 3.

European actions are intended to complement, not replace, national action: they must add to national public spending and must be carried out in close collaboration by the Commission, the member state involved and the competent national, local or other designated bodies. The amount of European funding varies from case to case and is often decided on the basis of the **Community Support Frameworks** (CSFs), which are drawn up for each country in cooperation with the country itself. The CSFs set out the priorities of the measures to be adopted, the form of intervention needed to implement these priorities and the funding for each form of intervention, divided among the various funding sources (Tsoukalis, 1997).

The structural funds are supplemented by the **Cohesion Fund**. Established in 1994, the Fund provides financing to member states whose *per capita* GDP is less than 90 per cent of the European average (the member states qualifying for the period 2000–6 are the same as for the previous period: Greece, Ireland, Portugal and Spain) for projects in the fields of environment and trans-European transport infrastructure networks – without burdening their public finances – in order to assist the member states in participating in economic and monetary union.

In addition to the structural funds, redistribution is also implemented through the **Common Agricultural Policy** (CAP) and social policy. The CAP is essentially a policy designed to *redistribute income to farmers*. Redistribution is effected partly through subsidies. However, the main instrument of CAP is still the fixing of **minimum prices** (intervention prices). These are set well above world market prices, which requires the levying of protectionist duties on non-EU agricultural imports (see section 18.8). In order to prevent overproduction, the intervention prices for some products (for example, milk) are supplemented by **output quotas** that each country allocates to individual producers.

Social policy consists of a set of rules that seek to harmonise the protection of workers in order to prevent **social dumping** and to promote wage equality between men and women. This policy has also had an impact on the distribution of income within the Union. The **European Social Fund** also ensures equality in vocational training (see Tsoukalis, 1997).

18.8 Industrial and trade policies

The European Union (and, before it, the EEC) has undertaken numerous industrial policy actions over the years (see Bianchi, 1999). Of special interest are the *sectoral initiatives* taken in the 1970s and 1980s, notably in the steel industry, for which a system of national quotas was developed. Little remains of this sectoral intervention, except in agriculture.

Beginning in the 1980s, the focus of industrial policy shifted towards *boosting R&D spending* as a proportion of GDP and fostering cooperation among the member states in the area of *technological innovation*. Early initiatives sought to encourage basic research, but they were subsequently broadened to applied research projects jointly proposed by firms, research centres and universities from different EU countries. Although in principle targeted at a wide variety of sectors (in that it was expected that the programmes would generate dynamic external economies in a range of areas), European research policy has in fact been selective, picking projects in sectors where it was felt appropriate to concentrate funding as circumstances dictated.

This approach has encompassed information technology (IT), with the ESPRIT programme, telecommunications (the RACE programme), new materials (BRITE) and energy (JET).[18]

In the area of environmental protection, the European Union established the European Environment Agency (EEA) in 1990, introduced the principle that polluters should bear the cost of external diseconomies and set uniform standards for improving the quality of water, air and certain products.

Apart from these fields, the EU's industrial policies have chiefly been passive in nature, taking a liberal approach to the market. The most important instrument of these policies has been the elimination of *non-tariff barriers* (NTBs) within the Union with measures aimed at creating the **Single Market**, which officially came into being on 1 January 1993. Specifically, these measures targeted the different consumer health and safety regulations established in the EU member states as well as rules mandating preferential treatment for national firms in calls for tender, licensing and public procurement.

The 'new approach' to technical standards, initiated in the 1980s, envisages that:

(1) **harmonisation** shall be focused on essential health and safety requirements, laid down in specific directives
(2) drafting of the *technical specifications* regarding the safety standards set by the Council shall be left to European standardisation organisations
(3) *new European standards* are voluntary but governments shall be required to presume that products manufactured to those standards are in conformity with essential safety requirements
(4) the principle of **mutual recognition** shall prevail, under which any product legally manufactured in one member state may move freely within the entire Union.

The European Union has liberalised many sectors, such as public-interest services, which were previously dominated by public monopolies (railways, energy, water, postal services), and financial services (banking, insurance and investment).[19]

Economic integration can be hampered or distorted by differences in *tax systems*, as far as indirect, income and capital taxes is concerned.

The European Community had long since adopted a unified system of taxation on consumption, based on the *value-added tax* (VAT). Its base and rates are harmonised

---

[18] The dilemmas of EU innovation policy are analysed in Borrás (2003).
[19] The reader will have noted that harmonisation and mutual recognition also underpinned the subsequent Commission effort to remove barriers between financial markets (see subsection 18.4.4).

to a large extent, starting from the 1977 Sixth Directive, and there are now limited interstate distortions as the tax is levied under the **destination principle** (exports free of taxes, imports taxed) (see however, Genser, 2003, for a discussion on the best VAT regime for the Single Market).

There are wider differences in excise taxes which stimulate cross-border shopping (e.g. for cigarettes, alcohol, perfumes) and induce differences in the production costs (e.g. for mineral oils).

The field in which the need for *tax coordination* is highest is that of capital taxation. Differences in corporate tax base and rates create obstacles to cross-border investment in the European Union and affect its location. Some types of income such as interest income can even escape taxation (Huizinga, 1994) or be arbitrarily divided as between different countries (Cnossen, 2003).

To deal with at least the most blatant divergences in capital taxation at the end of 1997 the Ecofin Council approved the 'Code of Conduct on Business Taxation' (European Commission, 1997). This is a non-binding agreement aimed at avoiding tax competition in the form of tax preferences to highly mobile investment activities, including foreign direct investment (FDI), and non-transparent administrative practices. The Code is, however, silent on competition in the form of uniformly low corporate income tax rates (Zodrow, 2003). Following the approval of the Code of conduct, the focus shifted to enhancing coordination among the member states, combined with a good dose of tax competition – for example, in the area of business taxation.

To remove obstacles to cross-border investment while favouring the creation of European business structures, the Bolkestein Report (2001), has more recently focused on *tax base uniformity* rather than tax rate harmonisation. It has proposed to establish a system of **common base taxation** (uniform rules for computing taxable profits for firms with cross-border operations) and a **home state taxation** (taxation of foreign operations in the member state where headquarters are located, on the basis of the principle of multilateral recognition).

More than a decade after its launch, the impact of the Single Market is difficult to assess, and despite a number of official efforts (see European Commission, 1996) we still lack a satisfactory evaluation. One attempt to provide an initial assessment of the effects of the creation of the Single Market, contained in Rondi and Sembenelli (1998), which assesses the changes introduced between 1987 and 1993,[20] reaches the following conclusions, which in part confirm previous studies (see Tsoukalis, 1997):

(1) the level of *economic integration* in the European Union has increased in terms of both trade and multinational activity
(2) the adjustment induced by the Single Market has not so much concerned the specialisation of production among the Member States as the *concentration of the ownership* of European firms in certain countries

[20] The focus on this period, prompted by data availability issues, is obviously a limitation of the study because presumably the market had still not felt (or anticipated) the full impact of the changes in 1993. Since the 1990s, market concentration appears to have increased sharply.

(3) the *economic concentration of production* has increased marginally[21]

(4) firms have expanded in different countries but reduced their *diversification*; meeting the competitive challenge has necessitated a return to their core businesses.

Given the close links between industrial policy and trade policy, we briefly examine the issue here, referring the reader to Tsoukalis (1997) for a more extensive treatment.

As we know, a *customs union* means setting a *common external tariff* (CET). The European Community set a common tariff from the very outset of the Common Market, although it has since been reduced as a result of international trade negotiations (see chapter 17 and table 19.7). It is currently equal to an average of 3.6 per cent for manufactured goods, with higher duties for so-called **'sensitive' products** (textiles, clothing, consumer electronics, etc.). Similarly, many NTBs to the importation of manufactured goods and services have also been removed as a result of multilateral agreements.

Agriculture, with the CAP, remains the most highly protected sector. The principle of **Community preference** that underlies the policy has given rise to:

- a system of **variable import duties**, calculated as the difference between the guaranteed price desired within the Union and the price of imports from non-EU countries, thereby ensuring that imports are not sold at lower prices than internally produced goods
- a system of **export refunds**, granted to EU producers when they sell outside the Union at (lower) world market prices.[22]

In addition to some former colonies,[23] preferential agreements were also reached with the transition countries in eastern Europe (the **Europe Agreements**). They were intended to create a *European free trade area* for manufactured goods, which for some transition economies was a prelude to accession to the enlarged European Union. Most imports of manufactures from the eastern European countries were liberalised, as were EU exports to those countries, albeit over a longer period of time.

18.9   Environmental policy

The Community has devoted attention to environmental policy since the early 1970s. Its objectives and instruments have evolved over time, however. The 5th EC Environment Action Programme, covering 1992–2000, established the **principle of integration**

---

[21] This appears to be an instance in which the study's findings are most affected by the limitations of the reference period.

[22] The mechanisms and goals of the CAP are described in detail in Tsoukalis (1997).

[23] These are the ACP countries – i.e. the African, Caribbean and Pacific countries which signed the Lomé Convention (1975) and its updates. In June 2000 a new agreement was signed in Cotonou (Benin) to establish a twenty-year partnership for development aid. The new ACP–EC partnership seeks to create a more favourable context for poverty reduction and sustainable development in the ACP countries (seventy-nine at the end of 2003). The aid is funded mainly by the European Development Fund. Regional integration among the ACP states themselves is an important objective.

The system of preferences granted to ACP countries – which sparked the 'banana war' between the European Union and the United States (see box 17.1) – will be gradually replaced by agreements based on the progressive and reciprocal removal of trade barriers.

of environmental policy into other policy areas as a necessary factor for sustainable development. To this end, all sectoral policies must be environmentally compatible and provide for an *environmental impact assessment* (see subsection 9.5.2). For the same reason, public aid for cooperation with developing and transition countries must be used for structural measures that are compatible with environmental protection.

The 6th Environment Action Programme of 2002, covering the period to 2010, set the following four priorities: achieving the greenhouse gas targets established in the Kyoto protocol; protecting nature and biodiversity; protecting health and the quality of life; ensuring the sustainable use of natural resources and improving waste management.

The six main instruments of Community environment policy are:

- *legislative measures*, such as regulations laying down standards, restrictions on the use of raw materials and plant, and limits on emissions
- *financial support* for demonstration projects and technical assistance for firms and local authorities, information, habitat conservation projects and technical assistance for non-EU countries
- *subsidies* for the development of clean technologies and emission abatement
- *environmental taxes*, although only a few countries have imposed these (primarily Denmark, Finland, Germany, the Netherlands and Sweden). As regards carbon dioxide emissions, the Commission's attempt to promote the adoption of a carbon tax was a failure: few countries imposed such a levy and even then only in a much milder form than that indicated by the Commission
- *tradable pollution permits*
- *voluntary agreements* to achieve environmental objectives, such as **Ecolabel** (a label providing consumers with information on the environmental compatibility of a product) and **Ecoaudit** (a systematic and documented assessment of the organisation, management and production processes of a firm aimed at verifying conformity with environmental policies).[24]

18.10 Summary

1 The process of *European integration* got under way in the early 1950s. After a pause in the 1970s and 1980s, it accelerated with the Single European Act (SEA) of 1987 (which amended the Treaty of Rome), the launch of European Monetary Union (EMU) in 1999 and the enlargement of the Union to other countries in 2004.

2 The chief objectives of the SEA were the completion of the Single Market, the extension of Community objectives to encompass environmental protection, the pursuit of economic and social cohesion as well as workplace safety and health. The SEA also envisaged a number of institutional changes.

3 A second impulse to the process of European integration was imparted by the drive to establish *monetary union*. A monetary union has benefits and costs for

[24] For more on European environmental policy, see European Agency for Environment (1999), Jordan (1999), Welfens and Hillebrand (2001), McCormick (2001, 2002).

its participants. The greatest fear is the possibility that asymmetric shocks could hit certain countries and that both independent market reaction and public re-equilibrating policies would be insufficient to cope with the consequences.

4   In Stage 3 of EMU, *monetary policy* is conducted by the European System of Central Banks (ESCB), which is guaranteed both political independence (in setting the primary objective of monetary stability) and operational independence.

5   The ESCB takes an *inflation targeting approach* and mainly uses open market operations (OMOs) in its conduct of monetary policy. Its role as a lender of last resort is limited, and banking regulation and supervision is conducted by national authorities.

6   In a possible conflict with the rules governing the independence of the European Central Bank (ECB), the latter is supposed to intervene in foreign exchange markets to pursue the *general exchange rate policy* established by the Council of Ministers.

7   The *Stability and Growth Pact* (SGP), which requires that the euro area countries maintain budgets in balance or surplus, has a restrictive nature, which is exacerbated by the lack of coordination among national fiscal policies.

8   The EU implements redistributive policies through the *structural funds* (which contribute to reducing social and economic disparities among the various regions of Europe), the Common Agricultural Policy (CAP) and social policy.

9   The EU's *industrial policy* is directed at fostering technological innovation and removing non-tariff barriers (NTBs) to trade in goods and services. This is implemented through liberalisation, harmonisation and mutual recognition of laws.

10   The EU has established the principle of *integration of environmental policy into other policy areas*. In order to pursue its environmental objectives – which include those set by the Kyoto protocol – it makes use of a variety of instruments.

VI Globalisation and the quest for a new institutional setting

19   The internationalisation of private institutions: the globalisation of markets and production

19.1   Forms of globalisation

Globalisation has been variously defined (for example, see Oman, 1996). Here we define it briefly as the expansion on a global scale of the interrelations among national economic and social systems through private economic institutions. Such expansion is associated with the increase in international movements of goods, 'financial' capital and labour (**shallow integration**, in the terminology used by UNCTAD, 1994) and with an increase in international production, mainly by multinational corporations (**deep integration**).[1] Globalisation is therefore a different phenomenon from (increased) competition in markets for goods and factors of production, although such an outcome is highly likely in certain stages of the globalisation process.

In order to grasp the scope and shape of globalisation, we first examine *international trade in goods*.

Overall, international trade expanded at a faster pace than GDP throughout the post-war period. The result was an increase in the degree of *international openness of economies* (defined as the ratio of exports to GDP),[2] as shown in table 19.1. Among the factors of production, *international capital movements* have expanded rapidly, especially bank capital (table 19.2). *International transactions in debt instruments and equities* have also grown much more than GDP (table 19.3).[3]

Total international migration flows have also increased since the Second World War: in 1990 about 120 million people were living outside their country of birth, compared with about 75 million in 1965. However, the ratio of such flows to population is broadly unchanged (World Bank, 1995, p. 52).

---

[1] By 'financial' capital we mean international capital movements different from FDI, which supports 'deep integration', as we will see.

   International production derives not only from the action of multinationals but also from licensing agreements, subcontracting arrangements, marketing agreements.

[2] The degree of *international openness* is often measured as the ratio of the sum of exports and imports to GDP.

[3] A more appropriate indicator would be the *ratio of external financial assets to total financial assets*. This has risen considerably in some countries. For instance, in Italy it rose from 6.7 per cent to 12.9 per cent between 1986 and 1997 (based on data in Banca d'Italia, 1998).

Table 19.1 *Exports as a percentage of GDP in selected developed countries, 1950, 1973, 1998*

	1950	1973	1998
France	7.6	15.2	28.7
Germany	6.2	23.8	38.9
Netherlands	12.2	40.7	61.2
United Kingdom	11.3	14.0	25.0
Spain	3.0	5.0	23.5
United States	3.0	4.9	10.1
Mexico	3.0	1.9	10.7
Brazil	3.9	2.5	5.4
China	2.6	1.5	4.9
India	2.9	2.0	2.4
Japan	2.2	7.7	13.4
World	**5.5**	**10.5**	**17.2**

Source: Maddison (2001).

Table 19.2 *International movements of bank capital as a percentage of world GDP, international trade and gross fixed capital formation (per cent) 1964, 1980, 1991*

	1964	1980	1991
As % of GDP	0.7	8.0	16.3
As % of international trade	7.5	42.6	104.6
As % of gross fixed capital formation	6.2	51.1	131.4

Source: UNCTAD (1994).

Table 19.3 *Cross-border transactions in bonds and equities as a percentage of GDP, 1975–1998*

	1975	1980	1985	1990	1995	1998
United States	4	9	35	89	135	230
Japan	2	8	62	119	65	91
Germany	5	7	33	57	172	334
France	–	5	21	54	187	415
Italy	1	1	4	27	253	640
Canada	3	9	27	65	187	331

Source: Bank for International Settlements (1999).

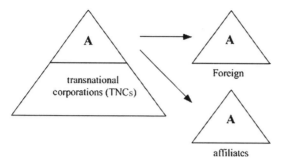

Figure 19.1
Source: UNCTAD (1994).

Deep integration is embodied in the **multinational (or transnational) corporation** (MNC). Such companies have production centres in a variety of countries, acquired through direct foreign investment (FDI). The reasons why a company would invest abroad are diverse:

* to gain a *foothold in an expanding market*
* to *adapt products to local demand* and endow them with a local image
* to lower *transport costs* and avoid import duties
* to lower *production costs*
* to increase *exports*
* to gain access to *new technologies.*[4]

The various determinants of FDI give rise to different types of multinational. There are three main categories.

The first is the **multidomestic multinational** (or stand-alone company).

For example, part **A** (see figure 19.1), which is often the final assembly stage, is replicated in foreign countries in order to reduce transport costs and import duties, adapt products to local tastes and exploit the potential for growth.

A second type is the **multinational with a simple integration strategy**. These are companies that shift one or more stages of the production process (see figure 19.2) or the manufacture of certain components to another country, chiefly to take advantage of lower labour costs or to use innovations introduced by foreign research labs in an innovative environment.

The third type is the **multinational with a complex integration strategy**, which has emerged in recent years under the stimulus of the need to reduce transport and communication costs and the liberalisation of trade. In this type of company, each affiliate is *specialised in certain functions* (for example, one would be specialised in manufacturing batteries for different car models, another in engines, and so on) in order to

---

[4] For a more detailed analysis of the determinants of FDI and the birth of the multinational firms, see Acocella (1975). On the broader problem of the expansion of international production and multinational corporations, see Cantwell (2000) and Ietto Gillies (2002).

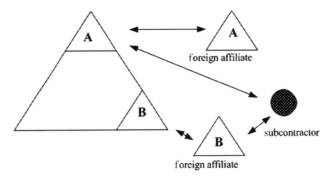

Figure 19.2
Source: UNCTAD (1994).

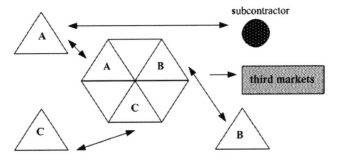

Figure 19.3
Source: UNCTAD (1994).

exploit *economies of scale* or to benefit from differences in the availability and cost of various types of labour or other factors of production. Some affiliates also assemble the components produced by the other units, as shown in figure 19.3 and box 19.1 (UNCTAD, 1994, 2001).

MNCs and FDI have expanded sharply since the 1950s (see table 19.4).

Box 19.1.   The division of labour within a transnational corporation

Integrated production systems have grown in regions that have reduced trade barriers between member countries and have strong industrial capabilities. The essence of this organisational form is geographical specialisation by different parts of a TNC production system (e.g. components, sub-assemblies, semi-finished products). In the European Union, for instance, TNCs in the automobile industry have built closely knit supply chains across several countries. A similar system is emerging in NAFTA, and increasingly in ASEAN (figure 19B.1).

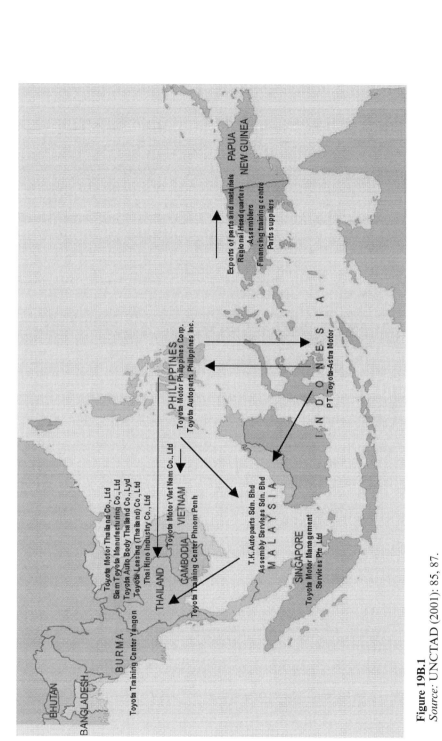

Figure 19B.1
Source: UNCTAD (2001): 85, 87.

Table 19.4 *Growth in FDI and multinational companies, 1960–2002*

	1960	1975	1990	2002
Stock of FDI ($ billion)	68	282	1874	7123
Employment in foreign affiliates of multinationals (million)	–	16	24	53
Turnover of foreign affiliates/world exports (%)	84	97	263	226

Source: UNCTAD, *World Investment Report* (various years).

Table 19.5 *Exports as a percentage of GDP in selected developed countries, 1870, 1913, 1929, 1998*

	1870	1913	1929	1998
France	4.9	7.8	8.6	28.7
Germany	9.5	16.1	12.8	38.9
Netherlands	17.4	17.3	17.2	61.2
United Kingdom	12.2	17.5	13.3	25.0
Spain	3.8	8.1	5.0	23.5
United States	2.5	3.7	3.6	10.1
Mexico	3.9	9.1	12.5	10.7
Brazil	12.2	9.8	6.9	5.4
China	0.7	1.7	1.8	4.9
India	2.6	4.6	3.7	2.4
Japan	0.2	2.4	3.5	13.4
World	**4.6**	**7.9**	**9.0**	**17.2**

Source: Maddison (2001).

19.2   The new features of globalisation

If we look at globalisation over a longer time horizon than the post-war years, we see that on some indicators (for example, the degree of trade integration) and for some countries (for example, the United Kingdom), the degree of internationalisation reached in recent years, which is greater than in the early 1950s as we saw, is not much higher than that on the eve of the First World War; for other countries, such as Brazil, India and Mexico, it is even lower now than in 1913 (see table 19.5).

Must we conclude that the much-heralded advance of globalisation is not a new phenomenon but rather a case of *dejà vu*? Is international integration a normal state of affairs for capitalist economies, and was the closure of economic systems in the period between the two world wars the real anomaly? For many reasons, the answer is 'no'.

First, the pattern of *economic development* shows that, at least for the most developed countries, an increasingly large part of GDP is accounted for by *services*, which by their very nature give rise to much smaller international trade flows than their domestic analogues as they are often not tradable. In other words, GDP growth in itself appears to be associated with a lower degree of trade integration. If, on the other hand, the total extent of integration (including tradable and non-tradable sectors) is in fact essentially unchanged, this means that international integration in tradable sectors is actually increasing. However, we must also consider the fact that since GDP is a measure of *value-added*: while exports and imports express the *overall value* of goods and services, the ratio of international trade to GDP tends to overstate international integration to an increasing degree as the division of labour increases.

Second, the *composition of international trade in goods and services* is very different from that before 1914. At the time, a significant or predominant part of trade involved the exchange of manufactured goods for raw materials between advanced and underdeveloped countries, respectively. Modern international trade is dominated by reciprocal flows of manufactured goods, often within the same industry (**intra-industry trade**, as against **inter-industry trade**, which involves flows of goods between different industries), both between advanced economies and between these and developing countries.

Moreover, international integration before the First World War necessarily had specific, limited effects, as it was largely conducted within the framework of the *colonial system*, which entailed specific bilateral relationships. A much larger number of countries are part of the global market today, even if many remain significantly removed from it (for example, much of sub-Saharan Africa, SSA).

Finally, *international capital movements* (both 'financial' movements and FDI) are now much more significant than they were in the period before the First World War, not only because of their size but also and above all because of their consequences for the productive specialisation of countries, for competitiveness and for the effectiveness of national economic policies.

While the international economic integration that has taken place since the Second World War represents to some extent the re-emergence of a phenomenon that has characterised the world economy for at least a century, the new integration has some new features that justify the use of the term 'globalisation' to describe it.

19.3   The causes of globalisation

Globalisation is a reality for the markets for goods, services and financial capital and for movements of 'productive' capital. This development has been driven by *technological progress* and *deliberate policy choices*:

(1) The first factor in the expansion of globalisation is *technical progress*, which has sharply lowered transport and communication costs in recent decades (see table 19.6). The reduction in these costs has helped shrink distances, thereby facilitating contacts between national economies with very different endowments of productive factors (and distributive variables, notably wages), technologies and preferences.

Table 19.6 *Changes in transport and communications costs, 1930–1990*

	1930	1950	1960	1970	1990
Air transport costs per passenger-mile	100	44	56	24	16
Cost of a three-minute telephone call between London and New York	100	22	19	13	1.4
Cost of using a satellite				100	8

Source: Based on IMF (1997).

Table 19.7 *Duties as a percentage of the value of manufactured goods, 1913, 1950, 1990, 2004*

	1913	1950	1990	2004
Germany	20	26	5.9	3.6
Japan	30	25	5.3	3.9
Italy	18	25	5.9	3.6
United States	44	14	4.8	4.0

Source: UNCTAD (1994); WTO (2004).

Specifically, lower transport and communication costs tend to:

(a) facilitate *productive specialisation* and international goods trade, as well as the international movement of factors of production

(b) facilitate the *transfer of production abroad* by multinationals, especially those of the second and third types we examined in section 19.1. This effect is connected with effect (a)

(c) increase the *price elasticity of supply and demand* for goods and factors of production, with an impact on income distribution. This helps explain the increase in wage differences in some countries, such as the United States.[5]

(2) The second factor driving globalisation is *economic policy*, which has primarily concentrated on gradually eliminating the obstacles to international trade previously erected by the developed countries. One example of these developments is provided by the duties levied by a selection of advanced countries (see table 19.7). It should be borne in mind that the most recent figures in the table have been modified by subsequent additional reductions after the conclusion of the Uruguay Round of trade negotiations and now average 4 per cent.

Reductions have been even larger within some regional blocs, such as the European Union (see chapter 18) or the North American Free Trade Area (NAFTA). Nevertheless, it is debatable whether the fall in duties in a given regional area creates new trade in that area (which would increase international trade) or simply diverts trade that would have taken place outside the area in any case (see Bairoch, 1993; UNCTAD, 1994).

[5] See UNCTAD (1994) and Rodrik (1997).

Table 19.8 *Trade barriers, convertibility and capital movement rules in the main developed countries in the twentieth century*

	Up to 1914	From 1914 to the end of the 1950s	From the end of the 1950s to the end of the 1980s	1990s
International goods movements	Relatively free	Considerable restrictions	Gradual liberalisation	Nearly complete freedom
Currency convertibility	Yes	No	Yes	Yes
International capital movements	Free	Restrictions	Restrictions	Free

The developing countries themselves radically altered their trade policy in the mid-1980s, moving away from protectionism and import substitution. There were many reasons for the change, such as the oil crises and the conditions imposed as part of the aid programmes of international organisations, which insisted on liberalising trade in goods (and capital movements), as we discussed in chapter 17.

Globalisation has also been fuelled by the spread of *currency convertibility*[6] and the *liberalisation of capital movements* by both the advanced and developing nations.

The reintroduction of convertibility between the currencies of the main industrial countries at the end of the 1950s, the OECD's adoption in 1961 of the Code of Liberalisation of Capital Movements and the Code of the Liberalisation of Current Invisible Operations, and a number of regional initiatives, such as those taken in European monetary union (EMU) (see chapter 16), were major strides towards the complete liberalisation of international movements of financial capital.

The restrictions on FDI imposed after the Second World War and at the end of the 1970s have also been eased considerably, with the drastic liberalisation of national rules beginning in the mid-1980s, numerous bilateral accords, regional liberalisation areas (such as the European Union and NAFTA), and multilateral trade negotiations, such as those undertaken within the OECD and the Uruguay Round (UNCTAD, 1994).

An additional boost to globalisation came from the opening of the *former Communist-bloc countries* to trade and international investment at the end of the 1980s.

Table 19.8 summarises international economic policy stances from the period before the First World War to 2000.

---

[6] In its simplest sense, **convertibility** means that economic agents can exchange the currency of their country of residence for the currency of another country. A country might restrict convertibility in order to reduce imports of goods and/or exports of capital. In chapter 16 we pointed out that in addition to the period between 1918 and 1939 currency restrictions were also used after 1945. In the post-war period, *non-resident convertibility* (see section 16.3) was a limitation of convertibility used to restrain capital movements without impeding international trade.

19.4   The impact of globalisation

Globalisation has had many consequences, given that it can essentially be likened to *changing the rules of the game*, which necessarily produces different outcomes, at least for those who continue to adopt old strategies. As we know, all economic phenomena can be assessed in terms of *efficiency* and *equity*. In a dynamic context, which is the most appropriate for globalisation, the impact of greater efficiency is primarily an increase in world economic growth. This is the result of the fact that globalisation increases specialisation (which parallels the increase in trade and FDI, especially FDI related to the second and third types of multinational). Among other things, specialisation enables firms to exploit economies of scale more effectively, thereby reducing costs and increasing the world economy's potential for growth.

One particular aspect of increased specialisation has been the **deindustrialisation** – i.e. the sharp fall in manufacturing's share of employment, of the developed countries since the 1970s. In the United States this share fell from 28 per cent in 1965 to 16 per cent in 1994; in the industrial countries as a whole the proportion fell from 27 per cent to about 18 per cent over the same period (IMF, 1997).

Some economists (see Wood, 1994) have attributed deindustrialisation to the *globalisation of markets and production*. The rise in developing countries' exports of manufactures due to the autonomous growth of certain of these countries and the simultaneous shifting of part of manufacturing by the developed countries to the developing world through direct investment or subcontracting and other similar arrangements could explain the (relative) loss of employment in manufacturing in the industrial world.

However, deindustrialisation can also be explained solely in terms of *demand and technological factors*. From the point of view of demand, the fall in the share of manufacturing employment might simply be a consequence of the higher **income elasticity of demand for services**: as income increases, the demand for services increases more than demand for manufactured and primary goods. On the technology front, we know that productivity rises more slowly in services than in manufacturing, which means that increased demand for services requires larger increases in employment than greater demand in industry. This therefore reduces the share of manufacturing employment in the total.

Empirical studies have so far not been able to resolve the debate between those who argue that deindustrialisation is caused by globalisation and those who instead attribute it to demand and technological factors. The prevailing view is that deindustrialisation is a normal feature of the growth of advanced countries, although it may generate adjustment or reconversion difficulties owing to the obstacles it may find in its path (low growth rates, institutional rigidities, barriers to entry in the services sector, etc.). Adjustment difficulties, which cause the unemployment rate to rise, can be worsened by increased competition from the developing countries. However, this would have only a small role in deindustrialisation (IMF, 1997) and is not the main cause of the rise in unemployment in many industrial countries in recent years. Future developments may however involve an expanded role for developing countries.

In addition to the division of benefits and costs among countries, globalisation also impacts the distribution within each country among different types of income and that within each category of income (for example, between skilled and unskilled workers).

As regards the impact of globalisation on the distribution of benefits among countries, the literature emphasises that the growth in trade and international capital movements has not only not helped to slow the marginalisation of some less developed countries in recent decades; it may in fact have reinforced the trend, for a variety of reasons: the elimination of tariff barriers erected by some of these countries to protect their vulnerable domestic industries; the removal of the tariff preferences accorded to them by some industrial countries; and the expected rise in the prices of agricultural products imported by many developing countries due to the elimination of the subsidies on these products in the industrial countries. As we saw in section 2.12, a centuries-long increase in world income inequality – with a deceleration of the process since the 1970s – has been detected. There is extensive discussion about the impact of globalisation on this both in the very long run and the short run.

Within individual countries, the benefits and costs of globalisation are not distributed uniformly. This depends in part on the impact of globalisation on *competitiveness*, which we discuss in section 19.5.[7]

19.5 Globalisation and competitiveness

Many of the repercussions of globalisation depend on its consequences for competitiveness.

It is difficult to deny that globalisation normally increases competition, at least in the short-to-medium term. However, in the longer term the fiercer competition that emerges in the initial stages may give way to the monopolisation of markets by firms that are not necessarily the most efficient[8]: the expansion of markets is accompanied by the expansion of firms through either internal or external growth.[9] In the broader global market, we can find a level of economic concentration or degree of monopoly that rivals that at the national level (box 19.2).

---

[7] A critical view of globalisation from a *distributive* point of view in a historical perspective is exposed in Milanovic (2003). An analysis of the effects of globalisation on social relations is provided in Amoroso (1996), who argues that the post-Fordian system of flexible specialisation, which has also been spread through globalisation, allows capitalist firms to control labour more efficiently.

[8] Under oligopoly, the outcome of competition among firms does not depend only on efficiency but also on the *capital* (and hence the size) of each. This is underscored by the **gambler's ruin problem**, which shows that in a game of chance each player's probability of being 'ruined' declines as the amount of initial capital increases (see Ross, 1993). Accordingly, it is possible that it will not be the most efficient firms that survive and grow, but instead the *largest* (and possibly less efficient). Similarly, competition at the system rather than firm level does not lead to the predominance of one or the other type of economic system (for example, the Anglo-American model over the German–Japanese model), for various historical, economic and political reasons (see Berger and Dore, 1996).

[9] This could be the main explanation for the pronounced concentration underway in various countries in the 1990s. Examples of a different impact on concentration of the entry of foreign firms in the UK market are given in box 19.2 (p. 432).

Box 19.2.   Transnational corporations, entry barriers and market concentration: three examples from the United Kingdom

Transnational corporations (TNCs) are often able to enter host country markets that are effectively barred to entry by domestic (non-TNC) firms, but the effects on concentration can differ. This is illustrated by three specific examples from recent years, for the United Kingdom.

The first example is the entry of *Mars* (United States) into the UK ice-cream market. The market for ice cream is dominated in many European countries by large TNCs, notably Unilever and Nestlé. In the United Kingdom, Unilever had a market share of over 60 per cent. Success on a national scale in this industry necessitates a strong brand image supported by heavy advertising (MMC, 1994). Given the fragmented nature of much of the retail market, it also requires a firm to have well-developed expertise and facilities in distribution. For many years, UK industry had not witnessed significant entry, presumably because of the large sunk costs which would be needed to support such entry. However, in 1989 there was a significant entrant – Mars, the US chocolate-bar manufacturer, a firm that had already incurred most of the relevant sunk costs in the adjacent chocolate-bar industry in both the United Kingdom and elsewhere. Importantly, the specific asset (a strong brand image and loyalty) was *transferable*, and Mars made significant inroads into the market, achieving a market share of 14 per cent within four years. Concentration clearly declined, with regard to both manufacturers and sellers. In addition, Mars expanded the ice-cream market considerably through the addition of new and upscale products, spurring Unilever to renew its focus on its world-wide activities in ice cream.

A second example, from the chocolate confectionary market, was the acquisition of one of the two largest UK manufacturers, Rowntree, by *Nestlé* (Switzerland) in 1989. Most informed opinion at the time interpreted the operation as a move to acquire the brand loyalty associated with two of Rowntree's strongest brands, Kit-Kat and Polo Mints. These complemented Nestlé's product range, placing it in a very strong market position in all product space segments in the United Kingdom and beyond. In this case, Nestlé was already selling in the United Kingdom market prior to the acquisition, and its entry effectively reduced the number of large competitors from four to three.

A third case is the mid-1980s entry of *Nissan*, the Japanese car manufacturer, through a large-scale greenfield investment, sinking considerable costs, in the UK market. Nissan had previously exported to the United Kingdom, but a combination of voluntary export restraints (VERs) and a welcoming attitude on the part of the British government induced it to invest in the country. Within a few years, it became a very prominent UK manufacturer, with a significant and increasing share of British production and sales. In this case, the concentration of manufacturers declined initially, while seller concentration remained the same. In the long run, Nissan's share of the UK market rose further, facilitated by the avoidance of tariffs and transport costs associated with exporting and a strengthening of its competitive position.

The full impact of these new entries in the longer term cannot, however, be understood without an appreciation of the changes under way in *competition and concentration at the global level*. This is especially the case with the automobile market, in which the British market (like that of most developed and many developing countries) is substantially integrated into the world market and in which firms are increasingly competing through innovation, relying on knowledge-based inter-firm networks for that purpose (Mytelka, 1999).

Source: UNCTAD (1997), p. 143.

The efficiency gains achieved in the short or medium term do generate benefits in terms of their stimulus to innovation and increased output in economic systems as a whole. Under appropriate conditions, innovation creates scope for producing more goods with the available resources. However, increased output is not a necessary result. Other conditions that must be satisfied include policies that do not depress demand.

Heightened competition increases the elasticity of labour demand, since for a given increase in wages in a country, firms will reduce output by more if they can easily find alternatives to national production (FDI, subcontracting abroad, etc.; see Slaughter and Swagel, 1997). The prices of goods and production factors therefore tend to decline, squeezing the rents that various economic agents may command (firms and workers in monopoly sectors). Obviously, while everyone may benefit as consumers by paying lower prices for goods and services, some will be equally harmed, especially those who have lost monopoly rents.

Globalisation thus benefits some and harms others in the short to medium term. Those who benefit the most – or are harmed the least – tend to be operators in sectors that are *sheltered from strong international competition*. This is the case in many service sectors (such as retailing and professional services), since such services cannot be delivered by foreigners unless they establish themselves directly in the country. Others who benefit – or suffer less harm – include highly skilled workers, for whom foreign competition is less pressing than it is for unskilled workers. It is clear that countries, sectors and people who are more exposed to competition will be harmed more or benefit less.

The people most vulnerable to globalisation are *unskilled workers* in the industrial countries, who are exposed to direct competition (through immigration from developing countries or the shifting abroad of unskilled labour-intensive manufacturing through FDI) and indirect competition (through imports of the goods produced using low-skill labour-intensive manufacturing processes).[10]

[10] An assessment of the effects of globalisation on labour markets is given in Greenaway and Nelson (2000) and in the papers in issue 2000 (3) of the *Oxford Review of Economic Policy*.

We have already discussed the impact of stiffer direct competition: it increases the *elasticity of labour demand*. The indirect effects manifest themselves simultaneously in the prices of goods and factors. The increased supply of low-skill labour-intensive products exported from developing countries lowers the relative price of such products and, therefore, the relative prices of the factor used most intensively in making them, namely unskilled labour (the **Stolper–Samuelson theorem**). This helps explain the appreciable increase in wage differences between skilled and unskilled labour in some developed countries, especially the United States and the United Kingdom (IMF, 1997). However, many economists argue that the main factor currently at work in the widening of wage differences is *technical progress*, which has increased the relative demand for skilled labour at the expense of unskilled labour.

In any case, the increase in wage differences would have permitted full employment to continue, whereas efforts to contain such disparities through labour market regulation, minimum wages and centralised bargaining have instead caused unemployment to rise (IMF, 1997). Not all are convinced by this argument, noting that there are other factors that could explain the increase in European unemployment, such as restrictive monetary and fiscal polices (see chapters 16 and 18).[11]

19.6   The consequences of globalisation for economic policy

In addition to its impact on income distribution, globalisation may also increase the exposure of economies to external shocks by increasing their degree of *international openness*. Since national economies are more interdependent, any decline in economic activity in one, whatever its cause, will be transmitted more easily to the others through the international ties that bind them together. For example, the negative consequences in Spain of a drop in aggregate demand in Germany are all the greater the larger is the share of Spanish output exported to Germany.

Globalisation may also reduce the *decisionmaking independence* of a country, since its economic conditions cannot diverge significantly from those in other economies. A specific aspect of this reduction in national policymakers' independence derives from the fact that almost no policy has only domestic effects (see sections 16.5 and 17.4). Exposure to the global market thus constrains divergent behaviour by public and private agents in the country in question. For example, *structural policies* that restrict the scope of action of economic agents (especially firms) in one country – e.g. environmental, competition or consumer protection rules, higher taxation – could encourage them to move to countries with fewer restrictions in even greater numbers than would be the case as a result of 'normal' productive specialisation. Countries are exposed to the negative consequences of *permissive economic policies* in other countries that seek to encourage consumers and firms to move in.

---

[11] For more on the benefits and drawbacks of low-wage labour as well as the impact of labour market institutions on employment levels, see Lucifora and Salverda (1998).

In addition, in a globalised international economy, the adoption of an expansionary policy (say, in France) in a context of stagnant growth in other countries would have serious adverse effects on France's balance of payments owing to the large rise in its net imports that would result. Similarly, action on the part of the ECB to lower interest rates in Europe when rates do not change in the rest of the world would trigger a balance of payments deficit for Europe as capital moved out of the area.

In general, each national government faces constraints in the short term on its freedom to expand demand or to adopt structural policy measures that increase the short-term costs of agents located in that country, even if such measures could produce positive effects in the long term.

The financial markets play the most important role in transmitting both the impact of *asymmetric shocks* that arise independently in one country and the effects of the *'abnormal' policies* that a country may adopt, since they tend to accentuate and accelerate the reaction of agents and have an essential role in the formation of expectations (see section 4.7). We discuss possible solutions to these problems in chapter 20.[12]

19.7 Summary

1 The term 'globalisation' refers to the increased *interdependence of economic and social systems* through the action of private institutions. We can distinguish between *shallow* globalisation, which concerns the growth in movements of goods, labour and financial capital, and *deep* globalisation, which is characterised by FDI and multinational firms.

2 The *expansion of globalisation* in the post-war period represents a resumption of a long-term growth trend in international transactions that was already present before the First World War but which stalled between 1918 and 1945. Unlike the trends before 1914, today's globalisation displays original features that justify using this term to describe it.

3 Globalisation has been fostered by *technological progress*, which has significantly reduced transport and communication costs in recent decades, and by the gradual removal of restrictions on the movement of goods and capital in the developed countries. Other factors have been the drastic change of direction in trade policy in the developing countries and the opening of the former socialist economies to international trade and investment.

4 The consequences of globalisation in terms of efficiency are mainly associated with *increased specialisation*, which tends to have a positive impact on the rate of growth of the world economy (and individual national economies).

   One alleged effect of globalisation is *deindustrialisation*. Considerable debate has also focused on the widening of wage differences between skilled and unskilled

---

[12] For the effects of globalisation on the national state's policies see Lee (2003).

workers, which many blame on the globalisation of markets and production, but which in fact appears so far to be largely the result of technological progress.

Globalisation tends to increase *competition* in the short to medium term. In the long term, the effects are less certain.

5 Globalisation increases the vulnerability of economies to *external shocks*. National governments have less scope to adopt measures to expand aggregate demand or structural measures that increase the short-term costs of economic agents in those countries, even if these measures will produce long-term benefits.

20 The challenges of globalisation for public policies

20.1 International payments imbalances since the 1970s

Despite the considerable tensions that emerged over the period and the absence of any considered and substantial reform, the international payment system was able to continue functioning without any further traumatic breakdowns after that of August 1971. This does not mean that problems did not arise, but rather that they were solved in some way, albeit often with partial, fortuitous or provisional adjustments. The problems that have emerged since the 1970s can be grouped into those specific to relationships between some groups of countries and those that concern all countries. Among the former are: the problem of disequilibria in countries that import raw materials (and oil in particular) owing to the rise in their prices during the 1970s; the problem of the foreign debt of developing countries; and that of the foreign debt of the East European countries around 1990, the foreign exchange and financial crises that hit some South-East Asian countries, Russia and Brazil in 1997–9 and Argentina in 2001–2. The more general problem concerns the strains that have been caused by *speculative capital movements*.

The sharp rise in raw materials prices in the 1970s created large *balance of payments disequilibria*. The IMF partially dealt with these by providing new special *facilities* (i.e. financing arrangements) and increasing the limit on *drawings* on existing funds.[1] The *conditional* nature of the credit, however, hindered more extensive use of the Fund as an intermediary to *recycle* the balance of payments surpluses accumulated by oil-exporting countries.

Recycling was thus largely left to *private institutions*: banks and other intermediaries in the eurocurrency market. In fact, the low (at times even negative) real interest rates prevailing in this market as a consequence of an excess supply of funds stimulated recourse to these forms of private credit by many developing countries during the 1970s. However, the lack of attention paid by both borrowers and lenders to borrowers' real capacity to **service** their foreign debt (payment of interest and principal) helped push

---

[1] Limits are reviewed periodically. Under the present guidelines, adopted in 1994, member access to the Fund is normally subject to an annual limit of 100 per cent of quota and a cumulative limit of 300 per cent of quota.

their debt situation towards the 'verge of unsustainability' even before 1979. In the first half of the 1980s a combination of circumstances led to a crisis in the financial situation of the developing countries and, with them, that of the lenders. First, the monetary restriction in the United States in 1979 caused real interest rates to rise sharply. The consequent appreciation of the dollar further increased the burden of debt servicing by requiring larger outlays of domestic currency to repay the principal. In addition, the recession that had hit the creditor nations in the early 1980s made it even more difficult to repay principal and interest.[2] The foreign debt crisis, which burst into the open with Mexico's declaration of a moratorium on debt payments in 1982, was only partially solved with the financial assistance of the IMF. A more comprehensive solution seems to have been found in measures that include:

(a) **voluntary debt reduction** by creditor countries through the granting of a subsidy for interest payments by international organisations (the Brady Plan)
(b) **debt buy-backs** at highly discounted prices (up to 90 per cent) by some developing countries
(c) **debt–equity swaps**, where debt is converted into shares, or **debt–nature swaps**, where debt is exchanged for land for investment in environmental projects.[3]

At the start of 1999, however, the foreign debt burden of some developing countries, especially the poorest, was still so large that it prompted renewed calls for the adoption of a French proposal to sell about 15 per cent of the IMF's gold holdings in support of highly indebted countries. After meeting fierce opposition from many countries, who argued that it was inappropriate to use the Fund's reserves in such a manner, the plan was eventually approved in June 1999 by the G7 countries.

At the end of the 1980s, foreign debt also became a problem in the former Soviet-bloc countries which abandoned central planning and changed their political orientation. Unlike the 1980s debt crisis in the developing countries, the problem did not pose a real threat to the stability of the international financial system. Most bank loans were backed by official guarantees and accompanied by sufficient provision for default. In addition, exposures, which were small in relation to lenders' capital and reserves, were not highly concentrated (BIS, 1992, p. 71). Nevertheless, foreign debt continued to severely affect the economic policy choices of the Eastern and Central European

---

[2] A country in recession tends to *reduce its imports*. In our case, the recession that hit creditor countries caused a reduction in the exports of debtor developing countries. Note that balance of payments equilibrium requires that the deficit on capital movements and investment income (in our case, associated with repayment of principal and interest) be offset by a surplus on (other) current transactions, essentially positive net exports. But this was precisely the problem in the developing countries. Note that only equilibrium (or a surplus, which would have even more drastic consequences) of the balance of payments of the developing countries would allow the debt to be repaid: a deficit would soon run down these countries' reserves and would not in any case be sustainable in the medium-to-long term.

[3] In some cases, these operations were used to encourage the return of *flight capital* that had left the country for economic or political reasons: thus, for example, someone who had exported capital from a developing country could acquire – usually at a discount – an existing credit with the country and then convert the credit into local currency with the central bank, using this to purchase shares or other equity interests within the country itself (*debt–equity swap*). In the case of debt–nature swaps, the purchaser of the foreign debt was an environmental association.

countries. For example, serious problems were caused by the drastic reduction in capacity[4] (with consequent shortages of even essential goods) and the simultaneous need to channel some output towards foreign markets in order to permit at least some debt servicing.

At the end of 1994 an unexpected currency crisis flared up in Mexico – initially for political reasons and later fuelled by the steady deterioration in the balance of payments – and spread to some degree to other Latin American countries. Despite the deployment of a package of measures,[5] large flows of speculative capital movements were triggered that caused the peso to depreciate sharply. This occurred despite the announcement of a massive programme of financial aid from the United States and various international organisations, including the IMF, until new and even more restrictive budget measures were taken.

In the summer of 1997 a serious currency crisis started in Thailand and rapidly spread, first to other countries in the area and then to countries outside it, notably Russia and Brazil. The foreign exchange crisis also triggered a financial crisis owing to the leap in bankruptcies caused by the depreciation of currencies, capital outflows, interest rate rises and tax policy restrictions. The crisis was sparked by current account deficits, aggravated by the appreciation of the dollar, which was the anchor currency of most minor South-East Asian currencies, and the adverse trend of world demand in the area's sectors of specialisation.

The spread of the crisis to other countries (**contagion**, for which see Kaminsky *et al.*, 2003) was due to a number of factors, among which three were prominent:

(1) the *depreciation of the currency* where the crisis originated tended to have an adverse impact on the current account of competitor countries, where it also generated speculative outflows
(2) the currency crisis was a signal of *macroeconomic disequilibria* shared by other countries: a crisis in one country tended to indicate a high probability of a crisis in other countries
(3) the *fall in GDP* (which was very large: 15 per cent in Indonesia in 1998, for example) in one country tended to reduce imports from other countries, thus lowering GDP in the latter.

The crisis in Argentina exploded in 2001 but its origins went back to the second half of the 1990s. The considerable appreciation of the dollar and the firm peg of the peso to it (through a currency board regime – see section 16.7) undermined the competitiveness of Argentine exports, depressed economic activity, eroded public finances, undermined the credibility of the currency regime, increased the risk premium and caused interest rates to rise. The financial crisis deepened until the end of 2001 and fears of devaluation

---

[4] This is due to a wide variety of factors, ranging from the disorganisation (or even chaos) caused by political upheaval to the fact that the sudden international opening of these countries has made production with often outdated (or, in any case, different) techniques unprofitable.
[5] These included interest rate increases, the issuing of indexed securities, substantial monetary authority intervention in the foreign exchange market, the widening of the fluctuation bands for the peso and subsequent floating of the currency, fiscal and credit squeezes and incomes policy agreements.

triggered a run on deposits and capital flight abroad. The introduction of restrictions on capital movements and withdrawals from bank accounts (*corralito*) caused severe political and social tensions.

At the start of 2002 the currency board was eliminated and a dual exchange rate regime (see section 16.5) installed. Over the year, plans for returning to normality were developed and implemented. The Argentine crisis resembled that in South-East Asia in certain respects but fortunately did not spread to Argentina's closest partners. This was partly due to the adoption of flexible exchange rate regimes by some of these countries (e.g. Brazil).

The spate of financial and currency crises provides useful lessons for domestic and international economic policy (box 20.1). In particular, they:

(a) suggest the adoption of *more incisive regulation and supervision* of domestic financial and credit markets, with the more extensive application of the capital adequacy requirements, prudential controls and disclosure rules formulated by the Basle Committee for Banking Supervision (BIS, 2001)
(b) identify cases in which it is not advisable to adopt fixed-*exchange rate systems*: although such regimes can help establish credibility during the initial stages of recovery from high inflation, countries with real or financial weaknesses find it difficult to maintain fixed exchange rates in the long run (Group of Ten, 1997)
(c) underscore the effects of the *liberalisation of international capital movements* in crises
(d) highlight the role of *international organisations*, especially the IMF.

We address point (c) in section 20.2, while point (d) is discussed in section 20.3.

20.2   The role of capital mobility

20.2.1   *Nature and size of international capital movements*

Let us examine the general problem posed by *speculative capital movements*. These are in large part fuelled by the existence of large international money markets that are not subject to any form of regulation, such as the **eurodollar** market. This market, which emerged in the 1960s and grew rapidly in the following years (see McKinnon, 1979, for a detailed discussion of the reasons for this growth), deals in US dollar deposits with banks of any nationality located in Europe. Analogous balances in other foreign currencies with banks resident in Europe are also possible and constitute the **eurocurrency** market. More generally, deposits in a currency different from that of the country (European or otherwise) where they are held are known as **xeno-currencies**.

How do these markets function? Assume that IBM has deposited $1 billion with Wells Fargo, a US bank, but feels that the interest rate it earns is too low. It may be more profitable for IBM to transfer the deposit to Barclays Bank in England by drawing a cheque for the amount against its balance with Wells Fargo for deposit with

Box 20.1.   Financial stability as a global public good and policy attitudes[a]

We want to show that:

(1) financial stability is a *global public good* (GPG)
(2) it creates *externalities* that cannot be cured by the market or by devising market solutions
(3) in order to ensure financial stability, carefully studied *public mechanisms* should be developed.

Financial stability

Financial stability is a GPG since its positive effects spread across countries. This is easier to show if we speak, as with other GPGs such as health and the environment, of its opposite, financial instability – i.e. 'excessive' volatility not justified by currently available information – which is a *global public bad*. Financial instability creates *costs* – in terms of bankruptcy of both financial and non-financial firms, and the reduction of GDP and asset prices. All of these phenomena tend to snowball, spreading from one individual to another and across countries, given the extent of the economic ties – especially international capital movements – in the age of globalisation (see section 19.1).

Externalities

Some externalities can be remedied through the market, with no policy intervention. This is the case of *pecuniary externalities,* i.e. externalities that are reflected in market prices, such as congestion in large cities, which at least in part raises the cost of transportation, rents, etc.,[b] thereby imposing a limit to their creation since a market mechanism is at work.

In other cases, there is no self-regulating mechanism to restrict the creation of externalities but a market can be made to operate through *public intervention*. In the case of water pollution, for example, there is no pecuniary externality by itself, but a market can be created if the state establishes a property right either for the polluter or for downstream residents when a few persons are involved and transaction costs are thus low (see section 2.8).

In still other cases there is neither a pecuniary externality nor can a market be created by the state, since the external effects are so diffuse as to make it impossible or very expensive to identify those who create them and those who are damaged. This is the case of financial instability, which resembles that of air pollution more than it does water pollution.

There are cases where pecuniary externalities are created: this happens, for example, when a country is rated negatively because of the high level of its external borrowing. However, rating agencies have failed in a number of high-profile cases, such as when they did not issue adequate warnings before the South-East Asia crisis in 1997.

Other negative externalities arising from financial instability are not pecuniary. Let us take bank runs. These can be cured only partially through markets or by such measures as deposit insurance,[c] since financial markets are prone to failures caused by moral hazard, adverse selection and multiple equilibria.[d] Bank runs are a typical manifestation of *herd behaviour* (see section 20.2). In the case of international capital movements, a financial crisis in one country tends to prompt lenders to withdraw from countries in a 'similar' position: the financial crisis is thus exported from one country to another, thus giving rise to the restriction of the extent of markets that typically occurs with adverse selection. Self-fulfilling attacks on exchange rates are a well-documented instance of multiple equilibria in a number of cases, from the EMS crises of 1992–3 to those of Mexico, South-East Asia in the late 1990s and so on. For such attacks to succeed the existence of some 'weakness' (often not involving the 'fundamentals') is a necessary, but not sufficient, condition: not all situations of weakness evolve into crises and in some cases these do not involve countries with bad 'fundamentals'.

Public mechanisms

In order to ensure financial stability appropriate measures should be taken at the national as well as the international level.

At the national level, adequate *macroeconomic and structural policies* – ensuring price stability, fiscal discipline, fundamental equilibrium of the balance of payments, a proper and efficient policy process and well-designed institutions, distortion-reducing taxation, efficient labour markets and efficient and deep financial markets – should be undertaken. As to *capital flows*, some limitation along the lines of the Tobin tax (see chapters 12 and 14 and section 20.2) would be appropriate in view of its ability to limit herd behaviour and other sources of instability.

Measures to be taken by international institutions include instability prevention through surveillance of national policies and selective granting of aid.

Notes:
a   This box is largely drawn from Wyplosz (1999).
b   We ignore other effects of congestion, such as pollution, which do not have a similar impact on prices.
c   This solution can only be partial: deposit insurance can give rise to moral hazard in the conduct of the banking activity.
d   We deal at length with moral hazard and adverse selection elsewhere in this book. Financial markets are also prone to *multiple equilibria*, where a bad equilibrium can coexist with a good one, depending on expectations.

Barclays. This operation (or, alternatively, a giro transfer from IBM's account with Wells Fargo to its account with Barclays) does not give rise to a physical transfer of funds, as it simply involves making accounting entries in the appropriate accounts: debiting IBM and crediting Barclays Bank in Wells Fargo's accounts; debiting Wells Fargo and crediting IBM in Barclays' accounts. The latter can transfer access to the dollar balance with Wells Fargo to some other European bank, again without any material movement of funds, in order to earn an acceptable interest rate. The scope for creating further *interbank deposits* is practically unlimited if:

(a) there are no reserve requirements for the dollar deposits received by Barclays and other banks in Europe (hence **eurobanks**)
(b) the dollar deposits remain within the eurobank system.

The first condition is normally met, since many monetary authorities do not require banks to meet reserve obligations for foreign currency deposits. The second condition is met to a varying degree, which cannot be known *a priori*: the deposit creation process ends when a eurobank makes a loan to a customer who converts his credit with Wells Fargo into cash rather than redepositing it with another eurobank.

The size of the eurocurrency market can be measured with reference to *gross and net stocks*: gross stocks include interbank deposits, while net stocks exclude them, comprising only transactions between eurobanks and the sources or final beneficiaries of the funds outside the eurobank system itself.

What characterises the market is not the specific nature of the operations – which are no different from normal bank transactions – but rather the *absence of any regulation by the monetary authorities*. This reduces the cost of fund-raising and allows banks to offer higher deposit rates and lower lending rates, thus stimulating the formation and growth of markets. The **spread** between lending and deposit rates can be very small (1/8 per cent, 1/4 per cent) and still be profitable.

The eurocurrency markets are very sensitive to *economic policies* (and more generally, economic conditions), especially in the countries that issue the currency in which the deposits are denominated, and tend to reduce the effectiveness of the policies themselves. For example, a tight monetary policy in the United States or some other country will induce US operators to raise funds on the eurodollar market, thereby circumventing the monetary tightening; similarly, an expansionary policy in the United States or another country may be undermined by an outflow of funds from that country. In addition, all countries (especially in Europe) are exposed to the backlash of events in these markets, which can cause sudden large flows of funds connected with arbitrage and speculative activities, fuelled by even small interest rate differentials or expectations of exchange rate changes. On the other hand, on various occasions (e.g. during the oil crisis) the eurocurrency market has enabled some countries to finance large balance of payments deficits.

These markets therefore have both positive and negative effects that countries cannot ignore. Among the problems that await solution within the framework of a reform of the international monetary system is the adequate regulation of the eurocurrency market.

The eurocurrency market has been flanked by the development of a **eurobond** market, which involves transactions in bearer bonds denominated in currencies different from that of the country in which they are issued or marketed. This market is not a simple extension of the eurocurrency market to different maturities. In the eurocurrency market, it is the banks, which are the major operators in it, that bear the risk of default, whereas in the eurobond market – as with securities transactions of any sort – the risk is borne only by the lender (Giddy, 1983, p. 4).

20.2.2 *Speculative capital movements and currency crises*

The free movement of large amounts of capital clearly facilitates and amplifies the spread of currency and financial crises. All of the countries involved in recent foreign exchange crises had previously liberalised international capital movements. In fact, a study by the Federal Reserve Board demonstrates that the incidence of banking crises is highly correlated with the degree to which capital markets are liberalised (Kaminsky and Reinhart, 1996).

It should be noted that once the crises were under way, a number of countries reacted by reimposing capital controls, but these failed to work. The ineffectiveness of reintroducing restrictions does not, however, demonstrate that controls are useless. On the contrary, it suggests that countries should not liberalise capital movement prematurely. In conditions of information asymmetry, premature liberalisation can attract substantial flows of capital that, at the moment controls are reinstated, can rapidly move out of the country since the very reintroduction of restrictions signals the gravity of the crisis itself.

The problem of *controlling outward capital movements* is closely linked to that of *regulating inflows*. Currency crises cannot be prevented by regulating capital outflows only. If tackled from this direction (or from this direction alone), the problem appears intractable because of the signalling effects we mentioned. However, if regulation is shaped so as to slow and select capital *inflows*, the negative effects can be prevented or attenuated. As Tobin (1978) argues, short-term inflows of capital can be discouraged by, for example, imposing some form of tax or additional reserve requirement on short-term deposits of foreign capital, as Chile and Colombia did.

The most common argument in favour of liberalising capital movements appeals to the resulting efficiency gains (McKinnon, 1973; Levine, 1997; IMF, 2002). It is correctly pointed out that freeing capital movements can produce efficient outcomes that complement those resulting from the liberalisation of international trade. The benefits of *capital account liberalisation* include a more efficient allocation of savings and improved productivity (e.g. through technology transfer in the case of FDI), expanded opportunities for portfolio diversification, risk-sharing, deeper financial markets and a greater division of labour (IMF, 2002, p. 32). The benefits of capital movements in an intertemporal framework should be stressed. From this point of view, international capital mobility makes it possible to redirect the use of resources from 'undesirable' countries (for example, those with low growth rates, high inflation or balance of payments deficits) to virtuous countries with sound **fundamentals** (that is, strong growth, low inflation, balance of payments equilibrium excluding short-term capital).

However, the efficiency of free capital movements is open to criticism from a number of points of view, especially as regards short-term capital movements:

(1) First, as shown by Keynes (1936, chapter 12), under uncertainty speculators are not so much concerned with identifying the highest long-term yields (which would give rise to behaviour directed at achieving an efficient allocation of resources) as they are with assessing the *prevailing mood of the markets and its changes*. Speculators' gains or losses on an option or futures contract (see section 13.1) depend solely on their ability to predict the *market price* more or less accurately than other investors. If everyone behaves this way, it is difficult to argue that the market price has any connection with the underlying long-term profitability of the asset.[6]

(2) The enormous volume of international capital movements (relative to countries' limited foreign reserves and financing available from multilateral organisations), the speed of those movements and the emergence of '**herd behaviour**' (which occurs when capital providers mindlessly follow the behaviour of those they think are best informed (see Bikhchandani and Sharma, 2000)) increase the possibility of *false or self-fulfilling expectations* (see Krugman, 1998; Jeanne, 1999), with little or no relationship with *economic fundamentals*.

(3) With regard to *information asymmetry*, financial liberalisation reduces the profit margins of financial intermediaries by increasing competition, at least in the short term, prompting them to expand their activities in new areas that are less familiar (increasing the possibility of adverse selection) and riskier (moral hazard).

(4) The liberalisation of capital movements increases **volatility** (i.e. erratic variations in prices) and hence uncertainty in financial and foreign exchange markets. Greater volatility has encouraged investors to take short-term (and therefore less uncertain) positions. However, short-term positions react more readily to signals, news, contingent impressions and rumours, which can increase volatility even further.

(5) The excessive variability of exchange rates hinders international trade. Short-term capital movements can also generate **misalignments** between exchange rates. This refers to the situation where exchange rates are systematically higher or lower than the value that would tend to ensure 'fundamental' equilibrium[7] in the balance of payments, with consequent costs for the *real economy*.

---

[6] According to Keynes (1936) financial and foreign exchange markets work like '**beauty contests**' in which contestants are asked to choose, for example, the six prettiest faces from among a hundred photographs. However, the winner of the contest is not the person who chooses those that he or she feels are the most attractive, but rather the person who comes closest to the *average opinion* of the contestants. They thus make their decisions not on the basis of their own assessments, but rather by employing second-order (or higher) reasoning about the most common judgement of the others.

In financial and foreign exchange markets, professional investors do not have their own opinions but rather formulate their expectations on the basis of the expectations of others. However, if this approach is widespread, price developments are completely undetermined, since they are driven by 'beliefs' that may have no basis in the real economy.

[7] The *equilibrium exchange rate* can be defined in a number of ways. One possible definition is the exchange rate that ensures equilibrium in the balance of payments (net of speculative components) and the desired level of employment in the country involved.

(6) As regards the potential that international capital movements have to induce 'virtuous' behaviour and performance, it must be noted, for the reasons given above, that the financial markets tend to provoke more a violent reaction than that needed to adjust countries' economic positions, thereby *worsening those very situations and increasing their fragility.*

20.3   The role of international institutions in recent currency crises

The IMF intervened heavily to support the countries embroiled in the recent currency and financial crises, allocating hundreds of billions of dollars in assistance. In order to bolster its financial resources, it borrowed from some countries and increased country quotas. The IMF developed adjustment programmes for the crisis countries that required them to meet a range of commitments (in particular, restrictive budgetary and monetary measures; privatisation and liberalisation programmes, adoption of fixed exchange rates) in exchange for loans (the *conditionality*[8] of credit).

The behaviour of the international institutions, and above all that of the IMF, in the recent foreign exchange crises has been widely criticised on many fronts:

(1) The intervention of an *international lender of last resort*, which some consider the IMF to be, reduces market discipline and self-assessment skills, accentuating the moral hazard of the various economic agents involved, who are encouraged to undertake even riskier transactions in the belief that the Fund will step in to prevent insolvency. However, the possibility that IMF action might give rise to moral hazard is considerably reduced by two circumstances:

(a) Intervention does not eliminate all harm to the parties involved in a financial transaction; it may prevent default but does not erase the *negative impact on reputation* caused by the inappropriate behaviour that prompted the intervention in the first place.

(b) The emergency intervention of the IMF also imposes penalties on borrowers who avoid insolvency. In particular, the interest rates charged by the Fund are higher than normal market rates and, above all, the Fund normally does not fully cover the *debtor country's losses*. The injection of liquidity into the economy is intended solely to prevent the spread of financial crises, not to soften the 'therapeutic' effects of the crisis itself, as argued by De Bonis, Giustiniani and Gomel (1999).

(2) A second criticism concerns the *inadequacy of the financial assistance* provided by the IMF. Expanding the IMF's role as a lender of last resort has been advocated by many authors (see Fischer, 1999, the Meltzer report cited in section 16.5 and Goodhart and Illing, 2002). This position is symmetrical to that in point (1). However, rejecting the argument that the presence of a lender of last resort undermines the self-discipline of economic agents does not necessarily mean that the Fund

---

[8] On conditionality see J. Williamson (1983), Spraos (1996).

should increase its lending. Paradoxically, market reaction to IMF intervention has been more severe the greater the amount of financing provided. This reaction is again attributable to the fact that given the considerable information asymmetry in financial markets, the size of the IMF's intervention is interpreted as an indicator of the gravity of the crisis.

(3) A third problem concerns the fact that the *conditions imposed* by the IMF on borrowers when it provides liquidity aggravate the crisis in certain respects. One of these conditions is that countries must restrict aggregate demand, which is often required in order to facilitate the adjustment of goods movements (thereby reducing the size of the devaluation needed to restore balance). However, this can lead to recession and unemployment and, in the short term, may worsen the financial situation, reducing the quality of banks' portfolios and making *debt service* more difficult. Sensitive to the financial problems involved, the Fund has recently sought to emphasise reforms of the financial sector and the balance sheets of firms in its adjustment programmes, in an attempt to improve the response to economic developments.

(4) Another debatable aspect of the conditions imposed by the IMF concerns the *liberalisation of international capital movements*. We have already seen that the freedom of capital movements can have a negative impact on systemic stability. It would therefore be advisable for the IMF, in accordance with the provisions of its original Articles (now amended) to permit countries to restrict liberalisation to medium- and long-term capital flows and retain some form of control over short-term flows, which may have a more significant speculative component. The weaker the financial structures of the countries involved, the greater this faculty should be.

In accepting some of the criticism levelled against it, the Fund has recently drafted plans to:

(a) Ensure *greater transparency* of the conditions and decisions of the individual countries as well as the policies and operations of the IMF itself (in particular, the IMF's bilateral surveillance and supported programmes).

(b) Strengthen the *financial sector* of the countries involved, especially less-developed countries (LDCs), by improving financial legislation and supervision and working to achieve closer international coordination.

(c) Increase *preventive measures and response capability*. From the point of view of preventive measures, the desirability of liberalising long-term capital flows (in particular, FDI) ahead of short-term flows has been suggested; in addition, a new credit facility for preventive action has been introduced.[9] Concerning response capability, there is the need to increase the IMF's capacity to assess the *sustainability* of

---

[9] This is the Contingent Credit Line, created in 1999 to enhance incentives for sound policies and provide a better safety net for good performers. It offers precautionary short-term financing under a *stand-by arrangement* to help a member overcome its balance of payments need arising from a sudden and disruptive loss of market confidence due to contagion and largely generated by circumstances beyond the member's control. This facility, however, was not used until mid-2003, most likely because countries with balance of payments problems did not want to signal their weak policies (IMF, 2003, p. 24).

a country's debt, to state in clear terms the policy on access to the Fund resources for members facing capital account crises as well as the mechanism for sovereign debt restructuring.

(d) Review rules for *conditionality* by emphasising that this must be applied in a way that reinforces national ownership and should focus on policies critical to achieving the macroeconomic goals of Fund-supported programs (IMF, 2002).

20.4   The case for international coordination[10]

Following Cooper (1969), we define **international coordination** as a situation in which each country adjusts its policy instruments so as to achieve the objectives of the Rest of the World as well as its own. The need for coordination may arise when there is interdependence between the different economies. In this case the non-coordinated action of the various countries would produce suboptimal outcomes.

Economic interdependence between different economies is expressed through the globalisation of markets and production (see chapter 19). Thus, events in one country, including those induced by government action, have repercussions in others. These repercussions can be positive or negative and therefore constitute *externalities* similar to those we discussed in chapters 2 and 6 (*spillovers*):

(1) In some cases the concepts of external economies and diseconomies and of (*global*) *public goods* can be applied directly, as we saw in chapter 2: pollution, for example, or the spread of knowledge through different means of communication. Financing or providing global public goods is a much more complex problem than performing the same task for public goods at a national level. In fact, in the case of global public goods the (nation) state can itself be free rider, and there is no supranational public entity to which the role of financing and/or providing global public goods can be attributed.

External effects at the international level and global public goods could be tackled through international coordinated policy action, but this is not easy to achieve. A first type of difficulty in international coordination to foster the production of *global public goods* is exemplified by the events relative to the ratification of the Kyoto protocol for pollution control. In 2001 the new US administration refused to ratify the protocol signed by the previous administration, while other countries reduced their obligations. This sort of difficulty has to do with the distribution of benefits and costs in the production of the global public good and the number of countries interested. More on this can be found in box 20.2.

Another kind of difficulty concerns the possible *substitutability* between one policy objective (in this case, environmental protection) and other goals of public policy (e.g. income distribution) at a global level. This question is addressed in box 20.3.[11]

---

[10] *International coordination* poses many problems. For reasons of space, we must limit our discussion here. A minor problem is semantic – it is worth stressing that in most of the literature the terms 'coordination' and 'cooperation' are used interchangeably. We will adopt this usage here.

[11] For more on the internationalisation of the economy and environmental policy options, see Welfens (2001).

Box 20.2.   International cooperation to protect the environment

Why was it so easy to reduce the output of ozone-depleting substances? And why is it so difficult to control greenhouse gas (GHGs) emissions? In the mid-1970s some scientists predicted that production of chlorofluorocarbons (CFCs) could cause a 7 per cent depletion of the ozone layer. This, in turn, would cause physical problems such as skin cancer and reduce productivity in agriculture and fishing. Some countries were motivated to unilaterally restrict production of CFCs and promote an international agreement. International cooperation led to the Montreal protocol in 1987. This required the signatory countries to halve production and consumption of CFCs by 1999 and was later tightened, by increasing the number of controlled substances and fully phasing out CFCs. The signatories, which were initially only thirty, rose to 165 in 1998. The protocol was effectively implemented and a number of recent studies appear to indicate an improvement in the ozone layer.

In 1988 an Intergovernmental Panel on Climate Change was formed to assess the possibility of climate change, its potential impact and policy actions. The Panel's report calculated that emissions of long-lived gases like carbon dioxide should be reduced by more than 60 per cent just to stabilise their concentration at the current level. Most OECD countries unilaterally committed to reducing their carbon dioxide emissions, but only a few stuck to their undertakings. After various attempts at international coordination, a protocol was finally signed in 1997 in Kyoto requiring industrial countries and European economies in transition to reduce or set limits on their emissions within a specified term. The protocol requires the developed and transition countries to reduce their emissions of GHGs by an average of 5.2 per cent from their 1990 levels by 2012. For the European Union and many of the Eastern European countries now candidates to join the Union, the required reduction is even larger (8 per cent); the percentages for the United States (7 per cent) and for Japan, Canada, Poland and Hungary (6 per cent) are not quite as large but are still above average. The reduction for Russia, Ukraine and New Zealand is nil, while Iceland, Australia and Norway can even increase their emissions. The mechanisms for achieving these objectives include increasing energy efficiency and conducting research into developing process innovations that reduce GHG emissions. The agreements also envisage a system of *tradable emission rights*. A change in US policy after the new administration took office in 2001 placed the United States in a free rider role, as it refused to ratify the protocol, making achievement of its initial objectives more difficult for the other signatories: in order to take effect, the protocol must be ratified by countries responsible for generating at least 55 per cent of global emissions. The much-delayed entry into force of the protocol has finally been guaranteed by Russia's ratification, which came in October 2004.

In order to understand the different fates of the CFC initiative and Kyoto protocol, we need to consider the differences in the characteristics of the *global public*

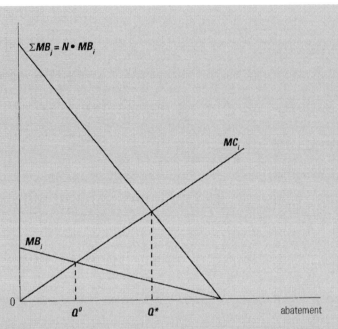

Figure 20B.1

goods (GPGs) involved in the two cases, independently of the impact (however significant) of the change in US policy on greenhouse gases.

First, the success of international cooperative initiatives depends in part on the number of countries involved in producing the GPG in question and, in addition, on the distribution of *benefits and costs of its production*. The characteristics of every public good, first and foremost non-rivalry in use, mean that it is to the advantage of individual players to engage in non-cooperative behaviour (that is, act as free riders). The result is a prisoners' dilemma situation (see section 2.10). In the non-cooperative solution, each country will produce GPG only in the amount for which the marginal cost and benefit are equal. In a cooperative solution, each country will equalise its marginal cost with the sum of the marginal benefits.

Assume we have *n* countries, each of which has a marginal cost for the production of the GPG equal to MC_i and a marginal benefit of MB_i. Figure 20B.1 indicates the various quantities of the public good produced in the cooperative solution (equal to $0Q_c$) and in the non-cooperative solution, $0Q_{nc}$. The larger the number of countries and the greater the symmetry of the positions of those countries (from the point of view of both costs and benefits), the more pronounced will be the free riding behaviour of each; in other words, the more the effective output of the public good will diverge from the optimal amount and the greater will be the difference between $0Q_c$ and $0Q_{nc}$. Conversely, if the number of countries producing the public good is relatively small – i.e. if the costs and benefits are concentrated in a small group of countries – each of them will find it advantageous to produce a quantity of the good closer to that which ensures allocative efficiency.

These characteristics of GPGs explain the different outcomes of international coordination in the two cases. Negotiations on CFCs were relatively straightforward and productive, as the number of countries involved in generating the environmental damage was small, replacement technologies were relatively inexpensive and the cost/benefit calculation (CBA) for protecting the ozone layer pointed to the clear benefits of both cooperative and unilateral action (USEPA 1988, cited by Barrett, 1999).

By contrast, the situation in the GHG case differed in important respects. First, the number of polluting countries was larger, which in itself reduced the chances of achieving an agreement unless some of these nations, for ethical or political reasons, were granted some sort of exemption. This eventually happened for the developing countries and emerging economies like China and Brazil, even though they were responsible for a significant amount of pollution. Moreover, the reduction of GHGs was expensive (in particular, the marginal cost increased rapidly) from the point of view of each country. The cost made it more difficult to achieve or maintain a balanced public budget (owing to government expenditure on pollution abatement: spending for subsidies to firms or direct expenditure on environmental innovation) and cut into the profits of private firms (the costs of regulation, taxation or the creation of pollution permits). This in turn eroded the competitiveness of the countries involved. For those who would have shouldered the lion's share of the burden of reducing emissions (partly owing to the exemptions granted to others), the cost might have been judged too high in relation to the more uncertain benefits it would generate.

International coordination in reducing GHGs was thus especially difficult due to the fact that some countries could, either immediately or subsequently, act as free riders. It was also a consequence of the absence of any *international authority* that (for global public goods) could mimic the role that national governments play in financing or supplying public goods at the domestic level. Without such an authority to internalise the positive effects of public goods, the task of achieving some sort of collectively beneficial outcome (in our case the financing or production of the public good) is left to international negotiations, which essentially simulate the market.

However, there are circumstances that facilitate international coordination. Sometimes, a relatively small number of countries can give an initial impulse to an agreement, to be joined subsequently by others.[a] This was the case with sulphur emissions, where an initial agreement among the Scandinavian countries was later extended to others (Musu, 2000). In other situations, the difficulty of coordinating environmental issues is reduced or eliminated if the countries involved do not focus solely on negotiations over emissions but also use other instruments (e.g. trade policy, foreign debt, development aid) to induce other countries to cooperate (Siniscalco, 1991).

Note:
a In fact, this also happened with the Kyoto protocol: some developing countries that had not approved the agreement initially later signed on, although as developing countries they were exempt from the restrictions imposed by the accord.
Source: The first part of this box draws extensively on S. Barrett, 'Montreal versus Kyoto, International Cooperation and the Global Environment', in Kaul, Grunberg and Stern (1999).

Box 20.3.   Complementarity or substitutability between protecting the environment and fighting hunger?

There are two facets to this issue: the first concerns the relationship between *environmental protection* and *food consumption*; the second regards that between *environmental protection* and *food production*. We address these in order.

A sound environment contributes to everyone's well-being in all circumstances. Nevertheless, the demand for environmental goods is highly elastic to income: poorer people or countries assign a lower value to the environment than others, even if they are fully aware of the negative consequences of pollution and other environmental damage. There are two reasons for this: first and foremost, the greatest *contingent* problem facing the poor is likely to be hunger; second, the fact that the environment is a (global) public good prompts free riding behaviour.

The preference expressed in many ways by developing countries for fighting hunger rather than protecting the environment is indicative that, *at least as things stand now*, the dominant concern is the *substitutability* (or trade-off) between – rather than complementarity of – protecting the environment and alleviating hunger. Many of these countries (sometimes under the influence of lobbies) have preferred deforestation to saving the environment. As noted above, this is partly due to the fact that the environment is a GPG. However, the revealed preferences of many inhabitants of developing nations who have migrated to the major cities in their own countries or to foreign countries with worse environmental conditions than in their region of origin clearly demonstrate the preference for food and other essential goods over the environment.

Instances of complementarity, *even in the short term*, between environmental protection and food consumption are few but deserve attention, since at least some tools in the fight against hunger require an appropriate environment to be effective. Powdered milk is a case in point: it cannot be used safely (because of the risk of intestinal infection) in areas without access to a supply of clean water. The availability of clean water is a problem for many developing countries for other reasons as well, given that it is essential for healthy and effective nutrition. Since in many countries, especially in Africa, 'food production is not only a source of food but also the main source of incomes for the majority of people facing food insecurity, it is impossible to understand the causes of . . . poverty and under-nutrition . . . unless we . . . [consider] factors responsible for the disappointing growth records of local food production' (Platteau, 1995, p. 448).

In addition to the substitutability of the preferences of many countries and people, there is also a major trade-off in agricultural production (FAO, 2000): increased agricultural output is achieved at the expense of environmental protection, such as when pollution-causing fertilisers are used to raise crop yields. The shorter the time horizon considered, the greater the trade-off between agricultural output and environmental protection. For example, using fertilisers in the short term does not produce the level of pollution that over time might reduce yields as a result of acid rain or contamination of the water table.

In some situations, however, environmental protection can complement agricultural production even in the short term: in certain cases the absence of environmental protection measures can have an adverse impact on the production of food in the span of a very few years. Sensitivity to environmental issues is a major feature of so-called sustainable agriculture (Pretty, 1995), which incorporates such complementarity between the environment and agriculture.

In some densely populated areas of Nepal, the effort to keep the soil fertile based on manure from cattle fed on forest products is threatened by deforestation.

The deforestation of the Amazon jungle through the use of itinerant agriculture (farmers cultivate land cleared of forest and then move on to other plots as soon as yields begin to drop significantly) destroys the organic matter contained in the soil, whereas cultivation that mimics the dense natural vegetation of the rain forest is sustainable in the long term.

The erosion of the soil on hillside fields poses a major threat to agricultural yields, with declines of between 8 per cent and 21 per cent in some areas between 1970 and 1995. More generally, environmentally sound farming techniques can have a positive impact on agricultural output and productivity (FAO, 2000).

In addition, *global warming*, which at least in the medium term may have a positive effect in developed countries at colder latitudes (Sandler, 1997), has a negative impact on many developing countries, especially in sub-Saharan Africa (SSA), and on temperate countries such as Argentina, Australia, Greece, Italy, New Zealand and Spain (Nordhaus, 1999; FAO, 2000).

Finally, many of the negative consequences of agriculture for the environment can be attenuated with an appropriate mix of policies and technological innovation (FAO, 2000; see also Pretty, 1995; Conway, 1997).

(2) In other cases, the effects are better represented in macroeconomic terms. In this section, we focus on macroeconomic effects.

Let us examine how these effects can emerge. Let there be two countries only, Germany and the United Kingdom. Let us assume that there are fixed exchange rates and the two economies are approximately the same size, there is only one policy instrument available (government expenditure) and there are flexible targets. More precisely, the governments seek to maximise a welfare function whose arguments are income and the balance of payments. For simplicity, we assume that welfare increases with both arguments of the function, at least within a certain range, as far as the balance of payments is concerned.

Given the policy followed by the United Kingdom, which we assume has government expenditure of G_{UK}^0, Germany adopts a fiscal policy that will cause income to grow but will not worsen (too much) the balance of payments.[12] Let G_D^0 be the level of this optimal policy; any more expansionary policy, *ceteris paribus*, will reduce German welfare. There is a similar situation in the United Kingdom: given the level of German government expenditure (e.g. G_D^0), the United Kingdom will set its own expenditure at a level, G_{UK}^0, that maximises its welfare function.

These are the optimal policies for each country *given* the non-expansionary behaviour of the other. However, for each country the optimal level of government expenditure would be higher if the other were to adopt a more expansionary policy: the United Kingdom could raise government expenditure above G_{UK}^0, thus increasing income without worsening its balance of payments if Germany were to adopt a more expansionary policy $(G_D > G_D^0)$. In this case, the increase in UK imports caused by the expansionary policy would be balanced by the rise in German imports (which represent UK exports) due to Germany's expansionary policy. The reason this does not occur is the *lack of coordination*: if each country fears that the other will not expand its economy enough, the outcome may be that neither expands.[13] Obviously, in the real world there are other facets to the problem. For example, asymmetry in the size of the economy or in the degree of international openness can make coordination difficult.

Thus in theory it is possible to increase the welfare of both countries, thereby achieving a Pareto superior outcome, by employing some form of *policy coordination*.

The **transmission** of the effects of one country's policy to another country may be negative rather than positive, as it was in our example. As there are negative external effects (such as actions that increase pollution) at an international level, there can be negative international macroeconomic effects of a 'beggar-thy-neighbour' sort. Examples of this are devaluations or other protectionist policies.[14]

---

[12] More precisely, we have an optimal policy when the marginal rate of substitution between the two objectives is equal to their marginal rate of 'transformation'.

[13] This is the classic prisoner's dilemma we discussed in section 2.9. In other cases, the situation may appear not as a prisoner's dilemma but as some other game (e.g. the stag-hunt game). This depicts a situation where *n* hunters surround a stag. If one defects to catch a passing rabbit, the stag will escape, with some gain for the defecting hunter and none for the others. If they all hunt for the stag, they will share it equally. Each hunter prefers 1*n* of a stag to one rabbit. According to Carraro (1989) this is an appropriate game to model international policy coordination.

[14] In some cases, as we pointed out in section 15.7, devaluation or protectionism, used together with other policy measures, may not constitute a 'beggar-thy-neighbour' policy.

Cooperation can also be beneficial when the two countries assign different weights to the various objectives. This is clearer if we consider the fact that coordination enables us to shift the efficiency frontier (i.e. the 'transformation' curve between two targets) outwards. We will return to this issue in section 20.5.

(3) An additional argument for policy coordination is to avoid a **race to the bottom** among governments that would hinder achievement of their shared objectives, to the detriment of all countries. This can occur in a wide variety of areas, such as environmental policy, competition policy, labour protection and taxation (see box 20.4).[15]

Box 20.4.   Globalisation and tax policy

As long as the volume of international trade and capital movements was limited, national tax authorities could set taxes without regard to the conflicting demands of authorities in other countries or the taxes applied in other jurisdictions. The 'principle of territoriality', which gives a state the right to tax all incomes and all activities in its territory, did not generate conflicts with other countries. Tax policies adopted abroad were of only marginal interest to domestic politicians since they did not affect the behaviour of a country's citizens.

In the age of globalisation, however, many domestic policies have an impact outside national borders, as we have seen in chapters 17 and 19. This has numerous implications for traditional national policies and institutions, which still largely reflect the environment and rationale of the closed economies that existed when such policies and institutions were first created. This box examines the repercussions of these developments for national tax policies.

In the current environment, many governments find themselves sharply constrained or, at the very least, highly influenced by the choices of other governments as taxation has had increasingly significant cross-border effects. This has created scope for some countries to exploit the new situation by bidding to attract a larger share of the world's tax base, thus exporting a bit of their tax burden. A few examples of the different types of taxes illustrate the key aspects of this phenomenon.

Sales taxes

A growing number of countries seek to attract foreign consumers to do a little shopping on their territory[a] by keeping excise and (above all) sales taxes low on expensive, easily transportable goods. This essentially *'exports' a part of a country's tax burden*, reducing the tax revenues of other countries while increasing

---

[15] In the area of taxation, countries with 'soft' policies are considered **tax havens**. Even the European Union has a number of them in its midst (Luxembourg, the Netherlands, Ireland). For more on EU efforts to eliminate harmful tax competition, see section 18.8. Problems associated with tax havens are discussed in box 20.4.

its own. Such initiatives are especially beneficial for small countries, which attract consumers from their larger neighbours.[b]

This development has inevitably reduced the ability of some countries to set taxes as they see fit. For example, when a Canadian province tried to raise cigarette taxes to discourage smoking, it was forced to backtrack because cigarette demand shifted across the border to the United States, where taxes, and hence prices, were lower.

Corporate income taxes

Like all taxpayers, multinationals (MNCs) try to *minimise their overall tax liability*. They can do so in a number of ways. The first is to locate production facilities in countries whose nominal tax rates are lower or which offer the most generous tax breaks. This explains why Ireland attracted so much foreign direct investment (FDI) in the 1980s and 1990s.

Both developed and developing countries have been generous in granting tax incentives to attract FDI. Here we give a very few examples out of the many such cases. In 1996, the chemical firm Dow received a subsidy of $3.4 million for every job created in Germany. In Alabama (USA) Honda Motor Co. received an incentive package in 2000 worth $158 million to help build a $400 million minivan assembly plant. Singapore has targeted incentives to encourage the expansion of multinationals in high technology industries by offering a ten-year tax holiday to 'pioneer firms' producing goods and services not currently produced in the country. Malaysia grants a similar exemption for five years. Bangladesh gives tax holidays and other incentives to export-oriented activities. China exempts foreign affiliates with contracts for operating periods of at least ten years from income tax for two years after making profit; grants a further 50 per cent reduction in their tax liability for the three subsequent years; and gives other sorts of reduction for technologically advanced foreign enterprises or localisation in special economic zones (see UNCTAD, 2002).

A second approach involves manipulating the costs of inputs imported from affiliates in other countries for tax purposes (*transfer pricing*). Such inputs, which account for a sizeable percentage of the value of the final product, are often manufactured by the foreign affiliate of an MNC for specific use in a given product. Thus, there is no genuine, objective, market-determined price that could serve as a reference for establishing the real cost of that input. Imputing the costs of licensing trademarks, parent company overheads, research and development (R&D) costs and loans between divisions of the same MNC create similar tax-manipulation opportunities. By setting transfer prices appropriately, MNCs can shift taxable profits to affiliates located in jurisdictions with low effective tax rates, moving them out of high-tax countries.[c]

The net effect of adjusting transfer prices is to reduce MNCs' total global tax liability and to change its distribution among the main countries. Some countries lose more tax revenues than others as a result of such behaviour, while others benefit.

The manipulation of transfer prices and the resulting erosion of tax revenues has become a fairly serious problem. Tax authorities in various countries have been forced to rely on estimates of such prices, thereby altering the nature of corporate income tax, distancing its actual connection with income.

Personal income taxes

With the rise of personal mobility, the spread of information technology (IT) and the increasing freedom to invest personal savings abroad, the total or comprehensive earnings of many people now include a large and growing amount of *income earned abroad*. It is likely that these people declare only a part (or none at all) of such income when they feel that the tax authorities in their country of residence will, realistically, not be able to discover it, especially if there is no exchange of information between tax authorities in different countries.

The existence of tax havens facilitates tax avoidance and evasion. In recent years, countries and territories that impose low or even no income taxes have proliferated in an attempt to attract individuals and firms to establish a tax residence through which they can channel their foreign earnings.

Finally, new financial instruments (derivatives and other exotic instruments) are creating complex problems for tax authorities and additional scope for tax competition. The questions facing tax authorities include:

- What transaction is to be taxed?
- Who is the taxpayer?
- When and to what extent must the income (or loss) be recognised?
- How much of profits must be declared in a given tax jurisdiction?

Tax authorities are finding it increasingly difficult to identify income, attribute it to a particular country or taxpayer and tax it. Taking a constructive attitude, one can follow different guidelines. Some authors (see Sinn, 1990; Tanzi and Bovenberg, 1990 and Tanzi, 1998) stress the negative impact deriving from increased tax competition on income redistribution and the allocation of resources between the different countries, asking for harmonisation of tax rates. Other authors (see, e.g. Frey and Eichenberger, 1996) argue that *tax competition* – as opposed to tax coordination – helps to reduce the 'political distortions' that arise from the tendency toward the overexpansion of the public sector stressed in the public choice literature and should thus be favoured. Existence of both pros and cons for tax harmonisation has led some (see, e.g. Zodrow, 2003) to suggest a cautious approach to tax coordination rather than sweeping attempts at full harmonisation of tax rates, especially of corporate tax rates. In particular, the efforts of international bodies should not focus on **harmful tax competition** (since any tax reduction causing capital outflows from other countries is perceived as harmful by these countries), but only on **unfair tax competition** (i.e. competition taking place under the form of bank secrecy laws, non-transparent or negotiable tax treatment, absence of information exchanges).

As a matter of fact, after efforts to limit tax competition and induce governments in **tax havens** to at least cooperate in cases of suspected tax evasion under the aegis of both the European Union (through its Code of Conduct on Business Taxation: see section 18.8) and the **Organisation for Economic Cooperation and Development**, OECD (see OECD, 1998),[d] a more reflexive attitude has emerged in recent years (see European Commission, 2001b).

Notes:
a   For example, airports are becoming enormous malls and major sales outlets sprout up in border areas.
b   This sort of competition is also common in federal states such as the United States and Brazil. A small country that can attract consumers from the rest of the world can easily offset the loss of tax revenues from its own citizens.
c   This is done by overstating costs and understating revenues of affiliates in high-tax jurisdictions and doing the opposite in low-tax jurisdictions. There is empirical evidence that US MNCs shift high profits to affiliates in countries with low effective taxation. (See US Department of Commerce, 1995). Obviously, much FDI derives from valid economic determinants, not just tax avoidance purposes.
d   This international organisation was established in 1961 and brings together thirty of the world's most advanced economies. The forerunner of the OECD was the Organisation for European Economic Cooperation (OEEC), which was established in 1948 to administer American and Canadian aid to Europe under the Marshall Plan for reconstruction after the Second World War. The OECD provides a forum for the discussion of policies aimed at promoting economic growth, free trade and foreign aid to less-developed countries (LDCs).
Source: Drawn mainly from Tanzi (2002), pp. 34–40.

As we discuss in section 20.5, international coordination normally improves achievement of a given objective *for the countries as a group*. However, it is not certain that *each country* will benefit from coordination nor, even if some benefit does accrue, that coordination is necessarily the best option, since defection from the agreement could generate a better result in the absence of retaliation on the part of the other countries.

In view of the foregoing, we can conclude that international coordination would be fostered by the presence of an effective system of *sanctions* for countries that try to act as free riders and of an adequate *compensation mechanism* for countries that have been harmed by their participation in a multilateral agreement.

Obviously, cooperation in this area requires dealing with the problem of safeguarding initial positions, especially for disadvantaged countries that might see their position worsen. In order to tackle this issue, international agreements often incorporate exceptions, delays, safeguard clauses and so on for the more vulnerable countries. However, the real problem is that these exceptions are often insufficient to allow less developed countries to emerge from their backward condition. Other measures that attack the roots of underdevelopment, which often exceed the capacity of individual backward countries, are essential.

The cases we have just examined concern a situation of **pure discretionary coordination** (the term was introduced by Schultze, 1988): the various countries decide on a case-by-case basis to internalise the externalities or benefit from macroeconomic interdependence and each country gains without losing anything. There are then cases of **discretionary coordination through compromise**, in which each country gains with reference to one objective but loses with respect to one or more other objectives, while still achieving a net gain.

Coordination can be implemented with **ad hoc concertation** (e.g. solution of trade disputes negotiated directly by the parties; temporary bilateral or multilateral agreements to stabilise exchange rates in flexible regimes), or through the adoption of rules that give rise to **institutionalised cooperation** (e.g. settlement of trade disputes among WTO members through its Dispute Settlement Body (DSB); an agreement to maintain fixed exchange rates, perhaps with the help of ad hoc institutions such as the IMF).

There are reasons for preferring institutionalised cooperation to ad hoc solutions. For example, the latter is more vulnerable to pressure from various interest groups. The need to repeat ad hoc negotiations before each concerted action also makes this approach inefficient, all the more so if there are problems of *political instability* in the negotiating countries, with a related turnover of negotiators.

On the other hand, an awareness of the difficulty of renegotiating rules established within the framework of institutionalised cooperation (rules that in theory should be complied with for an indefinite, or at least lengthy, period) may accentuate the difficulties of this sort of coordination. In addition, ad hoc (and hence discretionary) intervention may be required whenever the system has to cope with events that are not provided for in the rules of institutionalised cooperation or specific circumstances force policymakers to take different action than that contemplated by those rules.[16] Finally, such rules require regular review, which cannot be ignored simply to avoid slow and difficult negotiations. Without such revision, the discretion and flexibility needed to adapt to the evolution of the historical context would be provided by the technocrats of the institutions themselves, which could produce distortions.[17]

In general, the effectiveness of international cooperation is ensured by rules and public bodies that cover the global space in which private institutions (firms, markets) now operate. This could be done in two different ways. A first route is by establishing *world government*, or at least *regional (supranational) public authorities*, such as the European Union, that can remedy the efficiency or equity failures of the private sector.

---

[16] Institutional cooperation often provides for exceptions – or **safeguard clauses** – to the normal rules. For example, article 59 (formerly 73) of the Treaty of Rome establishing the (then) European Economic Community (EEC), which is still in force, allows a member state to adopt discretionary protectionist measures whenever capital movements jeopardise the operation of its capital markets.

[17] An example of such distortions is perhaps the decision to allow access to IMF resources for deficits caused by capital outflows. Access was first denied and then granted by the Fund bureaucrats without any change in the Fund's Articles of Agreement, with significant practical consequences.

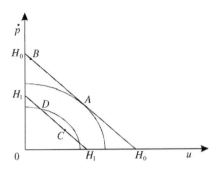

Figure 20.1

The difficulties of political representation, especially at the world level, are enormous, but the gains would be of a similar order of magnitude. A second – more modest, but also more feasible – way of ensuring global governance is by strengthening international rules and boosting existing international organisations or founding new ones in fields such as competition legislation or labour protection and movements.[18]

20.5   International coordination in formal terms

In this section we analyse problems of macroeconomic coordination (those under point (2) in section 20.4), which differ depending on whether targets are fixed or flexible. Let us first consider *fixed targets*. We know that a country, regardless of international coordination, can achieve any set of fixed targets as long as there are at least as many instruments as targets and as long as the targets are feasible (i.e. are within the set bounded by the 'transformation' curve). International coordination is beneficial simply because the frontier of possible targets (the 'transformation' curve) is shifted outwards (if the targets are 'goods') or inwards (if they are 'bads') for each country. This makes it possible to improve the attainable level of at least one of the two targets, leaving the other unchanged; alternatively, in the case of flexible targets, it will be possible to move to a higher indifference curve.

Take the case of the Phillips curve (e.g. for the United States), which we assume can be drawn like $H_0 H_0$ in figure 20.1. Let A be the initial position of the United States, which corresponds, by hypothesis, to the values of the targets that maximise its welfare. An expansionary policy would move the US *along* the curve to B, which is suboptimal. On closer examination, however, we see that the *position* of this curve depends on the level of demand in the Rest of the World: if foreign demand were higher, under flexible exchange rates the curve would shift downwards to, say, $H_1 H_1$.[19] The increase in foreign demand could worsen the terms of trade of the Rest of the

---

[18] The need for various types of international governance structures is stressed by De Martino (2000), Koenig-Archibugi (2003) and Panić (2003).
[19] For simplicity, we assume that the magnitude of the expansion is given. For brevity, we do not examine the change in the transformation curve under fixed exchange rates.

Table 20.1 *The benefits of cooperation in a 'prisoner's dilemma' setting*

		Rest of the World	
		Expand	Don't expand
United States	Expand	(D, D′)	(B, C′)
	Don't expand	(C, B′)	(A, A′)

World (through depreciation of the exchange rate) while improving those of the United States. Since the consumption basket of workers also includes foreign goods, which would become less expensive, workers could be satisfied with a smaller nominal wage increase for each given level of unemployment, since their real wages would increase by the same amount that they would have done if the Rest of the World had not adopted expansionary policies.

With the new Phillips curve H_1H_1 resulting from the expansion of demand abroad, it will be possible, for example, to reach C (if the United States does not expand) or D (if it does). Both are Pareto superior to A (remember that since we are dealing with 'bads', curves closer to the origin ensure greater welfare). Note that this is the case whatever the shape of the indifference curves (apart from their slope, which must be negative), which reflects the weights assigned to the two targets. The basic idea is that easing the constraint, which is reflected in the lowering of the Phillips curve, can benefit the country in any case.

The problem of coordination can be formulated in terms of *game theory*. If each country acts in a non-cooperative fashion, we may be faced with a prisoner's dilemma situation. If, instead, the game is cooperative, both countries may be able to achieve a better outcome. Let us see why. First assume that all of the considerations we have made with regard to the United States apply to the Rest of the World as well: the position of the latter can be plotted in exactly the same way as that of the United States in figure 20.1. In order to distinguish the two positions, the points referring to the Rest of the World will be marked with primes. Thus, A' will be the initial position of the Rest of the World if both it and the United States adopt restrictive policies. B' is the Rest of the World's position if it expands while the United States maintains its restrictive stance. C' is the position of the Rest of the World if it does not expand and the United States does, while D' denotes the Rest of the World's position if both adopt expansionary policies. The outcomes of the different possible combinations are given in table 20.1.

As we can see from figure 20.1, the preference ordering of the various positions for the United States is: C, D, A, B, where C provides the highest welfare and the other positions offer decreasing levels of satisfaction. Similarly for the Rest of the World.

Game theory shows that in a non-repeated game the non-cooperative equilibrium is (A, A′), which is suboptimal.[20] One of the ways to reach the efficient solution is to repeat the game: if the game is repeated an infinite number of times, it is possible that a Pareto superior outcome ((D, D′) in our example) will be reached. The repetitive nature of the relationship between the two countries may induce each of them to adopt a cooperative attitude and, therefore, build a reputation as being cooperative and as being willing to punish non-cooperative behaviour in others, even when this is not beneficial in the short run.[21] This would therefore be a form of cooperation that emerges implicitly from the unilateral actions of the various countries. However, bear in mind that the benefits of such cooperative behaviour decrease as the number of countries increases: a small country may have a strong incentive to adopt a non-cooperative stance (e.g. not expanding) that would enable it to achieve C, which is superior to D.

Introducing time and the related problems of time consistency may make the outcome of cooperation negative. Rogoff (1985),[22] for example, considers a situation in which domestic wages in each country depend on the expected price level. Without cooperation between monetary authorities, each will adopt restrictive policies to avoid the formation of inflationary expectations and higher wage setting stimulated by the possibility of a depreciation (or devaluation). If the various central banks cooperate, they can take an expansionary stance without fear of causing a depreciation, since all would expand at the same time. However, stronger demand would have inflationary effects. Fearing such effects, workers would increase their wage demands, thus fuelling inflation. The solution would be for the central banks to commit themselves to not expanding the money supply excessively once wages had been set. In the setting indicated, this is the only form of cooperation that will produce an outcome superior to that of independent policies. A set of more or less explicit assumptions are crucial to such a result. For example, policymakers are assumed to ignore inflationary expectations created among workers when they cooperate to expand their economies. This is a special case of a more general situation: cooperative solutions can be inferior if some policymakers do not know the 'true' model of the economy (Frankel and Rockett, 1986).

The uncertainty of the advantages of cooperation (as well as other economic policy measures in different contexts) underscores the need for extreme care in modelling any given problem: since different models can yield different conclusions, the results can be considered 'robust' only when they are supported by a wide range of models, as they do not change in relation to changes in the underlying hypotheses. Moreover, an effort must be made to capture the aspects of reality felt to be most significant, avoiding ad hoc hypotheses adopted merely for the sake of analytical expediency.

---

[20] A **'cooperative' game** is one in which the players can make *binding commitments*. In such games, the coordination of strategies is thus supported by the possibility of enforcement guaranteed by appropriate institutions.

[21] The classic example is a trade war by means of tariff reprisals.

[22] For a critique, see Carraro and Giavazzi (1991). The analysis employs game theory.

20.6   International coordination (multilateralism) and regionalism

While international global coordination (*multilateralism*) is generally beneficial, we must also assess the repercussions of the free trade areas (FTAs) and other regional integration initiatives that have emerged since the late 1980s (*regionalism*). In the 1990s, the process of European economic union accelerated, reaching out to encompass all the other countries on the continent and extending its scope to an ever-wider range of objectives beyond its initial aim of creating a common market (see chapter 18). Similarly, a free trade area (the North American Free Trade Area, NAFTA) is being consolidated in North America, which should lead to the abolition of tariff barriers and NTBs by 2009, while South America's Mercosur (between Argentina, Brazil, Paraguay and Uruguay) appears to being having more success than previous attempts at establishing a free trade area on that continent (see Estevadeordal, Goto and Saez, 2001). In April 2001, it was decided to work towards the formation of a Free Trade Area of the Americas (FTAA) that would include thirty-four countries on the two American continents; the area is scheduled to start in 2005.[23] Asia and Africa are also developing a number of regional integration initiatives (Asian Free Trade Area, Association of South-east Asia Nations; Communauté Economique des Etats de l'Afrique Central; Economic Community of West African States).

In parallel with the development of regional public institutions, there has been a significant increase in regional trade in goods and, to some extent, direct foreign investment (FDI). These flows – especially goods movements – have generally grown at a much faster pace within regional groupings than at the world level, thereby deepening regional integration even further (see UNCTAD, 1994).

The doubts raised about the real benefits of global coordination are even more relevant at the regional level. It has long been known that imposing a common external tariff (CET) at the regional level can give rise to problems associated with the *diversion of external trade flows*. Similar problems are also created by any technical standards, regulations and so on adopted with a regional area. The development of three large opposing regional blocs (Europe, America and Asia) can therefore be a source of concern. The likelihood that common tariffs, technical standards or regulations will be wielded for protectionist purposes is higher at the regional level, where preferential treatment is accorded to members, than at the non-discriminatory level of multilateral institutions such as the WTO. Some have also noted the slower pace of regionalism compared with the development of specialised global institutions (note that the creation of a Single European market took almost four decades).

Conversely, it has been argued that attempts to establish *regional harmonisation and aggregation initiatives* can be instrumental to the progressive globalisation of public institutions – i.e. a step forward in strengthening multilateral institutions. For example, negotiations on reducing barriers to the movement of goods, people and capital are easier when a smaller number of countries is involved. However, this holds only when

[23] The draft Agreements prepared for the various meetings are available on the official FTAA website (http://www.ftaa-alca.org).

the desire of regional institutions to discriminate against the outside world is weak or non-existent. Some scholars have noted that regional groupings can successfully help satisfy the demand for *global public goods* (for example, common standards, a single currency or monetary stability accords, joint measures to sustain economic activity, environmental protection) that has arisen with globalisation. Ultimately, multilateralism can be viewed as the limit towards which we can progress through successive enlargements of regional unions. Furthermore, regional integration is deeper, going beyond simple trade liberalisation and other purely economic issues.[24]

The arguments for and against regional integration all have a logical foundation. However, the practical import of each depends on historical processes and social and political aspects that go beyond the scope of this book.

20.7 Summary

1 There have been several *currency crises* after those caused by the rise in the prices of raw materials in the 1970s. The most recent hit the South-East Asian economies and Argentina. The crisis in South-East Asia was to a large extent caused by the liberalisation of capital movements. The Argentine crisis was a consequence of the strict pegging of the local currency to the dollar.

2 The causes of the crises were numerous. However, an especially prominent role was played by the *freedom of capital movements*, which are channelled through unregulated markets such as the eurocurrency markets. The operation of financial and foreign exchange markets can be characterised as a 'beauty contest' and for various reasons does not guarantee an efficient allocation of resources.

3 The role of *international organisations* in the crises has been the subject of heated debate. Some have argued that acting as lender of last resort diminishes market discipline and capacity for self-assessment, thus creating fertile ground for moral hazard. Conversely, others complain that the International Monetary Fund (IMF) does not have sufficient financial resources. Others have criticised the conditions imposed by the IMF on the beneficiaries of its financial assistance.

4 *International coordination* requires each country to adjust its policy instruments to achieve not only its own objectives but also those of the Rest of the World. The need for coordination derives from interdependence between economies and the possibility of achieving Pareto superior results.

5 Game theory shows cases in which international coordination (which can be represented in terms of a *cooperative game*) is beneficial or detrimental.

6 The process of *regional integration* accelerated sharply in the 1990s. It can be viewed either as a step towards multilateralism, or as antithetical to the development of coordination at the global level.

---

[24] A more detailed examination of multilateralism and regionalism is available in Winters (1999).

Bibliography

The date of the first edition of a work is usually quoted for works published before 1939; however, page references are to the most recent edition indicated.

Acocella, N. (1975). *Imprese multinazionali e investimenti diretti*, Milan: Giuffrè

(1992a). 'The Multinational Firm and the Theory of Industrial Organization', in A. Del Monte (ed.), *Recent Approaches to the Theory of Industrial Organization*, London: Macmillan

(1992b). 'Trade and Direct Investment within the EC: The Impact of Strategic Considerations', in J. Cantwell (ed.), *Multinational Investment in Modern Europe*, Cheltenham: Edward Elgar

(1998). *The Foundations of Economic Policy. Values and Techniques*, Cambridge: Cambridge University Press

(ed.) (1999). *Le istituzioni fra mercato e stato*, Rome: Carocci

Acocella, N. and G. Ciccarone (1994). 'Equilibrium Stagnation and Stagflation in a Policy Game', Dipartimento di Economia Pubblica, Università di Roma 'La Sapienza', Working Paper 1, July

Acocella, N. and G. Ciccarone (1995). 'Moderazione salariale e "scambio politico": un'analisi microfondata', *Rivista Italiana di Economia*, 0: 111–38

(1997). 'Trade Unions, Nonneutrality and Stagflation', *Public Choice*, 91: 161–78

Acocella, N. and G. Di Bartolomeo (2001). 'Robustness and Feasibility of Corporatism', Dipartimento di Economia Pubblica, Università di Roma 'La Sapienza', Working Paper, 44, July

(2003). 'Wage and Public Expenditure Setting in a Monetary Union', *Zagreb International Review of Economics and Business*, 6: 1–16

(2004). 'Non-Neutrality of Monetary Policy in Policy Games', *European Journal of Political Economy*, 20: 695–707

Aghion, P., E. Caroli and C. Garcìa-Peñalosa (1999). 'Inequality and Economic Growth: The Perspective of the New Growth Theories', *Journal of Economic Literature*, 37: 1615–60

Akerlof, G. (1970). 'The Market for Lemons, Uncertainty and the Market Mechanism', *Quarterly Journal of Economics*, 84: 488–500

Alchian, A. (1950). 'Uncertainty, Evolution and Economic Theory', *Journal of Political Economy*, 68: 211–21

(1987). 'Property Rights', in J. Eatwell, M. Milgate and P. Newman (eds.), *The New Palgrave. A Dictionary of Economics*, 3, London: Macmillan

Alesina, A. (1987). 'Macroeconomic Policy in a Two-Party System as a Repeated Game', *Quarterly Journal of Economics*, 102: 651–678; reprinted in J. Persson and G. Tabellini (eds.), *Monetary and Fiscal Policies*, 2, Cambridge, MA: MIT Press, 1994

Alesina, A. and G. Tabellini (1990). 'A Positive Theory of Fiscal Deficits and Government Debt', *Review of Economic Studies*, 57: 403–14

Alesina, A., G. D. Cohen and N. Roubini (1992). 'Macroeconomic Policy and Elections in OECD Democracies', *Economics and Politics*, 4: 1–30

Alt, J. E. (1991). 'Leaning into the Wind or Ducking out of the Storm: US Monetary Policy in the 1980s', in A. Alesina and G. Carliner (eds.), *Politics and Economics in the '80s*, Chicago: University of Chicago Press

Alt, J. E. and K. A. Chrystal (1983). *Political Economics*, Brighton: Wheatsheaf Books

Amoroso, B. (1996). *Della globalizzazione*, Barletta: Ed. La Meridiana

Aoki, M. and M. Canzoneri (1979). 'Sufficient Conditions for Control of Target Variables and Assignment of Instruments in Dynamic Macroeconomic Models', *International Economic Review*, 20: 605–16

Aoki, M. and R. Dore (eds.) (1994). *The Japanese Firm: The Sources of Competitive Strength*, Oxford and New York: Oxford University Press

Ardeni, P. G. and B. Wright (1992). 'The Prebisch–Singer Hypothesis: A Reappraisal Independent of Stationary Hypothesis', *Economic Journal*, 102: 803–12

Argy, V. (1988). 'A Post-War History of the Rules versus Discretion Debate', *Banca Nazionale del Lavoro Quarterly Review*, 165: 147–77

Arrow, K. J. (1962). 'The Economic Implications of Learning by Doing', *Review of Economic Studies*, 29: 155–73

Arrow, K. J. and G. Debreu (1954). 'Existence of an Equilibrium for a Competitive Economy', *Econometrica*, 22: 265–90

Arrow, K. J. and F. Hahn (1971). *General Competitive Analysis*, Edinburgh: Oliver & Boyd

Artis, M. J. and M. Buti (2000). 'Close-to-Balance or in Surplus': A Policy Maker's Guide to the Implementation of the Stability and Growth Pact', *Journal of Common Market Studies*, 38: 563–92

Atkinson, A. B. (1970). 'On the Measurement of Inequality', *Journal of Economic Theory*, 2: 244–63

(1993). 'Conclusions', in A B. Atkinson and G. V. Morgensen (eds.), *Welfare and Work Incentives: A North European Perspective*, Oxford: Clarendon Press

(1995). 'The Welfare State and Economic Performance', *National Tax Journal*, 48: 171–98

(2003). 'Income Inequality in OECD Countries: Data and Explanations', CESifo Working Paper, 881

Auerbach, A. J. (1988). *Corporate Takeovers: Causes and Consequences*, National Bureau of Economic Research, Chicago: University of Chicago Press

Auerbach, A. J. and M. Feldstein (eds.) (1987). *Handbook of Public Economics*, Amsterdam: North-Holland

Autorità garante della concorrenza e del mercato (2002). *Relazione annuale sull'attività svolta*, Rome: Istituto Poligrafico e Zecca dello Stato (http://www.agcm.it)

Averch, H. and L. Johnson (1962). 'Behaviour of the Firm Under Regulatory Constraint', *American Economic Review*, 52: 1052–69

Azariadis, C. (1975). 'Implicit Contracts and Underemployment Equilibria', *Journal of Political Economy*, 83: 1183–1202

Baily, M. N. (1974). 'Wages and Employment under Uncertain Demand', *Review of Economic Studies*, 41: 37–50

Bairoch, P. (1993). *Economics and World History: Myths and Paradoxes*, Chicago: University of Chicago Press

Balassone, F. and D. Franco (2001). *EMU Fiscal Rules: A New Answer to an Old Question?*, ECSPC–CIDEI meeting, May

Balassone, F. and D. Monacelli (2000). 'EMU Fiscal Rules: Is there a Gap?', Banca d'Italia, *Temi di discussione del Servizio Studi*, 375, July

Baldassarri, M., L. Paganetto and E. S. Phelps (eds.) (1996). *Equity, Efficiency and Growth; The Future of The Welfare State*, London: Macmillan

Baldwin, R. (1988). 'Hysteresis in Import Prices: The Beachhead Effect', *American Economic Review*, 78: 773–85

Banca d'Italia, (1998). *Relazione annuale del governatore all'assemblea dei partecipanti*, Rome

Bank for International Settlements (BIS) (1983). *53rd Annual Report*, Basle: Bank for International Settlements

  (1992). *62nd Annual Report*, Basle: Bank for International Settlements

  (1999). *Annual Report*, Basle: Bank for International Settlements

  (2001). *The New Basle Capital Accord*, Basle, 16 January, http://www.bis.org

Barca, F. (1994). *Imprese in cerca di padrone. Proprietà e controllo nel capitalismo italiano*, Bari: Laterza

  (1997). 'Le politiche del governo societario', in A. Ninni and F. Silva (eds.), *La politica industriale*, Bari: Laterza

Baron, D. P. and T. D. Besanko (1984). 'Regulation, Asymmetric Information and Auditing', *Rand Journal of Economics*, 15: 447–70

Barr, N. (1992). 'Economic Theory and the Welfare State: A Survey and Interpretation', *Journal of Economic Literature*, 30: 741–803

  (1993). *The Economics of the Welfare State*, Stanford: Stanford University Press, 1st edn., 1987

  (2001). *The Welfare State as a Piggy Bank. Information, Risk, Uncertainty and the Role of the State*, Oxford: Oxford University Press

Barrett, S. (1999). 'Montreal versus Kyoto. International Cooperation and the Global Environment', in I. Kaul, I. Grunberg and M. A. Stern, *Global Public Goods: International Co-operation in the 21st Century*, Oxford: Oxford University Press

Barro, R. (1974). 'Are Government Bonds Net Wealth?', *Journal of Political Economy*, 82: 1095–1118

  (1989). 'The Ricardian Approach to Fiscal Policy', in R. Barro (ed.), *Modern Business Cycle Theory*, Cambridge, MA: Harvard University Press

Barro, R. J. and D. Gordon (1983). 'Rules, Discretion and Reputation in a Model of Monetary Policy', *Journal of Monetary Economics*, 12: 101–121; reprinted in J. Persson and G. Tabellini (eds.), *Monetary and Fiscal Policies*, 1, Cambridge, MA: MIT Press, 1994

Barro, R. J. and H. I. Grossman (1971). 'A General Disequilibrium Model of Income and Employment', *American Economic Review*, 61: 82–93

Baumol, W. J. (1986). *Superfairness*, Cambridge, MA: MIT Press

Baumol, W. J., J. Panzar and R. D. Willig (1982). *Contestable Markets and the Theory of Industry Structure*, New York: Harcourt Brace Jovanovich

Baumol, W. J. and W. E. Oates (1975). *The Theory of Environmental Protection*, Englewood Cliffs: Prentice-Hall

Bénabou, R. (1996). 'Inequality and Growth', NBER Working Paper, 5583

Bénassy, J. P. (1992). *The Economics of Market Disequilibrium*, New York: Academic Press

Bentivogli, C. and S. Trento (1995). *Economia e politica della concorrenza,* Rome: La Nuova Italia Scientifica

Berger, S. and R. Dore (eds.) (1996). *National Diversity and Global Capitalism*, Ithaca: Cornell University Press

Bergstrom, T. (1971). 'On the Existence and Optimality of Competitive Equilibrium for a Slave Economy', *Review of Economic Studies*, 38: 23–36

Bernanke, B. and F. Mishkin (1992). 'Central Bank Behaviour and the Strategy of Monetary Policy: Observations from Six Industrialized Countries', in O. J. Blanchard, S. Fischer (eds.), *NBER Macroeconomics Annual 1992*, Cambridge, MA: MIT Press

Beveridge, W. (1942). *Social Insurance and Allied Services*, Cmnd 6404, London: HMSO

Bianchi, P. (1988). *Politiche della concorrenza e monopolizzazione*, in P. Bianchi (ed.), *Antitrust e gruppi industriali*, Bologna: Il Mulino

  (1999). *Le politiche industriali dell'Unione europea*, 2nd edn., Bologna: Il Mulino

Bikhchandani, S. and S. Sharma (2000). 'Herd Behaviour in Financial Markets', *IMF Staff Papers*, 47: 279–310

Bird, E. J. (2001). 'Does the Welfare State Induce Risk-Taking?', *Journal of Public Economics*, 80: 357–83

Bishop, M. and J. Kay (1993). *European Mergers and Merger Policy*, Oxford: Oxford University Press

Blackorby, C. and D. Donaldson (1988). 'Cash versus Kind, Self-Selection and Efficient Transfers', *American Economic Review*, 78: 691–700

Blair, M. M. (1995). *Ownership and Control: Rethinking Corporate Governance for the Twenty-First Century*, Washington, DC: The Brookings Institution

Blanchard, O. J. and N. Kiyotaki (1987). 'Monopolistic Competition and the Effects of Aggregate Demand', *American Economic Review*, 77: 647–66

Blanchard, O. J. and L. Summers (1986). 'Hysteresis and the European Employment Problem', *NBER Macroeconomic Annual*, in Stanley Fischer (ed.), vol. 1, Fall, Cambridge, MA: MIT Press: 15–78

Blank, R. M. (2002). Can Equity and Efficiency Complement Each Other?, NBER Working Paper, 8820, March

Blinder, A. S. and R. M. Solow (1973). 'Does Fiscal Policy Matter?', *Journal of Public Economics*, 2: 319–37

Boadway, R. W. and N. Bruce (1984). *Welfare Economics*, Oxford: Blackwell

Boiteux, M. (1956). 'Sur la Gestion des Monopoles Publics Astreints à l'Equilibre Budgètaire', *Econometrica*, 24: 22–40

Bolkestein Report (2001). *Company Taxation in the Internal Market*, COM (2001), 582 final, Brussels

Bordo, M. and A. Schwartz (1984). *A Retrospective on the Classical Gold Standard, 1821–1931*, Chicago: University of Chicago Press

Borrás, S. (2003). *The Innovation Policy of the European Union*, Cheltenham: Edward Elgar

Bös, D. (1989). 'Comments', in J. E. Stiglitz, *The Economic Role of the State*, Oxford: Blackwell (1991). *Privatization. A Theoretical Treatment*, Oxford: Clarendon Press

Boubakri, N. and J. C. Cosset (1998). 'The Financial and Operating Performance of Newly Privatised Firms. Evidence from Developing Countries', *Journal of Finance*, 53: 1081–1110

Boughton, J. M. (2001). *Silent Revolution: The International Monetary Fund, 1979–89*, Washington, DC: IMF

Bourguignon, F. and C. Morrisson (2002). 'Inequality among World Citizens: 1820–1992', *American Economic Review*, 92: 727–44

Bowles, S. (1985). 'The Production Process in a Competitive Economy: Walrasian, Neo-Hobbesian, and Marxian Models', *American Economic Review*, 75: 16–36

Brandolini, A. and N. Rossi (1997). *Income Distribution and Growth in Industrial Countries*, in V. Tanzi and K. Cho (eds.), *Income Distribution and High-Quality Growth*, Cambridge, MA: MIT Press

Brandolini, A., E. Granaglia and S. Scicchitano (2001). *Diritti di cittadinanza: l'assistenza sociale*, in L. Barca and M. Franzini (2001), *La cittadinanza difficile. Diritti e welfare*, Florence: Il Ponte

Bresciani Turroni, C. (1937). *The Economics of Inflation*, London: Allen & Unwin (1st Italian edn., 1931)

Breuss, F., S. Griller and E. Vranes (2003). *The Banana Dispute: An Economic and Legal Analysis*, Berlin and Heidelberg: Springer-Verlag

Brosnan, P. (2003). 'The Minimum Wage in a Global Context', in J. Michie (ed.), *The Handbook of Globalisation*, Cheltenham: Edward Elgar

Brusco, S. (1986). 'Small Firms and Industrial Districts: The Experience of Italy', in D. Keeble and E. Wever (eds.), *New Firms and Regional Development*, London: Croom Helm

Buchanan, J. M. (1965). 'An Economic Theory of Clubs', *Economica*, 32: 1–14

Buchanan, J. M. and G. Tullock (1962). *The Calculus of Consent: Logical Foundations of Constitutional Democracy*, Ann Arbor: University of Michigan Press

Buiter, W. H. (1980). 'The Macroeconomics of Dr. Pangloss. A Critical Survey of the New Classical Macroeconomics', *Economic Journal*, 90: 34–50

(1981). 'The Superiority of Contingent Rules over Fixed Rules in Models with Rational Expectations', *Economic Journal*, 91: 647–70; reprinted in W. H. Buiter, *Macroeconomic Theory and Stabilization Policy*, Manchester: Manchester University Press, 1989

Burrell, S. and M. Stutchbury (1994). *Australia Rebuilds: The Recovery we had to have*, Sydney: Financial Review Library

Burtless, G. and T. M. Smeeding (2001). *The Level, Trend, and Composition of Poverty*, in S. H. Danzinger and R. H. Haveman (eds.), *Understanding Poverty*, Cambridge, MA: Harvard University Press

Buti, M. and A. Sapir (eds.) (1998). *Economic Policy in the EMU. A Study by the European Commission Services*, Oxford: Oxford University Press

Caffè, F. (1948). 'La politica delle priorità e il pensiero degli economisti inglesi', *Critica Economica*, 5

(1966). *Politica economica: sistematica e tecniche di analisi*, 1. Turin: Boringhieri

(1990). *Lezioni di politica economica*, 5th edn. (1st edn., 1978), Turin: Boringhieri

Cagan, P. (1956). 'The Monetary Dynamics of Hyperinflation', in M. Friedman (ed.), *Studies in the Quantity Theory of Money*, Chicago: University of Chicago Press

Calabresi, G. (1968). 'Transaction Costs, Resource Allocation, and Liability Rules: A Comment', *Journal of Law and Economics*, 11: 67–73

Calmfors, L. (1993). 'Centralisation of Wage Bargaining and Macroeconomic Performance. A Survey', *OECD Economic Studies*, 21: 161–91

Cantwell, J. (2000). 'A Survey of Theories of International Production', in C. N. Pitelis and R. Sugden (eds.), *The Nature of the Transnational Firm*, 2nd edn., London: Routledge

Carillo, M. R. and A. Zazzaro (eds.) (2001). *Istituzioni, capitale umano e sviluppo del Mezzogiorno*, Naples: ESI

Carraro, C. (1989). *Modelling International Policy Coordination*, November, mimeo

Carraro, C. and F. Giavazzi (1991). 'Can International Policy Co-Ordination Really Be Counterproductive?', in C. Carraro and F. Giavazzi (eds.), *International Economic Policy Co-Ordination*, Oxford: Blackwell

Carraro, C. and D. Siniscalco (eds.) (1993). *The European Carbon Tax: An Economic Assessment*, Dordrecht: Kluwer Academic

Caselli, P. (1993). 'Prezzi all'esportazione e tassi di cambio: una verifica empirica', *Temi di discussione del Servizio Studi*, 213, Banca d'Italia, December

Cassel, G. (1918). 'Abnormal Deviations in International Exchanges', *Economic Journal*, 28: 413–15

Caves, R. E. (1989). 'Mergers, Takeovers and Economic Efficiency: Foresight vs. Hindsight', *International Journal of Industrial Economics*, 7: 151–74

Cecchini, P. (1988). *The European Challenge 1992. The Benefits of a Single Market*, Aldershot: Wildwood House

CEEP (1994). *Annales*, Paris

Chesnais, F. (1993). 'The French National System of Innovation', in R. Nelson (ed.), *National Innovation Systems. A Comparative Analysis*, Oxford: Oxford University Press

Chrystal, K. A. and S. Price (1994). *Controversies in Macroeconomics*, 3rd edn., Hemel Hempstead: Wheatsheaf

Claassen, E. M. (ed.) (1990). *International and European Monetary Systems*, New York: Praeger

Clower, R. (1965). 'The Keynesian Counterrevolution: A Theoretical Appraisal', in F. H. Hahn, F. and P. R. Brechling (eds.), *Theory of Interest Rates*, London: Macmillan

Cnossen, S. (2003). 'How Much Tax Coordination in the European Union?', *International Tax and Public Finance*, 10: 625–49

Coase, R. H. (1937). 'The Nature of the Firm', *Economica*, 4: 386–405; reprinted in K. E. Boulding and G. J. Stigler (eds.), *Readings in Price Theory*, London: Allen & Unwin, 1953 and in R. H. Coase, *The Firm, the Market and the Law*, Chicago: University of Chicago Press, 1988

  (1960). 'The Problem of Social Cost', *Journal of Law and Economics*, 3: 1–44; reprinted in R. H. Coase, *The Firm, the Market and the Law*, Chicago: University of Chicago Press, 1988

  (1988). *The Firm, the Market and the Law*, Chicago: University of Chicago Press

Coffey, P. (1984). *The European Monetary System. Past, Present and Future*, Dordrecht: Martinus Nijhoff

Coleman, J. S. (1990). *Foundations of Social Theory*, Cambridge: Cambridge University Press

Coles, J. L. and P. J. Hammond (1995). 'Walrasian Equilibrium without Survival: Existence, Efficiency and Remedial Policy', in P. Pattanaik and K. Suzumura (eds.), *Choice, Welfare Development: A Festschrift in Honour of Amartya Sen*, Oxford: Clarendon Press

Commission of the European Communities (1989). *Interim Report on a Specific Community Action Programme to Combat Poverty*, Brussels: European Commission

Commission of the European Communities, IMF, OECD, UN and World Bank (1993). *System of National Accounts*, rev. edn., Brussels: Commission of the European Communities

Committee on the Working of the Monetary System (1959). *Report,* Cmnd 827, HMSO

Conway, G. (1997). *The Doubly Green Revolution: Food for All in the 21st Century*, Ithaca: Cornell University Press

Cooper, J. and A. John (1988). 'Coordinating Coordination Failures in Keynesian Models', *Quarterly Journal of Economics*, 103: 441–63

Cooper, R. N. (1969). 'Macroeconomic Policy Adjustment in Interdependent Economies', *Quarterly Journal of Economics*, 83: 1–24

Cooter, R. (1982). 'The Cost of Coase', *Journal of Legal Studies*, 11: 1–33

Coricelli, F. (1990). 'Industrial Relations and Macroeconomic Performance: An Application to Spain', IMF Working Paper, October

Corlett, W. J. and D. C. Hague (1953). 'Complementarity and the Excess Burden of Taxation', *Review of Economic Studies*, 21: 21–30

Cornes, R. and T. Sandler (1996). *The Theory of Externalities, Public Goods, and Club Goods*, 2nd edn., Cambridge: Cambridge University Press

Cornwall, R. R. (1984). *Introduction to the Use of General Equilibrium Analysis*, Amsterdam: North-Holland

Costabile, L. (ed.) (1996). *Istituzioni e sviluppo economico nel Mezzogiorno*, Bologna: Il Mulino

Costabile, L. and A. Giannola (1996). Norme sociali e distribuzione dei posti di lavoro: Una parabola della corruzione nell'Italia meridionale, in L. Costabile (ed.), *Istituzioni e sviluppo economico nel Mezzogiorno*, Bologna: Il Mulino

Cottarelli, C. (1994). 'Should an "Independent" Central Bank Control Foreign Exchange Policy?', in T. J. T. Balino and C. Cottarelli (eds.), *Framework for Monetary Stability*, Washington, DC: IMF

Cozzi, G. (1997). 'Exploring Growth Trajectories', *Journal of Economic Growth*, 2: 1–14

Cripps, T. F. and W. Godley (1976). 'A Formal Analysis of the Cambridge Economic Policy Group Model', *Economica*, 43: 335–48

Crocker, D. A. (1992). 'Functioning and Capability. The Foundations of Sen's and Nussbaum's Development Ethics', *Political Theory*, 20: 584–612

Cummings, R. G., D. S. Brookshire and W. D. Schulze (1986). *Valuing Environmental Goods. An Assessment of the Contingent Valuation Method*, Totowa, NJ: Rowman & Allanheld

D'Souza, J. and W. L. Megginson (1999). 'The Financial and Operating Performance of Privatized Firms During the 1990s', *Journal of Finance*, 54: 1397–1438

Dabbah, M. M. (2003). *The Internationalisation of Antitrust Policy*, Cambridge: Cambridge University Press

Dales, J. H. (1968). *Pollution, Property and Prices. An Essay in Policy-Making and Economics*, Toronto: University of Toronto Press

Dam, K. W. (1970). *The GATT: Law and International Economic Organization*, Chicago: University of Chicago Press

Davidson, P. (1982–3). 'Rational Expectations: A Fallacious Foundation for Studying Crucial Decision Making Processes', *Journal of Post-Keynesian Economics*, 5: 182–98

De Bonis, R., A. Giustiniani and G. Gomel (1999). 'Crises, Bail-Outs of Banks and Countries: Linkages, Analogies, and Differences', *The World Economy*, 22: 55–86

De Cecco, M. (1995). 'Central Bank Cooperation in the Inter-War Period: A View from the Periphery', in J. Reis (ed.), *International Monetary Systems in Historical Perspective*, Basingstoke: Macmillan

De Fraja, G. and F. Delbono (1989). 'Alternative Strategies of a Public Enterprise in Oligopoly', *Oxford Economic Papers*, 41: 302–11

De Grauwe, P. (1990). 'The Cost of Disinflation and the European Monetary System', *Open Economies Review*, 1: 147–73

   (1998). *Economics of Monetary Union*, 5th edn., Oxford: Oxford University Press

De Martino, G. (2000). *Global Economy, Global Justice: Theoretical Objectives and Policy Alternatives to Neoliberalism*, London: Routledge

   (2003). 'Free Trade or Social Tariffs?', in J. Michie (ed.), *The Handbook of Globalisation*, Cheltenham: Edward Elgar

De Vries, M. G. (1976). *The International Monetary Fund, 1966–71: The System Under Stress*, 2 vols, Washington, DC: IMF

   (1985). *The International Monetary Fund, 1972–1978: Cooperation on Trial*, 3 vols, Washington, DC: IMF

De Vries, M. G. and J. K. Horsefield (1969). *The IMF, 1945–1965: Twenty Years of International Monetary Cooperation, 2: Analysis*, Washington, DC: IMF

Del Monte, A. (1996), *I fattori determinanti la corruzione nelle regioni italiane*, in L. Costabile (ed.), *Istituzioni e sviluppo economico nel Mezzogiorno*, Bologna: Il Mulino

Demsetz, H. (1968). 'The Cost of Transacting', *Quarterly Journal of Economics*, 82: 33–53

Dernburg, T. F. (1989). *Global Macroeconomics*, New York: Harper & Row

Desai, M. (1989). 'Potential Lifetime (PLT): A Proposal for an Index of Social Welfare', in F. Bracho (ed.), *Towards a New Way to Measure Development*, Caracas: Office of the South Commission

   (1991). 'Human Development: Concepts and Measurement', *European Economic Review*, 35: 350–7

Dilnot, A. W. (1995). 'The Assessment: The Future of Welfare State', *Oxford Review of Economic Policy*, 11: 1–10

Dixit, A. (1989). 'Entry and Exit Decisions under Uncertainty', *Journal of Political Economy*, 97: 620–38

   (1992). Investment and Hysteresis, *Journal of Economic Perspectives*, 6: 107–302

   (1996). *The Making of Economic Policy: A Transaction-Cost Politics Perspective*, Cambridge, MA: MIT Press

(1997). 'Power of Incentives in Private versus Public Organizations', *American Economic Review*, 87: 378–82

Domar, E. D. (1946). 'Capital Expansion, Rate of Growth and Employment', *Econometrica*, 14: 137–47

(1947). 'Expansion and Employment', *American Economic Review*, 37: 34–55

Donahue, J. D. (1997). 'Tiebout? Or not Tiebout? The Market Metaphor and America's Devolution Debate', *Journal of Economic Perspectives*, 11: 73–81

Donaldson, T. and Preston L. E. (1995). 'The Stakeholder Theory of the Corporation: Concepts, Evidence and Implications', *Academy of Management Review*, 20: 65–91

Dore, R. (1992). 'Japanese Capitalism, Anglo-Saxon Capitalism: How Will the Darwinian Contest Turn Out?', London School of Economics, Centre for Economic Performance, Occasional Paper, 26

(2000). *Stock Market Capitalism: Welfare Capitalism – Japan and Germany, versus the Anglo-Saxons*, Oxford: Oxford University Press

Dore, R., R. Boyer and Z. Mars (eds.) (1994). *The Return to Incomes Policy*, London: Pinter

Dornbusch, R. (1988). 'The European Monetary System, the Dollar and the Yen', in F. Giavazzi, S. Micossi and M. Miller (eds.), *The European Monetary System*, Cambridge: Cambridge University Press

Dornbusch, R. and S. Fischer (1994). *Macroeconomics*, 6th edn. (1st edn., 1978), New York: McGraw-Hill

Downs, A. (1957). *An Economic Theory of Good Decision-Making in Democracy*, New York: Harper & Row

(1967). *Inside Bureaucracy*, Boston: Little, Brown & Co.

Drèze, J. (1993). *Money and Uncertainty: Inflation, Interest, Indexation*, Paolo Baffi Lectures on Money and Finance, Banca d'Italia, Roma: Edizioni dell'Elefante

Drèze, J. and N. Stern (1987). *The Theory of Cost-Benefit Analysis*, in A. J. Auerbach and M. Feldstein, *Handbook of Public Economics*, Amsterdam: North-Holland

Driver, C. and G. Thompson (2002). 'Corporate Governance and Democracy: The Stakeholder Debate Revisited', *Journal of Management and Governance*, 6: 111–30

Drummond, M. F. (1980). *Principles of Economic Appraisal in Health Care*, Oxford: Oxford University Press

Dupuit, J. (1844). 'De l'Utilité et de sa Mesure', *Annales de Ponts et Chaussées* (English translation: 'On the Measurement of Utility of Public Works'), *International Economic Papers*, 1952, 2: 83–110

Economides N. (1996). The Economics of Networks, *International Journal of Industrial Organization*, 14: 673–99

Edwards, J. and M. Nibler (2000). 'Corporate Governance in Germany: The Role of Banks and Ownership Concentration', *Economic Policy: A European Forum*, 0: 237–60

Edwards, S. (2001). Dollarization: Myths and Realities, *Journal of Policy Modelling*, 23: 249–65

Eichengreen, B. (1992). *Golden Fetters: The Gold Standard and the Great Depression 1919–1939*, Oxford: Oxford University Press

Eichengreen, B. and C. Wyplosz (1993). 'The Unstable EMS', *Brookings Papers on Economic Activity*, 1: 51–124

Eijffinger, S. and E. Schaling (1993). 'Central Bank Independence in Twelve Industrial Countries', *Banca Nazionale del Lavoro Quarterly Review*, 184: 49–89

Esping-Andersen, G. (1990). *The Three Worlds of Welfare Capitalism*, Princeton: Princeton University Press

Estevadeordal, A., J. Goto and R. E. Saez (2001). 'The New Regionalism in the Americas: The Case of Mercosur', *Journal of Economic Integration*, 16: 180–202

European Agency for Environment (1999). *Environment in the European Union* 1995. *Report for the Review of the Fifth Environmental Action Programme*, Luxembourg: Office for Official Publications of the European Communities, OPOCE

European Central Bank (ECB) (2001). *The Monetary Policy of the ECB*, Frankfurt am Main
    (2003a). *Monthly Bulletin*, April
    (2003b). *TARGET Annual Report* 2002, April
    (2003c), 'The ECB's Monetary Policy Strategy', Press Release, 8 May (www.ecb.int)

European Commission (1970). *Industrial Policy in the European Community* (*Colonna Memorandum*), Brussels
    (1996). *European Economy: Reports and Studies*, Directorate General for Economic and Financial Affairs, Brussels, http://www.europa.eu.int/
    (1997). 'Towards Tax Coordination in the European Union: A Package to Tackle Harmful Tax Competition', COM (97), 495, http://europa.eu.int/comm/taxation_customs/publications/official_doc/com/taxation/com495_oct1997/en.pdf
    (2001a). *Final Report of the Committee of Wise Men on the Regulation of the European Securities Markets*, Brussels http://www.europa.eu.int/
    (2001b). 'Company Taxation in the Internal Market', COM (2001), 582, http://europa.eu.int/comm/taxation_customs/publications/official_doc/IP/ip1468/company_tax_study_en.pdf
    (2004). 'Public Finances in EMU – 2004', *European Economy*, 3

European Economic Advisory Group at CESifo (EEAG) (2003). *Report on the European Economy*, Munich: IFO, Institute for Economic Research

European Monetary Institution (EMI) (1997). *The Single Monetary Policy in Stage Three: General Documentation on ESCB Monetary Policy Instruments and Procedures*, September

Fehr, E. and K. M. Schmidt (1999). 'A Theory of Fairness, Competition and Cooperation', *Quarterly Journal of Economics*, 114: 817–68

Ferri, G., L. Liu and J. E. Stiglitz (1999). 'The Procyclical Role of Rating Agencies: Evidence from the East Asian Crisis', *Economic Notes*, 28: 335–55

Fetherston, M. and W. Godley (1978). 'New Cambridge Macroeconomics and Global Monetarism: Some Issues in the Conduct of UK Economic Policy', *Carnegie Rochester Conference Series on Public Policy*, 9: 33–65

Finger, J. M. and J. Nogués (2002). 'The Unbalanced Uruguay Round Outcome', *The World Economy*, 25: 321–40

Fink, R. (1982). *Supply-Side Economics*, Washington, DC: University Publications of America

Finsinger, J. and I. Vogelsang (1985). 'Strategic Management Behaviour under Reward Structures in a Planned Economy', *Quarterly Journal of Economics*, 100: 263–9

Fischer, F. (1974). 'Alcoa Revisited: Comment', *Journal of Economic Theory*, 9: 357–59

Fischer, S. (1990). 'Rules versus Discretion in Monetary Policy', in B. Friedman and F. Hahn (eds.), *Handbook of Monetary Economics*, 2, Amsterdam: North-Holland
    (1999). 'On the Need for an International Lender of Last Resort', *Journal of Economic Perspectives*, 13: 85–104

Fisher, F. M. (1983). *Disequilibrium Foundations of Equilibrium Economics*, Cambridge: Cambridge University Press

Fisher, I. (1932). *Booms and Depression*, New York: Adelphi
    (1933). 'The Debt–Deflation Theory of Great Depression', *Econometrica*, 1: 337–57

Flanagan, R. J., D. W. Soskice and L. Ulman (1983). *Unionism, Economic Stabilization and Incomes Policies: European Experience*, Washington, DC: The Brookings Institution

Fleming, J. M. (1962). 'Domestic Financial Policies under Fixed and under Floating Exchange Rates', *IMF Staff Papers*, 9: 369–80

Fleurbaey, M. and F. Maniquet (1999). 'Fair Allocation with Unequal Production Skills: The Solidarity Approach to Compensation', *Social Choice and Welfare*, 16: 569–83

Florio, M. (2004). *The Great Divestiture: Evaluating the Welfare Impact of the British Privatizations 1979–1997*, Cambridge, MA: MIT Press

Foley, D. (1970). 'Economic Equilibrium with Costly Marketing', *Journal of Economic Theory*, 2: 276–91

Food and Agriculture Organisation (FAO) (2000). *Agriculture: Towards 2015/30, Technical Interim Report*, Rome, April, http://www.fao.org

Foreman-Peck, J. and G. Federico (1999). *European Industrial Policy – The Twentieth-Century Experience*, Oxford: Oxford University Press

Forster, M. and M. Pearson (2002). 'Income Distribution and Poverty in the OECD Area: Trends and Driving Forces', *OECD Economic Studies*, 34: 7–39

Frankel, J. A. (1992). *Monetary Regime Choices for a Semi-Open Economy*, Berkeley, CA: University of California

Frankel, J. A. and K. Rockett (1986). 'International Macroeconomic Policy Coordination when Policy-Makers Disagree on the Model', *NBER Working Paper*, 2059

Franks, J., R. S. Harris and C. Mayer (1988). 'Means of Payment in Takeovers: Results for the United Kingdom and the United States?, in A. J. Auerbach, *Corporate Takeovers: Causes and Consequences*, NBER, Chicago: University of Chicago Press

Franzini, M. (1993). 'Corrupt Transactions', Paper presented at the Workshop on Economics and Politics, International School of Economic Research, Certosa di Pontignano, Siena, mimeo

(1997). 'Le organizzazioni tra opportunismo e adattamento: un riesame di exit e voice', in B. Jossa and U. Pagano (eds.), *Economie di mercato ed efficienza dei diritti di proprietà*, Turin: Giappichelli

(1999). 'Cooperazione, scelte pubbliche e sviluppo locale', *Meridiana*, 34–35, November

Franzini, M. and A. Nicita (eds.) (2002). *Economic Institutions and Environmental Policy*, London: Ashgate

Franzini, M. and F. R. Pizzuti (1994). 'La sfiducia nella politica e le scelte economiche', in F. R. Pizzuti (ed.), *L'economia italiana dagli anni '70 agli anni '90*, Milan: McGraw-Hill Libri Italia

Fratianni, M. and J. Von Hagen (1990). 'Asymmetries and Realignments in the EMS', in P. De Grauwe and L. Papademos (eds.), *The European Monetary System in the 1990's*, London: Longman

(1991). *The European Monetary System and European Monetary Union*, San Francisco: Westview Press

Freeman, R. B. (1995). 'The Large Welfare State as a System', *American Economic Review*, 85: 16–21

Freeman, R. B., R. Topel and B. Swedenborg (1997). *The Welfare State in Transition: Reforming The Swedish Model*, Chicago: University of Chicago Press

Frenkel, J. A. and H. G. Johnson (eds.) (1976). *The Monetary Approach to the Balance of Payments*, London: Allen & Unwin

(1978). *The Economics of the Exchange Rates: Selected Studies*, London: Addison-Wesley

Frey, B. and R. Eichenberger (1996). 'To Harmonize or to Compete? That's not the Question', *Journal of the Public Economics*, 60: 335–49

Friedman, B. M. (1979). 'Optimal Expectations and the Extreme Information Assumptions of "Rational Expectation" Macromodels', *Journal of Monetary Economics*, 5: 23–41

Friedman, J. W. (1990). *Game Theory with Applications to Economics*, Oxford: Oxford University Press

Friedman, M. (1953). *Essays in Positive Economics*, Chicago: Chicago University Press

(1968). 'The Role of Monetary Policy', *American Economic Review*, 58: 1–17

Fudenberg, D. and J. Tirole (1991). *Game Theory*, Cambridge, MA: MIT Press

Galal, A., L. Jones, P. Tandon and I. Vogelsang (1994). *Welfare Consequences of Selling Public Enterprises: An Empirical Analysis*, Oxford: Oxford University Press

Galor, O. and J. Zeira (1993). 'Income Distribution and Macroeconomics', *Review of Economic Studies*, 60: 35–52

Gandolfo, G. (1998). *International Trade Theory and Policy*, Berlin and Heidelberg: Springer-Verlag

(2001). *International Finance and Open-Economy Macroeconomics*, Berlin and Heidelberg: Springer-Verlag

Gaskins, D. W. (1974). 'Alcoa Revisited: The Welfare Implications of a Second Hand Market', *Journal of Economic Theory*, 7: 254–71

Genser, B. (2003). 'Coordinating VATs Between EU Member States', *International Tax and Public Finance*, 10: 735–52

Gerber, E. R. and J. E. Jackson (1993). 'Endogenous Preferences and the Study of Institutions', *American Political Science Review*, 87: 639–56

Gerlach, S. and P. A. Petri (eds.) (1990). *The Economics of the Dollar Cycle*, Cambridge, MA: MIT Press

Giavazzi, F. and A. Giovannini (1989). *Limiting Exchange Rate Flexibility. The European Monetary System*, Cambridge, MA: MIT Press

Giavazzi, F. and M. Pagano (1988). 'Capital Controls in the EMS', in D. E. Fair and C. de Boissieu (eds.), *International Monetary and Financial Integration: The European Dimension*, Dordrecht: Martinus Nijhoff

Giavazzi, F. and L. Spaventa (1990). 'The New EMS', in P. De Grauwe and L. Papademos (eds.), *The European Monetary System in the 1990's*, London: Longman

Giddy, I. H. (1983). 'The Eurocurrency Market', in A. M. George and I. H. Giddy (eds.), *International Finance Handbook*, 1, New York: Wiley

Gilbert, C. and D. Vines (2000). *The World Bank: Structure and Policies*, Cambridge: Cambridge University Press

Giotakos, D., L. Petit, G. Garnier and P. De Luyck (2001). 'General Electric/Honeywell – An Insight into the Commission's Investigation and Decision', *Competition Policy Newsletter*, 3: 5–13

Glaeser, E. L. (ed.) (2003). *The Governance of Non Profit Organizations*, Chicago: NBER and Chicago University Press

Glomm, G. and B. Ravikumar (1992). 'Public versus Private Investment in Human Capital: Endogenous Growth and Income Inequality', *Journal of Political Economy*, 100: 813–34

Glyn, A. and R. B. Sutcliffe (1972). *British Capitalism, Workers and the Profit Squeeze*, Harmondsworth: Penguin

Gnesutta, C. (1999). 'Le istituzioni finanziarie', in N. Acocella (ed.), *Le istituzioni fra mercato e stato*, Rome: Carocci

Goodhart, C. A. E. (1988). *The Evolution of Central Banks*, Cambridge, MA: MIT Press

Goodhart, C. and G. Illing (eds.) (2002). *Financial Crises, Contagion and the Lender of Last Resort*, Oxford: Oxford University Press

Goodin, R. E., B. Headey, R. Muffels and H. J. Dirven (1999). *The Real Worlds of Welfare Capitalism*, Cambridge: Cambridge University Press

Graziani, A. (2000). *Lo sviluppo dell'economia italiana*, Turin: Bollati Boringheri

Greenaway, D. and D. Nelson (2000). 'The Assessment: Globalization and Labour-Market Adjustment', *Oxford Review of Economic Policy*, 16: 1–11

Greenwald, B. and J. Stiglitz (1993). 'New and Old Keynesians', *Journal of Economic Perspectives*, 7: 23–44

Gregg, S. (2001). '"Stakeholder" Theory: What it means for Corporate Governance', *Policy*, 17: 33–8

Grilli, V., D. Masciandaro and G. Tabellini (1991). 'Political and Monetary Institutions and Public Finance Policies in the Industrial Countries', *Economic Policy*, 6: 342–392; reprinted in J. Persson and G. Tabellini (eds.), 2, *Monetary and Fiscal Policies*, Cambridge, MA: MIT Press, 1994, 2 vols.

Gronchi, S. (1984). 'On Karmel's Criterion for Optimal Truncation', Quaderni del Dipartimento di Economia Politica dell'Università di Siena, 26

Grossman, G. and E. Helpman (1991). *Innovation and Growth in the Global Economy*, Cambridge, MA: MIT Press

(2001). *Special Interest Politics*, Cambridge, MA and London: MIT Press

Grossman, S. and O. Hart (1986). 'The Costs and Benefits of Ownership: A Theory of Vertical and Lateral Integration', *Journal of Political Economy*, 94: 691–719

Group of Ten (1997). *Financial Stability in Emerging Market Economies*, Basle: Bank for International Settlements, April

Grubel, H. G. (1984). *The International Monetary System: Efficiency and Practical Alternatives*, 4th edn., Harmondsworth: Penguin

Guesnerie, R. (1995). 'The Genealogy of Modern Theoretical Public Economies: From First Best to Second Best', *European Economic Review*, 39: 353–81

Gui, B. (1993). 'The Economic Rationale for The "Third Sector"', in A. Ben-Ner and B. Gui (eds.), *The Nonprofit Sector in The Mixed Economy*, Ann Arbor: University of Michigan Press

Guiso, L. and D. Terlizzese (1998). 'Time Consistency and Subgame Perfection: The Difference between Promises and Threats', *Temi di Discussione*, 138, Banca d'Italia

Guiso, L., A. K. Kashyap, F. Panetta and D. Terlizzese (1999). 'Will a Common European Monetary Policy Have Asymmetric Effects?', *Federal Reserve Bank of Chicago Economic Perspectives*, 23: 56–75

Hahn, F. (1982). 'Reflections on the Invisible Hand', *Lloyds Bank Review*, 144: 1–21

(1985). 'Some Keynesian Reflections on Monetarism', in F. Vicarelli (ed.), *Keynes' Relevance Today*, London: Macmillan

Hall, B. J. and K. J. Murphy (2003). 'The Trouble with Stock Options', *Journal of Economic Perspectives*, 17: 49–71

Hammond, P. J. (1990). 'Theoretical Progress in Public Economics: A Provocative Assessment', *Oxford Economic Papers*, 42: 6–33

Hansmann, H. B. (1980). 'The Role of Nonprofit Enterprise', *Yale Law Journal*, 89: 835–901

Hardin, G. (1968). 'The Tragedy of Commons', *Science*, 162: 1243–8

Harris, J. R. and M. P. Todaro (1970). 'Migration, Unemployment and Development: A Two-Sector Analysis', *American Economic Review*, 60: 136–42

Harrod, R. F. (1939). 'An Essay in Dynamic Theory', *Economic Journal*, 49: 14–33

Hart, O. and J. Moore (1990). 'Property Rights and the Nature of the Firm', *Journal of Political Economy*, 98: 1119–58

Haveman, R. H. (1977). 'Evaluating Public Expenditures under Conditions of Unemployment', in R. H. Haveman and J. Margolis, *Public Expenditure and Policy Analysis*, Chicago: Rand McNally

Hay, D. A. and D. J. Morris (1991). *Industrial Economics and Organization. Theory and Evidence*, Oxford: Oxford University Press

Hayek, F. A. Von (1945). 'The Use of Knowledge in Society', *American Economic Review*, 35: 519–530; reprinted in F. A. Von Hayek, *Individualism and Economic Order*, Chicago: University of Chicago Press, 1948

Heintz, J. (2003). 'Global Labour Standards. Their Impact and Implementation', in J. Michie (ed.), *The Handbook of Globalisation*, Cheltenham: Edward Elgar

Heller, W. P. (1972). 'Transactions with Set Up Costs', *Journal of Economic Theory*, 4: 465–78

Helm, D. (1989). 'The Economic Borders of the State', in D. Helm (ed.), *The Economic Borders of the State*, Oxford: Oxford University Press

Helpman, E. and P. R. Krugman (1985). *Market Structure and Foreign Trade*, Cambridge, MA: MIT Press

Henderson, D. (2001). *Misguided Virtue. False Notions of Corporate Social Responsibility*, New Zealand Business Roundtable, June

Hibbs, D. A. (1977). 'Political Parties and Macroeconomic Policy', *American Political Science Review*, 71: 1467–87

(1992). 'Partisan Theory after Fifteen Years', *European Journal of Political Economy*, 8: 361–73

(2005). 'Voting and the Macroeconomy', in B. R. Weingast and D. Wittman (eds.), *The Oxford Handbook of Political Economy*, Oxford: Oxford University Press, forthcoming

Hicks, J. R. (1937). 'Mr. Keynes and the 'Classics': A Suggested Interpretation', *Econometrica*, 5: 147–59

Hills J. (1995), 'Funding the Welfare State', *Oxford Review of Economic Policy*, 11: 27–43

Hirschman, A. O. (1970). *Exit, Voice and Loyalty. Responses to Decline in Firms, Organizations and States*, Cambridge, MA: Harvard University Press

Holcombe, R. G. (1994). *The Economic Foundations of Government*, London: Macmillan

Holmstrom, B. and S. N. Kaplan (2001). 'Corporate Governance and Merger Activity in the United States: Making Sense of the 1980s and 1990s', *Journal of Economic Perspectives*, 15: 121–44

Horsefield, J. K. (ed.) (1969a). *The IMF, 1945–1965: Twenty Years of International Monetary Cooperation*, 1: Chronicle, Washington, DC: IMF

(ed.) (1969b). *The IMF, 1945–1965: Twenty Years of International Monetary Cooperation*, 3: Documents, Washington, DC: IMF

Hoshi, T., and A. Kashyap (2004). *Corporate Financing and Governance in Japan*, Cambridge, MA: MIT Press

Hotelling, H. (1938). 'The General Welfare in Relation to Problems of Taxation and of Railways and Utility Rates', *Econometrica*, 6: 242–69

Hovenkamp, H. (1999). *Federal Antitrust Policy. The Law of Competition and its Practice*, 2nd edn., St Paul, MN: West Publishing (Hornbook Series)

Hughes, A. (1993). 'Mergers and Economic Performance in the UK: A Survey of the Empirical Evidence 1950–1990', in M. Bishop and J. Kay, *European Mergers and Merger Policy*, Oxford: Oxford University Press

Huizinga, H. (1994). 'International Interest Withholding Taxation: Prospects for a Common European Policy', *International Tax and Public Finance*, 1: 277–91

Hume, D. (1739). *Treatise of Human Nature*, London: Everyman Library

Hunt, E. K. (1980). 'A Radical Critique of Welfare Economics', in E. Nell (ed.), *Growth, Profits and Property*, Cambridge: Cambridge University Press

Ietto Gillies, G. (2002). *Transnational Corporations: Fragmentation Amidst Integration*, London: Routledge

Ilzkovitz, F. and R. Meiklejohn (2001). 'European Merger Control: Do We Need an Efficiency Defence?', *European Economy*, 5

Inman, R. P. (1987). *Markets, Governments, and the 'New' Political Economy*, in A. J. Auerbach and M. Feldstein (eds.), *Handbook of Public Economics*, Amsterdam: North-Holland

International Monetary Fund (IMF) (1993). *Balance of Payments Manual*, 5th edn., Washington, DC: IMF

(1994). *International Trade Policies: The Uruguay Round and Beyond*, 2 vols., Washington, DC: IMF

(1997). *World Economic Outlook. Globalization: Opportunities and Challenges*, Washington, DC: IMF, May

(2002). *Annual Report* 2002, Washington, DC: IMF

(2003). *Annual Report* 2003, Washington, DC: IMF

IRI (2001). *Le privatizzazioni in Italia 1992–2000*, Rome: Edindustria, http://www.iri.it

James, H. (1996). *International Monetary Cooperation Since Bretton Woods*, Washington, DC and New York: IMF and Oxford University Press

Jeanne, O. (1999). *Currency Crises: A Perspective on Recent Theoretical Development*, CEPR Discussion Paper, 2170

Jenkinson T. and C. Mayer (1994). *Hostile Takeovers*, New York: McGraw-Hill

Johansen, L. (1978). *Lectures on Macro-Economic Planning, Part II*, Amsterdam: North-Holland

Jones-Lee, M. W. (1976). *The Value of Life: An Economic Analysis*, Chicago: University of Chicago Press

Jordan, A. (1999). 'Editorial Introduction: The Construction of Multilevel Environmental Governance System', *Environment and Planning C: Government and Policy*, 17: 1–17

Kaldor, N. (1939). 'Speculation and Economic Stability', *Review of Economic Studies*, 7(1): 1–27, reprinted in N. Kaldor, *Essays on Economic Stability and Growth*, London: G. Duckworth, 1960: 17–58

(1971). 'Conflicts in National Economic Objectives', *Economic Journal*, 81: 1–16

(1976). 'Inflation and Recession in the World Economy', *Economic Journal*, 86: 703–14

Kalecki, M. (1933). *Proba Teorji Konjuktury*, Warszaw: Ibkge; 1st chapter reprinted in M. Kalecki, *Studies in the Theory of Business Cycle*, Oxford: Blackwell, 1996

(1943). 'Political Aspects of Full Employment', *Political Quarterly*, October; reprinted in M. Kalecki, *Selected Essays on the Dynamics of the Capitalist Economy 1933–1970*, Cambridge: Cambridge University Press, 1971

Kaminsky, G. L. and C. M. Reinhart (1996). 'The Twin Crises: The Causes of Banking and Balance-of-Payments Problems', Board of Governors of the Federal Reserve System, International Finance, Discussion Paper, 544

Kaminsky, G. L., C. M. Reinhart and C. A. Végh (2003). 'The Unholy Trinity of Financial Contagion', *Journal of Economic Perspectives*, 17: 51–74

Kanbur, S. M. R. and G. D. Myles (1992). 'Policy Choice and Political Constraints', *European Journal of Political Economy*, 8: 1–29

Kareken, J. (1975). 'Lenders Preferences, Credit Rationing and the Effectiveness of Monetary Policy', *Review of Economics and Statistics*, 39: 292–302

Kaufman, G. G. (2000). 'Banking and Currency Crises and Systemic Risk: A Taxonomy and Review', *Financial Markets Institutions and Instruments*, 9: 69–131

Kaul I., I. Grunberg and M. A. Stern (eds.) (1999), *Global Public Goods: International Co-Operation in the 21st Century*, Oxford: UNDP and Oxford University Press

Kaul, I., P. Conceição, K. Le Goulven and R. U. Mendoza (eds.) (2003). *Providing Global Public Goods. Managing Globalization*, New York: UNDP and Oxford University Press

Kay, J. and A. Silberston (1995). 'Corporate Governance', *National Institute Economic Review*, 153: 84–97

Kay J. and J. Vickers (1990). 'Regulatory Reform: An Appraisal', in G. Majone (ed.), *Deregulation or Reregulation? Regulatory Reform in Europe and the US*, London: Pinter

Kelly, G., D. Kelly and A. Gamble (1997). *Stakeholder Capitalism*, London: Macmillan

Kenworthy, L. (1998). *Do Social Welfare Policies Reduce Poverty? A Cross National Assessment*, Working Paper, 188, Luxemburg Income Study

Keynes, J. M. (1924). *Tract on Monetary System*, London: Macmillan

(1936). *The General Theory of Employment, Interest and Money*, London: Macmillan; reprinted in *The Collected Writings*, VII, London: Macmillan, 1973

(1940). *How to Pay for the War*; reprinted in *The Collected Writings*, IX, London: Macmillan, 1972

Kirman, A. (1989). 'The Intrinsic Limits of Modern Economic Theory: The Emperor Has No Clothes', *Economic Journal*, Conference Issue, 99: 126–39

(1992). 'Whom or What Does the Representative Consumer Represent?', *Journal of Economic Perspectives*, 6: 117–36

Knight, F. H. (1952). 'Institutionalism and Empiricism in Economics', *American Economic Review*, 42: 45–55

Koenig-Archibugi, M. (2003). 'Global Governance', in J. Michie (ed.), *The Handbook of Globalisation*, Cheltenham: Edward Elgar

Kolm, S.-C. (1984). *La Bonne Economie: La Réciprocité Générale*, Paris: Presses Universitaire de France

Krueger, A. (1974). 'The Political Economy of the Rent-Seeking Society', *American Economic Review*, 64: 291–303

Krugman, P. R. (1998). *What Happened to Asia?*, http.//www.mit.edu/people/krugman

Kydland, F. E. and E. C. Prescott (1977). 'Rules Rather than Discretion: The Inconsistency of Optimal Plans', *Journal of Political Economy*, 85: 473–492; reprinted in Persson, J. and G. Tabellini (eds.), *Monetary and Fiscal Policies*, 1, Cambridge, MA: MIT Press, 1994, 2 vols.

La Porta, R. and F. Lopez-de-Silanes (1999). 'The Benefits of Privatization: Evidence from Mexico', *Quarterly Journal of Economics*, 114: 1193–1242

Ladd, H. F. (2002), 'School Vouchers: A Critical View', *Journal of Economic Perspectives*, 16: 3–22

Laffont, J. J. (1976). 'Decentralization with Externalities', *European Economic Review*, 7: 359–75

(2000). *Incentives and Political Economy*, Oxford: Oxford University Press

Laffont, J. J. and J. Tirole (1991). 'The Politics of Government Decision-Making: A Theory of Regulatory Capture', *Quarterly Journal of Economics*, 106: 1089–1127

Lal Das, B. (1999). *The World Trade Organization: A Guide to the Framework for International Trade*, London and New York: Zed Books

Lall, S. (1994). 'Does the Bell Toll for Industrial Strategy?', *World Development*, 22: 645–54

Lampman, R. J. (1984). *Social Welfare Spending: Accounting for Changes from 1950 to 1978*, New York: Academic Press

Layard, R. (1996). 'Subsidising Employment rather than Unemployment', in M. Baldassarri, L. Paganetto and E. S. Phelps (eds.), *Equity, Efficiency and Growth; The Future of the Welfare State*, London: Macmillan

Layard, R., S. Nickell and R. Jackman (1991). *Unemployment: Macroeconomic Performance and the Labour Market*, Oxford: Oxford University Press

Le Grand, J. (1987). 'The Middle-Class Use of the British Social Services', in R. E. Goodin and J. Le Grand (eds.), *Not only the Poor: The Middle Classes and the Welfare State*, London: Allen & Unwin

(1991). 'The Theory of Government Failure', *British Journal of Political Science*, 21: 423–42

Ledebur L. and W. Barnes (1992). *City Distress, Metropolitan Disparities and Economic Growth*, National League of Cities Research Report

Lee, S. (2003). 'The Political Economy of the Third Way: The Relationship between Globalisation and National Economic Policy', in J. Michie (ed.), *The Handbook of Globalisation*, Cheltenham: Edward Elgar

Leibenstein, H. (1966). 'Allocative Efficiency against "X-Efficiency"', *American Economic Review*, 56: 392–415

Leijonhufvud, A. (1968). *On Keynesian Economics and the Economics of Keynes. A Study in Monetary Theory*, Oxford: Oxford University Press

Lerner, A. P. (1978). 'A Wage-Increase Permit Plan to Stop Inflation', *The Brookings Papers on Economic Activity*, 2: 491–505

Lerner, A. P. and D. C. Colander (1980). *MAP, A Market Anti-Inflation Plan*, New York: Harcourt Jovanovich

Levine, R. (1997). 'Financial Development and Economic Growth: Views and Agenda', *Journal of Economic Literature*, 35: 688–726

Levinthal, D. (1996). 'Learning and Schumpeterian Dynamics', in G. Dosi and F. Malerba (eds.), *Organisation and Strategy in the Evolution of the Enterprise*, New York: Macmillan

Levy, F. (1987). *Dollars and Dreams: The Changing American Income Distribution*, New York: Basic Books

Lewis, W. A. (1954). 'Development with Unlimited Supply of Labour', *The Manchester School of Economic and Social Studies*, 22:139–91

Lindbeck, A. (1976). 'Stabilisation Policies in Open Economies with Endogenous Politicians', *American Economic Review*, 66: 1–19

(1995a). 'Hazardous Welfare-State Dynamics', *American Economic Review*, 85: 9–15

(1995b). 'Welfare State Disincentives with Endogenous Habits and Norms', *Scandinavian Journal of Economics*, 97: 477–94

Lindbeck, A. and D. J. Snower (1984). 'Involuntary Unemployment as an Insider-Outsider Dilemma', Seminar Paper, 282, Institute for International Economic Studies, University of Stockholm, reprinted in W. Beckerman (ed.), *Wage Rigidity and Unemployment*, London: Duckworth, 1986

Lipsey, R. G. and K. Lancaster (1956). 'The General Theory of Second Best', *Review of Economic Studies*, 24: 11–32

Littlechild, S. (1983). *Regulation of British Telecommunications Profitability*, London: HMSO

Lucas, R. E. (1973). 'Some International Evidence on Output–Inflation Tradeoffs', *American Economic Review*, 63: 326–34

(1976). 'Econometric Policy Evaluation: A Critique', in K. Brunner and A. Meltzer (eds.), *The Phillips Curve and Labour Markets*, 1, Carnegie–Rochester Conference Series on Public Policy, Amsterdam: North-Holland

(1988). 'On the Mechanism of Economic Development', *Journal of Monetary Economics*, 22: 3–42

Lucifora, C. and W. Salverda (eds.) (1998). *Policies for Low Wage Employment and Social Exclusion*, Milan: FrancoAngeli

Machlup, F. (1952). *The Political Economy of Monopoly*, Baltimore, MD: Johns Hopkins University Press

MacRae, C. D. (1977). 'A Political Model of the Business Cycle', *Journal of Political Economy*, 85: 239–63

Maddison, A. (1991). *Dynamic Forces in Capitalist Development. A Long-Run Comparative View*, Oxford: Oxford University Press

(2001). *The World Economy: A Millennial Perspective*, Paris: OECD

Maddock, R. and M. Carter (1982). 'A Child's Guide to Rational Expectations', *Journal of Economic Literature*, 20: 39–51

Madse, H. J. (1981). 'Partisanship and Macroeconomic Outcomes: A Reconsideration', in D. A. Hibbs and H. Fassbender (eds.), *Contemporary Political Economy*, Amsterdam: North-Holland

Magill, M. and M. Quinzii (1996). *Theory of Incomplete Markets*, Cambridge, MA: MIT Press

Malinvaud, E. (1977). *The Theory of Unemployment Reconsidered*, Oxford: Blackwell

(1984). *Mass Unemployment*, Oxford: Blackwell

Mankiw, N. G. (1985). 'Small Menu Costs and Large Business Cycles: A Macroeconomic Model of Monopoly', *Quarterly Journal of Economics*, 100: 529–538; reprinted in N. G. Mankiw and D. Romer (eds.), *New Keynesian Economics*, Cambridge, MA: MIT Press, 1991

Marselli, R. and M. Vannini (1996). La criminalità nelle regioni italiane: Il ruolo del sistema sanzionatorio, delle motivazioni economiche e del contesto sociale, in L. Costabile (ed.), *Istituzioni e sviluppo economico nel Mezzogiorno*, Bologna: Il Mulino

Marshall, A. (1890). *Principles of Economics*, 1st edn. (9th edn., 1920), London: Macmillan

Martimort D. (1996). 'The Multiprincipal Nature of Government', *European Economic Review*, 35: 673–86

Martin, S. and D. Parker (1997). *The Impact of Privatisation: Ownership and Corporate Performance in the UK*, London: Routledge

Martin, W. and L. A. Winters (1995). *The Uruguay Round*, Washington, DC: The World Bank

Martini, G. (1998). 'Recenti sviluppi dell'economia italiana: la politica della concorrenza: fatti stilizzati, teoria, evidenza empirica italiana', *Rivista internazionale di scienze sociali*, 106: 327–50

Marx, K. (1867). *Das Kapital, Kritik der Politische Ökonomie*, Hamburg: Meisner (English translation, *Capital*, New York: International Publishers, 1967)

Maskus, K. E. (1997). Should Core Labor Standards be Imposed through International Trade Policy', World Bank, Working Paper, 1817, August, http://econ.world bank.org

McCormick, J. (2001). *Environmental Policy in the European Union*, London: Macmillan
  (2002). *Understanding the European Union: A Concise Introduction*, 2nd edn., London: Macmillan

McCubbins, M. D. (1991). 'Party Governance and US Budget Deficits: Divided Government and Fiscal Stalemate', in A. Alesina and G. Carliner (eds.), *Politics and Economics in the Eighties*, Chicago; University of Chicago Press

McDonald, I. M. and Solow R. M. (1981). 'Wage Bargaining and Employment', *American Economic Review*, 71: 896–908

McKenzie, L. W. (1951). 'Ideal Output and the Interdependence of Firms', *Economic Journal*, 61: 785–803

McKinnon, R. I. (1973). *Money and Capital in Economic Development*, Baltimore, MD: John Hopkins University Press
  (1979). *Money in International Exchange: The Convertible Currency System*, Oxford: Oxford University Press

Meade, J. E. (1955). *Trade and Welfare*, Oxford: Oxford University Press

Megginson, W. L., R. C. Nash and M. Van Randenborgh (1994). 'The Financial and Operating Performance of Newly Privatized Firms: An International Empirical Analysis', *Journal of Finance*, 49: 403–52

Michie, J. (ed.) (2003). *The Handbook of Globalisation*, Cheltenham: Edward Elgar

Migué, J. L. and G. Bélanger (1974). 'Towards a General Theory of Managerial Discretion', *Public Choice*, 17: 27–34

Milanovic, B. (2003). 'The Two Faces of Globalization: Against Globalization as We Know It', *World Development*, 31: 667–83

Mill, J. S. (1848). *Principles of Political Economy*, London; reprinted Harmondsworth: Penguin, 1970

Miller, M. and A. Sutherland (1991). 'The "Walters Critique" of the EMS: A Case of Inconsistent Expectations', *Manchester School of Economics and Social Studies*, 59 (supplement): 23–37

Millward, R. and D. Parker (1983). *Public and Private Enterprise: Comparative Behaviour and Relative Efficiency*, in R. Millward, D. Parker, L. Rosenthal, M. T. Sumner and N. Topham (eds.), *Public Sector Economics*, London: Longman

Milone, L. M. (1993). *Libero scambio, protezionismo e cooperazione internazionale nel pensiero di Keynes*, Rome: La Nuova Italia Scientifica

Minsky, H. P. (1975). *John Maynard Keynes*, New York: Columbia University Press

Mishra, R. (1993). 'Typologies of the Welfare State and Comparative Analysis: The "Liberal" Welfare State', paper presented at the Seminar on Comparative Research on Welfare States in Transition, Oxford, 9–12 September

Mitchell, R. C. and R. T. Carson (1989). *Using Surveys to Value Public Goods: The Contingent Valuation Method*, Washington, DC: Resources for the future

Modigliani, F. (1944). 'Liquidity Preference and the Theory of Interest and Money', *Econometrica*, 12: 45–88

Modigliani, F., M. Baldassarri and F. Castiglionesi (1996). *Il miracolo possibile: un programma per l'economia italiana*, Bari: Laterza

Moffitt, R. (1992). 'Incentives Effects of the US Welfare System', *Journal of Economic Literature*, 30: 1–61

Monopolies and Mergers Commission, UK (MMC) (1994). *Annual Report*, London: HMSO

Mueller, D. C. (2003). *Public Choice III*, 3rd edn., Cambridge: Cambridge University Press

Mundell, R. A. (1961). 'A Theory of Optimal Currency Areas', *American Economic Review*, 51: 657–664, reprinted in R. A. Mundell, *International Economics*, London: Macmillan, 1968

(1962). 'The Appropriate Use of Monetary and Fiscal Policy for Internal and External Stability', *IMF Staff Papers*, 9: 70–79; reprinted in R. A. Mundell, *International Economics*, London: Macmillan, 1968

(1963). 'Capital Mobility and Stabilisation Policy under Fixed and Flexible Exchange Rates', *Canadian Journal of Economics and Political Science*, 29: 475–85; reprinted in R. A. Mundell, *International Economics*, London: Macmillan, 1968

Musgrave, R. A. (1959). *The Theory of Public Finance*, 1st edn., New York: McGraw-Hill

Mussa, M. (1997). 'IMF Surveillance', *American Economic Review, Papers and Proceedings*, 87: 28–31

Musu I. (2000). *Introduzione all'economia dell'ambiente*, Bologna: Il Mulino

Muth, J. F. (1961). 'Rational Expectations and the Theory of Price Movements', *Econometrica*, 29: 315–55

Myrdal, G. (1953). *The Political Element in the Development of Economic Theory*, London: Routledge & Kegan Paul

(1956). *An International Economy: Problems and Prospects*, London: Routledge & Kegan Paul

(1957). *Economic Theory and Underdeveloped Regions*, London: Duckworth (reprinted, London: University Paperbacks, Methuen and Co., 1969)

(1958). *Value in Social Theory*, New York: Harper

Mytelka, L. K. (ed.) (1999). *Competition, Innovation and Competitiveness in Developing Countries*, Paris: OECD Development Centre

National Economic Development Office (NEDO) (1976). *A Study of UK Nationalised Industries: Their Role in the Economy and Control in the Future*, Background Paper, London

Neal, D. (2002). 'How Vouchers Could Change the Market for Education', *Journal of Economic Perspectives*, 16: 25–44

Neumann, M. (2001). *Competition Policy. History, Theory and Practice*, Cheltenham: Edward Elgar

Newbery, D. M. and M. G. Pollitt (1997). 'The Restructuring and Privatisation of Britain's CEGB – Was it Worth it?', *Journal of Industrial Economics*, 45: 269–304

Newlyn, W. T. (1962). *Theory of Money*, Oxford: Clarendon Press

Niskanen, W. (1971). *Bureaucracy and Representative Government*, Chicago: Aldine

(1975). 'Bureaucrats and Politicians', *Journal of Law and Economics*, 38: 617–44

Nordhaus, W. D. (1975). 'The Political Business Cycle', *Review of Economic Studies*, 42: 169–90

(1999). 'Biens publics globaux et changement climatique', *Revue Française d'Economie*, 14: 11–32

North, D. C. (1990). 'A Transaction Cost Theory of Politics', *Journal of Theoretical Politics*, 2: 355–67

Nozick, R. (1974). *Anarchy, State and Utopia*, New York: Basic Books

Nurkse, R. (1953). *Problems of Capital Formation in Underdeveloped Countries*, Oxford: Oxford University Press

Oakland, W. H. (1987). 'Theory of Public Goods', in A. J. Auerbach and M. Feldstein (eds.), *Handbook of Public Economics*, Amsterdam: North-Holland

Oates, W. (1972). *Fiscal Federalism*, Harbrace Series in Business and Economics, New York: Harcourt Brace Jovanovich

Odagiri, H. and A. Goto (1993). 'The Japanese System of Innovation: Past, Present and Future', in R. Nelson (ed.), *National Innovation Systems: A Comparative Analysis*. Oxford: Oxford University Press

OECD (1990). *Economic Outlook*, December

(1998). *Harmful Tax Competition: An Emerging Global Issue*, Paris: Organisation for Economic Cooperation and Development

(2004). *Economic Outlook*, June

Office for National Statistics (ONS) (n.d.). *Statistics online*, http://www.statistics.gov.uk/statbase

Okun, A. M. (1962). 'Potential GNP: Its Measurement and Significance', in American Statistical Association, 'Proceedings of the Business and Economic Statistics Section'; reprinted (1970) in A. M. Okun, *The Political Economy of Prosperity*, Washington, DC: The Brookings Institution

(1975). *Equality and Efficiency*, Washington, DC: The Brookings Institution

Olson, M. (1965). *The Logic of Collective Action: Public Goods and Theory of Groups*, Cambridge, MA: Harvard University Press

(1982). *The Rise and Decline of Nations*, New Haven: Yale University Press

Oman, C. (1996). *The Policy Challenges of Globalisation and Regionalisation*, OECD, Policy Brief, 11

Ordover, J. A. and A. Weiss (1981). 'Information and the Law: Evaluating Legal Restrictions on Competitive Contracts', *American Economic Review*, 71: 399–404

Orszag, P. R. and J. E. Stiglitz (2001). 'Rethinking Pension Reform: Ten Myths about Social Security Systems', in R. Holman and J. Stiglitz (eds.), *New Ideas about Old Age Security*, Washington, DC: World Bank, pp. 27–56 (presented at the Conference on 'New Ideas about Old Age Security', World Bank, Washington, DC, 14–15 September 1999)

Padoa Schioppa, T. (2002). *Self vs Discipline in the Financial Field*, Lecture at the London School of Economics, 20 May, www.ecb.int/key/sp990224.htm

Pagano, U. (1992). 'Organizational Equilibria and Production Efficiency', *Metroeconomica*, 43: 227–47

Pagano, U. and R. Rowthorn (1997). 'Selezione di mercato e democrazia economica', in B. Jossa and U. Pagano (eds.), *Economie di mercato ed efficienza dei diritti di proprietà*, Turin: Giappichelli

Panić, M. (2003). 'A New Bretton Woods?', in J. Michie (ed.), *The Handbook of Globalisation*, Cheltenham: Edward Elgar

Pareto, V. (1906). *Manuale di economia politica*, Milan: Società Editrice Libraria; (reprinted Rome: Bizzarri, 1965; French translation, *Manuel d'Economie politique*, Paris: M. Giard, 1909; English translation, *Manual of Political Economy*, New York: A.M. Kelley, 1927)

Pasinetti, L. L. (1981). *Structural Change and Economic Growth*, Cambridge: Cambridge University Press

(1993). *Structural Economic Dynamics: A Theory of the Economic Consequences of Human Learning*, Cambridge: Cambridge University Press

Patinkin, D. (1956). *Money Interest and Prices*, Evanston: Roe Peterson; 2nd edn., New York: Harper & Row, 1965

Patnaik, P. and C. P. Chandrasekhar (1998). 'India, Dirigisme, Structural Adjustment, and the Radical Alternative', in D. Baker, G. Epstein and R. Pollin (eds.), *Globalization and Progressive Economic Policy*, Cambridge: Cambridge University Press

Pearce, D. W. and E. B. Barbier (2000). *Blueprint for a Sustainable Economy*, London: Earthscan Publications

Pearce, D. W. and R. K. Turner (1990). *Economics of Natural Resources and the Environment*, Baltimore, MD: Johns Hopkins University Press

Pearce, D. W., A. Markandya and E. B. Barbier (1989), *Blueprint for a Green Economy*, London: Earthscan Publications

Pencavel, J. (1981). 'The American Experience with Incomes Policy', in J. L. Fallick and R. F. Elliot (eds.), *Incomes Policy, Inflation and Relative Pay*, London: Allen & Unwin

Perotti, R. (1996). 'Growth, Income Distribution, and Democracy: What the Data Say', *Journal of Economic Growth*, 1: 149–87

Persson, J. and G. Tabellini (eds.) (1994). *Monetary and Fiscal Policies*, Cambridge, MA: MIT Press, 2 vols.

Persson, M. (1995). 'Why are Taxes so High in Egalitarian Societies?', *Scandinavian Journal of Economics*, 97: 569–80

Persson, T. and G. Tabellini (2000). *Political Economics: Explaining Economic Policy*, Cambridge, MA: MIT Press

Petersen, H. C. (1989). *Business and Government*, 3rd edn., New York: Harper & Row

Pezzoli, A. and R. Schiattarella (1999). 'Le autorità indipendenti', in N. Acocella (ed.), *Le istituzioni fra mercato e stato*, Rome: Carocci

Phelps, E. S. (1970). 'Introduction: The New Microeconomics of Unemployment and Inflation Theory', in E. S. Phelps *et al.* (eds.), *Microeconomic Foundations of Employment and Inflation Theory*, New York: Norton

Phillips A. C. (1958). 'The Relation Between Unemployment and the Rate of Change of Money Wage Rates in the United Kingdom, 1861–1957', *Economica*, 25: 283–99

Pieper, U. and L. Taylor (1998). 'The Revival of the Liberal Creed: The IMF, the World Bank and Inequality in a Globalized Economy', in D. Baker, G. Epstein and R. Pollin (eds.), *Globalization and Progressive Economic Policy*, Cambridge: Cambridge University Press

Piga, G. (2000). 'Dependent and Accountable: Evidence from the Modern Theory of Central Banking', *Journal of Economic Surveys*, 14: 563–93

Pigou, A. C. (1920). *The Economics of Welfare*, 1st edn. (4th edn., 1932), London: Macmillan (1928). *A Study in Public Finance*, 1st edn. (3rd edn., 1947), London: Macmillan

Platteau, J. P. (1995). 'The Food Crisis in Africa: A Comparative Structural Analysis', in J. Drèze, A. Sen and A. Hussain (eds), *The Political Economy of Hunger*, WIDER Studies in Development Economics, Oxford: Clarendon Press

Pollitt, C. and G. Bouckaert (2000). *Public Management Reform: A Comparative Analysis*, Oxford: Oxford University Press

Prebisch, R. (1950). *The Economic Development of Latin America and Its Principal Problems*, Lake Success, NY: United Nations

Preston, A. J. and A. R. Pagan (1982). *The Theory of Economic Policy. Statics and Dynamics*, Cambridge: Cambridge University Press

Pretty J. N. (1995). *Regenerating Agriculture, Policies and Practice for Sustainability and Self-Reliance*, Earthscan: London

Price, R. W. R. and J. C. Chouraqui (1983). 'Public Sector Deficits: Problems and Policy Implications', *OECD Economic Outlook, Occasional Studies*, June

Putnam, R. D. (ed.) (2002). *Democracies in Flux: The Evolution of Social Capital in Contemporary Society*, New York: Oxford University Press

Putterman L., J. E. Roemer and J. Silvestre (1998). 'Does Egalitarianism Have a Future?', *Journal of Economic Literature*, 36: 861–902

Pyke, F., G. Becattini and W. Sengenberger (1990). *Industrial Districts and Inter-Firm Cooperation in Italy*, Geneva: International Institute for Labour Studies

Qian, Y. and B. R. Weingast (1997). 'Federalism as a Commitment to Preserve Market Incentives', *Journal of Economic Perspectives*, 11: 83–92

Rajan, R. G. and L. Zingales (2000). 'The Governance of the New Enterprise', in X. Vives (ed.), *Corporate Governance: Theoretical and Empirical Perspectives*, Cambridge: Cambridge University Press

Ramsey, F. P. (1927). 'A Contribution to the Theory of Taxation', *Economic Journal*, 37: 47–61

Rasmusen, E. (1994). *Games and Information*, 1st edn. 1989, Oxford: Blackwell

Ravenscraft, D. J. and F. M. Scherer (1987). *Mergers, Selloffs and Economic Efficiency*, Washington, DC: Brookings Institution

Regan, D. H. (1972). 'The Problem of Social Cost Revisited', *Journal of Law and Economics*, 15: 427–37

Robinson, J. (1937). *Essays in the Theory of Employment*, London: Blackwell

   (1943). 'Planning Full Employment', *The London Times*, 22, 23 January; reprinted in *Collected Economic Papers*, 1, Oxford: Blackwell, 1951

   (1962a). *Essays in the Theory of Economic Growth*, London: Macmillan

   (1962b). 'Latter-Day Capitalism', *New Left Review*, July–August: 37–46; reprinted in *Collected Economic Papers*, III, Oxford: Blackwell, 1965

Rodrik, D. (1997). *Has Globalization Gone too Far?*, Washington, DC: Institute for International Economics

Roemer, J. E. (1994). 'The Strategic Role of Party Ideology when Voters Are Uncertain about How the Economy Works', *American Political Science Review*, 88: 327–35

   (1996). *Theories of Distributive Justice*, Cambridge, MA and London: Harvard University Press

Rogoff, K. (1985). 'Can International Monetary Policy Coordination Be Counterproductive?', *Journal of International Economics*, 18: 199–217

Rogoff, K. and A. Sibert (1988). 'Elections and Macroeconomic Policy Cycles', *Review of Economic Studies*, 55: 1–16

Romani, F. (1984). 'I limiti della politica economica', *Rassegna Economica*, 2 (reprinted in Società Italiana degli Economisti, *I limiti della politica economica*, Milan: Giuffrè, 1985)

Romer, D. (1993). 'The New Keynesian Synthesis', *Journal of Economic Perspectives*, 7: 5–22

Romer, P. (1986). 'Increasing Returns and Long-run Growth', *Journal of Political Economy*, 94: 1002–37

   (1987). 'Growth Based on Increasing Returns Due to Specialisation', *American Economic Review*, 77: 56–62

   (1990). 'Endogenous Technological Change', *Journal of Political Economy* (supplement), 98 (5) (part 2): S71–S102

Rondi, L. and A. Sembenelli (1998). 'Integrazione economica e aggiustamento strutturale nelle industrie e nelle imprese europee', *L'Industria*, 19: 733–55

Roosa, R. V. (1951). 'Interest Rates and the Central Bank', in R. V. Roosa, *Money, Trade and Economic Growth: In Honour of John Henry Williams*, New York: Macmillan

Rose-Ackerman, S. (1975). 'The Economics of Corruption', *Journal of Public Economics*, 4: 187–203

    (1986). 'Reforming Public Bureaucracy through Economic Incentives?', *Journal of Law, Economics and Organisation*, 2: 131–61

Rosen, S. (1985). 'Implicit Contracts', *Journal of Economic Literature*, 23: 1144–75

    (1997). 'Public Employment and The Welfare State in Sweden', in R. B. Freeman, R. Topel and B. Swedenborg, *The Welfare State in Transition: Reforming The Swedish Model*, Chicago: University of Chicago Press

Rosenstein-Rodan, P. N. (1943). 'Problems of Industrialization of Eastern and South Eastern Europe', *Economic Journal*, 53: 202–11

Ross, S. (1993). *Introduction to Probability Models*, New York: Academic Press

Rossi, E. and M. Sorge (2000). 'Will the Growth and Stability Pact Actually Work? A Critical Look at its underlying Rationale and Inconsistencies', *Rivista italiana degli economisti*, 5: 323–45

Rothschild, K. (1973). 'Politica dei redditi o politica economica', in D. Cavalieri (ed.), *La politica dei redditi*, Milan: Franco Angeli (Italian translation from 'Einkommenspolitik oder Wirtschaftspolitik', in *Probleme der Einkommenspolitik*, Kiel: Institut für Weltwirtschaft an der Universität, 1973: 63–80)

Roubini, N. and J. Sachs (1989). 'Political and Economic Determinants of Budget Deficits in the Industrial Democracies', *European Economic Review*, 33: 903–33

Rusk D. (1993). *Cities without Suburb*, Baltimore, MD: Johns Hopkins University Press

Salin, P. (1990). *The Role of the SDRs in the International Monetary System: Comment*, in E. M. Claassen (ed.), *International and European Monetary Systems*, New York: Praeger

Salvati, M. (1985). 'Commento alla relazione di Franco Romani', in Società Italiana degli Economisti, *I limiti della politica economica*, Milan: Giuffrè

Samuelson, P. A. (1954). 'The Pure Theory of Public Expenditure', *Review of Economics and Statistics*, November; reprinted in K. J. Arrow and T. Scitovsky (eds.), *Readings in Welfare Economics*, Homewood, IL: Irwin, 1969

    (1963). 'Problems of Methodology. Discussion', *American Economic Review*; reprinted in *Collected Scientific Papers*, Cambridge, MA: MIT Press, 1966

Sandler, T. (1997). *Global Challenges. An Approach to Environmental, Political and Economic Problems*, Cambridge: Cambridge University Press

Sandmo, A. (1991). 'Economists and the Welfare State', *European Economic Review*, 35: 213–39

Sarkar, P. and H. W. Singer (1991). 'Manufactured Exports of Developing Countries and their Terms of Trade since 1965', *World Development*, 19: 333–40

Scherer, F. M. (1980). *Industrial Market Structure and Economic Performance*, Boston: Houghton Mifflin

Schröder, J. (1990). *The Role of the SDRs in the International Monetary System*, in E. M. Claassen (ed.), *International and European Monetary Systems*, New York: Praeger

Schultze, C. L. (1988). 'International Macroeconomic Coordination. Marrying the Economic Models with Political Reality', in M. Feldstein (ed.), *International Economic Cooperation*, Chicago: University of Chicago Press

Schumpeter, J. A. (1934). *The Theory of Economic Development*, Cambridge, MA: Harvard University Press

    (1943). *Capitalism, Socialism and Democracy*, London: Allen & Unwin

Schwartz, A. J. (1975). 'Review of Kindleberger's *The World in Depression*', *Journal of Political Economy*, 83: 231–37

    (1981). 'Understanding 1929–1933', in K. Brunner (ed.), *The Great Depression Revisited*, Boston: Kluwer-Nijhoff

Seidman, L. S. (1978). 'Tax-Based Incomes Policy', *Brookings Papers on Economic Activity*, 2: 301–61

Sen, A. K. (1970a). *Collective Choice and Social Welfare*, Edinburgh: Oliver & Boyd
(ed.) (1970b). *Growth Economics: Selected Readings*, Harmondsworth: Penguin
(1980). 'Equality of What?', in S. McMurrin (ed.), *The Tanner Lectures on Human Values*, 1, Salt Lake City, University of Utah and Cambridge: Cambridge University Press; reprinted in A. K. Sen, *Choice, Welfare and Measurement*, Oxford: Blackwell, 1982
(1982). *Choice, Welfare and Measurement*, Oxford: Blackwell
(1987). *On Ethics and Economics*, Oxford: Blackwell
(1995). 'Rationality and Social Choice', *American Economic Review*, 85: 1–24

Sengenberger, W. and F. Pyke (eds.) (1992). *Industrial Districts and Local Economic Regeneration*, Geneva: International Institute for Labour Studies

Shapiro, C. and J. E. Stiglitz (1984). 'Equilibrium Unemployment as a Worker Discipline Device', *American Economic Review*, 74: 433–44

Shleifer, A. (1985). 'A Theory of Yardstick Competition', *Rand Journal of Economics*, 16: 319–27

Shleifer, A. and R. W. Vishny (1993). 'Corruption', *Quarterly Journal of Economics*, 108: 599–617
(1997). 'A Survey of Corporate Governance', *Journal of Finance*, 52: 737–83
(1998). *The Grabbing Hand: Government Pathologies and Their Cures*, Cambridge, MA: Harvard University Press

Shonfield, A. (1965). *Modern Capitalism: The Changing Balance between Public and Private Power*, London: Oxford University Press

Simon, H. A. (1976). 'From Substantive to Procedural Rationality', in S. Latsis (ed.), *Method and Appraisal in Economics*, Cambridge: Cambridge University Press

Singer, H. W. (1950). 'The Distribution of Gains between Investing and Borrowing Countries', *American Economic Review*, 40: 473–85

Singh, A. (1971). *Takeovers: Their Relevance to the Stock Market and the Theory of the Firm*, Cambridge: Cambridge University Press
(1975). 'Takeovers, Economic "Natural Selection", and the Theory of the Firm: Evidence from the Post–war UK Experience', *Economic Journal*, 85: 497–515
(1992). '*Corporate Takeovers*', in P. Newman, M. Milgate and J. Eatwell (eds.), *The New Palgrave Dictionary of Money and Finance*, 1, London: Macmillan

Singh, A. and A. Zammit (2003). 'Globalisation, Labour Standards and Economic Development', in J. Michie (ed.), *The Handbook of Globalisation*, Cheltenham: Edward Elgar

Siniscalco, D. (1991). *La protezione dei trans-national commons: accordi volontari o istituzioni*, in Osservatorio 'G. Dell'Amore' sui rapporti tra diritto ed economia, *Ambiente, etica, economia e istituzioni*, in 'Ufficio Studi, Notiziario della CARIPLO', suppl.: 5–6

Sinn, H.-W. (1990). 'Tax Harmonisation and Tax Competition in Europe', *European Economic Review*, 34: 489–504
(1995). 'A Theory of the Welfare State', *Scandinavian Journal of Economics*, 97: 495–526

Slaughter, M. J. and P. Swagel (1997). *The Effect of Globalization on Wages in the Advanced Economies*, IMF Working Paper 43, April

Smith, A. (1776). *An Inquiry into Nature and Causes of the Wealth of Nations*, 1st edn. London: Straham & Cadell (quotations from the edn. by R. H. Campbell A. S. Skinner and W. B. Todd, Oxford: Clarendon Press, 1976)

Snower, D. J. (1994). *What is the Domain of the Welfare State*, Centre for Economic Policy Research, Discussion Paper 1018, November (1994), reprinted in M. Baldassarri, L. Paganetto and E. S. Phelps (eds.), *Equity, Efficiency and Growth. The Future of the Welfare State*, London: Macmillan

Solow, R. (1956). 'A Contribution to the Theory of Economic Growth', *Quarterly Journal of Economics*, 70: 65–94

(1992). *An Almost Practical Step toward Sustainability*, Washington DC: RFF Press, Resources for the Future

Spiller, P. T. (1990). 'Politicians, Interest Groups and Regulators: A Multiple-Principals Agency Theory of Regulation, or "Let Them Be Bribed"', *Journal of Law and Economics*, 33: 65–101

Spraos, J. (1996). *IMF Conditionality: Ineffectual, Inefficient, Mistargeted*, Princeton, NJ: International Finance Section, Department of Economics, Princeton University

Spulber, D. F. (1989). *Regulation and Markets*, Cambridge, MA: MIT Press

Staniland, M. (1985). *What is Political Economy? A Study of Social Theory and Underdevelopment*, New Haven: Yale University Press

Starrett, D. A. (1972). 'Fundamental Non-Convexities in the Theory of Externalities', *Journal of Economic Theory*, 4: 180–99

(1988). *Foundations of Public Economics*, Cambridge: Cambridge University Press

Stevenson, A., V. Muscatelli and M. Gregory (1988). *Macroeconomic Theory and Stabilisation Policy*, New York: P. Allan

Stigler, G. J. (1966). *The Theory of Price*, 3rd edn. (1st edn., 1946), New York: Macmillan

Stiglitz, J. E. (1988). *Economics of the Public Sector*, 2nd edn., New York: Norton

(1989). *The Economic Role of the State*, Oxford: Blackwell

(1991). *Some Theoretical Aspects of Privatisation: Applications to Eastern Europe*, IPR-USAID Working Paper, September; reprinted in M. Baldassarri, L. Paganetto and E. S. Phelps (eds.), *Privatisation Processes in Eastern Europe*, New York: St Martin's Press, 1993

(1994). *Whither Socialism?*, Cambridge, MA: MIT Press

(2002). *Globalization and its Discontents*, London: Penguin Books

Stiglitz, J. E. and A. Weiss (1981). 'Credit Rationing in Markets with Imperfect Information', *American Economic Review*, 71: 393–410

Sullivan, L. A. and W. S. Grimes (2000). *The Law of Antitrust: An Integrated Handbook*, St Paul, MN: West Publishing (Hornbook series)

Summers, L. H. (1983). 'The Nonadjustment of Nominal Interest Rates: A Study of the Fisher Effect', in J. Tobin, (ed.), *Macroeconomics, Prices and Quantities: Essays in Memory of Arthur M. Okun*, Oxford: Blackwell

Sutherland, A. (1997). 'Fiscal Crises and Aggregate Demand: Can High Public Debt Reverse the Effects of Fiscal Policy?', *Journal of Public Economics*, 65: 147–62

Svensson, L. O. E. (1999). 'Inflation Targeting as a Monetary Policy Rule', *Journal of Monetary Economics*, 43: 607–54

(2003). *In the Right Direction, but Not Enough: The Modification of the Monetary-Policy Strategy of the ECB*, Briefing Paper for the Committee on Economic and Monetary Affairs (ECON) of the European Parliament, May, http://www.princeton.edu/svensson/

Svimez (2002), *Rapporto 2002 sull'economia del Mezzogiorno*, Bologna: Il Mulino, http://www.svimez.it

Sylos Labini, P. (1962). *Oligopoly and Technical Progress*, Cambridge, MA: Harvard University Press, 1st Italian edn., 1956

Tabellini, G. and A. Alesina (1990). 'Voting on the Budget Deficit', *American Economic Review*, 80: 37–49; reprinted in Persson, J. and G. Tabellini, *Monetary and Fiscal Policies*, 2, Cambridge, MA: MIT, 1994, 2 vols.

Tanzi, V. (1998). 'The Need for Tax Coordination in an Economically Integrated World', in P. Roberti (ed.), *Financial Markets and Capital Income Taxation in Global Economy*, New York: Elsevier

(2002). 'Globalizzazione e sistemi fiscali', Banca Etruria, Studi e Ricerche, Supplemento 58 di *Etruria Oggi*, Banca Popolare dell'Etruria e del Lazio: 34–40

Tanzi, V. and A. L. Bovenberg (1990). 'Is there a Need for Harmonizing Capital Income Taxes within EC Countries?', in H. Siebert (ed.), *Reforming Capital Income Taxation*, Tübingen: J.C.B. Mohr

Tarantelli, E. (1983). 'The Regulation of Inflation in Western Countries and the Degree of Neocorporatism', *Economia (Portuguese Catholic University)*, 7: 199–238

Temin, P. (1976). *Did Monetary Forces Cause the Great Depression?*, New York: Norton

Teulings, C. N. and J. Hartog (1998). *Corporatism or Competition: Labour Contracts, Institutions and Wage Structures in International Comparison*, Cambridge: Cambridge University Press

Theichroew, D., A. Robichek and M. Montalbano (1965). 'An Analysis of Criteria for Investment and Financial Decisions under Certainty', *Management Science*, 12: 151–79

Theil, H. (1964). *Optimal Decision Rules for Government and Industry*, Amsterdam: North-Holland

Tiebout, C. M. (1956). 'A Pure Theory of Local Expenditures', *Journal of Political Economy*, 64: 416–22

Tinbergen, J. (1952). *On the Theory of Economic Policy*, Amsterdam: North-Holland
    (1956). *Economic Policies. Principles and Design*, Amsterdam: North-Holland

Tirole, J. (1994). 'The Internal Organization of Government', *Oxford Economic Papers*, 46: 1–29

Tizzano, A. (2000). Quelques observations sur la coopération internationale en matière de concurrence, *Revue du Droit de l'Union Européenne*, 1: 75–100

Tobin, J. (1978). 'A Proposal for International Monetary Reform', *Eastern Economic Journal*, 4: 153–9

Traxler, F. (1995). 'Farewell to Labour Market Associations? Organised versus Disorganised Decentralisation as a Map for Industrial Relations', in C. J. Crouch and F. Traxler (eds.), *Organised Industrial Relations in Europe. What Future?*, Aldershot: Avebury

Triffin, R. (1960). *Gold and the Dollar Crisis*, New Haven: Yale University Press

Tsoukalis, L. (1997). *The New European Economy Revisited*, Oxford: Oxford University Press

Tullock, G. (1965). *The Politics of Bureaucracy*, Washington, DC: Public Affairs Press

US Congress (2000). *Commission Report*, International Financial Institutions Advisory Commission, March, http://www.house.gov/jec/imf/meltzer.htm

US Department of Commerce, Bureau of Economic Analysis (1995). *US Direct Investment Abroad, Operations of US Parent Companies and Their Affiliates*, Revised 1992 Estimates, Washington, DC, US Government Printing Office, June

ul Haq, M., I. Kaul and I. Grunberg (eds.) (1996). *The Tobin Tax: Coping with Financial Volatility*, Oxford: Oxford University Press

UNCTAD (1994). *World Investment Report 1994*, New York: United Nations
    (1997). *World Investment Report 1997: Transnational Corporations, Market Structure and Competition Policy*, New York and Geneva: United Nations
    (2001). *World Investment Report: Promoting Linkages*, New York and Geneva: United Nations
    (2002). *World Investment Report 2002: Transnational Corporations and Export Competitiveness*, New York and Geneva: United Nations

United Nations (UN) (1987). *Our Common Future*, World Commission on Environment and Development, Oxford University Press, Oxford, http://www.un.org
    (1990). *Human Development Report 1990*, Oxford: Oxford University Press
    (1993). *Human Development Report 1993*, Oxford: Oxford University Press
    (2000). Millennium Declaration, A/RES/55/2. 18 September, New York, http://www.un.org/millennium/declaration/ares552e.pdf.
    (2002). *Human Development Report, 2002*, Oxford: Oxford University Press

United Nations Development Programme (UNDP) (2002). *Human Development Report 2002*, Oxford: Oxford University Press
    (2003). *Human Development Report 2003*, Oxford: Oxford University Press

US Environmental Protection Agency (USEPA) (1988). *Regulatory Impact Analysis: Protection of Stratospheric Ozone*, Washington, DC

Van Meerhaeghe, M. A. G. (1992). *International Economic Institutions*, 6th edn., Dordrecht: Kluwer Academic

Van Ypersele, J. (1977). 'A Central Position for the SDR in the Monetary System', *Banca Nazionale del Lavoro Quarterly Review* 123: 381–97

   (1984). *The European Monetary System*, Brussels: European Communities

Vandenbroucke, F. (1985). 'Conflicts in International Economic Policy and the World Recession: A Theoretical Analysis', *Cambridge Journal of Economics*, 9: 15–42

Varian, H. R. (1987). *Intermediate Microeconomics: A Modern Approach*, New York: Norton

Veljanovski, C. (ed.) (1991). *Regulators and the Market: An Assessment of the Growth of Regulation in the UK*, London: Institute of Economic Affairs

Vercelli, A. (1991). *Methodological Foundations of Macroeconomics: Keynes and Lucas*, Cambridge: Cambridge University Press

Vernon, R. (1974). *Big Business and the State: Changing Relations in Western Europe*, London: Macmillan

Vicarelli, F. (1984). *Keynes: The Instability of Capitalism*, Philadelphia: University of Pennsylvania Press

Vickers, J. (1995). 'Concepts of Competition', *Oxford Economic Papers*, 47:1–23

Vickers, J. and G. Yarrow (1988). *Privatization: An Economic Analysis*, Cambridge, MA: MIT Press

Viner, J. (1950). *The Customs Union Issue*, New York: Carnegie Endowment for International Peace

Vines, D. and C. L. Gilbert (2003). *The IMF and its Critics: Reform of Global Financial Architecture*. Cambridge: Cambridge University Press

Viscusi, W. K. (1983). *Risk by Choice: Regulating Health and Safety in the Workplace*, Cambridge, MA: Harvard University Press

Visser, J. (2002). 'Unions, Wage Bargaining and Co-ordination in European Labour Markets – the Past Twenty Years and the Near Future', in P. Pochet (ed.), *Wage Policy in the Eurozone*, Brussels: PIE – Peter Lang: 39–78

Vives, X. (ed.) (2000). *Corporate Governance: Theoretical and Empirical Perspectives*, Cambridge: Cambridge University Press

Walsh, C. E. (2003). *Monetary Theory and Policy*, 2nd edn., Cambridge, MA: MIT Press

Wallich, H. and S. Weintraub (1971). 'Tax Based Incomes Policies', *Journal of Economic Issues*, 5: 1–17

Warshawsky, M. J. (1987). 'Determinants of Corporate Merger Activity: A Review of the Literature', Staff Study, 152, Board of Governors of the Federal Reserve System, Washington, DC, April; summarised in Federal Reserve Bulletin, 73(4): 270–1

Waterson, M. (1988). *Regulation of the Firm and Natural Monopoly*, Oxford: Blackwell

Weber, A. A. (1991). 'European Economic and Monetary Union and Asymmetries and Adjustment Problems in the European Monetary System: Some Empirical Evidence', *European Economy*, special edition, 1: 185–207

Weber, M. (1992). *Wirtschaft und Gesellschaft*, Mohr: Tübingen (English translation, *Economy and Society: An Outline of Interpretive Sociology*; translation of the 4th German edn., New York: Bedminster Press, 1968)

Weitzacker, C. C. (1975). *Political Limits of Traditional Stabilization Policy*, mimeo, 5 May

Weitzman, M. L. (1982). 'Increasing Returns and the Foundations of Unemployment Theory', *Economic Journal*, 92: 787–804

Welfens, P. J. J. (ed.) (2001). *Internationalization of the Economy and Environmental Policy Options*, Heidelberg and New York: Springer

Welfens, P. J. J. and R. Hillebrand (2001). 'Environmental Problems in the Single EU Market: Developments, Theory and New Policy Options', in P. J. J. Welfens (ed.), *Internationalization of the Economy and Environmental Policy Options*, Heidelberg and New York: Springer

Williamson, Jeffrey (2002). *Winners and Losers over Two Centuries of Globalisation*, National Bureau of Economic Research, Working Paper, 9161

Williamson, J. (1983). *IMF Conditionality*, Washington DC: Institute for International Economics

(1985). *The Exchange Rate System*, rev. edn., Washington, DC: Institute for International Economics

Williamson, O. E. (1975). *Markets and Hierarchies: Analysis and Antitrust Implications*, New York: Free Press

(1985). *The Economic Institutions of Capitalism*, New York: Free Press

(1989). 'Transaction Cost Economics', in R. Schmalensee and R. Willig (eds.), *Handbook of Industrial Organization*, 1, Amsterdam: North-Holland

Winters, A. (1999). *Regionalism versus Multilateralism*, in R. E. Baldwin, D. Cohen, A. Sapir and A. Venables (eds.), *Market Integration, Regionalism, and the Global Economy*, Cambridge: Cambridge University Press

Wolf, C. (1979). 'A Theory of Nonmarket Failure', *Journal of Law and Economics*, 22: 107–39

(1988). *Markets or Governments: Choosing between Imperfect Alternatives*, Cambridge, MA: MIT Press

Wood, A. (1994). *North–South Trade, Employment and Inequality: Changing Fortunes in a Skill-Driven World*, Oxford: Clarendon Press

Wood, G. (1991). 'Valuation Effects, Currency Contract Impacts and the J-Curve: Empirical Estimates', *Australian Economic Papers*, 30: 148–63

World Bank (1993). *The East Asian Miracle: Economic Growth and Public Policy*, Oxford: Oxford University Press

(1995). *World Development Report 1995: Workers in an Integrating World*, Oxford: Oxford University Press

(1997). *World Development Report 1997*, Oxford: Oxford University Press

(1998). *Culture in Sustainable Development*, http://www.worldbank.org/environment

(2002). *World Development Report 2003*, Oxford: Oxford University Press, http://www.worldbank.org

(2004). *Global Economic Prospects and the Developing Countries 2003*, Washington DC: World Bank, http://www.worldbank.org/prospects/gep2004, March

World Trade Organisation (WTO) (2004). *Annual Report*, Geneva

(various years) *Annual Report*, Geneva

Wyplosz, C. (1999). 'International Financial Instability', in I. Kaul, I. Grunberg and M. A. Stern (eds.), *Global Public Goods: International Co-Operation in the 21st Century*, Oxford: Oxford University Press

Young, A. (1928). 'Increasing Returns and Economic Progress', *Economic Journal*, 38: 527–42

Zazzaro, A. (2001). 'Nuova programmazione e sviluppo del Mezzogiorno: c'è ancora spazio per l'impresa pubblica?', in M. R. Carillo and A. Zazzaro (eds.), *Istituzioni, capitale umano e sviluppo del Mezzogiorno*, Naples: ESI

Zodrow, G. R. (2003). 'Tax Competition and Tax Coordination in the European Union', *International Tax and Public Finance*, 10: 651–71

Author index

Subject index

Printed in Great Britain
by Amazon.co.uk, Ltd.,
Marston Gate.